BLADE® PRESENTS

41st Edition

Knives
2021

Edited by Joe Kertzman

Published by

Gun Digest® Books, an imprint of Caribou Media Group, LLC
Gun Digest Media
5600 W. Grande Market Drive, Suite 100
Appleton, WI 54913
www.gundigest.com

To order books or other products call 920.471.4522 ext. 104
or visit us online at **www.gundigeststore.com**

CAUTION: Technical data presented here, particularly technical data on handloading and on firearms adjustment and alteration, inevitably reflects individual experience with particular equipment and components under specific circumstances the reader cannot duplicate exactly. Such data presentations therefore should be used for guidance only and with caution. Caribou Media accepts no responsibility for results obtained using these data.

ISBN: 978-1-951115-23-4

Edited by Joe Kertzman and Ben Sobieck

Printed in the United States of America

10 9 8 7 6 5 4 3 2 1

3 3988 10162 4648

Dedication and Acknowledgments

When I read *BLADE Magazine* Editor Steve Shackleford's online article, *A Look Back at BLADE Magazine Cutlery Hall of Fame® History* (https://bit.ly/3czphLx) it made me smile, but not because it was funny, off color or silly. It was as well-written and insightful as I thought it would be. Mine was a knowing smile, a prideful one and an "all's OK with the world" smile. Some things never change.

Steve has been an institution with *BLADE* for more than three decades. He has met some incredible people, learned from them, and has as much experience or more than any knife magazine editor on the planet. Little did Steve know that, shortly after penning the article, he himself would be inducted into the *BLADE* Magazine Cutlery Hall of Fame, along with renowned knifemakers Tony Bose and Mel Pardue. It is an incredibly well-deserved induction, and I acknowledge Steve, but he is not the only one I dedicate this 41st Anniversary Edition of the *KNIVES Annual* to. I am dedicating it to all the *BLADE* Magazine Cutlery Hall of Fame members. Doesn't that seem like an obvious choice?

It does, but I have never met many of the members, nor do I know much of their history in the knife industry. Though I spent nearly two decades with *BLADE*, its history came before me and has extended beyond my time there. I know enough, however, to realize we truly do "stand on the shoulders of giants," and that there would not be a collector market for handmade and production knives, and no dealers, purveyors or accessory manufacturers, if not for many of the Hall of Fame members.

Steve remembers when A.G. Russell of A.G. Russell Knives and Ken Warner, who wrote 19 editions of the *KNIVES* book, inducted each other in 1988. He fondly recalls Hubert Lawell's 1989 induction; how Col. Rex Applegate, B.R. Hughes and J. Bruce Voyles were all inducted together in 1993; and the memorable induction of Spyderco CEO Sal Glesser in 1999, specifically because Sal's wife, Gail, had a prior engagement but, unbeknownst to him, cancelled it and showed up and surprised him.

It is humbling to read the list of *BLADE* Magazine Cutlery Hall of Fame members, an inspirational group of dedicated and driven individuals who made a difference in this world. From Bo Randall, who was inducted into the Hall of Fame in 1983 and pioneered handmade knives at a time when no one else was considering it; up to the 2018 inductees, Dan Delavan and Phil Lobred, these are people who furthered an entire industry and ensured its viability. Delavan and his wife, Pam, ran the Plaza Cutlery retail knife shop in Costa Mesa, California, for 44 years as one of the world's most forward-thinking, brick-and-mortar cutlery stores. Lobred commissioned what is arguably the most important knife of the modern era: the King Tut Dagger Reproduction by fellow Hall-of-Famer Buster Warenski.

Current sitting Hall of Fame members nominate, vote on and induct new members, using the criteria of having demonstrated extraordinary service to the knife industry; displayed honesty, character and integrity; advanced the industry through creativity and originality of his or her works or contributions; furthered positive impact of the knife industry on the world stage as an ambassador or outstanding contributor; and demonstrated worthiness to be a member of the prestigious group.

The prestigious group includes such stalwarts as Uncle Henry and Albert M. Baer, M.H. Cole, James Lile, Robert Loveless, Pete Gerber; William Moran, Jr.; James Parker, George Herron, William Scagel, Gil Hibben, Harry McEvoy, Bernard Levine, C. Houston Price, Bill Adams, Jim Weyer; Al, Chuck and C.J. Buck; Blackie Collins, Frank Centofante, Ron Lake, Rudy Ruana, D'Alton Holder, Michael Walker, George "Butch" Winter, Tim Leatherman, Dan Dennehy, Ken Onion, Al Mar, Paul Bos, Kit Carson, Wayne Goddard, Goldie Russell and Chris Reeve.

There are many other names on the list, available at https://blademag.com/blade-magazine-cutlery-hall-of-fame, and there are plenty more deserving folks to be added in the future. For as long as there are makers and manufacturers who subscribe to a theory of building high-quality knives at a fair price, there will be a sound knife industry and market. If creative artists lend embellishments and technological wizards forever advance knife mechanics, the industry will thrive. With conscientious knife dealers, purveyors, proprietors, bloggers, suppliers, mentors, show coordinators, writers, editors, wholesalers and retailers promoting quality handmade and production knives, the knife world will benefit.

I dedicate this book, *KNIVES 2021*, to the BLADE Magazine Cutlery Hall of Fame members. □

Joe Kertzman

Contents

On The Cover

The stone-cold cutters on the cover of the *KNIVES 2021* book represent the best of the best in modern handmade blades. At left is a spotless slip-joint folder by Stephen Vanderkolff featuring a CPM 154 blade and a 416 stainless body with double integral bolsters. The blade includes snappy little gold Dellana Dots for grip when opening, and the handle is Mexican crazy lace agate with deep, psychedelic waves of shapes and color. Front-and-center stands a Dmitriy Popov piece that won "Best Chef's Knife" at the 2019 Sydney Knife Show. A smoky temper line is visible on the W2 blade, itself accompanied by a Gabon ebony bolster and Arizona desert ironwood handle. The James Beard Award cannot be far behind. Upon studying it, there are no straight lines on Ron Best's incredible "Curv-Jr." flipper folder at right, complete with a particularly pointed Damasteel blade, zirconium handle, brilliant titanium and Dichrolam (composite) inlays, and a titanium back bar and pocket clip. It is a trio worthy of all the accolades.

Introduction

It's like keeping a secret—not just a juicy piece of gossip, club handshake or password—but one that brings with it a feeling of incredible elation or ecstasy. It's knowing true joy that no one else within your age bracket or circle of friends could possibly understand. They wouldn't have any idea.

Insider information is so sweet, forbidden in the stock trading world, but treasured in just about any other facet of human experience.

It's how a knife collector feels after initiating an opening mechanism and feeling the silky-smooth action as a folding blade slides silently over ball bearings and snaps into position with an ever-so-slight "snick." The feeling is akin to running a finger across a scrimshawed ancient ivory handle, colors saturating the pores of a creamy white medium born from permafrost, where only the sturdiest reside.

The feeling extends to knife enthusiasts schooled in damascus, mosaic damascus, Timascus, Moku-Ti, powder metal and san mai steels; flipper mechanisms, out-the-front autos, spring assists, bowie/fighter combos, neck knives and fluted-handle daggers showcasing gold wire wraps; satin finishes and basket-woven leather sheaths.

It's the inner warmth experienced by a discerning collector who just obtained an authentic Bob Loveless ATS-34 chute knife sporting a green Micarta® handle, red fiber liners, brass washers and tube, with an original leather sheath. Few know what a lifelong knife fan goes through when they obtain a coveted W.F. Moran ST-23 damascus fighter featuring a hardwood handle, big brass double guard and pointed pommel.

No one could know. There's an inner peace followed by uninhibited joy.

The knife world is filled with people who have experienced similar feelings, as well as those who've gambled and lost their shirts, closed their businesses, taken their lumps and walked away. It's not an industry for the faint of heart, and even the most business savvy experience hard times, dark days, loss and regret. To know ecstasy is to understand pain and suffering.

It's so worth it! Knowing joy no one else has experienced, walking around with a cat-who-ate-the-canary look on one's face, a spring in the step, song in the heart and glint in the eye. That's what life is all about—the rush of the purchase and thrill of ownership, infatuation, a day trip that knife lovers hope will never end, a high in the middle of the afternoon.

In the ever-changing, constantly evolving world of custom, handmade knives, newness has become a working standard. Each year, within the pages of the *KNIVES Annual* book, new trends are revealed, materials exposed for the first time, and patterns and prowess debuted in full color. The glossy pages of the *KNIVES* book have been rubbed dull, dogeared, torn and tattered over the past 41 years. Wish lists were made, dreams born, promises made and ideas birthed. Some have bought knives they drooled over, others failed to acquire the funds and still more lost interest or moved on. Wives have been made aware of what husbands want for Christmas, birthdays, Father's Days and anniversaries.

The books have survived—40 previous editions of the *KNIVES Annual* residing in collections, on shelves, workbenches, nightstands and tabletops; some dusty, neglected and maybe even forgotten. It's not the writing, editing, layout or design that has made them staples of people's lives, but the handmade knives within—photos of craftsmanship many have aspired to, but few have achieved. The impeccable workmanship, hours of sweat and labor, hand finishing, embellishments and technical wizardry have saved the written tomes from recycling bins and garbage dumps.

The secret is the knives—those that evoke sensations of guilt, pleasure, ecstasy and remorse. The privileged few, keepers of the light and harbingers of secrets and knowledge, have a responsibility to pass it along as they see fit. The feeling is indescribable, as if touched by a higher power, anointed and granted access into a secret society.

Oh, what a feeling! □ *—Joe Kertzman*

2021
WOODEN SWORD AWARD

All images by Jim Cooper,
SharpByCoop.com

This one is for you, Trekkies!
Honestly, it is for every knife lover, because the U.S.S. Enterprise NCC-1701 model from Italian maker Corrado Moro is a special piece.

Corrado wanted to fashion the iconic Starship Enterprise from *Star Trek* in knife form. The model takes inspiration from various versions of the Starship Enterprise, essentially combining the design of the Enterprise NCC-1701-E from the movie *Star Trek: First Contact* and the latest ship from the 2009 franchise reboot by J.J. Abrams.

Trekkies will easily recognize the new style "nacelles" (outer casings of the spacecraft engine) and the old-style disc section combined in the unique knife. The registration number and name of the ship, U.S.S. ENTERPRISE NCC-1701, from the TV series, is also engraved in a few places on the knife.

The unique "Picard Lock" blade-opening and locking system is named in honor of Jean Luc Picard, the captain of the Enterprise portrayed by Sir Patrick Stewart in the *Next Generation* series. A complex hinge system allows the blade to swing open, pivoting over and to the front of the disc. It is then locked in place by four tabs from the side. Two of them lock the blade when it is open and two in the "rest" position (pointing backward). A small brace shaped like the Starfleet logo, between the nacelles, protects the edge and tip. The blade shape is reminiscent of the Starfleet logo in the latest *Star Trek* series.

Speaking of the blade, it is RWL-34 stainless combined with a titanium frame/body of the spaceship, 16 rubies in the nacelles' heads and a blue anodized titanium "shield generator" (hull of the ship). The ship/knife is parked in a special slip/case fashioned from black anodized 6000 aluminum that resembles a photon torpedo and doubles as a stand.

Suffice it to say, the U.S.S. Enterprise NCC-1701 goes boldly where no knife has gone before. □
Joe Kertzman

YOUNGER KNIFE FANS for BALISONGS

Balisongs Were Built For The Era Of Online Videos & Social Media

By David W. Jung

There are certain things that we learn in life, from not playing in traffic to keeping politics away from family gatherings. Throwing sharp knives up in the air certainly seems like it belongs in the list. Yet, that very behavior has been enthusiastically welcomed by attendees at recent BLADE Show and BLADE Show West events in Atlanta and Portland, Oregon, respectively.

While the shows are two of the premier knife events in the world, it quickly becomes apparent that the demographic for balisong fans trends younger than the typical BLADE Show attendee. Attracting a younger crowd that is passionate about knives can be a major plus for our overall knife community.

Who Flips?

It is difficult to categorize the average balisong flipper, in the same way that one would have trouble defining the average knife user. What is apparent from BLADE Show balisong flipping competitions is that newer flippers are far younger than the average knife enthusiast.

The availability of trainers is one reason.

Lucas Cao has taken a passion for flipping balisongs and combined it with his engineering education to create Squid Industries in Fremont, California. Using CNC (computer numerically controlled) machining and hand assembly, the company has hit the sweet spot in the balisong trainer market. *Photo by David W. Jung*

Parents who might not give a child or teen access to a live blade balisong have a hard time arguing against a trainer. Another reason for the influx is the huge numbers of flippers living through social media. Websites like Facebook, Instagram, Reddit and YouTube, as well as online balisong forums, attract young, tech-savvy users. When asked why they started flipping, most flippers point to online videos or seeing a friend with a balisong.

A huge factor that favors balisong skill development among young people is that they have more time to learn. Working a 9-5 job will afford you far less balisong flipping practice than a student with after-school time. If students have friends that also flip, they can work together to learn new tricks. It is the rare work environment that allows time for afternoon balisong flipping.

Another factor that favors youth is hand-eye coordination, which can be better at a young age than for an older beginner. Finger dexterity is important in performing advanced tricks. For better or worse, lack of fear or common sense also favors the young.

Do not think that being over 21 dooms your chance to learn how to flip. The same patience and ability to problem solve can come in handy when learning. Once again, the opportunity to learn with a trainer helps avoid some of the common injuries that come with manipulating a sharp blade. Flipping a balisong is very satisfying and is a great way to control one's desire to fidget. Another crossover hobby that attracts a similar crowd is competitive yo-yo playing, with many enthusiasts doing both. Dexterity and patience factor into each sport.

Flipping a balisong can be as simple as swinging a handle when opening the knife or as complicated as performing a complex aerial ballet. The knife can be tossed into the air only to be caught behind the back or even between the neck and shoulder. In between are twirls, spins, fanning, rollovers and more. Learning tricks is best done through observation and practice.

Watching accomplished flippers in person or through online videos is the best approach. Users are limited only by their imagination and aversion to risk. There can be an adrenaline rush when flipping a balisong, especially a live blade, and for some that is part of the allure.

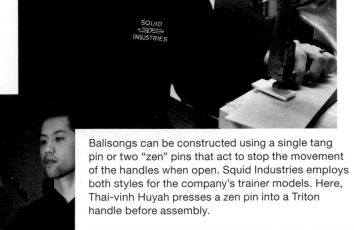

Balisongs can be constructed using a single tang pin or two "zen" pins that act to stop the movement of the handles when open. Squid Industries employs both styles for the company's trainer models. Here, Thai-vinh Huyah presses a zen pin into a Triton handle before assembly.

One of the more difficult balisong flipping maneuvers is the aerial. Flipping the blade into the air and safely catching it is a challenge. Here, Thai-vinh Huyah, who assembles and finetunes Squid Industries balisongs, is performing an aerial with a Krake Raken live blade. *Photo by David W. Jung*

Squid the Kid

Squid Industries, founded in 2016 by Lucas Cao in California, has put an emphasis on trainers without live blades to provide quality balisongs that flip well at a reasonable price point. Widely praised by the online flipper community, Squid balisongs are designed, assembled, tested and tuned by flippers.

Lucas, whose high school nickname inspired the company name, was often asked what flipper he might recommend to enthusiasts. In reply, he'd say there weren't any quality balisongs that were also affordable. Quality balisongs can easily range from $300 to $1,200, which is out of the range of many young flippers. Lucas developed a series of models starting under $100.

The Squiddy series is made up of CNC (computer numerically controlled)-machined balisongs made from CPVC (chlorinated polyvinyl chloride), which is a plastic designed to handle high temperatures and withstand impact without cracking. Because of their construction, balisongs in the Squiddy line are far less likely to damage anything when dropped.

Because Squiddy models are lighter than tradi-

tional balisongs, they are ideal for younger or beginner balisong enthusiasts. Given the lighter designs, don't assume they are not capable models. The balance of each is excellent, and the phosphorus bronze washers allow for one of the best trainers for first-time users or situations where a metal balisong would be unwelcome.

When asked whether a Squiddy would be welcome in schools, Lucas states, "I have heard of kids taking them to science class and having the teacher welcome them, as well as having a kid get in trouble with the front office for having one."

Plainly, it is not recommended that students take balisongs to school. Outside of school situations, Squiddys play nicely, and even though they are kid friendly, many grown-up "kids" flip them as well.

While the Squiddy series consists of entry-level Squids, there are also metal-handle models available. The Squid Industries Mako has a two-piece aluminum handle with optional Cerakote colors and a shark-faced bottle-opener blade. Once again, the balance allows for a good flipping experience in a

The Triton trainer is fashioned from aluminum handles with press-fit zen pins, phosphorus bronze washers and machine screws. The same person who assembles the trainer then flips it to determine function and play controlled by the Loctite®-secured screws. "Tap," which is side-to-side blade and handle play when the knife is closed, is also checked. *Photo by David W. Jung*

Philippines-style balisong manufacture in the United States and elsewhere took off in the 1980s. At top is a Taylor/Seto Manila Folder. The U.S.-based Taylor knife company had this model made in Japan. The middle knife is an early Bali-Song U.S.A. model made in California with a Weehawk-style blade and aluminum handles. Bali-song became Pacific Cutlery, which was reborn as Benchmade in Oregon. On the bottom is a Valor balisong, another imported model sold in the states. *Photo by David W. Jung*

reasonably priced, friendly design.

A step above the Mako is the Triton, featuring machined one-piece aluminum handles and a trainer blade. This allows for a more solid feel and sturdier construction. On the higher end of the spectrum is the Squidtrainer, which was first released in 2016. It has been refined since then and has grooved handles with tighter machining tolerances.

At the top of the line is the Nautilus with aluminum handles and laminated G-10 scales. As the top-of-the-line trainer, it boasts numerous refinements that provide high-end flipper construction and balance. As balisongs for the flipping purist, it should be noted that Squid models don't have latches or clips that would affect balance when flipping.

Squid Industries does make a live-blade knife, which is sold by a vendor outside of California. Originally called the Kraken, the name was changed to Krake Raken. The AEB-L steel blade is

based on an updated Squidtrainer. This allows enthusiasts to enjoy the live-blade experience and carry a Squid as a daily user or as a flipper with "bite." Squid Industries uses a "product drop" marketing model. Each Monday, the company announces online what is available for the week, and enthusiasts quickly buy out the inventory.

The Allure Is In The Design

The balisong, also known as a butterfly knife, is a simple design with two channeled handles and a sharp live blade or dull trainer blade. The base of the blade is attached by rivets or pins to pivoting handles, allowing sharpened steel to swing out to the open position or closed into the channeled grips.

If you can imagine how most multi-tools open, you can visualize how a balisong operates. The "bite-side" handle faces the sharpened blade side, while the "safe side" is adjacent to the dull spine. There are a few balisongs with double-edged blades, making for interesting collectables that are frightening to flip. With users often bouncing the dull spines off fingers in performing tricks, and if there are no dull spines, well, you get the picture.

In use, a balisong blade can be held in the open position by squeezing the handles closed in one's grip or through use of a latch. Usually the latch is on the bite-side handle, though not always. It's a good idea to check before you flip. Many balisongs do not have a latch, as it can affect the balance of the knife when flipping. When the balisong is carried for everyday use, the latch helps to keep the knife closed.

As with any knife, there is a wide range of

quality and materials that determine how well a balisong functions. There are imported trainers that are inexpensive and feel like it. Unfortunately, many users start with the cheap knives and lose interest due to the poor flipping quality. The best way to get a good balisong is to buy from someone who understands flipping, and the mechanics and physics of the balisong.

A Little Blood Never Hurt Anyone, Right?

It is important to discuss sharpened live blade balisongs versus non-sharp trainer blades. If you flip with a live blade, you *will* inevitably get cut or "bit." Even with experience, cuts will happen, so have a good supply of Band-Aid®s and super glue available. Some users put tape over a live-blade edge to start, but a trainer is a far safer way to begin.

Others argue that the chance of getting cut accelerates the learning curve, and the slight risk accentuates the experience. Still others feel that the safer nature of trainers encourages learning more dramatic tricks without the cautious restraint.

Most flippers who start by using trainer blades transition to live blades if they can, depending on local laws. Enthusiasts often revert to trainers in exploring tricky maneuvers, then switch back to live blades.

Regardless, there's something to be said for the element of danger present in a balisong. Perhaps that's what makes the knife so appealing to younger demographics. If balisongs were risk-free, what would there be to show off?

Contested History

Showing off wasn't how balisongs got their start, though. They were tools. That much is certain. However, less certain is the origin of balisongs. Some French knives dating back to the 1700s exhibited the traditional balisong shape. Enthusiasts in the Philippines claim a much earlier beginning, based on oral history. Perhaps European explorers in the Philippines brought the design over if it was not there already.

Regardless of the origin, the Philippines can proudly take credit for the development of the modern balisong flipping style as we know it. With quickly moving blades and handles, this style has given birth to the contemporary American balisong flipping movement. It should be noted that the style of flipping practiced in the Philippines encourages keeping the knife in a ready-to-use fighting posi-

Learning Tips for Flipping Balisongs

- Know what the laws are where you live. Use a trainer if needed.
- Be aware of small children and pets when flipping.
- Try to practice over carpet rather than concrete. Your knife will thank you.
- Tape up your live blade when starting out or use a trainer blade.
- Always wear shoes. Even experts sometimes drop balisongs.
- If you lose control of the balisong during an aerial trick, step back and let it drop. Don't try to catch the knife.
- Avoid flipping over glass tables, cell phones, flat screens or anything fragile.
- Slow your trick down first and learn it in stages. Assemble the stages later.
- If someone of unknown skill wants to try your knife, hand them a trainer.
- Loctite® is your friend. Balisongs undergo a lot of screw-loosening shocks.
- Learn from others in the balisong community— online forums are great.
- Spending a little more money on a better-quality balisong is a smart choice.
- Be wary of counterfeit balisongs. Know who you are buying from.
- Don't be discouraged when learning. Many tricks take hours of practice.
- Attend flipping competitions at venues like the BLADE Show or BLADE Show West.
- Have a safe place to store and transport your balisongs.
- When you are at a knife show, ask before you pick up and flip a seller's balisong.
- If you flip live blades, have a good first aid kit available. You will get cut.
- Know when and where to flip so you can be a positive image for the community.
- Have fun!

tion. American flipping as practiced competitively includes numerous maneuvers, with sleight of hand manipulation and style favored over a fighting stance.

Numerous balisong-style knives made in Europe and America appeared in cutlery catalogs in the 1900s, and Western patents date back to the late 1800s. Most were not designed for rapid flipping, but rather as a simple way to construct utility or

There are three basic variations on balisong handle types. At bottom is a Mako trainer exhibiting sandwich construction. Above it, the sliver one-piece channel design is more rigid and has less of a chance of loosening handles and blade. The red Nautilus features one-piece handles and a G-10 laminate for better grip. *Photo by David W. Jung*

hunting knives. From World War II to the Vietnam War, thousands of U.S. soldiers visited or were stationed in the Philippines. As a result, many knives made their way to the United States.

The Filipino knives came handmade from basic roadside workshops with whatever materials happened to be available. Some were crude, while others had high levels of fit and finish. These knives sparked the first wave of balisong enthusiasts in the States. Based on this exposure, American knifemakers and importers began to market balisong knives in the U.S.

Balisongs Hit the United States

In the 1980s, American knife companies such as Taylor and Valor contracted with Japanese manufacturers to bring balisongs to the American market. In 1979, Les de Asis began Bali-Song®, Inc., in California with the assistance of knifemaker Jody Samson, who ground the balisong blades. Mr. Samson developed the Weehawk blade shape in 1980 and was also a bladesmith on numerous Hollywood movies, before passing away in 2009. Bali-Song became Pacific Cutlery, which went out of business. Pacific Cutlery was replaced by Benchmade Knives, founded by de Asis, who relocated the company to Oregon.

If there is a legacy company in the balisong world, it is Benchmade Knife Company. Unlike many of the cheap imported models, the Benchmade balisongs quickly developed a reputation for quality construction and excellent flipping performance. Over the years, they have also earned collectable status, with some old and even newer models selling for thousands of dollars, though most current production models cost much less.

Benchmade still holds a special place on the balisong hierarchy. For the young flipper starting out, Benchmade balisongs score high on Christmas lists.

Other Balisong Businesses

There are many other makers that fill out the balisong market. Custom knifemaker Rick Hinderer and companies such as Bear & Sons Cutlery, Benchmark, Bradley Cutlery, Brous Blades, Cold Steel, Emerson Knives, Kershaw, Microtech, Schrade and Spyderco currently produce or have made or manufactured balisongs in the past.

Among the high-end makers are Blade Runner Systems, also known as BRS, as well as the standard bearer, Benchmade. Some companies sell only live blades, trainers or both, depending on customer demand or state laws and regulations where they are located.

Changing Perceptions About Balisongs

In recent history, automatic knives and balisongs have been targeted as weapons that threaten society with criminal chaos, especially among "troublesome teens." In the 1950s, using Hollywood films as evidence, the automatic, or switchblade, was labeled as a knife favored by gang members. The balisong knife was grouped with switchblades and labeled as a gravity or flick knife that could be opened by centrifugal/centripetal force for quick deployment.

In an ironic twist, those same teens may be playing an integral part in reversing that stigma by building online communities of flippers. It certainly isn't hurting. In recent years, many states have relaxed laws to allow the carry of automatic knives and balisongs. Unfortunately, in some states, even possession in your home is still illegal. The 1958 Federal Switchblade Act remains intact.

For a new, younger generation, balisongs present an exciting hobby that encourages skill and dexterity. Though the roots are from online groups, as these enthusiasts enter the knife community, it is important to welcome and encourage them. It is also critical to keep pressure on government officials to change laws for live blade balisong carry in all locales.

Keeping this fresh enthusiasm alive will benefit the overall knife community. Take a moment to watch a flipping competition and try to flip a balisong today. It's a lot of flipping fun. ☐

HOW MAKERS
DESIGN KNIVES
for
LARGE COMPANIES

By Ryan M. Johnson, RMJ Tactical, LLC

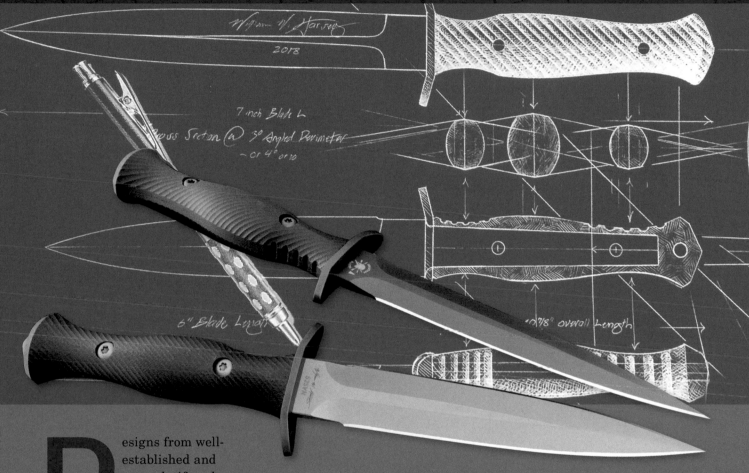

Designs from well-established and newer knifemakers are licensed to large knife companies so that a broad audience can access otherwise exclusive patterns. By bringing custom makers on board, the companies not only tap into proven designs, but also built-in fan bases and audiences that the makers have built up over time. It's easy to assume this process just happens, and new knives appear on shelves like apples on a tree. But how does this really work?

There hasn't been much written on the subject, so I hope to shed a little light here through interviews with three makers and designers I greatly admire: Bill Harsey, Les George and Tom Krein.

Bill Harsey states that the Spartan Blades "Harsey Dagger" is a culmination of 40 years of attempted knife design and a lot of paying attention. Note the detail in the original illustrated design.

While their work and designs vary greatly, their core design philosophies have a lot in common. These makers are some of the best in the business.

What do you draw on for inspiration?

Bill Harsey
It's a combination of a desire to make knives, a love of the outdoors and wanting to have something on

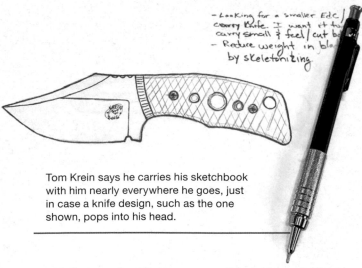

- Looking for a smaller Edc carry knife. I want it to carry small & feel / cut b...
- Reduce weight in bla... by skeletonizing

Tom Krein says he carries his sketchbook with him nearly everywhere he goes, just in case a knife design, such as the one shown, pops into his head.

me that works. Knives were a kind of magic thing when I was young; they were how stuff got done when fishing or hunting, and such tools included an axe when logging in the Oregon woods.

This evolved into a great respect for people, especially in the military and emergency services, who may need knives in critical situations. This has inspired me to try harder.

Les George

Sometimes I will think of a character from TV or a movie and try to design the knife that person would want to have on them. For example, Vin Diesel as a space marine is going to need a much different knife than Tommy Lee Jones as an FBI hostage negotiator. Ken Onion shared that technique with me years ago.

What I really like to do is take an old design from 70 or 80 years ago, research it all the way to the ground and try to uncover the intent the maker had back then. I refocus it through a lens of the ensuing three-quarters of a century that includes manufacturing technology and new materials. The V14 that I designed for Spartan Blades is a great example of that.

Tom Krein

Inspiration is one of those things that is not always 100 percent conscious. I feel like there is more than a little that is subconscious. We note things here and there that we like and then are influenced. I am what I would consider a very function-oriented designer. I think of a task or knife use and then envision myself doing that task.

Where do you come up with most of your designs?

Harsey

Most of my designs begin on the drafting table in the knifemaking shop. Certainly, that's where the work of further refinement happens when what I'm working on is brought into focus. I have always traveled with some form of small drawing book to make notes and sketches of concepts or parts of concepts. The belt grinder is not a good place to design knives, and cocktail napkin drawings are always suspect.

George

I will usually get an idea and roll it around in my head until I can't stand it anymore, and it must get out. This is a 24/7 kind of thing.

Krein

For me, personally, I have tended to design where I was. Inspiration is a strange thing. Sometimes everything I draw resonates with me, and other times I can't get an idea onto paper. In the past, it's hot or cold. Recently, I rearranged my office with a designated design area. I'm trying to train myself to design daily. I still carry my design journal pretty much everywhere I go, though, you know, just in case!

What is the process for how you design?

Harsey

I work with pencil in a drawing book.

George

These days, I will either start out with a paper sketch and bring it into a CAD (Computer Aided Design,

Les George's M3 model exhibits detail in design and execution.

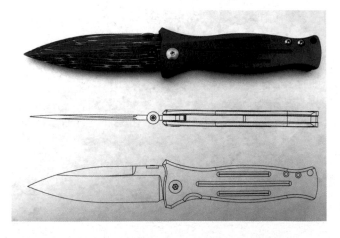

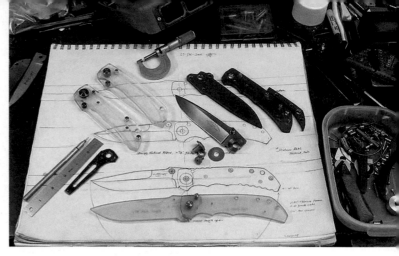

Plexiglas and steel prototypes lie atop original drawings of the Bill Harsey "Bench" knife.

SolidWorks) program, drawing over it with CAD and refining it from there, or sometimes I take an existing knife CAD drawing and start modifying it.

Krein

My design process is pretty low-tech. I think about it until I get the concept in mind and then I take it to paper. I do have some specifics, though. I must have a .5 mm mechanical pencil and an eraser. I am a sketch and refine designer. It can take days to get a design to where I'm happy with it, and some concepts never make it.

The Advocate is a design that I had in my mind for over a year before I was able to get it on paper to the point where I was happy with it.

How do you prototype a design?

Harsey

From a drawing, I transition to a hand-cut and shaped polycarbonate plastic like Lexan for a master pattern template. If the concept is holding up, then I hand build a working prototype with properly heat-treated parts. Prototypes should always be properly heat treated because someone will always have to test the prototype.

I believe in hand making a knife while designing for industry because we are making tools to be handheld. I learn things this way that I wouldn't on a computer screen.

When working with knife manufacturers, after we agree on a design, then the knife concept is sent to engineers who begin the CAD process with my continual review and oversight as part of the normal process.

I'm lucky to work with highly skilled folks who are good at what they do.

George

I love my CO_2 laser. With this, I can cut out plastic or wood mock-ups, and in the case of a folder, I can screw all the parts together and get a great idea of how the knife will work in metal. This is very useful for me, since I tend to misjudge the size of things on the computer screen. With a fixed blade, I can check the size and shape; everything but the weight can be determined.

Krein

Usually I get a drawing that I'm happy with, make a copy and then transition to steel. The drawings and prototypes are usually close, but I don't hesitate to make small changes to the steel as I make that first pattern. You are forced to make knives around the capacity of your tools.

Recently I've taken sketches to my CAD guy and had them go straight to the CNC (computer numerically controlled) machine. That was pretty crazy and surreal.

What designs do you look at from the past and admire?

Harsey

The single greatest influence on my work is Bob Loveless, who was so revolutionary in his time. Bob never deviated from his design path.

I was always in awe of whatever multi-blade pocketknife, usually a stockman pattern, my Grandpa Wes Harsey pulled out for any job, even if it was just sharpening a pencil in his cabinetmaking shop. It was *how* he used it that was the important part I remember, and that remains a huge inspiration to me.

George

The more I've studied the designs of the last century, the more I have seen how the makers all built on the work that came before them. I love the World War II knives because of how many different ones were made in those years and how well they did overall.

Krein

I admire pretty much all the classics—Scagel, Randall, Loveless—and so many others. It's extremely difficult to even put a name on them. I may not like the entire design and might take inspiration from a guard or blade shape, etc.

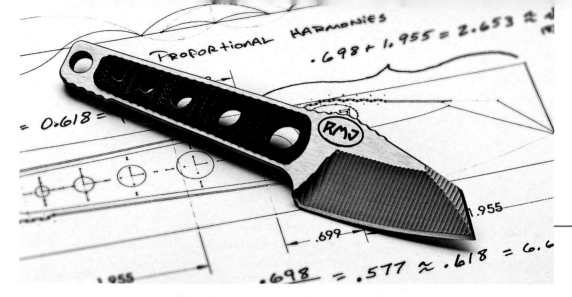

Ryan M. Johnson's "No Bother" knife, produced by CRKT, is a design based off a drawing by his daughter.

What advice do you have for someone interested in designing a knife?

Harsey

If you are designing a knife, it's best to be honest with yourself and ask, "Why am I doing this?" and then work at that. The goal should be to make a knife that works, not just to get attention. Knife designing, for me, is integral with knifemaking because it's tough to understand one without the other.

Learn about tool steels and heat-treating. Don't rely on the flavor of the day on the internet for any of this. Think for yourself.

George

Do not let the desire to be new and unique cloud your vision. Mankind has been making knives for over 5,000 years. If a thing has not been done by now, in some way or shape, you really need to stop and take a second look at it and make sure it hasn't been done because it's a bad idea. I would never try to say that it's all been done or there is no room for something truly new, but all the low hanging fruit has been picked to the bone.

Krein

Don't rush it. Don't try to reinvent the wheel, but don't be a tracer either! Think about the use, and it is helpful if you have used a knife for that task and better if you have used many knives for that task. Experience will tell you what does and doesn't work. One of my early design mantras was "form follows function."

What are the key things to keep in mind when designing a knife?

Harsey

It must function for its intended purpose and be scaled to the type of carry needed. For example, a machete is difficult to wear discreetly with office clothes. A knife needs to have a handle that will not wreck the hand in extensive cutting or be too slippery. Also important is if you can access the knife in complete darkness and know where the edge is just by the feel of the handle.

Choice of steel is important, especially for wet, tropical and/or marine environments. Sheath type is critical for fixed blades, especially for safe carry. The sheaths we provide with knives for military Spec Ops forces are "jump qualified" for airborne operations.

At all times, do the very best you can.

George

This question would take a whole book to answer completely! So instead of that, 30 years ago, if you wanted to see knives, you had to go to where they were, either a show or a store. Outside of mail order catalogs and magazines, this was the way, and you ended up putting knives in your hand, and the ones that stood out looked *and* felt good!

The tactile response is missing in a lot of knife interactions in this day of social media bombardments, so we try to stand out and visually stop people in their tracks, or at least stop scrolling and notice us.

Just do not let the desire to have visual impact detract from the core functionality of the knife.

Krein

Safety and comfort—think about how a knife will be carried/sheathed. What tasks will it be used for? Also keep in mind material and tooling constraints.

Which design of yours is your favorite?

Harsey

That's a tough one to answer, but the Pacific model fashioned for the 1st Special Forces Group Airborne and the Difensa for the Canadian Special Operations Regiment would be high on the list. The Yarborough might be top of class because of the honor it was to work with Chris Reeve Knives on that piece, which was designed for our Special Forces (Green Beret) soldiers.

The folding knife I hand-built for my son, who is currently a senior engineer at SpaceX, might just be most important to me. This pattern became the Impinda by Chris Reeve Knives.

The Spartan Harsey dagger is the result of my now 40 years of attempting to work at this stuff and trying to pay attention. This might be my other top favorite.

George

I like my Rockeye design the best. I love that it's simple and scalable. I have made variations with blades from 2.6 to 7.5 inches long. It's the first design that I licensed to a factory (Pro-Tech) and my first mid-tech design in the form of the VECP.

Krein

Probably my TK-1 Necker—I feel it was the start of my niche (small fixed blades). It's a design that has endured, and it's a *very big* small knife, a strange dichotomy that simply works.

What is expected of a knife designer in the industry?

Harsey

Make a company money.

George

The industry expects us to do good work. The companies I work with expect the same. It also helps to be able to communicate your design intent and ideas to the companies and customers. Companies expect you to communicate and deal with them in a timely, professional manner.

You will no doubt note how many times I mention communication. It is the hardest thing we do as human beings. When a company I am working with asks me for something, an idea to fix a problem, whatever it is, I try to do it right then and to send them three ideas if they asked for one. I try to be so "johnny on the spot" that if it's the eleventh hour

Bill Harsey says it was an honor to work with Chris Reeve Knives on the Yarborough, designed for and carried by Special Forces (Green Beret) soldiers. The prototype and drawings are shown.

and they need one more design right now, it just pops into their head to get it from me since I am so easy to work with.

Krein

After many years, I'm not sure I honestly know. I've had many conversations with different people from the companies I design for, and honestly, I'm not sure they know either. I think that is one of the most confusing things about trying to design for production companies.

What do you see is the biggest misconception about knife designing?

Harsey

That it's easy or not that important.

George

The biggest misconception I had when designing my own custom knives was thinking I was better than I was. It's easy for a popular knifemaker to build a knife that seems like it sells well, so it must be a great design. But a quality knife with, well, let's just call it a disjointed design, may sell very well in custom knife quantities, but not necessarily in production numbers necessary for it to be successful.

When you move into a marketplace where the knives are executed in a similar way, design is the only real separation, especially to the non-knife geeks. When your design needs to sell in the thousands versus dozens, you really start to get a feel for what matters.

Krein

Even if you have a working relationship with a company that will take your knife designs, it's a continual push and a lot of work to keep submitting ideas or patterns. Another misconception is the timeframe. These big companies tend to move very slowly. It can easily take two or three years for an approved project to happen.

What these makers don't say in their interviews

Bill Harsey indicates that the folding knife he hand-built for his son, who is currently a senior engineer at SpaceX, might just be most important to the maker. This pattern became the Impinda by Chis Reeve Knives.

The Shrike S13 tomahawk is one of Ryan M. Johnson's popular designs.

is that they all mentor and help other makers become excellent designers in their own rights. We are lucky that the knife industry helps their own.

As the years pass, hopefully new generations of designers will look back at classic models like the Difensa, Rockeye and TK-1, drawing inspiration for future knife designs and collaborations. □

Bill Harsey is a legend in the knife industry. He has designed for just about every company, but his most current work has been with Spartan Blades, Chris Reeves Knives and CRKT.

Les George is a former Marine EOD (Explosive Ordnance Disposal) tech turned knifemaker. He has a special knack for blending World War II-era blades with CNC technology to combine the best of both worlds. He designs for Kershaw, Pro-Tech and Spartan Blades.

Tom Krein is a knifemaker's knifemaker. A master at traditional knifemaking skills, he incorporates classic concepts into contemporary designs. He has designed for CRKT and Boker.

The author, Ryan Johnson, is the CEO of RMJ USA and builds custom tomahawks and knives at his Gold Point Forge shop. He designs for RMJ USA and CRKT.

Where Have the BLUE-CHIP MAKERS GONE?

There might be more out there than apparent if an investor knows where to look

By Les Robertson

R ecently, at a show, a group of collectors, makers and other individuals familiar with the industry were discussing the current state of the custom knife market. The question was posed, "What happened to all the blue-chip knifemakers?" The individual was inquiring about makers whose knives collectors and other enthusiasts can rely on to be solid investments, almost assured of making money should they decide to sell the work one day.

Have the blue-chip makers disappeared? The argument can be made that a trip to the Art Knife Invitational, held every two years in San Diego, would put a collector in a room full of blue-chip makers.

Most custom knives are made and bought with little or no thought given toward investment potential. Collectors collect. Collectors buy what they like, and for many of them, there are no such things as "investment-grade" knives.

Many makers start fashioning knives after handling one or more custom pieces and thinking to themselves, "I could make that" or "I could do better than this." A common trait among blue-chip makers is they think outside the box. Their craftsmanship goes beyond just building a knife. Often it is combining and creating new design elements or utilizing fresh materials and techniques to create knives that catch the eye. They create their own style that is easily recognizable as theirs.

Bill Ruple has positioned himself as one of the premier slip-joint makers in the world. Constant improvement and value pricing have increased his demand.

For a maker to create knives that appreciate monetarily, he or she must master the craftsmanship and business sides of the custom knife market. Certainly, supply and demand will help investment potential, but ultimately the maker's ability to create "buzz" about his or her knives is what creates a demand that is essential to success. The blue-chip status is achieved by the investment success of those who purchased their knives.

What separates the collector from the investor? Due diligence.

In the investment world, the term "due diligence" is defined as a comprehensive appraisal of a business undertaken by a prospective buyer, especially to establish its assets and liabilities and evaluate its commercial potential.

Doing Due Diligence

The prospective buyer is the collector. The business is that of the custom knifemaker. The homework of the buyer or collector is establishing the assets and liabilities of the knife before purchasing it. The mindset of the collector differs from that of the investor. Most collectors want to enjoy their hobby without the analysis that an investor would use.

The same can be said for most knifemakers. First and foremost, they enjoy creating knives.

In both scenarios, neither the collector nor the maker gives much thought to the investment potential of their knives. Most collectors do not expect knives they purchase to hold their value. Investors differ, as they expect a return on investment (ROI), thus why they do their homework.

There is an old axiom: you pay to go to school. While you may not realize it, every time you buy a custom knife, you have just written a tuition check. Did you buy the knife because you liked the looks, materials or maker? Were you influenced by the hype surrounding this maker or materials? Or did you do your homework?

Print and social media provide a wealth of information. Perhaps the greatest ally of the collector today is the internet. Searches can provide a collector with insight into makers and their knives, and thus a competitive edge when investing. No matter the source, I would caution collectors to research the standing and experience of so-called experts and do their due diligence.

What are the homework topics collectors should concentrate on? While there are many areas to investigate, I would start with researching a maker's position in the custom knife market and his or her pricing.

A knifemaker's position in the market is not always obvious. Early on, when I was primarily a collector, I noticed (after spending several thousand dollars) that just about every knife I bought and later sold lost money. Confused as to why this was happening, since I did a lot of homework, I realized that what I thought was homework turned out to

American Bladesmith Society (ABS) journeyman smith Josh Fisher combines quality, design elements and variety of materials, all at a value price!

As well as any journeyman smith in the world, Wess Barnhill's knives display the "Four F's" of fit, finish function and flow.

be picking my next favorite knife and not which knife would hold its value or even increase in value.

I was not then, nor am I now, one of those who believe custom knives should lose money. This inspired me to create what I called "Robertson's Maker Market Matrix" (RM3). I compared every maker who was in the *KNIVES 1992* book to other makers working in a similar category. They were then analyzed by variables I chose. Variables included materials, design elements, skills, reputation, price, etc. It was then that patterns and strata started to form in my market matrix. This matrix broke the makers into the top, middle and bottom thirds within a market.

Appropriate Pricing by Level

Important note: There is nothing wrong with buying a knife from a maker who is in the second or even third level *if the piece is priced appropriately for that level*. A third-level knife should not be priced the same as a first-level piece. If it is, then you must have the wherewithal to recognize that it is overpriced.

If your collection is comprised of knives from one market sector, you are probably familiar with the top three-to-five makers in that segment. While their knives may be sought after, their prices are likely at the top tier of the market. These artisans may or may not be blue-chip knifemakers. What is the maker doing to increase demand for his or her work? Is the aftermarket doing its part to keep the demand high?

Pricing is difficult. Often, new knifemakers rely on established craftsmen and women to give them pricing guidance. Others merely look at similar knives built by fellow makers and then estimate what theirs should sell for.

ABS journeyman smith Michael Deibert takes feather-pattern damascus to the next level. All his knives exhibit excellent craftsmanship and outside-the-box thinking at a value price.

This is exactly why it's incumbent upon the investor to know the maker's position in the market. Most collectors don't know the maker's position in the market. Subsequently, they often overpay for a knife. This doesn't become apparent until they enter the aftermarket

Knowing the maker's position in a market segment helps in understanding what his or her knife prices should be, even if they don't. This is where the collector and investor part ways. An investor looking at a potential blue-chip maker will know if the price is indicative of the current market and possibly the aftermarket. The investor has a higher degree of sensitivity to the maker's current status.

Understanding what variables are affecting a maker, positively or negatively, allows an investor to make a more informed decision based on facts and not the hype of the day. Determining a maker's position in the market provides the investor with the ability to judge if the knives are value priced. The ability to do this may encourage an investor to create his or her own matrix. In doing so, it is amazing how quickly a collector can determine investment potential and the possibility of a future blue-chip maker.

One variable that must be taken into consideration is the cyclical nature of custom knives. Imagine a circle with a line through it. Above the line are the words "fixed blades," and below the line, "folding knives." Within that circle are smaller circles that include "trends," "hot makers," "the latest and greatest steel," etc.

In 1993, a new category of knives appeared and took the custom knife world by storm. These were called tactical folders. They remained hot until 1999. In 2000, fixed blades, predominately forged blades, got hot. By 2010, they had given way to tactical folders again. In 2020, we find that fixed blades are now in more demand.

Cycles are an important variable for potential investment. Each of these cycles had three things in common:

1. Initially, the knives were inexpensive and plentiful.
2. As more collectors came into the market sector, demand for certain makers' knives rose, allowing collectors to sell them at a profit, sometimes a large profit. As the knives from these makers became more difficult to obtain, it opened the door for more makers and collectors buying their knives, all hoping to repeat previous successes.
3. Increased demand led to escalating prices. Many of the collectors did not recognize the signs of a maturing market, leaving them with knives they overpaid for and putting them in a position that hurt their chances of achieving an ROI.

Those who do not learn from history are doomed to repeat it. Yet, investors who chose to incorporate value pricing exited the overpriced market at the right time, selling their knives for a profit and looking for the next investment opportunity.

There is short- and long-term investing. Custom knives are best for short-term investing. This can help avoid cycles (unless you are coming in at the end, but your value pricing matrix should not allow you to do that). This can also help you to take advantage of or avoid trends. Short term can be anywhere from immediate re-sale to two or three years after purchase. During the last tactical folder cycle, knives would be bought from the maker, usually via lottery, then sold immediately to a collector who was not chosen in the lottery at a profit.

This led to collectors being shut out of that market sector. I have always stated that "collectors want to collect," meaning they want to add to their collections. If they can't participate in a market, they will turn their collectors' eyes to another style, leaving the bloated (prices) behind for knives that are priced on the maker's position in the market and not the hyped-up aftermarket.

Selling for a profit has its own set of nuances. As a custom knife investor, it is vital to buy the knife at the right price. Just as important is to know when it is time to sell the knife. The primary market is where you purchase directly from the maker. The aftermarket is when you purchase a previously owned custom knife. Utilizing the essential information available in the aftermarket is key to successful sales, as the aftermarket is where you will sell your knife.

The internet is an excellent place for anyone to track trends and identify strong performers. Internet sites are best used to identify knives and makers for a short-term ROI. However, searches allow you to go back for years. You can track how makers did with previous styles of knives over the years, helping you analyze not only the demand for their knives, but also which ones sold at the highest prices. This is the type of knowledge that can pay off big when working in niche markets.

Determine what percentage of the initial knife price is your ideal ROI. Once you do that, there is room for short- and long-term investment gains among knives.

Quick Flips

With the help of forums and social media, many investors are inclined to post knife images and information on their favorite sites and let the bidding begin. Short-term investing is a tempting proposition. As trends of the day move, it can be easier to cherry pick the more in-demand makers or knives. If the collector can get a custom knife directly from the market leader, it can be flipped for a quick profit. In investment circles, this is referred to as the time value of money. Getting back an initial investment and a small profit allows a collector to reinvest quickly and hopefully with the same results.

The long-term investment is usually what you hear about. The stories are out there for all to see or read. A collector bought the "famous maker's knife"

R.J. Martin has secured his position as one the best and most sought-after tactical folder makers in the world, partly due to the value pricing he has utilized over the last 30 years.

ABS master smith Russ Andrew's work is clean, precise and flawless. The author says he's worked with Russ for 18 years and has found his work to be value priced.

when he or she was a newcomer in the market. The maker became a legend and his or her custom knives now sell for several times more than they initially did. Generally, these custom knives have been held for 20-plus years.

Having set your ROI percentage, could you have sold these knives in the short term instead of holding onto them for decades and continued to buy more as opportunities presented themselves? Over 20-plus years, would you have made more money? It is interesting to contemplate which would have been a better investment strategy. Keep in mind, you don't hear the stories that most custom knives are worth significantly less 20-plus years later than they originally cost.

Any market experiences internal and external pressure, causing what appears to be the truth changing. Paying attention to the totality of the market will make your decisions of when to buy and sell easier, and this, in turn, will help to maximize your ROI.

Falling in love with a knife can cause you to miss an opportunity to sell, and that can be costly. At this point, you have two choices: hold onto the knife and hope the market for this maker returns; or realize you wrote another tuition check, sell the knife, take the loss and try not to make the same mistake again.

Budding Blue-Chip Maker

Knife artisans can get hot seemingly overnight and appear to be on the path to becoming blue-chip makers. Then, just as quickly, the once hot maker is no longer in demand. The truth as everyone knew it months ago has changed. At what point does the knife from the blue-chip maker stop being a blue-chip knife?

Becoming a budding blue-chip maker has its hazards. Raising prices too quickly, extending delivery times and missing them, attending fewer shows with less knives and limiting the buyer's ability to purchase a knife will open the door for competitors to gain clients. The aftermarket can sound the final death knell if a maker finds his or her knives selling for less than their current retail price.

Conversely, utilizing due diligence can lead you to the next blue-chip maker, allowing you to purchase a knife that can be looked at as a short- or long-term investment.

Final Thoughts

The practices of investing in and collecting custom knives don't have to be mutually exclusive. They can work hand in hand to develop a collection that, over time, becomes a sound investment. For those of us who collect knives, we know the joy of each addition to our collection. Now imagine that each knife you purchase, at a minimum, holds its value with the potential for a return on your investment.

ABS master smith Steve Randall's knives embody the epitome of value pricing.

An ABS journeyman smith, Shawn Ellis continues to evolve and diversify, providing his clients options most makers don't offer.

Buying what you like should influence your collection. I would suggest that combining due diligence with your knife purchase adds even more enjoyment to collecting. Buying what you like without doing due diligence can have the opposite effect when it's time to trade or sell the knife. Just because you thought it was an incredible knife does not mean everyone else agrees. You cannot buy what you like and expect the knife to become an investment when you want to sell it.

There are more blue-chip makers than investors realize. Granted, some are in the early or middle stages of being recognized at that level. Most of the legendary blue-chip knives were purchased from makers when they were in the beginning stages of their careers.

The blue-chip makers are out there. Using due diligence will help you identify them and purchase custom knives with the potential for a solid return on investment. □

Urban EDCs
Turn Heads Without Raising Eyebrows

The secret to their popularity is how well they blend into public settings

By Dexter Ewing
All photos by Marty Stanfield Photography

Folding knives are versatile carry pieces. They can be toted daily whether you are a mechanic, carpenter, plumber, police officer, firefighter, emergency medical technician, hunter, hiker, a member of the military or even an office worker in a corporate setting.

In an office, one needs to be careful with the selection of his or her EDC (everyday carry) knife. It's best to remain on the conservative side of things, not wanting to whip out a large tactical flipper folder for opening boxes or mail.

A new class of folding knife has emerged over the past few years that addresses environments such as this. The knives borrow traits that made tactical folders popular and distill them down to small and compact forms for easy carry and unobtrusiveness, particularly when blades are opened in public settings.

Urban EDC knives are easy to acquire and use once an enthusiast becomes familiar with the features and quality pieces available on the market. The knives blend in well in the office, but also have substance for tackling tough cutting chores. They are equally at home in a pair of dress slacks or jeans and can perform most daily cutting tasks.

Four modern Urban EDCs include, from top to bottom, the Rick Hinderer Knives XM Slippy, Zero Tolerance 0230, Enrique Pena Front Flipper Barlow and Quiet Carry IQ frame-lock folder.

Quiet Carry Lives Up to Its Name

Quiet Carry is a new knife brand that embodies the urban EDC trend. The company's IQ frame-lock folder is a slender and compact model that carries so easily, one's apt to forget it's there. The blade of the IQ is ground from ELMAX stainless steel and is a user-friendly sheepsfoot shape. Measuring 2.9 inches, the blade is just long enough to be compact and pocket-friendly but sports enough length to get work done.

Slight Belly

The IQ puts a unique spin on the tried-and-true sheepsfoot blade shape with the inclusion of a slight belly. Typically, sheepsfoot blades have straight-line edges, making them precise utility cutters. The slight belly of the IQ allows the knife to be an effective slicer even with the handle held at an upward angle when cutting media on a bench or tabletop.

The blade nests fully inside the handle in the closed position and is opened via a flipper. A small flipper tab protrudes from the end of the handle, with the blade riding on ceramic caged bearings to promote ultra-smooth rotation. The handle is 6AL-4V titanium, and the folder includes a travel limiter that prevents the lock bar from being pushed past the blade tang. There is also a steel wear pad on the end of the bar to provide secure steel-on-steel lockup. All these innovations are common to quality tactical frame-lock folders.

A small but sturdy

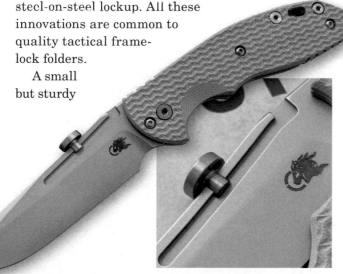

The Rick Hinderer Knives XM Slippy combines tactical folder styling and construction with the convenience of a slip-joint folder. One of the most rugged single-blade, slip-joint folders on the market, it comes with an elongated nail nick and a thumb disk that can be removed via a small hex wrench that's included.

Nick Timpson, who does business as Birdvis Knives, offers up his Lanny's Clip single-blade slip-joint in a variety of handle materials, with superb fit and finish.

titanium clip is attached to the handle of the IQ for tip-up pocket carry. Of deep-carry design, no part of the knife handle remains visible above the seam of a pants pocket. The clip is small but thick and sturdy, with no danger of springing through forced outward pressure while securing it to a pants pocket.

The IQ tested for this article sports a black PVD-coated handle, and the non-lock side has a carbon fiber overlay for a classy touch. Four tiny holes on each side of the handle are aesthetic and serve no functional purpose. Overall, the manufacturing quality of the knife is excellent with fine fit and finish. It is comfortable, thin and carries well, but those with large hands might consider it a bit awkward to use with little girth to the grip.

Regardless, the unique sheepsfoot blade makes this knife a workhorse. With its low profile, the IQ is a great candidate for an office carry piece and equally comfortable in a pair of jeans. It will slice cardboard, strip wire and cut webbing with ease. Don't let its slender profile fool you, this knife is built for work. The manufacturer's suggested retail price (MSRP) as of this writing is $198 for the black PVD-coated handle/carbon fiber overlay version, and $182 for a bead-blasted titanium handle piece. Orders can be placed through the company's website at quietcarry.com.

Front Flipper Barlow

Enrique Pena from Laredo, Texas, is one of the hottest custom knifemakers working today. Specializing in folding knives of the lock-blade variety, Pena's style merges the traditional with modern flair. Case in point, his Front Flipper Barlow looks like an average traditional folder, parading a 3-inch, modified clip-point blade and a substantial handle that fills the hand comfortably. Barlows are work knives, ideal for utilitarian knife chores.

Yet Pena's version showcases top-of-the-line materials all around. The blade is premium CPM-154 stainless steel for edge-holding power. When closed, the tang protrudes slightly and features deep finger notches. The design allows for thumb motion, like that in actuating a Bic lighter, to be used on the exposed tang, rolling it and causing the blade to rotate and snap into the open and locked position. The blade rides smoothly on caged ball bearings in the pivot area. The result is ultra-smooth action that needs to be experienced.

Pena offers the Barlow in an OD green handle with tan Micarta® single bolsters. Black titanium liners lend the knife some class and delineate the green and tan Micarta®. A propeller shield is a traditional touch on an otherwise modern piece. A LinerLock secures the blade in the open position, and a tan Micarta® handle spacer rounds out the handsome good looks.

The Front Flipper Barlow is a hot seller from a popular maker. The piece showcases Pena's eye for detail and superb craftsmanship. One of the things I liked was the ease of deploying the blade. With the average flipper folder, the opening tab protrudes from the bottom of the tang. Pena's flipper adopts a low profile with nothing protruding to disrupt the classic lines of the knife. And unlike classic flat-sided Barlows, contoured handle scales are palpably comfortable. A little over a half-inch wide, the knife naturally nestles in the user's palm.

The contoured handle scales also ride better in a pants pocket, making it feel less bulky and therefore more comfortable to carry. In this modern era of pocket clips, it's refreshing to see a knife that slides into a pants pocket for traditional carry. I found the front-flipper Barlow to be a pleasing intersection of the old (Barlow pattern) and new (one-hand flipper opening mechanism and Liner-Lock). Quick to deploy, the clip-point blade is utilitarian with a tip that can be used for cutting or scoring, and a bit of belly for slicing and cutting easily through any material.

Pena's custom Barlow adds flash and panache to a traditional design, as well as high utility

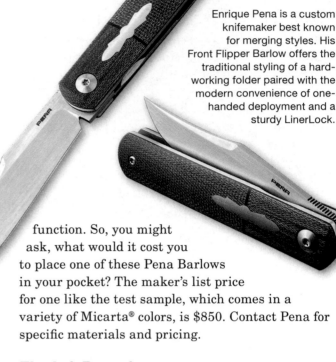

Enrique Pena is a custom knifemaker best known for merging styles. His Front Flipper Barlow offers the traditional styling of a hard-working folder paired with the modern convenience of one-handed deployment and a sturdy LinerLock.

function. So, you might ask, what would it cost you to place one of these Pena Barlows in your pocket? The maker's list price for one like the test sample, which comes in a variety of Micarta® colors, is $850. Contact Pena for specific materials and pricing.

Flash & Panache

The XM-18 has been the signature and best-selling folder line for Rick Hinderer Knives. Knife enthusiasts everywhere have come to describe the XM-18 with adjectives such as "overbuilt," "rugged," "built like a tank" and other descriptive terms that denote rock-solid engineering. Offering the XM-18 in several sizes, Hinderer also designed a slip-joint version—the XM Slippy.

The Quiet Carry IQ folder combines sleek styling with one-handed opening, a frame lock and high-performance blade steel. The knife's ultra-slim and compact form allows it to blend in easily and carry well in jeans or slacks.

Zero Tolerance's first slip-joint folder, the ZT 0230 is designed by Danish knifemaker Jens Anso with advanced materials like carbon fiber and CPM 20CV stainless steel, giving it a high-tech edge.

The XM Slippy takes the concept of a non-locking, slip-joint folder and gives it the same rugged, built-tough treatment that is a hallmark of the series.

Currently offered in 3-inch CPM-20CV stainless steel sheepsfoot and Spanto (Hinderer's own reinforced blade shape) versions, the ergonomic handle features 3-D-machined G-10 scales for a solid grip. Color choices include black, blue, gray, red and OD green, and Hinderer sent me a gray-handle XM Slippy with a sheepsfoot blade. Getting it in hand, I was immediately impressed by the excellent quality of the build. Everything fits together nicely, and the blade's action is smooth. A heavy-duty titanium pocket clip is easily mounted to either side of the handle for ambidextrous tip-up or tip-down carry.

For all intents and purposes, the Slippy looks much like the rest of the Rick Hinderer XM-18 models. Two options for blade deployment include pulling it open manually using a long nail nick like other slip-joint folders or via a thumb disc, the latter of which can be attached or detached from the blade spine using an included Allen wrench. Once open, there is more than enough spring pressure on the blade to secure it during use.

Which blade shape is for you? For general, all-around use, it's hard to beat the Spanto—a shape conducive to many uses with a reinforced tip that adds strength to the blade. The sheepsfoot is more of a working blade shape, something you can use on a job site stripping wires, opening packages and for other cutting tasks that come up. Overall, the Rick Hinderer Knives XM Slippy looks like a tactical knife, but upon closer inspection is an urban EDC for folks who will put the knife to work without hesitation about its durability over the long run. Be sure to check out the XM Slippy. Its MSRP: $275.

Wolf in Sheep's Clothing

The Zero Tolerance 0230 is a wolf in sheep's clothing. Slender and lightweight, it sports a 3-inch CPM-20CV stainless steel sheepsfoot blade and an extremely lightweight, durable, all-weather carbon fiber handle. Best known for high-end tactical folders, Zero Tolerance offers the 0230 slip-joint in high-tech materials and a no-nonsense working knife configuration.

Designed by Jens Anso, a popular custom maker from Denmark, the straight edge of the sheepsfoot blade is easy to sharpen and the blunt nose is non-threatening and eliminates accidental punctures. Instead of a traditional back spring, the 0230 slip-joint folder employs a special double ball-bearing detent system. Much like the ball bearing detents of LinerLock or frame-lock folders, the double detent system not only holds the blade closed, but also secures it in the open position. It does not lock the blade, but rather holds it open.

Cutting force is applied in the opposite direction from which the blade rotates, so regardless how hard you bear down on the blade, it should never accidentally close. Like traditional slip-joint folders, a half-stop pauses the blade when it's partially open, allowing the user to index and manipulate the blade without necessarily having to look at it.

In use, the 0230 is a capable cutter. The sheepsfoot blade is a great pull-cut tool and wire stripper that would make a fine companion on home improvement projects. It has no bulk in the pocket and carries exceptionally well. The only problem is that you may forget you even have it! The carbon fiber handle gives it a cool, futuristic look, and a blue anodized aluminum spacer adds a nice touch of color. If you are a fan of ZT knives, the 0230 will make a great old-school addition to your collection. Certainly, this knife will not disappoint. Available now through ZT dealers, the MSRP is $180.

Don't Stop Here

Urban EDC folders pair low-profile characteristics with modern materials and mechanisms, making them the perfect daily companions, particularly in office or corporate environments. Less bulky than tactical folders, urban EDCs are ideal for everyday carry and blend into any scenario. Having proper tools is a must for those who are serious about tackling daily tasks at home or in the office. □

How Knifemakers Develop Their
Signature Styles

Is style an accident, something intentional or a little of both?

By Kevin Cashen

When asked if I'd be interested in writing an article on how a knifemaker develops a signature style, I was initially a bit intimidated by a subject so far removed from my usual technical treatises.

However, having just finished a series of talks on elements of knife design, and reflecting on 25 years of wrestling with the concept of my responsibilities in the American Bladesmith Society, I found the idea of dissecting the topic rather intriguing.

Style is a commonly applied word in the custom knife business. Every maker is determined to have one, or believes they already do. But what is this elusive concept we call a "style?" Why do some individuals develop one that is so easily recognizable while others never really establish the same level of uniqueness in their knives?

Can a signature style be intentionally fashioned or is it something that must be recognized, if not almost conferred, by others who see a certain quality in a maker's work?

Most people are familiar with general definitions given for style in the dictionary, such as "a distinctive manner or technique by which something is done or created" or "a fashionable elegance, an effortless beauty or grace."

Because of the iconic styles of the knives, many enthusiasts can name the makers of these models by only looking at the silhouettes. Very few knifemakers possess such a strong sense of style.

Many knifemakers accomplish the first—a distinctive manner or technique—in their work, but few incorporate both meanings, combining the first with a fashionable elegance, or an effortless beauty or grace, and this includes makers whose work is admired. In other words, it is not so easy to accomplish a style that has *style*, or a *signature style*.

True Style Persists

We may be tempted to oversimplify a signature style by looking for clues or elements within one's work, such as favorite materials, finishes or treatments. But it is more in how a knifemaker uniquely brings the elements together in a way that is recognizably theirs. Nor can a signature style be confined to a specific genre of knife, as a maker with true style will display it in any piece that's fashioned, be it a hunter, bowie, sword or kitchen knife.

Perhaps it is easier to define style by what it is not. A memorable style is more than a flash in the pan or a transient marketing trend. The field of custom knives can be heavily driven by the fads of the market.

True styles are timeless and are not the result of chasing the fad of the day. Just leaf through the previous editions of this very book and you will clearly see the trends dominating custom knives from year to year. But, throughout it all, you will see makers who deftly ride those waves while never losing their own signature way of doing it.

This is important even if you are the trendsetter, for your achievement can be lost among legions of others rushing to cash in on an ensuing feeding frenzy before it is over. One who claims a fleeting trend as their signature style will not be remembered long in such an environment.

Another reason to separate the knife market from a maker's style is the ease of confusing an ability to sell knives with having an admirable style. It is easy for marketing ability, or marketability, to outshine one's reputation as a craftsman. This is particularly true in the present era of quick social media sales where invaluable feedback from discerning customers and fellow knifemakers who would otherwise handle and closely inspect your work is mostly lost.

Having people amazed at your knife sales, despite the level or quality of work, may seem flattering now, but in the long run, it becomes a stigma rather than a style.

So how does a knifemaker achieve a signature style? After a quarter century of teaching and judging aspiring American Bladesmith Society (ABS) journeyman and master smiths, one learns to recognize makers who are on their way to developing a style and those who are still struggling to work it out.

Ben Breda is one of several makers that the author has watched develop a signature style.
Caleb Royer photo

Such classic knives would include the Olsen Knife Company and Marble's Knives fixed blades shown here.
Jeff Baugher photos

No Beginner's Luck

First, if you have only made a dozen knives, you don't have a style. The sooner a budding knifemaker understands this, the sooner he or she can get on their way to finding it for real. Nobody starts with a style of their own, and it can't happen until the work is good enough to have style. Too many new makers become so fixated on having a style that they do not pay attention to fit, finish or design details that are essential to a good knife.

Some may struggle for years doing things just for the sake of being different before they stumble on a classic design element that they can expand upon, but that can't happen until the work reaches a certain level.

We are often told that we can't judge an applicant's style in the ABS judging room when determining if work is up to the standards of the coveted master and journeyman smith ratings. But poorly made or unfinished work is not a style; it is nothing more than a bad decision to settle for less that will keep a maker from developing a look worthy of being recognized.

The key is not to rush it; style is a classy thing that comes to those with aesthetic tastes and vision, not an affectation forced onto work for its own sake. It happens almost on its own as a result of one's personal way of allowing form to follow function.

A key element of a signature style that a maker's work exhibits is heavily influenced by how their hands manipulate their own tools. A given skill set is, after all, a result of intentionally created habits that can be reproduced without much conscious thought. This probably accounts for the indefinable nature of a maker's style; it is a product of how they work, without even thinking much about it, recorded in their knives.

It is why, when holding the work of someone with a distinctive style, you feel as though you've gotten to personally know them on some level.

You know a signature style when you see it.

Recognizable Qualities

How do you know when you've finally achieved your own signature style? One could say that a maker has a signature style when they no longer need to mark their blades with tang stamps or maker's marks for the admirable of qualities of their knives to be instantly recognized.

This can be particularly challenging for the maker of everyday working or using knives. In a quality tool, certain design necessities for meeting the pesky demands of actual performance can limit the artistic license in pursuing style. And when one considers that people have been fashioning metal into blades from 5,000 to 7,000 years now, it makes it difficult to come up with something new.

Is there room for new styles, or are we just redoing the same themes again and again?

Writer and founding member of the ABS, B.R. Hughes, has said that it is rare for a maker to have such an undeniable style that their work can be recognized from nothing more than a silhouette. I would agree that it is precious few who have shaped their blades so distinctively that they also shaped our idea of custom knives. One thing that makers who've achieved a signature style seem to have in common, in my own observation, is that it was, and is, easier for them to blaze a trail as a lone pioneer than it was as part of a multitude.

A maker today has their work cut out for them in coming up with a style that will allow him or her to stand out from a large field of craftsmen and women. The Custom Knifemaker Directory in the *KNIVES '81* book listed a little over 300 makers, many with their own unique styles. But the number of custom makers listed in the book you now hold in your hands is around 2,000, all hoping to stand out, not only from their contemporaries, but also from those who came before them, and there are only so many ways to make a knife.

Believe it or not, custom knifemaking has seen a lot of refinement in the last 40 years. The quality of work being done by new makers today would have been unheard of in the past. Along with this comes higher standards and tighter aesthetic expectations that make creating a unique style trickier than it has ever been. One can't just make a different looking knife in hopes of having it accepted as a coveted style.

Ben Breda reinforced this sentiment to me when he said how grateful he was that he got his foot in the door of knifemaking just before the social media- and pop culture-driven explosion of new makers over the past five years. I was interested in Ben's perspective because he is one of the makers that I've had an opportunity to watch develop a style.

As a beginner student in a basic knife class that I taught back in 2012, Ben caught my attention by how he was never in a hurry to move on before getting the details just right on his blade. Two years later, I served as a judge on a panel that gave him the ABS George Peck Award for the best work submitted by a journeyman smith. I had never seen a smith's skills develop so quickly.

Four years later, I was able to recognize Ben's work at a show before I was aware that he had a table there. Observing him obsessively removing every scratch from his still developing work told me that he had what it takes to stand out in today's competitive field.

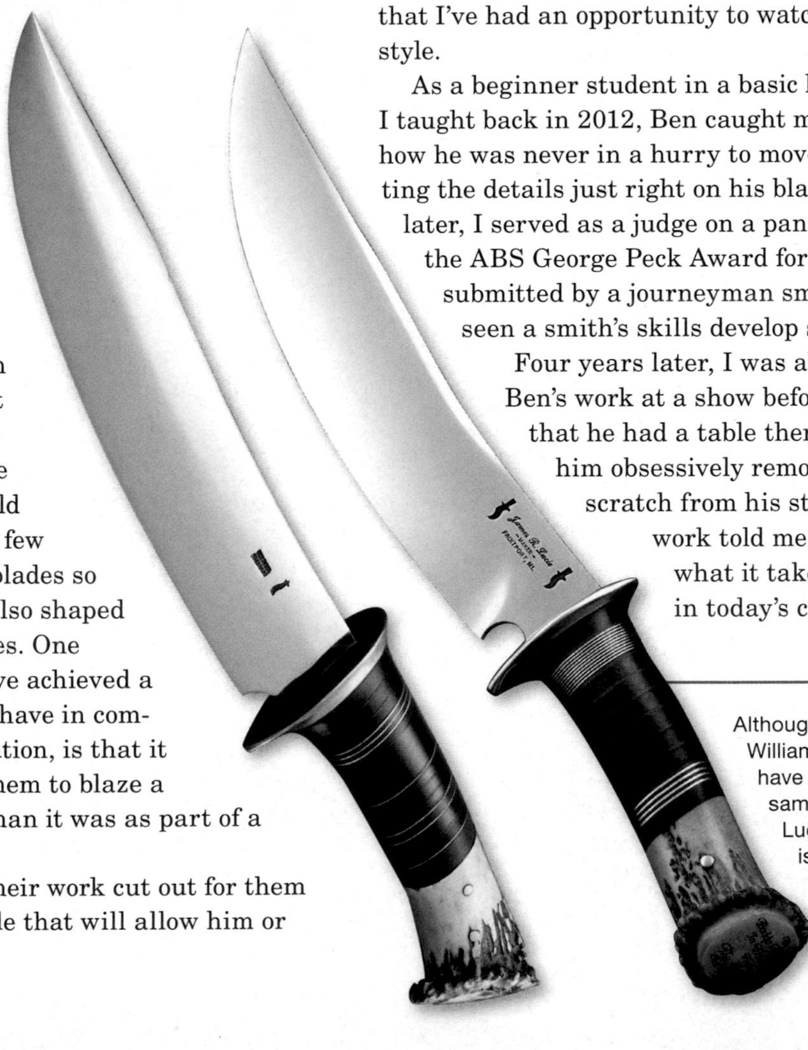

Although many emulate William W. Scagel, none have done it with the same style as Dr. Jim Lucie. A Scagel knife is shown at left with a Lucie piece to its right. *Buddy Thomason photos*

"My style is always evolving. I look at each build when it is done and figure out how I can make small changes that will improve my style," Ben says. "It might be a small detail on the guard or a slight change on the handle sculpting. There are always minor changes, but that's what it takes. It's all in the details."

His sentiments bring up another important point about having a true signature style. A successful style is a driving force that never stagnates or impedes your progression as a maker. It evolves with your skills to highlight an ever-growing quality of workmanship. If, in order to preserve your style, the knives you are making 25 years from now show no progress in the refinement of quality or techniques, that style probably has no *style*. Ben is in no danger of that.

From Homage to Inspiration

It is probably safe to say that any style developed by a knifemaker consists of elements from an already proven design that appealed to him or her in their early development as students of the craft. Even those who take pride in doing their own thing would have to give some credit to classic influences in their evolution as a knifemaker or artist.

Looking back, I can see common elements in my designs that harken back to the first knives that impressed me in my youth. As a child in the woods of Michigan, the home state of so many iconic outdoor blades, feeling the influence of classics like Marble's or Olsen knives was unavoidable. And when my best friend got his hands on a Western W49 Bowie, we used that knife for so many of our outdoor activities that it was ingrained in my mind as the quintessential using blade.

I wasn't aware of how much so until, years later, when I noticed that almost every knife that I made for outdoor use echoed that unmistakable, wide blade belly profile. But does that equate to a style in my work? I hope not, as I have since sought to refine my work by traveling the world to study and pay homage to the styles of true masters from a far more distant and richer past. To this day, I am not sure I am ready to say that I have a style. I feel it is for those who find my work uniquely appealing to decide.

Some makers are so strongly influenced by the iconic work of another that they decide to devote themselves entirely to that already established style. Following the tried and true is one way of assuring you are on the right track, but how does one stand out when your style is literally somebody else's? I guess the answer is by not doing it half-heartedly, or by attempted appropriation, but by honoring the original to such a level that the work takes on a value of its own. In other words, you must do it with style.

The best example of this that I can think of is Dr. Jim Lucie, who so immersed himself in honoring the legacy of William Scagel, from biographical research to using the very tools and materials from the original maker, that the closest you could get to a newly made Scagel knife was a Lucie model.

John Doyle credits ABS master smith Jon Christensen as a mentor, and the influence is seen in his style. At left is a Christensen piece, with a Doyle knife to its right. *Caleb Royer (left) and SharpByCoop photos*

Seeking Guidance

Short of adopting an existing style, the most common way of developing a signature style is still by finding an established maker's work that you admire and seeking guidance until finding a way to craft their influence into something of your own. This is seen most clearly in students from classes who have eerily similar blades to those of their instructors, until they begin developing new and independent skills in their own shops.

This also contributes to the phenomenon of regional styles, as makers learn heavily from the local talent. Some break out on their own, while others may get lost in the familial look. In contrast to this are more geographically separated makers, such as those from other countries, who hit the scene with work that is impossible to ignore and a style solidly their own.

Rather than other parts of the world, some makers come to the knife scene with a fresh look that they bring from another field of artistry. One such maker that quickly comes to my mind is Mardi Meshejian, who brought concepts from his jeweler experience with him when he began making knives. I first saw Mardi's work in the mid 1990s, and it immediately spoke to me as something original.

When I asked Mardi how he so effectively puts his own spin on it, he replied, "I am influenced by a lot of knives from different cultures. I like blending elements from all of them, but I don't feel the need to recreate them as they were originally made. I was never interested in copying a single style because those knives already exist. When I first started, I didn't have any boundaries, so my work was more radical. I just wanted to see what I could make. As I continued and my career progressed, I

Knifemaker Rodrigo Sfreddo's work is another example of how other parts of the world can produce styles loaded with style. *MuzenArt photo*

Mardi Meshejian is one maker who does it his way when it comes to style. *SharpByCoop photo*

Here in the United States, we can't wait to see what the incomparable style of Veronique Laurent will bring us from Belgium. *Caleb Royer photo*

made more conventional knives, but I always mixed influences and brought in non-traditional design elements, materials and color."

Despite the numbers, with something as individual and unique as a handmade knife, it may be inevitable that a maker with patience and creative vision will have a style emerge in their work that is valued by collectors.

A Legacy

But what is it that makes a signature style the goal of so many knifemakers? In the end, perhaps a style is our legacy, something we are remembered for, now or after we are gone. It is what sets us apart while still honoring those who have influenced us. It is taking mankind's oldest and most ubiquitous tool and making it our own in order to tell the world, "I made this." □

THE RESURGENT
BLADE Show West

After a hiatus, the West Coast knife event is back and better than ever

By Mike Haskew

t was well-heeded advice more than 150 years ago when the phrase "Go west young man!" became popular. Hoping to fulfill their destiny, many settlers did indeed set out for the western territory. The rest, as they say, is history.

For the knife industry, encompassing custom and factory knives, it had become apparent by the mid-1990s that there were opportunities out west as well. At the time, Krause Publications owned *BLADE* Magazine, and the associated BLADE Show, an icon among annual events in the industry, was thriving in Atlanta. But there were other opportunities, or so it seemed.

Krause publisher Dave Kowalski identified a pivotal demographic among the attendees of the Atlanta show, one that was cause for concern while at the same time full of potential.

"It began when Krause Publications bought the California Custom Knife Show from Dan and Pam Delavan," *BLADE* editor Steve Shackleford remembers. "Dave Kowalski was instrumental in acquiring the show for Krause. They wanted to bring the BLADE Show to a western audience that did not come to the BLADE Show in Atlanta."

The concept was sound, and so BLADE Show West was born, making an eight-year run in the Los Angeles area from 1996 to 2003 at venues in such locales as Costa Mesa, Irvine and Ontario before relocating to Portland, Oregon, in 2004, and ceasing to exist five years later.

BLADE Magazine staffer Melissa Miller poses with John Dingman of Big John Blades. Dingman garnered the "Best Custom EDC Tool Award" at the 2019 BLADE Show West for his Huntsman Hatchet, which he is holding. *(photo courtesy of Big John Blades)*

From left to right, Adam Drescher of Adam Unlimited, American Bladesmith Society master smith Steve Schwarzer and Larry Hirsch, knife purveyor and owner of Larry's Knives, all familiar faces in the knife industry, pose for a photo during BLADE Show West. *(photo courtesy of Larry Hirsch)*

Kolter Livengood, winner of the 2019 chef's division of the chef's knife cutting competition held during BLADE Show West, displays his dexterity with a suitable kitchen knife and an onion.

A Good Run Ends in 2009

Logically, along with the noble purposes of advancing the knife industry and introducing knives to a new audience, a necessary element of continuing success was to maintain the event's economic viability.

"After all, shows, like magazines, are a business," Shackleford observes. "The number one goal of any business is to stay in business. Bruce Voyles [former owner and publisher of *BLADE* Magazine] told me that once, and I believe he was right. The event brought a taste of the BLADE Show out west all right, and many seemed to enjoy it."

Was that enough to call the show a success?

"Though we made a lot of friends and spread the word about the BLADE Show and *BLADE* magazine to a new audience, since we eventually shut it down after a 10-year-plus run, I guess the answer would have to be 'no,'" Shackleford states frankly. "While the show broke even in terms of revenue, breaking even was not the goal. Making friends, selling knives and supporting the knife industry in that part of the country were all significant accomplishments, but in the end that wasn't enough to keep it going."

External pressure on BLADE Show West did the event in. A global economic downturn obviously had a negative impact on the event as budgets tightened. The Great Recession proved detrimental to many enterprises during those tough times, and that left BLADE Show West suspended after the 2009 event.

This likely didn't surprise too many exhibitors, already battered by a bad economy.

"I attended the 2008 and 2009 shows when they were at the Monarch Hotel in Portland," recalls custom knifemaker Mike Tyre. "It was a smaller show, maybe 50 to 70 tables. It had some great makers exhibiting, and I was lucky enough to have a table next to Wayne Goddard at both shows and absorbed a wealth of knowledge from him. Bruce Bump was another whose work stood above anything I had seen. I enjoyed great sales at the early shows, but attendance was small, and I feel the show was not profitable for management."

A Legacy That Never Went Away

Still, BLADE Show West left something that resonated with participants, a legacy of value that was undeniable. During its decade-plus run, the event attracted some of the greatest luminaries in the history of custom knives, including Goddard, Murray Carter, Bob Loveless, Jason Knight, Jot Singh Khalsa, Herman Schneider, Warren Thomas, Ed Fowler, Bill Herndon, Ron Lake and others.

From the factory side, Columbia River Knife & Tool, Kershaw, Pete Gerber, Tim Leatherman, Sal Glesser and Spyderco, Benchmade, Chris Reeve Knives, Ernest Emerson, Hogue Knives, Medford Knife and Tool, Microtech, SOG, TOPS Knives, White River Knives, We Knife, Work Sharp, Wicked Edge, and more, were regulars. Just gathering these titans of the knife world in the same place for

Custom knifemaking legends Bob Loveless (left) and Wayne Goddard compare notes during an early BLADE Show West event. Knifemaker Bill Herndon stands in the background wearing a yellow apron.

a brief period was of immense value.

BLADE Show West also left an indelible impression on Shackleford when the show took place in October 2001, following the tragedy of 9-11.

"One of the most memorable shows was the one right after 9-11," he relates. "A number of people wanted us to cancel the show because of the terrorist attacks, but we decided to go on with it. I'll never forget the plane ride out. It was a week or two after the attack, and the flight had about 10 passengers, if that many. Riding in that near-empty plane was an eerie feeling."

"However, the show was one of our better ones in the L.A. area," Shackleford qualifies. "It was well attended, and a number of exhibitors and patrons wore American flag t-shirts and armbands."

BLADE Show West Returns

Although it may not have seemed so at the time, when the painful decision was made to discontinue BLADE Show West in 2009, a firm foundation for the future had been laid that later paid off. The management of F+W Media, which acquired Krause in 2002, undertook a reevaluation of the prospects for success with BLADE Show West and revived the enterprise with a new and revitalized format in 2018, the same year that the *BLADE* franchise was sold to Caribou Media Group, previously known primarily for its publication of *Gun Digest*.

Raymond Richard puts on a forging demonstration in Portland, Oregon, during a past BLADE Show West. The event was revived in 2018 and is now receiving rave reviews.

Joyce Laituri of Spyderco and custom knifemaker Murray Carter share a moment during the 2019 BLADE Show West. Both are holding knives that received awards during the show.

"F+W Media believed giving the show another try in Portland was a good idea thanks to the proximity of a number of factory knife companies, such as Gerber, Kershaw, Columbia River Knife & Tool, Leatherman Tool, William Henry, Al Mar Knives and others," notes Shackleford, a 2019 inductee into the *BLADE* Magazine Cutlery Hall of Fame.

The original reason for the show remained valid, too.

"After doing an analysis of BLADE Show attendees in Atlanta, we discovered that most of our attendees came from the South and Midwest, along with the Eastern corridor, to attend that show," explains Alicia Newton, who currently serves as director for both the BLADE Show and its younger sibling, BLADE Show West.

According to Shackleford, the first reboot of

BLADE Show West in 2018 at the Oregon Convention Center in Portland "wasn't bad" for an initial effort. In 2019, though, the event may well have hit its stride.

"It seemed much better," he says, "with many more buyers than tire kickers. Also, new events such as the chef's knife cutting competition, a new seminar featuring knifemakers meeting with hobbyist knifemakers to critique their knives and tell them how to improve them, and others, were well received. The BLADE Show staff, spearheaded by Alicia Newton, has worked tirelessly to improve the show, and their efforts have paid off."

Reemergence of Western Event

Taking place in early October or early November, a schedule that's still settling, the show is well on its way to re-establishing itself.

"BLADE Show West is definitely fulfilling its purpose," relates Newton, "and as for growth, it is still a bit early to tell since 2019 was only our second year. We did have increased attendance, but like all new business ventures, it will probably take a good five years until we can really determine whether hosting this show in Portland will truly be a success."

Tweaks and enhancements are setting a new standard for BLADE Show West, setting it apart from other shows and blazing a new trail for those interested in venturing to Portland. In addition to the new competitions, other innovations are creating a buzz around the event.

"The show has changed because it takes place in a convention center and not a ballroom," explains Newton. "We have created its own logo, its own branding, its own identity, a different floor layout and a different product mix. We wanted to differentiate somewhat from Atlanta so that, as the show grows, some people will choose to come to both because there will be elements that take place at BLADE Show West that don't take place in Atlanta and vice versa."

Carter had attended the early version of BLADE Show West and acknowledges the convenience of the Portland location to his home in Vernonia, Oregon. "The significance of the show for me was that it allowed a public forum for my work right in the local area where I was relatively unknown. The show was a great marketing opportunity," he says. "It had the added advantage of being close enough that I could sleep in my own bed each night after the show."

For years, Carter has been a regular presenter at the BLADE Show and BLADE Show West, usually offering 60 minutes of discussion and demonstration on freehand knife sharpening, social media marketing and traditional Japanese bladesmithing techniques.

The reemergence of BLADE Show West has been a positive occurrence for him. "One obvious change is the shift in target demographics," he observes. "Historically, the knife buying population was predominantly older males, but now, thanks to

Jot Singh Kalsa wears an American flag arm band and holds one of his custom knives during the 2001 BLADE Show West. The show was held just weeks after the tragedy of 9-11.

TV programming concerning knives, the demographic is more co-ed and younger. BLADE Show West is a world class event and it is sure to spark interest and imagination in all who attend."

"The new owners of BLADE have decided to take a hands-on approach and make BLADE Show West a successful event," remarks Tyre. "It has exploded to over 200 tables of exhibitors. It is well organized and has been well attended by collectors. In previous Oregon shows, it seems most patrons were interested in learning to make knives, but at the 2018 and 2019 shows people were interested in purchasing knives."

Exceeding Expectations

Along with the strong custom knife emphasis, Shackleford sees a more comprehensive show that gives the factories significant opportunity as well. "It has gone from being largely custom knife based in the mid-'90s to more of an all-around approach with both factory and custom knives now," he says. "Also, the venue is much larger and more state-of-the-art than anything BLADE Show West had in the past. The cutting competition was well received, and we are looking at updating it for the next show."

Exceeding expectations is a continual challenge. Success is defined by the quality of the journey, and the roadmap is ready.

"BLADE Show West is evolving as we try to create an identity with it that is different from Atlanta," concludes Newton. "Atlanta is a pure traditional knife show. For our Portland show, we have allowed some more bushcraft, survival and other products not directly knife related but industry related. We also have different award categories for custom and factory knives in Portland than we do in Atlanta."

A reenergized vision, revitalized format and a surging demand from the broad base of the knife buying public have brought BLADE Show West back from the shadows to the forefront of the industry.

More than just a footnote on a forgotten page of knife history, BLADE Show West is already writing a new chapter all its own. ☐

THE PRICE OF
$LICE

$50 vs. $500
Tactical Knives
BY PAT COVERT

Two attractive folders, but an ocean apart in price. The Kershaw Eris (left) is for the budget-minded buyer, while the Chris Reeve Inkosi (right) is a high-end buyer's dream.

The gulf between expensive high-end knives and affordable ones is a wide one. Some knife users are aghast that anyone would pay $500 for a knife, while others stand in line to get them. Others are perfectly happy with a $50 blade to meet their everyday needs, and the market for these is voluminous. Here we explore the differences between a $500 tactical knife and a $50 one.

I chose to compare two very successful folding knives, one in each cost category. On the top end is Chris Reeve Knives' newest folder, the Inkosi, which (with black Micarta inserts) retails for $515.00.

Reeve's BLADE Show awards for Quality in Manufacturing over the past two decades are unparalleled. We'll compare the Inkosi to one of Kershaw's hottest sellers, the Eris, which checks in at $49.99 MSRP (manufacturer's suggested retail price). Both folders are of Integral Lock (also referred to as frame-lock) design and represent their price group well. There is no winner or loser here.

Larry Connelley is the founder of Knifeart.com, one of the premier internet sites for selling high-end knives — both custom and production. Connelley started Knifeart.com over 20 years ago and is very knowledgeable about what goes into the production of a knife. I asked Connelley his basic thoughts on why some knives cost more than others. "The price of a knife is determined by two key factors: labor costs and price of materials," he said. "The price of higher-end knives is directly related to these factors. The importance of precision in the design of a knife cannot be over-stated. High-quality American-made knives are usually produced by skilled manufacturers with a high attention to detail. The knife can be serviced domestically and provides the owner with a lifetime of service.

"The cost and quality of materials is a major factor in the final price to the con-sumer," Connelley added. "While the steel used for the blade and handle are major considerations, all of the other parts — such as the pivot, bushings and spacers — are just as important. All of the enhancements to materials used, along with not cutting corners on manufac-turing, provides a superior product."

Material Matters

Before a knife goes into production the manufacturer must choose the materials that will go into making the blade, handle and component parts. As Connelley noted, on a folding knife the choice of blade steel and frame alloy are the two most important factors in determining the cost and retail price of a knife. Most high-end folding knives have frames made of titanium while their low-budget counterparts utilize aluminum or stainless steel for cost savings. Compared to the latter two less expensive metals, titanium can easily cost a manufacturer 20–25 times the price per pound depending on the alloy, so it's easy to see how these choices can affect the price of a knife.

"In general, the material chosen to construct a knife's handle is indicative of its overall quality," Connelley notes. "The materials selected to construct a knife handle help to determine the weight and the strength of the knife itself. While the use of high-quality base materials raises the cost to the consumer, the use of high-quality handle materials will prolong the life of a knife.

Titanium or carbon fiber are frequently used in the construction of high-quality knives — they are very strong yet much lighter. If I can choose a stronger yet

(left) Note the difference between the frame thickness of the Eris at left versus the Inkosi at right. Not only do the thicker slabs on the Inkosi cost more, they provide a better grip.

(right) High-end knives tend to have much crisper machining and are held to tighter tolerances. At left is the Kershaw Eris, at right the Chris Reeve Inkosi.

Components also factor into the price of a knife. The Reeve Inkosi at left has an inset Titanium pocket clip that matches the frame, the Eris a stainless steel clip that doesn't.

lighter knife, I will make that selection every time. Heavy doesn't equal quality."

Titanium, as Connelley explained, has greater strength and withstands wear and tear better than less costly materials like stainless steel, polymers or alumi-num. The increased cost of titanium comes from longer machining times, thus greater machine shop costs.

The same goes for blade steels, which can easily drive the price of a knife higher. The modern tactical knife boom of the 1990s, spurred on by our country's involvement in the Gulf Wars, created a demand for higher-grade steels (such as ATS-34 and BG-42 stain-less). The blade steel equation got kicked up several notches with the development of S30V stainless, a proprietary powdered knife steel developed by Crucible Industries, LLC and Chris Reeve. The two entities col-laborated again and released a revised version, S35VN, which remains a top-shelf blade steel to this day. Once

The small things used in construction of a folder, such as screws, pivots and spacers, affect both its price and durability. The Kershaw Eris uses stainless steel components, which cost less and are not as durable as titanium.

The Kershaw Eris has features that the higher-priced Inkosi does not, such as the flipper opener shown here. It also employs spring assist to roll the blade out in a flash.

The Reeve Inkosi utilizes titanium in most of its fabrication. Here you can see the pivot, blade stop, and thumb stud — all made of the superior alloy. Note also that the pivot is much beefier than its lower-priced counterpart.

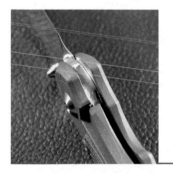

Thicker, beefier frame slabs like those found on the Inkosi, which includes the locking leaf for the blade, offer more surface area on the locking leaf, making for a solid lock-up as greater surface area blocks the tang of the blade.

Like handle materials, blade steels are determining factors in the cost of a knife. The Inkosi (top) employs top-shelf U.S.-made S35VN Crucible steel while the Eris (bottom) uses 8Cr13MoV manufactured in China.

Crucible's proprietary steels became popular, other manufacturers, such as domestic-based Carpenter Steel and Bohler-Uddeholm of Germany, jumped in. All of these manufacturers' steels add expense to a knife — especially in their early small batch stages.

Connelley gives insight into why high-end steels are so much better. "You simply cannot compare a high-alloy particle metallurgy steel blade to a low-grade steel one that is made offshore. You can't see the difference with your eyes, but a high-quality blade is the cornerstone of a dependable knife. Specialty steel manufacturers in the U.S., such as Crucible Industries, tend to employ CPM (Crucible Particle Metallurgy) performance steel that requires costly additional steps to produce. The result is a high-performance blade with more even distribution of carbides and a higher content of alloying elements. The end product is a tougher steel that retains its edge longer."

The Kershaw Eris' modified drop point blade is made of 8Cr13MoV stainless steel, the Chinese-made version of Japanese AUS-8 steel — a popular low-budget choice by manufacturers. While both are very adequate EDC budget steels, they don't hold a candle to the high-end proprietary metals such as the S35VN found on the Reeve Inkosi, and price-wise it isn't even close. In summary, all of the component materials that go into a knife, from frames to blades to pivot bearings and the cost of screws, add up when you consider the overall price of the knife.

Cost of Labor

Custom knifemaker Jim Hammond has been making knives for 41 years and has been involved in dozens of design collaborations with Columbia River Knife & Tool (CRKT) dating back to CRKT's inception in 1994. Hammond is very knowledgeable about the manufacturing end of cutlery production.

"From a manufacturing standpoint, two aspects loom large — ease of fabrication and final product cost," Hammond notes. "Premium steels can degrade tooling and blanking processes much sooner than lower-quality steels. Too, the factor of seven would often be applied with component costs, such as the steel pricing for each blade. For example, a company's steel cost per blade would commonly be multiplied by seven to determine its valuation in the final retail pricing of the knife. With a targeted price point often predetermined going in, the steel selection is often made — not just with the best steel in mind, but the best steel that be used to achieve the targeted retail price point for the knife."

As Connelley noted earlier, the cost of a knife is largely determined by the wages in the country in which the manufacturer is based. A recent article by Forbes magazine suggested factory wages in China have increased drastically in the past few years to an average of approximately $3.60 per hour. It would be only a guess where workers at cutlery factories fall in the entire job market since much of this type of information is protected, but we can assume they are less than, say, a worker at an automotive plant. Computerized machining technologies and robotics are a big factor in production in both low- to high-budget knives, but manufacturers still must have warm bodies running the equipment, inspecting the processes, and exercising quality control — not to mention some assembly. The average wage of the American factory worker is just north of $21.00 per hour at the time of this writing, so it's easy to see the grossly disproportionate amount of labor cost that goes into making a knife in the U.S. versus offshore.

Folding knives require many steps from start to finish, all of which determine the final product. The differences between the equipment used cutting, shaping, sanding and finishing parts for a knife make a difference for the simple reason that some machines hold tolerances better than others. Likewise, the workers running the equipment, inspecting the parts and doing any manual assembly are a factor as well. A manufacturer making thousands of low-budget knives in a single run can't be expected to have the same quality controls as one making smaller batches of higher-priced ones. In a nutshell, high-end knives cost more, and are better made, because superior equipment and more human hands-on time are spent in their fabrication.

Parts Specification Equation

Parts specifications, such as the thickness of blade steel and frame rails, play a large role in fabrication and determine the efficiency and cost of the folder. For instance, the Reeve Inkosi has a blade thickness of 0.140 inch and 0.1505-inch thick frame slabs. The Kershaw Eris' blade is 0.11-inch thick and its frame slabs are 0.09-inch thick. A beefier knife will outperform a lesser one but will cost more, which is the case with our subjects. Granted, the Inkosi is a slightly larger knife, but there are knives closer in size to the Eris with materials that spec closer to our Reeve subject. It should also be noted that Integral Locks with thicker

The Kershaw Eris will serve you well for everyday chores, having no trouble slicing corrugated board, paracord and 3/8-inch rappelling rope during light testing.

frame slabs like the Inkosi's offer more surface area on the locking leaf, making for a stronger lock-up because more surface area blocks the blade tang.

The quality of manufacture shows up in the crispness of the design and added elements to the whole package. Less expensive knives tend to have rounded contours and flat surfaces on the frame. More expensive knives will have beveling around the slab edges and design enhancements such as sculpting and inlays (like the Micarta inserts found on the Inkosi). While the overwhelming majority of pocket clips like those found on the Eris are stamped stainless steel, the Inkosi has a titanium one to match the frame. Such aesthetic value and features add to the cost of the knife due to the added time and materials they add to the manufacturing process, but these upscale elements are expected in an upscale knife.

However, the Kershaw Eris has design features the Reeve knife doesn't, and these should not be overlooked. The Eris folder opens by way of a blade flipper that protrudes out the top rear of the frame. Many prefer this over the somewhat dated thumb stud because it can be located quicker by the index finger (as opposed to the thumb) and takes only a quick flick to engage the blade. The icing on the Eris' cake is the addition of Kershaw's SpeedSafe spring-assisted opening mechanism, which can employ the blade in the blink of an eye — an important feature on any everyday carry blade for tactical or self-defense use.

Both knives have a comfortable grip with the wider frame on the Reeve Inkosi offering more comfort and better purchase. Both are good for everyday carry and are very adequate for self-defense, but the beefier Inkosi is more than willing to step out into the field for serious camp duty. Indeed, the forerunner Reeve Sebenza model, which shares many of the same traits as the Inkosi, has been serving military field operators for well over 25 years.

Designer Labels

Interestingly, you'll find a greater selection of collaborations with popular custom knifemakers among the lower-priced knives. While the Kershaw Eris is an in-house design — and a darn good one at that — the

company has had great success with custom knife-maker Rick Hinderer's designs in its standard line and in the more upscale Zero Tolerance line under the same KAI USA Ltd. corporate umbrella. Collaborations are a huge bonus for the knife customer who can't afford a custom knife by the same maker. The manufacturers also benefit by increased sales from designer collaborations. How popular are they? In this day and age you'd be hard-pressed to find a cutlery manufacturer who is not offering collaborations with custom knife-makers. Custom knifemakers are also well served as it gives them added exposure and royalty checks to pad their wallets.

Custom knifemaker Jim Hammond is familiar with such collaborations. "As President Kennedy once said, 'When the tide comes in, all the ships will rise.' This has proven true with benefits to everyone in the knife industry with the inflow of custom knifemakers now working with production companies. It's far easier to utilize creative vision, design understanding and proven manufacturing experience from a maker who's done it for over 40 years, such as myself, than to train someone for decades to hopefully achieve the same end. It brings expertise to the moment and ramps up every aspect of the process into real time from initial concepts to placing the finished knife into the customer's hand."

In the case of Chris Reeve, he is a legendary knifemaker dating back to when he only offered custom fare. His manufacturing designs have been popular dating back nearly 30 years when he introduced the Sebenza, which still sells like hotcakes along with other additions such as the Inkosi. Reeve is also considered the father of the integral lock design, which rules the roost among not only folder manufacturers but custom knifemakers as well.

A Place for Both

Despite such broad differences between low- and high-budget knives there is a strong case to be made for each. Budget knives offer a great opportunity for entry-level knife customers to use and enjoy a compe-

SPECIFICATIONS	
MODEL:	Kershaw Eris
BLADE STEEL:	8Cr13MoV stainless steel
OVERALL LENGTH:	7.50 in.
HANDLE LENGTH:	4.50 in.
HANDLE THICKNESS:	0.38 in.
BLADE TYPE:	Modified drop point
BLADE LENGTH:	3.0 in.
HANDLE MATERIAL:	Stainless steel
SPECIAL FEATURES:	Flipper opener/ Spring assist
CARRY:	Pocket clip/tip-up carry
WEIGHT:	4.70 oz.
MSRP:	$49.99
COUNTRY OF MANUFACTURE:	China

SPECIFICATIONS	
MODEL:	Chris Reeve Large Inkosi
BLADE STEEL:	S35VN Crucible stainless steel
OVERALL LENGTH:	8.40 in.
HANDLE LENGTH:	4.80 in.
HANDLE THICKNESS:	0.46 in.
BLADE TYPE:	Drop point
BLADE LENGTH:	3.60 in.
HANDLE MATERIAL:	Titanium/Micarta
SPECIAL FEATURES:	Micarta inlays/ lanyard
CARRY:	Pocket clip/tip-up carry
WEIGHT:	4.96 oz.
MSRP:	$515
COUNTRY OF MANUFACTURE:	USA

The Inkosi will have no trouble with field chores like carving and shaving seasoned wood. Like its older sibling the Chris Reeve Sebenza Model, these knives are made for hard use and have a lifetime guarantee.

tent knife at an affordable price, and the selection from the manufacturers is almost endless. Even counting average materials in low-end models compared to high-end knives, budget blades perform perfectly fine for the average user's everyday needs. And their fixed-blade brethren do well in the field as well. In fact, some knife users carry a budget folder as their EDC and switch to a more upscale option for special occasions. Budget knives don't offer the endurance of high-end knives, but many users will take that trade-off.

High-end folders are for those who prefer the best and can afford to pay the price. They have complete confidence in their knife and know with no uncertainty that it will perform to the extreme, will be less prone to fail, and will cut like a house afire with an edge that will hold its sharpness longer.

Better yet, there are a plethora of knives to be had between the low- and high-budget folders featured here. The cutlery market is burgeoning with knives for any budget, any taste and any need. You'll have no trouble finding one made just for you!

SOURCES

Chris Reeve Knives, 2949 S. Victory View Way, Boise, ID 83709. 208-375-0367 chrisreeve.com

Jim Hammond Knives & Designs, LLC, 104 Owens Parkway Suite M, Birmingham, AL 35244. 256-651-1376 jimhammondknives.com

Kershaw/Kai USA, 18600 Teton Avenue, Tualatin, OR 97062. 800-325-2891 kershawknives.com

KnifeArt.com, 13301 Pompano Drive, Little Rock, AR 72211. 800-564-3327 knifeart.com ☐

Knife Industry Copes with
COVID-19

Pandemic affected sales and practices, but not resilience of the blade business

By Mike Haskew

A.G. Russell Knives closed its retail store as a precaution against the spread of COVID-19, and management took steps to reopen with safety measures in place.

To protect our customers, staff and their families against the Coronavirus

Our Walk-in Retail Store is
CLOSED

We'll reopen as soon as possible.

Customer service lines will continue on our regular schedule

800-255-9034

We are continuing to take orders at 800-255-9034 and online. Shipping of orders is continuing on our regular schedule.

Since the novel coronavirus began to stretch its invisible tentacles around the world in early 2020, carrying with it the deadly COVID-19 illness, life as previously known and business as usual have been in limbo.

Upon publication of the *KNIVES 2021* book, a return to normal activity remained somewhat elusive since the definition of just what the new "normal" meant lingered as a work in progress. Every aspect of living has felt the impact of COVID-19, including the knife industry, from the custom maker's shop floor to the crowded bustle of well-known annual events and the leisurely browsing of retail store shelves—all long taken for granted. How is the knife industry handling a challenge that is simply like no other?

Knife Shows Skid to a Stop

Greatly anticipated annual events were cancelled or rescheduled. As of this writing, BLADE Show 2020 moved from its perennial June date to August. Details of the procedures, safeguards and protocols were still being developed.

For more than a decade, the Usual Suspects Network's Gathering took place on Labor Day weekend at Planet Hollywood in Las Vegas, and the show has grown to include more than 250 vendors. The USN event is renowned for its camaraderie, and its social aspect is precious to founder Larry Brahms of Bladeart. com.

"We have always taken precautions," related Brahms, "which include medical personnel on hand, and we have been very conscious of the well-being of the people who attend the show. We have always planned to do whatever it takes to adhere to any safety considerations."

For those attending the USN Gathering, the fabric of the event has been the atmosphere of a reunion, with friends who may not have seen

In the pre-COVID-19 days, the store at A.G. Russell Knives was always a crowded space.

The packing and shipping department at A.G. Russell Knives remained busy throughout the changing circumstances of the COVID-19 pandemic.

one another for a year meeting and greeting each other. Hugs and handshakes, friendships renewed, stories told, and ideas exchanged are hallmarks that Brahms has sought to preserve. In the era of COVID-19, those handshakes might look more like elbow bumps. Like other organizers, Brahams was still assessing the future of the USN Gathering as *Knives 2021* went to press.

Famed custom knifemaker Jerry Fisk has addressed concerns not only with his shop, but also with setting up tables at knife shows and an annual event that he hosts as well. "I haven't changed anything with my shop operations due to COVID-19 since I only have four or five visitors a year anyway and people have elected to stay in," he explained. "So that problem cured itself."

"I am nearing retirement age and had planned on slowing down my public shows starting at the end of 2020," he continued. "So, the virus changes nothing I had not already planned. I promote my own micro show each year, and yes, there will be changes with it. At this time, I am still in the planning stages, so I cannot say for sure what those would be."

Some Things Won't Change

The knife show of tomorrow will surely offer a different experience than in the past, but the core will undoubtedly remain the same. A custom knifemaker or knife company lays out their livelihoods on a table for attendees to inspect. Conversation and personal interaction can't be avoided as a result. How that looks is still up in the air.

Fisk admits the way forward is not yet well defined. "I am just not sure now," he observed. "I do feel attendance will be down at shows due to folks

hanging back. You have to face it that the majority of both makers and buyers are in a 45 years and older group of people, many of them 60-plus, so this problem will be very fluid as to how shows operate, and both makers and buyers will need to be able to figure out how to keep moving. This will hold true for collectors of art pieces, as art is always uplifting, and it will also hold true for tacticals as the need to use a knife is always there."

Custom knifemaker Dennis Friedly sees a limited number of visitors in his Wyoming shop but remains conscious of COVID-19. "Being a one-man operation like so many other knifemakers and living in the country, I'm not frequented by many visitors," he remarked. "Most drop-ins are friends, and we have been aware of social distancing both in the shop and outside."

For custom knifemakers, the key to the future is preparation. Taking time to review shop and show procedures and safety standards promotes confidence and eliminates anxiety among customers. Shop visitors may well be limited in number more than ever, required to wear masks and maintain social distancing, and even restricted on touching surfaces.

Business Skills

"To quote an old phrase," Fisk observed, "'The one who gets there firstest with the mostest' will come out okay through all of this. This COVID-19 event will cause many hobby makers to pull back from

A thick crowd gathers around knifemakers' tables at BLADE Show 2019, and vendors discuss the virtues of their everyday carry gear. At press time, changes were in the wind for BLADE Show 2020. Thousands have flocked to the annual event, one of the premiere happenings in the knife industry.

begun to enjoy a distinct sales advantage. During a period of uncertainty and limited physical proximity, a prospective purchaser is unable to handle a knife, feel the balance and examine fit and finish in person. Therefore, sharp photography and easily navigable websites have become more relevant every day.

"Internet-driven sales have gotten stronger and will continue to do so," Fisk concluded. "The COVID-19 pandemic will bump that harder to where some folks will rely on the internet more often than they did, but a show can never be fully replaced due to the interaction. We are animals by nature, and pack animals at that, so we like to gather around a 'kill' and celebrate. The internet is a remote animal standing on a hillside and watching others as they gather around the kill. He can neither smell nor taste. He can just see from a distance."

No less problematic is the new reality of the simple visit to a retail cutlery store, a pleasure that in the recent past took place without a second thought. The emphasis was on the fully stocked shelves, showroom cases and eye-catching displays. Now the ideas of health and safety share top billing.

knifemaking due to slower sales, and those with marginal business skills will be out of work due to fewer sales. Being able to make a knife does not mean you have good business skills. It just means you know how to make a knife. There are too many variables now to make a statement on what exactly to do next. If the economy worsens in this country and worldwide, makers need to have a Plan B just to make sure they survive."

"I have my Plan B," Fisk added, "that is already being put into a slow cycle and even a Plan C that I am kicking around. But that will be determined by each maker on their own, doing what is best for them as we all take a different approach."

Friedly stresses that well-attended shows are a must for the future health of the knife industry. He has implemented safeguards at his table, and they are becoming commonplace. "Hand sanitizer is being made available to the public on the table, as well as tissues," he advised. "I would also look to promoters to allow more space between exhibitors, at least until things calm down. After knives have been handled, it would be wise to wipe them before returning them to the table."

One logical conclusion is that custom knifemakers with a robust internet presence have already

Flattening the Curve

Smoky Mountain Knife Works has been a knife enthusiast destination for decades. One of the best-known and highly trafficked retail establishments in the industry, the Sevierville, Tennessee-based enterprise has not been immune from substantive change in the wake of COVID-19.

"We closed our 108,000-square-foot retail store at the end of March," related Chief Operating Officer Tyler Pipes, "not due to any sickness, but because we do get 1.5 million visitors annually. We felt that it was the right thing to do not only for our employees, but also for our customers, that we should be a part of the solution to help flatten the curve and not a part of the problem."

Technically, Smoky Mountain Knife Works could have remained open as an essential provider through its sales of firearms and ammunition. Still, the weeks wore on until the word was passed by the Tennessee state government that certain businesses could reopen in early May. Smoky Mountain executed its reopening plan in stages, and by mid-month, a limited number of customers were being allowed on the floor at a given time, while retail employees wore masks and gloves.

"All of our shopping carts are being cleaned after every use," Pipes added. "We have hand sanitizer stations at every counter and in common areas. We have installed Plexiglas at the registers to cut down on the potential spread of the virus through the air. We are cleaning all restrooms and door handles every hour to ensure the facility is as clean as it can be. Lastly, we have signs printed throughout the building reminding folks about social distancing."

Although circumstances varied from state to state, A.G. Russell Knives closed its Rogers, Arkansas, retail store to foot traffic on March 17. Arkansas was never under a general lockdown, but Goldie Russell assessed the situation and made the decision for the protection of everyone concerned.

"That was a Tuesday," she remembered. "I met with the store staff early that day and from the meeting found that most of the customers who were in the store on the previous day were traveling from out of state. That left us more exposed than we were comfortable with. So, we put up big signs and locked those doors. We tried to accommodate local customers by taking their order either online or by phone and taking it to them in the parking lot when they came to pick it up."

A.G. Russell Knives also planned a staged reopening by mid-May, incorporating similar precautions to those implemented at Smoky Mountain Knife Works. The closing of the retail operation necessitated the reduction of the workforce by 50 percent at A.G. Russell Knives, and Goldie met with each employee affected. The expectation was that everyone would return to work as soon as possible.

"We had no general lockdown, and we are fortunate to be located in Arkansas where the population density is low," Goldie continued. "By the end of April, most employees had returned to work with a few reassigned from one department to another. We were able to reorganize the inventory and create efficiencies in the warehouse, the shop and different departments that were needed but we seemed never to have time to accomplish."

Both A.G. Russell Knives and Smoky Mountain

Custom knifemaker Dennis Friedly pauses while working in his shop. Friedly takes steps to sanitize the area around his table at knife shows.

Knife Works have experienced changes with distribution and fulfillment since COVID-19 interfered with business as usual. The two companies have found their operations to be highly adaptable, and the impact on customers has been minimal.

Extra Precautions

"We have taken extra precautions at our distribution center to ensure that every packing station is cleaned on an hourly basis," commented Pipes, "that every tub is cleaned after every use, that every employee working in our facility is in good health before coming into the facility, and that our boxes and supplies are coming from suppliers who have similar measures in place."

Tyler sees these steps as permanent and asserts that any future changes will take place only to enhance them. "I believe these adaptations are nothing but positive. Obviously, the shutdown of our

The management of Smoky Mountain Knife Works has taken precautions to ensure the safety of crowds that frequent its retail store (shown pre-pandemic). Since the COVID-19 pandemic, steps have been implemented to maintain safety standards, including social distancing.

Positive Results

Although the positive elements may be somewhat hidden at first glance, a reflective Goldie appreciates the focus that resulted from the emergence of COVID-19. "It seems that for A.G. Russell as a company, a lot of positive results have come out of it. It caused our staff to function more effectively as a team, caused communication to improve and made everyone more appreciative of what they have. It has given us reason to evaluate how we do things. I think we will be a better company because of it."

A.G. Russell's gross sales were down a bit in April 2020 while the retail store was closed. It turns out that the decline was almost the same dollar amount that the retail store had generated in the same month a year earlier.

A degree of uncertainty remains amid the swirl of response to COVID-19. Even as the knife industry has been affected at every level, there have been other challenges in the past. The industry always survived, coming back even stronger.

"I believe, in the long run, the knife industry as a whole will be fine," related Pipes. "We are a part of one of the oldest industries known to man, and the only thing that has changed is how we go to market with our products. As with all things, he who can adapt the fastest will survive."

Considering the recent trials, every knife enthusiast can take heart. After all, adaptability and wondrous inventiveness have always been alive and well in the knife world. ☐

retail store had a significant impact on our overall revenue. However, we have shifted more focus toward our website, mail order catalog and dealers in our distribution business, and put more resources in to help emphasize those channels for us," he explained.

Still, Pipes acknowledges that there will always be a place for the retail store and knife show, even though change has come. "You just can't feel the craftsmanship of a custom knife through a picture," he said, "or test the sharpness of an edge looking at a computer screen."

A.G. Russell Knives has experienced a stronger response to email campaigns in recent months, and the average dollar amount per online order has increased.

"A larger percentage of orders started coming through our website than before," observed Goldie, "but if you were stuck at home and unable to go and do the things you normally do, I guess you might have time to get more comfortable using the internet and ordering online. That seems to have been happening here."

Attendees at the pre-pandemic 2019 BLADE Show gather close to one another during a demonstration.

How to Make Money MAKING KNIVE$

Success in knifemaking is more about the journey and less about the destination

By Murray Carter

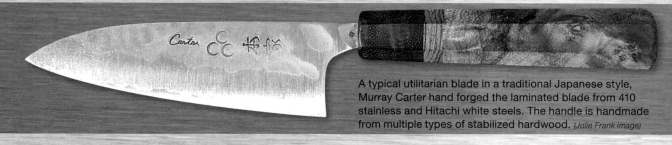

A typical utilitarian blade in a traditional Japanese style, Murray Carter hand forged the laminated blade from 410 stainless and Hitachi white steels. The handle is handmade from multiple types of stabilized hardwood. *(Jolie Frank image)*

Always treat new customers like they will become your best clients. This $6,000 custom damascus steak knife set, which was a collaboration between Murray Carter (left) and his assistant, Greyson Walker, was ordered by the most unlikely customer.

What is success? Generally, most people think that being famous and having a lot of money is what success is all about. While undeniably that is a common measure of success, when folks say things like, "If I were rich and famous, I would do so and so," that standard can be so daunting that common people become paralyzed when it comes to trying to achieve their own success.

People talk in defeatist terms as if true success is reserved for only the luckiest or most fortunate within society.

However, when we define success as the active and sustained pursuit towards a realistic, yet difficult long-term personal goal, success becomes within reach of every person seeking it. The measure of success is therefore as varied as there are individuals pursuing it.

For some, it might be becoming a published author, having a large passive income, creating a life-changing invention, being a star athlete, etc., while for others, it may be reuniting a broken family, learning how to walk again or staying sober as a recovering alcoholic.

Similarly, most people view the word success as if it were a final destination or only a net result. On the contrary, actual success happens as soon as we start to see fruit from the active pursuit of our own defined goals. For the person who is trying to reach

A practical belief at Carter Cutlery is that all tools are meant to be held in the hand while used, and knives should be hand sanded and finished. *(Amanda Robertson image)*

a net worth of $2 million, for example, success is experienced as early as the first year of investing, with perhaps only a few thousand dollars saved.

Similarly, success for the person who has a healthy body weight goal comes as soon as that person learns new habits regarding food and exercise and puts them into practice. For this person, habitually walking around the block after a modest dinner is a success, even if they still have lots of weight left to lose.

The important thing is that the person has a well-defined goal and detailed plan, and is actively working towards that plan, with the discipline and determination to finish.

Success in Knifemaking

For the sake of this article, I am going to assume that success in knifemaking for you is something along the lines of, "I want to be able to make high-quality knives; sell them for a premium price; keep long-term customers; make dealers, suppliers, and family happy; establish a reputation of being honest and trustworthy; and have some funds put aside for retirement or a rainy day."

Remember, success is more about the journey and less about the destination, so if you put together

a good plan and implement some of what you read in this book, success will be within your reach!

Selling knives, like any business, is about developing relationships based on trust and respect. Earning money making knives depends on the most crucial step in the process, and that is getting people to willingly give you some of their hard-earned cash. A successful business is one where the *same* people give you money over and over again. Therefore, it is imperative that your customers trust and respect you.

So, just who are these people who will willingly give you money over and over again? Is it the businessman standing at your trade show table inquiring about your knives? Is it your mother's best friend? Is it 10-year-old Johnny living down the street? Is it the person on the other end of the telephone line as it rings, disrupting your work in the knife shop? Honestly, it could very well be all these people. Initially, there is no way to know for sure. The answer is that you have to assume it is all of these people and treat them the same.

The strategy for long term success assumes that any one of these folks could be worth $10,000 to you, even little Johnny living down the street! You need to deal with each one of them the same way you would a longtime customer. You need to be polite, patient, be willing to educate them, share your enthusiasm for your job and answer all their questions with the understanding that, in many cases, it will be months, if not years, before any of them make a purchase.

As you know, trust and respect take time to develop. Little Johnny might end up going to med school and become a lifetime customer, and after 20 years, habitually buy dozens of knives to give away to all his family, friends and colleagues. Therefore,

The best knifemaking techniques are born out of sheer repetition. In this photo, Carter Cutlery's newest Muteki bladesmith, Chloe Kim, grinds her 70th blade, all 70 of which she made in under five months. *(Amanda Robertson image)*

The key to success: Stick to the plan! Murray Carter has forged and completed over 27,000 knives in 32 years. Here he holds a Jewel Damascus Funayuki with his signature Carter Elbow blade feature. *(Amanda Robertson image)*

treat every customer as if they will buy $10,000 worth of knives from you eventually, and don't ever neglect to answer a telephone call, return a voice mail or respond to an email inquiry. It can cost you $10,000!

In *The Legacy Journey*, Dave Ramsey says there's only one way to heal a selfish and greedy spirit: generosity. "Giving is the antidote for selfishness," he writes. "It's the hallmark character quality of those who win with money."

Giving & Receiving

I listen to Ramsey a lot on the radio, and from time to time I watch his short video clips online. I love his direct biblical approach to financial management. His ministry of Six Baby Steps has turned more people's financial lives around than many advisors have done in history. Of interest is that he advocates giving money away to earn more money! It sounds counter-intuitive. The answer lies in the fact that, according to Ramsey, more than 90 percent of the thousands of self-made millionaires that he has researched are extremely generous people.

They help those in need, give to their churches and to charities. They are cheerful givers, and that is the key: Cheerful givers are kind and happy people who are nice to be around and therefore they attract more lucrative opportunities to themselves. Furthermore, steady giving requires a degree of financial responsibility and budgeting, which has the bonus of ensuring the givers live well below their means and produce a surplus every month.

So, how can the knifemaker exercise this generosity? I believe that no matter what you bring in each month, a tenth of your income should be given away. You may be thinking, "Good grief! He doesn't

understand my financial situation. I'm in debt and I can't spare a penny!" If that is you, then learning generous responsibility is exactly what will help you turn your finances around permanently.

Another very specific way to be generous is by donating knives, teaching for free and giving T-shirts or promotional material away. These donations will gain you double returns because you will get your work out in front of more people, and large audiences will feel your goodwill. It's likely only a matter of time before a very wealthy customer contacts you to purchase something because they heard about your generous spirit.

Ultimately, these are the kind of customers you want to have anyway. Generosity engenders generosity. Generosity should also motivate you to manage your resources more wisely, and help you establish a monthly budget.

A word on donating knives: Before donating one of your handmade knives, try to discern if the actual fiscal value will be realized when the knife is auctioned, sold or raffled away. I have often just donated money instead of knives because it can cause some damage to the pricing of your knives

The way to success: Keep grinding that steel! Remember, only practice makes perfect. *(Amanda Robertson image)*

All the staff at Carter Cutlery works hard daily to produce high performance hand forged knives and deliver outstanding customer service. *(Tetsuo Carter image)*

if the edged model sells for a substantially lower value than your advertised price. My worst nightmare would be to witness one of my $500 knives auctioned off at a local charity function for a tenth of the value.

When you do take a chance and donate a handmade knife, be sure to follow up with the recipients and record what benefits the piece generated for them. That information will inform a decision when they come asking for a donation again.

Proper Vetting

In one instance, I gave $900 to a local advertising agency. They convinced me to print an advertisement in my children's high school sports program brochure. The phone call came when I was preoccupied with the daily challenges of running a business, and since they said they worked directly with my kids' school, I didn't vet them properly.

There was no brochure, and I lost my money to this scam. You should still practice giving because it is the *right* thing to do and does your spirit good. Learn from your mistakes, but don't let them keep you from being generous. If your customers get one scent of you being stingy, that will kill business faster than you would want to believe.

Efficiency

Making knives is fun and rewarding. The challenges are varied and unending. The most fun is making just one knife at a time and progressing through the individual steps until the

project is complete. As much fun as this process is, it is generally not an efficient use of time.

Since making knives includes many steps, using different machinery, there will be a lot of walking back and forth as you transition from one workstation to the next, from the forge to the sandblaster, to the grinders, drill press, back to the forge and grinders again. There is a lot of movement involved before the knife is done.

Then there is setting up the machinery for the work—putting the correct drill bit in the press, changing the sanding belt on the grinders or getting ready to epoxy handles. Making knives in batches, where each step can be completed on a bunch of knives at one time, increases efficiency. So how many knives should you make in a batch? Generally, the larger the batch of knives, the more efficient your use of time and resources.

However, if the batch is too large, forward progress through the multitude of steps to complete the knives will feel like it is taking forever. Ideally, find a compromise between making just one knife at a time and making too many in one batch.

It is my conclusion after having completed more than 28,000 knives in 32 years that the best knife batch size is between 10-30 knives. Another approach commonly used by my apprentices is to experiment with how many knives can be started on a Monday and completed by the end of the work week. This is the fastest way to keep new inventory offered to your customers, but it is not as efficient as making 10-30 knives in one batch, which will almost always take the better part of a month.

Ancient and modern married together, the Carter Cutlery damascus steel blades come with colored carbon fiber handles. *(Jolie Frank image)*

All the staff at Carter Cutlery works hard daily to produce high performance hand forged knives and deliver outstanding customer service.
(Tetsuo Carter image)

The fastest and most efficient way to improve your bladesmithing technique is to make small batches of knives, with one batch immediately succeeding the next. *(Amanda Robertson image)*

In the last few years, since my shop time has been reduced due to teaching and directing more than 10 employees, I have adopted the new practice of making upwards of 70-100 knives in one batch, and finishing them in about two to three months. It means that getting new inventory on the shelves is sporadic, but my time per knife ratio is extremely efficient.

Forward Progress

Another approach for efficiency, especially for the beginning knifemaker, is to focus not on perfection from knife to knife, but to rather focus on improvement from knife batch to knife batch. For the sake of clarity, let's assume that a knifemaker has adopted the technique of making 10 knives in every batch. With each step in the knifemaking process, the maker takes note of the average time it takes, a baseline as it were, to do the same step to three knives.

Take rough grinding of the knife profile, for example. If the average of three blades is 10 minutes each, then the knifemaker should set a literal timer (stopwatch or smartphone timer with a chime)

for each knife. When the timer rings, it is important to put that knife down, reset the timer and start on the next knife and so on until all knives are finished with that step. Now comes the important tip: Look at all 10 knives, but only take a few more minutes to touch up the three ugliest of them.

The concept here is that the timer keeps you making forward progress. The truth is that repeating the same step 10 times will develop more skills and muscle memory than spending endless time trying to make one knife perfect. Once you have performed the same step 10 times, you will be better equipped to improve upon the three knives needing it the most.

Having touched up the three knives, though, it is imperative that you move on to the next step and repeat the process of timing each knife, and then fixing only the worst three. This will ensure that you complete the whole batch of 10 knives and have something to sell. The goal is not to make perfect knives as a beginner, but to see improvement from batch to batch of 10 knives.

Make a Realistic Plan

In conclusion, the key to success is to determine what your exact goals are, to develop a challenging but realistic plan and to actively engage in that plan in a sustainable manner over time. That is the technical component; the other component has to do with the strength of your character as it relates to honesty, trustworthiness and integrity.

Since so much of our success in knifemaking comes as a result of interacting with others, it stands to reason that being of strong moral character will greatly enhance the level of success that you achieve. □

THE KNIFE OF THE 21ST CENTURY:
The Tactical Folder

A tactical folding knife is essential on a shortlist of survival gear

By James Morgan Ayres

The author used his Spyderco Military folder to fend off a pack of feral dogs on this very street in a Bulgarian village.

I was walking on a deserted street of abandoned buildings in Bulgaria when a pack of feral dogs came around the corner at a dead run. The leader of the pack, a European jackal the size of a German Shepard, complete with characteristic neck ruff, thick shoulders and long muzzle, was coming straight at me. The other three mongrels spread out to surround me.

For a flash of a second, I yearned for a shotgun, or the 10-inch bowie I'd been using. But the shotgun was at the cabin and the bowie had gone missing along with my luggage. As the pack closed on me, I got my back to a wall, reached for my tactical folder and …

The Spyderco Military is used to make a fish spear.

Folders such as the Spyderco Military model can be employed for all kitchen duties, including this past year when the author and his wife split a Thanksgiving turkey in two parts to fit it into a small oven.

I'll get back to this true story soon, one that happened to me two years ago. But, since this is a publication about knives, first a few words about my tactical folder and why you need one, aside from fighting feral dog packs, and why the tactical folder is the knife for the 21st century.

What Makes for a Good Tactical Folder

Most knife enthusiasts reserve fixed blades for wilderness use. Few can or will carry a fixed blade in urban areas, or even in rural spaces. Many people like myself, however, spend much time in cities and the surrounding countryside, and we need knives with us.

When my luggage disappeared, I found myself at a train station in Bucharest with only my day pack and a 12-year-old Spyderco Military clipped inside my waistband. I was more than a little annoyed at the disappearance of my other bag. But I had all essentials in my daypack and one good knife that was useful for urban and wilderness survival, bushcraft and everyday utility.

My Military, with its 4-inch blade, reliable lock, secure grip and strong clip is not the only excellent tactical folder but is surely one of the very best. This one has served me well during a dozen years of hard use, and I expect it to be good for many more.

A tactical folder should have these features:

- Robust construction, especially at the pivot point
- Strong and reliable lock to prevent closure on a

user's finger
- One-hand opening because the user might be injured, need to stabilize himself or hold onto a cutting medium
- A pocket clip to secure the folder from loss and make it readily available
- A 3- to 4-inch blade for utility, but smaller tactical folders with blades of 2 inches or less are also viable

A Matter of Survival

These reasons and one other are why I came to use tactical folders for survival and bushcraft. Twenty years ago, I witnessed a teenage boy die of hypothermia. He had been snowboarding off a piste, got lost and spent three nights exposed to the winter mountain weather before the search-and-rescue team found him.

He wore inadequate clothing and had no survival gear at all, not even a butane lighter. The team was too late to save him from fatal hypothermia. He was never more than a mile from the ski lodge. I watched the light fade from his eyes and felt his

A Spyderco Military is shown with a small flint stick and burning tinder.

Tactical folders like the Al Mar SERE can be used for such survival chores as cutting a sapling.

A Buck Tactical folder has such capabilities as slashing through sheet metal.

fear as he faced the unknown. I saw the anguish and despair on the faces of his parents and felt their pain as he slipped away. I experienced the frustration and sorrow of the medical team that tried to save him.

At that moment, I determined to do whatever I could to pass on knowledge that was once part of children's education, but which has faded with the urbanization of our culture.

In response to this tragedy, and upon learning the majority of accidental wilderness deaths that occur in the United States today are from hypothermia, I developed a one-day seminar and have offered it since that time to any and all on a pro bono basis. My special focus is on outreach to teenagers.

The only equipment used, other than proper clothing, is a top-quality survival/tactical folder, a butane lighter and a small flint stick. I chose this equipment because young people who use the outdoors for recreation will not, due to peer pressure, social norms or legal restrictions, carry a fixed blade. Nor will they carry any gear that their peers think isn't cool. A folder and a lighter can be tucked away out of sight and the flint stick goes unobtrusively on a key ring.

A lineup of tactical folders includes, from top to bottom, Kershaw, Fällkniven, Spyderco, Victorinox and Al Mar Knives models.

A CRKT tactical folder easily opens a cardboard box.

This minimal gear does not get in the way of snowboarding, skiing, backpacking, rafting or climbing, and draws little or no attention from others. In addition to teaching teens fire building skills and how *not* to get lost, I instruct them on the use of tactical folders for all survival/bushcraft tasks: making shelter, spears and fuzz sticks, and safely using a knife as a baton to bring down a small tree, split kindling and so on.

Maintenance Free

Few of the kids, or adults, I trained have any notion of equipment maintenance. So, I recommend folders with stainless blades that hold their edges during much use, and butane lighters and sparkers because they require no maintenance. From years of experience, and from teaching hundreds of people these methods, we have proven that a tactical folder, a fire starter and a little knowledge can save lives.

Knives Save Lives

I've also taught urban survival and self-defense to many people using only a tactical folder and a few other pocket-carry items. To illustrate the utility of a tactical folder in an urban survival situation, the following are a couple examples from dozens in my files of people using the folding blades in emergency situations that could happen to anyone.

A young woman was inside a shipping container in Manhattan taking inventory when the explosion of the World Trade Center flipped the container on its side, breaking her arm and trapping her. She was growing weak and in pain when a firefighter leaving the scene heard her cries. He had no tools with him other than his tactical folder. Using a chunk of broken concrete, he pounded the blade of his knife through the steel-walled container, cut an opening, freed the woman and took her to medical help.

During the earthquake in Haiti, a young backpacker was trapped in her hostel when the building collapsed. She used her tactical folder to dig her way to a small opening where rescuers could hear her calls for help. She was saved with only a few bruises and scratches.

Aside from urban and wilderness survival or bushcraft use, tactical folders can be employed for daily tasks and stand in for everyday tools, including kitchen knives. My wife, ML, and I spend a good part of each

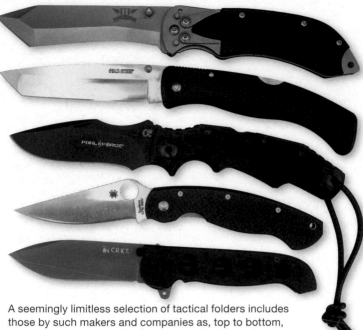

A seemingly limitless selection of tactical folders includes those by such makers and companies as, top to bottom, Mykel Hawke, Cold Steel, Pohl Force, Spyderco and CRKT.

year traveling and staying in rented holiday apartments and cabins. These places never have good kitchen knives. We travel light, without an array of cutlery, and use our folders or field knives if we have them for all kitchen duties, including this past year when splitting the Thanksgiving turkey into two parts to fit in a small oven.

I had to use a wooden mallet to baton the blade of my Military through the tough breastbone. After roasting, I carved the bird for the table. With our tactical folders, we also open packages, make fish traps, clean fish for campfire cooking, teach defensive and survival seminars, and with duct tape and needle and thread, repair equipment. For just such situations, a knife user should always have a tactical folder. Combined with convenience of carry, it's available in an emergency.

Back to the Dogs

Okay, back to the feral dog story.

As the pack closed on me, I got my back to a wall, reached for my tactical folder, dropped into a mobile stance, took a deep breath, steadied and waited the few seconds it took for them to get to me. When the alpha got within reach, about a foot from my front leg, I thrust my blade and caught him on the side of his muzzle with the point. His momentum combined with the strength of my thrust slashed him from muzzle down the side of his head through his ear. He broke to the side, howled, turned tail and ran,

spraying blood.

While this was happening, a brown medium-sized dog that had circled to my left tried to hamstring my left leg. I kicked at him while cutting the alpha, but to little effect. He snagged my pants and got a couple of teeth into my calf. The other two mutts hung back to my right between the alpha and the wall behind me and never got into the fight. All three broke and ran at once when the alpha howled and ran down the street.

The bite on my left leg, my only injury, was minor. The entire episode lasted only a couple of minutes. Luck was with me. The pack could have been more determined, or desperate, and I could have had a harder fight. If I had panicked, if I had not been ready and able to fight, if I had not had my Spyderco Military, I might have ended up like the American who was killed by a dog pack in Sofia, the capital city of Bulgaria, four years ago.

Feral dog packs, part jackal or otherwise, are a danger in the Balkans, most of Eastern Europe, Greece, Russia, India, Southeast Asia, and other parts of the world. Sofia, for example, is estimated to have over 10,000 stray dogs, some of which run

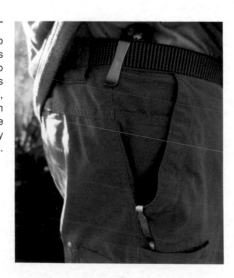

A pocket clip allows folders to be secured to pants pockets or waistbands, securing them from loss and making the edged tools readily available.

in packs and attack people. Four people have been killed by dog packs in the Balkans during the past year. A British woman was killed by a dog pack in Greece two years ago. There are many such accounts. The situation is worse in rural Asia and the Middle East.

I've not seen effective defensive tactics for this situation available anywhere else in print. So, here is some information on the subject that I have gained through experience. Many "experts" advise that if attacked by a dog or dogs, you should avoid eye contact and be submissive. The notion being that the dog will then leave you alone. This advice might get you killed.

A dog or pack of dogs attacking you, or about to attack, are not nice doggies. They have gone feral and will injure or kill you if they can. If they bring you down and kill you, and if no one stops them, they will eat you. Think of them as canine psychopathic cannibals.

Being submissive in the face of a dog attack can get you severely mauled, or killed, especially if attacked by a pack. You must dominate the dog, or dogs, and fight if necessary. I've been attacked by packs of feral dogs on several occasions, and as a result, have developed defensive tactics for this threat.

Some tips if you face a hostile canine pack:

1. Carry your knife so that it can be quickly accessed.
2. If attacked, accept that you will have to fight. Commit to doing so with full aggression.
3. If attacked, deploy your knife at once. Keep your blade between yourself and the threat. Do NOT attempt to use the so-called reverse grip with the blade extending from the lower part of your hand like an icepick. Hold your knife like a sword. Use controlled slashes and stabs as you advance, attack and retreat to cover.
4. If possible, get your back to a wall, tree, boulder, auto or anything that offers cover from rear attack. If you cannot get cover for your back, stay light on your feet, be prepared to spin. While doing so, keep awareness all around you. Beware of pack members circling to your back.
5. Attack the alpha if he's within reach. If you can wound or otherwise chase off the alpha, the others will follow. If you cannot reach the alpha, attack the dog closest to you.
6. Do not attempt to give a dog your weak arm, as experts advise. They are unlikely to go for

You never know when your Kershaw tactical folder will be called upon to peel an apple.

your arm. But if they do, the resulting pain and injury can be incapacitating. Moreover, while you're dealing with the one dog, jackal or wolf that has your arm and is trying to bring you down, the others will be circling and attacking in low line from all directions.
7. A pack can, and sometimes does, circle and continue to attack for an extended period. You may need to call on your reserves of endurance.
8. Yell at the dogs and call for help while fighting, but do not count on help arriving. Accept that you might have to overcome this attack on your own.

Other Threats

A tactical folder could also save your life from other feral creatures. For some years I provided self-defense training on a pro bono basis to people referred to me by the Los Angeles Rape Crisis Center. To some, I taught self-defense using a small folder, as I have done for Peace Corp volunteers, State Department personnel, NGO workers and others not allowed to be armed with anything else. Some of them have had to use this training and their small tactical folder to avoid being kidnapped, injured or killed.

The Knife of the 21st Century

However, even if you have no training whatever, a tactical folder, or even a not so tactical folder, could save your life. The tactical folder is the knife you can always have with you, conveniently clipped to your clothing, strong enough to stand in for the fixed blade, useful for everything a knife can be used. It is the knife for the 21st century. □

TRENDS

It is a lot to take in—the materials, mechanisms, functional makeup, just the colors and patterns. Knife styles and formations are limited only by the imaginations of the makers. There are no limits. People often ask if there can be anything new in the world of knives. The answer to that would be in the affirmative.

Yes, gold-, copper- and silver-infused carbon fiber has hit the floor running; chef's knives have evolved to the point of futuristic material makeup and specialized cutting tasks in the kitchen; balisongs fly and flip so fast, and to manipulate them has become a sport; bowie patterns have blended with fighters for an all-new SKU in the online knife store; and flipper folder blades open faster than spring-loaded switchblades.

The real question is, "What's not new in the world of knives?" And when you think about that, it is nothing short of spectacular. Credit the knifemakers themselves, the designers, engineers, material suppliers and manufacturers. No one rested on their laurels. When regulations limited blade lengths, opening mechanisms and patterns, makers objected, campaigned, testified, fought hard and emerged victorious.

When there were no materials at hand, they made or found them. When the mechanisms didn't work to their satisfaction, they fashioned new ones. When the patterns were stale, they reinvented them. When trends were tired, they created new categories. Can there really be anything new in the world of knives? Oh, yeah, there really can.

Double Jointed

⌃ BRUCE BARNETT
Twice the "River of Fire" damascus is doubly good on a two-blade folding slip joint with cream-toned ancient mammoth ivory handle slabs. *(BladeGallery.com image)*

⌃ BUBBA CROUCH
A world of discoveries in the confines of a trapper, the blade and bolster steel is Bill Poor's "Gorgon Flower Mosaic," the sambar stag handle of the amber kind, and double vine filework is found along the CPM 154 back spacers. *(SharpByCoop image)*

⌃ RAYMON E. HUNT
Not your daddy's two-blade trapper, flat-ground 154CM blades meet stainless bolsters engraved and gold inlaid by Alice Carter and mammoth ivory handle scales with peened and polished gold pins. *(SharpByCoop image)*

⌃ RICK NOWLAND
You couldn't color the Mokume bolsters or mammoth ivory handle scales better with crayons, and the two-blade damascus trapper is better for them. *(Cory Martin image)*

» PHIL JACOB
"Roman knot" file work spans the blade spines and back spacers of a CPM 154 folder with ancient mammoth ivory handle scales. *(SharpByCoop image)*

« TOBY HILL
Raindrop damascus and bark mammoth ivory are the one-two punch on a sunfish-pattern whaler's knife with elephant-toenail-style blades.
(BladeGallery.com image)

» TIM ROBERTSON
A Remington 1123 style folder is executed in CPM 154 blade steel, stainless, stag handle scales and a tri-colored (brass, copper and stainless) signature bullet shield. *(SharpByCoop image)*

» CHRIS SHARP
The flat-ground slip-joint folder features damascus blade steel, 416 stainless bolsters, ivory handle scales and a pierced shield.
(SharpByCoop image)

« TOBIN HILL
Not only it is a double-blade CPM-154 canoe-pattern folder in a pair of amber stag handle scales, but it's also a slip joint/lock-back combination. There's double everything.
(SharpByCoop image)

Melting Pot

The United States is and has been the melting pot of the world. People who call the country home are more culturally, ethnically and racially diverse, of mixed nationalities and removed from their ancestral roots than ever. Ancestry websites have sprung up and capitalized on peoples' desires to trace their family roots.

So why is cultural heritage still so important to people? Why hold onto the past?

It is the only way to move forward. Historical accuracy is inherent to progress, and knowledge is key to understanding the world in which we live. The ways of peoples' dress, style, religious beliefs, traditions, food, shelter, art, music, architecture, schools, tools, weaponry and understanding of the universe intertwine into a culture.

Knifemakers have embraced this, becoming the curators of edged tools and weapons, replicating centuries-old styles and studying traditional knifemaking methods, keeping historic models alive and advancing them into the 21st century.

» KEVIN CASHEN
The Medieval Knightly Sword looks its part, complete with a leather wrapped handle, wrought iron guard and pommel, and 32-inch double-fullered L6 blade.
(SharpByCoop image)

» PAUL DISTEFANO
A time capsule capturing early Japan, a 14-inch W2 blade with *hamon* (temper line) is accompanied by an etched wrought iron *tsuba* (guard) and traditionally wrapped, carved and textured Wenge wood handle.
(Caleb Royer photo)

« JOHN LUNDEMO
With obvious Roman gladius influences, the "Space Captain" navigates the galaxy in a leather-wrapped wood handle and a black DLC-coated CPM 3V blade.
(Whetstone Studio image)

« PETER DEL RASO
Righteously engraved by Marcello Pedini, the Persian fighter is regaled in an etched san mai blade of Takefu steel with a VG-10 core, and a giraffe bone handle set with several garnets.
(SharpByCoop image)

« HENRY HILDEN
The stacked handle of the damascus Nordic hunter is a combination of crosscut mammoth ivory, ironwood and Masur birch, complete with an inlaid sterling silver moose shield.
(BladeGallery.com image)

» PAR-OLOF EKLUND
The Sami-style half-horn hunter showcases a fitting "frost-pattern" Damasteel blade, and an engraved and carved reindeer antler handle.
(BladeGallery.com image)

» WILLIAM LLOYD
Plenty of carving went into the wolf jaw handle of a Viking seax that also sports a K.C. Lund damascus blade. *(Whetstone Studio image)*

》DAVID MIRABILE
The long, sleek body of the "Dragonfly Cutter" incorporates a 14.75-inch blade and a cord-wrapped stingray skin handle.
(SharpByCoop image)

《 TRISTEN KNIGHT
Though the blade of the "Meridian" model is forged from a Ford Model A axle, the Japanese influence is undeniable, particularly the cord-wrapped stingray skin handle. *(Whetstone Studio image)*

《 ANDREW FRANKLAND
The 10-inch Khyber Carver is a pointed affair in an ATS-34 blade, rope filework along the spine and tang, heat-blued titanium bolsters and an African cape buffalo horn handle.

《 DMITRIY POPOV
Damasteel and ebony dominate the maker's take on a tanto that also sports copper spacers. *(SharpByCoop image)*

» VINCE EVANS
The accurate rendering of a Scottish dirk includes a 5160 blade, brass furniture and carved walnut hilt.
(SharpByCoop image)

« MATTHEW STAGMER
A ribbon of stars wends its way across the mosaic damascus blade of a Roman Maine Gladius showcasing a Mexican rosewood handle; and silver, bronze and mosaic fittings.
(Whetstone Studio image)

» ARTUR SZYNGWELSKI
The differentially tempered O1 Japanese-style fixed blade has a rayon-wrapped stingray skin handle.
(Caleb Royer photo)

» RODRIGO ENGLERT
A fine example of a gaucho knife showcases a 9-inch Turkish damascus blade with integral guard, matching ferrule and pommel, and a giraffe bone handle. *(Caleb Royer photo)*

« MAURICIO DALETZKY
In a gaucho style, the damascus fixed blade features an integral front bolster, sterling silver spacers, a stabilized maple burl handle and matching sheath. *(BladeGallery.com image)*

≪ TIMOTHY STEINGASS
A takedown Kwaiken enlists a clad 1095 and stainless blade, and a twisted steel wire handle. *(SharpByCoop image)*

≪ KOJI HARA
Japanese Super Gold Damascus was a fitting choice for the tanto with copper bolsters and leather wrapped (Tsukamaki) stingray skin handle. *(SharpByCoop.com image)*

≪ DON SYLVEST
Nothing but the best for a Natchez fighter—maple burl handle scales, mosaic pins, CPM 154 blade, blue liners and a tapered tang—all the boxes are checked.
(Caleb Royer photo)

≪ MATT GREGORY
A matched set of bowies is fashioned after the "Weehawk Tantos" of Jody Samson, including Crucible Steel S7 blades, black Richlite and stainless bolsters; cord-wrapped stingray skin handles and sterling silver tiger *menuki* (handle charms).
(SharpByCoop image)

≪ KEITH FLUDDER
Let's talk about a tanto in a stingray skin handle with burn orange cord wrap, Mokume fittings and a W-2 blade that wears its *hamon* (temper line) like a badge.
(SharpByCoop image)

» JEREMY SPAKE
The puukko parades a Nitro V blade, nickel silver guard and textured spacer, and combination African blackwood and rosewood handle. *(SharpByCoop image)*

⌃ CHARLIE ELLIS
A traditionally styled folding knife native to Japan, the Higonokami friction folder sports a hand-forged damascus blade and a textured 304 stainless handle recovered from a beer keg. Now we can all respect that! *(BladeGallery.com image)*

» DAVID MCCONNELL
The maker's version of a Persian kard comes in an 8-inch W1 blade and a dyed and stabilized sambar stag handle. *(Whetstone Studio image)*

« SHAWN SHROPSHIRE
With obvious Malaysian keris influences, namely the 1084 blade, the exotic knife sports a Lignum Vitae handle and mild steel fittings. *(Whetstone Studio image)*

« DAVE PARTHEMORE
A keris-style dagger is done up in a 1084-and-15N20 damascus blade, mokume-gane guard and deer antler handle. *(SharpByCoop image)*

« JOHN COHEA
The American frontier hunter crosses the Plains dressed in a Chad Nichols raindrop damascus blade, and a mammoth ivory handle and thong bead. *(Caleb Royer photo)*

Gold-, Copper- & Silver-Infused Carbon Fiber

« KEN ONION
A CPM 154 folding dagger sashays a copper wire-infused "lightning strike" carbon fiber handle and titanium hardware colorfully engraved by the maker in a poker theme.
(SharpByCoop photo)

« ANDRE VAN HEERDEN and ANDRE THORBURN (A2)
A titanium handle inlaid with copper-shred carbon fiber highlights the san mai damascus flipper folder.
(BladeGallery.com image)

« RUBEM LORENZ
As if fashioning his own carbon fiber with gold and silver points for the handle of a damascus fixed blade wasn't impressive enough, the maker inlaid 10 pieces of meteorite into the eagle head that adorns the pommel. *(Caleb Royer photo)*

⌃ ANDRE THORBURN
A delight from tip to butt, the Damasteel flipper folder is fashioned with a gold dust-inlaid shred carbon fiber handle, and a zirconium bolster gold inlaid and engraved by Julien Marchal.

(SharpByCoop photo)

⌃ PETER MARTIN
Though it's tough to see past the "lava lamp" damascus blade and blacked-out Superconductor bolsters of the flipper folder, hints of copper and bronze dust in the carbon fiber handle are nice touches. *(Cory Martin image)*

Faithful to Their Masters

No, they're not dogs, but faithfulness isn't reserved for the *Canis lupus familiaris* . Humans are faithful servants, as well. Of all *Homo sapiens*, knifemakers tend to gravitate toward history and tradition, faithfully representing the craft they endeavor to pursue.

Does that mean knifemakers haven't changed with the times, upgraded, adopted technology and advanced? They certainly have done all those things, but blade builders haven't forgotten what the art of knifemaking was like before it evolved. Many speak of knives being man's oldest tools, chipped from rock and used to remove animal hides, cut meat and build shelter.

Few knifemakers walk around in leopard skins and fur boots, nor do they chip rocks. They do pay homage to everyone from Japanese bladesmiths who clay coated and differentially tempered blades, to the first makers who fashioned drop-point hunters, one-hand- and spring-assisted-opening folders, myriad legendary military and tactical knives, chute and boot knives, automatics, cross-draw models, hip huggers, neck knives and frame-lock flipper folders.

They are faithful to their masters, crediting those who have come before and doing the living and non-living legends proud.

» STEPHEN LELAND
The San Francisco masters of yesteryear would be proud of the walrus ivory-handle bowie with brass liners, and nickel silver guard and sheath.
(Caleb Royer photo)

» JOHN YOUNG
A Bob Loveless-style drop-point hunter has a slight recurve to the blade, as well as red liners and a stag handle. *(SharpByCoop image)*

« EDMUND DAVIDSON
The Bob Loveless-design fighter is fashioned using a Siberian mastodon ivory handle, CPM 154 blade and integral guard engraved by Jere Davidson.
(Whetstone Studio image)

» KEVIN STROUP
A Bob Loveless-style chute knife, this one is sent to market in a black canvas Micarta® handle, brass guard and 80CrV2 steel blade. *(Dirk Loots image)*

« RICHARD WRIGHT
A copy of a circa 1740-1790 folding knife owned by William J. McHenry, the maker kept his close to the original, shaping a hollow-ground Damasteel blade, a damascus shotgun barrel frame, file-worked back bar and an ivory blade stop.

« ADAM FROMHOLTZ
A barrel knife is a fun one to emulate, here in an ebony coffin-style handle, nickel silver bolsters and a Takefu blade. *(SharpByCoop image)*

« JIM SORNBERGER
Forging the san mai damascus blade was a feat in itself, not to mention fashioning the mokume-gane, synthetic tortoise shell and gold quartz handle of the San Francisco dagger. *(SharpByCoop image)*

《 MAMORU SHIGENO
One Loveless-style Big Bear and one chute knife in the ilk of Bob, they both sport ATS-34 blades, stainless guards and burgundy Micarta® handles. *(SharpByCoop image)*

《 TIM STEINGASS
Calling it a "Silver Bear" after a Bob Loveless Big Bear fighter, the maker's rendition involves a CPM 154 blade and a twisted stainless wire handle.
(SharpByCoop image)

《 FOREST "BUTCH" SHEELY
An Edwin Forrest Bowie is faithfully reproduced in a 12.25-inch 1095 blade, checkered Cuban mahogany handle and sterling silver fittings.
(Whetstone Studio image)

》 AKIO SHINOZAKI
A damascus fighter reminiscent of a Bob Loveless chute knife is handled in ironwood with a nickel silver guard.
(SharpByCoop image)

» JOHN APRIL
Green mammoth ivory almost steals the show on a Bob Loveless-style chute knife, but the CPM 154 blade is ground just so. *(SharpByCoop image)*

» MARCUS LIN
A Loveless-style semi skinner sports a Stellite 6K blade, black linen Micarta® handle scales, red liners and stainless fittings engraved by Alvin Chewiwi. *(Caleb Royer photo)*

» ROBERT APPLEBY
A faithfully executed Rudy Ruana-style Model 30A exhibits a hollow-ground, satin-finished 440C clip-point blade, a 6061-T6 aluminum handle and frame and sheep horn handle scales. *(Whetstone Studio image)*

» MACE VITALE
There's meteorite forged into the Wootz blade of the maker's antique bowie rendition, this with a nickel silver bolster and coffin-style blackwood handle. *(SharpByCoop image)*

» MAMORU SHIGENO
The maker fashions many knives in the style of the masterful R.W. Loveless, and this pretty piece is no exception. *(SharpByCoop image)*

Tactical in the True Sense

No matter how many times people say that "tactical" simply means the ability to manipulate something in one's hand, to be "tactile," to touch, maneuver or handle; it's simply not the full picture. They cut themselves short.

"Of or occurring at the battlefront," is another definition, as are "carefully planned to gain a specific military end" and "a tactical first strike." These are closer to what knifemakers and enthusiasts originally meant by "tactical folders" or "tactical fixed blades." They were designed to look and work like warrior blades, or as all-black, stealth and even camouflaged edged weapons. The designs were purposeful, and the blades meant for self-defense and tactical fighting. The locks were strong, the edges and tips wicked, and the handle materials practically indestructible.

Of course, the genre got away from that, and soon "tactical" meant any folder with a pocket clip, lock and one-hand opener. Tactical fixed blades were demoted to anything black or camo with sheaths designed for quick release and draw. Remember when all tactical fixed blade sheaths were Kydex? Whatever happened to that?

Some tactical fixed blades and folders have not only remained true to a military and self-defense form, but they've also progressed to being more reliable in the field, of higher quality materials and sporting duty-specific attributes. They're tactical in the true sense, at least as far as gaining a tactical advantage over an opponent or obstacle.

» DIRK LOOTS
A full takedown sub-hilt fighter, this puppy sports an antiqued 80CrV2 blade, blackened A2 fittings, an anodized titanium guard and frame, and a maple handle. *(Dirk Loots image)*

⌃ GARY CHELETTE
This refreshing take on a hollow-handle model features a CPM-154 blade, carbon fiber guard and a green cord wrap.
(Whetstone Studio image)

» BOB OHLEMANN
The black Cerakote coating on the recurved CPM 154 blade and hardware, combined with an olive drab Micarta® handle, makes this one a tactical in the true sense.
(SharpByCoop image)

« SOBRAL BROTHERS/ CAS KNIVES
The fighter comes to dance in a damascus blade, blued-steel guard and ironwood grip.
(SharpByCoop image)

« DOMINIC BINKERT
A collaboration with Marks Innovative Gear, the custom knife and pen set includes a hollow-ground CPM 154 blade and carbon fiber handle scales. *(SharpByCoop image)*

« MATT GASKILL
The rubberized carbon fiber grip is good on a 1095 trench knife with smoky temper line, knuckle guard and skull crusher pommel. *(Caleb Royer image)*

« FRANK HUNTER
Fashioned for a fellow law enforcement officer, the folder sports an Alabama Damascus blade and an OD green G-10 handle. *(SharpByCoop image)*

« RAMON CHAVEZ
The laser-engraved CPM-3V blade and titanium handle don't detract from the tactical nature of the Liberation frame-lock folder. *(Whetstone Studio image)*

« RIAAN MANSER
A ferocious-looking flipper folder is carried out in a multi-ground ELMAX blade, caged ceramic bearings and a black-and-white carbon fiber handle. *(BladeGallery.com image)*

« KUNIHIKO TAMATSU
A sleek integral fighter relies only on ATS-34 stainless steel, linen Micarta® and its own wits. *(SharpByCoop image)*

» PIERRE MEFFLIN
A dastardly dagger does its dirty deeds in W2 tool steel (complete with temper line), a G-10 handle and carbon fiber pins. *(SharpByCoop image)*

» ANDREW DEMKO
Donated to Knife Rights for the "2020 Ultimate Steel" fundraiser, this one's tactical "lock, stock and barrel."
(SharpByCoop image)

» TODD REXFORD
It might seem like a no-frills flipper, but the titanium frame-lock folder features a milled and groovy grip and a little pearl planted in the pivot head area.
(Cory Martin image)

» ARTHUR SZYGWELSKI
A slim, sharp stiletto enlists an M390 blade, a Juma (resin) handle, mosaic pin, and a G-10 guard and pommel. *(Caleb Royer image)*

« MICHAEL RAYMOND
Like windswept sands, the CarboQuartz handle of the Bohler M390 frame-lock folder makes for a desolate yet inviting landscape.
(SharpByCoop image)

« MAMORU SHIGENO
The Bob Loveless-style Big Bear fighter is locked and loaded via ATS-34 blade steel and brown Micarta®.
(SharpByCoop image)

« TOM KREIN
The maker's Alpha model sports an acid-washed CPM-154 asymmetrical folding dagger blade, titanium bolsters and "jungle camo" Fat Carbon handle scales. *(Whetstone Studio image)*

« ANTONY RICHARDS
Between the hollow-ground, recurved blade, the blue Micarta® handle and the Kydex sheath, she's a true tactical temptress. *(SharpByCoop image)*

» DILLON DEAN
"Caesar II" is outfitted in a 5.5-inch, recurved CPM 154 blade, canvas Micarta® handle and a "mountain viper"-pattern camo sheath. *(SharpByCoop image)*

« PAUL LEBATARD
Nothing fancy here—it's a clean PTK-4 model in a 5-inch, clip-point CPM 154 blade, 7075-T6 aluminum guard and brown canvas Micarta® handle. *(Whetstone Studio image)*

» NATHAN CAROTHERS
Practically indestructible, the integral CPM 3V dagger shows off a G-10 handle and deep blood groove (or fuller). *(SharpByCoop image)*

» R.J. MARTIN
The no-nonsense, frame-lock dress tactical folder leans heavily on a CPM S125V blade and a red/black Carboquartz handle. *(SharpByCoop image)*

« TYLER TURNER
The maker's version of an M3 trench knife does the pattern justice in an "Odin's Heimskringla"-pattern Damasteel blade, zirconium guard and carbon fiber handle. *(SharpByCoop image)*

True Blue Bowies

《 LUKE DELLMYER

From the tip of the low-layer damascus blade to the butt of the snakewood coffin-style handle, the bowie with clamshell S-guard is a rare beauty.

(Caleb Royer photo)

《 TANNER SASLOW

The takedown bowie boasts a W1 blade with *hamon* (temper line), a Mallee burl handle, wrought iron guard and copper spacer.

(Whetstone Studio image)

》 JOHN APRIL

Ball bearing damascus makes quite a showing, paired with a mammoth ivory handle for a bowie with a terraced coffin-style handle.

(SharpByCoop image)

》 JASON FRY

Circle the wagons—the maker forged a bowie sporting a san mai blade of wagon wheel wrought iron over a 1084 steel core, a wagon wheel wrought iron guard and an ash handle from the wagon tongue of his grandfather's wagon. *(SharpByCoop image)*

« ADAM MILLEA
A hand-forged 5160 bowie benefits from a damascus guard, a brass spacer and sculpted cherry burl handle.
(SharpByCoop image)

« JIM POLING
Lots of love went into the ladder-pattern damascus bowie with stag handle and nickel silver fittings, as evidenced by the impeccable fit and finish, and overall eye-popping appeal.
(Cory Martin image)

« CHARLES CARPENTER
The vision was a 5160 bowie in a cocobolo handle, nickel guard and bronze spacers, and it came to fruition.
(Whetstone Studio image)

» ANDREW BLOMFIELD
A bowie is beautifully executed in a "River of Fire" damascus blade, damascus D-guard and stag handle.
(SharpByCoop image)

» PAUL SAVAGE
A damascus D-guard bowie is the beneficiary of a hot-blued O-1 guard and a mammoth ivory handle.
(SharpByCoop image)

» KEN CARR and TOM MCGINNIS
A D-guard bowie is the beneficiary of a keen ladder-pattern damascus blade, damascus fittings and an amber stag handle. *(Caleb Royer image)*

» KEN HALL
Fifteen-plus inches of bowie encompass a damascus blade and guard and a stabilized curly Koa wood grip. *(SharpByCoop image)*

» SOBRAL BROTHERS/CAS KNIVES
The fuller along the damascus blade is enough to grab your attention, not to mention the blued steel guard and stag grip. *(SharpByCoop image)*

« GENE KIMMI
The maker's first S-guard bowie likely won't be his last. This one sports a 360-layer, raindrop-damascus blade; fluted and coined quilted maple spacers; a desert ironwood handle and black Micarta® pin. *(Caleb Royer photo)*

« DAVID LISCH
The "Mind Bender Damascus" blade is just the start of reality-altering elements of a split-penny, splitring D-guard bowie, with others including a gold-covered wrought iron guard and sambar stag handle. *(SharpByCoop image)*

» KEVIN ROOM
Everything is big—the 52100 blade, stag handle and the pommel fileworked to match the grooves of the handle. *(Caleb Royer photo)*

» JERRY FISK
The "Trail of Tears"-pattern damascus, catalpa wood handle, gold inlay and engraving of the true-blue bowie bespeak class and tradition.
(SharpByCoop image)

« DAN PETERS
The 16-inch CPM 154 bowie packs a wallop, outfitted in brass, African blackwood and amboyna burl.
(Whetstone Studio image)

« TRAVIS MOORE
The long, recurved 1095 blade with pronounced clip and integral finger guard is enough to get the juices flowing. Add the ironwood handle and turn into a puddle. *(Cory Martin image)*

« W. ALLEN SURLS
If you are hungry, feast on the Chad Nichols "scrambled eggs" damascus blade of the frontier bowie outfitted in an elkhorn handle and a rawhide-wrapped copper ferrule. *(Dirk Loots image)*

» ANDREW TAKACH
The bowie boasts a clay quenched W1 blade etched to reveal the *hamon* (temper line), a bronze guard and Steller's sea cow rib grip.
(Caleb Royer photo)

« RUSS ANDREWS
The Rio Grande Bowie features a foot-long, duplex-ladder-pattern damascus blade; a damascus guard, ferrule and finial; and a sambar stag handle. *(Caleb Royer photo)*

« ERIK FRITZ
A straightforward bowie showcases a 9.25-inch 5160 tool steel blade, a ringed Gidgee wood handle and mild steel fittings. *(Whetstone Studio image)*

« JACKSON RUMBLE
The flat-ground integral 5160 keyhole bowie boasts an ironwood grip.
(SharpByCoop image)

« KEVIN HARVEY
In addition to differentially heat treating the 9-inch 1070 blade and achieving a wispy temper line, the maker carved the desert ironwood handle in the style of an Enoch Drabble Sheffield bowie from the late 1830s. *(BladeGallery.com image)*

« TOMMY GANN
Between the mosaic damascus blade forged from high-carbon steels and a curly Koa handle, the maker plied plenty of pattern into the proper bowie. *(BladeGallery.com image)*

« DYLAN BRUGMAN
This classic bowie parades a 1075+Cr blade, a mild steel guard and spacer, and a stabilized walnut handle secured using a carbon fiber pin. *(Caleb Royer photo)*

» RUSSELL ROOSEVELT
Besides the traditional bowie pattern, there are eye-popping spalted maple and 1084-and-15N20 damascus. *(SharpByCoop image)*

» GREG KEITH
Why not give the damascus blade of a clip-point bowie a little swoosh? It was as good an idea as the desert ironwood grip. *(SharpByCoop image)*

Ancient Ivory & Steel

« WILLIAM MILLER
The camp knife is set up in a fossil walrus ivory handle, a "W's"-pattern damascus blade and damascus fittings.
(Whetstone Studio image)

« ARNO BERNARD SR.
Oh, that blue-green, bark-like ancient ivory, pinned properly to the full tang of a damascus drop-point hunter and appealing to so many tastes.
(BladeGallery.com image)

» JIM POOR
A LinerLock folder is executed to great effect in twist-pattern damascus and mammoth ivory. The maker forged matching damascus horse riding spurs as well, for good measure. *(SharpByCoop image)*

» PAUL LUSK
He endeavored to build the "Endeavor" hunter using an AEB-L blade, a stainless bolster and mammoth ivory handle scales, and succeed the maker did.
(SharpByCoop image)

« ANDERS HOGSTROM
Crosscut fossil walrus ivory more than suffices for the grip of "The Beaker" dagger in a Heimskringla-pattern Damasteel blade.
(SharpByCoop image)

« JOHN COHEA
Bark mammoth ivory crackles on a primitive drop-point hunter, guarded in copper and rawhide and given a leather sheath adorned in beadwork and horsehair tassels.
(Whetstone Studio image)

« LON HUMPHREY
Old meets new via artifact walrus ivory, brass, G-10 and a forge-finished 52100 steel blade.
(Caleb Royer image)

« TOBIN HILL
Mammoth ivory makes a statement on a three-blade lock-back whittler, and it's not "pamper me so I don't break."
(SharpByCoop image)

» DANIEL CHINNOCK
Mammoth ivory knife grips take wing on a drop-point hunter showcasing a nitre-blued damascus blade and 24k-gold screws.
(Whetstone Studio image)

» W. ALLEN SURLS
The walrus ivory was left *au natural* on a frontier hunter otherwise dressed in Alabama damascus and a rawhide-wrapped copper guard. *(Dirk Loots image)*

« SAMUEL LURQUIN
The sub-hilt fighter parades its W2 blade and wavy temper line with pride, pairing it up with a fossil walrus ivory grip. *(SharpByCoop image)*

« DON HANSON III
Between the ancient walrus ivory and W2 tool steel is some fantastic mosaic damascus, with a little left over for the thumb disc.
(SharpByCoop image)

A Blank Canvas
Micarta®

I love the old documentaries and movies about master artists in their studios, paintings covering every inch of wall and floor space, propped up on furniture, pigments and pallets strewn throughout; and some ingenious, wild-haired, crazy-eyed bohemian taking brush to canvas, seemingly unaware of his surroundings and lost in a world of creativity.

I'd feel bad about making the comparison to some knifemakers, but I've had several tell me that's exactly what their shops are like. For others, their knifemaking studios are as neat as pins, all machines wiped down, floor swept and tools in their places.

The similarity among all is the blank canvas—in this case, canvas Micarta®—a clean slate on which to build, a material that will make up the whole, upon which to create a design, add elements, push boundaries and make magic happen. Knifemakers are creative and utilitarian types, that rare breed of function meeting fashion, and they're taking canvas Micarta® to its limits, picking it up and laying it down for all to see in new and innovative ways.

» JIM TAYLOR
A front flipper folder sports a CPM 154 blade, titanium liners and a coffin-style vintage European Micarta® handle with an umbrella logo.
(SharpByCoop image)

» JOHN ARNOLD
It's not the OD green or the camouflage canvas Micarta®, but the creative combination of the two, that make the "Mini Simba" flipper folder a work of art, shown here in an M390 powdered-metallurgical stainless blade.
(BladeGallery.com image)

« MATT GASKILL
An upswept Persian design with a hidden tang, the O1 fixed blade is paired with a sculpted and cool black canvas Micarta® handle and pins, and an orange G-10 liner.
(Caleb Royer image)

» TAD LYNCH
The forge-finished W2 tool steel guardless hunter enlists a vintage Micarta® handle and wrought iron fittings.

(Whetstone Studio image)

» DAN BIDINGER
Bloodwood and green canvas Micarta® anchor and enliven an 8.5-inch, satin-finished AEB-L stainless chef's knife.

(BladeGallery.com image)

« ALISTAIR PHILLIPS
A three-blade stockman is constructed of CPM S35VN blade steel, titanium bolsters and liners, and green canvas Micarta® handle scales.

(SharpByCoop image)

« JOEY BERRY
He broke out the black canvas and burnt orange Westinghouse Micarta® for the Serbian chef's knife in an O1 blade featuring hammer-finished flats.

(Dirk Loots image)

» PIERRE MEFFLIN
Black G-10, antique linen Micarta® (a bit finer than canvas) and stainless pins make up the handle half of a W2 fighter with slight tapered tang.

« MIKE NELSON
Though he left the black canvas Micarta® blank, he bolted it to the full tang of a differentially tempered drop-point W2 blade. *(Caleb Royer image)*

« SHAWN MCINTYRE
Natural canvas Micarta® spacers set off the 52100 drop-point hunter in a black linen Micarta® handle and a stainless guard. *(SharpByCoop image)*

« LUCAS BURNLEY
The maker highlights the green canvas Micarta® handles of the "Willow" and "Thresh" knives by underlaying them with orange Glo liners. The knives also sport stonewashed Nitro V and AEB-L blades and brass and copper fittings. *(Whetstone Studio image)*

Flippers in G-10, Mokume, Titanium and Carbon Fiber

⌃ OLAMIC CUTLERY
The titanium handle of the "Wayfarer 247" flipper folder is given an entropic finish and paired with a flat-ground M390 blade. *(SharpByCoop image)*

⌃ JOHN ARNOLD
It takes a trained eye to know that the Moku-Ti bolsters and silver-strike carbon fiber handle scales would pair so nicely for a Damasteel flipper folder. *(BladeGallery.com image)*

⌃ HERECUS BLOMERUS
The pattern play on an LL14M flipper folder includes a Vinland damascus blade, Zladinox titanium damascus bolsters and carbon fiber handle scales.
(BladeGallery.com image)

⌃ TREVOR BURGER
Spalted oak is an inspired choice for the bolsters of a Bohler M390 stainless steel flipper folder with carbon fiber handle scales.
(BladeGallery.com image)

» STEVEN SKIFF
An impeccable frame-lock flipper folder regales its admirers in a 3D-machined titanium handle, a stainless Damasteel blade, and Timascus pivot discs and pocket clip. *(SharpByCoop image)*

» TIM KINGSFORD
A dimpled bolster is a nice touch on an RWL-34 front flipper with titanium frame. *(SharpByCoop image)*

» CORY MARTIN
It's good to have bolster choices—titanium or mokume-gane—on a flipper folder, such as this model in 12C27 stainless steel with carbon fiber handle scales. *(Cory Martin image)*

» JASON CLARK
Gray is good from tip to hilt on a stainless damascus (Chad Nichols) flipper folder that features zirconium bolsters and chatoyant carbon fiber handle scales. *(BladeGallery.com image)*

« ANDRE THORBURN
Ironwood inlaid into the G-10 handle frame is an inspired choice, as is the Takefu blade and zirconium pivot collar. *(SharpByCoop image)*

« PETER and CORY MARTIN
It took a father-son team to fashion a pair of nearly identical (one has blue-anodized liners) CFK flipper folders in 12C27 stainless blades and red G-10 handles. *(Cory Martin image)*

« KIRBY LAMBERT
Follow the lines of the flipper folder itself and the materials, a dizzying yet alluring blend of modern makeup and mechanical wizardry. *(SharpByCoop image)*

« RIAAN MANSER
Black G-10 outlines and frames the stabilized maple handle inlays of the T3 Flipper in a premium Bohler ELMAX stainless steel blade. *(BladeGallery.com image)*

« BRIAN TIGHE
Inlaying abalone into the carbon fiber handle was a stroke of genius, and the Damasteel blade and pocket clip, dual thumb studs and button lock of the flipper folder are not bad choices, either. *(SharpByCoop image)*

» TODD REXFORD
A damascus blade in a tight, subtle pattern is a nice counterpart to the inlaid titanium handle of a clean flipper folder.
(Cory Martin image)

« WILL ZERMENO
The foxy flipper is executed in a grooved titanium handle and a CPM S30V blade with integral guard.
(Whetstone Studio image)

« PHILIPPE JOURGET
A Tashi Bharucha design, the flipper folder parades a Damasteel blade, Moku-Ti bolster, bronze-anodized titanium liners and CarboQuartz handle scales. *(SharpByCoop image)*

« MANUELE MESSORI
Handles of the D2 flipper folders are combinations of heat-colored titanium and G-Tec, and anodized titanium and carbon fiber. *(SharpByCoop image)*

Bowie/Fighter Frenzy

Raised clips, slight clips, re-curves and elongated clips or no clip points at all. These are the attributes and features of bowie/fighters, those hybrid knives that are infusing the knife industry with new energy and creating a category all their own.

It makes sense. If you like vanilla ice cream and have a taste for some chocolate as well, then a vanilla/chocolate soft serve swirl isn't far behind. Is your mouth watering yet?

Bowie/fighters blend two of the tastiest knife styles the industry has to offer, a sweet concoction of the reaching, thin-blade, double guard or sub-hilt fighter, and the big-bladed bowie with clip point, hefty handle and deep, sweeping belly. They may even sport a little Spanish notch near the choil or a flat choil, a leather sheath, a cross-draw number or a fringed version.

It's a bowie/fighter frenzy, and the knifemakers can't fashion enough hybrids to ward off the masses of crazed fans in line to own one of the raised-, slight-, elongated- or sans-clip-point blades, properly honed, hafted and housed, of course.

» PAUL DISTEFANO
If you prefer your bowie to have a foot-long, flat-ground, 500-layer damascus blade, a damascus guard and walrus ivory handle, then you are in luck. *(SharpByCoop image)*

» MARK FLEMING
With 13.75 inches of ladder-pattern damascus to work with, the maker didn't disappoint, forging a mosaic damascus guard for the piece and building a white G-10 handle with stainless ferrule. *(SharpByCoop image)*

» TYLER HACKBARTH
The "Wolf River Warfighter" sports a 100-layer damascus blade clad with a W2 core, a buffalo horn and Koa wood handle, copper pins, and copper and G-10 liners. *(Whetstone Studio image)*

« SHAWN ELLIS
A large clip-point bowie with fighter characteristics, the san mai blade is forged from 1095 high-carbon steel sandwiched between layers of 416 stainless, joined by an S-guard and African blackwood handle. *(BladeGallery.com image)*

» JACKSON RUMBLE
The integral fighter is sent to market in equal parts dazzling damascus and desert ironwood.
(SharpByCoop image)

» KELLY FRASIER
The 11.5-inch 1075 high-carbon blade of the bowie exhibits a temper line and a false edge and is accompanied by a copper guard and ironwood handle.
(SharpByCoop image)

« TYLER HALL
The bowie/fighter features a big W2 blade with raised clip and smoky temper line, an iron guard, amboyna burl handle, and a copper spacer and pin. *(Caleb Royer photo)*

« JIM POLING
Black and brown hues are brought forth via a damascus blade, wrought iron guard, copper spacer and Sapele (Nigerian mahogany) handle.
(Cory Martin image)

» BUTCH DEVERAUX
Part bowie/part fighter, the parts include a convex-ground 52100 blade, a brass guard and sheep horn handle.

(SharpByCoop image)

» ELAND GREEN
At 12.75 inches overall, the W2 Texas toothpick has some reach, with wavy temper line spanning the blade and an ironwood burl handle secured via stainless pins.

(Caleb Royer photo)

⌃ BUBBA COX
A bowie/fighter with sharpened clip and file-worked spine blends a mammoth ivory handle with damascus blade and fittings, with Corby bolts to hold it all together.

(Whetstone Studio image)

» MOHAMMED ALSULAIBIKH
No dainty knife, the bowie boasts a 10-inch 1080 blade, a stainless guard and walnut handle.

(SharpByCoop image)

» JAMES RODEBAUGH
The camp knife fits the bowie/fighter category perfectly, here in an O1 blade, bronze and silver guard, and African blackwood handle.

(SharpByCoop image)

« W. ALLEN SURLS
The raised clip of the antiqued 80CrV2 blade gives it a fighter feel, furthered by the arrowhead guard, rawhide-wrapped copper ferrule and ancient walrus ivory handle.
(Dirk Loots image)

« BEN BREDA
The dramatic number showcases a W2 blade with pronounced *hamon* (temper line), a stainless guard, damascus collar and Hawaiian Koa wood handle.
(Caleb Royer photo)

« KENNETH KING
The dimpling of ivory, filing of the damascus blade spine and cabochon creation for the turquoise inset—these are the touches that make this bowie pop.
(SharpByCoop image)

« OLIVER GOLDSCHMIDT
Calling it an integral damascus "chopper fighter," a Koa wood handle, stainless pin and damascus buttcap anchor the wieldy piece.
(Whetstone Studio image)

« TERRY VANDEVENTER
The fighter features a W2 blade with wispy temper line, a sambar stag handle, and fittings of damascus and Argentium silver.
(Whetstone Studio image)

» STEPHEN LELAND
A Sheffield bowie is outfitted with a coffin-style elephant ivory handle (the material obtained from the San Francisco Zoo), a nickel silver guard, and leather sheath with nickel silver throat and tip.
(Caleb Royer photo)

» DAVE ARMOUR
Dressed in purple stabilized box elder burl and a 1084 blade with smoky temper line, the bowie stretches 15 ¾ inches overall, a safe distance, and incorporates a copper guard to keep fingers from harm's way.
(SharpByCoop image)

« DON SYLVEST
Desert ironwood burl begets a CPM 154 fighter blade, separated solely by stainless bolsters.
(Caleb Royer photo)

« MACE VITALE
The maker forged the damascus blade and guard of the "Thunderstruck" bowie/fighter, affixing a curly Koa handle to the powerful piece.
(SharpByCoop image)

« BURTON HARRUFF
The well-coordinated cutter includes an 8.5-inch ladder-pattern damascus blade, a wrought iron S-guard, old growth redwood burl handle; and copper, G-10 and black ash burl spacers.
(Caleb Royer photo)

» RYAN JACOBS
A sub-hilt bowie/fighter with through-tang construction, the W2 blade has a handsome *hamon* (temper line) and butts up against a gun-blued guard and curly maple handle.
(Caleb Royer photo)

» DAVID MCCONNELL
A foot-long 1075 bowie/ fighter wears its spalted beech stripes well.
(Whetstone Studio image)

« LEO POTTER
A 1075 blade with raised clip leaves a lasting impression furthered by the low-layer, striped-damascus guard and rosewood handle.
(Caleb Royer photo)

« ALEXANDER NOOT
Of the "Dragonslayer Bowie" ilk, it features a distal-tapered Nilox steel bade with swedge near the tip, a stainless guard, stabilized bog oak handle and mosaic pin. *(Caleb Royer photo)*

Fly Butterfly Knives

The boy in many men can remember flipping butterfly knives, and quite a few, yours truly included, were scared to death of cutting fingers in the process. There he stood, friends watching, twirling sharp steel (well, not real sharp—the $10 knife did not come ready to shave) and practically dropping it at every turn. It was more of a herky-jerky motion than smooth twirling, with starts and stops, grunts and gyrations.

Yet the mechanics of the thing stuck. There was and remains an appeal of a stripped-down folding knife that is nothing but blade, handles, pivot pin and possibly a locking mechanism. There are no scales, bolsters, shields, guards or holsters. And the knives are exotic, tracing roots to the balisongs of the Filipinos, used as self-defense and pocket utility knives. Hollow-ground balisongs also sufficed as straight razors before conventional shavers were available in the Philippines.

In the hands of a skilled butterfly knife user, the blade flips open, handle halves close, the edge is locked and ready to use in seconds. A few more flips and twirls might be in order, purely for show. Those less agile might just proceed with caution, slowly, until they get the hang of it.

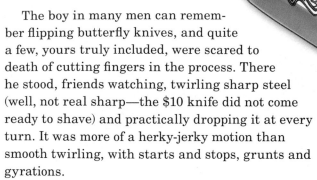

⌃ MICHAEL ZIEBA
The blade pattern, handle engraving and little skull inlays in the frame are equal parts impressive.
(SharpByCoop image)

» JOSHUA PRINCE
There really is something better than a butterfly knife—one with a Timascus handle and a bottle opener on the blade spine.
(SharpByCoop image)

⌃ DARRIEL CASTON
The grind of the M390 blade alone is enough to make the titanium-handle balisong fly, but before you let it loose, unlock the handle halves. *(SharpByCoop image)*

Utility Players

Sometimes they're the best ones on a team—the versatile few who can do anything asked of them, in a timely and efficient manner, and with no questions asked. They go about their tasks unfettered by outside influences or distractions.

Such knives are the utility players of the industry. They're multi-taskers with blade and handle shapes that allow for a multitude of cutting chores. Not too long, thick, curved or guarded, utility knives feel good in the hand, are easy to manipulate and cut straight and narrow.

They aren't slashers, choppers or stabbers, but slicers and dicers, incision makers, good for detail work but with enough heft to handle anything from animal skinning to tent stake shaping and rope cutting. They cut strings and leather with equal aplomb.

They are the utility players, and they're ready to get in the game whenever needed.

» STEPHEN LELAND
Some will admire the highly finished, 6-inch O-1 blade of the hunting/utility knife, others the oosik handle, and most will fall for both. *(Caleb Royer image)*

» ANDREW FRANKLAND
The "Otter Utility Knife" surfaces wearing an ATS-34 blade, stainless fittings and pins, and a "dead finish" (acacia) wood handle from the Australian outback.

« MARK FLEMING
The utilitarian design includes a water-quenched 5160 blade, stainless guard and Koa wood handle. *(SharpByCoop image)*

« RICK DARBY
He stuck to the straight and narrow with a CPM D2 deer hunter in a stag handle, tapering the tang to the end and sandwiching it in red liners. *(SharpByCoop image)*

» HARVEY HOLBROOK
A small game utility knife showcases a full-tang CPM-154 blade, a stabilized giraffe bone handle and Corby bolts. *(Whetstone Studio image)*

« JOHN COHEA
This one's more than utilitarian, encompassing a random pattern damascus blade, copper bolster, mammoth ivory handle and beautiful sheath work. *(SharpByCoop image)*

» JIM POLING
As straight as the grains are on the rosewood handle, just as chaotic is the patterning of the twist-damascus blade.
(Cory Martin image)

» BOB RANKIN
Don't leave home without the "Statesman," he dressed in damascus and stabilized buckeye burl.
(SharpByCoop image)

« SAMUEL LURQUIN
A palm-filling Koa wood handle is matched up with a big-bellied damascus blade for a fine utility knife. *(SharpByCoop image)*

» ULYSSE ROBERT
In the utility hunter realm, the piece sports a 3.75-inch forged 5160 blade, integral guard and rosewood handle. *(Caleb Royer image)*

» KUNIHIKO TAMATSU
In this case, true utility takes the form of an integral ATS-34 hunter with a linen Micarta® handle.
(SharpByCoop image)

« JOHN APRIL
Credited as a Bob Loveless-style utility hunter, the piece sports a CPM 154 blade, a stainless guard and righteous mammoth ivory handle.
(SharpByCoop image)

« LON HUMPHREY
It doesn't come more utilitarian than a pierced drop-point neck knife and Kydex sheath.
(Cory Martin image)

« JIM PERKINS
The handle of a CPM 154 fixed-blade utility knife is a combination of stabilized curly white oak with white camel bone, blue G-10 and black vulcanized spacers.
(SharpByCoop image)

« ALEX RUIZ
The maker says the hand-forged 5160 blade of a mahogany-handle utility knife is courtesy of his friend, Ray Kirk. *(Caleb Royer image)*

« TIGERLILY KNIGHT
It's not just an EDC, but an African blackwood-handle everyday carry knife with a damascus blade and integral guard. *(Whetstone Studio image)*

« KEN HALL
A good "Trail Thorn" should have a circa-5.5-inch damascus blade, stainless guard, and a curly Koa handle, and so she does. *(SharpByCoop image)*

« JERRY FISK
Quite possibly the prettiest utility knife in the drawer, it's amazing what one does with damascus, stag, stainless and engraving. *(SharpByCoop image)*

« JORDAN BORSTELMANN
A forge-finished 1095 blade is the beneficiary of a Brazilian hardwood handle and copper bolster. *(SharpByCoop image)*

« BUTCH DEVERAUX
Complementing the sheep horn handle and spacer, brass guard, and red, white and blue spacers, is a low-temp-forged, triple-tempered, convex-ground 52100 blade. *(SharpByCoop image)*

Hunters in the Woods

⌃ **ANDREW FRANKLAND**
Tasmanian myrtle burl anchors the 440C drop-point hunter with tapered tang and stainless bolsters. *(SharpByCoop image)*

⌃ **TOM BUCKNER**
Really, is there anything better than a drop-point hunter with a high, hollow grind? Perhaps one with a curly Koa handle and mosaic pins would exceed such expectations. *(BladeGallery.com image)*

⌃ **CRAIG BROSMAN**
A small bird and trout knife has big features, including a ball bearing and powder damascus blade, and a ringed Gidgee handle. *(SharpByCoop image)*

⌃ **DEREK LEE**
The stonewashed 1084 blade has almost as much character as the dyed box elder burl handle to which it is attached. *(Caleb Royer photo)*

⌃ **TONY ROED**
A birch hull holds 'er steady as she blows along an angry ocean of damascus. *(Cory Martin image)*

JACKSON RUMBLE
The keyhole hunter is all duded up in a 1075-and-15N20 damascus blade, and a Zircote wood handle. *(SharpByCoop image)*

HARVEY HOLBROOK
A utility/hunter/fighter all-purpose knife incorporates a satin-finished CPM-154 blade, a stabilized curly oak handle, stainless Corby bolts and a mosaic pin. *(Caleb Royer photo)*

KEVIN SLATTERY
If you want it put a ringed Gidgee handle on it, and a Takefu stainless san mai blade. *(SharpByCoop image)*

JORDAN LAMOTHE
One might assume it is "just art," but avoid telling that to the maker who forged the damascus blade with integral guard and added the tulipwood handle for the clip-point hunter. *(SharpByCoop image)*

JOSH FISHER
The temper line shows where the W2 blade was differentially heat treated, the fittings where they were heat blued and the spalted maple burl where the hand is placed. *(Caleb Royer photo)*

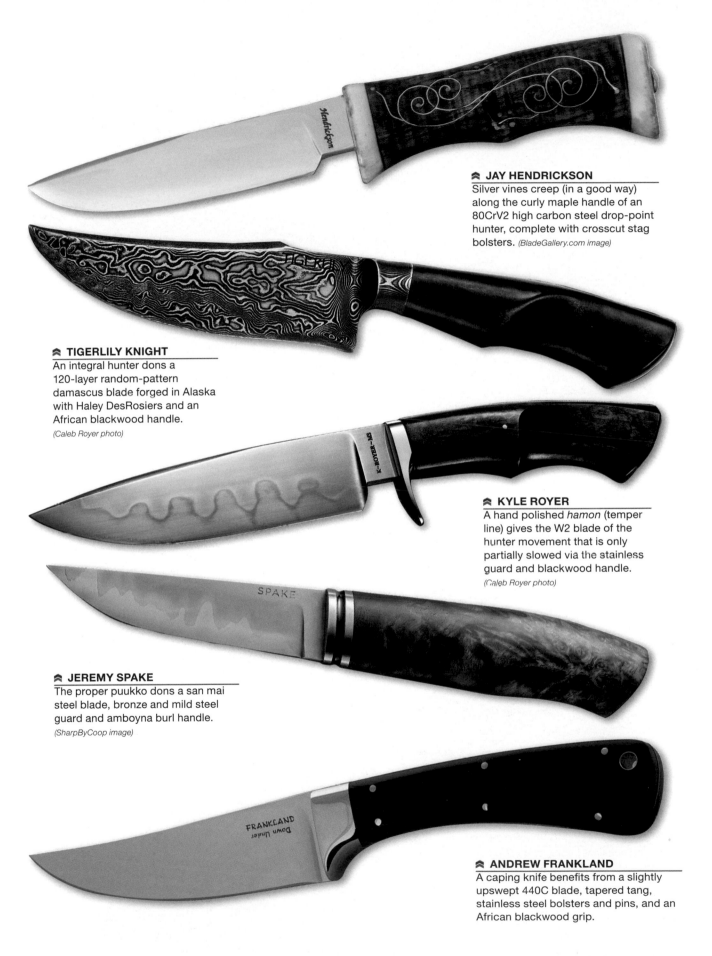

JAY HENDRICKSON
Silver vines creep (in a good way) along the curly maple handle of an 80CrV2 high carbon steel drop-point hunter, complete with crosscut stag bolsters. *(BladeGallery.com image)*

TIGERLILY KNIGHT
An integral hunter dons a 120-layer random-pattern damascus blade forged in Alaska with Haley DesRosiers and an African blackwood handle.
(Caleb Royer photo)

KYLE ROYER
A hand polished *hamon* (temper line) gives the W2 blade of the hunter movement that is only partially slowed via the stainless guard and blackwood handle.
(Caleb Royer photo)

JEREMY SPAKE
The proper puukko dons a san mai steel blade, bronze and mild steel guard and amboyna burl handle.
(SharpByCoop image)

ANDREW FRANKLAND
A caping knife benefits from a slightly upswept 440C blade, tapered tang, stainless steel bolsters and pins, and an African blackwood grip.

⌃ JESS HOFFMAN

Big and little skinning knives are busted out in 12C27 stainless steel blades with sharpened clips, and Budgeroo burl and spalted oak handles, the latter dyed green.

(Cory Martin image)

⌃ JIM PROVOST

The cryogenically quenched CPM 154, hollow-ground hunters sport a colorful array of stabilized pinecone handles.

(SharpByCoop image)

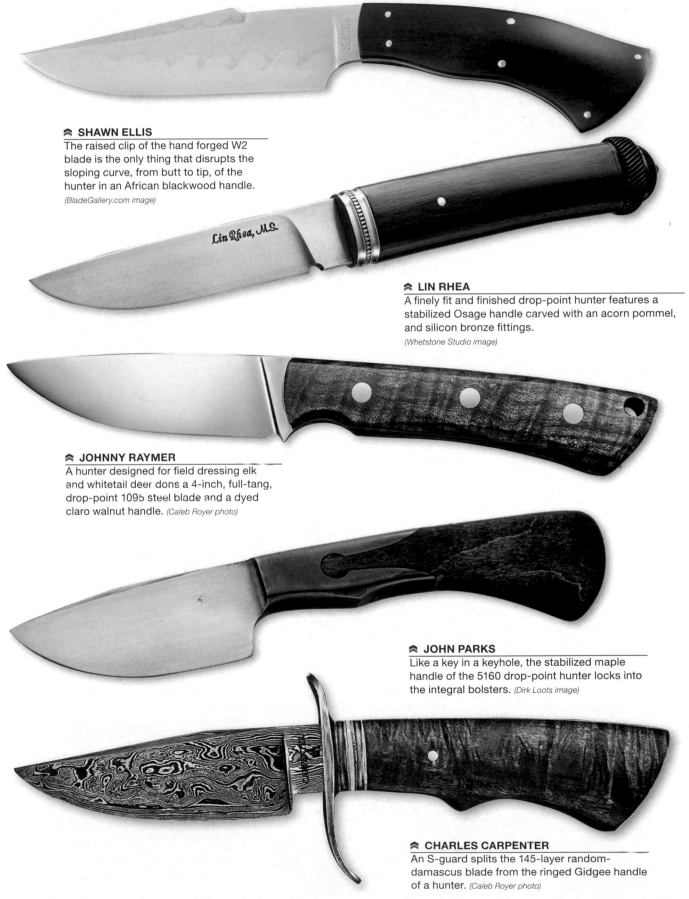

SHAWN ELLIS
The raised clip of the hand forged W2 blade is the only thing that disrupts the sloping curve, from butt to tip, of the hunter in an African blackwood handle.

(BladeGallery.com image)

LIN RHEA
A finely fit and finished drop-point hunter features a stabilized Osage handle carved with an acorn pommel, and silicon bronze fittings.

(Whetstone Studio image)

JOHNNY RAYMER
A hunter designed for field dressing elk and whitetail deer dons a 4-inch, full-tang, drop-point 1095 steel blade and a dyed claro walnut handle. *(Caleb Royer photo)*

JOHN PARKS
Like a key in a keyhole, the stabilized maple handle of the 5160 drop-point hunter locks into the integral bolsters. *(Dirk Loots image)*

CHARLES CARPENTER
An S-guard splits the 145-layer random-damascus blade from the ringed Gidgee handle of a hunter. *(Caleb Royer photo)*

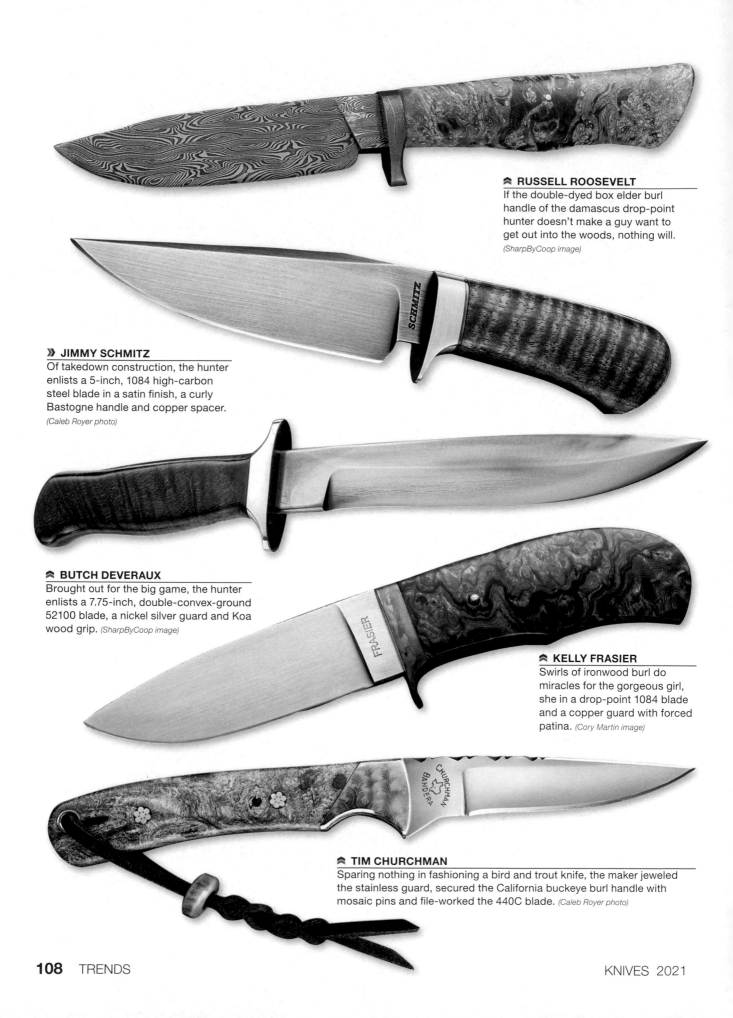

⌃ RUSSELL ROOSEVELT
If the double-dyed box elder burl handle of the damascus drop-point hunter doesn't make a guy want to get out into the woods, nothing will.
(SharpByCoop image)

» JIMMY SCHMITZ
Of takedown construction, the hunter enlists a 5-inch, 1084 high-carbon steel blade in a satin finish, a curly Bastogne handle and copper spacer.
(Caleb Royer photo)

⌃ BUTCH DEVERAUX
Brought out for the big game, the hunter enlists a 7.75-inch, double-convex-ground 52100 blade, a nickel silver guard and Koa wood grip. *(SharpByCoop image)*

⌃ KELLY FRASIER
Swirls of ironwood burl do miracles for the gorgeous girl, she in a drop-point 1084 blade and a copper guard with forced patina. *(Cory Martin image)*

⌃ TIM CHURCHMAN
Sparing nothing in fashioning a bird and trout knife, the maker jeweled the stainless guard, secured the California buckeye burl handle with mosaic pins and file-worked the 440C blade. *(Caleb Royer photo)*

Swords Drawn

» BEN ABBOTT
A full 53 inches long, the claymore enlists a 42-inch pattern-welded 15N20 and 1084 blade, a leather-over-wood handle, wrought iron fittings and 24k-gold inlays. *(Whetstone Studio image)*

« KEVIN CASHEN
Silver fittings, including a horsehead pommel, add to the shiny appeal of a Revolutionary War officer's sword outfitted in a 32-inch L6 blade and a wire-wrapped ivory handle.

⌃ TREVOR RIDEOUT
How about a sawback hunting sword done up in a damascus blade, a brass-coated and antiqued clamshell-style wrought iron guard and desert ironwood handle? *(SharpByCoop image)*

⌃ KEN HALL
The maker says the balancing point of the damascus Viking sword is 5.75 inches in front of the bronze guard, and who is to argue? That is a twisted copper wire handle, by the way. *(SharpByCoop image)*

⌃ BRENT STUBBLEFIELD
The hand-and-a-half long sword incorporates a 36-inch 5160 blade, a fluted African blackwood hilt and damascus guard and pommel. *(Whetstone Studio image)*

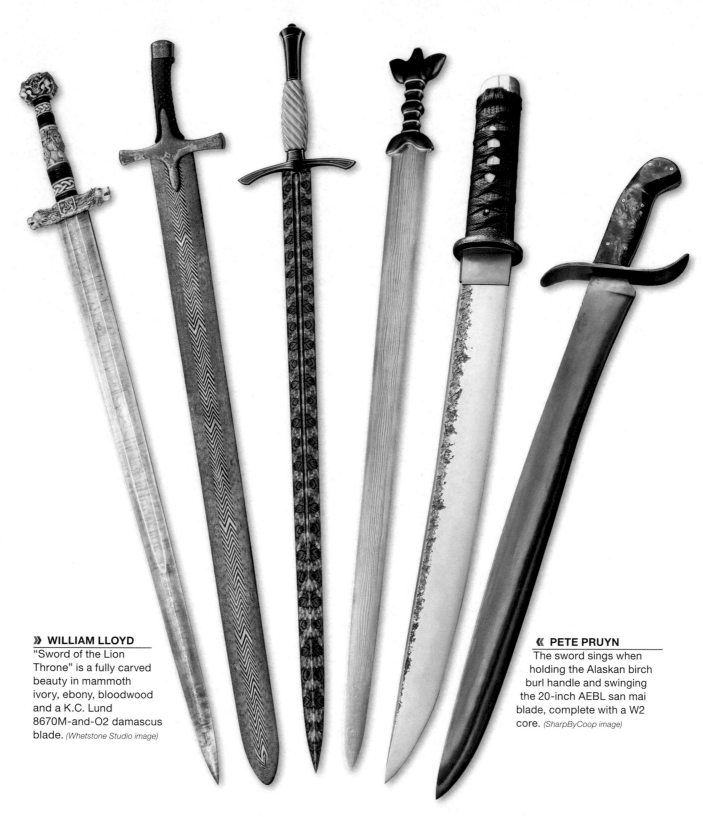

» WILLIAM LLOYD
"Sword of the Lion Throne" is a fully carved beauty in mammoth ivory, ebony, bloodwood and a K.C. Lund 8670M-and-O2 damascus blade. *(Whetstone Studio image)*

« PETE PRUYN
The sword sings when holding the Alaskan birch burl handle and swinging the 20-inch AEBL san mai blade, complete with a W2 core. *(SharpByCoop image)*

⌃ TOM WARD
He forged a 40-inch chevron damascus blade clad with W's mosaic damascus, outfitted it with a twist- and mosaic-damascus guard, and affixed a maple and goat hide handle. *(SharpByCoop image)*

⌃ KYLE ROYER
Thirty-six inches of complex mosaic "Nebula"-pattern damascus is a feat unto itself, not to mention the fluted fossil walrus ivory hilt of "Orion's Sword," or the gold-inlaid fittings in a black mirror finish. *(Caleb Royer image)*

⌃ COLLIN MILLER
Wouldn't it be fun to wield the "Epona" sword, grabbing the bog oak and bronze handle and lashing out at imaginary enemies using a pattern-welded blade? *(Whetstone Studio image)*

⌃ DAVID MIRABILE
A 21.75-inch tool steel sword is outfitted in a carbon fiber-over-Alaskan yellow cedar hilt, copper habaki and wrought iron *tsuba* (guard). *(SharpByCoop image)*

Mammoth Molar Mittfuls

⌃ ARNO BERNARD
A mammoth molar inlay breaks up the titanium and steel hues of the Orca frame-lock flipper folder in a Bohler M390 blade. *(BladeGallery.com image)*

⌃ CARL MICHAEL ALMQUIST
Imagine this beauty in the belt sheath—the crosscut mammoth ivory peeking out and the stainless Damasteel blade waiting to be called up for duty. *(BladeGallery.com image)*

⌃ SAL MANARO
Mammoth tooth makes a statement on a clip-point, frame-lock folder featuring a Takefu Super Gold 2 blade. *(SharpByCoop image)*

⌃ TODD FISCHER
It's not just that the flipper folder is fashioned from damascus, Moku-Ti and mammoth tooth, but that the patterns blow you over like a tropical monsoon coming ashore. *(Cory Martin image)*

Thank goodness we don't have molars like the ancient, calcified beauties of wooly mammoths. It would be cool as heck, and there'd certainly be no need for gold teeth, but with the black market the way it is, I'm afraid there'd be an underground criminal tooth trade and painful consequences from evil opportunists.

Certain materials—translucent pearl, marble, highly figured wood, abalone and ivory—appeal to discerning tastes, evoking elegance and style. In knives, the parts must be stable and pliable, comfortable and sturdy.

That's why, when Mother Nature provides a substance like mammoth molar, preserved in permafrost and allowed to age and mature, it is a gift from the gods. Opportunists in and of themselves, though rarely evil, knifemakers never pass up the chance to employ an aesthetically superior, utilitarian handle material. Thank goodness it is only the wooly mammoths with teeth like that.

» BLAINE STEPHENSON
Mammoth tooth handle scales put plenty of pop in a chef's knife with file-worked blade and stainless bolsters. *(Caleb Royer image)*

» WALTER BREND
It speaks volumes that the maker decked out a CPM 154 dagger celebrating his 40th anniversary of knifemaking in a mammoth tooth handle.
(Whetstone Studio image)

» LUKE DELLMYER
Between the damascus blade of the fighter and the mammoth molar handle is a mild steel guard to keep the peace.
(SharpByCoop image)

» IAN ROGERS
The 9 ½-inch integral chef's knife is served up in a hand-forged stainless raindrop-damascus blade and an amboyna burl grip with mammoth molar inlays.
(BladeGallery.com image)

Pot-Stirring Kitchen Knives

⌃ TOM BUCKNER
Not your ordinary paring knife, the 4-inch CPM S30V stunner comes in a dyed and stabilized snakeskin sycamore handle, a mosaic pin and even a custom maple sheath. *(BladeGallery.com image)*

⌃ MIKE NELSON
The forge-finished look of the W2 high-carbon tool steel blade also extends the length of the handle.
(Caleb Royer image)

⌃ JERRY GOETTIG
Satin-finished 52100 high-carbon blade steel is as good as it gets for a chef's knife, not to mention exhibition-grade snakewood handle scales secured with copper Loveless-style rivets. *(BladeGallery. com image)*

⌗ ALLEN NEWBERRY
A pretty addition to the kitchen cutlery, the 7.5-inch damascus chef's knife is served up in an African blackwood handle and stainless hardware. *(Caleb Royer image)*

JASON ELLARD
Don't misplace the chef's knife with "murder of crows" mosaic damascus blade and ringed Gidgee handle or it might disappear into someone else's collection.
(Caleb Royer image)

KEVIN CROSS
A chef's knife showcases a Raffir stabilized wood handle with a carbon fiber bolster, and an impressively patterned Damasteel blade. *(SharpByCoop image)*

WES DETRICK
Stirring the pot is an 88-layer damascus kitchen knife with bronze bolster and stabilized redwood burl handle.
(Caleb Royer image)

TOBIAS BOCKHOLT
Ingredients of a chef's and paring knife set include san mai blades of damascus over W-Nr 1.2562 steel, and Arizona ironwood, Micarta® and African blackwood handles.
(SharpByCoop image)

SCOTT FOX
The prettily patterned Kiritsuke gets its good looks from damascus, spalted tamarind and cocobolo. *(Caleb Royer image)*

IAN RONALD

Red and black and steel all over is a "K-tip Gyuto" featuring a single-bevel stainless blade, a Brazilian bloodwood handle and resin-based Juma Carbon spacer. *(SharpByCoop image)*

ISAIAH SCHROEDER

Clad in a "Vinland" Damasteel blade, a Koa wood handle and matching sheath, the kitchen knife even comes with its own matching chopsticks. *(Cory Martin image)*

ADAM ROGERS

Stirring up the pot is a chef's knife derived from 1084-and-15N20 damascus, a York gum burl handle and a buffalo horn spacer. *(SharpByCoop image)*

JUSTIN MEYER

A pair of 440C chef's knives don purple and orange Burlatex Micarta® handle slabs combined with black Micarta® for contrast.

(Dirk Loots image)

MATT PARKINSON

There is so much sweetness in the damascus chef's knife with integral ferrule and maple burl handle, it might best be reserved for dessert. *(SharpByCoop image)*

KEVIN SLATTERY
Now here's a chef's set that will get your pot stirring, in Takefu blades, pine handles; and mammoth ivory, G-10 and nickel silver spacers.
(SharpByCoop image)

MERT TANSU
The clean, keen kitchen knife is an integral Damasteel piece parading a kingwood handle with G-10 and nickel silver spacers. *(SharpByCoop image)*

TYLER HALL
Ready to cleave what's for dinner, the 6-inch "lava flow" damascus blade is accompanied by a stabilized curly Koa handle and silicone bronze and G-10 spacers. *(Caleb Royer image)*

NEIL KAMIMURA
A 1095-and-15N20-damascus blade and hexagonal walnut burl handle populate a 14.75-inch chef's knife.
(Caleb Royer image)

TREVOR NICHOL
Every kitchen should have an 8-inch AEB-L chef's knife in the block, one with a stabilized Koa handle, carbon pins and red G-10 liners.
(Caleb Royer image

» ROB FRENCH
The Gyuto Japanese chef's knife is forged in Takefu Suminagashi clad Vtoku2 steel and features a zebrawood handle, and reconstituted stone and white G-10 spacers.
(Caleb Royer image)

JODY HALE
Amenities of this handsome kitchen knife include a Hitachi Super Blue blade with stainless steel outer layers, a Honduran Rosewood burl handle and a musk ox horn spacer. *(Cory Martin image)*

SHINICHI WATANABE
A convex-ground damascus cooking knife includes a cassia wood handle, sculpted bronze pins and a mokume-gane bolster.
(SharpByCoop image)

GARRETT and MIKE ELTING
Calling them "Kitchen Petty" (or utility) knives, the pair sports low-contrast damascus blades, stabilized redwood burl handles and green-dyed redwood and bronze spacers.
(SharpByCoop image)

STATE OF THE ART

There are more chapters in the State of the Art section of the *KNIVES 2021* book than there have been in past years. Makers are raising the level of artistry, and it is more apparent than ever. In a world where businesses and craftspeople alike compete for the almighty dollar, or whatever currency is exchanged, there is more emphasis on quality, aesthetics and sometimes down-right eye-catching beauty today than in the past.

Innovation is likewise alive and well—blade builders taking cues from furniture makers and combining resins or acrylics with wood, or using precious and igneous stones for knife handles, Timascus in art folders and feather damascus patterning that follows the lines of the edged tools and weapons.

There are "Next-Level Steel Laminates," "Town Square-Worthy Sculptures," "Gallery-Ready Engraving," and "Basilica-Level Mosaics," not to mention fluted daggers, gentlemen's knives, carving and checkering, damascus pattern plying and a "Scrimshander Showcase."

There is no denying the pure skill, innovation and tenacity of knifemakers who refuse to be pigeon-holed into categories of workmanship or levels of quality. In an industry where art and utility are weighed equally, the knives and makers do not disappoint.

Only the best of the best is paraded before the discerning eyes of *KNIVES* book readers. There are not many apparent flaws in the knives, character or artistry of the makers. Enjoy flipping through the pages and admiring their work.

Fluted Daggers

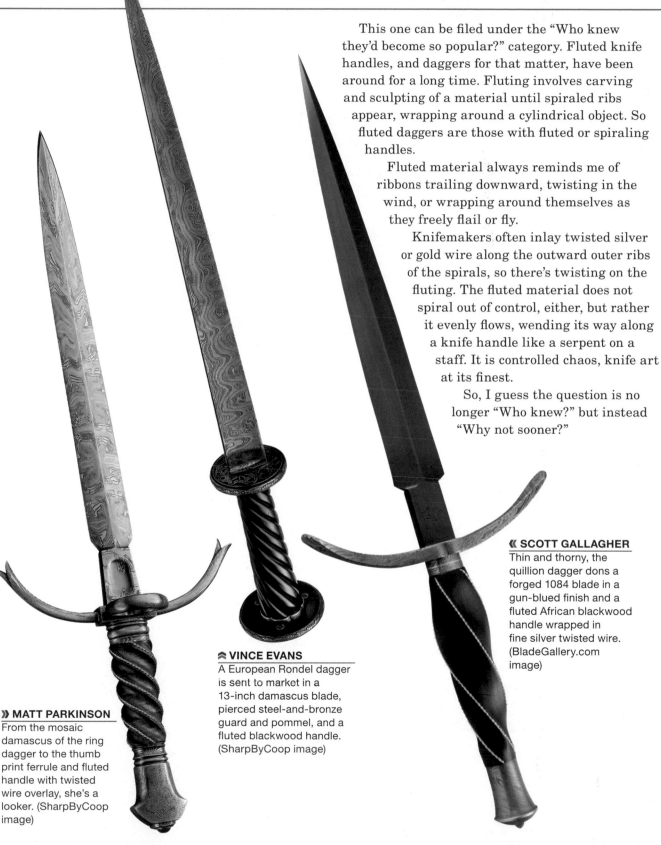

This one can be filed under the "Who knew they'd become so popular?" category. Fluted knife handles, and daggers for that matter, have been around for a long time. Fluting involves carving and sculpting of a material until spiraled ribs appear, wrapping around a cylindrical object. So fluted daggers are those with fluted or spiraling handles.

Fluted material always reminds me of ribbons trailing downward, twisting in the wind, or wrapping around themselves as they freely flail or fly.

Knifemakers often inlay twisted silver or gold wire along the outward outer ribs of the spirals, so there's twisting on the fluting. The fluted material does not spiral out of control, either, but rather it evenly flows, wending its way along a knife handle like a serpent on a staff. It is controlled chaos, knife art at its finest.

So, I guess the question is no longer "Who knew?" but instead "Why not sooner?"

» MATT PARKINSON
From the mosaic damascus of the ring dagger to the thumb print ferrule and fluted handle with twisted wire overlay, she's a looker. (SharpByCoop image)

⌃ VINCE EVANS
A European Rondel dagger is sent to market in a 13-inch damascus blade, pierced steel-and-bronze guard and pommel, and a fluted blackwood handle. (SharpByCoop image)

« SCOTT GALLAGHER
Thin and thorny, the quillion dagger dons a forged 1084 blade in a gun-blued finish and a fluted African blackwood handle wrapped in fine silver twisted wire. (BladeGallery.com image)

JOHN DAVIS
The dagger is imperially fashioned from Starburst damascus, fluted Gamelia burl with a nickel silver wire wrap, a wrought iron guard and abalone-inlaid pommel. (Cory Martin image)

JOSH FISHER
The damascus blade, hot-blued fittings and fluted ebony handle give the dagger that dark demeanor the maker was striving to achieve. (Caleb Royer image)

KYLE ROYER
Featuring a 17-plus-inch complex mosaic damascus blade, other highlights including 24k-gold scroll inlays, and a twisted-gold-wire-wrapped, fluted fossil walrus ivory handle. (Caleb Royer image)

WAYNE BARRETT
A thin, sparkling clean dagger looks dashing in a chrome vanadium blade, fluted Gidgee wood handle, a mild steel guard and a little crosscut Mulga (acacia) thrown in for good measure. (SharpByCoop image

HUGO ALMEIDA
Twisted silver wire wraps its way around the fluted ebony handle of an O1 tool steel dagger. (Caleb Royer image)

Handsome Handles

Talk about hands on—nowhere does art meet utility and a craftsman's work matter more than on a knife handle. This is where the hand meets the grip. The knifemaker only has one shot at it—if the handle does not feel right, the collector walks away. If the grip is not attractive to an enthusiast in the first place, the deal is done before it has begun.

There is only one thing more important than how a knife handle feels when using it, and that is how the blade cuts. So, it is cutting and then handling. Even if the blade slices and dices with aplomb, if the hand is sore afterward, another edge will do next time, thank you.

But knifemakers are not satisfied with how a handle feels, at least not custom blade builders—they want it to look good, too. Many are accomplished at one or the other, and only a select few master both. Meet the masters on this and the following pages. They build comfortable handles dashingly.

» ROBERT BURNS
A dimpled water buffalo horn handle gives way to a wrought iron guard with melted gold accents and a 10.5-inch damascus blade. (Caleb Royer image)

⌄ ANDREW MEERS
The art dagger exhibits equal parts blade—1084- and 15N20 damascus— and handle craft, complete with carving, engraving and gold gilding. (SharpByCoop image)

⌃ KEN STEIGERWALT
The ground, sculpted and cleverly crafted Art Deco fixed blade parades black-lip pearl cutouts and gold inlays. (SharpByCoop image)

⌃ CARL RECHSTEINER
A war club with point forged from a saw blade features an incredible gun stock haft embellished with a horsehair tassel, and brass tacks, moon and stars. (Dirk Loots image)

KOJI HARA
In this case, the dashing handle of a mirror-polished Cowry Y flipper folder is made up of 30 black-lip mother-of pearl sections (15 to a side) separated by stainless spacers. (BladeGallery.com image)

ADAM FROMHOLTZ
The sweet steampunk dagger is sent to market in a damascus blade, Australian hardwood handle, and brass, copper, bronze, mokume-gane and some cogs thrown in for good measure. (SharpByCoop image)

KEITH BAGLEY
A 405-layer damascus dagger is decked out in an African blackwood handle and a "Fordyce" stone spacer. (Whetstone Studio image)

SCOTT GALLAGHER
If you've got it, flaunt it, and that's what the maker did with the red and green dinosaur bone for the handle of a damascus folder. (SharpByCoop image)

DIRK LOOTS
The claw-like appendage of "Red Mantis" is W2 tool steel, while its body is raindrop damascus and red maple burl. (Dirk Loots image)

» MATTHEW LERCH
Sometimes you just sit back and soak it in—the Art Deco form, gold inlays, stepped frame and damascus blade. (SharpByCoop image)

« JERRY MCCLURE
"Big Daddy" rolls with an "electric chicken feather" damascus blade, a diamond thumb stud, jeweled pivot and a sterling silver handle fused with 22-karat gold. (Caleb Royer image)

⨄ TOMMY CARROLL
Certain knife models call for carved "dragon scales knotwork" in elk bone, not to mention wicked damascus blades and Labradorite crystal fittings. (Whetstone Studio image)

» JIM SORNBERGER
He kept piling the handle material onto the CPM 154 flipper folder, first titanium, then mokume-gane and finally gold quartz. (SharpByCoop image)

⨃ JIM PROVOST
You don't see too many hollow-ground CPM 154 fixed blades spruced up in spruce cone handles, but apparently one should. (SharpByCoop image)

» STEVE WEIS
The "parent" member of the integral keyhole-style damascus fixed blade family was fashioned in collaboration with Rodrigo Sfreddo, and the "siblings" are solo-maker affairs. (SharpByCoop image)

« JOHNNY STOUT
Highlighted by Alice Carter gold inlay and engraving, the LinerLock also features a Jerry Rados damascus blade, Robert Eggerling mosaic damascus bolsters and white mother-of-pearl handle scales. (SharpByCoop image)

» BRIAN HOESE
OK, now that is just cool how he sculpted the copper bolsters to match the highly figured vintage stag handle on a LinerLock folder with Devin Thomas basketweave-pattern damascus blade. (SharpByCoop image)

⌃ LON HUMPHREY
Sometimes hammered-steel hunters call for fleur-de-lis bolsters puzzle-pieced together with wood handles … sometimes. (Cory Martin image)

« JAY HENDRICKSON
Not all Alaskan ulu hunters sport silver wire-inlaid curly redwood and stag handles, and brass guards and pommels—just the special ones. (BladeGallery.com image)

» **JEREMY SPAKE**
The old "Witch Finger" is fashioned using a san mai damascus blade, dyed stabilized burl handle, and bronze liner, spacer and pin. (SharpByCoop image)

« **JOHNNY STOUT**
While the business end is Doug Ponzio Turkish twist damascus, the handle half parades Brian Bump gold inlay and engraving, as well as a fluted mammoth ivory grip. (SharpByCoop image)

» **VLADIMIR KOLENKO**
The time was well spent inlaying mother-of-pearl dots into the Gabon ebony handle of a Turkish twist damascus dagger. Other amenities include 14-karat gold, sterling silver, garnets and pearl. (SharpByCoop image)

» **DAN PETERSON**
The handle of the 6-inch 15N20-and-W2-damascus hunter is vitreous enamel on metal, and that is up to snuff. (Whetstone Studio image)

» **C. GRAY TAYLOR**
Engraving, sculpting and inlays embellish the antique tortoise shell handle of a sweet bartender's or sommelier's knife. (SharpByCoop image)

« **BRIAN TIGHE**
Brian's sculpted, inlaid and multi-ground flipper folders usually leave the other makers green with envy. (SharpByCoop image)

» KEVIN KLEIN
The handle of the damascus fixed blade is carved African blackwood with silver spacers, a mokume-gane ferrule and cast Shibuichi guard. (SharpByCoop image)

« PETER MARTIN
The 12C27 folding dagger looks dashing in a handle of red carbo-quartz (carbon layered with monocrystalline sand), and Chad Nichols Moku-Ti bolsters and pocket clip. (Cory Martin image)

« HYENA
Brass claws protrude from the stabilized burl wood handle of "The Gator" that also sports an Alabama damascus blade and mosaic pins. (Whetstone Studio image)

» MARDI MESHEJIAN
The hollow-ground damascus folding dagger sports a superconductor-inlaid titanium bolster and a mammoth ivory grip. (SharpByCoop image)

» MICHAEL ZIEBA
In envisioning his flipper folder, the maker saw koi fish, carbon fiber, damascus and Japanese-themed engraving, a vision that came to fruition. (SharpByCoop image)

Next-Level Steel Laminates

"Well, I wanted a hard edge that wouldn't break, and maybe some blade patterning—you know, more than just a temper line or damascus. So, I sandwiched a high-carbon steel core between layers of nickel damascus for the outer layers, and after welding it all together, I ground, finished and etched the steel to bring out the pattern."

This is not the statement of someone who pays to have their lawn mowed, driveway paved or bathroom remodeled. No, knifemakers are a do-it-yourself hearty bunch who do not shy away from a challenge.

Similar comments include, "I couldn't find screws or pins that fit, so I made my own;" "I wasn't satisfied with the locking mechanism and figured I could build one where the frame slams against the blade tang and secures it;" or "I've never worked with leather, but none of the sheaths I saw on the market met my criteria, so I taught myself to shape and stitch one, and then did a little embossing and beadwork on it."

No, next-level steel laminates are not bought at the steel mill. They are forged that way by makers who take things to the next level and are not satisfied until they get results.

❯ A2-ANDRE THORBURN and ANDRE VAN HEERDON
One highlight is a "Damacore San Mai" blade forged by Damasteel, and the other being a heat-colored MokuTi handle. (BladeGallery.com image)

❮❮ TOBIAS BOCKHOLT
The impressive steel mashup of the chef's knife includes "twisted W's" damascus over 15N20 and W-Nr 1.2562, while the handle recipe calls for Arizona ironwood, Micarta® and African blackwood. (SharpByCoop image)

❮❮ SHANE ATWOOD
An "Atomic Folder" sports a Chad Nichols "San Mai Boomerang" damascus blade with XHP core, zirconium bolsters, India stag handle scales and titanium hardware. (Caleb Royer image)

❯ JOHN FISHER
The smokin' hot blade is 416 stainless steel with a 1095 high-carbon core, combined with a desert ironwood handle and hot-blued fittings. (Caleb Royer image)

》 BILL BEHNKE
Canvas and ivory Micarta® are properly paired with a Takefu Samagushi Damascus blade in an appealing ladder pattern. (Cory Martin image)

《 HERUCUS BLOMERUS
So, you've got a "scramble"-pattern Zircuti damascus handle, and what do you do? Forge a san mai damascus blade with an SG2 powdered metallurgical stainless core, of course. (BladeGallery.com image)

⌃ TIMOTHY FORD
Let loose of that bad boy in a Takefu san mai blade of damascus over a VG-10 core, and a stabilized Huon pine and African blackwood handle. (SharpByCoop image)

⌃ JOHN GULSO
The san mai blade of the Texas bowie is ladder-pattern damascus with a 4600KC powder inlay accompanied by a damascus guard and ivory G-10 handle. (SharpByCoop image)

《 SHAWN MCINTYRE
The fire was hot forging the 1095 and stainless san mai blade of the utility knife, leaving black marks on the blade to match the bolsters and dimpled Micarta® handle. (SharpByCoop image)

« BILL BURKE
Presentation-grade ironwood is a fitting counterpart to a 52100 core and 416 stainless san mai blade, all within the confines of a Gyuto chef's knife. (BladeGallery.com image)

⌃ ROBERT BURNS
Balancing out a 9-inch san mai blade are a fossilized walrus ivory handle and a wrought iron guard covered in melted gold. (Caleb Royer image)

⌃ DMITRIY POPOV
Clever combinations include a V-Toku2 high-carbon and stainless san mai blade, and a spalted tamarind and African ebony handle. (SharpByCoop image)

⌃ CARL COLSON
In Texas, fixed blade hunters come in Damacore DC18N blades, stainless steel guards and black linen Micarta® handles, or at least this one does. (SharpByCoop image)

» JOHN PHILLIPS
The san mai Nakiri vegetable knife is forged from a sawmill blade and wrought iron, then given a proper black palm handle with a mokume-gane ferrule. (Whetstone Studio image)

» CARL ALMQUIST
With a name like Muonionalusta Meteorite Space Shark, you'd better have a Magnus Jonsson damascus blade forged from carbon steels and meteorite, and a Vladic Daniluk twist-pattern damascus handle. It comes, by the way, with an ancient mammoth ivory sheath. (BladeGallery.com image)

« BURT FOSTER and MATT GREGORY
One of six in a series with identical san mai blades, the tanto also dons a Turk's head knot bolster, a wrapped stingray skin handle and a gold cherry blossom *menuki* (handle charm). (SharpByCoop image)

» ALISTAIR PHILLIPS
The edge is easily distinguishable from the damascus pattern of the Takefu Super Gold blade of a folder sporting a marbled carbon fiber handle and Timascus fittings. (SharpByCoop image)

» TIM JOHNSON
The knife exhibits a Mike Norris stainless ladder-pattern damascus blade over an XHP core, an M3 bolster and amboyna burl handle. (SharpByCoop image)

« WILL MANNING
The maker forged stainless and 1095 high-carbon steels, added nickel, and outfitted the "Gran Monstrua" with a copper bolster, G-10 frame and stabilized cedar burl handle. (Caleb Royer image)

⌄ PETER MARTIN
Quicksilver damascus dips down to the high-carbon steel core and edge of the QSB flipper folder, outfitted in a zirconium frame and "tire tread" damascus handle. (Cory Martin image)

« JORDAN BERTHELOT
An 8-inch Nessmuk model makes its way in a Chad Nichols Boomerang damascus blade with a CTS-XHP core, and a blue angel step maple handle. (Caleb Royer image)

» JOE EDSON
It is like choosing between two sons. Which is more handsome: the san mai blade forged from Shirogami #2 carbon steel and damascus, or the dyed maple burl handle? (BladeGallery. com image)

« TOM WARD
Steels making up the head of the "DaneAx of the Varangian Guard" include chevron, wolf's-tooth and Zanjir damascus, complemented by a curly ash, hickory and bronze haft. (SharpByCoop image)

» ETHAN LEE
One san mai hunter comes in a 203E blade with 1095 core, a stabilized maple handle and stainless fittings. (Whetstone Studio image)

Precious & Igneous Stone Handles

☙ SCOTT GALLAGHER
An engraved handle inlaid with jade makes for an incredible first impression, one furthered by a harpoon-tip mosaic damascus blade and Dellana gold dots. (BladeGallery.com image)

» BLAINE STEPHENSON
A skinning knife sashays its stainless bolsters and Nebula stone handle scales. (Caleb Royer image)

» DENNIS FRIEDLY
In starts and stops, one stares unabashedly at the Picasso marble handle, damascus blade, Gil Rudolph gold inlay and engraving of the art dagger. (SharpByCoop image)

« GRANT CHAMBERS
Twisted gold wire wraps around the granite grip—as should the hands of many collectors and enthusiasts—of a damascus dagger.

« VLADIMIR KOLENKO
Garnets grace the blade, ferrule and pommel of a damascus dagger also adorned in gold, silver and mammoth ivory. (SharpByCoop image)

« BETHANY TUSSING
Whether the Greek goddess of love or just a girl, Freya comes to life on the stag handle of a Viking seax with damascus blade and carnelian stone insets. (Whetstone Studio image)

» DAVID LANDIS SR.
Pipestone, or catlinite, a brownish-red mudstone named for its use by Native American tribes for making ceremonial smoking pipes, is used to effect here for the spacer of a damascus fixed blade with nickel silver guard and bloodwood handle. (SharpByCoop image)

» JOHN YOUNG
An impeccably clean 440C stainless dagger is treated to a purple charoite handle. (SharpByCoop image)

The Gentlemen's Quarters

Refinement does not equate to snobbery in the knife industry and excludes no utilitarian-minded individuals. Rather, refinement is the further finishing of an object, tweaking of the fit between parts, the smoothness of operation and exacting of material matchup.

It is the smoothing out of all rough surfaces, sanding off the edges, rounding the corners, paying attention to details, meshing of mechanisms and seamless transitioning of materials.

Gent's folders bespeak refinement of the knives themselves. One does not have to be dressed in suitcoat and slacks to carry a gentleman's knife, but simply have a taste for the finer things in life, an appreciation for quality and aesthetics.

The knives will cut with the best of them—makers of gentlemen's knives not only refine the looks but also the utilitarian aspects of the blades, bolsters, handles and hardware. These knives belong to the gentlemen's quarters, and they are meant to be used and admired.

» ADAM FROMHOLTZ
So you're in your smoking jacket at the men's club and you pull out this steampunk folder fashioned from a 1095 blade clad with copper and nickel, and a red gum wood handle, with a brass frame, liners and guard, the latter made using old clock parts. I am thinking it turns a few clean-cut heads. (SharpByCoop image)

≪ ALISTAIR PHILLIPS
The "Trick Lock" is tricked out for the gents via a Damasteel blade, stainless bolsters and mammoth ivory handle scales. (SharpByCoop image)

≋ BUTCH BALL
The colossal and colorful cutter is done up in a Damasteel blade and a precious stone inlaid Timascus handle. (Whetstone Studio image)

≪ RON BEST
While the ladies cross their legs at the table and sip wine, the gent pulls out his damascus flipper folder with Timascus and pearl handle inlays to clip a thread on his suitcoat. (SharpByCoop image)

» R.J. MARTIN
A dress tactical folder features a CTS XHP blade, a titanium frame and blue CarboQuartz handle, all fully weight reduced to 66 grams. (SharpByCoop image)

« CLIFF PARKER
The walrus ivory handle is bookended by Art Deco mosaic damascus bolsters, all leading up to the random-pattern damascus blade with ivory-inset thumb stud. (Caleb Royer image)

« KOJI HARA
Yes, you are seeing that correctly—black-lip pearl is laid in a bamboo pattern over the dimpled stainless handle of a gent's folder, complete with a Tamahagane blade forged by Hiromune Takaba. (BladeGallery. com image)

» RON LAKE
Ron knows a bit about gent's folders, this one executed in Devin Thomas damascus, a stainless frame, sambar stag handle inlays, and rose gold screws and escutcheon. (SharpByCoop image)

« ISAO OHBUCHI
Let's face it, no one is likely carrying this pearl-handle multi-blade beauty around in a pants pocket, but it's so much fun to display in a case. (SharpByCoop image)

JAMIN BRACKETT
The dress locking folder shows off its fashion sense in a Robert Eggerling damascus blade and bolster, titanium frame and carbon fiber handle scales. (SharpByCoop image)

» JIM DUNLAP
It is nice to see a lock-back trapper in the mix, this in a CPM 154 blade, stainless acorn shield and stag handle slabs. (Whetstone Studio image)

» SCOTT GALLAGHER
Black jade and pearl inlays highlight the stainless handle of a damascus dress locking folder. (SharpByCoop image)

» RAPHAEL DURAND
The "Special Boxer" is fashioned from a semi-hollow-ground Adam Desrosiers damascus blade, a Sam Lurquin damascus bolster and fossil walrus ivory handle scales. (SharpByCoop image)

« BOB OHLEMANN
He brought his gent's folder vision to life in Mike Norris damascus, etched bronze and marbled carbon fiber. (SharpByCoop image)

« HERUCUS BLOMERUS
The san mai blade, zirconium bolster and Julien Marchal engraving are downright gorgeous, and the Westinghouse Micarta® handle soothing to the senses. (SharpByCoop image)

⍖ EUGENE SHADLEY
No less than six implements fit within and pivot from the handle frame of a neatly finished multi-blade folder. (SharpByCoop image)

« DWAYNE DUSHANE
Gold-plated screws and twisted 24k-gold wire cover the sculpted Devin Thomas damascus bolsters and carved pearl handle of a fine Damasteel folder. (Caleb Royer image)

» LARRY NEWTON
Such a fine folding dagger she is, dressed in a damascus blade with gold dots, gold-inlaid bolster, tiger coral handle, and file-worked liners and back spacer. (SharpByCoop image)

» FRANK HUNTER
A gentleman's everyday-carry folder features an AEB-L blade, Ultrex G-10 handle and a synthetic mother-of-pearl bolster (SharpByCoop image)

JIM GRIZZARD
The maker's "Auto Clasp" model comes in a heat-blued damascus blade and a choice of elk antler (shown) or mammoth ivory handle scales. (Whetstone Studio image)

RICHARD WRIGHT
A damascus bolster-release switchblade is treated to gold-lip-pearl handle scales with hues that match the mokume-gane bolsters.

BILL RUPLE
Fine fit and finish has never been more apparent than on this CPM 154 lock-back whittler showcasing stainless bolsters and pearl-inlaid carbon fiber handle scales. (SharpByCoop image)

CHRIS SHARP
The ivory handle with pierced acorn shield is a stunning choice for the flat-ground CPM 154 slip-joint folder. (SharpByCoop image)

MARDI MESHEJIAN
Damascus friction folders with curly tangs wear mammoth ivory and copper-inlaid carbon fiber handles. (SharpByCoop image)

《 TYLER TURNER
The Coke bottle pattern pocketknife exudes style via a hollow-saber-ground CPM 154 steel blade, stainless bolsters and jigged bone handle scales. (SharpByCoop image)

《 JOSH SMITH
The purple and beige hues of the blade bring out those of the ancient ivory handle. (SharpByCoop image)

》 BRUCE BARNETT
The pearl, shark's-tooth damascus and stainless steel of a three-blade sowbelly play so nicely together, highlighted by file-worked liners. (SharpByCoop image)

》 BRIAN HOESE
A custom front flipper folder receives a Devin Thomas basketweave-pattern damascus blade and blue mammoth ivory handle scales. (SharpByCoop image)

⌃ TANNER COUCH
The South Texas Trapper dons a CPM 154 blade, stainless bolsters, mill-relieved liners, and carved bone handle scales resembling amber stag. (SharpByCoop image)

» JOE EDSON
The high-class way to start the day is by shaving with a dragon-themed straight razor featuring a Mareko Maumasi mosaic damascus blade with a fire-breathing tail for a tang and crosscut mammoth ivory handle scales. (SharpByCoop image)

⩗ MICHAEL RAYMOND
Clean and colossal, the Galaxis gent's folder is stripped down to its bare essentials—a Bohler M390 blade, titanium frame and rose gold pivot inlays and thumb stud. (SharpByCoop image)

» LUCAS BURNLEY
It is the jade-anodized titanium handle, carved in a rose pattern, that stands out; but the duplex-ground, stonewashed CTS-Xhosa blade holds its own. (Whetstone Studio image)

« TOBIN HILL
Five Devin Thomas raindrop-damascus blades called for one heck of a mammoth ivory slab from which to fashion handle scales. (SharpByCoop image)

« MIKE TYRE
A beavertail model enlists a 1084-and-15N20-damascus blade in a Turkish twist pattern, mokume-gane bolsters and musk ox handle scales. (SharpByCoop image

Timascus Art Folders

⌄ CLYDE CHALLENOR
The modern materials of a front flipper folder include a stainless Damacore san mai blade forged by Damasteel, a titanium handle frame and Timascus inlays. (BladeGallery.com image)

» TODD FISCHER
Executed in Damasteel and Timascus, the "Archangel" flipper folder lifts the spirits. (Cory Martin image

» JEREMY KRAMMES
There's not a straight line on the flipper folder, the curvy gal dressed in a Chad Nichols san mai blade, titanium frame and Timascus handle inlay. (SharpByCoop image)

« DIRK LOOTS
Fashioned in a stingray theme, the folder parades an RWL-34 blade, Timascus fittings and different textures of titanium to form the appealing handle frame pattern. (Dirk Loots image)

REESE WEILAND
Take a gander at the "Wolverine" dual automatic executed in damascus, Timascus, ivory, abalone and a lot of fine folder crafting. (Cory Martin image)

RON BEST
He fired off the "Fire Hawk" in a wide but pointed, recurved, plain-old hot Damasteel blade; a zirconium frame and pearl and Timascus inlays. (Cory Martin image)

BRIAN TIGHE
The sculpted handle with Timascus inlay further invigorates an already lively "Tighe Down" Damasteel flipper folder. (SharpByCoop image)

LES VOORHIES and PETER MARTIN
"Lava lamp" damascus by Peter Martin (blade) and "bubble" damascus by Les Voorhies (handle frame) give the "VAMPersian" some bite. (Cory Martin image)

Gallery-Ready Engraving

⍆ **PETER DEL RASO**
If I had a dollar for every mother-of-pearl handle integral 440C fixed blade gorgeously engraved by Marcello Pedini and inset with garnets, I'd have a buck. (SharpByCoop image)

⌃ **GRANT CHAMBERS**
Gold and copper flowers sprout along the engraved guard of a 1095 bowie hafted in box elder burl.

《 **VINCE EVANS**
If all damascus Schiavona swords had such stop-you-in-your-tracks engraved baskets like this, there may never have been late 17th-century wars. (SharpByCoop image)

》 **LEE LERMAN**
Engraving and gold inlays by Pedro Villarrubia give the pearl-handle Vinland-pattern damascus flipper folder the pop it deserves. (Caleb Royer image)

》 **KOJI HARA**
When the maker can do gold overlay and engraving like that on a black-lip pearl handle, and then dimple the bolsters and build the folder, the rest just sit back and stare. (SharpByCoop image)

EDMUND DAVIDSON
One of the maker's integral masterpieces is executed in CPM 154 steel, including blade, guard and pommel engraving by Jere Davidson, and a Siberian mastodon handle. (Whetstone Studio image)

CHRISTIAN MATHIESON
Engraver Danae Cresswell invited some wildcats to sidle up to the bolster of a D2 dagger in a carbon fiber handle. (SharpByCoop image)

STAN BUZEK
The Alice Carter gold inlay and bolster engraving tie the Randy Hass feather damascus and mammoth ivory together on a Texas trapper. (SharpByCoop image)

ISRAEL FRANCO
Ghosts of years past are immortalized in ATX engraving on the bolsters of a 1095 folder with blue Corian handle scales. (Caleb Royer image)

TOM PLOPPERT
Joe Mason gold inlay and engraving on the bolsters and shield highlight the pearl-handle, five-blade stockman folder. (SharpByCoop image)

ENRIQUE PENA
The titanium frame of a CPM 154 flipper folder served as Carlos DeLao's blank canvas, and upon it he engraved a masterpiece. (SharpByCoop image)

ANDRE THORBURN
The flipper folder checks all the boxes—a Takefu blade, zirconium bolster engraving by Marietjie Thorburn and carbon fiber handle scales. (SharpByCoop image)

LUKE SWENSON
Putting pop in a LinerLock are a Bill Burke feather-damascus blade, a mammoth ivory handle and Alice Carter bolster engraving. (SharpByCoop image)

HARVEY DEAN
Of sole authorship and presented in all its splendor, the dog-bone bowie features a gold-inlaid and engraved damascus blade and bolsters, and a fossil walrus ivory handle with domed pins. (SharpByCoop image)

DEW HARA
The engraved copper handle of a damascus flipper folder is patinaed using a Kuroyogoshi technique and depicts a samurai standing below a cherry tree with drawn sword. (BladeGallery.com image)

⌄ HERUCUS BLOMERUS
Planted between the Damasteel blade and marbled carbon fiber handle of the flipper folder is a zirconium bolster engraved by Julien Marchal in a floral motif with gold inlays. (SharpByCoop image)

≫ JOHNNY STOUT
With a mammoth ivory handle and Veronique Laurent feather damascus blade, the folder was passed to Julie Warenski who engraved a bee, flowers and honeycomb. (SharpByCoop image)

⌃ ALEKSEYEV ILYA
A bastard sword, stupendously sculpted and engraved in an archangel Gabriel and dragon motif, enlists a cornucopia of materials, including wood, silver, copper, rubies, damascus, amethyst and gold. (Whetstone Studio image)

≪ RICHARD WRIGHT
One dragon with a ruby eye is carved into the red bronze bolster of an ambidextrous bolster-release auto sporting sambar stag handle scales.

≪ BRETT NOAKE
The Joe Mason inlay and engraving of the damascus fixed blade matches so well with the mammoth ivory handle, it is exquisite. (SharpByCoop image)

⯆ PRO-TECH
A Pro-Tech "Dark Angel" front-opening dress automatic folder is smartly engraved in a dragon motif by Andrew Lee Adams. (SharpByCoop image)

» JEAN-LOUIS REGEL
"La Vie en Rose" showcases a wootz steel blade, mammoth ivory handle and a black iron guard embellished with green gold, 24k-gold and platinum flowers. (SharpByCoop image)

« BUBBA CROUCH
Not your average trapper. The folder features Bill Burke feather-damascus blades, stag handle scales, Alice Carter engraved and gold-inlaid bolsters, knapped springs and liners, and a custom arrowhead shield. (SharpByCoop image)

» BRUCE BUMP
An art dagger is orchestrated in a rust-brown, san mai damascus blade, mammoth ivory handle and niter-blued fittings that are engraved and gold inlaid by Ray Cover Jr. (SharpByCoop image)

» ALLEN SURLS and DIRK LOOTS
What scroll engraving does for the bolster, Damasteel does for the blade and mammoth ivory for the grip of the folder. (Dirk Loots image)

» KEVIN HARVEY
Inspired by American folklore, the Mississippian dirk boasts a six-bar composite damascus blade, a dyed and stabilized giraffe shin bone handle and a heat-colored titanium pommel engraved in a mythical half-alligator, half-horse motif. (BladeGallery.com image)

PETER CAREY
From clover-like images to fleur-de-lis and vines, the David Riccardo gold inlay and engraving on the flipper folder is all-encompassing. (SharpByCoop image)

MICHAEL ANDERSSON
While texturing lends palpability and grip to the maple burl handle, Celtic knotwork adds appeal to the bolster of a composite damascus hunter. (BladeGallery.com image)

BRETT SELLEY
Simply stunning is a W2 straight razor showing off a temper line and Danae Creswell engraving that's infilled with blue instead of traditional black. (SharpByCoop image)

JOHN HORRIGAN
A 2.5-year project, the maker engraved and inlaid 99 gold leaves into the Turkish twist damascus blade and blued-steel guard of a Persian art knife in an African blackwood handle. (SharpByCoop image)

KEVIN CASHEN
Between the wire-wrapped haft and the engraved hilt, the 16th century rapier reproduction could be carried by the likes of Christian I, Elector of Saxony. (SharpByCoop image)

JERRY FISK
Deep relief or raised engraving, gold inlay, walrus ivory, damascus and a lot of love went into the knives. (SharpByCoop image)

Basilica-Level Mosaics

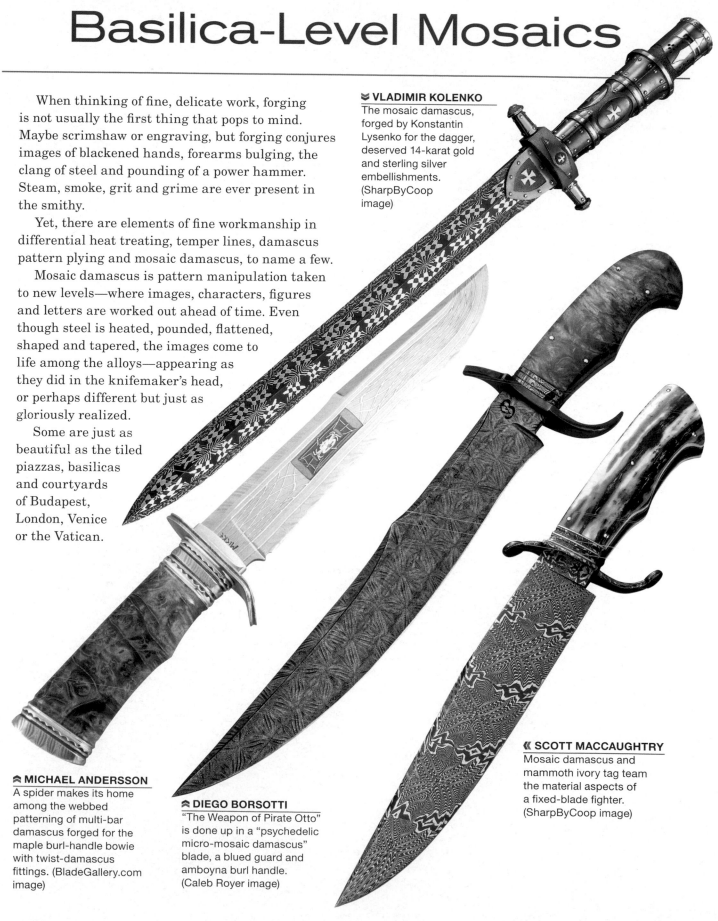

When thinking of fine, delicate work, forging is not usually the first thing that pops to mind. Maybe scrimshaw or engraving, but forging conjures images of blackened hands, forearms bulging, the clang of steel and pounding of a power hammer. Steam, smoke, grit and grime are ever present in the smithy.

Yet, there are elements of fine workmanship in differential heat treating, temper lines, damascus pattern plying and mosaic damascus, to name a few.

Mosaic damascus is pattern manipulation taken to new levels—where images, characters, figures and letters are worked out ahead of time. Even though steel is heated, pounded, flattened, shaped and tapered, the images come to life among the alloys—appearing as they did in the knifemaker's head, or perhaps different but just as gloriously realized.

Some are just as beautiful as the tiled piazzas, basilicas and courtyards of Budapest, London, Venice or the Vatican.

⌄ VLADIMIR KOLENKO
The mosaic damascus, forged by Konstantin Lysenko for the dagger, deserved 14-karat gold and sterling silver embellishments. (SharpByCoop image)

⌃ MICHAEL ANDERSSON
A spider makes its home among the webbed patterning of multi-bar damascus forged for the maple burl-handle bowie with twist-damascus fittings. (BladeGallery.com image)

⌃ DIEGO BORSOTTI
"The Weapon of Pirate Otto" is done up in a "psychedelic micro-mosaic damascus" blade, a blued guard and amboyna burl handle. (Caleb Royer image)

« SCOTT MACCAUGHTRY
Mosaic damascus and mammoth ivory tag team the material aspects of a fixed-blade fighter. (SharpByCoop image)

》ANDREW BLOMFIELD
This breakout bowie gets the job done in a mosaic damascus blade, tool steel guard and ringed Gidgee wood handle. (SharpByCoop image)

》DIONATAM FRANCO
Micro explosions of mosaic damascus leave indelible marks on the blade of a clip-point hunter handled in rosewood and gifted with a gold-inlaid guard. (BladeGallery.com image)

》DON HANSON III
A collector asked to have his "Scary Tacs" photographed featuring the maker's signature mosaic damascus bolsters. (SharpByCoop image)

》JASON "TOWBALL" WEIGHTMAN
If long, tightly patterned mosaic damascus blades are your thing, look no further than this fossilized walrus ivory-handle piece. (SharpByCoop image)

》ROBERT BURNS
Equally mesmerizing are the mosaic damascus blade, Minnesota birch burl ferrule and water buffalo horn handle. (Caleb Royer image)

▼ TERRY VENDEVENTER
The mosaic damascus power play involves the blade, guard and escutcheon plate of an elk antler-handled fighter. (Whetstone Studio image)

« KYLE ROYER
After a knock on the noggin, one might see the stars and bells inherent to the mosaic damascus blade of a fighter featuring 24-karat gold, blued fittings and a walrus ivory handle. (Caleb Royer image)

» JOSHUA PRINCE
He worked his culinary knife magic via 1080-15N20-and-nickel damascus and African blackwood. (SharpByCoop image)

⌃ JAMES RODEBAUGH
Ribbons of mosaic damascus crisscross the blade of a mammoth ivory-handle hunter featuring a bronze frame, and silicon bronze and nickel silver guard. (SharpByCoop image)

» SHAWN MCINTYRE
There is a storm brewing in the "hurricane" mosaic damascus blade of a bowie that also sports a twist-damascus guard and sambar stag handle. (SharpByCoop image)

⍦ GREGER FORSELIUS
The living, breathing Mattias Styrefors mosaic damascus blade of the long hunter nicely complements the patterns of black ash burl and mammoth molar. (BladeGallery.com image)

⌃ DANIELE IBBA
Twenty-seven rubies are set on the mother-of-pearl handle, titanium frame and pommel of a dagger that also showcases a Vlad Matveev mosaic damascus blade and matching guard. (SharpByCoop image)

≫ CODY HOFSOMMER
A 2.5-year project, the The contrasting mosaic damascus blade and walrus ivory handle make for a pretty pairing. (SharpByCoop image)

≪ CHRIS SHARP
Does anyone see a pattern here? No matter the damascus blade, pierced shield or mammoth ivory handle, it is all hot. (SharpByCoop image)

≪ JASON ELLARD
A low-layer-count mosaic damascus blade makes a good first impression on a chef's knife that also boasts a Tasmanian timber (Huon pine) handle and sheath. (Caleb Royer photo)

» JEFFREY WAGENAAR
Mosaic damascus spans the blade, guard, spacer and frame of a camel-bone-handle dagger with nickel silver pins. (Caleb Royer image)

« PETER MARTIN
Blued mosaic damascus and bronze-zirconium mokume-gane provide patterning and color for the QSB flipper folder with zirconium pocket clip. (Cory Martin image)

» RAY RYBAR
The cast brown bear immortalized on the pommel left tracks across the blade and even one of his bones for the grip. (SharpByCoop image)

» CLIFF PARKER
Imagine gifting the gent's folder with swordfish bill handle and swordfish-themed mosaic damascus blade to a fisherman. (SharpByCoop image)

» MATT PARKINSON
The mosaic damascus and bog oak fixed blade is brilliantly executed. (SharpByCoop image)

» JOELITON SATIUQ
A powerful pattern highlights a mosaic damascus bowie fashioned with a file-worked and sculpted guard and pommel, and a giraffe bone handle. (Caleb Royer image)

Town Square-Worthy Sculptures

⌄ ALISTAIR BASTIAN
The damascus blade, Timascus handle and pocket clip, and titanium liners are all sculpted, accompanied by a mother-of-pearl inlay. (SharpByCoop image)

⌃ STEVEN LICATA
Not your average blade grind. The dagger dips a little here and protrudes some over there, paired up nicely with a Chris Kravitt leather sheath. (SharpByCoop image)

» HYENA
The "Cutting Heat" model sashays around in a sculpted mokume-gane handle and an Alabama Damascus blade. The wood and acrylic stand is not bad, either. (Whetstone Studio image)

« CLAES LOFGREN
It is not just the aged bronze frame and guard that's sculpted, but also the 15N20-and-20C damascus blade and even the stabilized birch handle. (SharpByCoop image)

≫ DOUG NOREN
Francine Larstein is credited for the sculpted and engraved 18k-gold-plated nickel silver guard, pommel and shield of the pearl-handle George Wostenholm & Sons IXL-style Washington hunting knife. (Whetstone Studio image)

⌃ STUART KERR
The only straight line lies along the edge of a sculpted damascus straight razor in a stabilized and dyed maple burl handle. (SharpByCoop image)

≫ VERONIQUE LAURENT
A random-pattern damascus art dagger, the "Valentine" is delivered in a lovingly carved RWL-34 frame with mother-of-pearl and brass highlights. (SharpByCoop image)

≫ CORRADO MORO
It took two pierced blades, a grooved handle, black mother-of-pearl inlays, spiral bolsters and a lot of ingenuity to land at this knife. (SharpByCoop image)

≫ CORY MARTIN
All carving and finishing work on the "Megalodon" was done by hand, including the titanium handle, copper ribs, and copper and blackened titanium back bar. (Cory Martin image)

Carving and Checkering

» HERB DERR
A couple stag-handle damascus fixed blades are colossally carved with amphibian subjects making the gripping material their homes. (SharpByCoop image)

» KEITH FLUDDER
The copacetic counterparts of the Khanbar model are stippled and carved African blackwood and mosaic damascus. (SharpByCoop image)

« WILLIAM LLOYD
The "Green Man," complete with emerald eyes, comes to life on a short sword, carved in elk antler and dyed maple. K.C. Lund is credited for the damascus blade. (Whetstone Studio image)

» ANDREW BLOMFIELD
The carved, sculpted, engraved and dapper dagger enlists a feather damascus blade, tool steel guard and ebony handle. (SharpByCoop image)

⌃ GRANT CHAMBERS
From the upcurved, sweeping tip of the O1 tool steel Persian pirate's knife to the blood groove, gold inlay, engraving and carved African blackwood handle, this one's worth all the looting and pillaging.

» JOSH FISHER
A little handle checkering in desert ironwood goes a long way on a differentially heat treated W2 high carbon steel fixed blade. (Caleb Royer image)

» ARNO BERNARD
Warthogs are immortalized as they traverse the carved warthog ivory handle of a 440C fixed blade. (SharpByCoop image)

» RICHARD WRIGHT
The ambidextrous bolster-release switchblade relies on a Bob Eggerling mosaic damascus blade and bolsters and a checkered mammoth ivory handle.

» MARDI MESHEJIAN
The carving extends from the damascus blade to the fossil walrus ivory handle, with only a Shibuichi guard in between. (SharpByCoop image)

« PAUL DISTEFANO
The ladder-pattern damascus blade and sweeping guard get things going, while a carved ancient walrus ivory handle provides the finishing touch. (Caleb Royer image)

« STEVE HILL
In carving out a knife handle, one could do worse than a swordfish bill, matched with a "pool" damascus blade, heat-colored bolster and a pyrope garnet set in the thumb stud. (SharpByCoop image)

« TOMMY CARROLL
A bear jaw carved in Celtic knotwork more than suffices for the handle of a stingingly beautiful knife featuring a sculpted damascus blade by Aaron Schwartz. (Whetstone Studio image)

Damascus Pattern Plying

» DANIELE IBBA
With three types of damascus—Robert Eggerling, Zladinox and Doug Ponzio—plenty of white mother-of-pearl, 18-karat gold, blue diamonds and bluer bolsters, she was putting them out in pairs. (SharpByCoop image)

» MATT PARKINSON
The pattern of the mosaic damascus dagger starts near the coffin-style maple handle and points toward the tip. (SharpByCoop image)

» STEPHEN LELAND
The fine utility knife is adorned in damascus, nickel silver and buffalo horn. (Caleb Royer image)

» WENDON SHARMAN
The "laddered-W's"-pattern damascus blade is complemented by a damascus guard and pommel, and a mammoth ivory handle. (Caleb Royer image)

« JAMES RODEBAUGH
A French lock folder is kissed by "Mitosis" damascus for the blade and radial pattern damascus for the bolsters, as well as stag and titanium. (SharpByCoop image)

∀ BILL BURKE
The scroll engraving mimics the Spirograph damascus patterning, each making room for the exhibition-grade mammoth ivory handle. (BladeGallery.com image)

» JOHN PHILLIPS
The damascus patterning of the integral Gyuto chef's knife is dangerously endearing, complemented by a cherry burl handle and mokume-gane spacer. (Whetstone Studio image)

∧ JERRY FISK
The way the fossil walrus ivory feels in the hand, the damascus pattern splays out from spine to edge and the deep relief of the golden inlay looks, it's all good. (SharpByCoop image)

« BRUCE BARNETT
It's not easy navigating the "River of Fire" damascus blade pattern, but the mammoth ivory handle is clean and straightforward. (SharpByCoop image

» MERT TANSU
A highly patterned, 1084- and 15N20-damascus kitchen knife is handled in amboyna burl with chrome and G-10 spacers. (SharpByCoop image)

⌄ BUTCH BALL
Hello heat-colored Mike Norris damascus blade and Timascus handle, it's so nice to see you. (Whetstone Studio image)

» JERRY McCLURE
The art deco folder features a "star fighter" damascus blade, moissanite thumb stud, meteorite handle scales, and 18k-gold moon faces (each side) and pins. (Caleb Royer image)

« LES VOORHIES and PETER MARTIN
There's "bubble" damascus on the blade and back bar forged by Martin, and a Voorhies bubble damascus pocket clip and inlays, all adding lots of fizz. (Cory Martin image)

» ADAM PARKER
Damasteel looks dashing on a hefty fixed blade in a stag handle and red vulcanized liners. (SharpByCoop image)

» CURTIS HAALAND
The carved, sculpted, They are coming in pairs—a fighter hunter set—showcasing 80CrV2-and-15N20 damascus blades, wrought iron guards and blackwood handles with zirconium spacers. (SharpByCoop image

☆ THOMAS LOFGREN
That colossal blade is Zladinox high carbon damascus, the bolsters forged by Vlad Mateeu; and the handle of sterling silver, blackwood and stabilized maple burl. (SharpByCoop image)

☆ WILLIAM PORTO
A gaucho knife is the recipient of a Turkish Spirograph damascus blade with false edge, a walrus ivory handle and gold inlays. (Caleb Royer image)

☆ SHANE P. ATWOOD
Donated to The Friends of the NRA Banquet, the folder is done up in Chad Nichols raindrop damascus, a desert ironwood grip, twill carbon fiber bolsters and copper pivot collars. (Caleb Royer image)

☆ TOM WARD
The "Relic of the Fishspeakers" fighter parades a clad chevron and W's-pattern damascus blade, a carved mammoth ivory handle and a black-lip-pearl inlay. (SharpByCoop image)

☆ ADAM FROMHOLTZ
Forged from 15N20 and 1075 steels, the keyhole-style damascus fixed blade sports a rosewood handle for good measure. (SharpByCoop image)

☆ BROOK TURNER
If you can peel your eyes away from the Damasteel blade of the slicer, take a gander at the Arizona ironwood handle. (SharpByCoop image)

JOSH SMITH
The blade and bolster patterning mesmerizes, while the mammoth ivory handle scales add further depth and dimension. (SharpByCoop image)

PAUL SAVAGE
A buffalo horn-handle quillon dagger wears its damascus stripes with pride. (SharpByCoop image)

PAUL DISTEFANO
Like rungs of a ladder, the damascus pattern climbs the blade, leading to a textured S-guard and a carved blackwood handle. (Caleb Royer image)

WILL FREEMAN
A fighter enters the ring in a "twisted W's" multi-bar damascus blade, ironwood burl handle and wrought iron ferrule. (Whetstone Studio image)

BRIAN SELLERS
He just kept forging the damascus, for the 10-inch blade, split ring and sub-hilt of the fighter, which is handled in ironwood burl. (Whetstone Studio image)

PEYTON RAMM
The matching blade and bolsters of a dress locking folder are 1095-and-15N20 damascus accompanied by giraffe bone handle scales. (SharpByCoop image)

RICH RICHARDSON
What better for a hunting knife than a "predator-pattern"-damascus blade, carbon fiber guard and butt cap, and fossilized walrus tusk handle? (Caleb Royer image)

FRANCK SOUVILLE
The wide blade—a design by Tashi Bharucha—is the perfect medium for showing off the damascus pattern, paired with a stainless bolster and ironwood grip. (SharpByCoop image)

OLIVER GOLDSCHMIDT
The pattern might be random, but it was well planned and executed for an integral chopper sporting a Hawaiian Koa wood handle. (BladeGallery.com image)

ANDREW BLOMFIELD
The damascus patterning pops on a keyhole-style fixed blade with Gidgee wood handle. (SharpByCoop image

JORDAN BERTHELOT
Stare at the blade long enough and you'll see the boomerangs for which the damascus pattern is named, and then gaze upon that teal box elder burl handle. (Caleb Royer image)

STEVE RANDALL
Dark bronzed titanium, fossil walrus ivory and "W's"-pattern damascus achieve the desired effect for a sub-hilt fighter. (SharpByCoop image)

RUSSELL ROOSEVELT
Don't let the damascus distract you; just hold onto the California buckeye burl handle when cutting. (SharpByCoop image)

HENRY HILDEN
A Swedish bowie displays a hand forged, multi-bar damascus blade, a mosaic damascus guard and an ironwood handle with mammoth ivory spacers. (BladeGallery.com image)

TIM ROBERTSON
They finally figured out what all the buzz was about: Chris Marks "wasp nest" damascus handled in Sambar stag with a federal shield. (SharpByCoop image)

PAUL LUSK
The push dagger is wrought from 416-layer carbon damascus and given a simple yet effective stainless-steel palm. (Caleb Royer image)

DAVID KULIS
You know the heat coloring of the Doug Ponzio damascus blade achieved its mission when it matched the dyed and stabilized wood grip. (SharpByCoop image)

JUSTIN BURTON
Low-layer mosaic damascus makes an appearance on a fantastical fighter complete with curly Koa handle and copper pins. (Caleb Royer image)

ROBERT BURNS
Twelve inches of Turkish twist damascus get the party started on an ironwood-handle bowie with wrought iron guard. (Caleb Royer image)

KEVIN CASHEN
Rome would have never fallen had the soldiers carried Spatha swords such as the 1084-and-15N20 damascus blade hafted in cocobolo and bronze. (SharpByCoop image)

GENE KIMMI
All damascus—the 39-layer blade and 55-layer guard and pommel, is hand hammered and finished with a coffee etch. That will wake you up in the morning. (Caleb Royer image)

LARRY HOSTETLER
Chad Nichols "iguana" stainless damascus was just the ticket for a bolster-release auto in a mammoth ivory handle. (SharpByCoop image)

ANDREW MEERS
A collaboration with David Lisch, the makers forged the damascus blade and guard of the gold-inlaid, walrus-ivory-handle art dagger. (SharpByCoop image)

» GREGER FORSELIUS
It's not just the intricate, tight pattern of the Damasteel blade that impresses, but the way the lines follow the edge, the file-worked spine complements the columns of curves, and how spalted birch is a perfect counterpart. (BladeGallery.com image)

» JOSHUA WISOR
The ladder-pattern damascus blade is as palpable and palatable as the Hawaiian curly Koa handle. (Caleb Royer image)

» BOBBY GARZA
Who knew the combination of Alabama Damascus and amboyna burl would have such a calming effect? Apparently, the maker did. (Caleb Royer image)

« H.K. DERR
The hand-forged, heat-colored, bird's-eye-pattern damascus blade is the beneficiary of a Steller's sea cow rib handle, buckeye burl spacer and a nickel silver guard. (BladeGallery.com image)

⍖ ISMAEL BIEGELMEIER
Turkish "Spirograph" damascus makes a power play on a giraffe bone-handled forged fixed blade. (Caleb Royer image)

⍖ GARY ELLIS
Low layer-number ladder pattern damascus results in a dramatic look proper for a Bocote-handle fixed blade. (Caleb Royer image)

» CHRIS SHARP
The maker outdid himself in fashioning the damascus blade of a dress slip-joint folder, complete with a jigged bone handle and pierced shield. (SharpByCoop image)

» MICHAEL TYRE
Of cosmic duality are the O-1 and L-6 damascus blade and bolsters, in a Yin and Yang pattern, of course, and interdependent of the mammoth ivory handle. (SharpByCoop image)

TYLER TURNER
Waves of "Draupner" pattern Damasteel splash across the blade and handle of the "Merlin" frame-lock folder featuring titanium hardware and a custom pivot. (SharpByCoop image)

ANDREW SMITH
The damascus head of the spike tomahawk is just as handsome as the curly maple haft. (SharpByCoop image)

RUDY DEAN
Hafted in handsome red oak, the shining star of the combat tomahawk is the 336-layer damascus head that's heat treated and tempered to purple, green, blue and gold hues. (Caleb Royer image)

RUDY DEAN
The power comes from all sides—the Honduran rosewood handle, mild steel guard and that heat-colored 585-layer damascus blade. (SharpByCoop image)

JOSEPH SCHRUM
A little creative blacking and etching goes a long way for the "Phoenix" damascus fixed blade in a bog oak handle. (SharpByCoop image)

Knives of a Feather Together

❯ ROBERT FLYNT
Forged by Konstantin Lysenko, the blade of the Koa-wood-handle bowie combines feather damascus with a firecracker pattern along the edge and spine. (BladeGallery.com image)

⌃ CODY HOFSOMMER
Ah, my fine-feathered friend, he who would be sporting a bronze guard, stag handle and ringed Gidgee wood spacer. (SharpByCoop image)

❯ JOEL WORLEY
Handled in curly Koa wood, the feather damascus pattern splays out from edge to spine in spectacular fashion. (Cory Martin image)

❯ HARVEY DEAN
The "Wings of Honor" bowie offers a feather-damascus blade, a sterling silver guard displaying actual 1st lieutenant bars worn during World War II in Europe, and a blue-white mammoth ivory handle. (SharpByCoop image)

《 MIKE DEIBERT

If feather damascus tickles your fancy, look no further than the fixed blades with blued guards and natural handle materials. (SharpByCoop image)

》 TERRY DICKEY

A dapper dagger is done up in feather damascus, mammoth ivory and African blackwood. (Cory Martin image)

《 LUKE SWENSON

The long-pull, lockback folder features an equally handsome sambar stag handle and Bill Burke feather damascus blade. (SharpByCoop image

Resin and Acrylic Handle Craft

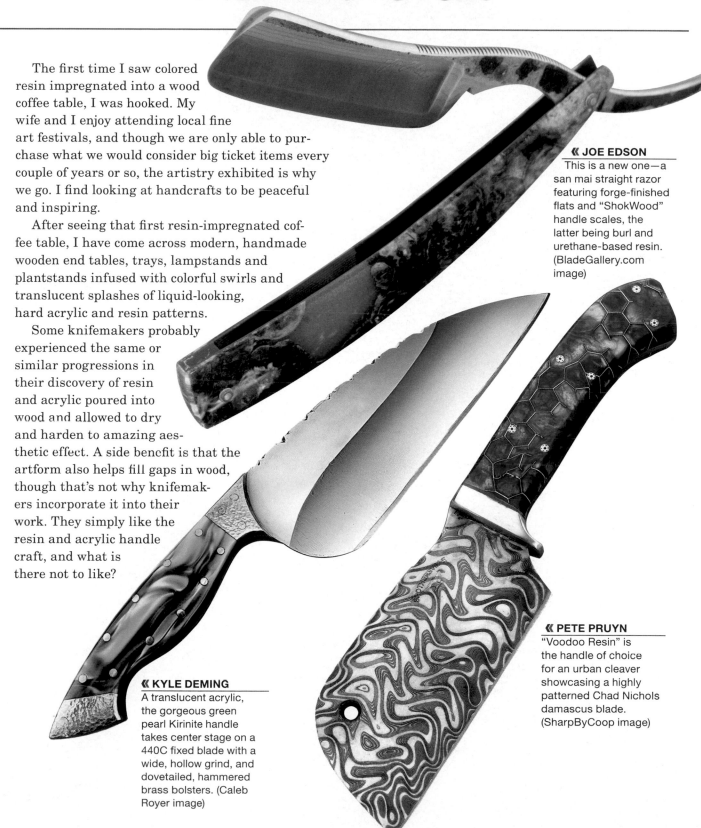

The first time I saw colored resin impregnated into a wood coffee table, I was hooked. My wife and I enjoy attending local fine art festivals, and though we are only able to purchase what we would consider big ticket items every couple of years or so, the artistry exhibited is why we go. I find looking at handcrafts to be peaceful and inspiring.

After seeing that first resin-impregnated coffee table, I have come across modern, handmade wooden end tables, trays, lampstands and plantstands infused with colorful swirls and translucent splashes of liquid-looking, hard acrylic and resin patterns.

Some knifemakers probably experienced the same or similar progressions in their discovery of resin and acrylic poured into wood and allowed to dry and harden to amazing aesthetic effect. A side benefit is that the artform also helps fill gaps in wood, though that's not why knifemakers incorporate it into their work. They simply like the resin and acrylic handle craft, and what is there not to like?

« JOE EDSON
This is a new one—a san mai straight razor featuring forge-finished flats and "ShokWood" handle scales, the latter being burl and urethane-based resin. (BladeGallery.com image)

« PETE PRUYN
"Voodoo Resin" is the handle of choice for an urban cleaver showcasing a highly patterned Chad Nichols damascus blade. (SharpByCoop image)

« KYLE DEMING
A translucent acrylic, the gorgeous green pearl Kirinite handle takes center stage on a 440C fixed blade with a wide, hollow grind, and dovetailed, hammered brass bolsters. (Caleb Royer image)

» KEVIN CROSS
The Damasteel cleaver is carried via a maple and acrylic handle, complete with carbon fiber guard and G-10 liners. (SharpByCoop image)

« DAVID MCCONNELL
The bowie's assembled cast of characters includes a 1075 hammer-finished blade, wrought iron guard and hybrid maple and green resin handle. (Cory Martin image)

» PAUL LEBATARD
All fillet knives should come standard with MOP Aluminite resin handles, CPM 154 blades and 7075-T6 aluminum Corby bolts. (Whetstone Studio image)

» MIKE WITHAM
Forging a five-layer "Gomai" blade of 1095 and nickel foil, the maker added a black resin handle inlaid with aluminum foil that he thought tied the piece together. Agreed! (Caleb Royer image)

RON BEST
The carbon fiber handle of the Damasteel "Fire Hawk" flipper folder is inlaid with "Black Sea" Dichrolam—polymer layers of laminated glass, burls and resins. (Cory Martin image)

» GAVIN DICKERSON
While the blade is hollow ground from N690 stainless steel, the handle is pinecone suspended in green acrylic resin. How cool is that? (BladeGallery.com image)

» ALEXANDER NOOT
One forged damascus "White Rapids Seax" knife is pictured multiple times to illustrate how the colors of the Raffir handle brighten as the temperature warms. (Caleb Royer image)

⌃ NICK WATSON and ZACK WORRELL
Not only is the serrated bread knife forged from stainless damascus, but it also sports a cholla cactus and black resin handle with a white G-10 bolster. (Whetstone Studio image)

Scrimshander Showcase

⌄ JOHN COHEA
A mammoth bark handle scrimshawed in a Native American motif that includes a wolf and a horse, the copper-etched damascus blade and copper fittings with rawhide wrap give the knife and sheath package a frontier-like look and feel. (Whetstone Studio image)

» TOMMY LEE
A "Turkish twist"-damascus dagger got the full embellishing treatment—gold inlay and bolster engraving by Martin Butler and a Roni Dietrich scrimshawed mammoth tusk handle. (SharpByCoop image)

⌃ PAUL BAKER
The handsome gent is rendered via needle and ink on the ivory handle of a sleek 1084 high carbon steel bowie. (Caleb Royer image)

« STEVE MULLIN
Whale scrimshaw on blue mammoth ivory by Matt Stothart is nestled in a damascus frame for an ATS-34 dress locking-liner folder. (SharpByCoop image)

» ANDERS HOGSTROM
Some will gravitate toward the Colt 1911 pistol-style fossil mammoth ivory grip scrimshawed by Rickard Perman in a "tumbling skulls" motif, and others to the swooping Damasteel blade with Spanish notch. Neither would be wrong. (SharpByCoop image)

« BILL KENNEDY
The mammoth ivory handle scales of a saddle-horn trapper were the perfect showcase for Linda Karst Stone Native American scrimshaw, and the bolsters a canvas for Alice Carter engraving. (SharpByCoop image)

« EDMUND DAVIUDSON
The integral 440C sub-hilt fighter, created as a fundraiser for the 116th Infantry Stonewall Brigade Museum Foundation, commemorates the history of the 116th from its beginnings in 1741 through the D-Day invasion to present. Jere Davidson is responsible for the hand-cut engravings. (Whetstone Studio image)

FACTORY TRENDS

It seemingly does not matter what type of cutting edge an enthusiast is in the market for, modern production knife companies supply whatever the heart desires.

Sounds like a commercial, doesn't it? Except it is the truth. In today's highly competitive marketplace, traditional pocketknife and sporting cutlery enterprises offer everything from machetes and axes to bolos, slip-joint folders, hunting and tactical fixed blades, flipper folders, kitchen knives, fillets and caping numbers, neck knives, and everything from edges under two inches in length to big burly blades.

There are categories of knives that were never in the Sears, Roebuck & Co., Herter's or Cabela's catalogs. A person could Google "locking folders" and come up with a dozen or more types of mechanisms for folding knives. There are hundreds of handle materials and blade steels today, and more sheath, rigging and carry systems than there are knives in the world's largest collections.

Honestly, it is a bit intimidating to seek out quality yet affordable knives. They are not all made in America, and yet not every Chinese knife is a cheap knockoff, either. There is quality coming out of countries far and wide, and ethnic influence has not been lost on today's knife companies. Like everything else in the modern era, there are choices, and variety can be the spice of life if one is willing to do a little research and find what is right for him or her. Or just take one of everything. There are folks doing that, too.

A Classic Never Goes out of Style

The Swiss Army Classic is a collectible little knife with a big reputation

By Evan F. Nappen, Esq.

It is widely contended that the most popular everyday carry (EDC) knife on the planet is the Victorinox 58mm Swiss Army Classic. It adorns key rings, and sits in uncountable pockets and purses throughout the world.

As a reasonably priced and incredibly handy knife containing a small blade, file with small screwdriver (Classic SD), scissors, toothpick, tweezers and lanyard ring, it has proven to be an almost magical combination of beloved features. The Swiss Victorinox factory makes over 45,000 pocketknives per day. They are sold worldwide in over 120 countries. You can bet that a good percentage of these knives are Classics.

The Victorinox Swiss Army Classic even comes in tie-dye handles.

For that reason, it is also the most confiscated pocketknife in the world, as folks go through more and more security screenings in our post 9-11 world. Airports have seized tens of thousands of these little darlings. Your author personally knows this, having purchased from the government boxfuls of such knives and found some outstanding rarities.

These finds include Classics presented by U.S. presidents in ceremonies or as awards, models with sterling silver handle scales (some made especially for Tiffany & Co.®), Classics with gold bar inlays, others given away by companies and government agencies, special edition Classics with unique designs and those commemorating various events and occasions.

Of course, airports are not the only places where knives are confiscated. After teaching a seminar on knife law at the BLADE Show in Atlanta, an attendee from the United Kingdom (UK) came up to me and said, "Let me tell you how bad it is where I'm from. I was sitting in a coffee shop, having a cup and opening my mail with my Swiss Army Classic. A bobby came up to me and said I was upsetting customers who were frightened over my knife and that he could arrest me under The Knife Act. He decided to only advise me, and he promptly confiscated my knife. The anti-knife movement in my country is in full force. There are knife surrender bins and even an effort to get rid of 'pointy kitchen knives.'"

My new UK friend pleaded with me not to let it happen here in the United States.

Historically, the first two-sided multi-tool was Karl Elsener's original Swiss Army Knife. In the 1890's, Elsener invented a method for both ends of a folding knife to utilize the same spring and hold two blades, one on either end. His knives not only contained blades but also tools, such as screwdrivers and cork screws. This invention allowed for double the number of features in a pocketknife, as compared to other multi-tool pocketknives at the time.

Victoria + Inox = Victorinox

Elsener's company was eventually called Victorinox. It was named after his mother, Victoria, and *Inox* which is the French abbreviated form of *acier inoxydable*, or stainless steel. "Victoria" and "inox" were joined to make the word "Victorinox" in 1921.

That famous name lives on to this day.

There is a dispute as to whether the first Classic was offered in a 1935 Victorinox sales catalog or if it originated from a patent, number 2,718,695, filed by Elsener on November 8, 1952, which was granted on September 27, 1955. Neither the 1935 nor the 1955 knife resemble—no toothpick, tweezers or lanyard ring—the Classic we know and love today with all its features. It was not until the late 1970's that the Swiss Army Knife catalog actually showed a knife called the "Classic" with features that make a Classic, well, a classic. The Classic SD (screwdriver tip on the file blade) was not added until 1987.

Today, the Classic version with red handle scales and the Swiss Army Knife logo is instantly recognizable throughout the world. However, numerous fascinating variations have been produced, making the 58mm Victorinox Classic with seemingly endless varieties a great knife to collect.

Classics are a popular marketing medium for thousands of companies worldwide that have advertised their logos and products on the handle scales. There are several ways Victorinox can imprint advertising on their knives. My favorite is by metal inlay. According to the factory catalog, metal inlay is described as follows: "The logos and wording are created photochemically with chromium steel and then pressed at high temperatures into the scales. This imprinting method features long-lasting durability and a high-quality appearance." This is a more expensive process than other forms of imprinting."

The most common way of imprinting is pad printing. Victorinox explains, "Today, over 90 percent of the printing jobs we carry out at Victorinox use the tampon print process (pad printing). Whether it is spot color printing using up to six colors, or four-color photo printing (CMYK), your logo will meet your CI (corporate identity) guidelines exactly. In both procedures, color is lifted with an elastic stamp from a steel plate (with an etched-in image)

Among variations of the Swiss Army Classic, the knife at far left is from the Victorinox 125th Anniversary Jubilee series.

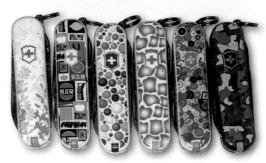

Pop art handle designs feature splashes of color across Swiss Army Classics.

and transferred to the object to be printed."

Victorinox also uses digital printing in conjunction with their pad printing process. The company notes, "We have used this procedure to successfully enhance our pad printing process for some time now. This new printing solution is most suitable for full-panel printing and halftones and/or finely detailed prints. It is mainly used for the areas where pad printing reaches the limits of its capability. Since pre-printing procedures such as the development of color separations or plates are unnecessary, this process is eco-friendly. Moreover, digital information can be stored or modified more easily. Digital prints are also treated with our benchmark protective lacquer technology, which enables an increase in the abrasion …"

Even 3-D printing is utilized with digital haptic: "It was only recently, with the introduction of clear ink, that new enhancement options became possible. Raised surfaces that feel realistic to the touch, such as canvas, leather, animal skin, convey a completely new tactile look and a 3-D experience, while maintaining the benefits of regular digital printing. High gloss is now a must, since the lacquer also comes in a semi-gloss and matt finish."

Laser Engraving

There is also laser engraving which, "… is suitable for a range of surfaces. On wood and rubber, this decoration method creates a perception of depth, making it perceptible to the touch. On metal, the lettering and logos appear on the surface in an

The no-frills Classic SD is one of the most popular knives in the world.

The Boy Scouts of America has commissioned Classics made for the organization.

anthracite/grey color. In general, the laser engraving features high wear resistance."

Victorinox also explains, "Hot Stamping a design is done with the help of a brass die stamp and stamp transfer foil, as well as with heat and pressure. It is suitable for one-color reproduction of simple logos and narrow fonts."

Finally, Classics can, of course, be engraved. With engraving, according to Victorinox, "A tool cuts the letters into the material. On plastic surfaces, the engraving cavity is then filled with a contrasting color. This method is also ideal for decorating blades and wood scales with individual names in our standard font. Engraving is suitable for small runs."

Every U.S. president since Lyndon B. Johnson has issued their guests an original Victorinox Swiss Army Knife. These Presidential Victorinox Classics have a metal inlay of the signature of the president. Both President Ronald Reagan and Vice President Dan Quayle had such knives for their guests. Even the Republican National Committee commissioned a Classic to be made. These Classics are not only collectable as knives, but also as political items.

Tiffany offered some of the highest priced Classics. The knives showcase thick sterling silver handle scales and the world-renowned name of Tiffany & Co. However, the inner workings of the Classic are all Victorinox. Tiffany marketing sterling silver-handle knives is nothing new. Theodore Roosevelt carried a beautiful Tiffany & Co. fixed-blade hunting knife, in the 1880's, with a silver handle. The Tiffany tradition of silver-handled

knives is well established.

The Swiss Army Knife is every bit as much associated with Switzerland as chocolate and gold. In fact, there are chocolate bars wrapped in foil made to look like Swiss Army Knives. There is a Victorinox Classic model featuring a 1-gram genuine Swiss gold bar in the handle. It's hard to get more Swiss than that.

The Boy Scouts of America (BSA) has commissioned Classics made for the organization. Considering that the BSA motto is "Be Prepared," it is an appropriate knife. The BSA Classic has been made for Boy Scouts, Cub Scouts and Eagle Scouts.

A fantastic resource for information on Swiss Army Knives is the website SAKWiki.com. The public knowledge base has the most detailed information and is better than any book available about the subject of Swiss Army Knives. According to SAKWiki, variations of the Classic are described as and include:

"The Classic comes in two main tool variations: The Classic and the Classic SD. The only difference is that the Classic has a nail cleaner at the tip of the nail file blade, while the Classic SD has a small slot-head screwdriver at the tip. The Classic SD seems to be the more common model these days.

The Alox Classic removes the toothpick and tweezers but offers metal scales that have also been produced in different colors. Initial colors were red, blue, green, black and silver.

2007 Euro colors (later released in North America) were turquoise-blue, lime green, hot pink, orange and silver, while 2013 France Limited Edition colors were red, brown, blue and dark blue (gunmetal blue).

The Classic is also available with an Emergency Blade instead of the pen blade. This blade variation is rarer than the standard or SD versions.

Around 2015/2016, a variation of the Classic was released with a push pin tool for removing a watch strap, replacing the nail file. It was sold in a set that included a military-style

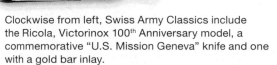

Clockwise from left, Swiss Army Classics include the Ricola, Victorinox 100th Anniversary model, a commemorative "U.S. Mission Geneva" knife and one with a gold bar inlay.

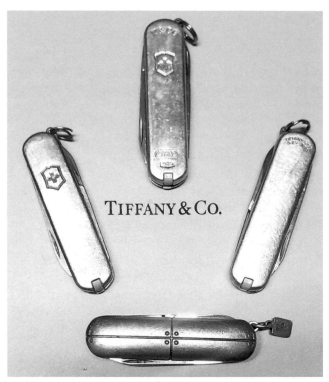

Swiss Army Classic models with sterling silver handle scales were made especially for Tiffany & Co.®

From left to right, Swiss Army Classic handle materials include wood, pearl and leather.

watch strap. It was also gifted with the purchase of a watch from the Victorinox I.N.O.X. line. At least two versions of the push pin tool exist, with the newer version having a slimmer profile.

Classics can be found with a few different logos and handles:

1. the Victorinox logo in a standard metal inlay or hot-stamped styles
2. Star of David: a blue classic with a Star of David (six-pointed star)
3. Shamrock: a green Classic or Classic SD with a shamrock printed, or inlaid, on the scales. The earlier Shamrock Classic had lighter green scales.
4. The 125th Anniversary Limited Edition Classic SD was part of the Jubilee series. (Note: This is not the same as advertising or branded knives, which are custom production knives that may, or may not, also have the Victorinox logo.)
5. Gold Bar Classics: four Gold Bar Classics were introduced in 1996, each with a 1-gram gold bar inlaid in the handle scales. Each knife is accompanied with a certificate of authenticity for 1 gram of pure gold. These models do not include a toothpick, although sometimes they are reported to. Their model numbers indicate a toothpick is present!
6. 2012+ Crowdstorm Annual Classic SD Limited Edition. In 2012, Victorinox initiated an exciting new approach to designing their Classics. Each year there is a competition open to the general public to submit designs for the Classic Swiss Army Knife. Victorinox shortlists several designs and then the general public votes on the shortlist. The most popular 10 designs go into production. This has resulted in some very creative, attractive and innovative scales for the Classic.
7. Since 2015, Victorinox has released an Alox Classic SD as a part of an Annual Alox Limited Editions set, consisting of three colored Alox knives: a Pioneer, Cadet and Classic. Each year's limited edition comes in a different color.
8. From 2015 on, Victorinox made special scales on standard knives for the Ukraine Victorinox Ukraine Edition.
9. In 2018 and 2019, Victorinox released a set of 12 Classic SD models with white and gold drawings on red scales featuring the animals from the Chinese Zodiac.

This section lists some of the key variations of the Classic. When scale colors and materials, and custom and advertising knives are considered, the variations run into many thousands!"

Given the seemingly endless variety of colors, scale materials and imprints, the Victorinox 58mm Swiss Army Classic is an ideal collectible. It is a little knife with a big reputation for being there when you need it. It has done everything from cleaning fingernails to saving lives. Regardless of why you'll need yours, one thing is certain, you'll end up using it, and that alone explains why the Classic is so enormously popular. □

No-Slack Slip Joints

BEAR & SON CUTLERY
The Bear & Son Model 61530 penknife is a traditional design with updated, textured, anodized-aluminum, two-tone dark red and black handle scales. *(Abe Elias image)*

CASE KNIVES
The Case Bose Locking Lanny's Clip comes in a flat-ground 154CM blade, fluted bolsters and a selection of handle materials with a chess-pawn-shaped shield.

BOKER USA
Handled in oak from the Schloss Burg castle built in 1113, the Boker Castle Series Trapper features a 3.35-inch blade of O1 tool steel in an acid-washed finish.

WE KNIFE CO.
A through-notch in the blade of the We Knife Co. Scamp makes it an ambidextrous one-hand-opening, slip-joint folder. *(Abe Elias image)*

ZERO TOLERANCE KNIVES
The ZT 0230 is a fair size yet sits well in the pocket, including a Wharncliffe blade that lends itself to daily cutting chores. (Abe Elias image)

Big Burly Blades

≫ BUCK KNIVES

The Buck Talon has a blunt forward spine for batoning, a saw blade, lashing points, an extended hammer pommel and a partially serrated convex edge that excels in cutting, sawing and slicing.

⌃ COLD STEEL

With one stroke, the Cold Steel Slant Tip Machete 18 Inch slices easily through such media as watermelon.

(Marty Stanfield image)

≫ KIZLYAR

With a 7-inch D2 tool steel blade and G-10 handle, the Kizlyar Survivalist X Full Tang D2 TW lives up to its lengthy name.

TOPS KNIVES
If you are going to use the TOPS Knives Bestia, eat a full bowl of Wheaties beforehand. The cutting edge is 12.75 inches and the knife tips the scales at 31.5 ounces.

MEDFORD KNIFE & TOOL
The blade length and shape, and handle ergonomics of the Medford Machete all converge, making it an excellent all-around tool for chopping saplings and clearing brush. *(Marty Stanfield image)*

HALFBREED BLADES
Sporting a 5.7-inch Bohler K110 D2 tool steel blade, the Halfbreed LBK-01 Large Bush Knife tips the scales at 17.46 ounces.

GERBER LEGENDARY BLADES
The ergonomic handle of the Gerber Golok features a forward finger recess to help index the blade, along with a bird's beak pommel to prevent slippage in use. *(Marty Stanfield image)*

CAS IBERIA
Based on Chinese models, the CAS Iberia APOC Butterfly Knives are designed to be used in each hand simultaneously in the martial arts discipline of Wing Chun.

Hatchets that Hack It!

» TODAY'S TOP HATCHETS
are as diverse as the day is
long. From left to right are the
ESEE Gibson Axe, Puma XP
Packable Camping Hatchet,
TOPS Knives Grandpa's
Ax and CRKT/Ruger Black
Powder.

Fine Factory Folders

《 CRKT LINCHPIN

Featuring the Deadbolt lock designed by Flavio Ikoma, the CRKT Linchpin flipper folder has a 3.73-inch blade of 1.4116 stainless steel and a glass-reinforced nylon handle. Weight: 6.2 ounces. Closed length: 5.26 inches. MSRP: $135 ($145 with Veff Serrations). Available: Now.

《 GIANTMOUSE CLYDE

A 3-inch blade of Elmax stainless steel in a stonewash finish operating on bronze washers and a green canvas Micarta® handle with wire pocket clip and bronze furniture highlight the Clyde linerlock folder from GiantMouse. Weight: 2.5 ounces. Closed length: 3.94 inches. Country of origin: Italy. MSRP: $154, Available: Now.

⌃ BENCHMADE TENGU FLIPPER

Old world knives meet the new with the Benchmade Tengu Flipper designed by Jared Oeser. The 2.77-inch tanto blade is CPM 20CV stainless steel and the handle is black contoured G-10 with a white G-10 base layer. Closed length: 3.85 inches. MSRP: $220.

》 SPYDERCO WATU

A 3.26-inch blade of CPM 20CV stainless steel provides the business end of the Spyderco Watu folder. Weight: 3 ounces. Closed length: 4.17 inches. Country of origin: Taiwan. MSRP: $260. A portion of the receipts of each Watu sold goes to Keep a Child Alive, an organization dedicated to providing life-saving anti-retroviral treatment, care and support services to HIV/AIDS-afflicted children and their families in Africa and the developing world.

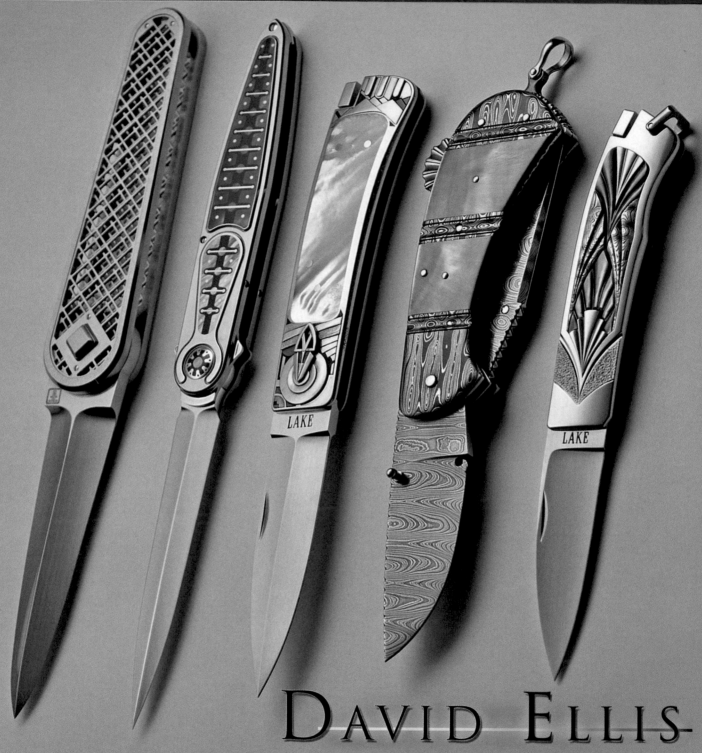

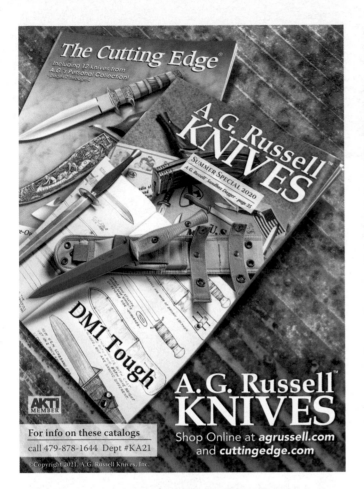

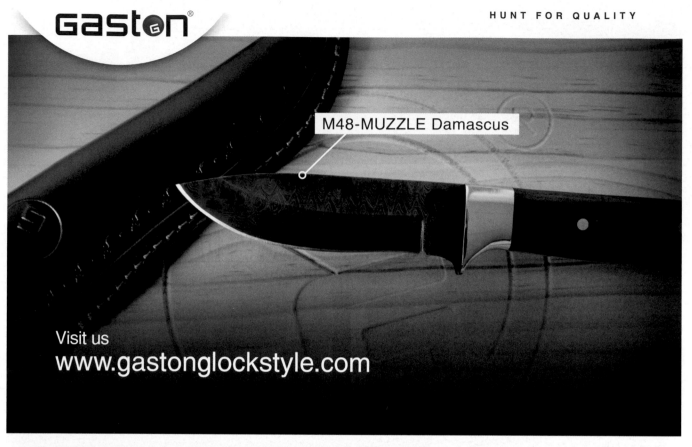

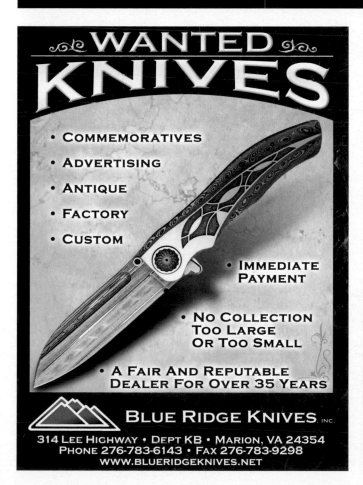

Directory

A

ABEGG, ARNIE
5992 Kenwick Cr, Huntington Beach, CA 92648 **Contact:** 714-848-5697

ABERNATHY, LANCE
Sniper Bladeworks, 1924 Linn Ave., North Kansas City, MO 64116 **Contact:** 816-585-1595, lanceabernathy@sbcglobal.net, sniperbladeworks.com
Specialties: Tactical frame-lock and locking-liner folding knives.

ACCAWI, FUAD
130 Timbercrest Dr., Oak Ridge, TN 37830 **Contact:** 865-414-4836, gaccawi@comcast.net, acremetalworks.com, Instagram @fuadaccawi
Specialties: Create one of a kind pieces from small working knives to performance blades and swords. **Patterns:** Styles include, and not limited to hunters, bowies, daggers, swords, folders and camp knives. **Technical:** I forge primarily 5160, produces own damascus and does own heat treating. **Prices:** $195 and up. **Remarks:** Full-time bladesmith. I enjoy producing Persian and historically influenced work. **Mark:** My mark is an eight sided Middle Eastern star with initials FA in the center.

ACKERSON, ROBIN E
119 W Smith St, Buchanan, MI 49107 **Contact:** 616-695-2911

ADAMS, JIM
1648 Camille Way, Cordova, TN 38016 **Contact:** 901-326-0441, jim@JimAdamsKnives.com jimadamsknives.com
Specialties: Fixed blades in classic design. **Patterns:** Hunters, fighters, and bowies. **Technical:** Grinds damascus, O1, others as requested. **Prices:** Starting at $150. **Remarks:** Full-time maker. **Mark:** J. Adams, Cordova, TN.

ADAMS, LES
3516 S.W. 2nd St., Cape Coral, FL 33991 **Contact:** 786-999-3060
Specialties: Working straight knives of his design. **Patterns:** Fighters, tactical folders, law enforcing autos. **Technical:** Grinds ATS-34, 440C and D2. **Prices:** $100 to $500. **Remarks:** Part-time maker, first knife sold in 1989. **Mark:** First initial, last name, Custom Knives.

ADDISON, KYLE A
588 Atkins Trail, Hazel, KY 42049-8629 **Contact:** 270-492-8120, kylest2@yahoo.com
Specialties: Hand forged blades including bowies, fighters and hunters. **Patterns:** Custom leather sheaths. **Technical:** Forges 5160, 1084, and his own damascus. **Prices:** $175 to $1500. **Remarks:** Part-time maker, first knife sold in 1996. ABS member. **Mark:** First and middle initial, last name under "Trident" with knife and hammer.

ADKINS, RICHARD L
138 California Ct, Mission Viejo, CA 92692-4079

ADKINS, WES
Adkins Wood & Knife 303 Lori Lane Council Bluffs, IA 51503 **Contact:** 402.250.5289, wes@adkinswoodandknife.com, www.adkinswoodandknife.com
Patterns: Fixed blade knives and tools.

AKIN, BEN
26-7 Narimasu 2-chome, Itabashi-ku, Tokyo, JAPAN 175-0094 **Contact:** 81-3-3939-0052, (fax) 81-3-3939-0058, Web: http://riverside-land.com/
Specialties: High-tech working straight knives and folders of his design. **Patterns:** bowies, lockbacks, hunters, fighters, fishing knives, boots. **Technical:** Grinds CV-134, ATS-34, buys damascus, works in traditional Japanese fashion for some handles and sheaths. **Prices:** $700 to $1200, some higher. **Remarks:** Full-time maker, first knife sold in 1978. **Mark:** Initial logo and Riverside West.

AIDA, YOSHIHITO
26-7 Narimasu 2-chome, Itabashi-ku, Tokyo, JAPAN 175-0094 **Contact:** 81-3-3939-0052, (fax) 81-3-3939-0058, Web: http://riverside-land.com/
Specialties: High-tech working straight knives and folders of his design. **Patterns:** bowies, lockbacks, hunters, fighters, fishing knives, boots. **Technical:** Grinds CV-134, ATS-34, buys damascus, works in traditional Japanese fashion for some handles and sheaths. **Prices:** $700 to $1200, some higher. **Remarks:** Full-time maker, first knife sold in 1978. **Mark:** Initial logo and Riverside West.

ALBERT, STEFAN
U Lucenecka 434/4, Filakovo 98604, SLOVAKIA, albert@albertknives.com albertknives.com
Specialties: Art Knives, Miniatures, Scrimshaw, Bulino. **Prices:** From USD $500 to USD $25000. **Mark:** Albert

ALCORN, DOUGLAS A.
14687 Fordney Rd., Chesaning, MI 48616 **Contact:** 989-845-6712, daalcornknives@gmail.com
Specialties: Gentleman style military, tactical and presentation knives. **Patterns:** Hunters, miniatures, and military type fixed blade knives and axes. **Technical:** Blades are stock removal and forged using best quality stainless, carbon, and damascus steels. Handle materials are burls, ivory, pearl, leather and other exotics. **Prices:** $200 and up. **Motto:** Simple, Rugged, Elegant, Handcrafted **Remarks:** Knife maker since 1989 and full time since 1999, Knife Makers Guild (voting member), member of the Bladesmith Society. **Mark:** D.A. Alcorn, Maker, Chesaning, MI.

ALDERMAN, ROBERT
2655 Jewel Lake Rd., Sagle, ID 83860 **Contact:** 208-263-5996
Specialties: Classic and traditional working straight knives in standard patterns or to customer specs and his design, period pieces. **Patterns:** bowies, fighters, hunters and utility/camp knives. **Technical:** Casts, forges and grinds 1084, forges and grinds L6 and O1. Prefers an old appearance. **Prices:** $100 to $350, some to $700. **Remarks:** Full-time maker, first knife sold in 1975. Doing business as Trackers Forge. Knife-making school. Two-week course for beginners, covers forging, stock removal, hardening, tempering, case making. All materials supplied, $1250. **Mark:** Deer track.

ALDRICH, MARC
16 Cheryl St., Chestnut Ridge, NY 10977-6508 **Contact:** 845-920-1092, Aldrich.kt@outlook.com, aldrichknifeandtool.com
Specialties: Working straight knives of his own design. **Patterns:** bowies, camp, fighters, hunters, skinners and kitchen knives. **Technical:** Forging and stock removal methods. Uses O1, 1075, 1084, 80CrV2, 1095, 5160, A2, W2 and AEB-L blade steels. Uses stainless, salvage wrought iron, brass and copper for fittings. Handle materials include stabilized and natural domestic and exotic figured woods, durable synthetics, stacked leather. Makes own sheaths. **Prices:** $300 and up. **Remarks:** Part-time maker. First knife sold in 2013. Doing business as Aldrich Knife & Tool. Emphasis put on clean lines, fit and finish and performance. **Mark:** An arched ALDRICH.

ALDRIDGE, DONALD
5731 University Blvd SE, Albuquerque, NM 87106 **Contact:** 505-366-4741, aldridgeknives@gmail.com, www.aldridgeknives.com.
Patterns: Hunters, utility, camp, and tactical forged knives. **Technical:** Hand-forged and worked blades. Hand-shaped handles of natural or synethic materials. Prefers 5160, 1084, 1080 steels. **Prices:** $200 to $500. **Mark:** Steel stamped "ALDRIDGE" or electroplated "Aldridge Knives" with anvil and crossed hammer design.

ALEXANDER, EUGENE
Box 540, Ganado, TX 77962-0540 **Contact:** 512-771-3727
Alexander,, Oleg, and Cossack Blades
15460 Stapleton Way, Wellington, FL 33414 **Contact:** 443-676-6111, cossackblades.com
Technical: All knives are made from hand-forged damascus (3-4 types of steel are used to create the damascus) and have a HRC of 60-62. Handle materials are all natural, including various types of wood, horn, bone and leather. Embellishments include the use of precious metals and stones, including gold, silver, diamonds, rubies, sapphires and other unique materials. All knives include hand-made leather sheaths, and some models include wooden presentation boxes and display stands. **Prices:** $395 to over $10,000, depending on design and materials used. **Remarks:** Full-time maker, first knife sold in 1993. **Mark:** Rectangle enclosing a stylized Cyrillic letter "O" overlapping a stylized Cyrillic "K."

ALLAN, TODD
TODD ALLAN KNIVES, 6525 W. Kings Ave., Glendale, AZ 85306 **Contact:** 623-210-3766, todd@toddallanknives.com, toddallanknives.com
Patterns: Fixed-blade hunters and camp knives. **Technical:** Stock-removal method of blade making using 154CM, high-carbon damascus, stainless damascus, 5160 and 1095 blade steels. Handle materials include various Micartas, stabilized woods and mammoth ivory. **Prices:** $175 to $1,000. **Remarks:** Full-time maker.

ALLEN, JIM
Three Sisters Forge, LLC, 18830 Macalpine Loop, Bend, OR 97702, knives@threesistersforge.com, threesistersforge.com
Specialties: Folders with titanium frames, and stainless steel blades and fixtures. **Technical:** Stock-removal method of blade making using CPM S35VN steel for now, but always evaluating latest steels. **Prices:** $200 to $300. **Remarks:** Ninety percent of knives go to police and military. Special features such as anodizing and Cerakote coated blades available. **Mark:** The sun setting over the Three Sisters Mountains (the view from the maker's shop).

ALLRED, BRUCE F
1764 N. Alder, Layton, UT 84041 **Contact:** 801-825-4612, allredbf@msn.com
Specialties: Custom hunting and utility knives. **Patterns:** Custom designs that include a unique grind line, thumb and mosaic pins. **Technical:** ATS-34, 154CM and 440C. **Remarks:** The handle material includes but not limited to Micarta (in various colors), natural woods and reconstituted stone.

ALLRED, ELVAN
31 Spring Terrace Court, St. Charles, MO 63303 **Contact:** 636-936-8871, allredknives@yahoo.com, allredcustomknives.com
Specialties: Innovative sculpted folding knives designed by Elvan's son Scott that are mostly one of a kind. **Patterns:** Mostly folders but some high-end straight knives. **Technical:** ATS-34 SS, 440C SS, stainless damascus, S30V, 154cm, inlays are mostly natural materials such as pearl, coral, ivory, jade, lapis, and other precious stone. **Prices:** $500 to $4000, some higher. **Remarks:** Started making knives in the shop of Dr. Fred Carter in the early 1990s. Full-time maker since 2006, first knife sold in 1993. Take some orders but work mainly on one-of-a-kind art knives. **Mark:** Small oval with signature Eallred in the center and handmade above.

ALVERSON, TIM (R.V.)
209 Spring Rd. SE, Arab, AL 35016 **Contact:** 256-200-8031, alvie35@yahoo.com, cwknives.blogspot.com
Specialties: Fancy working knives to customer specs, other types on request. **Patterns:** bowies, daggers, folders and miniatures. **Technical:** Grinds 440C, ATS-34, buys some damascus. **Prices:** Start at $100. **Remarks:** Full-time maker, first knife sold in 1981. **Mark:** R.V.A. around rosebud.

AMERI, MAURO
Via Riaello No. 20, Trensasco St Olcese, Genova, ITALY 16010 **Contact:** 010-8357077, mauro.ameri@gmail.com
Specialties: Working and using knives of his design. **Patterns:** Hunters, bowies and utility/camp knives. **Technical:** Grinds 440C, ATS-34 and 154CM. Handles in wood or Micarta, offers sheaths. **Prices:** $200 to $1200. **Remarks:** Spare-time maker, first knife sold in 1982. **Mark:** Last name, city.

AMMONS, DAVID C
6225 N. Tucson Mtn. Dr, Tucson, AZ 85743 **Contact:** 520-471-4433, dcammons@msn.com
Specialties: Will build to suit. **Patterns:** Yours or his. **Prices:** $250 to $2000. **Mark:** AMMONS.

AMOS, CHRIS
PO Box 1519, Riverton, WY 82501 **Contact:** 520-271-9752, caknives@yahoo.com
Specialties: HEPK (High Endurance Performance Knives). **Patterns:** Hunters, fighters, bowies, kitchen knives and camp knives. **Technical:** Hand-forged, high rate of reduction 52100 and 5160 steel. **Prices:** $150 to $1,500. **Remarks:** Part-time maker since 1997, full time since 2012. Coach/instructor at Ed Fowler's Knifemaking School. HEPK mastersmith rating, 2013. **Mark:** Early mark: CAK stamped, current mark: Amos on right side.

AMOUREUX, A W
PO Box 776, Northport, WA 99157 **Contact:** 509-732-6292
Specialties: Heavy-duty working straight knives. **Patterns:** bowies, fighters, camp knives and hunters for world-wide use. **Technical:** Grinds 440C, ATS-34 and 154CM. **Prices:** $80 to $2000. **Remarks:** Full-time maker, first knife sold in 1974. **Mark:** ALSTAR.

ANDERS, DAVID
157 Barnes Dr, Center Ridge, AR 72027 **Contact:** 501-893-2294
Specialties: Working straight knives of his design. **Patterns:** bowies, fighters and hunters. **Technical:** Forges 5160, 1080 and damascus. **Prices:** $225 to $3200. **Remarks:** Part-time maker, first knife sold in 1988. Doing business as Anders Knives. **Mark:** Last name/MS.

ANDERS, JEROME
14560 SW 37th St, Miramar, FL 33027 **Contact:** 305-613-2990, andersknives.com
Specialties: Case handles and pin work. **Patterns:** Layered and mosiac steel. **Prices:** $275 and up. **Remarks:** All his knives are truly one-of-a-kind. **Mark:** J. Anders in half moon.

ANDERSEN, HENRIK LEFOLII
Jagtvej 8, Groenholt, Fredensborg, DENMARK 3480 **Contact:** 0011-45-48483026
Specialties: Hunters and matched pairs for the serious hunter. **Technical:** Grinds A2, uses materials native to Scandinavia. **Prices:** Start at $250. **Remarks:** Part-time maker, first knife sold in 1985. **Mark:** Initials with arrow.

ANDERSEN, KARL B.
20200 TimberLodge Rd., Warba, MN 55793 **Contact:** 218-398-4270, Karl@andersenforge.com andersenforge.com
Specialties: Hunters, bowies, fighters and camp knives forged from high carbon tool steels and Andersen Forge damascus. **Technical:** All types of materials used. Styles include hidden-tang and full-tang fixed blades, Brut de Forge, integrals and frame-handle construction. **Prices:** Starting at $450 and up. **Remarks:** Full-time maker. ABS journeyman smith. All knives sole authorship. Andersen Forge was instrumental in paving the way for take-down knife construction to be more recognized and broadly accepted in knifemaking today. **Mark:** Andersen in script on obverse. J.S. on either side, depending on knife.

ANDERSON, GARY D
2816 Reservoir Rd, Spring Grove, PA 17362-9802 **Contact:** 717-229-2665
Specialties: From working knives to collectors quality blades, some folders. **Patterns:** Traditional and classic designs, customer patterns welcome. **Technical:** Forges damascus carbon and stainless steels. Offers silver inlay, mokume, filework, checkering. **Prices:** $250 and up. **Remarks:** Part-time maker, first knife sold in 1985. Some engraving, scrimshaw and stone work. **Mark:** GAND, MS.

ANDERSON, MEL
29505 P 50 Rd, Hotchkiss, CO 81419-8203 **Contact:** 970-872-4882, (fax) 970-872-4882, artnedge@tds.net, melsscratchyhand@aol.com, scratchyhand.com
Specialties: Full-size, miniature and one-of-a-kind straight knives and folders of his design. **Patterns:** Tantos, bowies, daggers, fighters, hunters and pressure folders. **Technical:** Grinds 440C, 5160, D2, 1095. **Prices:** Start at $175. **Remarks:** Knifemaker and sculptor, full-time maker, first knife sold in 1987. **Mark:** Scratchy Hand.

ANDERSON, TOM
Artistry In Titanium. 955 Canal Rd. Extd., Manchester, PA 17345 **Contact:** 717-266-6475, andersontech1@comcast.net, artistryintitanium.com
Specialties: Battle maces and war hammers.

ANDRADE, DON CARLOS
CALIFORNIA CUSTOM KNIVES, 1824 Sunny Hill Ave., Los Osos, CA 93402 **Contact:** 805-528-8837 or 805-550-2324, andradeartworks@gmail.com, californiacustomknives.com
Specialties: Chef knife specialist, also integrally forged personal knives and camp knives. **Technical:** Forges to shape, and a small number of stain-resistant, stock-removal blades. All heat-treating in house. Uses 1095, W2, W1, 1084, 52100, 1065, 1070 and 13C26 blade steels. **Prices:** $250 to $1,650. **Remarks:** Full-time maker, first knife made in 2006 under tutorship of mentor Tai Goo. **Mark:** Initials "DCA" and two circles with a strike running through them (maker's version of infinity/continuity.)

ANDREWS, ERIC
132 Halbert Street, Grand Ledge, MI 48837 **Contact:** 517-627-7304
Specialties: Traditional working and using straight knives of his design. **Patterns:** Full-tang hunters, skinners and utility knives. **Technical:** Forges carbon steel, heat-treats. All knives come with sheath, most handles are of wood. **Prices:** $80 to $160. **Remarks:** Part-time maker, first knife sold in 1990. Doing business as The Tinkers Bench.

ANDREWS, RUSS
PO Box 7732, Sugar Creek, MO 64054 **Contact:** 816-252-3344, russandrews@sbcglobal.net, russandrewsknives.com
Specialties: Hand forged bowies & hunters. **Remarks:** ABS master smith. **Mark:** E. R. Andrews II. ERAII.

ANGELL, JON
22516 East C R1474, Hawthorne, FL 32640 **Contact:** 352-475-5380, syrjon@aol.com

ANKROM, W.E.
14 Marquette Dr, Cody, WY 82414 **Contact:** 307-587-3017, weankrom@hotmail.com
Specialties: Best quality folding knives of his design. bowies, fighters, chute knives, boots and hunters. **Patterns:** Tacticals, flipper folders, lock backs, LinerLocks and single high art. **Technical:** All high-tech steels, including ATS-34, commercial damascus, CPM 154 steel. **Prices:** $500 and up. **Remarks:** Full-time maker, first knife sold in 1975. **Mark:** Name or name, city, state.

ANSO, JENS
GL. Skanderborgvej 116, Sporup, DENMARK 8472 **Contact:** 45 86968826, info@ansoknives.com, ansoknives.com
Specialties: Working knives of his own design. **Patterns:** Balisongs, swords, folders, drop-points, sheepsfoots, hawkbill, tanto, recurve. **Technical:** Grinds RWL-34 Damasteel S30V, CPM 154CM. Handrubbed or beadblasted finish. **Prices:** $400 to $1200, some up to $3500. **Remarks:** Full-time maker since January 2002. First knife sold 1997. Doing business as ANSOKNIVES. **Mark:** ANSO and/or ANSO with logo.

APELT, STACY E
8076 Moose Ave, Norfolk, VA 23518 **Contact:** 757-583-5872, sapelt@cox.net
Specialties: Exotic wood and burls, ivories, bowies, custom made knives to order. **Patterns:** bowies, hunters, fillet, professional cutlery and Japanese style blades and swords. **Technical:** Hand forging, stock removal, scrimshaw, carbon, stainless and damascus steels. **Prices:** $65 to $5000. **Remarks:** Professional Goldsmith. **Mark:** Stacy E. Apelt - Norfolk VA.

APLIN, SPENCER
5151 County Rd. 469, Brazoria, TX 77422 **Contact:** 979-964-4448, spenceraplin@aol.com, stacustomknives.com
Specialties: Custom skinners, fillets, bowies and kitchen knives. **Technical:** Stainless steel powder metals, stainless damascus. Handles include stabilized woods, various ivory and Micarta. Guard and butt-cap materials are brass, copper, nickel silver and Mokume. **Prices:** $450 and up. **Remarks:** First knife sold in 1989. Knives made to order only, nothing is pre-made. All blades are hand drawn, then cut from sheet stock. No two are exactly the same. **Mark:** Signature and date completed.

APPLEBY, ROBERT
746 Municipal Rd, Shickshinny, PA 18655 **Contact:** 570-864-0879, applebyknives@yahoo.com, applebyknives.com
Specialties: Working using straight knives and folders of his own and popular and historical designs. **Patterns:** Variety of straight knives and folders. **Technical:** Hand forged or grinds O1, 1084, 5160, 440C, ATS-34, commercial damascus, makes own sheaths. **Prices:** Starting at $75. **Remarks:** Part-time maker, first knife sold in 1995. **Mark:** APPLEBY over SHICKSHINNY, PA.

APPLETON, RON
315 Glenn St, Bluff Dale, TX 76433 **Contact:** 254-396-9328, ronappleton@hotmail.com, appletonknives.com
Specialties: One-of-a-kind folding knives. **Patterns:** Unique folding multi-locks and high-tech patterns. **Technical:** All parts machined, D2, S7, 416, 440C, 6A14V et.al. **Prices:** Start at $32,000 U.S.. **Remarks:** Full-time maker, first knife sold in 1996. **Mark:** Initials in anvil or initials in arrowhead. Usually only shows at the Art Knife Invitational every 2 years in San Diego, CA.

ARBUCKLE, JAMES M
114 Jonathan Jct, Yorktown, VA 23693 **Contact:** 757-867-9578, a_r_buckle@hotmail.com
Specialties: One-of-a-kind of his design, working knives. **Patterns:** Mostly chef's knives and hunters. **Technical:** Forged and stock removal blades using exotic hardwoods, natural materials, Micarta and stabilized woods. Forge 5160 and 1084, stock removal D2, ATS-34, 440C and 154CM. Makes own pattern welded steel. **Prices:** $195 to $700. **Remarks:** Forge, grind, heat-treat, finish and embellish all knives himself. Does own leatherwork. Part-time maker. ABS Journeyman smith 2007, ASM member. **Mark:** J. Arbuckle or J. ARBUCKLE MAKER.

ARCHER, RAY AND TERRI
4207 South 28 St., Omaha, NE 68107 **Contact:** 402-505-3084, archerrt@cox.net
Specialties: Basic high-finish working knives. **Patterns:** Hunters, skinners camp knives. **Technical:** Flat grinds various steels like 440C, ATS-34 and CPM-S30V. **Prices:** $75 to $500. **Remarks:** Makes own sheaths, first knife sold 1994. **Mark:** Last name over knives.

ARDWIN, COREY
2117 Cedar Dr., Bryant, AR 72019 **Contact:** 501-413-1184, ardwinca@gmail.com

custom knifemakers

ARM-KO KNIVES
PO Box 76280, Marble Ray , KZN, SOUTH AFRICA 4035 **Contact:** 27 31 5771451, arm-koknives.co.za, arm-koknives.co.za

Specialties: They will make what your fastidious taste desires. Be it cool collector or tenacious tactical with handles of mother-of-pearl, fossil & local ivories. Exotic dye/stabilized burls, giraffe bone, horns, carbon fiber, g10, and titanium etc. **Technical:** Via stock removal, grinding Damasteel, carbon & mosaic. damascus, ATS-34, N690, 440A, 440B, 12C27, RWL34 and high carbon EN 8, 5160 all heat treated in house. **Prices:** From $200 and up. **Remarks:** Father a part-time maker for well over 10 years and member of Knifemakers Guild in SA. Son full-time maker over 3 years. **Mark:** Logo of initials A R M and H A R M "Edged Tools."

ARMOUR, DAVE
61 Sugar Creek Hills, Auburn, IL 62615 **Contact:** 217-741-0246, dave@armourcutlery.com, armourcutlery.com

Specialties: Hunters, utilities and occasional camp and bowie knives. **Technical:** Forges blades from 1084 and 80CrV2, with occasional san mai and damascus steels. **Prices:** $100 to $160 for most knives, up to $250 for dressier pieces. **Remarks:** Part-time maker, knives described as "deliberately casual" with a focus on working knives, performance, individuality and affordability. Field-grade knives usually using copper, stainless or bronze with horn (deer, elk or water buffalo), stabilized wood, Micarta or G-10 handles. Dressier knives often use wrought iron or Mokume with stag or oosic. **Mark:** Armour.

ARMS, ERIC
11153 7 Mile Road, Tustin, MI 49688 **Contact:** 231-829-3726, ericarms@netonecom.net

Specialties: Working hunters, high performance straight knives. **Patterns:** Variety of hunters, scagel style, Ed Fowler design and drop point. **Technical:** Forge 52100, 5160, 1084 hand grind, heat treat, natural handle, stag horn, elk, big horn, flat grind, convex, all leather sheath work. **Prices:** Starting at $150 **Remarks:** Part-time maker **Mark:** Eric Arms

ARNOLD, JOE
47 Patience Cres, London, ON, CANADA N6E 2K7 **Contact:** 519-686-2623, arnoldknivesandforge@bell.net

Specialties: Traditional working and using straight knives of his design and to customer specs. **Patterns:** Fighters, hunters and bowies. **Technical:** Grinds 440C, ATS-34, 5160, and Forges 1084-1085 **Prices:** $75 to $500, some to $2500. **Remarks:** Full-time maker, first knife sold in 1988. **Mark:** Last name, country.

ARROWOOD, DALE
556 Lassetter Rd, Sharpsburg, GA 30277 **Contact:** 404-253-9672

Specialties: Fancy and traditional straight knives of his design and to customer specs. **Patterns:** bowies, fighters and hunters. **Technical:** Grinds ATS-34 and 440C, forges high-carbon steel. Engraves and scrimshaws. **Prices:** $125 to $200, some to $245. **Remarks:** Part-time maker, first knife sold in 1989. **Mark:** Anvil with an arrow through it, Old English "Arrowood Knives."

ASCOLESE, SAL
Sal Ascolese Custom Knives PO Box 11354, New Brunswick, NJ 08906-1354 **Contact:** 732-710-2301, sal@salascolesecustomknives.com, www.salascolesecustomknives.com

Patterns: Fixed blade tactical knives. **Technical:** High-carbon and stainless steel blades. Exotic woods, bone, horn, Micarta and G10 handles. Hand stitched leather and handmade Kydex sheaths.

ASHBY, DOUGLAS
Doug Ashby Custom Knives. 10123 Deermont Trail, Dallas, TX 75243 **Contact:** 214-929-7531, doug@ashbycustomknives.com, ashbycustomknives.com

Specialties: Traditional and fancy straight knives and folders of his design or to customer specs. **Patterns:** Skinners, hunters, utility/camp knives, locking linner folders. **Technical:** Grinds ATS-34, commercial damascus, and other steels on request. **Prices:** $125 to $1000. **Remarks:** Part-time maker, first knife sold in 1990. **Mark:** Name, city.

ASHWORTH, BOYD
1510 Bullard Place, Powder Springs, GA 30127 **Contact:** 404-583-5652, boydashworthknives@comcast.net, boydashworthknives.com

Specialties: Gentlemen's and figurative folders. **Patterns:** Fighters, hunters and gents. **Technical:** Forges own damascus, offers filework, uses exotic handle materials. **Prices:** $500 to $5,000. **Remarks:** Part-time maker, first knife sold in 1993. **Mark:** Last name.

ATHEY, STEVE
3153 Danube Way, Riverside, CA 92503 **Contact:** 951-850-8612, stevelonnie@yahoo.com

Specialties: Stock removal. **Patterns:** Hunters & bowies. **Prices:** $100 to $500. **Remarks:** Part-time maker. **Mark:** Last name with number on blade.

ATKINSON, DICK
General Delivery, Wausau, FL 32463 **Contact:** 850-638-8524

Specialties: Working straight knives and folders of his design, some fancy. **Patterns:** Hunters, fighters, boots, locking folders in interframes. **Technical:** Grinds A2, 440C and 154CM. Likes filework. **Prices:** $85 to $300, some exceptional knives. **Remarks:** Full-time maker, first knife sold in 1977. **Mark:** Name, city, state.

AYARRAGARAY, CRISTIAN L.
Buenos Aires 250, Parana, Entre Rios, ARGENTINA 3100 **Contact:** 043-231753

Specialties: Traditional working straight knives of his design. **Patterns:** Fishing and hunting knives. **Technical:** Grinds and forges carbon steel. Uses native Argentine woods and deer antler. **Prices:** $150 to $250, some to $400. **Remarks:** Full-time maker, first

knife sold in 1980. **Mark:** Last name, signature.

AYLOR, ERIN LUTZER
10519 Highland School Rd., Myersville, MD 21773 **Contact:** 240-397-3820, erinlutzeraylor@gmail.com, erinaylor.com

Specialties: Custom knives with an Old World feel using mostly pattern-welded (damascus) steel in ladder, twist and random patterns made from 1084, 1075, 15N20 and 1095 with a core of 5100 or 1095. **Patterns:** Many styles of knives, including hunters, fighters, bowies, Japanese and standard kitchen cutlery, folding knives and woodworking chisels. **Technical:** All blades are coal forged. **Prices:** $300 to $3,500. **Remarks:** Full-time artisan working mostly in metal, wood and silver. Studied at The Appalachian Center for Crafts in Cookeville, Tennessee, where he made his first chisel and knife in 1992. **Mark:** Last name, "AYLOR," with earlier work stamped "ELA."

B

BAARTMAN, GEORGE
PO Box 1116, Bela-Bela, LP, SOUTH AFRICA 0480 **Contact:** 27 14 736 4036, (fax) 086 636 3408, thabathipa@gmail.com

Specialties: Fancy and working LinerLock® folders of own design and to customers specs. Specialize in pattern filework on liners. **Patterns:** LinerLock® folders. **Technical:** Grinds 12C27, ATS-34, and damascus, prefer working with stainless damasteel. Hollow grinds to hand-rubbed and polished satin finish. Enjoys working with mammoth, warthog tusk and pearls. **Prices:** Folders from $380 to $1000. **Remarks:** Part-time maker. Member of the Knifemakers Guild of South Africa since 1993. **Mark:** BAARTMAN.

BACHE-WIIG, TOM
N-5966, Eivindvik, NORWAY **Contact:** 475-778-4290, (fax) 475-778-1099, tom.bache-wiig@enivest.net, tombachewiig.com

Specialties: High-art and working knives of his design. **Patterns:** Hunters, utility knives, hatchets, axes and art knives. **Technical:** Grinds Uddeholm Elmax, powder metallurgy tool stainless steel. Handles made of rear burls of Nordic woods stabilized with vacuum/high-pressure technique. **Prices:** $430 to $900, some to $2300. **Remarks:** Part-time maker, first knife sold 1988. **Mark:** Etched name and eagle head.

BAGLEY, R. KEITH
OLD PINE FORGE, 4415 Hope Acres Dr, White Plains, MD 20695 **Contact:** 301-932-0990, keithbagley14@verizon.net, oldpineforge.com

Specialties: Folders. **Technical:** Use ATS-34, 5160, O1, 1085 and 1095. **Patterns:** Ladder-wave lightning bolt. **Prices:** $275 to $750. **Remarks:** Farrier for 37 years, blacksmith for 37 years, knifemaker for 25 years. **Mark:** KB inside horseshoe and anvil.

BAILEY, I.R.
Lamorna Cottage, Common End, Colkirk, ENGLAND NR 21 7JD **Contact:** 01-328-856-183, admin@grommitbaileyknives.com, grommitbaileyknives.com

Specialties: Hunters, utilities, bowies, camp knives, fighters. Mainly influenced by Moran, Loveless and Lile. **Technical:** Primarily stock removal using flat ground 1095, 1075, and 80CrV2. Occasionally forges including own basic damascus. Uses both native and exotic hardwoods, stag, Leather, Micarta and other synthetic handle materials, with brass or 301 stainless fittings. Does some filework and leather tooling. Does own heat treating. **Remarks:** Part-time maker since 2005. All knives and sheaths are sole authorship. **Mark:** Last name stamped.

BAILEY, JOSEPH D.
3213 Jonesboro Dr, Nashville, TN 37214 **Contact:** 615-889-3172, jbknfemkr@aol.com

Specialties: Working and using straight knives, collector pieces. **Patterns:** bowies, hunters, tactical, folders. **Technical:** 440C, ATS-34, damascus and wire damascus. Offers scrimshaw. **Prices:** $85 to $1200. **Remarks:** Part-time maker, first knife sold in 1988. **Mark:** Joseph D Bailey Nashville Tennessee.

BAIR, MARK
415 E. 700N, Firth, ID 83236 **Contact:** 208-681-7534, markbair@gmail.com

Specialties: Fixed blades. Hunters, bowies, kitchen, utility, custom orders. **Technical:** High-end damascus, San Mai steel, stainless steel and 52100. Also mammoth ivory and other exotic handles, custom hand filework, and works with high-end custom engravers. **Prices:** $300 to $7,500. **Remarks:** Part-time maker, first knife made in 1988. **Mark:** MB Custom Knives.

BAKER, HERB
14104 NC 87 N, Eden, NC 27288 **Contact:** 336-627-0338

BAKER, RAY
PO Box 303, Sapulpa, OK 74067 **Contact:** 918-224-8013

Specialties: High-tech working straight knives. **Patterns:** Hunters, fighters, bowies, skinners and boots of his design and to customer specs. **Technical:** Grinds 440C, 1095 spring steel or customer request, heat-treats. Custom-made scabbards for any knife. **Prices:** $125 to $500, some to $1000. **Remarks:** Full-time maker, first knife sold in 1981. **Mark:** First initial, last name.

BAKER, TONY
707 Lake Highlands Dr, Allen, TX 75002 **Contact:** 214-543-1001, tonybakerknives@yahoo.com

Specialties: Hunting knives, integral made **Technical:** 154cm, S30V, and S90V**Prices:** Starting at $500. **Prices:** $200-$1200 **Remarks:** First knife made in 2001

BAKER, WILD BILL
Box 361, Boiceville, NY 12412 **Contact:** 914-657-8646

Specialties: Primitive knives, buckskinners. **Patterns:** Skinners, camp knives and bowies. **Technical:** Works with L6, files and rasps. **Prices:** $100 to $350. **Remarks:** Part-time maker, first knife sold in 1989. **Mark:** Wild Bill Baker, Oak Leaf Forge, or both.

BALL, BUTCH
2161 Reedsville Rd., Floyd, VA 24091 **Contact:** 540-392-3485, ballknives@yahoo.com
Specialties: Fancy and Tactical Folders and Automatics. **Patterns:** Fixed and folders. **Technical:** Use various damascus and ATS34, 154cm. **Prices:** $300 - $1500. **Remarks:** Part-time maker. Sold first knife in 1990. **Mark:** Ball or BCK with crossed knives.

BALL, KEN
127 Sundown Manor, Mooresville, IN 46158 **Contact:** 317-834-4803
Specialties: Classic working/using straight knives of his design and to customer specs. **Patterns:** Hunters and utility/camp knives. **Technical:** Flat-grinds ATS-34. Offers filework. **Prices:** $150 to $400. **Remarks:** Part-time maker, first knife sold in 1994. Doing business as Ball Custom Knives. **Mark:** Last name.

BALLESTRA, SANTINO
via D. Tempesta 11/17, Ventimiglia, ITALY 18039 **Contact:** 0184-215228, ladasin@libero.it
Specialties: Using and collecting straight knives. **Patterns:** Hunting, fighting, skinners, bowies, medieval daggers and knives. **Technical:** Forges ATS-34, D2, O2, 1060 and his own damascus. Uses ivory and silver. **Prices:** $500 to $2000, some higher. **Remarks:** Full-time maker, first knife sold in 1979. **Mark:** First initial, last name.

BALLEW, DALE
PO Box 1277, Bowling Green, VA 22427 **Contact:** 804-633-5701
Specialties: Miniatures only to customer specs. **Patterns:** bowies, daggers and fighters. **Technical:** Files 440C stainless, uses ivory, abalone, exotic woods and some precious stones. **Prices:** $100 to $800. **Remarks:** Part-time maker, first knife sold in 1988. **Mark:** Initials and last name.

BANAITIS, ROMAS
84 Winthrop St., Medway, MA 02053 **Contact:** 774-248-5851, rbanaitis@verizon.net
Specialties: Designing art and fantasy knives. **Patterns:** Folders, daggers and fixed blades. **Technical:** Hand-carved blades, handles and fittings in stainless steel, sterling silver and titanium. **Prices:** Moderate to upscale. **Remarks:** First knife sold in 1996. **Mark:** Romas Banaitis.

BANKS, DAVID L.
99 Blackfoot Ave, Riverton, WY 82501 **Contact:** 307-856-3154/Cell: 307-851-5599, blackfootforge@bresnan.net
Specialties: Heavy-duty working straight knives. **Patterns:** Hunters, bowies and camp knives. **Technical:** Forges damascus 1084-15N20, L6-W1 pure nickel, 5160, 52100 and his own damascus, differential heat treat and tempers. Handles made of horn, antlers and exotic wood. Hand-stitched harness leather sheaths. **Prices:** $300 to $4,000. **Remarks:** Part-time maker. **Mark:** Banks, Blackfoot Forge, Dave Banks.

BAREFOOT, JOE W.
1654 Honey Hill, Wilmington, NC 28442 **Contact:** 910-641-1143
Specialties: Working straight knives of his design. **Patterns:** Hunters, fighters and boots, tantos and survival knives. **Technical:** Grinds D2, 440C and ATS-34. Mirror finishes. Uses ivory and stag on customer request only. **Prices:** $50 to $160, some to $500. **Remarks:** Part-time maker, first knife sold in 1980. **Mark:** Bare footprint.

BARKER, JOHN
5725 Boulder Bluff Dr., Cumming, GA 30040 **Contact:** 678-357-8586, barkerknives@bellsouth.net barkerknives.com
Specialties: Tactical fixed blades and folders. **Technical:** Stock removal method and CPM and Carpenter powdered technology steels. **Prices:** $150 and up. **Remarks:** First knife made 2006. **Mark:** Snarling dog with "Barker" over the top of its head and "Knives" below.

BARKER, REGGIE
40 Columbia Rd. 254, Taylor AR 71861 **Contact:** 318-539-2958, rbarker014@gmail.com, reggiebarkerknives.com
Specialties: Hunters. **Patterns:** Pocketknives, fighters, camp knives and bowies. **Technical:** Forges carbon steel, stainless steel for pocketknives and uses own damascus. **Prices:** $300 and up. **Remarks:** Full-time maker. Three-time World Cutting Champion with over 15 wins. Winner of Best Value of Show 2001, Arkansas Knife Show and Journeyman Smith. Border Guard Forge. **Mark:** Barker JS.

BARKER, ROBERT G.
2311 Branch Rd., Bishop, GA 30621 **Contact:** 706-769-7827
Specialties: Traditional working/using straight knives of his design. **Patterns:** bowies, hunters and utility knives, ABS Journeyman Smith. **Technical:** Hand forged carbon and damascus. Forges to shape high-carbon 5160, cable and chain. Differentially heat-treats. **Prices:** $200 to $500, some to $1000. **Remarks:** Spare-time maker, first knife sold in 1987. **Mark:** BARKER/J.S.

BARKER, STUART
51 Thorpe Dr., Wigston, Leicester, ENGLAND LE18 1LE **Contact:** +447887585411, sc_barker@hotmail.com barkerknives.co.uk
Specialties: Fixed blade working knives of his design. **Patterns:** Kitchen, hunter, utility/camp knives. **Technical:** Grinds O1, Rw134 & Damasteel, hand rubbed or shot blast finishes. **Prices:** $150 - $1,000. **Remarks:** Part-time maker, first knife sold 2006. **Mark:** Last initial or last name.

BARKES, TERRY
14844 N. Bluff Rd., Edinburgh, IN 46124 **Contact:** 812-526-6390, terrybarkes@outlook.comt, http://my.hsonline.net/wizard/TerryBarkesKnives.htm

---

Specialties: Traditional working straight knives of his designs. **Patterns:** Drop point hunters, boot knives, skinning, fighter, utility, all purpose, camp, and grill knives. **Technical:** Grinds 1095 - 1084 - 52100 - 01, Hollow grinds and flat grinds. Hand rubbed finish from 400 to 2000 grit or High polish buff. Hard edge and soft back, heat treat by maker. Likes File work, natural handle material, bone, stag, water buffalo horn, wildbeast bone, ironwood. **Prices:** $200 and up **Remarks:** Full-time maker, first knifge sold in 2005. Doing business as Barkes Knife Shop. **Marks:** Barkes - USA, Barkes Double Arrow - USA

BARLOW, JANA POIRIER
3820 Borland Cir, Anchorage, AK 99517 **Contact:** 907-243-4581

BARNES, AUBREY G.
11341 Rock Hill Rd, Hagerstown, MD 21740 **Contact:** 301-223-4587, a.barnes@myactv.net
Specialties: Classic Moran style reproductions and using knives of his own design. **Patterns:** bowies, hunters, fighters, daggers and utility/camping knives. **Technical:** Forges 5160, 1085, L6 and damascus, Silver wire inlays. **Prices:** $500 to $5000. **Remarks:** Full-time maker, first knife sold in 1992. Doing business as Falling Waters Forge. **Mark:** First and middle initials, last name, M.S.

BARNES, GREGORY
266 W Calaveras St, Altadena, CA 91001 **Contact:** 626-398-0053, snake@annex.com

BARNES, JACK
PO Box 1315, Whitefish, MT 59937-1315 **Contact:** 406-862-6078

BARNES, MARLEN R.
904 Crestview Dr S, Atlanta, TX 75551-1854 **Contact:** 903-796-3668, MRBlives@worldnet.att.net
Specialties: Hammer forges random and mosaic damascus. **Patterns:** Hatchets, straight and folding knives. **Technical:** Hammer forges carbon steel using 5160, 1084 and 52100 with 15N20 and 203E nickel. **Prices:** $150 and up. **Remarks:** Part-time maker, first knife sold 1999. **Mark:** Script M.R.B., other side J.S.

BARNES, ROGER
BC Cutlery Co., 314 Rosemarie Pl., Bay Point, CA 94565 **Contact:** 925-483-6982 or 925-231-4367, bccutlerycompany@gmail.com, Facebook.com/bc cutlery co. **Mark:** BC usa.

BARNES, ROGER
BC Cutlery Co., 314 Rosemarie Pl., Bay Point, CA 94565, bccutlerycompany@gmail.com
Specialties: Various styles of fixed-blade knives with an emphasis on quality in performance and simple aesthetics. **Patterns:** Karambits, Bob Loveless-inspired drop-point hunters and choppers. **Technical:** Uses 52100, 1095, 5160, AEB-L and CPM-3V blade steels, and Micartas, carbon fiber and G-10 handle scales, all USA-made materials. **Prices:** $75 to $500. **Remarks:** Wait time two weeks to one month.

BARNES, WENDELL
PO Box 272, Clinton, MT 59825 **Contact:** 406-825-0908
Specialties: Working straight knives. **Patterns:** Hunters, folders, neck knives. **Technical:** Grinds 440C, ATS-34, D2 and damascus. **Prices:** Start at $75. **Remarks:** Spare-time maker, first knife sold in 1996. **Mark:** First initial, split heart, last name.

BARNES JR., CECIL C.
141 Barnes Dr, Center Ridge, AR 72027 **Contact:** 501-893-2267

BARNETT, BRUCE
PO Box 447, Mundaring, WA, AUSTRALIA 6073 **Contact:** 61-4-19243855, bruce@barnettcustomknives.com, barnettcustomknives.com
Specialties: Most types of fixed blades, folders, carving sets. **Patterns:** Hunters, bowies, Camp Knives, Fighters, Lockback and Slipjoint Folders. **Prices:** $200 up **Remarks:** Part time maker. Member Australian Knifemakers Guild and ABS journeyman smith. **Mark:** Barnett + J.S.

BARNETT, VAN
BARNETT INT'L INC, P.O. Box 111, Gallipolis Ferry, WV 25515 **Contact:** 304-727-5512, 775-513-6969, 775-686-9084, ImATimeMachine@gmail.com & illusionknives@gmail.com, VanBarnettArt.com
Specialties: Collector grade one-of-a-kind / embellished high art daggers and art folders. **Patterns:** Art daggers and folders. **Technical:** Forges and grinds own damascus. **Prices:** Upscale. **Remarks:** Designs and makes one-of-a-kind highly embellished art knives using high karat gold, diamonds and other gemstones, pearls, stone and fossil ivories, carved steel guards and blades, all knives are carved and or engraved, does own engraving, carving and other embellishments, sole authorship, full-time maker since 1981. Does one high art collaboration a year with Dellana. Member of ABS. Member Art Knife Invitational Group (AKI) **Mark:** VBARNETT

BARNHILL, WESS
5846 Meadows Run, Spotsylvania, VA 22551 **Contact:** 540-582-8758, wess.barnhill@gmail.com, wessbarnhillknives.com
Specialties: High-art, collectible and functional straight knives. **Patterns:** bowies, hunters, camp knives and others. **Technical:** Hand forges high-carbon and damascus steel. Applied art in the forms of engraving, carving and filework. Offers functional leather sheaths in exotic leather. **Prices:** Start at $250. **Remarks:** Sole authorship on all knives, ABS journeyman smith. **Mark:** Last name followed by J.S..

BARR, JUDSON C.
1905 Pickwick Circle, Irving, TX 75060 **Contact:** 214-724-0564, judsonbarrknives@yahoo.com
Specialties: bowies. **Patterns:** Sheffield and Early American. **Technical:** Forged carbon steel

custom knifemakers

and damascus. Also stock removal. **Remarks:** Journeyman member of ABS. **Mark:** Barr.

BARRETT, RICK L. (TOSHI HISA)
18943 CR 18, Goshen, IN 46528 **Contact:** 574-533-4297, barrettrick@hotmail.com
Specialties: Japanese-style blades from sushi knives to katana and fantasy pieces. **Patterns:** Swords, axes, spears/lances, hunter and utility knives. **Technical:** Forges and grinds damascus and carbon steels, occasionally uses stainless. **Prices:** $250 to $4000+. **Remarks:** Full-time bladesmith, jeweler. **Mark:** Japanese mei on Japanese pieces and stylized initials.

BARRON, BRIAN
123 12th Ave, San Mateo, CA 94402 **Contact:** 650-341-2683
Specialties: Traditional straight knives. **Patterns:** Daggers, hunters and swords. **Technical:** Grinds 440C, ATS-34 and 1095. Sculpts bolsters using an S-curve. **Prices:** $130 to $270, some to $1500. **Remarks:** Part-time maker, first knife sold in 1993. **Mark:** Diamond Drag "Barron."

BARRY, SCOTT
4402 Comanche Dr., Laramie, WY 82072 Comment: 307-399-2646, scottyb@uwyo.edu
Specialties: Currently producing mostly folders, also make fixed blade hunters & fillet knives. **Technical:** Steels used are ATS 34, 154CM, CPM 154, D2, CPM S30V, Damasteel and Devin Thomas stainless damascus. **Prices:** Range from $300 $1000. **Remarks:** Part-time maker. First knife sold in 1972. **Mark:** DSBarry, etched on blade.

BARRY III, JAMES J.
115 Flagler Promenade No., West Palm Beach, FL 33405 **Contact:** 561-832-4197
Specialties: High-art working straight knives of his design also high art tomahawks. **Patterns:** Hunters, daggers and fishing knives. **Technical:** Grinds 440C only. Prefers exotic materials for handles. Most knives embellished with filework, carving and scrimshaw. Many pieces designed to stand unassisted. **Prices:** $500 to $10,000. **Remarks:** Part-time maker, first knife sold in 1975. Guild member (Knifemakers) since 1991. **Mark:** Branded initials as a J and B together.

BARTH, J.D.
101 4th St, PO Box 186, Alberton, MT 59820 **Contact:** 406-722-4557, mtdeerhunter@blackfoot.net, jdbarthcustomknives.com
Specialties: Working and fancy straight knives of his design. LinerLock® folders, stainless and damascus, fully file worked, nitre bluing. **Technical:** Grinds ATS-34, 440-C, stainless and carbon damascus. Uses variety of natural handle materials and Micarta. Likes dovetailed bolsters. Filework on most knives, full and tapered tangs. Makes custom fit sheaths for each knife. **Mark:** Name over maker, city and state.

BARTLETT, MARK
102 Finn Cir., Lawrenceburg, TN 38464 **Contact:** 931-477-5444, moosetrax@live.com
Specialties: Mostly hunters and small bowies, but moving into larger bowies. **Technical:** Forges for the most part, with some stock removal, primarily using 1095, 1084 and 52100 blade steels. Has started damascus recently. Uses hardwoods and Micarta mostly for handles. **Prices:** $200 to $500, with some recent orders booked at $900-$1,000. **Remarks:** Part-time maker, first knife made in September 2013. **Mark:** Last name with a dagger through the middle "T."

BASKETT, BARBARA
427 Sutzer Ck Rd, Eastview, KY 42732 **Contact:** 270-862-5019, bgbaskett@yahoo.com, baskettknives.com
Specialties: Hunters and LinerLocks. **Technical:** 440-C, CPM 154, S30V. **Prices:** $250 and up. **Mark:** B. Baskett.

BASKETT, LEE GENE
427 Sutzer Ck. Rd., Eastview, KY 42732 **Contact:** 270-862-5019, (fax) Cell: 270-766-8724, baskettknives@hotmail.com baskettknives.com
Specialties: Fancy working knives and fancy art pieces, often set up in fancy desk stands. **Patterns:** Fighters, bowies, and Survial Knives, lockback folders and liner locks along with traditional styles. Cutting competition knives. **Technical:** Grinds O1, 440-c, S30V, power CPM154, CPM 4, D2, buys damascus. Filework provided on most knives. **Prices:** $250 and up. **Remarks:** Part-time maker, first knife sold in 1980. **Mark:** Baskett

BASSETT, DAVID J.
P.O. Box 69-102, Glendene, Auckland, NEW ZEALAND 0645 **Contact:** 64 9 818 9083, (fax) 64 9 818 9013, david@customknifemaking.co.nz, customknifemaking.co.nz
Specialties: Working/using knives. **Patterns:** Hunters, fighters, boot, skinners, tanto. **Technical:** Grinds 440C, 12C27, D2 and some damascus via stock removal method. **Prices:** $150 to $500. **Remarks:** Part-time maker, first knife sold in 2006. Also carries range of natural and synthetic handle material, pin stock etc. for sale. **Mark:** Name over country in semi-circular design.

BATDORF, JASON
Delaney Knives 200 Airport Hwy Wauseon, OH 43567 **Contact:** 419-583-7238, Delaneyknives.com, Facebook: DelaneyKnives
Patterns: Integral art knives, bowies, folders, American-styled blades and miniatures. **Technical:** Makes own damascus and stabilizes all wood materials.

BATSON, JAMES
1316 McClung Ave., Huntsville, AL 35801 **Contact:** 256-971-6860, james.1.batson@gmail.com
Specialties: Forged damascus blades and fittings in collectible period pieces. **Patterns:** Integral art knives, bowies, folders, American-styled blades and miniatures. **Technical:** Forges carbon steel and his damascus. **Prices:** $150 to $1800, some to $4500. **Remarks:**

Semi retired full-time maker, first knife sold in 1978. **Mark:** Name, bladesmith with horse's head.

BATSON, RICHARD G.
6591 Waterford Rd, Rixeyville, VA 22737 **Contact:** 540-937-2318, mbatson6591@comcast.net
Specialties: Military, utility and fighting knives in working and presentation grade. **Patterns:** Daggers, combat and utility knives. **Technical:** Grinds O1, 1095 and 440C. Etches and scrimshaws, offers polished, Parkerized finishes. **Prices:** From $400. **Remarks:** Very limited production to active-dute military and vets only. First knife sold in 1958. **Mark:** Bat in circle, hand-signed and serial numbered.

BATTS, KEITH
500 Manning Rd, Hooks, TX 75561 **Contact:** 903-277-8466, kbatts@cableone.net
Specialties: Working straight knives of his design or to customer specs. **Patterns:** bowies, hunters, skinners, camp knives and others. **Technical:** Forges 5160 and his damascus, offers filework. **Prices:** $245 to $895. **Remarks:** Part-time maker, first knife sold in 1988. **Mark:** Last name.

BAUCHOP, ROBERT
PO Box 330, Munster, KN, SOUTH AFRICA 4278 **Contact:** +27 39 3192449
Specialties: Fantasy knives, working and using knives of his design and to customer specs. **Patterns:** Hunters, swords, utility/camp knives, diver's knives and large swords. **Technical:** Grinds Sandvick 12C27, D2, 440C. Uses South African hardwoods red ivory, wild olive, African blackwood, etc. on handles. **Prices:** $200 to $800, some to $2000. **Remarks:** Full-time maker, first knife sold in 1986. Doing business as Bauchop Custom Knives and Swords. **Mark:** Viking helmet with Bauchop (bow and chopper) crest.

BAXTER, DALE
291 County Rd 547, Trinity, AL 35673 **Contact:** 256-355-3626, dale@baxterknives.com
Specialties: bowies, fighters, and hunters. **Patterns:** No **patterns:** all unique true customs. **Technical:** Hand forge and hand finish. Steels: 1095 and L6 for carbon blades, 1095/L6 for damascus. **Remarks:** Full-time bladesmith and sold first knife in 1998. **Mark:** Dale Baxter (script) and J.S. on reverse.

BEAM, JOHN R.
1310 Foothills Rd, Kalispell, MT 59901 **Contact:** 406-755-2593
Specialties: Classic, high-art and working straight knives of his design. **Patterns:** bowies and hunters. **Technical:** Grinds 440C, damascus and scrap. **Prices:** $175 to $600, some to $3000. **Remarks:** Part-time maker, first knife sold in 1950. Doing business as Beam's Knives. **Mark:** Beam's Knives.

BEATTY, GORDON H.
121 Petty Rd, Seneca, SC 29672 **Contact:** 867-723-2966
Specialties: Working straight knives, some fancy. **Patterns:** Traditional patterns, mini-skinners and letter openers. **Technical:** Grinds ATS-34, makes knives one-at-a-time. **Prices:** $185 and up. **Remarks:** Part-time maker, first knife sold in 1982. **Mark:** Name.

BEATY, ROBERT B.
CUTLER, 1995 Big Flat Rd, Missoula, MT 59804 **Contact:** 406-549-1818
Specialties: Plain and fancy working knives and collector pieces, will accept custom orders. **Patterns:** Hunters, bowies, utility, kitchen and camp knives, locking folders. **Technical:** Grinds D-2, ATS-34, Dendritie D-2, makes all tool steel damascus, forges 1095, 5160, 52100. **Prices:** $150 to $600, some to $1100. **Remarks:** Full-time maker, first knife sold 1995. **Mark:** Stainless: First name, middle initial, last name, city and state. Carbon: Last name stamped on Ricasso.

BEAUCHAMP, GAETAN
125 de la Rivire, Stoneham, QC, CANADA G3C 0P6 **Contact:** 418-848-1914, (fax) 418-848-6859, knives@gbeauchamp.ca, gbeauchamp.ca
Specialties: Working knives and folders of his design and to customer specs. **Patterns:** Hunters, fighters, fantasy knives. **Technical:** Grinds ATS-34, 440C, damascus. Scrimshaws on ivory, specializes in buffalo horn and black backgrounds. Offers a variety of handle materials. **Prices:** Start at $250. **Remarks:** Full-time maker, first knife sold in 1992. **Mark:** Signature etched on blade.

BEAVER, DIRK
BEAVER CUSTOM BLADES, Ellijay, GA **Contact:** 706-633-7884, dirk@beavercustomblades.com, beavercustomblades.com
Specialties: Enjoys doing custom orders and working with his customers, making skinners, tactical fighters, neck knives and folders, anything a customer wants. **Technical:** Uses stock removal and forging methods of blade making, depending on style of knife, and works with high-carbon steel and damascus. **Remarks:** Full-time maker, first knife made in 2009.

BEERS, RAY
2501 Lakefront Dr, Lake Wales, FL 33898 **Contact:** 443-841-4143, rbknives@copper.net

BEETS, MARTY
390 N 5th Ave, Williams Lake, BC, CANADA V2G 2G4 **Contact:** 250-392-7199
Specialties: Working and collectable straight knives of his own design. **Patterns:** Hunter, skinners, bowies and utility knives. **Technical:** Grinds various steels-does all his own work including heat treating. Uses a variety of handle material specializing in exotic hardwoods, antler and horn. **Prices:** $125 to $400. **Remarks:** Wife, Sandy does handmade/hand stitched sheaths. First knife sold in 1988. Business name Beets Handmade Knives.

BEGG, TODD M.

1341 N. McDowell Blvd., Ste. D, Petaluma, CA 94954 **Contact:** 707-242-1790, info@beggknives.com, beggknives.net

Specialties: High-grade tactical folders and fixed blades. **Patterns:** Folders, integrals, fighters. **Technical:** Specializes in flipper folders using "IKBS" (Ikoma Korth Bearing System). **Prices:** $400 - $15,000. **Remarks:** Uses modern designs and materials.

BEHNKE, WILLIAM

8478 Dell Rd, Kingsley, MI 49649 **Contact:** 231-649-4993, bill@billbehnkeknives.com billbehnkeknives.com

Specialties: Fabricates carbide file/grinding guides, LinerLock folders. **Patterns:** Traditional styling in moderate-sized straight and folding knives. **Technical:** Forges own damascus, prefers W-2. **Prices:** $150 to $2,000. **Remarks:** Full-time maker. **Mark:** "Behnke".

BEHRING, JAMES

Behring Made Knives, POB 17317, Missoula, MT 59808 **Contact:** 406-926-1193, behringmadeknives@gmail.com, behringmade.com

Specialties: Custom handmade fixed blades for users and collectors alike. **Patterns:** Include, but are not limited to, hunters, skinners, bird & trout knives, fighters, kitchen cutlery, pocketknives, hatchets, etc. **Technical:** High-carbon steels (O1, 5160, 1095), CPM S30V, D2 and 440C stainless steel. Copper, nickel silver and brass fittings. Stag, Micarta, wide variety of wood, various horn (buffalo, musk ox, kudu), fossil and artifact walrus, etc. Open to new mediums upon request. **Prices:** $250 to $1,500. **Mark:** "B" logo with crossed hammer and knife, J. Behring Jr. Montana.

BELL, DON

Box 98, Lincoln, MT 59639 **Contact:** 406-362-3208, dlb@linctel.net

Patterns: Folders, hunters and custom orders. **Technical:** Carbon steel 52100, 5160, 1095, 1084. Making own damascus. Flat grinds. Natural handle material including fossil. ivory, pearl, & ironwork. **Remarks:** Full-time maker. First knife sold in 1999. **Mark:** Last name.

BELL, DONALD

2 Division St, Bedford, NS, CANADA B4A 1Y8 **Contact:** 902-835-2623, donbell@accesswave.ca, bellknives.com

Specialties: Fancy knives: carved and pierced folders of his own design. **Patterns:** Locking folders, pendant knives, jewelry knives. **Technical:** Grinds damascus, pierces and carves blades. **Prices:** $500 to $2000, some to $3000. **Remarks:** Spare-time maker, first knife sold in 1993. **Mark:** Bell symbol with first initial inside.

BELL, GABRIEL

88321 North Bank Lane, Coquille, OR 97423 **Contact:** 541-396-3605, gabriel@dragonflyforge.com, dragonflyforge.com & tomboyama.com

Specialties: Full line of combat quality Japanese swords. **Patterns:** Traditional tanto to katana. **Technical:** Handmade steel and welded cable. **Prices:** Swords from bare blades to complete high art $1500 to $28,000. **Remarks:** Studied with father Michael Bell. Instruction in sword crafts. Working in partnership with Michael Bell. **Mark:** Dragonfly In shield or kunitoshi.

BELL, MICHAEL

88321 N Bank Lane, Coquille, OR 97423 **Contact:** 541-396-3605, michael@dragonflyforge.com, Dragonflyforge.com & tomboyama.com

Specialties: Full line of combat quality Japanese swords. **Patterns:** Traditional tanto to katana. **Technical:** Handmade steel and welded cable. **Prices:** Swords from bare blades to complete high art $1500 to $28,000. **Remarks:** Studied with Japanese master Nakajima Muneyoshi. Instruction in sword crafts. Working in partnership with son, Gabriel. **Mark:** Dragonfly in shield or tombo kunimitsu.

BELL, TONY

PO Box 24, Woodland, AL 36280 **Contact:** 256-449-2655, tbell905@aol.com

Specialties: Hand forged period knives and tomahawks. Art knives and knives made for everyday use. **Technical:** Makes own damascus. Forges 1095, 5160,1080,L6 steels. Does own heat treating. **Prices:** $75-$1200. **Remarks:** Full time maker. **Mark:** Bell symbol with initial T in the middle.

BENJAMIN JR., GEORGE

3001 Foxy Ln, Kissimmee, FL 34746 **Contact:** 407-846-7259

Specialties: Fighters in various styles to include Persian, Moro and military. **Patterns:** Daggers, skinners and one-of-a-kind grinds. **Technical:** Forges O1, D2, A2, 5160 and damascus. Favors Pakkawood, Micarta, and mirror or Parkerized finishes. Makes unique para-military leather sheaths. **Prices:** $150 to $600, some to $1200. **Remarks:** Doing business as The Leather Box. **Mark:** Southern Pride Knives.

BENNETT, BRETT C

420 Adamstown Rd., Reinholds, PA 17569 **Contact:** 307-220-3919, brett@bennettknives.com, bennettknives.com

Specialties: Hand-rubbed satin finish on all blades. **Patterns:** Mostly fixed-blade patterns. **Technical:** ATS-34, D-2, 1084/15N20 damascus, 1084 forged. **Mark:** "B.C. Bennett" in script or "Bennett" stamped in script.

BENNETT, GLEN C

5821 S Stewart Blvd, Tucson, AZ 85706

BENNETT, PETER

PO Box 143, Engadine, NSW, AUSTRALIA 2233 **Contact:** 02-520-4975 (home), (fax) 02-528-8219 (work)

Specialties: Fancy and embellished working and using straight knives to customer specs and in standard patterns. **Patterns:** Fighters, hunters, bird/trout and fillet knives. **Technical:** Grinds 440C, ATS-34 and damascus. Uses rare Australian desert timbers for

handles. **Prices:** $90 to $500, some to $1500. **Remarks:** Full-time maker, first knife sold in 1985. **Mark:** First and middle initials, last name, country.

BENNICA, CHARLES

11 Chemin du Salet, Moules et Baucels, FRANCE 34190 **Contact:** +33 4 67 73 42 40, cbennica@bennica-knives.com, bennica-knives.com

Specialties: Fixed blades and folding knives, the latter with slick closing mechanisms with push buttons to unlock blades. Unique handle shapes, signature to the maker. **Technical:** 416 stainless steel frames for folders and ATS-34 blades. Also specializes in damascus.

BENSINGER, J. W.

583 Jug Brook Rd., Marshfield, VT 05658 **Contact:** 802-917-1789, jwbensinger@gmail.com vermontbladesmith.com

Specialties: Working hunters, bowies for work and defense, and Finnish patterns. Occasional folders. **Technical:** High performance handforged knives in 5160, 52100, 1080, and in-house damascus. **Prices:** Range from $130 for simple bushcraft knives to $500 for larger knives. damascus prices on request. **Remarks:** First knife made in 1980 or so. Full-time maker. Customer designs welcome. **Mark:** "JWB" and year in cursive.

BENSON, DON

2505 Jackson St #112, Escalon, CA 95320 **Contact:** 209-838-7921

Specialties: Working straight knives of his design. **Patterns:** Axes, bowies, tantos and hunters. **Technical:** Grinds 440C. **Prices:** $100 to $150, some to $400. **Remarks:** Spare-time maker, first knife sold in 1980. **Mark:** Name.

BENTLEY, C L

2405 Hilltop Dr, Albany, GA 31707 **Contact:** 912-432-6656

BER, DAVE

656 Miller Rd, San Juan Island, WA 98250 **Contact:** 206-378-7230

Specialties: Working straight and folding knives for the sportsman, welcomes customer designs. **Patterns:** Hunters, skinners, bowies, kitchen and fishing knives. **Technical:** Forges and grinds saw blade steel, wire damascus, O1, L6, 5160 and 440C. **Prices:** $100 to $300, some to $500. **Remarks:** Full-time maker, first knife sold in 1985. **Mark:** Last name.

BERG, LEE

PO Box 458, Roseburg, OR 97470, leeandlanny@gmail.com

Specialties: One-of-a-kind and investment-quality straight knives of his own design, incorporating traditional, period, Near East and Asian influence. **Patterns:** Daggers, fighters, hunters, bowies, short swords, full size and miniature. **Technical:** Stock removal with file, damascus, meteorite, O1, D2 and ATS-34. **Prices:** $200 and up. **Remarks:** Part-time maker, first knife sold in 1972. **Mark:** Full name.

BERG, LOTHAR

37 Hillcrest Ln, Kitchener ON, CANADA NZK 1S9 **Contact:** 519-745-3260, 519-745-3260

BERGER, MAX A.

5716 John Richard Ct, Carmichael, CA 95608 **Contact:** 916-972-9229, bergerknives@aol.com

Specialties: Fantasy and working/using straight knives of his design. **Patterns:** Fighters, hunters and utility/camp knives. **Technical:** Grinds ATS-34 and 440C. Offers fileworks and combinations of mirror polish and satin finish blades. **Prices:** $200 to $600, some to $2500. **Remarks:** Part-time maker, first knife sold in 1992. **Mark:** Last name.

BERGH, ROGER

Dalkarlsa 291, Bygdea, SWEDEN 91598 **Contact:** 469-343-0061, knivroger@hotmail.com, rogerbergh.com

Specialties: Collectible all-purpose straight-blade knives. damascus steel blades, carving and artistic design knives are heavily influenced by nature and have an organic hand crafted feel.

BERGLIN, BRUCE

17441 Lake Terrace Place, Mount Vernon, WA 98274 **Contact:** 360-333-1217, bruce@berglins.com

Specialties: Working fixed blades and folders of his own design. **Patterns:** Hunters, boots, bowies, utility, liner locks and slip joints some with vintage finish. **Technical:** Forges carbon steel, grinds carbon steel. Prefers natural handle material. **Prices:** Start at $300. **Remarks:** Part-time maker since 1998. **Mark:** (2 marks) 1. Last name, or 2. First initial, second initial & last name, surrounded with an oval.

BERTOLAMI, JUAN CARLOS

Av San Juan 575, Neuquen, ARGENTINA 8300, fliabertolami@infovia.com.ar

Specialties: Hunting and country labor knives. All of them unique high quality pieces and supplies collectors too. **Technical:** Austrian stainless steel and elephant, hippopotamus and orca ivory, as well as ebony and other fine woods for the handles.

BERTUZZI, ETTORE

Via Partigiani 3, Seriate, Bergamo, ITALY 24068 **Contact:** 035-294262, (fax) 035-294262

Specialties: Classic straight knives and folders of his design, to customer specs and in standard patterns. **Patterns:** bowies, hunters and locking folders. **Technical:** Grinds ATS-34, D3, D2 and various damascus. **Prices:** $300 to $500. **Remarks:** Part-time maker, first knife sold in 1993. **Mark:** Name etched on ricasso.

BESEDICK, FRANK E

1257 Country Club Road, Monongahela, PA 15063-1057 **Contact:** 724-292-8016, bez32@comcast.net

Specialties: Traditional working and using straight knives of his design. **Patterns:** Hunters, utility/camp knives and miniatures, buckskinner blades and tomahawks. **Technical:** Forges and grinds 5160, O1 and damascus. Offers filework and scrimshaw. **Prices:** $75 to $300, some to $750. **Remarks:** Part-time maker, first knife sold in 1990. **Mark:** Name or initials.

BESHARA, BRENT (BESH)
PO BOX 557, Holyrood, NL, CANADA A0A 2R0, BESH@beshknives.com beshknives.com
Specialties: Fixed blade tools and knives. **Patterns:** BESH Wedge tools and knives. **Technical:** Custom design work, grinds 0-1, D-2, 440C, 154cm. Offers kydex sheathing **Prices:** Start at $250. **Remarks:** Inventor of BESH Wedge geometry, custom maker and designer since 2000. Retired (24yrs) Special Forces, Special Operations Navy bomb disposal diver. Lifelong martial artist. **Mark:** "BESH" stamped.

BEST, RON
1489 Adams Lane, Stokes, NC 27884 **Contact:** 252-714-1264, ronbestknives@msn.com, ronbestknives.com
Specialties: Folders and automatics. **Patterns:** Everything including butterfly knives. **Technical:** Grinds 440C, D-2 and ATS-34. **Prices:** $600 to $8000.

BEUKES, TINUS
83 Henry St, Risiville, Vereeniging, GT, SOUTH AFRICA 1939 **Contact:** 27 16 423 2053
Specialties: Working straight knives. **Patterns:** Hunters, skinners and kitchen knives. **Technical:** Grinds D2, 440C and chain, cable and stainless damascus. **Prices:** $80 to $180. **Remarks:** Part-time maker, first knife sold in 1993. **Mark:** Full name, city, logo.

BEVERLY II, LARRY H
Beverly Knives. PO Box 741, Spotsylvania, VA 22553 **Contact:** 540-846-5426, beverlyknives@aol.com
Specialties: Working straight knives, slip-joints and liner locks. Welcomes customer designs. **Patterns:** bowies, hunters, guard less fighters and miniatures. **Technical:** Grinds 440C, A2 and O1. **Prices:** $125 to $1000. **Remarks:** Part-time maker, first knife sold in 1986. **Mark:** Initials or last name in script.

BEZUIDENHOUT, BUZZ
PO BOX 28284, Malvern, KZN, SOUTH AFRICA 4055 **Contact:** 031-4632827, (fax) 031-4632827, buzzbee@mweb.co.za
Specialties: Working and Fancy Folders, my or customer design.**Patterns:** Boots, hunters, kitchen knives and utility/camp knives. **Technical:** Use 12-C-27 + stainless damascus, some carbon damascus. Uses local hardwoods, horn: kudu, impala, buffalo, giraffe bone and ivory for handles.
Prices: $250 to upscale. **Remarks:** Part-time maker, first knife sold in 1985. Member S.A. Knife Makers Guild**Mark:** First name with a bee emblem.

BIGGIN, PAT
N7109 County Rd. O, Elkhorn, WI 53121 **Contact:** 608-391-0324, biggincustomknives@gmail.com, facebook.com/Howling-Wolf-Knifeworks-180648362962553/?ref=bookmarks
Specialties: Hunting, camping, bowies and utility knives. **Patterns:** Drop points, harpoon points, bowies, machetes and dirks. **Technical:** Forges 80CrV2, W2, W1, 5160, 10 series and damascus. **Stock removal steels:** 52100, O1, W2 and 80CrV2. **Remarks:** Part-time maker who hand forges majority of blades, doing stock removal for orders of multiple, identical blades. Made first knife in 2005 from an old spring. **Prices:** $90 to $600. **Mark:** Tribal-style wolf's head howling. Goes by business name of Howling Wolf Knifeworks, changed from Biggin Custom Knives.

BIRDWELL, IRA LEE
PO Box 1448, Congress, AZ 85332 **Contact:** 928-925-3258, heli.ira@gmail.com
Specialties: Special orders. **Mark:** Engraved signature.

BISH, HAL
9347 Sweetbriar Trace, Jonesboro, GA 30236 **Contact:** 770-477-2422, hal-bish@hp.com

BISHER, WILLIAM (BILL)
1015 Beck Road, Denton, NC 27239 **Contact:** 336-859-4686, blackturtleforge@wildblue.net,blackturtleforge.com
Specialties: Period pieces, also contemporary belt knives, friction folders. **Patterns:** Own design, hunters, camp/utility, bowies, belt axes, neck knives, carving sets. **Technical:** Forges straight high carbon steels, and own damascus, grinds ATS34 and 154CM. Uses natural handle materials (wood, bone, stag horn), micarta and stabilized wood.**Prices:** Starting at $75 - $2500. **Remarks:** Past president of North Carolina Custom Knifemakers Guild, member ABS, Full-time maker as of 2007, first knife made 1989, all work in house, blades and sheaths **Mark:** Last name under crown and turtle

BIZZELL, ROBERT
145 Missoula Ave, Butte, MT 59701 **Contact:** 406-782-4403, patternweld@yahoo.com
Specialties: damascus bowies. **Patterns:** Composite, mosaic and traditional. **Technical:** Fixed blades & LinerLock® folders. **Prices:** Fixed blades start at $275. Folders start at $500. **Remarks:** Currently not taking orders. **Mark:** Hand signed.

BLACK, EARL
3466 South, 700 East, Salt Lake City, UT 84106 **Contact:** 801-466-8395
Specialties: High-art straight knives and folders, period pieces. **Patterns:** Boots, bowies and daggers, lockers and gents. **Technical:** Grinds 440C and 154CM. Buys some damascus. Scrimshaws and engraves. **Prices:** $200 to $1800, some to $2500 and higher.

Remarks: Full-time maker, first knife sold in 1980. **Mark:** Name, city, state.

BLACK, SCOTT
27100 Leetown Rd, Picayune, MS 39466 **Contact:** 601-799-5939, copperheadforge@telepak.net
Specialties: Friction folders, fighters. **Patterns:** bowies, fighters, hunters, smoke hawks, friction folders, daggers. **Technical:** All forged, all work done by him, own hand-stitched leather work, own heat-treating. **Prices:** $100 to $2200. **Remarks:** ABS Journeyman Smith. Cabel / damascus/ High Carbone. **Mark:** Hot Mark - Copperhead Snake.

BLACK, TOM
921 Grecian NW, Albuquerque, NM 87107 **Contact:** 505-344-2549, blackknives@comcast.net
Specialties: Working knives to fancy straight knives of his design. **Patterns:** Drop-point skinners, folders, using knives, bowies and daggers. **Technical:** Grinds 440C, 154CM, ATS-34, A2, D2, CPM-154 and damascus. Offers engraving and scrimshaw. **Prices:** $250 and up, some over $8500. **Remarks:** Full-time maker, first knife sold in 1970. **Mark:** Name, city.

BLACKWELL, ZANE
PO BOX 234, Eden, TX 76837 **Contact:** 325-869-8821, blackwellknives@hotmail.com, blackwellknives.com
Specialties: Hunters, slip-joint folders and kitchen knives. **Patterns:** Drop-point and clip-point hunters, and classic slip-joint patterns like single-blade trappers. **Technical:** CPM 154, ATS-34, 440C and D2 blade steels, and natural handle materials. **Prices:** Single-blade folders start at $400. **Remarks:** Six-month back log. **Mark:** Zane Blackwell Eden Texas.

BLADOWSKI, JANUSZ
U1. Ogrodowa 8, 62-080 Sady, POLAND, Janusz.bladowski@gmail.com, Instagram and Facebook: Bladowski Custom Works
Specialties: High-end, professional kitchen knives, utility knives and classical folding knives. **Technical:** Grinds all kinds of steel, forges W2 and 52100. **Prices:** $75 and up. **Remarks:** Making knives as a hobby since 1995, full-time maker since 2008. **Mark:** Name.

BLAUM, ROY
ROY'S KNIFE & ARCHERY SHOP, 319 N Columbia St, Covington, LA 70433 **Contact:** 985-893-1060
Specialties: Working straight knives and folders of his design, lightweight easy-open folders. **Patterns:** Hunters, boots, fishing and woodcarving/whittling knives. **Technical:** Grinds A2, D2, O1, 154CM and ATS-34. Offers leatherwork. **Prices:** $40 to $800, some higher. **Remarks:** Full-time maker, first knife sold in 1976. **Mark:** Engraved signature or etched logo.

Bloodworth Custom Knives
3502 W. Angelica Dr., Meridian, ID 83646 **Contact:** 208-888-7778
Patterns: Working straight knives, hunters, skinners, bowies, utility knives of his designs or customer specs. Scagel knives. Period knives and traditional frontier knives and sheaths. **Technical:** Grinds D2, ATS34, 154CM, 5160, 01, damascus, Heat treats, natural and composite handle materials. **Prices:** $185.00 to $1,500. **Remarks:** Roger Smith knife maker. Full-time maker, first knife sold in 1978 **Mark:** Sword over BLOODWORTH.

BLOOMER, ALAN T
PO Box 154, 116 E 6th St, Maquon, IL 61458 **Contact:** Cell: 309-371-8520, alant.bloomer@winco.net
Specialties: Folders & straight knives & custom pen maker. **Patterns:** All kinds. **Technical:** Does own heat treating. **Prices:** $400 to $1000. **Remarks:** Part-time maker. No orders. **Mark:** Stamp Bloomer.

BLUM, KENNETH
1729 Burleson, Brenham, TX 77833 **Contact:** 979-836-9577
Specialties: Traditional working straight knives of his design. **Patterns:** Camp knives, hunters and bowies. **Technical:** Forges 5160, grinds 440C and D2. Uses exotic woods and Micarta for handles. **Prices:** $150 to $300. **Remarks:** Part-time maker, first knife sold in 1978. **Mark:** Last name on ricasso.

BLYSTONE, RONALD L.
231 Bailey Road, Creekside, PA 15732 **Contact:** 724-397-2671, taxibly@hotmail.com
Specialties: Traditional forged working knives. **Patterns:** Hunting utility and skinners of his own design. **Technical:** Forges his own pattern welded damascus using carbon steel. **Prices:** Starting at $150. **Remarks:** Spare-time maker.**Mark:** Initials - upsidedown R against the B, inside a circle, over the word FORGE

BOARDMAN, GUY
39 Mountain Ridge R, New Germany, KZN, SOUTH AFRICA 3619 **Contact:** 031-726-921
Specialties: American and South African-styles. **Patterns:** bowies, American and South African hunters, plus more. **Technical:** Grinds Bohler steels, some ATS-34. **Prices:** $100 to $600. **Remarks:** Part-time maker, first knife sold in 1986. **Mark:** Name, city, country.

BOCHMAN, BRUCE
183 Howard Place, Grants Pass, OR 97526 **Contact:** 541-471-1985, 183bab@gmail.com
Specialties: Hunting, fishing, bird and tactical knives. **Patterns:** Hunters, fishing and bird knives. **Technical:** ATS34, 154CM, mirror or satin finish. damascus. **Prices:** $250 to $350, some to $750. **Remarks:** Part-time maker, first knife sold in 1977. **Mark:** Custom Knives by B. Bochman

BODEN, HARRY
Via Gellia Mill, Bonsall Matlock, Derbyshire, ENGLAND DE4 2AJ **Contact:** 0629-825176
Specialties: Traditional working straight knives and folders of his design. **Patterns:** Hunters, locking folders and utility/camp knives. **Technical:** Grinds Sandvik 12C27, D2 and O1. **Prices:** £70 to £150, some £300. **Remarks:** Full-time maker, first knife sold in 1986. **Mark:** Full name.

BODOLAY, ANTAL
Rua Wilson Soares Fernandes #31, Planalto, Belo Horizonte, MG, BRAZIL MG-31730-700 **Contact:** 031-494-1885
Specialties: Working folders and fixed blades of his design or to customer specs, some art daggers and period pieces. **Patterns:** Daggers, hunters, locking folders, utility knives and Khukris. **Technical:** Grinds D6, high-carbon steels and 420 stainless. Forges files on request. **Prices:** $30 to $350. **Remarks:** Full-time maker, first knife sold in 1965. **Mark:** Last name in script.

BOECK, SANDRO EDUARDO
St. Eduardo Macedo de Oliveira, 300, Cachoeira do Sul - RS, BRAZIL CEP - 96 505 - 610 **Contact:** 55-51-99559106, sandroboeck@gmail.com, sandroboeck.com.br
Specialties: Fixed blades, integrals, gaucho style, bowies, hunters, dirks and swords. **Technical:** Forges his own damascus, mosaic damascus and high-carbon steel. Constructs integral knives. **Prices:** $500 to $2,000. **Remarks:** Part-time maker, IBO founding member, ABS journeyman smith, SBC lawyer consultant. **Mark:** S.Boeck JS.

BOEHLKE, GUENTER
Parkstrasse 2, 56412 Grobholbach, GERMANY **Contact:** (49) 2602-5440, (fax) (49) 2602-5491, Boehlke-Messer@t-online.de, boehlke-messer.de
Specialties: Classic working/using straight knives of his design. **Patterns:** Hunters, utility/camp knives and ancient remakes. **Technical:** Grinds damascus, CPM-T-440V and 440C. Inlays gemstones and ivory. **Prices:** $220 to $700, some to $2000. **Remarks:** Spare-time maker, first knife sold in 1985. **Mark:** Name, address and bow and arrow.

BOHRMANN, BRUCE
61 Portland St, Yarmouth, ME 04096 **Contact:** 207-846-3385, bbohr@maine.rr.com, Bohrmannknives.com
Specialties: Fixed-blade sporting, camp and hunting knives. **Technical:** Stock-removal maker using 13C26 Sandvik stainless steel hardened to 58-60 Rockwell. **Prices:** $499 for each model. Also, special "Heritage" production using historic certified woods (from Washington's, Jefferson's, Madison's and Henry's Plantations) - $1,250. **Remarks:** Full-time maker, first knife made in 1955. Always developing new models and concepts, such as steak knives, fixed blades and miniatures with special pocket sheaths. **Mark:** The letter "B" connected to and lying beneath deer antlers.

BOJTOS, ARPAD
Dobsinskeho 10, 98403 Lucenec, SLOVAKIA **Contact:** 00421-47 4333512, Cell: 00421-91 5875066, bojtos@stonline.sk, arpadbojtos.sk
Specialties: Art knives, including over 100 folders. **Patterns:** Daggers, fighters and hunters. **Technical:** Grinds ATS-34 and stainless damascus. Carves on steel, handle materials and sheaths. **Prices:** $5000 to $10,000, some over. **Remarks:** Full-time maker, first knife sold in 1990. **Mark:** AB.

BOLDUC, GARY
1419 Tanglewood Dr., Corona, CA 92882 **Contact:** 951-739-0137, gary@stillwaterwoods.com, bolducknives.com
Specialties: Fish fillet knives (larger sizes), medium 8" to large 10"-plus. Replica making of primitive Native Alaskan hunting and cutting tools, kitchen cutlery. **Patterns:** Hunters, skinners, fillet, boning, spear points and kitchen cutlery. **Technical:** High-quality stainless steel, mainly CTS-XHP, CPM-154 and CPM-S35VN for improved edge design. **Prices:** $200-$400 and up. **Remarks:** Full-time maker, first knife sold in 2007. **Mark:** First initial, last name with USA under, or grizzly bear with Bolduc Knives underneath.

BOLEWARE, DAVID
PO Box 96, Carson, MS 39427 **Contact:** 601-943-5372
Specialties: Traditional and working/using straight knives of his design, to customer specs and in standard patterns. **Patterns:** bowies, hunters and utility/camp knives. **Technical:** Grinds ATS-34, 440C and damascus. **Prices:** $85 to $350, some to $600. **Remarks:** Part-time maker, first knife sold in 1989. **Mark:** First and last name, city, state.

BOLEY, JAMIE
PO Box 477, Parker, SD 57053 **Contact:** 605-297-0014, jamie@polarbearforge.com
Specialties: Working knives and historical influenced reproductions. **Patterns:** Hunters, skinners, scramasaxes, and others.**Technical:** Forges 5160, O1, L6, 52100, W1, W2 makes own damascus. **Prices:** Starts at $125. **Remarks:** Part-time maker. **Mark:** Polar bear paw print with name on the left side and Polar Bear Forge on the right.

BONASSI, FRANCO
Via Nicoletta 4, Pordenone, ITALY 33170 **Contact:** 0434-550821, frank.bonassi@alice.it
Specialties: Fancy and working one-of-a-kind folder knives of his design. **Patterns:** Folders, linerlocks and back locks. **Technical:** Grinds CPM, ATS-34, 154CM and commercial damascus. Uses only titanium foreguards and pommels. **Prices:** Start at $350. **Remarks:** Spare-time maker, first knife sold in 1988. Has made cutlery for several celebrities, Gen. Schwarzkopf, Fuzzy Zoeller, etc. **Mark:** FRANK.

BOOCO, GORDON
175 Ash St, PO Box 174, Hayden, CO 81639 **Contact:** 970-276-3195

Specialties: Fancy working straight knives of his design and to customer specs. **Patterns:** Hunters and bowies. **Technical:** Grinds 440C, D2 and A2. Heat-treats. **Prices:** $150 to $350, some $600 and higher. **Remarks:** Part-time maker, first knife sold in 1984. **Mark:** Last name with push dagger artwork.

BOOS, RALPH
6018-37A Avenue NW, Edmonton, AB, CANADA T6L 1H4 **Contact:** 780-463-7094
Specialties: Classic, fancy and fantasy miniature knives and swords of his design or to customer specs. **Patterns:** bowies, daggers and swords. **Technical:** Hand files O1, stainless and damascus. Engraves and carves. Does heat bluing and acid etching. **Prices:** $125 to $350, some to $1000. **Remarks:** Part-time maker, first knife sold in 1982. **Mark:** First initials back to back.

BOOTH, PHILIP W
301 S Jeffery Ave, Ithaca, MI 48847 **Contact:** 989-601-6045, pbooth@charter.net, Instagram @philipboothknives, Facebook: Phil Booth Knives and Weird Stuff
Specialties: Automatic knives using many various mechanisms including lever lock, button locks, scale release and more. **Patterns:** Many patterns including small pocket carry automatics; Minnow, Twerp flippers. Larger titanium frame flipper knives. **Technical:** Phil is a grinder not a forger. Uses CPM154, 1095 and commercial damascus in both SS and carbon. Offers hot gun blue finish on various pieces. **Prices:** $450 and up. **Remarks:** Full-time maker, first knife sold in 1991. **Mark:** Either last name stamped in, or whole name with state of Michigan etched logo. Previous: Last name or name with city and map logo.

BORGER, WOLF
Benzstrasse 8, Graben-Neudorf, GERMANY 76676 **Contact:** 07255-72303, (fax) 07255-72304, wolf@messerschmied.de, messerschmied.de
Specialties: High-tech working and using straight knives and folders, many with corkscrews or other tools, of his design. **Patterns:** Hunters, bowies and folders with various locking systems. **Technical:** Grinds 440C, ATS-34 and CPM. Uses stainless damascus. **Prices:** $250 to $900, some to $1500. **Remarks:** Full-time maker, first knife sold in 1975. **Mark:** Howling wolf and name, first name on damascus blades.

BOSE, REESE
8810 N. County Rd. 375 E, Shelburn, IN 47879 **Contact:** 812-397-5114
Specialties: Traditional working and using knives in standard patterns and multi-blade folders. **Patterns:** Multi-blade slip-joints. **Technical:** ATS-34, D2, 154CM and CPM 440V. **Prices:** $600 to $3,000. **Remarks:** Full-time maker, first knife sold in 1992. Photos by Jack Busfield. **Mark:** R. Bose.

BOSE, TONY
7252 N. County Rd, 300 E., Shelburn, IN 47879-9778 **Contact:** 812-397-5114
Specialties: Traditional working and using knives in standard patterns, multi-blade folders. **Patterns:** Multi-blade slip-joints. **Technical:** Grinds commercial damascus, ATS-34 and D2. **Prices:** $400 to $1200. **Remarks:** Full-time maker, first knife sold in 1972. **Mark:** First initial, last name, city, state.

BOSSAERTS, CARL
Rua Albert Einstein 906, Ribeirao Preto, SP, BRAZIL 14051-110 **Contact:** 016 633 7063
Specialties: Working and using straight knives of his design, to customer specs and in standard patterns. **Patterns:** Hunters, fighters and utility/camp knives. **Technical:** Grinds ATS-34, 440V and 440C, does filework. **Prices:** 60 to $400. **Remarks:** Part-time maker, first knife sold in 1992. **Mark:** Initials joined together.

BOST, ROGER E
30511 Cartier Dr, Palos Verdes, CA 90275-5629 **Contact:** 310- 541-6833, rogerbost@cox.net
Specialties: Hunters, fighters, boot, utility. **Patterns:** Loveless-style. **Technical:** ATS-34, BG-42, 440C, 59-61RC, stock removal and forge. **Prices:** $300 and up. **Remarks:** First knife in 1990. Cal. Knifemakers Assn., ABS. **Mark:** Diamond with initials inside and Palos Verdes California around outside.

BOSWORTH, DEAN
329 Mahogany Dr, Key Largo, FL 33037 **Contact:** 305-451-1564, DLBOZ@bellsouth.net
Specialties: Free hand hollow ground working knives with hand rubbed satin finish, filework and inlays. **Patterns:** Bird and Trout, hunters, skinners, fillet, bowies, miniatures. **Technical:** Using 440C, ATS-34, D2, Meier damascus, custom wet formed sheaths. **Prices:** $250 and up. **Remarks:** Part-time maker, first knife made in 1985. Member Florida Knifemakers Assoc. **Mark:** BOZ stamped in block letters.

BOURBEAU, JEAN YVES
15 Rue Remillard, Notre Dame, Ile Perrot, QC, CANADA J7V 8M9 **Contact:** 514-453-1069
Specialties: Fancy/embellished and fantasy folders of his design. **Patterns:** bowies, fighters and locking folders. **Technical:** Grinds 440C, ATS-34 and damascus. Carves precious wood for handles. **Prices:** $150 to $1000. **Remarks:** Part-time maker, first knife sold in 1994. **Mark:** Interlaced initials.

BOYD, FRANCIS
1811 Prince St, Berkeley, CA 94703 **Contact:** 510-841-7210
Specialties: Folders and kitchen knives, Japanese swords. **Patterns:** Push-button sturdy locking folders, San Francisco-style chef's knives. **Technical:** Forges and grinds, mostly uses high-carbon steels. **Prices:** Moderate to heavy. **Remarks:** Designer. **Mark:** Name.

BOYE, DAVID
PO Box 1238, Dolan Springs, AZ 86441 **Contact:** 800-853-1617, (fax) 928-767-

4273, boye@cltlink.net, boyeknives.com
Specialties: Folders and Boye Basics. Forerunner in the use of dendritic steel and dendritic cobalt for blades. **Patterns:** Lockback folders and fixed blade sheath knives in cobalt. **Technical:** Casts blades in cobalt. **Prices:** From $129 to $360. **Remarks:** Part-time maker, author of Step-by-Step Knifemaking. **Mark:** Name.

BOYES, TOM
2505 Wallace Lake Rd., West Bend, WI 53090 **Contact:** 262-391-2172
Specialties: Hunters, skinners and fillets. **Technical:** Grinds ATS-34, 440C, O1 tool steel and damascus. **Prices:** $60 to $1000. **Remarks:** First knife sold in 1998. Doing business as R. Boyes Knives.

BOYSEN, RAYMOND A
125 E St Patrick, Rapid Ciy, SD 57701 **Contact:** 605-341-7752
Specialties: Hunters and bowies. **Technical:** High performance blades forged from 52100 and 5160. **Prices:** $200 and up. **Remarks:** American Bladesmith Society Journeyman Smith. Part-time bladesmith. **Mark:** BOYSEN.

BRACH, PAUL
4870 Widgeon Way, Cumming, GA 30028 **Contact:** 770-595-8952, brachknives.com
Specialties: Standard and one-of-a-kind straight knives and locking folders. Nickel silver sheath fittings and gemstone settings used on high-end pieces. **Patterns:** Hunters, bowies, daggers, antique bowies and titanium-frame folders. **Technical:** Grinds CPM-154 and forges high-carbon steel. Usually flat or full convex grinds. **Prices:** $150 to $1,000+. **Remarks:** Part-time maker, first knife sold in 1984. **Mark:** Etched "Paul Brach maker Cumming, GA" or "Brach" stamped.

BRACKETT, JAMIN
PO Box 387, Fallston, NC 28042 **Contact:** 704-718-3304, jaminbrackett@bellsouth.net, brackettknives.com
Specialties: Hunting, camp, fishing, tactical, and general outdoor use. Handmade of my own design or to customer specs. **Patterns:** Drop point, tanto, fillet, and small EDC the "Tadpole", as well as large camp and tactical knives. **Technical:** CPM154CM. Stock removal method, ATS-34 steel cryogenically treated to HRC 59-61. Mirror polish and bead blasted finishes. Handle materials include exotic woods, stag, buffalo horn, colored laminates, Micarta, and G-10. Some hand stitched 8-9 OZ leather sheaths treated in beeswax saddle oil mixture. Tactical models include reinforced tactical nylon sheaths Mollie system compatible. **Prices:** Standard models $150-$325. Personalized engraving available, for gifts and special occasions. **Remarks:** Part-time maker. First knife made in 2009. Member of NC Custom Knifemakers Guild.**Mark:** "Brackett", in bold. Each knife and sheath numbered.

BRADBURN, GARY
BRADBURN CUSTOM CUTLERY, 1714 Park Place, Wichita, KS 67203 **Contact:** 316-640-5684, gary@bradburnknives.com, bradburnknives.com
Specialties: Specialize in clay-tempered Japanese-style knives and swords. **Patterns:** Also bowies and fighters. **Technical:** Forge and/or grind carbon steel only. **Prices:** $150 to $1200. **Mark:** Initials GB stylized to look like Japanese character.

BRADFORD, GARRICK
582 Guelph St, Kitchener, ON, CANADA N2H-5Y4 **Contact:** 519-576-9863

BRADLEY, DENNIS
178 Bradley Acres Rd, Blairsville, GA 30512 **Contact:** 706-745-4364, dbbrad@windstream.net, dennisbradleyknives.com
Specialties: Working straight knives and folders, some high-art. **Patterns:** Hunters, boots and daggers, slip-joints and two-blades. **Technical:** Grinds CPM 154, CPM S35VN, ATS-34, D2, 440C and commercial damascus. **Prices:** $100 to $500, some to $2000. **Remarks:** Part-time maker, first knife sold in 1973. **Mark:** BRADLEY KNIVES in double heart logo.

BRADLEY, GAYLE
1383 Old Garner Rd., Weatherford, TX 76088-8720 **Contact:** 817-504-2262, bradleysblades@aol.com, bradleysblades.com
Specialties: High-end folders with wedge locks of maker's own design or lock backs, and work/utility knives. Uses high-end materials, including lapidary work and black-lip-pearl handle inlays. **Technical:** Grinds blades from bar stock, performs own heat treating. **Remarks:** Full-time maker, first knife made in 1988.

BRADLEY, JOHN
PO Box 33, Pomona Park, FL 32181 **Contact:** 386-649-4739, johnbradleyknives@yahoo.com
Specialties: Fixed-blade using and art knives, primitive folders. **Patterns:** Skinners, bowies, camp knives and primitive knives. **Technical:** Forged and ground 52100, 1095, O1 and damascus. **Prices:** $250 to $2000. **Remarks:** Full-time maker, first knife sold in 1988. **Mark:** Last name.

BRANDSEY, EDWARD P
4441 Hawkridge Ct, Janesville, WI 53546 **Contact:** 608-868-9010, ebrandsey@centurytel.net
Patterns: Large bowies, hunters, neck knives and buckskinner-styles. Native American influence on some. An occasional tanto, art piece. Does own scrimshaw. See Egnath's second book. Now making locking liner folders. **Technical:** ATS-34, CPM154, 440-C, 0-1 and some damascus. Paul Bos heat treating past 20 years. **Prices:** $350 to $800, some to $4,000. **Remarks:** Full-time maker, first knife sold in 1973. **Mark:** Initials connected.

BRANDT, MARTIN W
833 Kelly Blvd, Springfield, OR 97477 **Contact:** 541-954-2168, oubob747@aol.com
Specialties: Specializing in fur trapper-era knives, Scandanavian knives, and Indigenous knives.

BRANTON, ROBERT
PO BOX 807, Awendaw, SC 29429 **Contact:** 843-928-3624, brantonknives.com
Specialties: Working straight knives of his design or to customer specs, throwing knives. **Patterns:** Hunters, fighters and some miniatures. **Technical:** Grinds ATS-34, A2 and 1050, forges 5160, O1. Offers hollow- or convex-grinds. **Prices:** $25 to $400. **Remarks:** Part-time maker, first knife sold in 1985. Doing business as Pro-Flyte, Inc. **Mark:** Last name, or first and last name, city, state.

BRASCHLER, CRAIG W.
HC2 Box 498, Zalma, MO 63787 **Contact:** 573-495-2203
Specialties: Art knives, bowies, utility hunters, slip joints, miniatures, engraving. **Technical:** Flat grinds. Does own selective heat treating. Does own engraving. **Prices:** Starting at $200. **Remarks:** Full-time maker since 2003. **Mark:** Braschler over Martin Oval stamped.

BRATCHER, BRETT
11816 County Rd 302, Plantersville, TX 77363 **Contact:** 936-894-3788, (fax) (936) 894-3790, brett_bratcher@msn.com
Specialties: Hunting and skinning knives. **Patterns:** Clip and drop point. Hand forged. **Technical:** Material 5160, D2, 1095 and damascus. **Prices:** $200 to $500. **Mark:** Bratcher.

BRAY JR., W LOWELL
6931 Manor Beach Rd, New Port Richey, FL 34652 **Contact:** 727-846-0830, brayknives@aol.com brayknives.com
Specialties: Traditional working and using straight knives and collector pieces. **Patterns:** One of a kind pieces, hunters, fighters and utility knives. **Technical:** Grinds 440C and ATS-34, forges 52100 and damascus. **Prices:** $125 to $800. **Remarks:** Spare-time maker, first knife sold in 1992. **Mark:** Lowell Bray Knives in shield or Bray Primative in shield.

BREDA, BEN
56 Blueberry Hill Rd., Hope, ME 04847 **Contact:** 207-701-7777, bredaknives@gmail.com
Specialties: High-carbon-steel bowies, fighters, hunters chef's knives and LinerLock folders. **Technical:** Forges W2, W1 and 10xx series steels for blades, using natural and stabilized handle materials. **Prices:** Start at $300. **Remarks:** Part-time maker, ABS journeyman smith.

BREED, KIM
733 Jace Dr, Clarksville, TN 37040 **Contact:** 931-980-4956, sfbreed@yahoo.com
Specialties: High end through working folders and straight knives. **Patterns:** Hunters, fighters, daggers, bowies. His design or customers. Likes one-of-a-kind designs. **Technical:** Makes own Mosiac and regular damascus, but will use stainless steels. Offers filework and sculpted material. **Prices:** $150 to $2000. **Remarks:** Full-time maker. First knife sold in 1990. **Mark:** Last name.

BREND, WALTER
415 County Rd. 782, Etowah, TN 37331 **Contact:** 256-736-3520, 256-736-3474 (fax), walterbrend@outlook.com or walter@brendknives.com, brendknives.com
Specialties: Tactical-style knives, fighters, automatics. **Technical:** Grinds D-2 and 440C blade steels, 154CM steel. **Prices:** Micarta and titanium handles.

BRENNAN, JUDSON
PO Box 1165, Delta Junction, AK 99737 **Contact:** 907-895-5153, (fax) 907-895-5404
Specialties: Period pieces. **Patterns:** All kinds of bowies, rifle knives, daggers. **Technical:** Forges miscellaneous steels. **Prices:** Upscale, good value. **Remarks:** Muzzle-loading gunsmith, first knife sold in 1978. **Mark:** Name.

BRENNAN, PATRICK
Brandon, Chapel Hill, Thomastown, Kilkenny, Republic of Ireland **Contact:** 003353868798888, sales@brennanknives.com, www.brennanknives.com, Facebook: Brennan Knives, Instagram: Brennan Knives
Patterns: High-performance knives.

BRESHEARS, CLINT
1261 Keats, Manhattan Beach, CA 90266 **Contact:** 310-372-0739, (fax) 310-372-0739, breshears1@verizon.net, clintknives.com
Specialties: Working straight knives and folders. **Patterns:** Hunters, bowies and survival knives. Folders are mostly hunters. **Technical:** Grinds 440C, 154CM and ATS-34, prefers mirror finishes. **Prices:** $125 to $750, some to $1800. **Remarks:** Part-time maker, first knife sold in 1978. **Mark:** First name.

BREUER, LONNIE
PO Box 877384, Wasilla, AK 99687-7384
Specialties: Fancy working straight knives. **Patterns:** Hunters, camp knives and axes, folders and bowies. **Technical:** Grinds 440C, AEB-L and D2, likes wire inlay, scrimshaw, decorative filing. **Prices:** $60 to $150, some to $300. **Remarks:** Part-time maker, first knife sold in 1977. **Mark:** Signature.

BREWER, CRAIG
425 White Cedar, Killeen, TX 76542 **Contact:** 254-634-6934, craig6@embarqmail.com
Specialties: Folders, slip joints, some lock backs and an occasional liner lock. **Patterns:** I like the old traditional patterns. **Technical:** Grinds CPM steels most being CPM-154, 1095 for carbon and some damascus. **Prices:** $500 and up. **Remarks:** Full-time maker, first knife sold in 2005.**Mark:** BREWER.

BRITTON, TIM
5645 Murray Rd., Winston-Salem, NC 27106 **Contact:** 336-923-2062, tim@

timbritton.com, timbritton.com

Specialties: Small and simple working knives, sgian dubhs, slip joint folders and special tactical designs. **Technical:** Forges and grinds stainless steel. **Prices:** $165 to ???. **Remarks:** Veteran knifemaker. **Mark:** Etched signature.

BROADWELL, DAVID

PO Box 3373, Wichita Falls, TX 76301 **Contact:** 940-782-4442, david@broadwellstudios.com, broadwellstudios.com

Specialties: Sculpted high-art straight and folding knives. **Patterns:** Fighters and sub hilts, daggers, folders, sculpted art knives, and some bowies. **Technical:** Grinds mostly damascus, carves, prefers natural handle materials, including stone. Some embellishment. **Prices:** $700 to $5000, some higher. **Remarks:** Full-time maker since 1989, first knife sold in 1981. **Mark:** Stylized emblem bisecting "B"/with last name below.

BROCK, KENNETH L

PO Box 375, 207 N Skinner Rd, Allenspark, CO 80510 **Contact:** 303-747-2547, brockknives@nedernet.net

Specialties: Custom designs, full-tang working knives and button lock folders of his design. **Patterns:** Hunters, miniatures and minis. **Technical:** Flat-grinds D2 and 440C, makes own sheaths, heat-treats. **Prices:** $75 to $800. **Remarks:** Full-time maker, first knife sold in 1978. **Mark:** Last name, city, state and serial number.

BRODZIAK, DAVID

27 Stewart St, PO Box 1130, Albany, WA, AUSTRALIA 6331 **Contact:** 61 8 9841 3314, brodziak3@bigpond.com, brodziakcustomknives.com

BROMLEY, PETER

BROMLEY KNIVES, 1408 S Bettman, Spokane, WA 99212 **Contact:** 509-534-4235 or 509-710-8365, (fax) 509-536-2666, bromleyknives@q.com

Specialties: Period bowies, folder, hunting knives, all sizes and shapes. **Patterns:** bowies, boot knives, hunters, utility, folder, working knives. **Technical:** High-carbon steel (1084, 1095 and 5160). Stock removal and forge. **Prices:** $85 to $750. **Remarks:** Almost full-time, first knife sold in 1987. A.B.S. Journeyman Smith. **Mark:** Bromley, Spokane, WA.

BROOKER, DENNIS

55858 260th Ave., Chariton, IA 50049 **Contact:** 641-862-3263, dbrooker@dbrooker.com dbrooker.com

Specialties: Fancy straight knives and folders of his design. Obsidian and glass knives. **Patterns:** Hunters, folders and boots. **Technical:** Forges and grinds. Full-time engraver and designer, instruction available. **Prices:** Moderate to upscale. **Remarks:** Part-time maker. Takes no orders, sells only completed work. **Mark:** Name.

BROOKS, BUZZ

2345 Yosemite Dr, Los Angles, CA 90041 **Contact:** 323-256-2892

BROOKS, MICHAEL

2811 64th St, Lubbock, TX 79413 **Contact:** 806-438-3862, chiang@clearwire.net

Specialties: Working straight knives of his design or to customer specs. **Patterns:** Martial art, bowies, hunters, and fighters. **Technical:** Grinds 440C, D2 and ATS-34, offers wide variety of handle materials. **Prices:** $75 & up. **Remarks:** Part-time maker, first knife sold in 1985. **Mark:** Initials.

BROOKS, STEVE R

1610 Dunn Ave, Walkerville, MT 59701 **Contact:** 406-782-5114, (fax) 406-782-5114, steve@brooksmoulds.com, brooksmoulds.com

Specialties: Working straight knives and folders, period pieces. **Patterns:** Hunters, bowies and camp knives, folding lockers, axes, tomahawks and buckskinner knives, swords and stilettos. **Technical:** damascus and mosaic damascus. Some knives come embellished. **Prices:** $400 to $2000. **Remarks:** Full-time maker, first knife sold in 1982. **Mark:** Lazy initials.

BROOME, THOMAS A

1212 E. Aliak Ave, Kenai, AK 99611-8205 **Contact:** 907-283-9128, tomlei@ptialaska.ent, alaskanknives.com

Specialties: Working hunters and folders **Patterns:** Traditional and custom orders. **Technical:** Grinds ATS-34, BG-42, CPM-S30V. **Prices:** $175 to $350. **Remarks:** Full-time maker, first knife sold in 1979. Doing business as Thom's Custom Knives, Alaskan Man O, Steel Knives. **Mark:** Full name, city, state.

BROTHERS, DENNIS L.

2007 Kent Rd., Oneonta, AL 35121 **Contact:** 205-466-3276, blademan@brothersblades.com brothersblades.com

Specialties: Fixed blade hunting/working knives of maker's deigns. Works with customer designed specifications. **Patterns:** Hunters, camp knives, kitchen/utility, bird, and trout. Standard patterns and customer designed. **Technical:** Stock removal. Works with stainless and tool steels. SS cryo-treatment. Hollow and flat grinds. **Prices:** $200 - $400. **Remarks:** Sole authorship knives and customer leather sheaths. Part-time maker. Find on facebook "Brothers Blades by D.L. Brothers" **Mark:** "D.L. Brothers, 4B, Oneonta, AL" on obverse side of blade.

BROUS, JASON

POB 550, Buellton, CA 93427 **Contact:** 805-717-7192, jbrous@live.com or brousblades@outlook.com, brousblades.com

Patterns: Tactical mid-tech folders, production and customized. **Technical:** Stock removal method using D2 steel. **Prices:** $99 - $700. **Remarks:** Started May 2010.

BROUWER, JERRY

Vennewaard 151, 1824 KD, Alkmaar, NETHERLANDS **Contact:** 00-31-618-774146, brouwern1@hotmail.nl, brouwerknives.com

Specialties: Tactical fixed blades with epoxy-soaked Japanese wrapped handles, tactical and outdoor knives with Micarta or G-10 handles, tactical frame-lock folders. Fine, embellished knives for the demanding VIP. **Patterns:** Fixed-blade tantos, drop points, either V-ground or chisel ground, hunting knives, outdoor knives, folders, desk knives, pocket tools. **Technical:** Stock removal, only premium powder metallurgy steels and fine stainless damascus. **Prices:** $100 to $1,000. **Remarks:** Part-time maker, first knife sold in 2010. **Mark:** Laser etched "Brouwer" with a jack-o-lantern logo.

BROWER, MAX

2016 Story St, Boone, IA 50036 **Contact:** 515-432-2938, jmbrower@mchsi.com

Specialties: Hunters. Working/using straight knives. **Patterns:** Hunters. **Technical:** Grinds ATS-34. **Prices:** $300 and up. **Remarks:** Spare-time maker, first knife sold in 1981. **Mark:** Last name.

BROWN, DOUGLAS

1500 Lincolnshire Way, Fort Worth, TX 76134, debrownphotography.com

BROWN, HAROLD E

3654 NW Hwy 72, Arcadia, FL 34266 **Contact:** 863-494-7514, brknives@strato.net

Specialties: Fancy and exotic working knives. **Patterns:** Folders, slip-lock, locking several kinds. **Technical:** Grinds D2 and ATS-34. Embellishment available. **Prices:** $175 to $1000. **Remarks:** Part-time maker, first knife sold in 1976. **Mark:** Name and city with logo.

BROWN, JIM

1097 Fernleigh Cove, Little Rock, AR 72210

BROWN, ROB E

PO Box 15107, Emerald Hill, Port Elizabeth, EC, SOUTH AFRICA 6011 **Contact:** 27-41-3661086, (fax) 27-41-4511731, rbknives@global.co.za

Specialties: Contemporary-designed straight knives and period pieces. **Patterns:** Utility knives, hunters, boots, fighters and daggers. **Technical:** Grinds 440C, D2, ATS-34 and commercial damascus. Knives mostly mirror finished, African handle materials. **Prices:** $100 to $1500. **Remarks:** Full-time maker, first knife sold in 1985. **Mark:** Name and country.

BROWNE, RICK

980 West 13th St, Upland, CA 91786 **Contact:** 909-985-1728

Specialties: Sheffield pattern pocket knives. **Patterns:** Hunters, fighters and daggers. No heavy-duty knives. **Technical:** Grinds ATS-34. **Prices:** Start at $450. **Remarks:** Part-time maker, first knife sold in 1975. **Mark:** R.E. Browne, Upland, CA.

BROWNING, STEVEN W

3400 Harrison Rd, Benton, AR 72015 **Contact:** 501-316-2450

BRUCE, RICHARD L.

13174 Surcease Mine Road, Yankee Hill, CA 95965 **Contact:** 530-532-0880, richardkarenbruce@yahoo.com

Specialties: Working straight knives. Prefers natural handle material, stag bone and woods. Admires the classic straight knife look. **Patterns:** Hunters, Fighters, Fishing Knives. **Technical:** Uses 01, 1095, L6, W2 steel. Stock removal method, flat grind, heat treats and tempers own knives. Builds own sheaths, simple but sturdy. **Prices:** $150-$400. **Remarks:** Sold first knife in 2006, part-time maker. **Mark:** RL Bruce.

BRUNCKHORST, LYLE

COUNTRY VILLAGE, 23706 7th Ave SE Ste B, Bothell, WA 98021 **Contact:** 425-402-3484, bronks@bronksknifeworks.com, bronksknifeworks.com

Specialties: Forges own damascus with 1084 and 15N20, forges 5160, 52100. Grinds CPM 154 CM, ATS-34, S30V. Hosts Biannual Northwest School of Knifemaking and Northwest Hammer In. Offers online and in-house sharpening services and knife sharpeners. Maker of the Double L Hoofknife. Traditional working and using knives, the new patent pending Xross-Bar Lock folders, tomahawks and irridescent RR spike knives. **Patterns:** damascus bowies, hunters, locking folders and featuring the ultra strong locking tactical folding knives. **Prices:** $185 to $1500, some to $3750. **Remarks:** Full-time maker, first knife made in 1976. **Mark:** Bucking horse or bronk.

BRUNER, FRED JR.

BRUNER BLADES, E10910W Hilldale Dr, Fall Creek, WI 54742 **Contact:** 715-225-8017, fredbruner200@gmail.com

Specialties: Tomahawks, pipe tomahawks and period pieces. **Patterns:** Drop point hunters, long knives, French and working knives. **Technical:** Steels used include 1095, 52100, CPM 154 and 5160. **Prices:** $120 to $1,500. **Remarks:** Made knives for Herters into the 1980s. **Mark:** F.C. Bruner Jr.

BUCHANAN, THAD

THAD BUCHANAN CUSTOM KNIVES, 16401 S.W. Ranchview Rd., Powell Butte, OR 97753, buchananblades@gmail.com, buchananblades.com

Specialties: Fixed blades. **Patterns:** Various hunters, trout, bird, utility, boots & fighters, including most Loveless patterns. **Technical:** Stock removal, high polish, variety handle materials. **Prices:** $450 to $2000. **Remarks:** 2005 and 2008 Blade Magazine handmade award for hunter/utility. 2006 Blade West best fixed blade award, 2008 Blade West best hunter/utility. 2010 and 2011 Best Fixed Blade at Plaza Cutlery Show. **Mark:** Thad Buchanan - maker

BUCHANAN, ZAC

168 Chapel Dr., Eugene, OR 97404 **Contact:** 541-815-6706, zacbuchananknives@gmail.com, zacbuchananknives.com

Specialties: R.W. Loveless-style fixed blades. **Technical:** Stock-removal knifemaker using CPM-154 blade steel, 416 stainless steel fittings and pre-ban elephant ivory, mammoth ivory, buffalo horn, stag and Micarta handles. **Prices:** $500 to $2,000. **Remarks:** Full-time maker, first knife sold in 2009. **Mark:** Zac Buchanan Eugene, Oregon.

BUCHARSKY, EMIL

23 Linkside Pl., Spruce Grove, Alberta, CANADA T7X 3C5 **Contact:** 587-341-5066, ebuch@telus.net, ebuchknives.com

Specialties: Fancy working utility hunters and art folders, usually carved with overlays or inlays of damascus, hidden frames and screws. **Patterns:** Folders, hunters, bowies of maker's own design. **Technical:** Forges own damascus using 1095, 1084, 15N20 and nickel, stock-removal steels from Crucible, CPM alloys and UHB Elmax, natural handle materials of pearl, ancient ivory, bone, stabilized woods and others such as carbon fiber, titanium, stainless steel, mokume gane and gemstones. **Prices:** $400 to $1,000, art knives $1,500 and up. **Remarks:** Full-time maker, first knife made in 1989. **Mark:** Name, city and province in oval on fixed blades. Hand-engraved first name, initial and last name with year, in lower case, on folders.

BUCHNER, BILL

PO Box 73, Idleyld Park, OR 97447 **Contact:** 541-498-2247, blazinhammer@earthlink.net, home.earthlin.net/~blazinghammer

Specialties: Working straight knives, kitchen knives and high-art knives of his design. **Technical:** Uses W1, L6 and his own damascus. Invented "spectrum metal" for letter openers, folder handles and jewelry. Likes sculpturing and carving in damascus. **Prices:** $40 to $3000, some higher. **Remarks:** Full-time maker, first knife sold in 1978. **Mark:** Signature.

BUCKNER, TOM

5539 Meadowood Ln. NE, Olympia, WA 98502 **Contact:** 360-970-1668, tbuckner1967@gmail.com, bucknerknives.com

Specialties: Kitchen knives with custom wooden sayas (sheaths) and folding knives. **Patterns:** Chef's, Santoku, boning, paring and folding knives fashioned using various types of material, all with titanium liners. **Technical:** Blade steels include CPM 154, CPM S30V, CPM S35VN, AEB-L, stainless damascus and high-carbon damascus. Maker heat treats and cryogenically heats and quenches all the listed steels. **Prices:** $200 to $2,000. **Mark:** Tom Buckner Maker Olympia, WA.

BRYSON, DAVID

PO Box 106, Jarrell, TX 76537 **Contact:** 512-818-0516, dcbryson33@gmail.com **Remarks:** Founding member and Lone Star Member of the Texas Knife Makers Guild.

BUDELL, MICHAEL

3733 Wieghat Ln., Brenham, TX 77833 **Contact:** 979-836-3148, mbbudell@att.net **Specialties:** Slip Joint Folders. **Technical:** Grinds 01, 440C. File work springs, blades and liners. Natural material scales giraffe, mastadon ivory, elephant ivory, and jigged bone. **Prices:** $175 - $350. **Remarks:** Part-time maker, first knife sold 2006. **Mark:** XA

BUEBENDORF, ROBERT E

108 Lazybrooke Rd, Monroe, CT 06468 **Contact:** 203-452-1769 **Specialties:** Traditional and fancy straight knives of his design. **Patterns:** Hand-makes and embellishes belt buckle knives. **Technical:** Forges and grinds 440C, O1, W2, 1095, his own damascus and 154CM. **Prices:** $200 to $500. **Remarks:** Full-time maker, first knife sold in 1978. **Mark:** First and middle initials, last name and MAKER.

BULLARD, BENONI

4416 Jackson 4, Bradford, AR 72020 **Contact:** 501-344-2672, benandbren@earthlink.net **Specialties:** bowies and hunters. **Patterns:** Camp knives, bowies, hunters, slip joints, folders, lock blades, miniatures, Hawks Tech. **Technical:** Makes own damascus. Forges 5160, 1085, 15 N 20. Favorite is 5160. **Prices:** $150 - $1500. **Remarks:** Part-time maker. Sold first knife in 2006. **Mark:** Benoni with a star over the letter i.

BULLARD, RANDALL

7 Mesa Dr., Canyon, TX 79015 **Contact:** 806-655-0590 **Specialties:** Working/using straight knives and folders of his design or to customer specs. **Patterns:** Hunters, locking folders and slip-joint folders. **Technical:** Grinds O1, ATS-34 and 440C. Does file work. **Prices:** $125 to $300, some to $500. **Remarks:** Part-time maker, first knife sold in 1993. Doing business as Bullard Custom Knives. **Mark:** First and middle initials, last name, maker, city and state.

BULLARD, TOM

117 MC 8068, Flippin, AR 72634 **Contact:** 870-656-3428, tbullard8@live.com **Specialties:** Traditional folders and hunters. **Patterns:** bowies, hunters, single and 2-blade trappers, lockback folders. **Technical:** Grinds 440C, A2, D2, ATS-34 and O1. **Prices:** $175 and up. **Remarks:** Offers filework and engraving by Norvell Foster and Terry Thies. Does not make screw-together knives. **Mark:** T Bullard.

BUMP, BRUCE D.

1103 Rex Ln, Walla Walla, WA 99362 **Contact:** 509-386-8879, brucebump1@gmail.com, brucebumpknives.com

Specialties: Slip joints, bowies and muzzle-loading pistol-knife combinations. **Patterns:** Maker's own damascus patterns including double mosaics. **Technical:** One-of-a-kind pieces. **Prices:** Please email for prices. **Remarks:** Full-time maker, ABS master smith since 2003. **Mark:** Bruce D. Bump "Custom", Bruce D. Bump "MS".

BURDEN, JAMES

405 Kelly St, Burkburnett, TX 76354

BURGER, FRED

Box 436, Munster, KZN, SOUTH AFRICA 4278 **Contact:** 27 82 9265785, info@swordcane.com, swordcane.com

Specialties: Quality sword canes, custom canes and range of hiking staffs. **Patterns:** 440C and damascus blades. **Technical:** Double hollow ground and Poniard-style blades. **Prices:** $550 to $3000. **Remarks:** Full-time maker with son, Barry, since 1987. Member South African Guild. **Mark:** Last name in oval pierced by a dagger.

BURGER, PON

12 Glenwood Ave, Woodlands, Bulawayo, ZIMBABWE 75514 **Specialties:** Collector's items. **Patterns:** Fighters, locking folders of traditional styles, buckles. **Technical:** Scrimshaws 440C blade. Uses polished buffalo horn with brass fittings. Cased in buffalo hide book. **Prices:** $450 to $1100. **Remarks:** Full-time maker, first knife sold in 1973. Doing business as Burger Products. **Mark:** Spirit of Africa.

BURGER, TIAAN

69 Annie Botha Ave, Riviera,, Pretoria, GT, SOUTH AFRICA, tiaan_burger@hotmail.com **Specialties:** Sliplock and multi-blade folder. **Technical:** High carbon or stainless with African handle materials **Remarks:** Occasional fixed blade knives.

BURKE, BILL

20 Adams Ranch Rd., Boise, ID 83716 **Contact:** 208-336-3792, billburke@bladegallery.com

Specialties: Hand-forged working knives. **Patterns:** Fowler pronghorn, clip point and drop point hunters. **Technical:** Forges 52100 and 5160. Makes own damascus from 15N20 and 1084. **Prices:** $450 and up. **Remarks:** Dedicated to fixed-blade high-performance knives. ABS Journeyman. Also makes "Ed Fowler" miniatures. **Mark:** Initials connected.

BURNLEY, LUCAS

1005 La Font Rd. SW, Albuquerque, NM 87105 **Contact:** 505-814-9964, burnleyknives@comcast.net, burnleyknives.com

Specialties: Contemporary tactical fixed blade, and folder designs, some art knives. **Patterns:** Hybrids, neo Japanese, defensive, utility and field knives. **Technical:** Grinds CPM154, A2, D2, BG42, Stainless damascus as well as titanium and aerospace composites. **Prices:** Most models $225 to $1,500. Some specialty pieces higher. **Remarks:** Full-time maker, first knife sold in 2003. **Mark:** Last name or BRNLY.

BURNS, ROBERT

104 W. 6th St., Carver, MN 55315 **Contact:** 412-477-4677, wildernessironworks@gmail.com, wildernessironworks.org

Specialties: Utility knives, fighters, axes, pattern-welded axes and Viking swords. **Technical:** Trained as a blacksmith in Colonial style, forges 1095, 1090, 1084, 15N20, 5160, W1, W2, D2, 440C and wrought iron. **Prices:** $135 to $3,000-plus. **Remarks:** Full-time maker, first knife made in 2005. **Mark:** A compass rose with all of the cardinal directions, and underneath, in cursive, "Wilderness Ironworks."

BURRIS, PATRICK R

1263 Cty. Rd. 750, Athens, TN 37303 **Contact:** 423-336-5715, burrispr@gmail.com **Specialties:** Traditional straight knives and locking-liner folders. **Patterns:** Hunters, bowies, locking-liner folders. **Technical:** Flat grinds high-grade stainless and damascus. **Remarks:** Offers filework, embellishment, exotic materials and damascus **Mark:** Last name in script.

BURROWS, CHUCK

WILD ROSE TRADING CO, 289 La Posta Canyon Rd, Durango, CO 81303 **Contact:** 970-259-8396, chuck@wrtcleather.com, wrtcleather.com

Specialties: Presentation knives, hawks, and sheaths based on the styles of the American frontier incorporating carving, beadwork, rawhide, braintan, and other period correct materials. Also makes other period style knives such as Scottish Dirks and Moorish jambiyahs. **Patterns:** bowies, Dags, tomahawks, war clubs, and all other 18th and 19th century frontier style edged weapons and tools. **Technical:** Carbon steel only: 5160, 1080/1084, 1095, O1, damascus-Our Frontier Shear Steel, plus other styles available on request. Forged knives, hawks, etc. are made in collaborations with bladesmiths. Gib Guignard (under the name of Cactus Rose) and Mark Williams (under the name UB Forged). Blades are usually forge finished and all items are given an aged period look. **Prices:** $500 plus. **Remarks:** Full-time maker, first knife sold in 1973. 40+ years experience working leather. **Mark:** A lazy eight or lazy eight with a capital T at the center. On leather either the lazy eight with T or a WRTC makers stamp.

BURROWS, STEPHEN R

1020 Osage St, Humboldt, KS 66748 **Contact:** 816-921-1573 **Specialties:** Fantasy straight knives of his design, to customer specs and in standard patterns, period pieces. **Patterns:** Fantasy, bird and trout knives, daggers, fighters and hunters. **Technical:** Forges 5160 and 1095 high-carbon steel, O1 and his damascus. Offers lost wax casting in bronze or silver of cross guards and pommels. **Prices:** $65 to $600, some to $2000. **Remarks:** Full-time maker, first knife sold in 1983. Doing business as Gypsy Silk. **Mark:** Etched name.

BUSBIE, JEFF

John 316 Knife Works, 170 Towles Rd., Bloomingdale, GA 31302 **Contact:** 912-656-8238, jbusbie@comcast.net, john316knifeworks.com

Specialties: Working full-tang and hidden-tang fixed blades, locking-liner folders and hard-use knives. **Patterns:** bowies, skinners, fighters, neck knives, work knives, bird knives, swords, art knives and other creations. **Technical:** Stock-removal maker using Alabama damascus, CPM stainless steels and D2. Handles from hardwoods, G-10, ivory, bone and exotic materials. **Prices:** $100 to $800 and up. **Remarks:** Part-time maker building 150 to 200 knives a year, first knife sold in 2008. **Mark:** john 316 knife works with a cross in the middle.

BUSCH, STEVE

1989 Old Town Loop, Oakland, OR 97462 **Contact:** 541-459-2833, steve@buschcustomknives.com, buschcustomknives.blademakers.com

Specialties: D/A automatic right and left handed, folders, fixed blade working mainly in damascus file work, functional art knives, nitrate bluing, heat bluing most all scale materials. **Prices:** $150 to $2000. **Remarks:** Trained under Vallotton family 3 1/2 years on own since 2002. **Mark:** Signature and date of completion on all knives.

BUSFIELD, JOHN
153 Devonshire Circle, Roanoke Rapids, NC 27870 **Contact:** 252-537-3949, (fax) 252-537-8704, busfield@charter.net
Specialties: Investor-grade folders, high-grade working straight knives. **Patterns:** Original price-style and trailing-point interframe and sculpted-frame folders, drop-point hunters and semi-skinners. **Technical:** Grinds 154CM and ATS-34. Offers interframes, gold frames and inlays, uses jade, agate and lapis. **Prices:** $275 to $2000. **Remarks:** Full-time maker, first knife sold in 1979. **Mark:** Last name and address.

BUSSE, JERRY
11651 Co Rd 12, Wauseon, OH 43567 **Contact:** 419-923-6471
Specialties: Working straight knives. **Patterns:** Heavy combat knives and camp knives. **Technical:** Grinds D2, A2, INFI. **Prices:** $1100 to $3500. **Remarks:** Full-time maker, first knife sold in 1983. **Mark:** Last name in logo.

BUTLER, BART
822 Seventh St, Ramona, CA 92065 **Contact:** 760-789-6431

BUTLER, JOHN
777 Tyre Rd, Havana, FL 32333 **Contact:** 850-539-5742
Specialties: Hunters, bowies, period. **Technical:** damascus, 52100, 5160, L6 steels. **Prices:** $80 and up. **Remarks:** Making knives since 1986. Journeyman (ABS). **Mark:** JB.

BUTLER, JOHN R
20162 6th Ave N E, Shoreline, WA 98155 **Contact:** 206-362-3847, rjjjrb@sprynet.com

BUXTON, BILL
155 Oak Bend Rd, Kaiser, MO 65047 **Contact:** 573-348-3577, camper@yhti.net, billbuxtonknives.com
Specialties: Forged fancy and working straight knives and folders. Mostly one-of-a-kind pieces. **Patterns:** Fighters, daggers, bowies, hunters, linerlock folders, axes and tomahawks. **Technical:** Forges 52100, 0-1, 1080. Makes own damascus (mosaic and random patterns) from 1080, 1095, 15n20, and powdered metals 1084 and 4800a. Offers sterling silver inlay, n/s pin patterning and pewter pouring on axe and hawk handles. **Prices:** $300 to $2,500. **Remarks:** Full-time maker, sold first knife in 1998. **Mark:** First initial and last name.

BUZEK, STANLEY
PO Box 621, Caldwell TX 77836 **Contact:** 346-412-2532, stan@sbuzekknives.com, sbuzekknives.com
Specialties: Traditional slip-joint pocketknives, LinerLocks and frame-lock folders, and fixed-blade hunters and skinners. **Technical:** Grinds, heat treats and Rockwell tests CPM-154, and some traditional folders in O1 tool steel. Hand-rubbed finishes. Dyed jigged bone, mammoth ivory and fine stabilized woods. **Prices:** $250 and up. **Remarks:** Serious part-time maker, first knife sold in 2006. **Mark:** S. Buzek on riccasso.

BYBEE, BARRY J
795 Lock Rd. E, Cadiz, KY 42211-8615
Specialties: Working straight knives of his design. **Patterns:** Hunters, fighters, boot knives, tantos and bowies. **Technical:** Grinds ATS-34, 440C. Likes stag and Micarta for handle materials. **Prices:** $125 to $200, some to $1000. **Remarks:** Part-time maker, first knife sold in 1968. **Mark:** Arrowhead logo with name, city and state.

BYRD, WESLEY L
189 Countryside Dr, Evensville, TN 37332 **Contact:** 423-775-3826, w.l.byrd@worldnet.att.net
Specialties: Hunters, fighters, bowies, dirks, sgian dubh, utility, and camp knives. **Patterns:** Wire rope, random patterns. Twists, W's, Ladder, Kite Tail. **Technical:** Uses 52100, 1084, 5160, L6, and 15n20. **Prices:** Starting at $180. **Remarks:** Prefer to work with customer for their design preferences. ABS Journeyman Smith. **Mark:** BYRD, WB <X.

C

CABRERA, SERGIO B
24500 Broad Ave, Wilmington, CA 90744

CAFFREY, EDWARD J
2608 Central Ave West, Great Falls, MT 59404 **Contact:** 406-727-9102, caffreyknives@gmail.com, caffreyknives.net
Specialties: One-of-a-kind using and collector quality pieces. Will accept some customer designs. **Patterns:** bowies, folders, hunters, fighters, camp/utility, tomahawks and hatchets. **Technical:** Forges all types of damascus, specializing in Mosaic damascus, 52100, 5160, 1080/1084 and most other commonly forged steels. **Prices:** Starting at $185, typical hunters start at $400, collector pieces can range into the thousands. **Remarks:** Offers one-on-one basic and advanced bladesmithing classes. ABS Mastersmith. Full-time maker. **Mark:** Stamped last name and MS on straight knives. Etched last name with MS on folders.

CALDWELL, BILL
255 Rebecca, West Monroe, LA 71292 **Contact:** 318-323-3025
Specialties: Straight knives and folders with machined bolsters and liners. **Patterns:** Fighters, bowies, survival knives, tomahawks, razors and push knives. **Technical:** Owns and operates a very large, well-equipped blacksmith and bladesmith shop with six large forges and eight power hammers. **Prices:** $400 to $3500, some to $10,000. **Remarks:** Full-time maker and self-styled blacksmith, first knife sold in 1962. **Mark:** Wild Bill and Sons.

CALLAHAN, F TERRY
PO Box 880, Boerne, TX 78006 **Contact:** 210-260-2378, ftclaw@gvtc.com
Specialties: Custom hand-forged edged knives, collectible and functional. **Patterns:** bowies, folders, daggers, hunters & camp knives . **Technical:** Forges damascus and 5160. Offers filework, silver inlay and handmade sheaths. **Prices:** $150 to $500. **Remarks:** First knife sold in 1990. ABS/Journeyman Bladesmith. **Mark:** Initial "F" inside a keystone.

CALVERT JR., ROBERT W (BOB)
911 Julia, Rayville, LA 71269 **Contact:** 318-348-4490, rcalvert1@gmail.com
Specialties: Using and hunting knives, your design or his. Since 1990. **Patterns:** Forges own damascus, all patterns. **Technical:** 5160, D2, 52100, 1084. Prefers natural handle material. **Prices:** $250 and up. **Remarks:** TOMB Member, ABS. Journeyman Smith. ABS Board of directors **Mark:** Calvert (Block) J S.

CAMBRON, HENRY
169 Severn Way, Dallas, GA 30132-0317 **Contact:** 770-598-5721, worldclassknives@bellsouth.net, worldclassknives.com
Specialties: Everyday carry, working and small neck knives. **Patterns:** Hunters, bowies, camp, utility and combat. **Technical:** Forge and stock removal, filework, and I do the heat treatment on all my high carbon blades. No folders at this time. **Prices:** $95 and up **Remarks:** Full-time maker, member Georgia Custom Knifemakers' Guild **Mark:** First and last name over USA on blades. HC on sheaths.

CAMERER, CRAIG
3766 Rockbridge Rd, Chesterfield, IL 62630 **Contact:** 618-753-2147, craig@camererknives.com, camererknives.com
Specialties: Everyday carry knives, hunters and bowies. **Patterns:** D-guard, historical recreations and fighters. **Technical:** Most of his knives are forged to shape. **Prices:** $100 and up. **Remarks:** Member of the ABS and PKA. Journeymen Smith ABS.

CAMERON, RON G
PO Box 183, Logandale, NV 89021 **Contact:** 702-398-3356, rntcameron@mvdsl.com
Specialties: Fancy and embellished working/using straight knives and folders of his design. **Patterns:** bowies, hunters and utility/camp knives. **Technical:** Grinds ATS-34, AEB-L and Devin Thomas damascus or own damascus from 1084 and 15N20. Does filework, fancy pins, mokume fittings. Uses exotic hardwoods, stag and Micarta for handles. Pearl & mammoth ivory. **Prices:** $175 to $850 some to $1000. **Remarks:** Part-time maker, first knife sold in 1994. Doing business as Cameron Handmade Knives. **Mark:** Last name, town, state or last name.

CAMPBELL, DICK (R.C.)
196 Graham Rd, Colville, WA 99114 **Contact:** 509-684-6080, dicksknives@aol.com
Specialties: Working straight knives, folders and period pieces. **Patterns:** Hunters, fighters, boots and 19th century bowies. **Technical:** Grinds 440C and 154CM. **Prices:** $350 to $4,500. **Remarks:** Full-time maker. First knife sold in 1975. **Mark:** Initials. Previous: Name.

CAMPBELL, DOUG
46 W Boulder Rd., McLeod, MT 59052 **Contact:** 406-222-8153, dkcampbl@yahoo.com
Specialties: Sole authorship of fixed blades and folding knives. **Patterns:** Fixed blades, LinerLocks and frame-lock folders. **Technical:** Forged high-carbon, pattern-welded damascus, Elmax and CPM 154 steels. **Prices:** $300-$1,300. **Remarks:** ABS journeyman smith. **Mark:** Grizzly track surrounded by a "C," or "Campbell" etched on spine.

CAMPOS, IVAN
R. Stelio M. Loureiro, 206, Tatuí, SP, Brazil, 18270-810 **Contact:** 55-15-997120993, (fax) 00-55-15-2594368, ivan@ivancampos.net, ivancampos.net
Specialties: carbon steel and damascus kitchen knives. **Price:** $100 to $1,000 USD **Remarks:** making knives since 2000 **Mark:** "IC" in box, year and steel type

CANDRELLA, JOE
1219 Barness Dr, Warminster, PA 18974 **Contact:** 215-675-0143
Specialties: Working straight knives, some fancy. **Patterns:** Daggers, boots, bowies. **Technical:** Grinds 440C and 154CM. **Prices:** $100 to $200, some to $1000. **Remarks:** Part-time maker, first knife sold in 1985. Does business as Franjo. **Mark:** FRANJO with knife as J.

CANTER, RONALD E
96 Bon Air Circle, Jackson, TN 38305 **Contact:** 731-668-1780, canterr@charter.net
Specialties: Traditional working knives to customer specs. **Patterns:** Beavertail skinners, bowies, hand axes and folding lockers. **Technical:** Grinds 440C, Micarta & deer antler. **Prices:** $75 and up. **Remarks:** Spare-time maker, first knife sold in 1973. **Mark:** Three last initials intertwined.

CANTRELL, KITTY D
19720 Hwy 78, Ramona, CA 92076 **Contact:** 760-788-8304

CAPDEPON, RANDY
553 Joli Rd, Carencro, LA 70520 **Contact:** 318-896-4113, (fax) 318-896-8753
Specialties: Straight knives and folders of his design. **Patterns:** Hunters and locking folders. **Technical:** Grinds ATS-34, 440C and D2. **Prices:** $200 to $600. **Remarks:** Part-time maker, first knife made in 1992. Doing business as Capdepon Knives. **Mark:** Last

CAPDEPON, ROBERT
829 Vatican Rd, Carencro, LA 70520 **Contact:** 337-896-8753, (fax) 318-896-8753
Specialties: Traditional straight knives and folders of his design. **Patterns:** Boots, hunters and locking folders. **Technical:** Grinds ATS-34, 440C and D2. Hand-rubbed finish on blades. Likes natural horn materials for handles, including ivory. Offers engraving. **Prices:**

$250 to $750. **Remarks:** Full-time maker, first knife made in 1992. **Mark:** Last name.

CAREY, PETER
P.O. Box 4712, Lago Vista, TX 78645 **Contact:** 512-358-4839, careyblade.com
Specialties: Tactical folders, Every Day Carry to presentation grade. Working straight knives, hunters, and tactical. **Patterns:** High-tech patterns of his own design, Linerlocks, Framelocks, Flippers. **Technical:** Hollow grinds CPM154, CPM S35VN, stainless damascus, Stellite. Uses titanium, zirconium, carbon fiber, G10, and select natural handle materials. **Prices:** Starting at $450. **Remarks:** Full-time maker, first knife sold in 2002. **Mark:** Last name in diamond.

CARLISLE, JEFF
PO Box 282 12753 Hwy 200, Simms, MT 59477 **Contact:** 406-264-5693

CARPENTER, RONALD W
Rt. 4 Box 323, Jasper, TX 75951 **Contact:** 409-384-4087

CARR, JOSEPH E.
W183 N8974 Maryhill Drive, Menomonee Falls, WI 53051 **Contact:** 262-253-1374, carsmith1@SBCGlobal.net
Specialties: JC knives. **Patterns:** Hunters, bowies, fighting knives, every day carries. **Technical:** Grinds ATS-34 and damascus. **Prices:** $200 to $750. **Remarks:** Full-time maker for 2 years, being taught by Ron Hembrook.

CARR, TIM
3660 Pillon Rd, Muskegon, MI 49445 **Contact:** 231-766-3582, tim@blackbearforgemi.com, blackbearforgemi.com
Specialties: Hunters, camp knives. **Patterns:** His or yours. **Technical:** Hand forges 5160, 52100 and damascus. **Prices:** $125 to $700. **Remarks:** Part-time maker. **Mark:** The letter combined from maker's initials TRC.

CARRILLO, DWAINE
C/O AIRKAT KNIVES **Contact:** 405-503-5879, tripwire7@cox.net, airkatknives.com

CARROLL, CHAD
12182 McClelland, Grant, MI 49327 **Contact:** 231-834-9183, CHAD724@msn.com
Specialties: Hunters, bowies, folders, swords, tomahawks. **Patterns:** Fixed blades, folders. **Prices:** $100 to $2000. **Remarks:** ABS Journeyman May 2002. **Mark:** A backwards C next to a forward C, maker's initials.

CARTER, FRED
5219 Deer Creek Rd, Wichita Falls, TX 76302 **Contact:** 904-723-4020, fcarter40@live.com
Specialties: High-art investor-class straight knives, some working hunters and fighters. **Patterns:** Classic daggers, bowies, interframe, stainless and blued steel folders with gold inlay. **Technical:** Grinds a variety of steels. Uses no glue or solder. Engraves and inlays. **Prices:** Generally upscale. **Remarks:** Full-time maker. **Mark:** Signature in oval logo.

CARTER, MIKE
2522 Frankfort Ave, Louisville, KY 40206 **Contact:** 502-387-4844, mike@cartercrafts.com cartercrafts.com
Remarks: Voting Member Knifemakers Guild.

CARTER, MURRAY M
2038 N.E. Aloclek Dr. #225, Hillsboro, OR 97124 **Contact:** 503-466-1331, murray@cartercutlery.com, cartercutlery.com
Specialties: Traditional Japanese kitchen knives, utilizing San soh ko (three layer) or Kata-ha (two layer) blade construction. Laminated neck knives, traditional Japanese etc. **Patterns:** Works from over 200 standard Japanese and North American designs. **Technical:** Hot forges and cold forges Hitachi white steel #1, Hitachi blue super steel exclusively. **Prices:** $400 to $4,000. **Remarks:** Owns and operates North America's most exclusive traditional Japanese bladesmithing school and Apprentice Program, web site available at which viewers can subscribe to 10 free knife sharpening and maintenance reports. **Mark:** Name in cursive, often appearing with Japanese characters. **Other:** Offers the world's finest video instruction on sharpening.

CARTER, SHAYNE
5302 Rosewood Cir., Payson, UT 84651 **Contact:** 801-913-0181, shaynemcarter@hotmail.com
Specialties: Fixed blades. **Patterns:** Hunters, bowies and fighters. **Technical:** Flat grinds, hand finishes, forges blade steel, including own damascus, some 1084, 52100 and 5160. **Remarks:** Part-time maker, first damascus made in 1984.

CASEY, KEVIN
4 Broken Arrow Rd., Lander, WY 82520 **Contact:** 269-719-7412, kevinvecasey@gmail.com, kevincaseycustomknives.com, Instagram @kcaseyknives
Specialties: forges feather pattern damascus steel for fixed blades and folders **Patterns:** forges damascus and carbon steel. **Technical:** Forges damascus and carbon steels. **Prices:** Starting at $450. **Remarks:** dedicated to feather damascus steel **Mark:** KCaseyKnives

CASHEN, KEVIN R
Matherton Forge, 5615 Tyler St., Hubbardston, MI 48845 **Contact:** 989-981-6780, kevin@cashenblades.com, cashenblades.com
Specialties: User-oriented straight knives and medieval and renaissance period European swords and daggers. **Patterns:** Hunters and skinners, bowies and camp knives, swords and daggers. **Technical:** Hand forged blades of O1, L6 and maker's own O1-L6-and-O2 damascus, occasionally W2 or 1095, or bloomery steel which he smelts himself from raw ore, all heat-treated to exacting metallurgical standards. **Prices:** $300 for small hunters to $10,000+ for museum-quality swords, with an average range of $400-$2,000.

Remarks: Full-time maker, instructor/speaker/consultant; first knife sold in 1985. **Mark:** Gothic "K.C." with master smith stamp. On period pieces, a crowned castle encircled with "Cashen."

CASTEEL, DIANNA
PO Box 63, Monteagle, TN 37356 **Contact:** 931-212-4341, ddcasteel@charter.net, casteelcustomknives.com
Specialties: Small, delicate daggers and miniatures, most knives one-of-a-kind. **Patterns:** Daggers, boot knives, fighters and miniatures. **Technical:** Grinds 440C. Offers stainless damascus. **Prices:** Start at $350, miniatures start at $250. **Remarks:** Full-time maker. **Mark:** Di in script.

CASTELLUCIO, RICH
220 Stairs Rd, Amsterdam, NY 12010 **Contact:** 518-843-5540, rcastellucio@nycap.rr.com
Patterns: bowies, push daggers, and fantasy knives. **Technical:** Uses ATS-34, 440C, 154CM. I use stabilized wood, bone for the handles. Guards are made of copper, brass, stainless, nickle, and mokume.

CASTON, DARRIEL
125 Ashcat Way, Folsom, CA 95630 **Contact:** 916-539-0744, darrielc@gmail.com

CASWELL, JOE
173 S Ventu Park Rd, Newbury, CA 91320 **Contact:** 805-499-0707, caswellknives.com
Specialties: Historic pattern welded knives and swords, hand forged. Also high precision folding and fixed blade "gentleman" and "tactical" knives of his design, period firearms. Inventor of the "In-Line" retractable pocket clip for folding knives. **Patterns:** Hunters, tactical/utility, fighters, bowies, daggers, pattern welded medieval swords, precision folders. **Technical:** Forges own damascus especially historic forms. Sometimes uses modern stainless steels and damascus of other makers. Makes some pieces entirely by hand, others using the latest CNC techniques and by hand. Makes sheaths too.**Prices:** $100-$5,500. **Remarks:** Full time makers since 1995. Making mostly historic recreations for exclusive clientele. Recently moving into folding knives and 'modern' designs. **Mark:** CASWELL or CASWELL USA Accompanied by a mounted knight logo.

CATOE, DAVID R
4024 Heutte Dr, Norfolk, VA 23518 **Contact:** 757-480-3191
Technical: Does own forging, damascus and heat treatments. **Prices:** $200 to $500, some higher. **Remarks:** Part-time maker, trained by Dan Maragni 1985-1988, first knife sold 1989. **Mark:** Leaf of a camellia.

CECCHINI, GUSTAVO T.
2841 XV Novembro, Sao Jose Rio Preto SP, BRAZIL 15015110 **Contact:** +55 17 997725457, tomaki@terra.com.br, gtcknives.com
Specialties: Tactical and HiTech folders. **Technical:** Stock removal. Stainless steel fixed blades. S30V, S35Vn, S90V, CowryX, Damasteel, Chad Nichols SS damascus, RWL 34, CPM 154 CM, BG 42. **Prices:** $500 - $1500. **Remarks:** Full-time since 2004. **Mark:** Tang Stamp "GTC"

CEPRANO, PETER J.
213 Townsend Brooke Rd., Auburn, ME 04210 **Contact:** 207-786-5322, bpknives@gmail.com
Specialties: Traditional working/using straight knives, tactical/defense straight knives. Own designs or to a customer's specs. **Patterns:** Hunters, skinners, utility, bowies, fighters, camp and survival, neck knives. **Technical:** Forges 1095, 5160, W2, 52100 and old files, grinds CPM154cm, ATS-34, 440C, D2, CPMs30v, damascus from other makes and other tool steels. Hand-sewn and tooled leather and Kydex sheaths. **Prices:** Starting at $125. **Remarks:** Full-time maker, first knife sold in 2001. Doing business as Big Pete Knives. **Mark:** Bold BPK over small BigPeteKnivesUSA.

CHAFFEE, JEFF L
14314 N. Washington St, PO Box 1, Morris, IN 47033 **Contact:** 812-212-6188
Specialties: Fancy working and utility folders and straight knives. **Patterns:** Fighters, dagger, hunter and locking folders. **Technical:** Grinds commercial damascus, 440C, ATS-34, D2 and O1. Prefers natural handle materials. **Prices:** $350 to $2000. **Remarks:** Part-time maker, first knife sold in 1988. **Mark:** Last name.

CHAMBERLAIN, JON A
15 S. Lombard, E. Wenatchee, WA 98802 **Contact:** 509-884-6591
Specialties: Working and kitchen knives to customer specs, exotics on special order. **Patterns:** Over 100 patterns in stock. **Technical:** Prefers ATS-34, D2, L6 and damascus. **Prices:** Start at $50. **Remarks:** First knife sold in 1986. Doing business as Johnny Custom Knifemakers. **Mark:** Name in oval with city and state enclosing.

CHAMBERLIN, JOHN A
11535 Our Rd., Anchorage, AK 99516 **Contact:** 907-346-1524, (fax) 907-562-4583
Specialties: Art and working knives. **Patterns:** Daggers and hunters, some folders,. **Technical:** Grinds ATS-34, 440C, A2, D2 and damascus. Uses Alaskan handle materials such as oosic, jade, whale jawbone, fossil ivory. **Prices:** Start at $200. **Remarks:** Favorite knives to make are double-edged. Does own heat treating and cryogenic deep freeze. Full-time maker, first knife sold in 1984. **Mark:** Name over English shield and dagger.

CHAMBERS, GRANT
Ottawa, Ontario, CANADA **Contact:** doctorviggen@gmail.com, knifechambers.com, Instagram: Doctorviggen
Specialties: Carved and engraved collectible art knives, tactical and fancy folding knives. Leather sheath inlays. **Patterns:** Sub-hilt fighters, bowies, daggers, Persians and some Japanese-style knives. **Technical:** Stock removal, precious metal inlays. Prefers natural materials. Engraving, heat treating, leather work, etc., all by maker.

Prices: $500 and above. **Remarks:** Goldsmith by profession, knifemaker by passion. Knives meticulously detailed from top to bottom, aimed at the collector or an heirloom to be passed down the family. **Mark:** Gold, rose gold or silver medallion with hand engraved "G.C.".

CHAMBERS, RONNY
1900 W. Mississippi St., Beebe, AR 72012 **Contact:** 501-288-1476, chambersronny@yahoo.com, chamberscustomknives.net

CHAMBLIN, JOEL
960 New Hebron Church Rd, Concord, GA 30206 **Contact:** 678-588-6769, chamblinknives@yahoo.com, chamblinknives.com
Specialties: Fancy and working folders. **Patterns:** Fancy locking folders, traditional, multi-blades and utility. **Technical:** Uses ATS-34, CPM 154, and commercial damascus. Offers filework. **Prices:** Start at $400. **Remarks:** Full-time maker, first knife sold in 1989. **Mark:** Last name.

CHAMPION, ROBERT
7001 Red Rock Rd., Amarillo, TX 79118 **Contact:** 806-622-3970, rchampknives@gmail.com, rchampknives.com
Specialties: folders, automatics, fixed blades. **Patterns:** Hunters, skinners, camp knives, bowies and daggers. **Technical:** Stock removal using a variety of stainless steels, carbon and stainless damascus. **Prices:** $200 to $2,000. **Remarks:** Full-time maker; first knife sold in 1979. **Mark:** Last name with dagger logo, city and state.

CHAPO, WILLIAM G
45 Wildridge Rd, Wilton, CT 06897 **Contact:** 203-544-9424
Specialties: Classic straight knives and folders of his design and to customer specs, period pieces. **Patterns:** Boots, bowies and locking folders. **Technical:** Forges stainless damascus. Offers filework. **Prices:** $750 and up. **Remarks:** Full-time maker, first knife sold in 1989. **Mark:** First and middle initials, last name, city, state.

CHARD, GORDON R
104 S. Holiday Lane, Iola, KS 66749 **Contact:** 620-365-2311, (fax) 620-365-2311, gchard@cox.net
Specialties: High tech folding knives in one-of-a-kind styles. **Patterns:** Liner locking folders of own design. Also fixed blade Art Knives. **Technical:** Clean work with attention to fit and finish. Blade steel mostly ATS-34 and 154CM, some CPM440V Vaso Wear and damascus. **Prices:** $150 to $2500. **Remarks:** First knife sold in 1983. **Mark:** Name, city and state surrounded by wheat on each side.

CHASE, JOHN E
217 Walnut, Aledo, TX 76008 **Contact:** 817-441-8331, jchaseknives@sbcglobal.net
Specialties: Straight working knives in standard patterns or to customer specs. **Patterns:** Hunters, fighters, daggers and bowies. **Technical:** Grinds D2 and O1, offers mostly satin finishes. **Prices:** Start at $325. **Remarks:** Part-time maker, first knife sold in 1974. **Mark:** Last name in logo.

CHAUVIN, JOHN
200 Anna St, Scott, LA 70583 **Contact:** 337-237-6138, (fax) 337-230-7980
Specialties: Traditional working and using straight knives of his design, to customer specs and in standard patterns. **Patterns:** bowies, fighters, and hunters. **Technical:** Grinds ATS-34, 440C and O1 high-carbon. Paul Bos heat treating. Uses ivory, stag, oosic and stabilized Louisiana swamp maple for handle materials. Makes sheaths using alligator and ostrich. **Prices:** $200 and up. bowies start at $500. **Remarks:** Part-time maker, first knife sold in 1995. **Mark:** Full name, city, state.

CHAVEZ, RAMON
314 N. 5th St., Belen, NM 87002 **Contact:** 505-453-6008, ramon@chavesknives.com, chavesknives.com
Specialties: Frame-lock folding knives and fixed blades. **Patterns:** Hunters, skinners, bushcraft, tactical, neck knives and utility. **Technical:** Grind/stock removal of CPM D2, D2 and CPM 3V. Handles are mostly titanium and Micarta. Thermal molding plastic for sheaths. **Prices:** Start at $225. **Remarks:** Full-time maker, first knife made in 1993, first knife sold in 2010. **Mark:** CHAVES USA with skeleton key.

CHELETTE, GARY
PO Box 636, Laveen, AZ 85339 **Contact:** 602-237-2786, blademan76@aol.com
Specialties: Working straight knives and folders. **Patterns:** Hunters, fighters, boots and axes, locking folders. **Technical:** Grinds 440C. **Prices:** $150 to $350, exceptional knives to $600. **Remarks:** Full-time maker, first knife sold in 1976. **Mark:** Name, city, state.

CHERRY, FRANK J
3412 Tiley N.E., Albuquerque, NM 87110 **Contact:** 505-883-8643

CHEW, LARRY
3025 De leon Dr., Weatherford, TX 76087 **Contact:** 817-573-8035, chewman@swbell.net, voodooinside.com
Specialties: High-tech folding knives. **Patterns:** Double action automatic and manual folding patterns of his design. **Technical:** CAD designed folders utilizing roller bearing pivot design known as "VooDoo." Double action automatic folders with a variety of obvious and disguised release mechanisms, some with lock-outs. **Prices:** Manual folders start at $475, double action autos start at $750. **Remarks:** Made and sold first knife in 1988, first folder in 1989. Full-time maker since 1997. **Mark:** Name and location etched in blade, damascus autos marked on spring inside frame. Earliest knives stamped LC.

CHILDERS, DAVID
1193 Rocky Creek Ranch Rd., Lampasas, TX 76550 **Contact:** 281-797-7717, childersdavid@att.net, davidchildersknives.com

CHINNOCK, DANIEL T.
380 River Ridge Dr., Union, MO 63084 **Contact:** 314-276-6936, DanChinnock.com, email: Sueanddanc@cs.com
Specialties: One of a kind folders in damascus and Mammoth Ivory. Performs intricate pearl inlays into snake wood and giraffe bone. Makes matchingt ivory pistol grips for colt 1911's and Colt SAA. **Patterns:** New folder designs each year, thin ground and delicate gentleman's folders, large "hunting" folders in stainless damascus and CPM154. Several standard models carried by Internet dealers. **Prices:** $500-$1500 **Remarks:** Full-time maker in 2005 and a voting member of the Knifemakers Guild. Performs intricate file work on all areas of knife. **Mark:** Signature on inside of backbar, starting in 2009 blades are stamped with a large "C" and "Dan" buried inside the "C".

CHOMILIER, ALAIN AND JORIS
20 rue des Hauts de Chanturgue, Clermont-Ferrand, FRANCE 63100 **Contact:** + 33 4 73 25 64 47, jo_chomilier@yahoo.fr
Specialties: One-of-a-kind knives, exclusive designs, art knives in carved patinated bronze, mainly folders, some straight knives and art daggers. **Patterns:** Liner-lock, side-lock, button-lock, lockback folders. **Technical:** Grind carbon and stainless damascus, also carve and patinate bronze. **Prices:** $400 to $3000, some to $4000. **Remarks:** Spare-time makers, first knife sold in 1995, Use fossil stone and ivory, mother-of-pearl, (fossil) coral, meteorite, bronze, gemstones, high karat gold. **Mark:** A. J. Chomilier in italics.

CHRISTENSEN, JON P
516 Blue Grouse, Stevensville, MT 59870 **Contact:** 406-697-8377, jpcknives@gmail.com, jonchristensenknives.com
Specialties: Hunting/utility knives, folders, art knives. **Patterns:** Mosaic damascusTechnical:** Sole authorship, forges 01, 1084, 52100, 5160, damascus from 1084/15N20. **Prices:** $220 and up. **Remarks:** ABS Mastersmith, first knife sold in 1999. **Mark:** First and middle initial surrounded by last initial.

CHURCHMAN, T W (TIM)
475 Saddle Horn Drive, Bandera, TX 78003 **Contact:** 210-240-0317, tim.churchman@nustarenergy.com
Specialties: Fancy and traditional straight knives. Bird/trout knives of his design and to customer specs. **Patterns:** Bird/trout knives, bowies, daggers, fighters, boot knives, some miniatures. **Technical:** Grinds 440C, D2 and 154CM. Offers stainless fittings, fancy filework, exotic and stabilized woods, elk and other antler, and hand sewed lined sheaths. Also flower pins as a style. **Prices:** $350 to $450, some to $2,250. **Remarks:** Part-time maker, first knife made in 1981 after reading "KNIVES '81." Doing business as "Custom Knives Churchman Made." **Mark:** "Churchman" over Texas outline, "Bandera" under.

CIMMS, GREG
Kayne Custom Knife Works, 2297 Rt. 44, Ste. B, Pleasant Valley, NY 12569 **Contact:** 845-475-7220, cimms1@aol.com
Patterns: Kitchen knives, hunters, bowies, fighters, small swords, bird-and-trout knives, tactical pieces, tomahawks, axes and bushcraft blades. **Technical:** damascus and straight-carbon-steel cutlery, with some mosaic-damascus and powder-metal pieces. **Prices:** $300 to $4,000. **Remarks:** Full-time maker since 2014, first knife made in 2013. **Mark:** A compass with a "K" in the middle.

CLAIBORNE, JEFF
1470 Roberts Rd, Franklin, IN 46131 **Contact:** 317-736-7443, jeff@claiborneknives.com, claiborneknives.com
Specialties: Multi blade slip joint folders. All one-of-a-kind by hand, no jigs or fixtures, swords, straight knives, period pieces, camp knives, hunters, fighters, ethnic swords all periods. Handle: uses stag, pearl, oosic, bone ivory, mastadon-mammoth, elephant or exotic woods. **Technical:** Forges high-carbon steel, makes damascus, forges cable grinds, 01, 1095, 5160, 52100, L6. **Prices:** $250 and up. **Remarks:** Full-time maker, first knife sold in 1989. **Mark:** Stylized initials in an oval.

CLAIBORNE, RON
2918 Ellistown Rd, Knox, TN 37924 **Contact:** 615-524-2054, bowie@icy.net
Specialties: Multi-blade slip joints, swords, straight knives. **Patterns:** Hunters, daggers, folders. **Technical:** Forges damascus: mosaic, powder mosaic. Prefers bone and natural handle materials, some exotic woods. **Prices:** $125 to $2500. **Remarks:** Part-time maker, first knife sold in 1979. Doing business as Thunder Mountain Forge Claiborne Knives. **Mark:** Claiborne.

CLARK, D E (LUCKY)
413 Lyman Lane, Johnstown, PA 15909-1409
Specialties: Working straight knives and folders to customer specs. **Patterns:** Customer designs. **Technical:** Grinds D2, 440C, 154CM. **Prices:** $100 to $200, some higher. **Remarks:** Part-time maker, first knife sold in 1975. **Mark:** Name on one side, "Lucky" on other.

CLARK, HOWARD F
115 35th Pl, Runnells, IA 50237 **Contact:** 515-966-2126, howard@mvforge.com, mvforge.com
Specialties: Currently Japanese-style swords. **Patterns:** Katana. **Technical:** Forges L6 and 1086. **Prices:** $1200 to 5000. **Remarks:** Full-time maker, first knife sold in 1979. Doing business as Morgan Valley Forge. Prior **Mark:** Block letters and serial number on folders, anvil/initials logo on straight knives. Current **Mark:** Two character kanji "Big Ear."

CLARK, JASON
24896 77th Rd., O'Brien, FL 32071 **Contact:** 386-935-2922, jclark@clarkcustomknives.com, clarkcustomknives.com
Specialties: Frame-lock and LinerLock folders. **Patterns:** Drop points, tantos, Persians, clip points, razors and wharncliffes. **Technical:** Sole authorship of knives, constructing

100 percent in house, including designing, cutting, shaping, grinding, heat treating, fitting and finishing. Top quality materials and components, as well as hand-rubbed finishes, media blasting, stonewashing, anodizing and polishing. Licensed to use IKBS (Ikoma Korth Bearing System). **Remarks:** Part-time maker. **Mark:** Cross with initials incorporated.

CLARKE, ED
Ed Clarke Knives Hampstead, Md., 21074 **Contact:** 443-604-8297, www. EdClarkeKnives.com
Specialties: Sole authorship. **Patterns:** Hand-forged knives, swords, tomahawks and sheaths. **Remarks:** Journeyman Smith in the ABS. The shop manager and a director of the William F. Moran, Jr., Museum & Foundation.

CLEVELAND, MIKE
Half Life Knives, 329 W. Strasburg Way, Mustang, OK 73064 **Contact:** 405-627-6097, lawdawg3006@yahoo.com
Specialties: Stock removal fixed-blade knives, multi-ground tactical, hunting, chef's knives and tactical 'hawks. **Patterns:** Multi-ground tactical, hunting, kitchen knives and 'hawks. **Technical:** Stock-removal method of blade making, including 80CrV2, 1095, 1084, 1075, 5160, 52100, CPM M4 REX and damascus steels. **Remarks:** Full-time maker, 'hawk maker. **Mark:** Half skull with half Life Knives circling it.

CLINCO, MARCUS
821 Appelby Street, Venice, CA 90291 **Contact:** 818-610-9640, marcus@ clincoknives.com, clincoknives.com
Specialties: I make mostly fixed blade knives with an emphasis on everyday working and tactical models. Most of my knives are stock removal with the exception of my sole authored damascus blades. I have several integral models including a one piece tactical model named the viper. **Technical:** Most working knife models in ATS 34. Integrals in O-1, D-2 and 440 C. damascus in 1080 and 15 N 20. Large camp and bowie models in 5160 and D-2. Handle materials used include micarta, stabilized wood, G-10 and occasionally stag and ivory. **Prices:** $200 - $600.

COATS, KEN
317 5th Ave, Stevens Point, WI 54481 **Contact:** 715-544-0115
Specialties: Does own jigged bone scales **Patterns:** Traditional slip joints - shadow patterns **Technical:** ATS-34 Blades and springs. Milled frames. Grinds ATS-34, 440C. Stainless blades and backsprings. Does all own heat treating and freeze cycle. Blades are drawn to 60RC. Nickel silver or brass bolsters on folders are soldered, neutralized and pinned. Handles are jigged bone, hardwoods antler, and Micarta. Cuts and jigs own bone, usually shades of brown or green. **Prices:** $300 and up

COCKERHAM, LLOYD
1717 Carolyn Ave, Denham Springs, IA 70726 **Contact:** 225-665-1565

COFFEE, JIM
2785 Rush Rd., Norton, OH 44203 **Contact:** 330-631-3355, jcoffee735@aol.com
Specialties: Stock Removal, hunters, skinners, fighters. **Technical:** bowie handle material - stabilized wood, micarta, mammoth ivory, stag. Full tang and hidden tang. Steels - 0-1, d-2, 5160, damascus **Prices:** $150 to $500 and up. **Remarks:** Part-time maker since 2008.**Mark:** full name in a football etch.

COFFEY, BILL
68 Joshua Ave, Clovis, CA 93611 **Contact:** 559-299-4259, williamccoffey@comcast. net
Specialties: Working and fancy straight knives and folders of his design. **Patterns:** Hunters, fighters, utility, LinerLock® folders and fantasy knives. **Technical:** Grinds 440C, ATS-34, A-Z and commercial damascus. **Prices:** $250 to $1000, some to $2500. **Remarks:** Full-time maker. First knife sold in 1993. **Mark:** First and last name, city, state.

COFFMAN, DANNY
541 Angel Dr S, Jacksonville, AL 36265-5787 **Contact:** 256-435-1619
Specialties: Straight knives and folders of his design. Now making liner locks for $650 to $1200 with natural handles and contrasting damascus blades and bolsters. **Patterns:** Hunters, locking and slip-joint folders. **Technical:** Grinds damascus, 440C and D2. Offers filework and engraving. **Prices:** $100 to $400, some to $800. **Remarks:** Spare-time maker, first knife sold in 1992. Doing business as Customs by Coffman. **Mark:** Last name stamped or engraved.

COHEA, JOHN M
114 Rogers Dr., Nettleton, MS 38858 **Contact:** 662-322-5916, jhncohea@hotmail. com, http://jmcohea.blademakers.com
Specialties: Frontier style knives, hawks, and leather. **Patterns:** bowies, hunters, patch/ neck knives, tomahawks, and friction folders. **Technical:** Makes both forged and stock removal knives using high carbon steels and damascus. Uses natural handle materials that include antler, bone, ivory, horn, and figured hardwoods. Also makes rawhide covered sheaths that include fringe, tacks, antique trade beads, and other period correct materials. **Prices:** $100 - $1500, some higher. **Remarks:** Part-time maker, first knife sold in 1999. **Mark:** COHEA stamped on riccasso.

COHEN, N J (NORM)
2408 Sugarcone Rd, Baltimore, MD 21209 **Contact:** 443-929-5008, inquiry@ njcknives.com, njcknives.com
Specialties: Working class knives. **Patterns:** Hunters, skinners, bird knives, push daggers, boots, kitchen and practical customer designs. **Technical:** Stock removal 440C, ATS-34, CPM 154 and D2. Handles of Micarta, Corian and stabilized woods. **Prices:** $50 to $250. **Remarks:** Part-time maker, first knife sold in 1982. **Mark:** NJC engraved.

COLE, JAMES M
505 Stonewood Blvd, Bartonville, TX 76226 **Contact:** 817-430-0302, dogcole@swbell.

COLEMAN, JOHN A
7325 Bonita Way, Citrus Heights, CA 95610-3003 **Contact:** 916-335-1568, slimsknifes@yahoo.com
Specialties: Minis, hunters, bowies of his design or yours. **Patterns:** Plain to fancy file back working knives. **Technical:** Grinds 440C, ATS-34, 145CM, D2, 1095, 5160, 01. Some hand-forged blades. Exotic woods bone, antler and some ivory. **Prices:** $100 to $500. **Remarks:** Does some carving in handles. Part-time maker. First knife sold in 1989. OKCA 2010 Award winner for best mini of show. **Mark:** Cowboy setting on log whittling Slim's Custom Knives above cowboy and name and state under cowboy.

COLLINS, LYNN M
138 Berkley Dr, Elyria, OH 44035 **Contact:** 440-366-7101
Specialties: Working straight knives. **Patterns:** Field knives, boots and fighters. **Technical:** Grinds D2, 154CM and 440C. **Prices:** Start at $200. **Remarks:** Spare-time maker, first knife sold in 1980. **Mark:** Initials, asterisks.

COLTER, WADE
PO Box 2340, Colstrip, MT 59323 **Contact:** Shop: 406-748-2010, (fax) Cell: 406-740-1554
Specialties: Fancy and embellished straight knives, folders and swords of his design, historical and period pieces. **Patterns:** bowies, swords and folders. **Technical:** Hand forges 52100 ball bearing steel and L6, 1090, cable and chain damascus from 5N20 and 1084. Carves and makes sheaths. **Prices:** $250 to $3500. **Remarks:** SemiRetired, first knife sold in 1990. Doing business as "Colter's Hell" Forge. **Mark:** Initials on left side ricasso.

COLWELL, KEVIN
Professor's Forge, 15 Stony Hill Rd., Cheshire, CA 06410 **Contact:** 203-439-2223, colwellk2@southernct.edu
Specialties: Swords (Dao, jian, seax, messer, baurnwehr, etc.) and knives (puukko, Viking-style, hunters, skinners, bowies, fighters and chef's knives). **Technical:** Forges blades, vivid pattern welding or subtle pattern welding with beautiful hamon and grain structure. **Prices:** $175 to $500, swords $900 and up, depending upon what customer wants in adornment. **Remarks:** Associate professor of psychology.

CONKLIN, GEORGE L
Box 902, Ft. Benton, MT 59442 **Contact:** 406-622-3268, (fax) 406-622-3410, 7bbgrus@3rivers.net
Specialties: Designer and manufacturer of the "Brisket Breaker." **Patterns:** Hunters, utility/camp knives and hatchets. **Technical:** Grinds 440C, ATS-34, D2, 1095, 154CM and 5160. Offers some forging and heat-treats for others. Offers some jewelling. **Prices:** $65 to $200, some to $1000. **Remarks:** Full-time maker. Doing business as Rocky Mountain Knives. **Mark:** Last name in script.

CONLEY, BOB
1013 Creasy Rd, Jonesboro, TN 37659 **Contact:** 423-753-3302
Specialties: Working straight knives and folders. **Patterns:** Lockers, two-blades, gents, hunters, traditional-styles, straight hunters. **Technical:** Grinds 440C, 154CM and ATS-34. Engraves. **Prices:** $250 to $450, some to $600. **Remarks:** Full-time maker, first knife sold in 1979. **Mark:** Full name, city, state.

CONN JR., C T
206 Highland Ave, Attalla, AL 35954 **Contact:** 205-538-7688
Specialties: Working folders, some fancy. **Patterns:** Full range of folding knives. **Technical:** Grinds O2, 440C and 154CM. **Prices:** $125 to $300, some to $600. **Remarks:** Part-time maker, first knife sold in 1982. **Mark:** Name.

CONNOLLY, JAMES
2486 Oro-Quincy Hwy, Oroville, CA 95966 **Contact:** 530-534-5363, rjconnolly@ sbcglobal.net
Specialties: Classic working and using knives of his design. **Patterns:** Boots, bowies, daggers and swords. **Technical:** Grinds ATS-34, BG42, A2, 01. **Prices:** $100 to $500, some to $1500. **Remarks:** Part-time maker, first knife sold in 1980. Doing business as Gold Rush Designs. **Mark:** First initial, last name, Handmade.

CONNOR, JOHN W
PO Box 12981, Odessa, TX 79768-2981 **Contact:** 915-362-6901

CONNOR, MICHAEL
Box 502, Winters, TX 79567 **Contact:** 915-754-5602
Specialties: Straight knives, period pieces, some folders. **Patterns:** Hunters to camp knives to traditional locking folders to bowies. **Technical:** Forges 5160, O1, 1084 steels and his own damascus. **Prices:** Moderate to upscale. **Remarks:** Spare-time maker, first knife sold in 1974. ABS Master Smith 1983. **Mark:** Last name, M.S.

CONTI, JEFFREY D
POB 16, Judith Gap, MT 59453 **Contact:** 253-569-6303, Facebook at JL Knives
Specialties: Working straight knives. **Patterns:** Tactical, survival, hunting, campting, fishing and kitchen knives. **Technical:** Grinds D2, 154CM, 440C and O1. Engraves. **Prices:** Start at $150. **Remarks:** Part-time maker, first knife sold in 1980. Does own heat treating. **Mark:** Electrical etch: "JG Knives."

CONWAY, JOHN
13301 100th Place NE, Kirkland, WA 98034 **Contact:** 425-823-2821, jcknives@ Frontier.com
Specialties: Folders, working and damascus. Straight knives, camp, utility and fighting knives. **Patterns:** LinerLock® folders of own design. Hidden tang straight knives of own

design. **Technical:** Flat grinds forged carbon steels and own damascus steel, including mosaic. **Prices:** $300 to $850. **Remarks:** Part-time maker since 1999. **Mark:** Oval with stylized initials J C inset.

COOGAN, ROBERT
1560 Craft Center Dr, Smithville, TN 37166 **Contact:** 615-597-6801, http://iweb.tntech.edu/rcoogan/
Specialties: One-of-a-kind knives. **Patterns:** Unique items like ulu-style Appalachian herb knives. **Technical:** Forges, his damascus is made from nickel steel and W1. **Prices:** Start at $100. **Remarks:** Part-time maker, first knife sold in 1979. **Mark:** Initials or last name in script.

COOK, CHUCK
Chuck Cook Scout Knives 1017 SW View Crest Dr., Dundee, OR 97115 **Contact:** 503-554-5613, scout_knives@yahoo.com, scout-knives.synthasite.com
Patterns: Hunting, bushcraft, kitchen knives, and folding knives. **Technical:** Forges 1084 and high-carbon damascus. **Technical:** Handmade high carbon, damascus and tool steel blades.

COOK, JAMES R
455 Anderson Rd, Nashville, AR 71852 **Contact:** 870 845 5173, jr@jrcookknives.com, jrcookknives.com
Specialties: Working straight knives and folders of his design or to customer specs. **Patterns:** bowies, hunters and camp knives. **Technical:** Forges 1084 and high-carbon damascus. **Prices:** $800 to $20,000. **Remarks:** Full-time maker, first knife sold in 1986. **Mark:** First and middle initials, last name.

COOK, LOUISE
475 Robinson Ln, Ozark, IL 62972 **Contact:** 618-777-2932
Specialties: Working and using straight knives of her design and to customer specs, period pieces. **Patterns:** bowies, hunters and utility/camp knives. **Technical:** Forges 5160. Filework, pin work, silver wire inlay. **Prices:** Start at $50/inch. **Remarks:** Part-time maker, first knife sold in 1990. Doing business as Panther Creek Forge. **Mark:** First name and Journeyman stamp on one side, panther head on the other.

COOK, MIKE
475 Robinson Ln, Ozark, IL 62972 **Contact:** 618-777-2932
Specialties: Traditional working and using straight knives of his design and to customer specs. **Patterns:** bowies, hunters and utility/camp knives. **Technical:** Forges 5160. Filework, pin work. **Prices:** Start at $50/inch. **Remarks:** Spare-time maker, first knife sold in 1991. **Mark:** First initial, last name and Journeyman stamp on one side, panther head on the other.

COOK, MIKE A
10927 Shilton Rd, Portland, MI 48875 **Contact:** 517-242-1352, macook@hughes.net artofishi.com
Specialties: Fancy/embellished and period pieces of his design. **Patterns:** Daggers, fighters and hunters. **Technical:** Stone bladed knives in agate, obsidian and jasper. Scrimshaws, opal inlays. **Prices:** $60 to $300, some to $800. **Remarks:** Part-time maker, first knife sold in 1988. Doing business as Art of Ishi. **Mark:** Initials and year.

COOKE, MARK
LongDog Forge, 21619 Slippery Creek Ln., Spring, TX 77388, markcooke5@gmail.com, longdogforge.com
Specialties: One-off handforged blades featuring bold design, technical processes, sole authorship and an emphasis on a clean, complete package. **Technical:** Presently working with mono steel blades via W2, 1084, 80CrV2, as well as others upon request. **Remarks:** Enjoys challenging commissions that push the boundaries of the maker's skill set. All work done under the same roof, from initial forging of the blade to stitching of the sheath to ensure quality and adherence to the original design. Combines Old World techniques with modern design elements to achieve balance between form and function. **Mark:** Dachshund (LongDog) mark typically located on the spine of the blade.

COOMBS JR., LAMONT
546 State Rt 46, Bucksport, ME 04416 **Contact:** 207-469-3057, theknifemaker@hotmail.com, knivesby.com/coombs-knives.html
Specialties: Classic fancy and embellished straight knives, traditional working and using straight knives. Knives of his design and to customer specs. **Patterns:** Hunters, folders and utility/camp knives. **Technical:** Hollow- and flat-grinds ATS-34, 440C, A2, D2 and O1, grinds damascus from other makers. **Prices:** $100 to $500, some to $3500. **Remarks:** Full-time maker, first knife sold in 1988. **Mark:** Last name on banner, handmade underneath.

COON, RAYMOND C
21135 S.E. Tillstrom Rd, Damascus, OR 97089 **Contact:** 503-658-2252, Raymond@damascusknife.com, damascusknife.com
Specialties: Working straight knives in standard patterns. **Patterns:** Hunters, bowies, daggers, boots and axes. **Technical:** Forges high-carbon steel and damascus or 97089. **Prices:** Start at $235. **Remarks:** Full-time maker, does own leatherwork, makes own damascus, daggers, first knife sold in 1995. **Mark:** First initial, last name.

COOPER, PAUL
9 Woods St., Woburn, MA 01801 **Contact:** 781-938-0519, byksm@yahoo.com
Specialties: Forged, embellished, hand finished fixed-blade knives. **Patterns:** One of a kind designs, often inspired by traditional and historic pieces. **Technical:** Works in tool steel, damascus and natural materials. **Prices:** $500 - $2000. **Remarks:** Part-time maker, formally apprenticed under J.D. Smith. Sold first piece in 2006. **Mark:** Letter C inside bleeding heart.

COPELAND, THOM
136 Blue Bayou Ests., Nashville, AR 71852, tcope@cswnet.com
Specialties: Hand forged fixed blades, hunters, bowies and camp knives. **Remarks:** Member of ABS and AKA (Arkansas Knifemakers Association). **Mark:** Copeland.

COPPINS, DANIEL
700 S. 9th St., Cambridge, OH 43725 **Contact:** 740-995-9009, info@battlehorseknives.com, battlehorseknives.com
Specialties: Bushcraft knives, tacticals, hunting. **Technical:** Grinds 440C, D2. Antler handles. **Patterns:** Many. **Prices:** $40 to $600. **Remarks:** Sold first knife in 2002, formerly Blind Horse Knives. **Mark:** Horse-Kicking Donkey.

CORBY, HAROLD
218 Brandonwood Dr, Johnson City, TN 37604 **Contact:** 423-926-9781
Specialties: Large fighters and bowies, self-protection knives, art knives. Along with art knives and combat knives, Corby now has a all new automatic MO.PB1, also side lock MO LL-1 with titanium liners G-10 handles. **Patterns:** Sub-hilt fighters and hunters. **Technical:** Grinds 154CM, ATS-34 and 440C. **Prices:** $200 to $6000. **Remarks:** Full-time maker, first knife sold in 1969. Doing business as Knives by Corby. **Mark:** Last name.

CORDOVA, JOEY
1594 S. Hill Rd., Bernalillo, NM 87004 **Contact:** 505-410-3809, joeyscordova@gmail.com, joelouiknives.com
Patterns: High-carbon full-tang knives and hidden-tang bowies, as well as small neck knives. **Technical:** Differentially heat-treats blades producing hamons (temper lines). **Prices:** $120 and up. **Remarks:** Full-time knifemaker and part-time ring maker.

CORDOVA, JOSEPH G
1450 Lillie Dr, Bosque Farms, NM 87068 **Contact:** 505-869-3912, kcordova@rt66.com
Specialties: One-of-a-kind designs, some to customer specs. **Patterns:** Fighter called the 'Gladiator', hunters, boots and cutlery. **Technical:** Forges 1095, 5160, grinds ATS-34, 440C and 154CM. **Prices:** Moderate to upscale. **Remarks:** Full-time maker, first knife sold in 1953. Past chairman of American Bladesmith Society. **Mark:** Cordova made.

CORICH, VANCE
POB 97, Morrison, CO 80465 **Contact:** 303-999-1553, vancecorichcutlery@gmail.com, https://sites.google.com/site/vancesproject/
Specialties: Fixed blades, usually 2 to 7 inches, recurved blades, locking-liner folders and friction folders. **Technical:** Differential heat treating on high-carbon steels. **Prices:** $150 to $1,000. **Remarks:** Part-time maker working on going full time. **Mark:** Stamped "VCC" or VANCE.

CORKUM, STEVE
34 Basehoar School Rd, Littlestown, PA 17340 **Contact:** 717-359-9563, sco7129849@aol.com, hawknives.com

CORNETT, BRIAN
1511 N. College St., McKinney, TX 75069 **Contact:** 972-310-7289, devildogdesign@tx.rr.com, d3devildogdesigns.com
Patterns: Tactical, hunting, neck knives and personal-defense tools. **Technical:** Stock removal of 1095, O1 tool steel, 52100, D2, CPM 154 and damascus. **Prices:** $50 to $300. **Remarks:** Full-time maker, first knife made in 2011. **Mark:** D3.

CORNWELL, JEFFREY
Treasure Art Blades, PO Box 244014, Anchorage, AK 99524 **Contact:** 907-887-1661, cornwellsjej@alaska.net
Specialties: Organic, sculptural shapes of original design from damascus steel and mokume gane. **Technical:** Blade creations from Robert Eggerling damascus and Mike Sakmar mokume. **Remarks:** Free-time maker. **Mark:** Stylized J inside a circle.

COSTA, SCOTT
409 Coventry Rd, Spicewood, TX 78669 **Contact:** 830-693-3431
Specialties: Working straight knives. **Patterns:** Hunters, skinners, axes, trophy sets, custom boxed steak sets, carving sets and bar sets. **Technical:** Grinds D2, ATS-34, 440 and damascus. Heat-treats. **Prices:** $225 to $2000. **Remarks:** Full-time maker, first knife sold in 1985. **Mark:** Initials connected.

COTTRILL, JAMES I
1776 Ransburg Ave, Columbus, OH 43223 **Contact:** 614-274-0020
Specialties: Working straight knives of his design. **Patterns:** Caters to the boating and hunting crowd, cutlery. **Technical:** Grinds O1, D2 and 440C. Likes filework. **Prices:** $95 to $250, some to $500. **Remarks:** Full-time maker, first knife sold in 1977. **Mark:** Name, city, state, in oval logo.

COUSINO, GEORGE
7818 Norfolk, Onsted, MI 49265 **Contact:** 517-467-4911, cousinoknives@yahoo.com, cousinoknives.com
Specialties: Hunters, bowies using knives. **Patterns:** Hunters, bowies, buckskinners, folders and daggers. **Technical:** Grinds 440C. **Prices:** $95 to $300. **Remarks:** Part-time maker, first knife sold in 1981. **Mark:** Last name.

COVER, JEFF
11355 Allen Rd, Potosi, MO 63664 **Contact:** 573-749-0008, jeffcovercustomknives@hotmail.com
Specialties: Folders and straight knives. **Patterns: Technical:** Various knife steels and handle materials. **Prices:** $70 to $500.**Mark:** Jeff Cover J.C. Custom Knives.

COVER, RAYMOND A
16235 State Hwy. U, Mineral Point, MO 63660 **Contact:** 573-749-3783

custom knifemakers

Specialties: High-tech working straight knives and folders in working patterns. **Patterns:** Slip joints, lockbacks, multi-blade folders. **Technical:** Various knife steels and handle materials. **Prices:** Swords from bare blades to complete high art $200 to $600. **Mark:** "R Cover"

COWLES, DON
1026 Lawndale Dr, Royal Oak, MI 48067 **Contact:** 248-541-4619, don@cowlesknives.com, cowlesknives.com
Specialties: Straight, non-folding pocket knives of his design. **Patterns:** Gentlemen's pocket knives. **Technical:** Grinds CPM154, S30V, damascus, Talonite. Engraves, pearl inlays in some handles. **Prices:** Start at $300. **Remarks:** Full-time maker, first knife sold in 1994. **Mark:** Full name with oak leaf.

COX, LARRY
701 W. 13th St, Murfreesboro, AR 71958 **Contact:** 870-258-2429, (fax) Cell: 870-557-8062, cox870@windstream.net
Specialties: Forges his own "ghost flame" damascus. **Patterns:** Skinners, hunters, camp knives and bowies. **Technical:** Forges 5160, 1084, and L6 with 1084 and 5160 for damascus, as well as doing own heat treating. **Prices:** $300 and up. **Remarks:** Sole ownership of knives. Part-time maker, first knife sold in 2007. Member ABS and Arkansas Knifemakers Association. **Mark:** "L U" over "COX."

COX, SAM
1756 Love Springs Rd, Gaffney, SC 29341 **Contact:** 864-489-1892, coxworks.com
Remarks: Started making knives in 1981 for another maker. 1st knife sold under own name in 1983. Full-time maker 1985-2009. Retired in 2010. Now part time. **Mark:** Different logo each year.

COYE, BILL
PO Box 470684, Tulsa, OK 74147 **Contact:** 918-232-5721, info@coyeknives.com, coyeknives.com
Specialties: Tactical and utility knives. **Patterns:** Fighters and utility. **Technical:** Grinds CPM154CM, 154CM, CTS-XHP and Elmax stainless steels. **Prices:** $210 to $320. **Remarks:** Part-time maker. First knife sold in 2009. **Mark:** COYE.

CRADDOCK, MIKE
300 Blythe Dr., Thomasville, NC 27360 **Contact:** 336-382-8461, ncbladesmith@gmail.com
Specialties: Fighters, bowies. **Patterns:** Hunters and working knives. **Technical:** Forges and grinds high-carbon steel, and does own damascus. **Prices:** $350 to $1,500. **Mark:** CRADDOCK.

CRAIG, ROGER L
2617 SW Seabrook Ave, Topeka, KS 66614 **Contact:** 785-249-4109
Specialties: Working and camp knives, some fantasy, all his design. **Patterns:** Fighters, hunter. **Technical:** Grinds 1095 and 5160. Most knives have file work. **Prices:** $50 to $250. **Remarks:** Part-time maker, first knife sold in 1991. Doing business as Craig Knives. **Mark:** Last name-Craig.

CRAMER, BRENT
PO BOX 99, Wheatland, IN 47597 **Contact:** 812-881-9961, Bdcramer@juno.com, BDCramerKnives.com
Specialties: Traditional and custom working and using knives. **Patterns:** Traditional single blade slip-joint folders and standard fixed blades. **Technical:** Stock removal only. Pivot bushing construction on folders. Steel: D-2, 154 CM, ATS-34, CPM-D2, CPM-154CM, 0-1, 52100, A-2. All steels heat treated in shop with LN Cryo. Handle Material: Stag, Bone, Wood, Ivory, and Micarta. **Prices:** $150 - $550. **Remarks:** Part-time maker. First fixed blade sold in 2003. First folder sold in 2007. **Mark:** BDC and B.D.Cramer.

CRAWFORD, PAT AND WES
205 N. Center, West Memphis, AR 72301 **Contact:** 870-732-2452, patcrawford1@earthlink.com, crawfordknives.com
Specialties: Stainless steel damascus. High-tech working self-defense and combat types and folders. **Patterns:** Tactical-more fancy knives now. **Technical:** Grinds S30V. **Prices:** $400 to $2000. **Remarks:** Full-time maker, first knife sold in 1973. **Mark:** Last name.

CRAWLEY, BRUCE R
16 Binbrook Dr, Croydon, VIC, AUSTRALIA 3136
Specialties: Folders. **Patterns:** Hunters, lockback folders and bowies. **Technical:** Grinds 440C, ATS-34 and commercial damascus. Offers filework and mirror polish. **Prices:** $160 to $3500. **Remarks:** Part-time maker, first knife sold in 1990. **Mark:** Initials.

CRENSHAW, AL
Rt 1 Box 717, Eufaula, OK 74432 **Contact:** 918-452-2128
Specialties: Folders of his design and in standard patterns. **Patterns:** Hunters, locking folders, slip-joint folders, multi blade folders. **Technical:** Grinds 440C, D2 and ATS-34. Does filework on back springs and blades, offers scrimshaw on some handles. **Prices:** $150 to $300, some higher. **Remarks:** Part-time maker, first knife sold in 1981. Doing business as A. Crenshaw Knives. **Mark:** First initial, last name, Lake Eufaula, state stamped, first initial last name in rainbow, Lake Eufaula across bottom with Okla. in middle.

CREWS, RANDY
627 Cricket Trail Rd., Patriot, OH 45658 **Contact:** 740-379-2329, randy.crews@sbcglobal.net
Specialties: Fixed blades, bowies and hunters. **Technical:** 440C, Alabama damascus, 1095 with file work. Stock removal method. **Prices:** Start at $150. **Remarks:** Collected knives for 30 years. Part-time maker, first knife made in 2002. **Mark:** Crews Patriot OH.

CRIST, ZOE
2274 Deep Gap Rd., Flat Rock, NC 28731 **Contact:** 828-275-6689, zoe@zoecristknives.com zoecristknives.com

Specialties: San mai and stainless steel. Custom damascus and traditional damascus working and art knives. Also makes Mokume. Works to customer specs. **Patterns:** All damascus hunters, bowies, fighters, neck, boot and high-end art knives. **Technical:** Makes all his own damascus steel from 1095, L6, 15n20. Forges all knives, heat treats, filework, differential heat treating. **Prices:** $150 - $2500. **Remarks:** Full-time maker, has been making knives since 1988, went full-time 2009. Also makes own leather sheaths. **Mark:** Small "z" with long tail on left side of blade at ricasso.

CROCKFORD, JACK
1859 Harts Mill Rd, Chamblee, GA 30341 **Contact:** 770-457-4680
Specialties: Lockback folders. **Patterns:** Hunters, fishing and camp knives, traditional folders. **Technical:** Grinds A2, D2, ATS-34 and 440C. Engraves and scrimshaws. **Prices:** Start at $175. **Remarks:** Part-time maker, first knife sold in 1975. **Mark:** Name.

CROSS, KEVIN
5 Pear Orchard Rd., Portland, CT 06480 **Contact:** 860-894-2385, kevincross@comcast.net, kevincrossknives.com
Specialties: Working/using and presentation grade fixed-blade knives and custom kitchen knives. **Patterns:** Hunters, skinners, fighters, bowies, camp knives. **Technical:** Stock removal maker. Uses O1, 1095, 154 CPM as well as damascus from Eggerling, Ealy, Donnelly, Nichols, Thomas and others. Most handles are natural materials such as burled and spalted woods, stag and ancient ivory. **Prices:** $200 - $1,200. **Remarks:** Part-time maker. First knife sold around 1997. **Mark:** Name.

CROSS, ROBERT
RMB 200B, Manilla Rd, Tamworth, NSW, AUSTRALIA 2340 **Contact:** 067-618385

CROTTS, DAN
PO Box 68, Elm Springs, AR 72728 **Contact:** 479-422-7874, dancrottsknives@yahoo.com facebook.com/dancrottsknives
Specialties: User grade, hunting, tactical and folders. **Technical:** High-end tool steel. **Prices:** $2200. **Remarks:** Specializes in making performance blades. **Mark:** Crotts.

CROUCH, BUBBA
POB 461, Pleasanton, TX 78064 **Contact:** 210-846-6890, tommycrouch69@gmail.com, Facebook: Crouch Custom Knives
Specialties: Slip joints, straight blades. **Patterns:** Case style. Offers filework. **Technical:** ATS-34, CPM 154 and commercial damascus. Using stag, bone and mammoth ivory handle material. **Prices:** $250 to $1,200. **Remarks:** Part-time maker, first knife sold in 2010. **Mark:** Crouch.

CROWDER, GARY L
112480 S. 4614 Rd., Sallisaw, OK 74955 **Contact:** 918-775-9009, gcrowder99@yahoo.com
Specialties: Folders, multi-blades. **Patterns:** Traditional with a few sheath knives. **Technical:** Flat grinds ATS-34, D2 and others, as well as damascus via stock-removal. **Prices:** $150 to $600. **Remarks:** Retired, part-time maker. First knife sold in 1994. **Mark:** small acid-etched "Crowder" on blade.

CROWDER, ROBERT
Box 1374, Thompson Falls, MT 59873 **Contact:** 406-827-4754
Specialties: Traditional working knives to customer specs. **Patterns:** Hunters, bowies, fighters and fillets. **Technical:** Grinds ATS-34, 154CM, 440C, Vascowear and commercial damascus. **Prices:** $225 to $500, some to $2500. **Remarks:** Full-time maker, first knife sold in 1985. **Mark:** R Crowder signature & Montana.

CROWELL, JAMES L
676 Newnata Cutoff, Mtn. View, AR 72560 **Contact:** 870-746-4215, crowellknives@yahoo.com, crowellknives.com
Specialties: Bowie knives, fighters and working knives. **Patterns:** Hunters, fighters, bowies, daggers and a few folders. Period pieces: War hammers, Japanese and European. **Technical:** Forges 10 series carbon steels as well as O1, L6, W2 and his own damascus. "Flame painted" hamons (temper lines). **Prices:** $525 to $5,500, some to $8,500. **Remarks:** Full-time maker, first knife sold in 1980. Earned ABS master smith in 1986. ABS Hall of Fame. Certified ABS teacher. **Mark:** A shooting star.

CROWL, PETER
5786 County Road 10, Waterloo, IN 46793 **Contact:** 260-488-2532, pete@petecrowlknives.com, petecrowlknives.com
Specialties: bowie, hunters. **Technical:** Forges 5160, 1080, W2, 52100. **Prices:** $200 and up. **Remarks:** ABS Journeyman smith. **Mark:** Last name in script.

CROWNER, JEFF
2621 Windsor Pl., Plano, TX 75075 **Contact:** 541-201-3182, (fax) 541-579-3762
Specialties: Custom knife maker. I make some of the following: wilderness survival blades, martial art weapons, hunting blades. **Technical:** I differentially heat treat every knife. I use various steels like 5160, L-6, Cable damascus, 52100, 6150, and some stainless types. I use the following for handle materials: TeroTuf by Columbia Industrial products and exotic hardwoods and horn. I make my own custom sheaths as well with either kydex or leather.

CROWTHERS, MARK F
PO Box 4641, Rolling Bay, WA 98061-0641 **Contact:** 206-842-7501

CUCCHIARA, MATT
387 W. Hagler, Fresno, CA 93711 **Contact:** 559-917-2328, matt@cucchiaraknives.com cucchiaraknives.com
Specialties: I make large and small, plain or hand carved Ti handled Tactical framelock folders. All decoration and carving work done by maker. Also known for my hand carved Ti pocket clips. **Prices:** Start at around $400 and go as high as $1500 or so.

CULHANE, SEAN K.
8 Ranskroon Dr., Horizon, Roodepoort, 1740, SOUTH AFRICA **Contact:** +27 82 453-1741, skculhane9@gmail.com, culhaneknives.co.za
Specialties: Traditional working straight knives and folders in standard patterns and to customer specifications. **Patterns:** Fighters, hunters, kitchen cutlery, utility and Scottish dirks and sgian dubhs. **Technical:** Hollow grinding Sandvik 12C27 and commercial damascus. Full process, including heat treating and sheaths done by maker. **Prices:** From $180 up, depending on design and materials. **Remarks:** Full-time maker, first knife sold in 1988. **Mark:** First and surname in Gothic script curved over the word "Maker."

CULVER, STEVE
5682 94th St, Meriden, KS 66512 **Contact:** 785-230-2505, culverart.com, Facebook: Steve Culver Knives, YouTube: SteveCulverMS1
Specialties: Edged weapons. Spiral-welded damascus gun barrels, collectible and functional. **Patterns:** bowies, daggers, hunters, folders and combination weapons. **Technical:** Forges carbon steels and his own damascus. Stock removal of stainless steel for some folders. **Prices:** $500 to $50,000. **Remarks:** Full-time maker, also builds muzzle-loading pistols. **Mark:** Last name, MS.

CUMMING, BOB
CUMMING KNIVES, 35 Manana Dr, Cedar Crest, NM 87008 **Contact:** 505-286-0509, cumming@comcast.net, cummingknives.com
Specialties: One-of-a-kind exhibition grade custom bowie knives, exhibition grade and working hunters, bird & trout knives, salt and fresh water fillet knives. Low country oyster knives, custom tanto's plains Indian style sheaths & custom leather, all types of exotic handle materials, scrimshaw and engraving. Added folders in 2006. Custom oyster knives. **Prices:** $95 to $3500 and up. **Remarks:** Mentored by the late Jim Nolen, sold first knife in 1978 in Denmark. Retired U.S. Foreign Service Officer. Member NCCKG. **Mark:** Stylized CUMMING.

CURTISS, DAVID
Curtiss Knives, PO Box 902, Granger, IN 46530 **Contact:** 574-651-2158, david@curtissknives.com, curtissknives.com
Specialties: Specialize in custom tactical-style folders and flipper folders, with some of the best sellers being in the Nano and Cruze series. The Nano is now being produced by Boker Knives. Many new knife designs coming soon.

CURTISS, STEVE L
PO Box 448, Eureka, MT 59914 **Contact:** 406-889-5510, (fax) 406-889-5510, slc@bladerigger.com, bladerigger.com
Specialties: True custom and semi-custom production (SCP), specialized concealment blades, advanced sheaths and tailored body harnessing systems. **Patterns:** Tactical/personal defense fighters, swords, utility and custom patterns. **Technical:** Grinds A2 and Talonite®, heat-treats. Sheaths: Kydex or Kydex-lined leather laminated or Kydex-lined with Rigger Coat™. Exotic materials available. **Prices:** $50 to $10,000. **Remarks:** Full-time maker. Doing business as Blade Rigger L.L.C. Martial artist and unique defense industry tools and equipment. **Mark:** For true custom: Initials and for SCP: Blade Rigger.

D

DAILEY, G E
577 Lincoln St, Seekonk, MA 02771 **Contact:** 508-336-5088, gedailey@msn.com, gedailey.com
Specialties: One-of-a-kind exotic designed edged weapons. **Patterns:** Folders, daggers and swords. **Technical:** Reforges and grinds damascus, prefers hollow-grinding. Engraves, carves, offers filework and sets stones and uses exotic gems and gold. **Prices:** Start at $1100. **Remarks:** Full-time maker. First knife sold in 1982. **Mark:** Last name or stylized initialed logo.

DAKE, C M
19759 Chef Menteur Hwy, New Orleans, LA 70129-9602 **Contact:** 504-254-0357, (fax) 504-254-9501
Specialties: Fancy working folders. **Patterns:** Front-lock lockbacks, button-lock folders. **Technical:** Grinds ATS-34 and damascus. **Prices:** $500 to $2500, some higher. **Remarks:** Full-time maker, first knife sold in 1988. Doing business as Bayou Custom Cutlery. **Mark:** Last name.

DAKE, MARY H
Rt 5 Box 287A, New Orleans, LA 70129 **Contact:** 504-254-0357

DALEY, MARK
P.O. Box 427, Waubaushene, Ontario, CANADA L0K 2C0 **Contact:** 705-543-1080, mark@markdaleyknives.com
Specialties: Art knives with handles made of stainless steel, bronze, gold, silver, pearl and Shibuichi. Many of the maker's knives are also textured and/or carved. **Mark:** Engraved "Mark Daley" or chiseled initials "MD."

DALLYN, KELLY
124 Deerbrook Place S.E., Calgary, AB, CANADA T2J 6J5 **Contact:** 403-475-3056, info@dallyn-knives.com, dallyn-knives.com
Specialties: Kitchen, utility, and hunting knives

DALY, MICHAEL
9728 3rd Ave., Brooklyn, NY 11209 **Contact:** 718-748-7796, sifubayridge@aol.com
Specialties: Tactical/utility and EDC (everyday carry) fixed blades. **Technical:** Stock removal method of blade making using ATS-34 and 154CM steels, and linen and paper Micarta handles. **Remarks:** Began making knives as a hobby in 2009 under the guidance of Marcus Clinco and Bill Herndon. Member of the California Knifemakers Association.

Mark: Last name in a Chinese seal.

DAMLOVAC, SAVA
10292 Bradbury Dr, Indianapolis, IN 46231 **Contact:** 317-839-4952
Specialties: Period pieces, fantasy, Viking, Moran type all damascus daggers. **Patterns:** bowies, fighters, daggers, Persian-style knives. **Technical:** Uses own damascus, some stainless, mostly hand forges. **Prices:** $150 to $2500, some higher. **Remarks:** Full-time maker, first knife sold in 1993. Specialty, Bill Moran all damascus dagger sets, in Moran-style wood case. **Mark:** "Sava" stamped in damascus or etched in stainless.

D'ANDREA, JOHN
8517 N Linwood Loop, Citrus Springs, FL 34433-5045 **Contact:** 352-489-2803, shootist1@tampabay.rr.com
Specialties: Fancy working straight knives and folders with filework and distinctive leatherwork. **Patterns:** Hunters, fighters, daggers, folders and an occasional sword. **Technical:** Grinds ATS-34, 154CM, 440C and D2. **Prices:** $220 to $1000. **Remarks:** Part-time maker, first knife sold in 1986. **Mark:** First name, last initial imposed on samurai sword.

D'ANGELO, LAURENCE
14703 NE 17th Ave, Vancouver, WA 98686 **Contact:** 360-573-0546
Specialties: Straight knives of his design. **Patterns:** bowies, hunters and locking folders. **Technical:** Grinds D2, ATS-34 and 440C. Hand makes all sheaths. **Prices:** $100 to $200. **Remarks:** Full-time maker, first knife sold in 1987. **Mark:** Football logo—first and middle initials, last name, city, state, Maker.

DANIEL, TRAVIS E
PO Box 1223, Thomaston, GA 30286 **Contact:** 706-601-6418, dtravis405@gmail.com
Specialties: Traditional working straight knives of his design or to customer specs. **Patterns:** Hunters, fighters and utility/camp knives. **Technical:** Grinds ATS-34, 440-C, 154CM, forges his own damascus. Stock removal. **Prices:** $125 to $500. **Remarks:** Full-time maker, first knife sold in 1976. **Mark:** TED.

DARBY, DAVID T
30652 S 533 Rd, Cookson, OK 74427 **Contact:** 918-457-4868, knfmkr@fullnet.net
Specialties: Forged blades only, all styles. **Prices:** $350 and up. **Remarks:** ABS Journeyman Smith. **Mark:** Stylized quillion dagger incorporates last name (Darby).

DARBY, JED
7878 E Co Rd 50 N, Greensburg, IN 47240 **Contact:** 812-663-2696
Specialties: Traditional working/using straight knives of his design and to customer specs. **Patterns:** bowies, hunters and utility/camp knives. **Technical:** Grinds 440C, ATS-34 and damascus. **Prices:** $70 to $550, some to $1000. **Remarks:** Full-time maker, first knife sold in 1992. Doing business as Darby Knives. **Mark:** Last name and year.

DARBY, RICK
71 Nestingrock Ln, Levittown, PA 19054
Specialties: Working straight knives. **Patterns:** Boots, fighters and hunters with mirror finish. **Technical:** Grinds 440C and CPM440V. **Prices:** $125 to $300. **Remarks:** Part-time maker, first knife sold in 1974. **Mark:** First and middle initials, last name.

DARCEY, CHESTER L
1608 Dominik Dr, College Station, TX 77840 **Contact:** 979-696-1656, DarceyKnives@yahoo.com
Specialties: Lockback, LinerLock® and scale release folders. **Patterns:** bowies, hunters and utilities. **Technical:** Stock removal on carbon and stainless steels, forge own damascus. **Prices:** $200 to $1000. **Remarks:** Part-time maker, first knife sold in 1999. **Mark:** Last name in script.

DARK, ROBERT
2218 Huntington Court, Oxford, AL 36203 **Contact:** 256-831-4645, dark@darkknives.com, darknives.com
Specialties: Fixed blade working knives of maker's designs. Works with customer designed specifications. **Patterns:** Hunters, bowies, camp knives, kitchen/utility, bird and trout. Standard patterns and customer designed. **Technical:** Forged and stock removal. Works with high carbon, stainless and damascus steels. Hollow and flat grinds. **Prices:** $175 to $750. **Remarks:** Sole authorship knives and custom leather sheaths. Full-time maker. **Mark:** "R Dark" on left side of blade.

DARPINIAN, DAVE
PO Box 2643, Olathe, KS 66063 **Contact:** 913-244-7114, darpo1956@yahoo.com kansasknives.org
Specialties: Hunters and Persian fighters with natural handle materials. **Patterns:** Full range of straight knives including art daggers. **Technical:** Art grinds own damascus and purchased damascus. Creates clay-tempered hamon on 1095 blade steel. **Prices:** $300 to $1000. **Remarks:** First knife sold in 1986, part-time maker, member of ABS and KCKA. **Mark:** Last name on the spline.

DAVIDSON, EDMUND
3345 Virginia Ave, Goshen, VA 24439 **Contact:** 540-997-5651, davidson.edmund@gmail.com, edmunddavidson.com
Specialties: High class art integrals. **Patterns:** Many hunters and art models. **Technical:** CPM 154-CM. **Prices:** $100 to infinity. **Remarks:** Full-time maker, first knife sold in 1986. **Mark:** Name in deer head or custom logos.

DAVIDSON, SCOTT
SOLID ROCK KNIVES, 149 Pless Cir., Alto, GA 30510 **Contact:** 678-316-1318, (fax) 770-869-0882, solidrockknives@bellsouth.net
Specialties: Tactical knives, some hunters, skinners, bird-and-trout and neck knives. **Technical:** Stock-removal method of blade making, using CPM S30V, 440C and ATS-34

steels, also 01 and 1095HC tool steels. **Prices:** $100 to $1,200, depending on materials used. **Remarks:** Part-time maker, first knife made in 1996. **Mark:** "Ichthys," the Christian fish, with maker's name and address in or around the fish.

DAVIS, BARRY L
4262 US 20, Castleton, NY 12033 **Contact:** 518-477-5036, daviscustomknives@yahoo.com

Specialties: Collector grade damascus folders. Traditional designs with focus on turn-of-the-century techniques employed. Sole authorship. Forges own damascus, does all carving, filework, gold work and piquet. Uses only natural handle material. Enjoys doing multi-blade as well as single blade folders and daggers. **Prices:** Prices range from $2000 to $7000. **Remarks:** First knife sold in 1980.

DAVIS, CHARLIE
ANZA KNIVES, PO Box 457, Lakeside, CA 92040-9998 **Contact:** 619-561-9445, (fax) 619-390-6283, sales@anzaknives.com, anzaknives.com

Specialties: Fancy and embellished working straight knives of his design. **Patterns:** Hunters, camp and utility knives. **Technical:** Grinds high-carbon files. **Prices:** $20 to $185, custom depends. **Remarks:** Full-time maker, first knife sold in 1980. Now offers custom. **Mark:** ANZA U.S.A.

DAVIS, DON
8415 Coyote Run, Loveland, CO 80537-9665 **Contact:** 970-669-9016, (fax) 970-669-8072

Specialties: Working straight knives in standard patterns or to customer specs. **Patterns:** Hunters, utility knives, skinners and survival knives. **Technical:** Grinds 440C, ATS-34. **Prices:** $75 to $250. **Remarks:** Full-time maker, first knife sold in 1985. **Mark:** Signature, city and state.

DAVIS, JESSE W
3853 Peyton Rd., Coldwater, MS 38618 **Contact:** 901-849-7250, jessewdavis@yahoo.com

Specialties: Working straight knives and boots in standard patterns and to customer specs. **Patterns:** Boot knives, daggers, fighters, subhilts & bowies. **Technical:** Grinds A2, D2, 440C and commercial damascus. **Prices:** $125 to $1000. **Remarks:** Full-time maker, first knife sold in 1977. Former member Knifemakers Guild (in good standing). **Mark:** Name or initials.

DAVIS, JOEL
74538 165th, Albert Lea, MN 56007 **Contact:** 507-377-0808, joelknives@yahoo.com

Specialties: Complete sole authorship presentation grade highly complex pattern-welded mosaic damascus blade and bolster stock. **Patterns:** To date Joel has executed over 900 different mosaic damascus patterns in the past four years. Anything conceived by maker's imagination. **Technical:** Uses various heat colorable "high vibrancy" steels, nickel 200 and some powdered metal for bolster stock only. Uses 1095, 1075 and 15N20. High carbon steels for cutting edge blade stock only. **Prices:** 15 to $50 per square inch and up depending on complexity of pattern. **Remarks:** Full-time mosaic damascus metal smith focusing strictly on never-before-seen mosaic patterns. Most of maker's work is used for art knives ranging between $1500 to $4500.

DAVIS, JOHN
235 Lampe Rd, Selah, WA 98942 **Contact:** 509-697-3845, 509-945-4570, jdwelds@charter.net

Specialties: damascus and mosaic damascus, working knives, working folders, art knives and art folders. **Technical:** Some ATS-34 and stainless damascus. Embellishes with fancy stabilized wood, mammoth and walrus ivory. **Prices:** Start at $150. **Remarks:** Part-time maker, first knife sold in 1996. **Mark:** Name city and state on damascus stamp initials, name inside back RFR.

DAVIS, JOHN H.
N. State Road 135 Freetown, IN 47235 **Contact:** 209-740-7125, johndavis@custom-knifemaker.com, custom-knifemaker.com

Patterns: daggers, bowies, drop-point hunters, bird & trout knives, folding knives and custom orders. **Technical:** Forged knives primarily, but does some stock removal, makes own damascus steel using 1095 and 15N20, and uses 52100, W2, CPM 154 stainless steel and 440C. **Prices:** $250 and up. **Remarks:** Part-time maker, first knife made in high school in 1977. Voting member of the Knifemakers' Guild and an ABS member, also president and former treasurer for the Florida Knifemakers' Association. **Mark:** JD with a cross bar for the "H" between the "JD" and "Davis" under it.

DAVIS, STEVE
3370 Chatsworth Way, Powder Springs, GA 30127 **Contact:** 770-427-5740, bsdavis@bellsouth.net

Specialties: Gents and ladies folders. **Patterns:** Straight knives, slip-joint folders, locking-liner folders. **Technical:** Grinds ATS-34 forges own damascus. Offers filework, prefers hand-rubbed finishes and natural handle materials. Uses pearl, ivory, stag and exotic woods. **Prices:** $250 to $800, some to $1500. **Remarks:** Full-time maker, first knife sold in 1988. Doing business as Custom Knives by Steve Davis. **Mark:** Name engraved on blade.

DAVIS JR., JIM
5129 Ridge St, Zephyrhills, FL 33541 **Contact:** 813-779-9213 813-469-4241 Cell, jimdavisknives@aol.com

Specialties: Presentation-grade fixed blade knives w/composite hidden tang handles. Employs a variety of ancient and contemporary ivories. **Patterns:** One-of-a-kind gents, personal, and executive knives and hunters w/unique cam-lock pouch sheaths and display stands. **Technical:** Flat grinds ATS-34 and stainless damascus w/most work by hand w/assorted files. **Prices:** $300 and up. **Remarks:** Full-time maker, first knives sold in 2000. **Mark:** Signature w/printed name over "HANDCRAFTED."

DAVISON, TODD A.
230 S. Wells St., Kosciusko, MS 39090 **Contact:** 662-739-7440, crazyknifeblade@yahoo.com, tadscustomknives.com

Specialties: Making working/using and collector folders of his design. All knives are truly made one of a kind. Each knife has a serial number inside the liner. **Patterns:** Single and double blade traditional slip-joint pocket knives. **Technical:** Free hand hollow ground blades, hand finished. Using only the very best materials possible. Holding the highest standards to fit & finish and detail. Does his own heat treating. ATS34 and D2 steel. **Prices:** $450 to $900, some higher. **Remarks:** Full time maker, first knife sold in 1981. **Mark:** T.A. DAVISON USA.

DAWKINS, DUDLEY L
221 NW Broadmoor Ave., Topeka, KS 66606-1254 **Contact:** 785-817-9343, dawkind@reagan.com or dawkind@sbcglobal.net

Specialties: Stylized old or "Dawkins Forged" with anvil in center. New tang stamps. **Patterns:** Straight knives. **Technical:** Mostly carbon steel, some damascus-all knives forged. **Prices:** Knives: $275 and up, Sheaths: $95 and up. **Remarks:** All knives supplied with wood-lined sheaths. ABS Member, sole authorship. **Mark:** Stylized "DLD or Dawkins Forged with anvil in center.

DAWSON, BARRY
7760 E Hwy 69, Prescott Valley, AZ 86314 **Contact:** 928-255-9830, dawsonknives@yahoo.com, dawsonknives.com

Specialties: Samurai swords, combat knives, collector daggers, tactical, folding and hunting knives. **Patterns:** Offers over 60 different models. **Technical:** Grinds 440C, ATS-34, own heat-treatment. **Prices:** $75 to $1500, some to $5000. **Remarks:** Full-time maker, first knife sold in 1975. **Mark:** Last name, USA in print or last name in script.

DAWSON, LYNN
7760 E Hwy 69 #C-5 157, Prescott Valley, AZ 86314 **Contact:** 928-713-2812, lynnknives@yahoo.com, lynnknives.com

Specialties: Swords, hunters, utility, and art pieces. **Patterns:** Over 25 patterns to choose from. **Technical:** Grinds 440C, ATS-34, own heat treating. **Prices:** $80 to $1000. **Remarks:** Custom work and her own designs. **Mark:** The name "Lynn" in print or script.

DE BRAGA, JOSE C.
1341 9e Rue, Trois Rivieres, QC, CANADA G8Y 2Z2 **Contact:** 418-948-5864, josedebraga@cgocable.ca

Specialties: Art knives, fantasy pieces and working knives of his design or to customer specs. **Patterns:** Knives with sculptured or carved handles, from miniatures to full-size working knives. **Technical:** Grinds and hand-files 440C and ATS-34. A variety of steels and handle materials available. Offers lost wax casting. **Prices:** Start at $300. **Remarks:** Full-time maker, wax modeler, sculptor and knifemaker, first knife sold in 1984. **Mark:** Initials in stylized script and serial number.

DE MARIA JR., ANGELO
12 Boronda Rd, Carmel Valley, CA 93924 **Contact:** 831-659-3381, (fax) 831-659-1315, angelodemaria1@mac.com

Specialties: damascus, fixed and folders, sheaths. **Patterns:** Mosiac and random. **Technical:** Forging 5160, 1084 and 15N20. **Prices:** $200+. **Remarks:** Part-time maker. **Mark:** Angelo de Maria Carmel Valley, CA etch or AdM stamp.

DE MESA, JOHN
1565 W. Main St., STE. 208 #229, Lewisville, TX 75057 **Contact:** 972-310-3877, TogiArts@me.com, togiarts.com and togiarts.com/CSC/index.html

Specialties: Japanese sword polishing. **Technical:** Traditional sword polishing of Japanese swords made by sword makers in Japan and U.S. **Prices:** Starting at $75 per inch. **Remarks:** Custom Swords Collaborations IN collaboration with Jose De Braga, we can mount Japanese style sword with custom carved handles, sword fittings and scabbards to customer specs.

DE WET, KOBUS
2601 River Road, Yakima, WA 98902 **Contact:** 509-728-3736, kobus@moderndamascus.com, moderndamascus.com

Specialties: Working and art knives **Patterns:** Every knife is unique. Fixed blades and folders. Hunting, bowie, Tactical and Utility knives. **Technical:** I enjoy forging my own damascus steel, mainly from 15N20 and 1084. I also use stock removal and stainless steels. **Prices:** Starting at $200 **Remarks:** Part time maker, started in 2007 **Mark:** Circled "K" / Modern damascus - Kobus de Wet

DEAN, HARVEY J
3266 CR 232, Rockdale, TX 76567 **Contact:** 512-446-3111, (fax) 512-446-5060, dean@tex1.net, harveydean.com

Specialties: Collectible, functional knives. **Patterns:** bowies, hunters, folders, daggers, swords, battle axes, camp and combat knives. **Technical:** Forges 1095, O1 and his damascus. **Prices:** $350 to $10,000. **Remarks:** Full-time maker, first knife sold in 1981. **Mark:** Last name and MS.

DEBAUD, JAKE
1309 Glyndon Dr., Plano, TX 75034 **Contact:** 972-741-6280, jake@debaudblades.com, debaudknives.com

Specialties: Custom damascus art knives, hunting knives and tactical knives. **Technical:** A2, D2, 01, 1095 and some stainless if requested ATS-34 or 154CM and S30V. **Remarks:** Full-time maker. Have been making knives for three years.

DEBRAGA, JOVAN
141 Notre Dame des Victoir, Quebec, CANADA G2G 1J3 **Contact:** 418-997-

0819/418-877-1915, jovancdebraga@msn.com
Specialties: Art knives, fantasy pieces and working knives of his design or to customer specs. **Patterns:** Knives with sculptured or carved handles, from miniatures to full-sized working knives. **Technical:** Grinds and hand-files 440C, and ATS-34. A variety of steels and handle materials available. **Prices:** Start at $300. **Remarks:** Full time maker. Sculptor and knifemaker. First knife sold in 2003. **Mark:** Initials in stylized script and serial number.

DEDOMINICIS, RONNIE
DeDominicis Knives Huntsville, TX **Contact:** 936-577-8898, rk.na.dk@gmail.com, www.dedominicisknives.com, www.etsy.com/shop/DeDominicisKnives, www.facebook.com/DeDominicisKnives
Patterns: Bowies.

DEIBERT, MICHAEL
7570 Happy Hollow Rd., Trussville, AL 35173 **Contact:** 205-612-2359, mike@deibertknives.com, deibertknives.com
Specialties: Working straight knives in full or hidden tangs, in mono or damascus steel. **Patterns:** Choppers, bowies, hunters and bird-and-trout knives. **Technical:** Makes own damascus, forges all blades and does own heat treating. **Remarks:** ABS journeyman smith, part-time maker. **Mark:** Flaming "D" over an anvil.

DEL RASO, PETER
28 Mayfield Dr, Mt. Waverly, VIC, AUSTRALIA 3149 **Contact:** 613 98060644, delraso@optusnet.com.au
Specialties: Fixed blades, some folders, art knives. **Patterns:** Daggers, bowies, tactical, boot, personal and working knives. **Technical:** Grinds ATS-34, commercial damascus and any other type of steel on request. **Prices:** $200 to $3000. **Remarks:** Part-time maker, first show in 1993. **Mark:** Maker's surname stamped.

DELAROSA, JIM
502 Fairview Cir., Waterford, WI 53185 **Contact:** 262-422-8604, D-knife@hotmail.com
Specialties: Working straight knives and folders of his design or customer specs. **Patterns:** Hunters, skinners, fillets, utility and locking folders. **Technical:** Grinds ATS-34, 440-C, D2, O1 and commercial damascus. **Prices:** $100 to $500, some higher. **Remarks:** Part-time maker. **Mark:** First and last name.

DELL, WOLFGANG
Am Alten Berg 9, Owen-Teck, GERMANY D-73277 **Contact:** 49-7021-81802, wolfgang@dell-knives.de, dell-knives.de
Specialties: Fancy high-art straight of his design and to customer specs. **Patterns:** Fighters, hunters, bowies and utility/camp knives. **Technical:** Grinds ATS-34, RWL-34, Elmax, damascus (Fritz Schneider). Offers high gloss finish and engraving. **Prices:** $500 to $1000, some to $1600. **Remarks:** Full-time maker, first knife sold in 1992. **Mark:** Hopi hand of peace.

DELLANA
STARLANI INT'L INC, P.O. Box 111, Gallipolis Ferry, WV 25515 **Contact:** (702) 569-7827, DellanaKnives@gmail.com, DellanaKnives.com
Specialties: Collector grade fancy/embellished high art folders and art daggers. **Patterns:** Locking folders and art daggers. **Technical:** Forges her own damascus and W-2. Engraves, does stone setting, filework, carving and gold/platinum fabrication. Prefers exotic, high karat gold, platinum, silver, gemstone and mother-of-pearl handle materials. **Prices:** Upscale. **Remarks:** Sole authorship, full-time maker, first knife sold in 1994. Also does one high art collaboration a year with Van Barnett. Member: Art Knife Invitational and ABS. **Mark:** First name.

DELONG, DICK
PO Box 1024, Centerville, TX 75833-1024 **Contact:** 903-536-1454
Specialties: Fancy working knives and fantasy pieces. **Patterns:** Hunters and small skinners. **Technical:** Grinds and files O1, D2, 440C and damascus. Offers cocobolo and Osage orange for handles. **Prices:** Start at $50. **Remarks:** Part-time maker. Member of Art Knife Invitational. Voting member of Knifemakers Guild. Member of ABS. **Mark:** Last name, some unmarked.

DEMENT, LARRY
PO Box 1807, Prince Fredrick, MD 20678 **Contact:** 410-586-9011
Specialties: Fixed blades. **Technical:** Forged and stock removal. **Prices:** $75 to $200. **Remarks:** Affordable, good feelin', quality knives. Part-time maker.

DENNEHY, JOHN D
The Wild Irish Rose Custom Leatherworks. 1142 52 Ave. Ct., Greeley, CO 80634 **Contact:** 970-218-7128, jddennehy@yahoo.com, thewildirishrose.com
Specialties: Working straight knives, throwers, and leatherworker's knives. **Technical:** 440C, & O1, heat treats own blades, part-time maker, first knife sold in 1989. **Patterns:** Small hunting to presentation bowies, leatherworks round and head knives. **Prices:** $200 and up. **Remarks:** Custom leather work, now making DAN-D trademarked knives (Dan Dennehy)

DENNING, GENO
CAVEMAN ENGINEERING, 135 Allenvalley Rd, Gaston, SC 29053 **Contact:** 803-794-6067, cden101656@aol.com, cavemanengineering.com
Specialties: Mirror finish. **Patterns:** Hunters, fighters, folders. **Technical:** ATS-34, 440V, S-30-V D2. **Prices:** $100 and up. **Remarks:** Full-time maker since 1996. Sole income since 1999. Instructor at Montgomery Community College (Grinding Blades). A director of SCAK: South Carolina Association of Knifemakers. **Mark:** Troy NC.

DERESPINA, RICHARD
derespinaknives@yahoo.com, derespinaknives.com
Specialties: Custom fixed blades and folders, Kris and Karambit. **Technical:** I use the

stock removal method. Steels I use are S30V, 154CM, D2, 440C, BG42. Handles made of G10 particularly Micarta, etc. **Prices:** $150 to $550 depending on model. **Remarks:** Full-time maker. **Mark:** My etched logos are two, my last name and Brooklyn NY mark as well as the Star/Yin Yang logo. The star being both representative of various angles of attack common in combat as well as being three triangles, each points to levels of metaphysical understanding. The Yin and Yang have my company initials on each side D & K. Yin and Yang shows the ever present physics of life.

DERINGER, CHRISTOPH
625 Chemin Lower, Cookshire, QC, CANADA J0B 1M0 **Contact:** 819-345-4260, cdsab@sympatico.ca
Specialties: Traditional working/using straight knives and folders of his design and to customer specs. **Patterns:** Boots, hunters, folders, art knives, kitchen knives and utility/camp knives. **Technical:** Forges 5160, O1 and damascus. Offers a variety of filework. **Prices:** Start at $500. **Remarks:** Full-time maker, first knife sold in 1989. **Mark:** Last name stamped/engraved.

DERR, HERBERT
413 Woodland Dr, St. Albans, WV 25177 **Contact:** 304-727-3866
Specialties: damascus one-of-a-kind knives, carbon steels also. **Patterns:** Birdseye, ladder back, mosaics. **Technical:** All styles functional as well as artistically pleasing. **Prices:** $90 to $175 carbon, damascus $250 to $800. **Remarks:** All damascus made by maker. **Mark:** H.K. Derr.

DESAULNIERS, ALAIN
100 Pope Street, Cookshire, QC, CANADA J0B 1M0, pinklaperez@sympatico.ca desoknives.com
Specialties: Mostly Loveless style knives. **Patterns:** Double grind fighters, hunters, daggers, etc. **Technical:** Stock removal, ATS-34, CPM. High-polished blades, tapered tangs, high-quality handles. **Remarks:** Full-time. Collaboration with John Young. **Prices:** $425 and up. **Mark:** Name and city in logo.

DESROSIERS, ADAM
PO Box 1954, Petersburg, AK 99833 **Contact:** 907-518-4570, adam@alaskablades.com alaskablades.com
Specialties: High performance, forged, carbon steel and damascus camp choppers, and hunting knives. Hidden tang, full tang, and full integral construction. High performance heat treating. Knife designs inspired by life in Alaskan bush. **Technical:** Hand forges tool steels and damascus. Sole authorship. Full range of handle materials, micarta to Ivory. Preferred steels: W-2, O-1, L-6, 15n20, 1095. **Prices:** $200 - $3000. **Remarks:** ABS member. Has trained with Masters around the world. **Mark:** DrsRosiers over Alaska, underlined with a rose.

DESROSIERS, HALEY
PO Box 1954, Petersburg, AK 99833 **Contact:** 907-518-1416, haley@alaskablades.com alaskablades.com
Specialties: Hunting knives, integrals and a few choppers, high performance.**Technical:** Hand forged blades designed for hard use, exotic wood, antler and ivory handles. **Prices:** $300 - $1500. **Remarks:** Forged first knife in 2001. Part-time bladesmith all year except for commercial fishing season. **Mark:** Capital HD.

DETMER, PHILLIP
14140 Bluff Rd, Breese, IL 62230 **Contact:** 618-526-4834, jpdetmer@att.net
Specialties: Working knives. **Patterns:** bowies, daggers and hunters. **Technical:** Grinds ATS-34 and D2. **Prices:** $60 to $400. **Remarks:** Part-time maker, first knife sold in 1977. **Mark:** Last name with dagger.

DEUBEL, CHESTER J.
6211 N. Van Ark Rd., Tucson, AZ 85743 **Contact:** 520-440-7255, cjdeubel@yahoo.com, cjdeubel.com
Specialties: Fancy working straight knives and folders of his or customer design, with intricate file work. **Patterns:** Fighters, bowies, daggers, hunters, camp knives, and cowboy. **Technical:** Flat guard, hollow grind, antiqued, all types damascus, 154cpm Stainsteel, high carbon steel, 440c Stainsteel. **Prices:** From $250 to $3500. **Remarks:** Started making part-time in 1980, went to full-time in 2000. Don Patch is my engraver. **Mark:** C.J. Deubel.

DEVERAUX, BUTCH
PO Box 1356, Riverton, WY 82501 **Contact:** 307-851-0601, bdeveraux@wyoming.com, deverauxknives.com
Specialties: High-performance working straight knives. **Patterns:** Hunters, fighters, EDC's, miniatures and camp knives. **Technical:** Forged 52100 blade steel, brass guards, sheep-horn handles, as well as stag, cocobolo, she-oak and ironwood. **Prices:** $400 to $3,000. **Remarks:** Part-time maker, first knife sold in 2005. **Mark:** Deveraux on right ricasso.

DEYONG, CLARENCE
8716 Camelot Trace, Sturtevant, WI 53177 **Contact:** 630-465-6761, cmdeyong@yahoo.com, deyongknives.com
Specialties: Affordable quality straight knives of his or customer's design. **Patterns:** Hunters, skinners, fighters, bowies and camp knives. **Technical:** Uses old rasps and files for blade material, along with damascus and a variety of high carbon steels. Does stock removal and forging. Places an emphasis on natural handle materials. Custom makes his own fitted, leather sheaths. **Prices:** $150 and up. **Remarks:** Making knives since 1981. **Mark:** DeYong and sequential blade # engraved on the blade.

DIAZ, JOSE
409 W. 12th Ave, Ellensburg, WA 98926, jose@diaztools.com diaztools.com

custom knifemakers

Specialties: Affordable custom user-grade utility and camp knives. Also makes competition cutting knives. **Patterns:** Mas. **Technical:** Blade materials range from high carbon steels and damascus to high performance tool and stainless steels. Uses both forge and stock removal methods in shaping the steel. Handle materials include Tero Tuf, Black Butyl Burl, Micarta, natural woods and G10. **Prices:** $65-$700. **Remarks:** Part-time knife maker, made first knife in 2008. **Mark:** Reclining tree frog with a smile, and "Diaz Tools."

DICK, DAN
P.O. Box 2303, Hutchinson, KS 67504-2303 **Contact:** 620-669-6805, Dan@DanDickKnives.com, dandickknives.com
Specialties: Traditional working/using fixed bladed knives of maker's design. **Patterns:** Hunters, skinners and utility knives. **Technical:** Stock removal maker using CTS-XHP and D2. Prefers such materials as exotic and fancy burl woods. Makes his own sheaths, all leather with tooling. **Prices:** $150 and up. **Remarks:** Part-time maker since 2006. **Marks:** Name in outline border of Kansas.

DICKERSON, GAVIN
15 Anzac St., Primrose Ext. 2, Germiston, Gauteng, SOUTH AFRICA
Contact: +2784 250 1050, (fax) +27 011-965-0988, gavin.dickerson@denel.co.za
Specialties: Straight knives of his design or to customer specs. **Patterns:** Hunters, skinners, fighters and bowies. **Technical:** Hollow-grinds D2, 440C, ATS-34, 12C27 and damascus upon request. Prefers natural handle materials, offers synthetic handle materials. **Prices:** $190 to $2500. **Remarks:** Part-time maker, first knife sold in 1982. **Mark:** Name in full.

DICKISON, SCOTT S
179 Taylor Rd, Portsmouth, RI 02871 **Contact:** 401-855-1791, squared22@gmail.com, sqauredknives.com
Specialties: Straight knives, locking folders of his design. **Patterns:** Primarily Sgian Dubh knives. **Technical:** Forges and grinds commercial damascus, D2, and Sandvik stainless. **Prices:** $400 to $1200, some higher. **Remarks:** Part-time maker, first knife sold in 1989. **Mark:** Stylized initials.

DICRISTOFANO, ANTHONY P
10519 Nevada Ave., Melrose Park, IL 60164 **Contact:** 847-845-9598, sukemitsu@sbcglobal.net namahagesword.com or sukemitsu.com
Specialties: Japanese-style swords. **Patterns:** Katana, Wakizashi, Otanto, Kozuka. **Technical:** Tradition and some modern steels. All clay tempered and traditionally hand polished using Japanese wet stones. **Remarks:** Part-time maker. **Prices:** Varied, available on request. **Mark:** Blade tang signed in "SUKEMITSU."

DIETZ, HOWARD
421 Range Rd, New Braunfels, TX 78132 **Contact:** 830-885-4662
Specialties: Lock-back folders, working straight knives. **Patterns:** Folding hunters, high-grade pocket knives. ATS-34, 440C, CPM 440V, D2 and stainless damascus. **Prices:** $300 to $1000. **Remarks:** Full-time gun and knifemaker, first knife sold in 1995. **Mark:** Name, city, and state.

DIETZEL, BILL
779 Baycove Ct., Middleburg, FL 32068 **Contact:** 904-282-1091, wdms97@bellsouth.net
Specialties: Forged straight knives and folders. **Patterns:** His interpretations. **Technical:** Forges his damascus and other steels. **Prices:** Middle ranges. **Remarks:** Likes natural materials, uses titanium in folder liners. Master Smith (1997). **Mark:** Name.

DIGANGI, JOSEPH M
PO Box 257, Los Ojos, NM 87551 **Contact:** 505-929-2987, (fax) 505-753-8144, digangidesigns.com
Specialties: Kitchen and table cutlery. **Patterns:** French chef's knives, carving sets, steak knife sets, some camp knives and hunters. Holds patents and trademarks for "System II" kitchen cutlery set. **Technical:** Grinds ATS-34. **Prices:** $150 to $595, some to $1200. **Remarks:** Full-time maker, first knife sold in 1983. **Mark:** DiGangi Designs.

DILL, ROBERT
1812 Van Buren, Loveland, CO 80538 **Contact:** 970-667-5144, (fax) 970-667-5144, dillcustomknives@msn.com
Specialties: Fancy and working knives of his design. **Patterns:** Hunters, bowies and fighters. **Technical:** Grinds 440C and D2. **Prices:** $100 to $800. **Remarks:** Full-time maker, first knife sold in 1984. **Mark:** Logo stamped into blade.

DINTRUFF, CHUCK
306 East S.R. 60, Plant City, FL 33567 **Contact:** 813-381-6916, DINTRUFFKNIVES@aol.com, dintruffknives.com, spinwellfab.com

DION, GREG
3032 S Jackson St, Oxnard, CA 93033 **Contact:** 519-981-1013
Specialties: Working straight knives, some fancy. Welcomes special orders. **Patterns:** Hunters, fighters, camp knives, bowies and tantos. **Technical:** Grinds ATS-34, 154CM and 440C. **Prices:** $85 to $300, some to $600. **Remarks:** Part-time maker, first knife sold in 1985. **Mark:** Name.

DIONATAM, FRANCO
Sebastiao Jacinto de Amorim goncalves n 277, Filadelfia, Ibitinga-SP, BRAZIL 14940-000, francofacasartesanais@hotmail.com
Patterns: bowies, hunters, camp knives, utilitarian and chef's knives. **Technical:** Uses 5160, 1070, 52100 and several damascus steel patterns. Knife handle materials include stabilized wood, natural wood, mammoth ivory, deer horn and exotic materials. **Prices:** $700 to $6,000. **Remarks:** ABS journeyman smith who prefers working from orders. **Mark:** Franco.

DIOTTE, JEFF
DIOTTE KNIVES, 159 Laurier Dr, LaSalle, ON, CANADA N9J 1L4 **Contact:** 519-978-2764

DIPPOLD, AL
90 damascus Ln, Perryville, MO 63775 **Contact:** 573-547-1119, adippold@midwest.net
Specialties: Fancy one-of-a-kind locking folders. **Patterns:** Locking folders. **Technical:** Forges and grinds mosaic and pattern welded damascus. Offers filework on all folders. **Prices:** $500 to $3500, some higher. **Remarks:** Full-time maker, first knife sold in 1980. **Mark:** Last name in logo inside of liner.

DISKIN, MATT
PO Box 653, Freeland, WA 98249 **Contact:** 360-730-0451, info@volcanknives.com, volcanknives.com
Specialties: damascus autos. **Patterns:** Dirks and daggers. **Technical:** Forges mosaic damascus using 15N20, 1084, 02, 06, L6, pure nickel. **Prices:** Start at $500. Remarks, Full-time maker. **Mark:** Last name.

DIXON JR., IRA E
PO Box 26, Cave Junction, OR 97523, iraisknives@yahoo.com
Specialties: Straight knives of his design. **Patterns:** All patterns include art knives. **Technical:** Grinds CPM materials, damascus and some tool steels. **Prices:** $275 to $2000. **Remarks:** Full-time maker, first knife sold in 1993. **Mark:** First name, Handmade.

DOBRATZ, ERIC
25371 Hillary Lane, Laguna Hills, CA 92653 **Contact:** 949-233-5170, knifesmith@gmail.com
Specialties: Differentially quenched blades with Hamon of his design or with customer input. **Patterns:** Hunting, camp, kitchen, fighters, bowies, traditional tanto, and unique fixed blade designs. **Technical:** Hand-forged high carbon and damascus. Prefers natural material for handles, rare/exotic woods and stag, but also uses micarta and homemade synthetic materials. **Prices:** $150 - $1500. **Remarks:** Part-time maker, first knife made in 1995. **Mark:** Stylized Scarab beetle.

DOBSON, RICHARD
Richard Dobson Custom Knives 658 River Bluff Ln Gainesville, TX 76240 **Contact:** 940-902-9052, Facebook: Richard Dobson Custom Knives
Patterns: Hunters, skinners, bowies, fighters, and kitchen knives.

DODD, ROBERT F
4340 E Canyon Dr, Camp Verde, AZ 86322 **Contact:** 928-567-3333, rfdknives@commspeed.net, rfdoddknives.com
Specialties: Folders, fixed blade hunter/skinners, bowies, daggers. **Patterns:** Drop point. **Technical:** ATS-34 and damascus. **Prices:** $250 and up. **Remarks:** Hand tooled leather sheaths. **Mark:** R. F. Dodd, Camp Verde AZ.

DOIRON, DONALD
6 Chemin Petit Lac des Ced, Messines, QC, CANADA J0X-2J0 **Contact:** 819-465-2489

DOMINY, CHUCK
PO Box 593, Colleyville, TX 76034 **Contact:** 817-498-4527
Specialties: Titanium LinerLock® folders. **Patterns:** Hunters, utility/camp knives and LinerLock® folders. **Technical:** Grinds 440C and ATS-34. **Prices:** $250 to $3000. **Remarks:** Full-time maker, first knife sold in 1976. **Mark:** Last name.

DOOLITTLE, MIKE
13 Denise Ct, Novato, CA 94947 **Contact:** 415-897-3246
Specialties: Working straight knives in standard patterns. **Patterns:** Hunters and fishing knives. **Technical:** Grinds 440C, 154CM and ATS-34. **Prices:** $125 to $200, some to $750. **Remarks:** Part-time maker, first knife sold in 1981. **Mark:** Name, city and state.

DORNELES, DAVE
7404 NW 30th St, Bethany, OK 73008 **Contact:** 405-789-0750
Specialties: Folders of his design. **Patterns:** Various patterns. **Technical:** Hand-grinds 440C, ATS-34. Offers engraving and filework on all folders. **Prices:** Starting at $450. **Remarks:** Full-time maker, first knife sold in 1987. **Mark:** First initial, last name.

DORNELES, LUCIANO OLIVERIRA
Rua 15 De Novembro 2222, Nova Petropolis, RS, BRAZIL 95150-000 **Contact:** 011-55-54-303-303-90, tchebufalo@hotmail.com
Specialties: Traditional "true" Brazilian-style working knives and to customer specs. **Patterns:** Brazilian hunters, utility and camp knives, bowies, Dirk. A master at the making of the true "Faca Campeira Gaucha," the true camp knife of the famous Brazilian Gauchos. A Dorneles knife is 100 percent hand-forged with sledge hammers only. Can make spectacular damascus hunters/daggers. **Technical:** Forges only 52100 and his own damascus, can put silver wire inlay on customer design handles on special orders, uses only natural handle materials. **Prices:** $250 to $1000. **Mark:** Symbol with L. Dorneles.

DOTSON, TRACY
1280 Hwy C-4A, Baker, FL 32531 **Contact:** 850-537-2407
Specialties: Folding fighters and small folders. **Patterns:** LinerLock® and lockback folders. **Technical:** Hollow-grinds ATS-34 and commercial damascus. **Prices:** Start at $250. **Remarks:** Part-time maker, first knife sold in 1995. **Mark:** Last name.

DOUCETTE, R
CUSTOM KNIVES, 19 Evelyn St., Brantford, ON, CANADA N3R 3G8 **Contact:** 519-756-9040, randy@randydoucetteknives.com, randydoucetteknives.com
Specialties: High-end tactical folders with filework and multiple grinds. **Patterns:** Tactical

folders. **Technical:** All knives are handmade. The only outsourcing is heat treatment. **Prices:** $900 to $2,500. **Remarks:** Full-time knifemaker, 2-year waiting list. Maker is proud to produce original knife designs every year!Im **Mark:** R. Doucette

DOURSIN, GERARD
Chemin des Croutoules, Pernes les Fontaines, FRANCE 84210
Specialties: Period pieces. **Patterns:** Liner locks and daggers. **Technical:** Forges mosaic damascus. **Prices:** $600 to $4000. **Remarks:** First knife sold in 1983. **Mark:** First initial, last name and I stop the lion.

DOUSSOT, LAURENT
1008 Montarville, St. Bruno, QC, CANADA J3V 3T1 **Contact:** 450-441-3298, doussot@skalja.com, skalja.com, doussot-knives.com
Specialties: Fancy and embellished folders and fantasy knives. **Patterns:** Fighters and locking folders. **Technical:** Grinds ATS-34 and commercial damascus. Scale carvings on all knives, most bolsters are carved titanium. **Prices:** $350 to $3000. **Remarks:** Part-time maker, first knife was sold in 1992. **Mark:** Stylized initials inside circle.

DOWNIE, JAMES T
1295 Sandy Ln., Apt. 1208, Sarnia, Ontario, CANADA N7V 4K5 **Contact:** 519-491-8234
Specialties: Serviceable straight knives and folders, period pieces. **Patterns:** Hunters, bowies, camp knives, fillet and miniatures. **Technical:** Grinds D2, 440C and ATS-34, Damasteel, stainless steel damascus. **Prices:** $195 and up. **Remarks:** Full-time maker, first knife sold in 1978. **Mark:** Signature of first and middle initials, last name.

DOWNING, LARRY
12268 State Route 181 N, Bremen, KY 42325 **Contact:** 270-525-3523, larrydowning@bellsouth.net, downingknives.com
Specialties: Working straight knives and bowies. **Patterns:** From mini-knives to daggers, folding lockers to interframes. **Technical:** Grinds 154CM, CPM154, damascus. **Prices:** $250 to $2000, some higher. **Remarks:** Semi-retired, first knife sold in 1979. **Mark:** Name in arrowhead.

DOWNING, TOM
2675 12th St, Cuyahoga Falls, OH 44223 **Contact:** 330-923-7464
Specialties: Working straight knives, period pieces. **Patterns:** Hunters, fighters and tantos. **Technical:** Grinds 440C, ATs-34 and CPM-T-440V. Prefers natural handle materials. **Prices:** $150 to $900, some to $1500. **Remarks:** Part-time maker, first knife sold in 1979. **Mark:** First and middle initials, last name.

DOWNS, JAMES F
2247 Summit View Rd, Powell, OH 43065 **Contact:** 614-766-5350, jfdowns1@yahoo.com, downshandmadeknives.com
Specialties: Working straight knives of his design or to customer specs. **Patterns:** Folders, bowies, boot, hunters, utility. **Technical:** Grinds 440C and other steels. Prefers mastodon ivory, all pearls, stabilized wood and elephant ivory. **Prices:** $75 to $1200. **Remarks:** Full-time maker, first knife sold in 1980. **Mark:** Last name.

DOX, JAN
Zwanebloemlaan 27, Schoten, BELGIUM B 2900 **Contact:** 32 3 658 77 43, jan.dox@scarlet.be, http://doxblades.weebly.com
Specialties: Working/using knives, from kitchen to battlefield. **Patterns:** Own designs, some based on traditional ethnic patterns (Scots, Celtic, Scandinavian and Japanese) or to customer specs. **Technical:** Grinds D2/A2 and stainless, forges carbon steels, convex edges. Handles: Wrapped in modern or traditional patterns, resin impregnated if desired. Natural or synthetic materials, some carved. **Prices:** $50 and up. **Remarks:** Spare-time maker, first knife sold 2001. **Mark:** Name or stylized initials.

DOYLE, JOHN
3334 McCulloch Rd. Beaverton, Michigan 48612 **Contact:** 989-802-9470, jdoyleknives@gmail.com
Specialties: Hunters, camp knives and bowies. **Technical:** Forges 1075, 1080, 1084, 1095 and 5160. Will practice stock-removal method of blademaking on small knives at times. **Remarks:** Full-time maker, first knife made in 2009. **Mark:** J. Doyle in "Invitation" style print font

DOZIER, BOB
Dozier Knives and Arkansas Made Dozier, PO Box 1941, Springdale, AR 72765 **Contact:** 888-823-0023/479-756-0023, (fax) 479-756-9139, info@dozierknives.com, dozierknives.com
Specialties: Folding knives and collector-grade knives (Dozier Knives) and hunting and tactical fixed blades (Arkansas Dozier Made). **Technical:** Uses D2. **Prices:** Start at $205 (Arkansas Made Dozier) or $500 (Dozier Knives). **Remarks:** Full-time maker, first knife sold in 1965. **Mark:** Dozier with an arrow through the D and year over arrow for foldiers, or R.L. Dozier, maker, St. Paul, AR in an oval for the collector-grad knives (Dozier Knives), and Arkansas, Made, Dozier in a circle (Arkansas Dozier Made).

DRAPER, AUDRA
#10 Creek Dr, Riverton, WY 82501 **Contact:** 307-856-6807, audknives@gmail.com, draperknives.info
Specialties: Daggers, hunters, and one-of-a-kind straight and folding knives. Also make pendants, earring and bracelets of damascus. **Patterns:** Damascus blades of various patterns. Design custom knives, using knives, and minis. **Technical:** Forge damascus, heat-treats all knives. **Prices:** Vary depending on item. **Remarks:** Full-time maker, and instructor of bladesmithing courses, master bladesmith in the ABS. **Mark:** Audra

DRAPER, MIKE
#10 Creek Dr, Riverton, WY 82501 **Contact:** 307-856-6807, adraper@wyoming.com

Specialties: Mainly folding knives in tactical fashion, occasonal fixed blade. Custom titanium-lined damascus rings. Titanium spatulas. **Patterns:** Hunters, bowies and camp knives, tactical survival. **Technical:** Grinds S30V stainless steel. **Prices:** Starting at $250+. **Remarks:** Full-time maker, first knife sold in 1996. **Mark:** Initials M.J.D. or name, city and state.

DREW, GERALD
213 Hawk Ridge Dr, Mill Spring, NC 28756 **Contact:** 828-713-4762
Specialties: Blade ATS-34 blades. Straight knives. **Patterns:** Hunters, camp knives, some bowies and tactical. **Technical:** ATS-34 preferred. **Prices:** $65 to $400. **Mark:** GL DREW.

DRISCOLL, MARK
4115 Avoyer Pl, La Mesa, CA 91941 **Contact:** 619-670-0695, markdriscoll91941@yahoo.com
Specialties: High-art, period pieces and working/using knives of his design or to customer specs, some fancy. **Patterns:** Swords, bowies, fighters, daggers, hunters and primitive (mountain man-styles). **Technical:** Forges 52100, 5160, O1, L6, 1095, 15n20, W-2 steel and makes his own damascus and mokume, also does multiple quench heat treating. Uses exotic hardwoods, ivory and horn, offers fancy file work, carving, scrimshaws. **Prices:** $150 to $550, some to $1500. **Remarks:** Part-time maker, first knife sold in 1986. Doing business as Mountain Man Knives. **Mark:** Double "M."

DROST, JASON D
Rt 2 Box 49, French Creek, WV 26218 **Contact:** 304-472-7901
Specialties: Working/using straight knives of his design. **Patterns:** Hunters and utility/camp knives. **Technical:** Grinds 154CM and D2. **Prices:** $125 to $5000. **Remarks:** Spare-time maker, first knife sold in 1995. **Mark:** First and middle initials, last name, maker, city and state.

DROST, MICHAEL B
Rt 2 Box 49, French Creek, WV 26218 **Contact:** 304-472-7901
Specialties: Working/using straight knives and folders of all designs. **Patterns:** Hunters, locking folders and utility/camp knives. **Technical:** Grinds ATS-34, D2 and CPM-T-440V. Offers dove-tailed bolsters and spacers, filework and scrimshaw. **Prices:** $125 to $400, some to $740. **Remarks:** Full-time maker, first knife sold in 1990. Doing business as Drost Custom Knives. **Mark:** Name, city and state.

DRUMM, ARMIN
Lichtensteinstrasse 33, Dornstadt, GERMANY 89160 **Contact:** +49-174-8018018, armin@drumm-knives.de, drumm-knives.de
Specialties: One-of-a-kind forged and damascus fixed blade knives and folders. **Patterns:** Classic bowie knives, daggers, fighters, hunters, folders, swords. **Technical:** Forges own damascus and carbon steels, filework, carved handles. **Prices:** $250 to $800, some higher. **Remarks:** First knife sold in 2001, member of the German Knifemakers Guild. **Mark:** First initial, last name.

DUCKER, BRIAN
Lamorna Cottage, Common End, Colkirk, ENGLAND NR21 7JD **Contact:** 01-328-856-183, admin@grommitbaileyknives.com, grommitbaileyknives.com
Specialties: Hunters, utility pieces, bowies, camp knives, fighters and folders. **Technical:** Stock removal and forged 1095, 1075 and 80CrV2. Forging own damascus, using exotic and native hardwoods, stag, leather, Micarta and other synthetic materials, with brass and 301 stainless steel fittings. Own leatherwork and heat treating. **Remarks:** Part-time maker since 2009, full time Dec. 2013. All knives and sheaths are sole authorship. **Mark:** GROMMIT UK MAKER & BAILEY GROMMIT MAKERS.

DUFF, BILL
2801 Ash St, Poteau, OK 74953 **Contact:** 918-647-4458
Specialties: Straight knives and folders, some fancy. **Patterns:** Hunters, folders and miniatures. **Technical:** Grinds 440-C and commercial damascus. **Prices:** $250 and up. **Remarks:** First knife sold in 1976. **Mark:** Bill Duff.

DUFOUR, ARTHUR J
8120 De Armoun Rd, Anchorage, AK 99516 **Contact:** 907-345-1701
Specialties: Working straight knives from standard patterns. **Patterns:** Hunters, bowies, camp and fishing knives—grinded thin and pointed. **Technical:** Grinds 440C, ATS-34, AEB-L. Tempers 57-58R, hollow-grinds. **Prices:** $135, some to $250. **Remarks:** Part-time maker, first knife sold in 1970. **Mark:** Prospector logo.

DUGDALE, DANIEL J.
11 Eleanor Road, Walpole, MA 02081 **Contact:** 508-404-6509, dlpdugdale@comcast.net
Specialties: Button-lock and straight knives of his design. **Patterns:** Utilities, hunters, skinners, and tactical. **Technical:** Falt grinds D-2 and 440C, aluminum handles with anodized finishes. **Prices:** $150 to $500. **Remarks:** Part-time maker since 1977. **Mark:** Deer track with last name, town and state.

DUNCAN, RON
5090 N. Hwy. 63, Cairo, MO 65239 **Contact:** 660-263-8949, duncanmadeknives.com
Remarks: Duncan Made Knives

DUNKERLEY, RICK
PO Box 601, Lincoln, MT 59639 **Contact:** 406-210-4101, dunkerleyknives@gmail.com dunkerleyknives.com
Specialties: Mosaic damascus folders and carbon steel utility knives. **Patterns:** One-of-a-kind folders, standard hunters and utility designs. **Technical:** Forges 52100, damascus and mosaic damascus. Prefers natural handle materials. **Prices:** $200 and up. **Remarks:** Full-time maker, first knife sold in 1984, ABS Master Smith. Doing business as Dunkerley Custom Knives. Dunkerley handmade knives, sole authorship. **Mark:** Dunkerley, MS.

DUNLAP, JIM
800 E. Badger Lee Rd., Sallisaw, OK 74955 **Contact:** 918-774-2700, dunlapknives@gmail.com
Specialties: Traditional slip-joint folders. **Patterns:** Single- and multi-blade traditional slip joints. **Technical:** Grinds ATS-34, CPM-154 and damascus. **Prices:** $250 and up. **Remarks:** Part-time maker, first knife sold in 2009. **Mark:** Dunlap.

DUNN, STEVE
376 Biggerstaff Rd, Smiths Grove, KY 42171 **Contact:** 270-563-9830, dunnknives@windstream.net, stevedunnknives.com
Specialties: Working and using straight knives of his design, period pieces. Offers engraving and gold inlay. **Patterns:** Hunters, skinners, bowies, fighters, camp knives, folders, swords and battle axes. **Technical:** Forges own damascus, 1075, 15N20, 52100, 1084, L6. **Prices:** Moderate to upscale. **Remarks:** Full-time maker, first knife sold in 1990. **Mark:** Last name and MS.

DURAN, JERRY T
PO Box 9753, Albuquerque, NM 87119 **Contact:** 505-873-4676, jtdknives@hotmail.com, google.com/profiles/jtdknivesLLC
Specialties: Tactical folders, bowies, fighters, liner locks, autopsy and hunters. **Patterns:** Folders, bowies, hunters and tactical knives. **Technical:** Forges own damascus and forges carbon steel. **Prices:** Moderate to upscale. **Remarks:** Full-time maker, first knife sold in 1978. **Mark:** Initials in elk rack logo.

DURBIN, JERRY
Durbin's Forge, LLC P.O. Box 1037, Middleton, ID 83644 **Contact:** (208) 890-3873, durbinsforge@gmail.com, www.durbinsforge.com
Specialties: Leather and Kydex sheaths. **Patterns:** Kitchen and hunting knives. **Technical:** High-carbon steel shaped by forging or stock removal.

DURHAM, KENNETH
BUZZARD ROOST FORGE, 10495 White Pike, Cherokee, AL 35616 **Contact:** 256-359-4287, home.hiwaay.net/~jamesd/
Specialties: bowies, dirks, hunters. **Patterns:** Traditional patterns. **Technical:** Forges 1095, 5160, 52100 and makes own damascus. **Prices:** $85 to $1600. **Remarks:** Began making knives about 1995. Received Journeyman stamp 1999. Got Master Smith stamp in 2004. **Mark:** Bull's head with Ken Durham above and Cherokee AL below.

DURIO, FRED
144 Gulino St, Opelousas, LA 70570 **Contact:** 337-948-4831/cell 337-351-2652, fdurio@yahoo.com
Specialties: Folders. **Patterns:** Liner locks, plain and fancy. **Technical:** Makes own damascus. **Prices:** Moderate to upscale. **Remarks:** Full-time maker. **Mark:** Last name-Durio.

DUVALL, FRED
10715 Hwy 190, Benton, AR 72015 **Contact:** 501-778-9360
Specialties: Working straight knives and folders. **Patterns:** Locking folders, slip joints, hunters, fighters and bowies. **Technical:** Grinds D2 and CPM440V, forges 5160. **Prices:** $100 to $400, some to $800. **Remarks:** Part-time maker, first knife sold in 1973. **Mark:** Last name.

DWYER, DUANE
565 Country Club Dr., Escondido, CA 92029 **Contact:** 760-471-8275, striderguys@striderknives.com, striderknives.com
Specialties: Primarily tactical. **Patterns:** Fixed and folders. **Technical:** Primarily stock removal specializing in highly technical materials. **Prices:** $100 and up, based on the obvious variables. **Remarks:** Full-time maker since 1996.

DYER, DAVID
4531 Hunters Glen, Granbury, TX 76048 **Contact:** 817-573-1198
Specialties: Working skinners and early period knives. **Patterns:** Customer designs, his own patterns. **Technical:** Coal forged blades, 5160 and 52100 steels. Grinds D2, 1095, L6. **Prices:** $150 for neck knives and small (3" to 3-1/2"). To $600 for large blades and specialty blades. **Mark:** Last name DYER electro etched.

DYESS, EDDIE
1005 Hamilton, Roswell, NM 88201 **Contact:** 505-623-5599, eddyess@msn.com
Specialties: Working and using straight knives in standard patterns. **Patterns:** Hunters and fighters. **Technical:** Grinds 440C, 154CM and D2 on request. **Prices:** $150 to $300, some higher. **Remarks:** Spare-time maker, first knife sold in 1980. **Mark:** Last name.

E

EAKER, ALLEN L
416 Clinton Ave Dept KI, Paris, IL 61944 **Contact:** 217-466-5160
Specialties: Traditional straight knives and folders of his design. **Patterns:** Hunters, locking folders and slip-joint folders. **Technical:** Grinds 440C, inlays. **Prices:** $200 to $500. **Remarks:** Spare-time maker, first knife sold in 1994. **Mark:** Initials in tankard logo stamped on tang, serial number and surname on back.

EALY, DELBERT
PO Box 121, Indian River, MI 49749 **Contact:** 231-238-4705

EATON, FRANK L JR
5365 W. Meyer Rd., Farmington, MO 63640 **Contact:** 703-314-8708, eatontactical@me.com, frankeatonknives.com
Specialties: Full tang/hidden tang fixed working and art knives of his own design. **Patterns:** Hunters, skinners, fighters, bowies, tacticals and daggers. **Technical:** Stock removal maker, prefer using natural materials. **Prices:** $175 to $400. **Remarks:** Part-time maker - Active Duty Airborn Ranger-Making 4 years. **Mark:** Name over 75th Ranger Regimental Crest.

EATON, RICK
Rick Eaton Knives & Engraving. 313 Dailey Rd, Broadview, MT 59015 **Contact:** 406-667-2405, rick@eatonknives.com, eatonknives.com
Specialties: Interframe folders and one-hand-opening side locks. **Patterns:** bowies, daggers, fighters and folders. **Technical:** Grinds 154CM, ATS-34, 440C and other maker's damascus. Makes own mosaic damascus. Offers high-quality hand engraving, Bulino and gold inlay. **Prices:** Upscale. **Remarks:** Not taking orders. Full-time maker, first knife sold in 1982. AKI member since 2007. **Mark:** Full name or full name and address.

EBISU, HIDESAKU
3-39-7 Koi Osako, Nishi Ku, Hiroshima, JAPAN 733 0816

ECHOLS, RODGER
2853 Highway 371 W, Nashville, AR 71852-7577 **Contact:** 870-845-9173 or 870-845-0400, blademanechols@aol.com, echolsknives.com
Specialties: Liner locks, auto-scale release, lock backs. **Patterns:** His or yours. **Technical:** Autos. **Prices:** $500 to $1700. **Remarks:** Likes to use pearl, ivory and damascus the most. Made first knife in 1984. Part-time maker, tool and die maker by trade. **Mark:** Name.

EDDY, HUGH E
211 E Oak St, Caldwell, ID 83605 **Contact:** 208-459-0536

EDGE, TOMMY
1244 County Road 157, Cash, AR 72421 **Contact:** 870-897-6150, tedge@tex.net
Specialties: Fancy/embellished working knives of his design. **Patterns:** bowies, hunters and utility/camping knives. **Technical:** Grinds 440C, ATS-34 and D2. Makes own cable damascus, offers filework. **Prices:** $70 to $250, some to $1500. **Remarks:** Part-time maker, first knife sold in 1973. **Mark:** Stamped first initial, last name and stenciled name, city and state in oval shape.

EDMONDS, WARRICK
Adelaide Hills, SOUTH AUSTRALIA **Contact:** 61-8-83900339, warrick@riflebirdknives.com riflebirdknives.com
Specialties: Fixed blade knives with select and highly figured exotic or unique Australian wood handles. Themed collectors knives to individually designed working knives from damascus, RWL34, 440C or high carbon steels. **Patterns:** Hunters, utilities and workshop knives, cooks knives with a Deco to Modern flavour. Hand sewn individual leather sheaths. **Technical:** Stock removal using only steel from well known and reliable sources. **Prices:** $250Aust to $1000Aust. **Remarks:** Part-time maker since 2004. **Mark:** Name stamped into sheath.

EDWARDS, MITCH
303 New Salem Rd, Glasgow, KY 42141 **Contact:** 270-404-0758 / 270-404-0758, medwards@glasgow-ky.com, traditionalknives.com
Specialties: Period pieces. **Patterns:** Neck knives, camp, rifleman and bowie knives. **Technical:** All hand forged, forges own damascus O1, 1084, 1095, L6, 15N20. **Prices:** $200 to $1000. **Remarks:** Journeyman Smith. **Mark:** Broken heart.

EHRENBERGER, DANIEL ROBERT
1213 S Washington St, Mexico, MO 65265 **Contact:** 573-633-2010
Specialties: Affordable working/using straight knives of his design and to custom specs. **Patterns:** 10" western bowie, fighters, hunting and skinning knives. **Technical:** Forges 1085, 1095, his own damascus and cable damascus. **Prices:** $80 to $500. **Remarks:** Full-time maker, first knife sold 1994. **Mark:** Ehrenberger JS.

EKLUND, MAIHKEL
Fone Stam V9, Farila, SWEDEN 82041, info@art-knives.com, art-knives.com
Specialties: Collector-grade working straight knives. **Patterns:** Hunters, bowies and fighters. **Technical:** Grinds ATS-34, Uddeholm and Dama steel. Engraves and scrimshaws. **Prices:** $200 to $2000. **Remarks:** Full-time maker, first knife sold in 1983. **Mark:** Initials or name.

ELDRIDGE, ALLAN
7731 Four Winds Dr, Ft. Worth, TX 76133 **Contact:** 817-370-7778, Cell: 817-296-3528
Specialties: Fancy classic straight knives in standard patterns. **Patterns:** Hunters, bowies, fighters, folders and miniatures. **Technical:** Grinds O1 and damascus. Engraves silver-wire inlays, pearl inlays, scrimshaws and offers filework. **Prices:** $50 to $500, some to $1200. **Remarks:** Spare-time maker, first knife sold in 1965. **Mark:** Initials.

ELISHEWITZ, ALLEN
1659 W State Highway 46, Suite 115 #610, New Braunfels, TX 78132 **Contact:** 830-885-3099, allen@elishewitzknives.com, elishewitzknives.com
Specialties: Collectible high-tech working straight knives and folders of his design. **Patterns:** Working, utility and tactical knives. **Technical:** Designs and uses innovative locking mechanisms. All designs drafted and field-tested. **Prices:** $600 to $1000. **Remarks:** Full-time maker, first knife sold in 1989. **Mark:** Gold medallion inlaid in blade.

ELLEFSON, JOEL
PO Box 1016, 310 S 1st St, Manhattan, MT 59741 **Contact:** 406-284-3111
Specialties: Working straight knives, fancy daggers and one-of-a-kinds. **Patterns:** Hunters, daggers and some folders. **Technical:** Grinds A2, 440C and ATS-34. Makes own mokume in bronze, brass, silver and shibuishi, makes brass/steel blades. **Prices:** $100 to $500, some to $2000. **Remarks:** Part-time maker, first knife sold in 1978. **Mark:** Stylized last initial.

ELLERBE, W B
3871 Osceola Rd, Geneva, FL 32732 **Contact:** 407-349-5818

Specialties: Period and primitive knives and sheaths. **Patterns:** bowies to patch knives, some tomahawks. **Technical:** Grinds Sheffield O1 and files. **Prices:** Start at $35. **Remarks:** Full-time maker, first knife sold in 1971. Doing business as Cypress Bend Custom Knives. **Mark:** Last name or initials.

ELLIOTT, JERRY
4507 Kanawha Ave, Charleston, WV 25304 **Contact:** 304-925-5045, elliottknives@gmail.com

Specialties: Classic and traditional straight knives and folders of his design and to customer specs. **Patterns:** Hunters, locking folders and bowies. **Technical:** Grinds ATS-34, 154CM, O1, D2 and T-440-V. All guards silver-soldered, bolsters are pinned on straight knives, spot-welded on folders. **Prices:** $80 to $265, some to $1000. **Remarks:** Full-time maker, first knife sold in 1972. **Mark:** First and middle initials, last name, knife maker, city, state.

ELLIS, WILLIAM DEAN
2767 Edgar Ave, Sanger, CA 93657 **Contact:** 559-314-4459, urleebird@comcast.net, billysblades.com

Specialties: Classic and fancy knives of his design. **Patterns:** Boots, fighters and utility knives. **Technical:** Grinds ATS-34, D2 and damascus. Offers tapered tangs and six patterns of filework, tooled multi-colored sheaths. **Prices:** $250 to $1500 **Remarks:** Part-time maker, first knife sold in 1991. Doing business as Billy's Blades. Also make shave-ready straight razors for actual use. **Mark:** "B" in a five-point star next to "Billy," city and state within a rounded-corner rectangle.

ELLIS, WILLY B
1025 Hamilton Ave., Tarpon Springs, FL 34689 **Contact:** 727-942-6420, willyb.com

Specialties: One-of-a-kind high art and fantasy knives of his design. Occasional customs full size and miniatures. **Patterns:** bowies, fighters, hunters and others. **Technical:** Grinds 440C, ATS-34, 1095, carbon damascus, ivory bone, stone and metal carving. **Prices:** $175 to $15,000. **Remarks:** Full-time maker, first knife made in 1973. Member Knifemakers Guild and FEGA. Jewel setting inlays. **Mark:** Willy B. or WB'S C etched or carved.

ELROD, ROGER R
58 Dale Ave, Enterprise, AL 36330 **Contact:** 334-347-1863

EMBRETSEN, KAJ
FALUVAGEN 67, Edsbyn, SWEDEN 82830 **Contact:** 46-271-21057, (fax) 46-271-22961, kay.embretsen@telia.com, embretsenknives.com

Specialties: damascus folding knives. **Patterns:** Uses mammoth ivory and some pearl. **Technical:** Uses own damascus steel. **Remarks:** Full time since 1983. **Prices:** $2500 to $8000. **Mark:** Name inside the folder.

EMERSON, ERNEST R
1234 W. 254th, Harbor City, CA 90710 **Contact:** 310-539-5633, info@emersonknives.com, emersonknives.com

Specialties: High-tech folders and combat fighters. **Patterns:** Fighters, LinerLock® combat folders and SPECWAR combat knives. **Technical:** Grinds 154CM and damascus. Makes folders with titanium fittings, liners and locks. Chisel grind specialist. **Prices:** $550 to $850, some to $10,000. **Remarks:** Full-time maker, first knife sold in 1983. **Mark:** Last name and Specwar knives.

EMMERLING, JOHN
POB 2080, Gearheart, OR 97138 **Contact:** 503-738-5434, gearhartironwerks@gmail.com, gearhartironwerks.com

ENCE, JIM
145 S 200 East, Richfield, UT 84701 **Contact:** 435-896-6206

Specialties: High-art period pieces (spec in California knives) art knives. **Patterns:** Art, boot knives, fighters, bowies and occasional folders. **Technical:** Grinds 440C for polish and beauty boys, makes own damascus. **Prices:** Upscale. **Remarks:** Full-time maker, first knife sold in 1977. Does own engraving, gold work and stone work. Guild member since 1977. Founding member of the AKI. **Mark:** Ence, usually engraved.

ENGLAND, VIRGIL
1340 Birchwood St, Anchorage, AK 99508 **Contact:** 907-274-9494, hardfistdown@gmail.com, virgilenglandshetlandarmory.com

Specialties: Edged weapons and equipage, one-of-a-kind only. **Patterns:** Axes, swords, lances and body armor. **Technical:** Forges and grinds as pieces dictate. Offers stainless and damascus. **Prices:** Upscale. **Remarks:** A veteran knifemaker. No commissions. **Mark:** Stylized initials.

ENGLE, WILLIAM
16608 Oak Ridge Rd, Boonville, MO 65233 **Contact:** 816-882-6277

Specialties: Traditional working and using straight knives of his design. **Patterns:** Hunters, bowies and fighters. **Technical:** Grinds 440C, ATS-34 and 154 CM. **Prices:** $250 to $500, some higher. **Remarks:** Part-time maker, first knife sold in 1982. All knives come with certificate of authenticity. **Mark:** Last name in block lettering.

ENGLISH, JIM
14586 Olive Vista Dr, Jamul, CA 91935 **Contact:** 619-669-0833

Specialties: Traditional working straight knives to customer specs. **Patterns:** Hunters, bowies, fighters, tantos, daggers, boot and utility/camp knives. **Technical:** Grinds 440C, ATS-34, commercial damascus and customer choice. **Prices:** $130 to $350. **Remarks:** Part-time maker, first knife sold in 1985. In addition to custom line, also does business as Mountain Home Knives. **Mark:** Double "A," Double "J" logo.

ENNIS, RAY
1220S 775E, Ogden, UT 84404 **Contact:** 800-410-7603, (fax) 501-621-2683, nifmakr@hotmail.com, ennis-entrekusa.com

ENOS III, THOMAS M
12302 State Rd 535, Orlando, FL 32836 **Contact:** 407-239-6205, tmenos3@att.net

Specialties: Heavy-duty working straight knives, unusual designs. **Patterns:** Swords, machetes, daggers, skinners, filleting, period pieces. **Technical:** Grinds 440C. **Prices:** $75 to $1500. **Remarks:** Full-time maker, first knife sold in 1972. No longer accepting custom requests. Will be making his own designs. Send SASE for listing of items for sale. **Mark:** Name in knife logo and year, type of steel and serial number.

EPTING, RICHARD
4976 Drake Dr. Co, College Station, TX 77845 **Contact:** 979-255-2161, rgeknives@hotmail.com, eptingknives.com

Specialties: Folders and working straight knives. **Patterns:** Hunters, bowies, and locking folders. **Technical:** Forges high-carbon steel and his own damascus. **Prices:** $200 to $800, some to $1800. **Remarks:** Part-time maker, first knife sold 1996. **Mark:** Name in arch logo.

ERDLAC JR. RICHARD J.
Caldre Knives 4900 Thomason Dr., Midland, TX 79703 **Contact:** 432-699-5288, rjerdlac@att.net

Specialties: Combining woodworking with knifemaking and leather work. **Remarks:** Started making in 2005. Part-time maker. Geologist by profession.

ERICKSON, DANIEL
Ring Of Fire Forge, 20011 Welch Rd., Snohomish, WA 98296 **Contact:** 206-355-1793, ringoffireforge.com

Specialties: Likes to fuse traditional and functional with creative concepts. **Patterns:** Hunters, fighters, bowies, folders, slip joints, art knives, the Phalanx. **Technical:** Forges own pattern-welded damascus blades (1080/15N20), 5160, CruForgeV, 52100 and W2. Uses figured burls, stabilized woods, fossil ivories and natural and unique materials for handles. Custom stands and sheaths. **Prices:** $250 to $1,500. **Remarks:** Sole authorship, designer and inventor. Started making in 2003, first knife sold in 2004. ABS journeyman smith. **Mark:** "Ring of Fire" with Erickson moving through it.

ERICKSON, L.M.
1379 Black Mountain Cir, Ogden, UT 84404 **Contact:** 801-737-1930

Specialties: Straight knives, period pieces. **Patterns:** bowies, fighters, boots and hunters. **Technical:** Grinds 440C, 154CM and commercial damascus. **Prices:** $200 to $900, some to $5000. **Remarks:** Part-time maker, first knife sold in 1981. **Mark:** Name, city, state.

ERICKSON, WALTER E.
22280 Shelton Tr, Atlanta, MI 49709 **Contact:** 989-785-5262, wberic@src-milp.com

Specialties: Unusual survival knives and high-tech working knives. **Patterns:** Butterflies, hunters, tantos. **Technical:** Grinds ATS-34 or customer choice. **Prices:** $150 to $500, some to $1500. **Remarks:** Full-time maker, first knife sold in 1981. **Mark:** Using pantograph with assorted fonts (no longer stamping).

ERIKSEN, JAMES THORLIEF
dba VIKING KNIVES, 3830 Dividend Dr, Garland, TX 75042 **Contact:** 972-494-3667, (fax) 972-235-4932, VikingKnives@aol.com

Specialties: Heavy-duty working and using straight knives and folders utilizing traditional, Viking original and customer specification patterns. Some high-tech and fancy/embellished knives available. **Patterns:** bowies, hunters, skinners, boot and belt knives, utility/camp knives, fighters, daggers, locking folders, slip-joint folders and kitchen knives. **Technical:** Hollow-grinds 440C, D2, ASP-23, ATS-34, 154CM, Vascowear. **Prices:** $150 to $300, some to $600. **Remarks:** Full-time maker, first knife sold in 1985. Doing business as Viking Knives. For a color catalog showing 50 different models, mail $5 to above address. **Mark:** VIKING or VIKING USA for export.

ERNEST, PHIL (PJ)
PO Box 5240, Whittier, CA 90607-5240 **Contact:** 562-556-2324, hugger883562@yahoo.com, ernestcustomknives.com

Specialties: Fixed blades. **Patterns:** Wide range. Many original as well as hunters, camp, fighters, daggers, bowies and tactical. Specialzin in Wharncliff's of all sizes. **Technical:** Grinds commercial damascus, Mosaid damascus. ATS-34, and 440C. Full Tangs with bolsters. Handle material includes all types of exotic hardwood, abalone, peal mammoth tooth, mammoth ivory, damascus steel and Mosaic damascus. **Remarks:** Full time maker. First knife sold in 1999. **Prices:** $200 to $1800. Some to $2500. **Mark:** Owl logo with PJ Ernest Whittier CA or PJ Ernest.

ESPOSITO, EMMANUEL
Via Reano 70, Buttigliera Alta TO, ITALY 10090 **Contact:** 39-011932-16-21, emmanuelmaker.it

Specialties: Folding knife with his patent system lock mechanism with mosaic inlay.

ESSEGIAN, RICHARD
7387 E Tulare St, Fresno, CA 93727 **Contact:** 309-255-5950

Specialties: Fancy working knives of his design, art knives. **Patterns:** bowies and some small hunters. **Technical:** Grinds A2, D2, 440C and 154CM. Engraves and inlays. **Prices:** Start at $600. **Remarks:** Part-time maker, first knife sold in 1986. **Mark:** Last name, city and state.

ESTABROOK, ROBBIE
1014 Madge Ct., Conway, SC 29526 **Contact:** 843-489-2331, r1956e@hotmail.com

Specialties: Traditional working straight knives. **Patterns:** Hunters and fishing knives. **Technical:** Hand grinds ATS 34 and D2. **Prices:** $100 and up. **Remarks:** Part-time maker. **Mark:** ESTABROOK.

ETZLER, JOHN
11200 N Island, Grafton, OH 44044 **Contact:** 440-748-2460, jetzler@bright.net, http://members.tripod.com/~etzlerknives/

custom knifemakers

Specialties: High-art and fantasy straight knives and folders of his design and to customer specs. **Patterns:** Folders, daggers, fighters, utility knives. **Technical:** Forges and grinds nickel damascus and tool steel, grinds stainless steels. Prefers exotic, natural materials. **Prices:** $250 to $1200, some to $6500. **Remarks:** Full-time maker, first knife sold in 1992. **Mark:** Name or initials.

EVANS, BRUCE A
409 CR 1371, Booneville, MS 38829 **Contact:** 662-720-0193, beknives@avsia.com, bruceevans.homestead.com/open.html

Specialties: Forges blades. **Patterns:** Hunters, bowies, or will work with customer. **Technical:** 5160, cable damascus, pattern welded damascus. **Prices:** $200 and up. **Mark:** Bruce A. Evans Same with JS on reverse of blade.

EVANS, CARLTON
PO Box 72, Fort Davis, TX 79734 **Contact:** 817-223-8556, carlton@carltonevans.com, carltonevans.com

Specialties: High end folders and fixed blades. **Technical:** Uses the stock removal methods. The materials used are of the highest quality. **Remarks:** Full-time knifemaker, voting member of Knifemakers Guild, member of the Texas Knifemakers and Collectors Association.

EVANS, PHIL
594 SE 40th, Columbus, KS 66725 **Contact:** 620-249-0639, phil@glenviewforge.com glenviewforge.com

Specialties: Working knives, hunters, skinners, also enjoys making bowies and fighters, high carbon or damascus. **Technical:** Forges own blades and makes own damascus. Uses all kinds of ancient Ivory and bone. Stabilizes own native hardwoods. **Prices:** $150 - $1,500. **Remarks:** Part-time maker. Made first knife in 1995. **Mark:** EVANS.

EVANS, RONALD B
209 Hoffer St, Middleton, PA 17057-2723 **Contact:** 717-944-5464

EVANS, VINCENT K AND GRACE
PO Box 3604, Show Low AZ 85902 **Contact:** 809-443-8198, evansvk@gmail.com picturetrail.com/vevans

Specialties: Period pieces, swords. **Patterns:** Scottish, Viking, central Asian. **Technical:** Forges 5160 and his own damascus. **Prices:** $700 to $4000, some to $8000. **Remarks:** Full-time maker, first knife sold in 1983. **Mark:** Last initial with fish logo.

EWING JR, JOHN H
3276 Dutch Valley Rd, Clinton, TN 37716 **Contact:** 865-457-5757, johnja@comcast.net

Specialties: Working straight knives, hunters, camp knives. **Patterns:** Hunters. **Technical:** Grinds 440-D2. Forges 5160, 1095 prefers forging. **Prices:** $150 and up. **Remarks:** Part-time maker, first knife sold in 1985. **Mark:** First initial, last name, some embellishing done on knives.

F

FAIRLY, DANIEL
2209 Bear Creek Canyon Rd, Bayfield, CO 81122, danielfairlyknives@gmail.com, danielfairlyknives.com

Specialties: "Craftsmanship without compromise. **Patterns:** Ultralight titanium utilities, everyday carry, folders, kitchen knives, Japanese-influenced design. **Technical:** Grinds mostly tool steel and carbidized titanium in .050" to .360" thick material. Uses heavy duty handle materials and flared test tube fasteners or epoxy soaked wrapped handles. Most grinds are chisel, flat convex and hollow grinds used. **Prices:** $85 to $1,850. **Remarks:** Full-time maker since first knife sold in Feb. 2011. **Mark:** Fairly written in all capitals with larger F.

FANT JR., GEORGE
1983 CR 3214, Atlanta, TX 75551-6515 **Contact:** (903) 846-2938

FARID, MEHR R
8 Sidney Close, Tunbridge Wells, Kent, ENGLAND TN2 5QQ **Contact:** 011-44-1892 520345, farid@faridknives.com, faridknives.com

Specialties: Hollow handle survival knives. High tech folders. **Patterns:** Flat grind blades & chisel ground LinerLock® folders. **Technical:** Grinds 440C, CPMT-440V, CPM-420V, CPM-15V, CPM5125V, and T-1 high speed steel. **Prices:** $550 to $5000. **Remarks:** Full-time maker, first knife sold in 1991. **Mark:** First name stamped.

FARR, DAN
6531 E. Poleline Ave., Post Falls, ID 83854 **Contact:** 585-721-1388

Specialties: Hunting, camping, fighting and utility. **Patterns:** Fixed blades. **Technical:** Forged or stock removal. **Prices:** $150 to $750.

FASSIO, MELVIN G
420 Tyler Way, Lolo, MT 59847 **Contact:** 406-544-1391, fassiocustomknives@gmail.com, fassiocustomknives.com

Specialties: Working folders to customer specs. **Patterns:** Locking folders, hunters and traditional-style knives. **Technical:** Grinds 440C. **Prices:** $125 to $350. **Remarks:** Part-time maker, first knife sold in 1975. **Mark:** Name and city, dove logo.

FAUCHEAUX, HOWARD J
PO Box 206, Loreauville, LA 70552 **Contact:** 318-229-6467

Specialties: Working straight knives and folders, period pieces. Also a hatchet with capping knife in the handle. **Patterns:** Traditional locking folders, hunters, fighters and bowies. **Technical:** Forges W2, 1095 and his own damascus, stock removal D2. **Prices:** Start at $200. **Remarks:** Full-time maker, first knife sold in 1969. **Mark:** Last name.

FAUST, JOACHIM
Kirchgasse 10, Goldkronach, GERMANY 95497

FELIX, ALEXANDER
PO Box 4036, Torrance, CA 90510 **Contact:** 310-320-1836, sgiandubh@dslextreme.com

Specialties: Straight working knives, fancy ethnic designs. **Patterns:** Hunters, bowies, daggers, period pieces. **Technical:** Forges carbon steel and damascus, forged stainless and titanium jewelry, gold and silver casting. **Prices:** $110 and up. **Remarks:** Jeweler, ABS Journeyman Smith. **Mark:** Last name.

FELLOWS, MIKE
P.O. Box 184, Riversdale 6670, SOUTH AFRICA **Contact:** 27 82 960 3868, karatshin@gmail.com

Specialties: Miniatures, art knives and folders with occasional hunters and skinners. **Patterns:** Own designs. **Technical:** Uses own damascus. **Prices:** Upon request. **Remarks:** Uses only indigenous materials. Exotic hardwoods, horn and ivory. Does all own embellishments. **Mark:** "SHIN" letter from Hebrew alphabet over Hebrew word "Karat." **Other:** Member of Knifemakers Guild of South Africa.

FERGUSON, JIM
4652 Hackett St., Lakewood, CA 90713 **Contact:** 562-342-4890, jim@twistednickel.com, twistednickel.com, howtomakeaknife.net

Specialties: bowies and push blades. **Patterns:** All styles. **Technical:** Flat and hollow grinds. Sells in U.S. and Canada. **Prices:** $100 to $1,200. **Mark:** Push blade with "Ferguson-USA." Also makes swords, battle axes and utilities.

FERGUSON, JIM
3543 Shadyhill Dr, San Angelo, TX 76904 **Contact:** 325-655-1061

Specialties: Straight working knives and folders. **Patterns:** Working belt knives, hunters, bowies and some folders. **Technical:** Grinds ATS-34, D2 and Vascowear. Flat-grinds hunting knives. **Prices:** $200 to $600, some to $1000. **Remarks:** Full-time maker, first knife sold in 1987. **Mark:** First and middle initials, last name.

FERGUSON, LEE
1993 Madison 7580, Hindsville, AR 72738 **Contact:** 479-443-0084, info@fergusonknives.com, fergusonknives.com

Specialties: Straight working knives and folders, some fancy. **Patterns:** Hunters, daggers, swords, locking folders and slip-joints. **Technical:** Grinds D2, 440C and ATS-34, heat-treats. **Prices:** $50 to $600, some to $4000. **Remarks:** Full-time maker, first knife sold in 1977. **Mark:** Full name.

FERRIER, GREGORY K
3119 Simpson Dr, Rapid City, SD 57702 **Contact:** 605-342-9280

FERRY, TOM
16005 SE 322nd St, Auburn, WA 98092 **Contact:** 253-939-4468, tomferryknives@Q.com, tomferryknives.com

Specialties: Presentation grade knives. **Patterns:** Folders and fixed blades. **Technical:** Specialize in damascus and engraving. **Prices:** $500 and up. **Remarks:** DBA: Soos Creek Ironworks. ABS Master Smith. **Mark:** Combined T and F in a circle and/or last name.

FINCH, RICKY D
1179 Hwy 844, West Liberty, KY 41472 **Contact:** 606-743-7151, finchknives@mrtc.com, finchknives.com

Specialties: Traditional working/using straight knives of his design or to customer spec. **Patterns:** Hunters, skinners and utility/camp knives. LinerLock® of his design. **Technical:** Grinds 440C, ATS-34 and CPM154, hand rubbed stain finish, use Micarta, stabilized wood, natural and exotic. **Prices:** $85 to $225. **Remarks:** Part-time maker, first knife made 1994. Doing business as Finch Knives. **Mark:** Last name inside outline of state of Kentucky.

FINLEY, JON M.
3921 W. 142nd Dr., Leawood, KS 66224 **Contact:** 913-707-0016, jon66224@hotmail.com

Specialties: Fancy hunters with mosaic handles and channel inlays, with much use of exotic woods, mammoth ivory and gemstones. **Technical:** Stock-removal method of blade making using high-carbon damascus steel. **Prices:** $200 to $1,000. **Remarks:** Part-time maker, first knife made in 2012. **Mark:** Logo and last name.

FINNEY, GARETT
7181 Marcob Way, Loomis, CA 95650 **Contact:** 650-678-7332, garett@finneyknives.com, finneyknives.com

Specialties: Customizes knives utilizing materials that couldn't be used for handle materials until the maker casts them into acrylic. He then combines the cast items with exotic natural materials via inlays in order to create unique, one-of-a-kind works of art. **Technical:** Most knives are mirror polished with fileworked blade spines and engraved bolsters. **Prices:** $80 to $900, depending on knife and materials. **Remarks:** Full-time maker. **Mark:** Maker signs his name via engraving, and also uses a stamp for stock-removal or forged pieces.

FISHER, JAY
1405 Edwards, Clovis, NM 88101, jayfisher@jayfisher.com JayFisher.com

Specialties: High-art, working and collector's knives of his design and client's designs. Military working and commemoratives. Gemstone handles. Locking combat sheaths. **Patterns:** Hunters, daggers, folding knives, museum pieces and high-art sculptures. **Technical:** 440C, ATS-34, CPMS30V, D2, 01, CPM154CM, CPMS35VN. Prolific maker of stone-handled knives and swords. **Prices:** $850 to $150,000. **Remarks:** Full-time maker, first knife sold in 1980. High resolution etching, computer and manual engraving. **Mark:** Signature "JaFisher"

FISHER, JOSH
JN Fisher Knives, 8419 CR 3615, Murchison, TX 75778 **Contact:** 903-203-2130, fisherknives@aol.com, jnfisherknives.com
Specialties: Frame-handle fighters. **Technical:** Forge 5160 and 1084 blade steels. **Prices:** $125 to $1,000. **Remarks:** Part-time maker, first knife made in 2007. ABS journeyman smith. **Mark:** Josh Fisher etched. "JS" also etched on the reverse.

FISHER, LANCE
9 Woodlawn Ave., Pompton Lakes, NJ 07442 **Contact:** 973-248-8447, lance.fisher@sandvik.com
Specialties: Wedding cake knives and servers, forks, etc. Including velvet lined wood display cases. **Patterns:** Drop points, upswept skinners, bowies, daggers, fantasy, medieval, San Francisco style, chef or kitchen cutlery. **Technical:** Stock removal method only. Steels include but are not limited to CPM 154, D2, CPM S35VN, CPM S90V and Sandvik 13C26. Handle materials include stag, sheep horn, exotic woods, micarta, and G10 as well as reconstituted stone. **Prices:** $350 - $2000. **Remarks:** Part-time maker, will become full-time on retirement. Made and sold first knife in 1981 and has never looked back. **Mark:** Tang stamp.

FISK, JERRY
10095 Hwy 278 W, Nashville, AR 71852 **Contact:** 870-845-4456, jerry@jerryfisk.com, jerryfisk.com or Facebook: Jerry Fisk, MS Custom Knives
Specialties: Edged weapons, collectible and functional. **Patterns:** bowies, daggers, swords, hunters, camp knives and others. **Technical:** Forges carbon steels and his own pattern welded steels. **Prices:** $1100 to $20,000. **Remarks:** National living treasure. **Mark:** Name, MS.

FISTER, JIM
PO Box 307, Simpsonville, KY 40067
Specialties: One-of-a-kind collectibles and period pieces. **Patterns:** bowies, camp knives, hunters, buckskinners, and daggers. **Technical:** Forges, 1085, 5160, 52100, his own damascus, pattern and turkish. **Prices:** $150 to $2500. **Remarks:** Part-time maker, first knife sold in 1982. **Mark:** Name and MS.

FITCH, JOHN S
45 Halbrook Rd, Clinton, AR 72031-8910 **Contact:** 501-893-2020

FITZ, ANDREW A. SR. AND JR.
63 Bradford Hwy., Milan, TN 38358 **Contact:** 731-420-0139, fitzknives@yahoo.com
Specialties: Tactical utility flipper folders and fixed blades of the makers' designs. **Patterns:** High-tech utility/defense folders and fixed blades. **Technical:** Grinds CPM 154, CTS B75P, PSF27, Elmax and CTS XHP. Titanium and carbon fiber handles, or G-10 on tactical utility folders. **Prices:** $600 to $1,300 (Andrew Sr.) and $200 to $500 (Andrew Jr.). **Remarks:** Fitz Sr. made and sold first knife in 2002. Fitz Jr. made first knife in 2013 and sold first knife in 2014. **Mark:** Fitz Sr.: Last name Fitz, and Fitz Jr.: Last name with Jr. in the Z.

FITZGERALD, DENNIS M
4219 Alverado Dr, Fort Wayne, IN 46816-2847 **Contact:** 219-447-1081
Specialties: One-of-a-kind collectibles and period pieces. **Patterns:** Skinners, fighters, camp and utility knives, period pieces. **Technical:** Forges 1085, 1095, L6, 5160, 52100, his own pattern and Turkish damascus. **Prices:** $100 to $500. **Remarks:** Part-time maker, first knife sold in 1985. Doing business as The Ringing Circle. **Mark:** Name and circle logo.

FIVECOAT, ROCKY
603 Midway RD Seagoville, TX 75159 **Contact:** 214-794-2144
Patterns: Traditional fixed blade hunting knives. **Technical:** D-2 and 440c steel. **Remarks:** Lone Star member of Texas Knifemakers' Guild.

FLANAGAN, BURT
Burt Flanagan Custom Knives, P.O. Box 594, Tom Bean, TX 75489 **Contact:** Facebook: Burt Flanagan Custom Knives, Instagram: @burtflanagan
Patterns: Traditional slipjoint folders, fixed blade hunting knives.

FLEMING, MARK
Fleming Knives P.O. Box 164, Washington, AR 71862
Specialties: Hand-forged custom knives. **Patterns:** Damascus and carbon steel knives.

FLINT, ROBERT
2902 Aspen, Anchorage, AK 99517 **Contact:** 907-243-6706
Specialties: Working straight knives and folders. **Patterns:** Utility, hunters, fighters and gents. **Technical:** Grinds ATS-34, BG-42, D2 and damascus. **Prices:** $150 and up. **Remarks:** Part-time maker, first knife sold in 1998. **Mark:** Last name, stylized initials.

FLOURNOY, JOE
5750 Lisbon Rd, El Dorado, AR 71730 **Contact:** 870-863-7208, flournoy@ipa.net
Specialties: Working straight knives and folders. **Patterns:** Hunters, bowies, camp knives, folders and daggers. **Technical:** Forges only high-carbon steel, steel cable and his own damascus. **Prices:** $350 Plus. **Remarks:** First knife sold in 1977. **Mark:** Last name and MS in script.

FLUDDER, KEITH
3 Olive Ln., Tahmoor, New South Wales, AUSTRALIA 2573 **Contact:** 612 46843236 or 61 412687868, keith@knifemaker.com.au, bladesmith.com.au
Specialties: damascus and carbon steel fixed blades and art knives. **Patterns:** bowies, fighters, hunters, tantos, wakizashis, katanas and kitchen knives. **Technical:** Forges and makes own damascus, including mosaics and multi-bars from 1075 and 15N20. Also uses 1084, W2, O1, 52100 and 5160. **Prices:** $275 to $3,000. **Remarks:** Full-time maker since 2000, ABS journeyman smith since 2014, first knife made in 1989. **Mark:** Reverse K on F centered in Southern Cross constellation. Fludder on spine.

FLYNT, ROBERT G
Flynt Knives. 15173 Christy Lane, Gulfport, MS 39503 **Contact:** 228-265-0410, robertflynt@cableone.net, flyntstoneknifeworks.com
Specialties: All types of fixed blades: drop point, clip point, trailing point, bull-nose hunters, tactical, fighters and bowies. LinerLock, slip-joint and lockback folders. **Technical:** Using 154CM, CPM-154, ATS-34, 440C, CPM-3V and 52100 steels. Most blades made by stock removal, hollow and flat grind methods. Forges some cable damascus and uses numerous types of damascus purchased in billets from various makers. All filework and bluing done by the maker. Various wood handles, bone and horn materials, including some with wire inlay and other embellishments. Most knives sold with custom-fit leather sheaths, most include exotic skin inlay when appropriate. **Prices:** $150 and up, depending on embellishments on blade and sheath. **Remarks:** Full-time maker, first knife made in 1966. **Mark:** Last name in cursive letters or a knife striking a flint stone.

FOGARIZZU, BOITEDDU
via Crispi 6, Pattada, ITALY 07016
Specialties: Traditional Italian straight knives and folders. **Patterns:** Collectible folders. **Technical:** forges and grinds 12C27, ATS-34 and his damascus. **Prices:** $200 to $3000. **Remarks:** Full-time maker, first knife sold in 1958. **Mark:** Full name and registered logo.

FONTENOT, GERALD J
901 Maple Ave, Mamou, LA 70554 **Contact:** 318-468-3180

FORREST, BRIAN
FORREST KNIVES, PO Box 611, Descanso, CA 91916 **Contact:** 619-445-6343, forrestforge@gmail.com, forrestforge.biz
Specialties: Forged tomahawks, working knives, big bowies. **Patterns:** Traditional and extra large bowies. **Technical:** Hollow grinds: 440C, 1095, S160 damascus. **Prices:** $125 and up. **Remarks:** Member of California Knifemakers Association. Full-time maker. First knife sold in 1971. **Mark:** Forrest USA/Tomahawks marked FF (Forrest Forge).

FORTHOFER, PETE
5535 Hwy 93S, Whitefish, MT 59937 **Contact:** 406-862-2674
Specialties: Interframes with checkered wood inlays, working straight knives. **Patterns:** Traditional-style hunting knives. **Technical:** Grinds D2, 440C, 154CM and ATS-34, and prefers mammoth ivory handles and mokume guards. **Prices:** $650 to $850. **Remarks:** Part-time maker, full-time gunsmith. First knife sold in 1979. **Mark:** Name and logo.

FOSTER, AL
118 Woodway Dr, Magnolia, TX 77355 **Contact:** 936-372-9297
Specialties: Straight knives and folders. **Patterns:** Hunting, fishing, folders and bowies. **Technical:** Grinds 440-C, ATS-34 and D2. **Prices:** $100 to $1000. **Remarks:** Full-time maker, first knife sold in 1981. **Mark:** Scorpion logo and name.

FOSTER, BURT
23697 Archery Range Rd, Bristol, VA 24202 **Contact:** 276-669-0121, burt@burtfoster.com, burtfoster.com
Specialties: Working straight knives, laminated blades, and some art knives of his design. **Patterns:** bowies, hunters, daggers. **Technical:** Forges 52100, W-2 and makes own damascus. Does own heat treating. **Remarks:** ABS MasterSmith. Full-time maker, believes in sole authorship. **Mark:** Signed "BF" initials.

FOSTER, JARED
2970 N Hwy. 208 Colorado City, TX 79512 **Contact:** 325-370-5707, fosterforge31@gmail.com
Patterns: Hunters, bowies, straight knives, cleavers, kitchen knives. **Technical:** Forges; 5160, 1080, W-2, and makes own Damascus. **Prices:** $200 to $1000; some higher. **Remarks:** Part-time maker, first knife sold in 2009. **Mark:** J. L. Foster

FOSTER, NORVELL C
7945 Youngsford Rd, Marion, TX 78124-1713 **Contact:** 830-914-2078
Specialties: Engraving, ivory handle carving. **Patterns:** American-large and small scroll-oak leaf and acorns. **Prices:** $25 to $400. **Remarks:** Have been engraving since 1957. **Mark:** N.C. Foster - Marion - Tex and current year.

FOSTER, RONNIE E
95 Riverview Rd., Morrilton, AR 72110 **Contact:** 501-354-5389
Specialties: Working, using knives, some period pieces, work with customer specs. **Patterns:** Hunters, fighters, bowies, liner-lock folders, camp knives. **Technical:** Forge-5160, 1084, O1, 15N20-makes own damascus. **Prices:** $200 (start). **Remarks:** Part-time maker. First knife sold 1994. **Mark:** Ronnie Foster MS.

FOSTER, TIMOTHY L
723 Sweet Gum Acres Rd, El Dorado, AR 71730 **Contact:** 870-863-6188

FOWLER, CHARLES R
226 National Forest Rd 48, Ft McCoy, FL 32134-9624 **Contact:** 904-467-3215

FOWLER, ED A.
Willow Bow Ranch, PO Box 1519, Riverton, WY 82501 **Contact:** 307-856-9815
Specialties: High-performance working and using straight knives. **Patterns:** Hunter, camp, bird, and trout knives and bowies. New model, the gentleman's Pronghorn. **Technical:** Low temperature forged 52100 from virgin 5-1/2 round bars, multiple quench heat treating, engraves all knives, all handles domestic sheep horn processed and aged at least 5 years. Makes heavy duty hand-stitched waxed harness leather pouch type sheaths. **Prices:** $800 to $7000. **Remarks:** Full-time maker. First knife sold in 1962. **Mark:** Initials connected.

custom knifemakers

FOWLER, STEPHAN

98 Due West Court, Dallas, GA 30157 **Contact:** 678-323-9283, stephan@fowlerblades.com, fowlerblades.com

Specialties: bowies. **Patterns:** bowies, hunters, chef's knives (American and Japanese style). **Technical:** Primarily W2 blade steel, also 52100, 1084, 1095 and various damascus patterns. **Prices:** $200 and up. **Remarks:** Part-time maker since 2004. **Mark:** Fowler.

FRALEY, D B

1355 Fairbanks Ct, Dixon, CA 95620 **Contact:** 707-678-0393, dbtfnives@sbcglobal.net, dbfraleyknives.com

Specialties: Usable gentleman's fixed blades and folders. **Patterns:** Four locking-liner and frame-lock folders in four different sizes. **Technical:** Grinds CPM S30V, 154CM and 6K Stellite. **Prices:** $250 and up. **Remarks:** Part-time maker. First knife sold in 1990. **Mark:** First and middle initials, last name over a buffalo.

FRAMSKI, WALTER P

24 Rek Ln, Prospect, CT 06712 **Contact:** 203-758-5634

FRANCE, DAN

Box 218, Cawood, KY 40815 **Contact:** 606-573-6104

Specialties: Traditional working and using straight knives of his design. **Patterns:** Hunters, bowies and utility/camp knives. **Technical:** Forges and grinds O1, 5160 and L6. **Prices:** $35 to $125, some to $350. **Remarks:** Spare-time maker, first knife sold in 1985. **Mark:** First name.

FRANCIS, JOHN D

FRANCIS KNIVES, 18 Miami St., Ft. Loramie, OH 45845 **Contact:** 937-295-3941, jdfrancis72@gmail.com

Specialties: Utility and hunting-style fixed bladed knives of 440 C and ATS-34 steel, Micarta, exotic woods, and other types of handle materials. **Prices:** $90 to $150 range. **Remarks:** Exceptional quality and value at factory prices. **Mark:** Francis-Ft. Loramie, OH stamped on tang.

FRANK, HEINRICH H

3323 N.E. Avery St., Newport, OR 97365 **Contact:** 541-265-8683

Specialties: High-art investor-class folders, handmade and engraved. **Patterns:** Folding daggers, hunter-size folders and gents. **Technical:** Grinds 07 and O1. **Prices:** $2,100 to $16,000. **Remarks:** Full-time maker, first knife sold in 1965. Doing business as H.H. Frank Knives. **Mark:** Name, address and date.

FRANKLIN, LARRY

Mya Knives, 418 S. 7th St., Stoughton, WI 53589 **Contact:** 608-719-2758

Specialties: Fixed-blade hunters, kitchen knives and bird-and-trout knives. **Technical:** Forges 20 percent of blades and uses stock-removal method of blade making on the other 80 percent, with favorite steels being 1095, D2, 440C and 14-4 CrMo steels. **Prices:** $85 to $500. **Remarks:** Started making knives around 2005. **Mark:** Daughter's name with a leaf for her favorite season.

FRANKLIN, MIKE

7033 Utopia Way Maysville, KY 41056 **Contact:** 606-407-0029, mikefranklin2013@gmail.com

Specialties: Hunters of all sizes, neck knives and tacticals ranging from small to fighter size. **Patterns:** Hunters with all blade shapes, lots of tactical tanto blades, some radical. **Technical:** Mostly full-tang knives, some with tapered tangs and others narrow tangs. **Prices:** $150 to $1,000+. **Remarks:** Retired to Florida and makes knives he desires to make on a limited basis. **Mark:** Franklin made (with an Old English "F.")

FRAPS, JOHN R

3810 Wyandotte Tr, Indianapolis, IN 46240-3422 **Contact:** 317-849-9419, jfraps@att.net, frapsknives.com

Specialties: Working and collector grade LinerLock® and slip joint folders. **Patterns:** One-of-a kind linerlocks and traditional slip joints. **Technical:** Flat and hollow grinds ATS-34, damascus, Talonite, CPM S30V, 154Cm, Stellite 6K, hand rubbed or mirror finish. **Prices:** $200 to $1500, some higher. **Remarks:** Voting member of the Knifemaker's Guild, Full-time maker, first knife sold in 1997. **Mark:** Cougar Creek Knives and/or name.

FRAZIER, JIM

6315 Wagener Rd., Wagener, SC 29164 **Contact:** 803-564-6467, jbfrazierknives@gmail.com, jbfrazierknives.com

Specialties: Hunters, semi skinners, oyster roast knives, bird and trout, folders, many patterns of own design with George Herron/Geno Denning influence. **Technical:** Stock removal maker using CPM-154, ATS-34, CPM-S30V and D2. Hollow grind, mainly mirror finish, some satin finish. Prefer to use natural handle material such as stag, horn, mammoth ivory, highly figured woods, some Micarta, others on request. Makes own leather sheaths on 1958 straight needle stitcher. **Prices:** $125 to $600. **Remarks:** Part-time maker since 1989. **Mark:** JB Frazier in arch with Knives under it. Stamp on sheath is outline of state of SC, JB Frazier Knives Wagener SC inside outline.

FRED, REED WYLE

3149 X S, Sacramento, CA 95817 **Contact:** 916-739-0237

Specialties: Working using straight knives of his design. **Patterns:** Hunting and camp knives. **Technical:** Forges any 10 series, old files and carbon steels. Offers initialing upon request, prefers natural handle materials. **Prices:** $30 to $300. **Remarks:** Part-time maker, first knife sold in 1994. Doing business as R.W. Fred Knifemaker. **Mark:** Engraved first and last initials.

FREDEEN, GRAHAM

16499 Ida Center Dr., Petersburg, MI 49270 **Contact:** 719-964-3353, fredeenblades@hotmail.com, fredeenblades.com

Specialties: Working class knives to high-end custom knives. Traditional pattern welding and mosaic damascus blades. **Patterns:** All types: bowies, fighters, hunters, skinners, bird and trout, camp knives, utility knives, daggers, etc. Occasionally swords, both European and Asian. **Technical:** Differential heat treatment and Hamon. damascus steel rings and jewelry. Hand forged blades and damascus steel. High carbon blade steels: 1050, 1075/1080, 1084, 1095, 5160, 52100, W1, W2, O1, 15n20 **Prices:** $100 - $2,000. **Remarks:** Sole authorship. Part-time maker. First blade produced in 2005. Member of American Bladesmith Society and Professional Knifemaker's Association **Mark:** "Fredeen" etched on the ricasso or on/along the spine of the blade.

FREDERICK, AARON

272 Brooks Ln, West Liberty, KY 41472-8961 **Contact:** 606-743-2015, aaronf@mrtc.com, frederickknives.com

Specialties: Makes most types of knives, but as for now specializes in the damascus folder. Does all own damascus and forging of the steel. Also prefers natural handle material such as ivory and pearl. Prefers 14k gold screws in most of the knives he do. Also offer several types of file work on blades, spacers, and liners. Has just recently started doing carving and can do a limited amount of engraving.

FREEMAN, MATT

Fresno, CA 93720 **Contact:** 559-375-4408, cmftwknives@gmail.com, youtube.com/cmftwknives

Specialties: Fixed blades and butterfly knives. **Technical:** Using mostly 1084, 154CM, D2 and file steel, works in any requested materials via stock removal. Also does knife modifications and leather/Kydex work. Three months or less waiting list. **Prices:** $75+. **Mark:** CMFTW.

FREER, RALPH

114 12th St, Seal Beach, CA 90740 **Contact:** 562-493-4925, (fax) same, ralphfreer@adelphia.net

Specialties: Exotic folders, liner locks, folding daggers, fixed blades. **Patters:** All original. **Technical:** Lots of damascus, ivory, pearl, jeweled, thumb studs, carving ATS-34, 420V, 530V. **Prices:** $400 to $2500 and up. **Mark:** Freer in German-style text, also Freer shield.

FREY JR., W FREDERICK

305 Walnut St, Milton, PA 17847 **Contact:** 570-742-9576, wffrey@ptd.net

Specialties: Working straight knives and folders, some fancy. **Patterns:** Wide range miniatures, boot knives and lock back folders. **Technical:** Grinds A2, O1 and D2, vaseo wear, cru-wear and CPM S90V. **Prices:** $100 to $250, some to $1200. **Remarks:** Spare-time maker, first knife sold in 1983. All knives include quality hand stitched leather sheaths. **Mark:** Last name in script.

FRIEDLY, DENNIS E

12 Cottontail Lane E, Cody, WY 82414 **Contact:** 307-527-6811, friedlyknives@hotmail.com friedlyknives.com

Specialties: Fancy working straight knives and daggers, lock back folders and liner locks. Also embellished bowies. **Patterns:** Hunters, fighters, short swords, minis and miniatures, new line of full-tang hunters/boots. **Technical:** Grinds 440C, commercial damascus, mosaic damascus and ATS-34 blades, prefers hidden tangs and full tangs. Both flat and hollow grinds. **Prices:** $350 to $2500. Some to $10,000. **Remarks:** Full-time maker, first knife sold in 1972. **Mark:** D.E. Friedly-Cody, WY. Friedly Knives

FRIESEN, DAVE J

Qualicum Beach, British Columbia, CANADA **Contact:** 250-927-4113, info@islandblacksmith.ca, islandblacksmith.ca

Specialties: Charcoal-forged classical tanto and fusion-style takedown knives crafted by hand from reclaimed and natural materials using traditional techniques.

FRIGAULT, RICK

1189 Royal Pines Rd, Golden Lake, ON, CANADA K0J 1X0 **Contact:** 613-401-2869, rfrigaultknives.ca

Specialties: Fixed blades. **Patterns:** Hunting, tactical and large bowies. **Technical:** Grinds ATS-34, 440-C, D-2, CPMS30V, CPMS60V, CPMS90V, BG42 and damascus. Use G-10, Micarta, ivory, antler, ironwood and other stabilized woods for carbon fiber handle material. Makes leather sheaths by hand. Tactical blades include a Concealex sheath made by "On Scene Tactical." **Prices:** Sold first knife in 1997. Member of Canadian Knifemakers Guild. **Mark:** RFRIGAULT.

FRITZ, ERIK L

837 River St Box 1203, Forsyth, MT 59327 **Contact:** 406-351-1101, tacmedic45@yahoo.com

Specialties: Forges carbon steel 1084, 5160, 52100 and damascus. **Patterns:** Hunters, camp knives, bowies and folders as well as forged tactical. **Technical:** Forges own Mosaic and pattern welded damascus as well as doing own heat treat. **Prices:** A$200 and up. **Remarks:** Sole authorship knives and sheaths. Part time maker first knife sold in 2004. ABS member. **Mark:** E. Fritz in arc on left side ricasso.

FRITZ, JESSE

900 S. 13th St, Slaton, TX 79364 **Contact:** 806-828-5083

Specialties: Working and using straight knives in standard patterns. **Patterns:** Hunters, utility/camp knives and skinners with gut hook, bowie knives, kitchen carving sets by request. **Technical:** Grinds 440C, O1 and 1095. Uses 1095 steel. Fline-napped steel design, blued blades, filework and machine jewelling. Inlays handles with turquoise, coral and mother-of-pearl. Makes sheaths. **Prices:** $85 to $275, some to $500. **Mark:** Last name only (FRITZ).

FRIZZELL, TED

14056 Low Gap Rd, West Fork, AR 72774 **Contact:** 501-839-2516, mmhwaxes@aol.com mineralmountain.com

Specialties: Swords, axes and self-defense weapons. **Patterns:** Small skeleton knives to large swords. **Technical:** Grinds 5160 almost exclusively—1/4" to 1/2"— bars some O1 and A2 on request. All knives come with Kydex sheaths. **Prices:** $45 to $1200. **Remarks:**

Full-time maker, first knife sold in 1984. Doing business as Mineral Mountain Hatchet Works. Wholesale orders welcome. Ted Frizzell is owner, Kyel Kidder is maker. **Mark:** A circle with line in the middle, MM and HW within the circle.

FRIZZI, LEONARDO
Via Kyoto 31, Firenze, ITALY 50126 **Contact:** 335-344750, postmaster@frizzi-knives.com, frizzi-knives.com
Specialties: Fancy handmade one-of-a kind folders of his own design, some fixed blade and dagger. **Patterns:** Folders liner loch and back locks. **Technical:** Grinds rwl 34, cpm 154, cpm s30v, stainless damascus and the best craft damascus, own heat treating. I usually prefer satin finish the flat of the blade and mirror polish the hollow grind, special 18k gold, filework. **Prices:** $600 to $4,000. **Remarks:** Part-time maker, first knife sold in 2003. **Mark:** Full name, city, country, or initial, last name and city, or initial in square logo.

FRONEFIELD, DANIEL
Meteor Forge. 20270 Warriors Path, Peyton, CO 80831 **Contact:** 719-749-0226, dfronfld@hiwaay.com, MeteorForge.net
Specialties: Fixed and folding knives featuring meteorites and other exotic materials. **Patterns:** San-mai damascus, custom damascus. **Prices:** $500 to $3000.

FROST, DEWAYNE
1016 Van Buren Rd, Barnesville, GA 30204 **Contact:** 770-358-1426, lbrtyhill@aol.com
Specialties: Working straight knives and period knives. **Patterns:** Hunters, bowies and utility knives. **Technical:** Forges own damascus, cable, etc. as well as stock removal. **Prices:** $150 to $500. **Remarks:** Part-time maker ABS Journeyman Smith. **Mark:** Liberty Hill Forge Dewayne Frost w/liberty bell.

FRUHMANN, LUDWIG
Stegerwaldstr 8, Burghausen, GERMANY 84489
Specialties: High-tech and working straight knives of his design. **Patterns:** Hunters, fighters and boots. **Technical:** Grinds ATS-34, CPM-T-440V and Schneider damascus. Prefers natural handle materials. **Prices:** $200 to $1500. **Remarks:** Spare-time maker, first knife sold in 1990. **Mark:** First initial and last name.

FRY, DEAN
1569 Balsam Rd., Wellsboro, PA 16901 **Contact:** 570-948-9019, fireflycollection@yahoo.com, balsamridgeknives.com
Specialties: User-type fixed blades, including hunters, bird & trout, neck knives, drop points and everyday carry pieces. **Technical:** Hollow, Scandi and flat grinds using CPM 154 and Alabama damascus steels. Exotic wood, antler and composite handles, and leather and Kydex sheaths made in house. **Prices:** $95 to $250. **Remarks:** Part-time maker, first knife sold in 2007. **Mark:** Initials in script stamped on blade.

FRY, JASON
720 8th St., Wolfforth, TX 79382 **Contact:** 325-669-4805, frycustomknives@gmail.com, frycustomknives.com, @frycustomknives on Instagram
Specialties: Traditional hunting patterns in native Texas materials. **Patterns:** Primarily EDC and hunting/skinning knives under 8 inches, slip-joint folders and art knives. **Technical:** Stock removal and forging of 1080 carbon steel, D2 tool steel and 154CM stainless. **Prices:** $150 to $3,000. **Remarks:** Part-time maker since July 2008, and 2015 voting member of the Knifemakers' Guild. 2015 president of the Texas Knifemakers Guild. **Mark:** Jason Fry over Abilene, TX (2015 and prior), and Jason Fry over Hawley, TX (2015 and forward).

FUEGEN, LARRY
617 N Coulter Circle, Prescott, AZ 86303 **Contact:** 928-776-8777, fuegen@cableone.net, larryfuegen.com
Specialties: High-art folders and classic and working straight knives. **Patterns:** Forged scroll folders, lockback folders and classic straight knives. **Technical:** Forges 5160, 1095 and his own damascus. Works in exotic leather, offers elaborate filework and carving, likes natural handle materials, now offers own engraving. **Prices:** $1,200 to $26,000. **Remarks:** Full-time maker, first knife sold in 1975. Sole authorship on all knives. ABS Mastersmith. **Mark:** Initials connected or last name engraved.

FUJIKAWA, SHUN
Sawa 1157, Kaizuka, Osaka, JAPAN 597 0062 **Contact:** 81-724-23-4032, (fax) 81-726-23-9229
Specialties: Folders of his design and to customer specs. **Patterns:** Locking folders. **Technical:** Grinds his own steel. **Prices:** $450 to $2500, some to $3000. **Remarks:** Part-time maker.

FUKUTA, TAK
38-Umeagae-cho, Seki-City, Gifu, JAPAN **Contact:** 0575-22-0264
Specialties: Bench-made fancy straight knives and folders. **Patterns:** Sheffield-type folders, bowies and fighters. **Technical:** Grinds commercial damascus. **Prices:** Start at $300. **Remarks:** Full-time maker. **Mark:** Name in knife logo.

FULLER, BRUCE A
3366 Ranch Rd. 32, Blanco, TX 78606 **Contact:** 832-262-0529, fullcoforg@aol.com
Specialties: One-of-a-kind working/using straight knives and folders of his designs. **Patterns:** bowies, hunters, folders, and utility/camp knives. **Technical:** Forges high-carbon steel and his own damascus. Prefers El Solo Mesquite and natural materials. Offers filework. **Prices:** $200 to $500, some to $1800. **Remarks:** Spare-time maker, first knife sold in 1991. Doing business as Fullco Forge. **Mark:** Fullco, M.S.

FULLER, JACK A
7103 Stretch Ct, New Market, MD 21774 **Contact:** 719-395-3374, coloradojack2003@yahoo.com
Specialties: Forging straight knives. **Patterns:** Fighters, camp knives, hunters and

tomahawks. **Technical:** damascus, silver wire inlay, does own leather work, wood lined big sheaths. **Prices:** $400 and up. **Remarks:** Master Smith in ABS since 1990, first knife sold in 1979. **Mark:** Fuller's Forge MS.

FULTON, MICKEY
406 S Shasta St, Willows, CA 95988 **Contact:** 530-934-5780
Specialties: Working straight knives and folders of his design. **Patterns:** Hunters, bowies, lockback folders and steak knife sets. **Technical:** Hand-filed, sanded, buffed ATS-34, 440C and A2. **Prices:** $65 to $600, some to $1200. **Remarks:** Full-time maker, first knife sold in 1979. **Mark:** Signature.

G

GABRIEL, BASTIAN
BG Blades LLC Houston, TX **Contact:** 832-381-6922, customknives@bg-blades.com
Patterns: Tactical, hunting and kitchen knives.

GADBERRY, EMMET
82 Purple Plum Dr, Hattieville, AR 72063 **Contact:** 501-354-4842

GADDY, GARY LEE
205 Ridgewood Lane, Washington, NC 27889 **Contact:** 252-946-4359
Specialties: Working/using straight knives of his design, period pieces. **Patterns:** bowies, hunters, utility/camp knives, oyster knives. **Technical:** Grinds ATS-34, O1, forges 1095. **Prices:** $175+ **Remarks:** Spare-time maker, first knife sold in 1991. No longer accepts orders. **Mark:** Quarter moon stamp.

GAETA, ANGELO
Rua: Saldanha Marinho, 1281, Centro Jau, SP-CEP: 14.201310, BRAZIL 17201-310, e.a.gaeta@gmail.com, Facebook: cutelaria.a.gaeta@gmail.com
Specialties: Straight using knives to customers' specs. **Patterns:** Hunters, fighters, daggers, belt push daggers. **Technical:** Grinds ATS-34 and 440C stainless steel. All knives are unique pieces. **Prices:** $400 and up. **Remarks:** Full-time maker, first knife sold in 1992. **Mark:** First initial, last name.

GAHAGAN, KYLE
200 Preachers Bottom Dr., Moravian Falls, NC 28654 **Contact:** 919-359-9220, kylegahagan78@yahoo.com, gahaganknives.com
Specialties: bowies and fighters. **Patterns:** Custom designs from maker or customer. **Technical:** Forges 1095, W2, 1075, 1084 and damascus blade steels. **Prices:** $200 and up. **Remarks:** Full-time bladesmith, sold first knife in 2011. **Mark:** Gahagan crest with Gahagan underneath.

GAINES, BUDDY
GAINES KNIVES, 155 Red Hill Rd., Commerce, GA 30530, gainesknives.com
Specialties: Collectible and working folders and straight knives. **Patterns:** Folders, hunters, bowies, tactical knives. **Technical:** Forges own damascus, grinds ATS-34, D2, commercial damascus. Prefers mother-of-pearl and stag. **Prices:** Start at $200. **Remarks:** Part-time maker, sold first knife in 1985. **Mark:** Last name.

GAINEY, HAL
904 Bucklevel Rd, Greenwood, SC 29649 **Contact:** 864-223-0225, scak.org
Specialties: Traditional working and using straight knives and folders. **Patterns:** Hunters, slip-joint folders and utility/camp knives. **Technical:** Hollow grinds ATS-34 and D2, makes sheaths. **Prices:** $95 to $145, some to $500. **Remarks:** Full-time maker, first knife sold in 1975. **Mark:** Eagle head and last name.

GALLAGHER, BARRY
POB 892, 130 Main St., Lincoln, MT 59639 **Contact:** 406-366-6248, gallagherknives.com
Specialties: One-of-a-kind damascus folders. **Patterns:** Folders, utility to high art, some straight knives, hunter, bowies, and art pieces. **Technical:** Forges own mosaic damascus and carbon steel, some stainless. **Prices:** $400 to $5000+. **Remarks:** Full-time maker, first knife sold in 1993. Doing business as Gallagher Custom Knives. **Mark:** Last name.

GALLAGHER, SCOTT
335 Winston Manor Rd., Santa Rosa Beach, FL 32459 **Contact:** 850-865-8264, scottgallagher04@gmail.com, Facebook: SGallagherKnives
Specialties: Traditional hunters, bowies, fighters and camp knives. **Technical:** Forged-to-shape 1075, 80CrV2, 5160 and W2 blade steels. **Prices:** $300 to $1,500. **Remarks:** Serious part-time maker, first knife sold in 2014. **Mark:** S. Gallagher (with Anvil & Hammer).

GAMBLE, ROGER
18515 N.W. 28th Pl., Newberry, FL 32669, ROGERLGAMBLE@COX.NET
Specialties: Traditional working/using straight knives and folders of his design. **Patterns:** Liner locks and hunters. **Technical:** Grinds ATS-34 and damascus. **Prices:** $150 to $2000. **Remarks:** Part-time maker, first knife sold in 1982. Doing business as Gamble Knives. **Mark:** First name in a fan of cards over last name.

GANN, TOMMY
2876 State Hwy. 198, Canton, TX 75103 **Contact:** 903-848-9375
Specialties: Art and working straight knives of my design or customer preferences/design. **Patterns:** bowies, fighters, hunters, daggers. **Technical:** Forges damascus 52100 and grinds ATS-34 and D2. **Prices:** $200 to $2500. **Remarks:** Full-time knifemaker, first knife sold in 2002. ABS journey bladesmith. **Mark:** TGANN.

GANSHORN, CAL
123 Rogers Rd., Regina, SK, CANADA S4S 6T7 **Contact:** 306-584-0524, cganshorn@accesscomm.ca or cganshorn@myaccess.ca

custom knifemakers

Specialties: Working and fancy fixed blade knives. **Patterns:** bowies, hunters, daggers, and filleting. **Technical:** Makes own forged damascus billets, ATS, salt heat treating, and custom forges and burners. **Prices:** $250 to $1500. **Remarks:** Part-time maker. **Mark:** Last name etched in ricasso area.

GARAU, MARCELLO
Via Alagon 27, Oristano, ITALY 09170 **Contact:** 00393479073454, marcellogarau@libero.it knifecreator.com
Specialties: Mostly lock back folders with interframe. **Technical:** Forges own damascus for both blades and frames. **Prices:** 200 - 2,700 Euros. **Remarks:** Full-time maker, first knife made in 1995. Attends Milano Knife Show and ECCKSHOW yearly. **Mark:** M.Garau inside handle.

GARCIA, MARIO EIRAS
Rua Edmundo Scannapieco 300, Caxingui, SP, BRAZIL 05516-070 **Contact:** 011-37218304, (fax) 011-37214528
Specialties: Fantasy knives of his design, one-of-a-kind only. **Patterns:** Fighters, daggers, boots and two-bladed knives. **Technical:** Forges car leaf springs. Uses only natural handle material. **Prices:** $100 to $200. **Remarks:** Part-time maker, first knife sold in 1976. **Mark:** Two "B"s, one opposite the other.

GARDNER, ROBERT
13462 78th Pl. N, West Palm Beach, FL 33412
Specialties: Straight blades, forged and clay hardened or differentially heat treated. Kydex and leather sheath maker. **Patterns:** Working/using knives, some to customer specs, and high-end knives, daggers, bowies, ethnic knives, and Steelhead and Lil' Chub woodland survival/bushcraft knife set with an elaborate, versatile sheath system. Affordable hard-use production line of everyday carry belt knives, and less-expensive forged knives, neck knives and "wrench" knives. **Technical:** Grinds, forges and heat treats high-carbon 1084, 1095, 1075, W1, W2, 5160 and 52100 steels, some natural handle materials and Micarta for full-tang knives. **Prices:** $60 and up, sheaths $30 and up. **Remarks:** Full-time maker since 2010, first knife sold in 1986. **Mark:** Initials in angular script, stamped, engraved or etched.

GARNER, GEORGE
7527 Calhoun Dr. NE, Albuquerque, NM 87109 **Contact:** 505-797-9317, razorbackblades@msn.com razorbackblades.com
Specialties: High art locking liner folders and Daggers of his own design. Working and high art straight knives. **Patterns:** bowies, daggers, fighters and locking liner folders. **Technical:** Grinds 440C, CPM-154, ATS34 and others. damascus, Mosaic damascus and Mokume. Makes own custom leather sheaths. **Prices:** $150 - $2,500. **Remarks:** Part-time maker since 1993. Full-time maker as of 2011. Company name is Razorback Blades. **Mark:** GEORGE GARNER.

GARVOCK, MARK W
RR 1, Balderson, ON, CANADA K1G 1A0 **Contact:** 613-833-2545, (fax) 613-833-2208, garvock@travel-net.com
Specialties: Hunters, bowies, Japanese, daggers and swords. **Patterns:** Cable damascus, random pattern welded or to suit. **Technical:** Forged blades, hi-carbon. **Prices:** $250 to $900. **Remarks:** CKG member and ABS member. Shipping and taxes extra. **Mark:** Big G with M in middle.

GATLIN, STEVE
3812 Arroyo Seco, Schertz, TX 78154 **Contact:** 229-328-5074, stevegatlinknives@hotmail.com, stevegatlinknives.com
Specialties: Loveless-style knives, double-ground fighters and traditional hunters. Some tactical models of maker's design. Fixed blades only. **Technical:** Grinds CPM-154, ATS-34 and 154CM. **Prices:** $450 to $1,500 on base models. **Remarks:** Voting member of Knifemakers' Guild since 2009, first knife sold in 2008. **Mark:** Typical football shape with name on top and city below.

GEDRAITIS, CHARLES J
GEDRAITIS HAND CRAFTED KNIVES, 444 Shrewsbury St, Holden, MA 01520 **Contact:** 508-963-1861, gedraitisknives@yahoo.com, gedraitisknives.com
Specialties: One-of-a-kind folders & automatics of his own design. **Patterns:** One-of-a-kind. **Technical:** Forges to shape mostly stock removal. **Prices:** $300 to $2500. **Remarks:** Full-time maker. **Mark:** Signature of last name. Previous - 3 scallop shells with an initial inside each one: CJG.

GENOVESE, RICK
17802 South Oak Drive, Peeples Valley, AZ 86332 **Contact:** 916-693-3979, genoveseknives@hotmail.com, rickgenoveseknives.com
Specialties: Interframe-style folders. **Patterns:** Sleek folders in gentleman's designs. Also folding dirks and daggers. **Technical:** Main blade material is CPM 154. Also uses damascus by Devin Thomas and Jerry Rados. Inlays gemstones such as lapis lazuli, jade, opal, dinosaur bone, tiger eye, jasper, agate, malachite, petrified wood, as well as various pearls. **Prices:** $1,500-$10,000. **Remarks:** Full-time maker, first knife sold in 1975. **Mark:** Genovese in stylized letters.

GEORGE, HARRY
3137 Old Camp Long Rd, Aiken, SC 29805 **Contact:** 803-649-1963, hdkk-george@scescape.net
Specialties: Working straight knives of his design or to customer specs. **Patterns:** Hunters, skinners and utility knives. **Technical:** Grinds ATS-34. Prefers natural handle materials, hollow-grinds and mirror finishes. **Prices:** Start at $70. **Remarks:** Part-time maker, first knife sold in 1985. Trained under George Herron. Member SCAK. Member Knifemakers Guild. **Mark:** Name, city, state.

GEORGE, LES
1072 CR 185, Blue Springs, MS 38828 **Contact:** 662-598-5396, les@georgeknives.com, georgeknives.com
Specialties: Tactical and art folders and historical daggers. **Patterns:** Folders, balisongs, and daggers. **Technical:** CPM154, S30V, Chad Nichols damascus. **Prices:** $200 to $800. **Remarks:** Full-time maker, first knife sold in 1992. Doing business as georgeknives.com. **Mark:** Last name over logo.

GEORGE, TOM
550 Aldbury Dr, Henderson, NV 89014, tagmaker@aol.com
Specialties: Working straight knives, display knives, custom meat cleavers, and folders of his design. **Patterns:** Hunters, bowies, daggers, buckskinners, swords and folders. **Technical:** Uses D2, 440C, ATS-34 and 154CM. **Prices:** $500 to $13,500. **Remarks:** Custom orders not accepted "at this time". Full-time maker. First knife1982, first 350 knives were numbered, after that no numbers. Almost all his knives today are bowies and swords. Creator and maker of the "Past Glories" series of knives. **Mark:** Tom George maker.

GEPNER, DON
2615 E Tecumseh, Norman, OK 73071 **Contact:** 405-364-2750
Specialties: Traditional working and using straight knives of his design. **Patterns:** bowies and daggers. **Technical:** Forges his damascus, 1095 and 5160. **Prices:** $100 to $400, some to $1000. **Remarks:** Spare-time maker, first knife sold in 1991. Has been forging since 1954, first edged weapon made at 9 years old. **Mark:** Last initial.

GERNER, THOMAS
PO Box 301, Walpole, WA, AUSTRALIA 6398, gerner@bordernet.com.au, deepriverforge.com
Specialties: Forged working knives, plain steel and pattern welded. **Patterns:** Tries most patterns heard or read about. **Technical:** 5160, L6, O1, 52100 steels, Australian hardwood handles. **Prices:** $220 and up. **Remarks:** Achieved ABS Master Smith rating in 2001. **Mark:** Like a standing arrow and a leaning cross, T.G. in the Runic (Viking) alphabet.

GHIO, PAOLO
4330 Costa Mesa, Pensacola, FL 32504-7849 **Contact:** 850-393-0135, paologhio@hotmail.com
Specialties: Folders, fillet knives and skinners. **Patterns:** Maker's own design, or will work from a customer's pattern. **Technical:** Stock removal, all work in house, including heat treat. **Prices:** $200 to $500. **Mark:** PKG.

GIAGU, SALVATORE AND DEROMA MARIA ROSARIA
Via V Emanuele 64, Pattada (SS), ITALY 07016 **Contact:** 079-755918, (fax) 079-755918, coltelligiagupattada@tiscali.it culterpattada.it
Specialties: Using and collecting traditional and new folders from Sardegna. **Patterns:** Folding, hunting, utility, skinners and kitchen knives. **Technical:** Forges ATS-34, 440, D2 and damascus. **Prices:** $200 to $2000, some higher. **Mark:** First initial, last name and name of town and muflon's head.

GIBERT, PEDRO
Los Alamos 410, San Martin de los Andes, Neuquen, ARGENTINA 8370 **Contact:** 054-2972-410868, rosademayo@infovia.com.ar
Specialties: Hand forges: Stock removal and integral. High quality artistic knives of his design and to customer specifications. **Patterns:** Country (Argentine gaucho-style), knives, folders, bowies, daggers, hunters. Others upon request. **Technical:** Blade: Bohler k110 Austrian steel (high resistance to waste). Handles: (Natural materials) ivory elephant, killer whale, hippo, walrus tooth, deer antler, goat, ram, buffalo horn, bone, rhea, sheep, cow, exotic woods (South America native woods) hand carved and engraved guards and blades. Stainless steel guards, finely polished: semi-matte or shiny finish. Sheaths: Raw or tanned leather, hand-stitched, rawhide or cotton yarn embroidered. Box: One wood piece, hand carved. Wooden hinges and locks. **Prices:** $600 and up. **Remarks:** Full-time maker. Made first knife in 1987. **Mark:** Only a rose logo. Buyers initials upon request.

GIBO, GEORGE
PO Box 4304, Hilo, HI 96720 **Contact:** 808-987-7002, geogibo@hilo808.net
Specialties: Straight knives and folders. **Patterns:** Hunters, bird and trout, utility, gentlemen and tactical folders. **Technical:** Grinds ATS-34, BG-42, Talonite, Stainless Steel damascus. **Prices:** $250 to $1000. **Remarks:** Spare-time maker, first knife sold in 1995. **Mark:** Name, city and state around Hawaiian "Shaka" sign.

GILBERT, CHANTAL
291 Rue Christophe-Colomb est #105, Quebec City, QC, CANADA G1K 3T1 **Contact:** 418-525-6961, (fax) 418-525-4666, gilbertc@medion.qc.ca, chantalgilbert.com
Specialties: Straight art knives that may resemble creatures, often with wings, shells and antennae, always with a beak of some sort, fixed blades in a feminine style. **Technical:** ATS-34 and damascus. Handle materials usually silver that she forms to shape via special molds and a press, ebony and fossil ivory. **Prices:** Range from $500 to $4000. **Remarks:** Often embellishes her art knives with rubies, meteorite, 18k gold and similar elements.

GILBREATH, RANDALL
55 Crauswell Rd, Dora, AL 35062 **Contact:** 205-648-3902
Specialties: damascus folders and fighters. **Patterns:** Folders and fixed blades. **Technical:** Forges damascus and high-carbon, stock removal stainless steel. **Prices:** $300 to $1500. **Remarks:** Full-time maker, first knife sold in 1979. **Mark:** Name in ribbon.

GILJEVIC, BRANKO
35 Hayley Crescent, Queanbeyan 2620, New South Wales, AUSTRALIA 0262977613
Specialties: Classic working straight knives and folders of his design. **Patterns:** Hunters, bowies, skinners and locking folders. **Technical:** Grinds 440C. Offers acid etching, scrimshaw and leather carving. **Prices:** $150 to $1500. **Remarks:** Part-time maker, first

knife sold in 1987. Doing business as Sambar Custom Knives. **Mark:** Company name in logo.

GINGRICH, JUSTIN
5329 Anna Belle Ln., Wade, NC 28395 **Contact:** 507-230-0398, justin@gingrichtactical.com gingrichtactical.com
Specialties: Anything from bushcraft to tactical, heavy on the tactical. **Patterns:** Fixed blades and folders. **Technical:** Uses all types of steel and handle material, method is stock-removal. **Prices:** $30 - $1000. **Remarks:** Full-time maker. **Mark:** Tang stamp is the old Ranger Knives logo.

GIRTNER, JOE
409 Catalpa Ave, Brea, CA 92821 **Contact:** 714-529-2388, conceptsinknives@aol.com
Specialties: Art knives and miniatures. **Patterns:** Mainly damascus (some carved). **Technical:** Many techniques and materials combined. Wood carving knives and tools, hunters, custom orders. **Prices:** $55 to $3000. **Mark:** Name.

GITTINGER, RAYMOND
6940 S Rt 100, Tiffin, OH 44883 **Contact:** 419-397-2517

GLASSER, ROGER CESAR
Av. Ceci, 679 - Sao Paulo - SP, BRAZIL 04065-001 **Contact:** +55-11-974615357, roger.glasser@gmail.com, mostrainternacionaldecutelaria.com
Specialties: Fixed blades, military knives, fighters and hunters. **Prices:** $300 to $1,000. **Remarks:** Part-time maker, IBO founder, ABS member, SBC member and CKCA member. Creator and manager of the biggest knife show in Latin America: Mostra Internacional de Cutelaria, a.k.a. Brazil Knife Show. **Mark:** R.Glasser.

GLOVER, RON
5896 Thornhill Ave., Cincinnati, OH 45224 **Contact:** 513-404-7107, r.glover@zoomtown.com
Specialties: High-tech working straight knives and folders. **Patterns:** Hunters to bowies, some interchangeable blade models, unique locking mechanisms. **Technical:** Grinds 440C, 154CM, buys damascus. **Prices:** $70 to $500, some to $800. **Remarks:** Part-time maker, first knife sold in 1981. **Mark:** Name in script.

GLOVER, WARREN D
dba BUBBA KNIVES, PO Box 475, Cleveland, GA 30528 **Contact:** 706-865-3998, (fax) 706-348-7176, warren@bubbaknives.net, bubbaknives.net
Specialties: Traditional and custom working and using straight knives of his design and to customer request. **Patterns:** Hunters, skinners, bird and fish, utility and kitchen knives. **Technical:** Grinds 440, ATS-34 and stainless steel damascus. **Prices:** $75 to $400 and up. **Remarks:** Full-time maker, sold first knife in 1995. **Mark:** Bubba, year, name, state.

GODDARD, STEVE
Goddard Knife Works 4325 Commerce St, #111-344, Eugene OR 97402 **Contact:** 541-870-6811 or 541-968-1845, www.goddardknifeworks.com
Patterns: EDC of all styles. **Remarks:** Continuing the tradition of Wayne Goddard's knifemaking.

GODDARD, WAYNE
473 Durham Ave, Eugene, OR 97404 **Contact:** 541-689-8098, wgoddard44@comcast.net
Specialties: Working/using straight knives and folders. **Patterns:** Hunters and folders. **Technical:** Works exclusively with wire damascus and his own-pattern welded material. **Prices:** $250 to $4000. **Remarks:** Full-time maker, first knife sold in 1963. **Mark:** Blocked initials on forged blades, regular capital initials on stock removal.

GODLESKY, BRUCE F.
1002 School Rd., Apollo, PA 15613 **Contact:** 724-840-5786, brucegodlesky@yahoo.com, birdforge.com
Specialties: Working/using straight knives and tomahawks, mostly forged. **Patterns:** Hunters, birds and trout, fighters and tomahawks. **Technical:** Most forged, some stock removal. Carbon steel only. 5160, O-1, W2, 10xx series. Makes own damascus and welded cable. **Prices:** Starting at $75. **Mark:** BIRDOG FORGE.

GOERS, BRUCE
3423 Royal Ct S, Lakeland, FL 33813 **Contact:** 941-646-0984
Specialties: Fancy working and using straight knives of his design and to customer specs. **Patterns:** Hunters, fighters, bowies and fantasy knives. **Technical:** Grinds ATS-34, some damascus. **Prices:** $195 to $600, some to $1300. **Remarks:** Part-time maker, first knife sold in 1990. Doing business as Vulture Cutlery. **Mark:** Buzzard with Initials.

GOLDBERG, DAVID
321 Morris Rd, Ft Washington, PA 19034 **Contact:** 215-654-7117, david@goldmountainforge.com, goldmountainforge.com
Specialties: Japanese-style designs, will work with special themes in Japanese genre. **Patterns:** Kozuka, Tanto, Wakazashi, Katana, Tachi, Sword canes, Yari and Naginata. **Technical:** Forges his own damascus and his own handmade tamehagane steel from straw ash, iron, carbon and clay. Uses traditional materials, carves fittings handles and cases. Hardens all blades in traditional Japanese clay differential technique. **Remarks:** Full-time maker, first knife sold in 1987. Japanese swordsmanship teacher (jaido) and Japanese self-defense teach (aikido). **Mark:** Name (kinzan) in Japanese Kanji on Tang under handle.

GONCALVES, LUIZ GUSTAVO
R Alberto Gebara, 124A -Sao Paulo SP, BRAZIL 04611-060 **Contact:** +55-11-98336-0001, lgustavo@lgustavo.com, lgustavo.com
Specialties: Most types of fixed blades of his own designs or to customer specs. **Patterns:** Hunters, fighters, bowies, gaucho, utility, camp and kitchen knives. **Technical:** Forges and grinds carbon steel (5160, 52100, O1) and his own damascus in random, ladder, raindrop, W's and other patterns. Heat treatment in electronically controlled kiln to obtain maximum control. Natural handle materials, including hardwood, stabilized wood, giraffe bone, deer stag, merino horn and others. Flat and hollow grinds. **Prices:** $400 to $1,300. **Remarks:** Part-time maker, ABS apprentice, first knife sold in 2012. **Mark:** LGustavo.

GONZALEZ, LEONARDO WILLIAMS
Ituzaingo 473, Maldonado, URUGUAY 20000 **Contact:** 598 4222 1617, (fax) 598 4222 1617, willyknives@hotmail.com, willyknives.com
Specialties: Classic high-art and fantasy straight knives, traditional working and using knives of his design, in standard patterns or to customer specs. **Patterns:** Hunters, bowies, daggers, fighters, boots, swords and utility/camp knives. **Technical:** Forges and grinds high-carbon and stainless Bohler steels. **Prices:** $100 to $2500. **Remarks:** Full-time maker, first knife sold in 1985. **Mark:** Willy, whale, R.O.U.

GOO, TAI
5920 W Windy Lou Ln, Tucson, AZ 85742 **Contact:** 520-282-9541, taigoo@msn.com, taigooknives.com, taigoo.com
Specialties: High art, neo-tribal, bush and fantasy. **Technical:** Hand forges, does own heat treating, makes own damascus. **Prices:** $250 to $2,500 and higher. **Remarks:** Full-time maker, first knife sold in 1978. **Mark:** Chiseled signature.

GOOD, D.R.
Custom Knives and Weaponry, 6125 W. 100 S., Tipton, IN 46072 **Contact:** 765-963-6971, drntammigood@bluemarble.net
Specialties: Working knives, own design, Scagel style, "critter" knives, carved handles. **Patterns:** bowies, large and small, neck knives and miniatures. Offers carved handles, snake heads, eagles, wolves, bear, skulls. **Technical:** damascus, some stelite, 6K, pearl, ivory, moose. **Prices:** $150 - $1500. **Remarks:** Full-time maker. First knife was bowie made from a 2-1/2 truck bumper in military. **Mark:** D.R. Good in oval and for minis, DR with a buffalo skull.

GOODE, BEAR
BEAR KNIVES, PO Box 6474, Navajo Dam, NM 87419 **Contact:** 505-632-8184, beargood58@gmail.com
Specialties: Working/using straight knives of his design and in standard patterns. **Patterns:** bowies, hunters and utility/camp knives. **Technical:** Grinds 440C, ATS-34, 154-CM, forges and grinds 1095, 5160 and other steels on request, uses damascus. **Prices:** $150 and up. **Remarks:** Full-time maker since 2010, first knife made in 1975 and first knife sold in 1993. Doing business as Bear Knives. **Mark:** First and last name with a three-toed paw print.

GOODE, BRIAN
203 Gordon Ave, Shelby, NC 28152 **Contact:** 704-434-6496, bgoodeknives.com
Specialties: Flat ground working knives with etched/antique or brushed finish. **Patterns:** Field, camp, hunters, skinners, survival, kitchen, maker's design or yours. Currently full tang only with supplied leather sheath. **Technical:** 0-1, D2 and other ground flat stock. Stock removal and differential heat treat preferred. Etched antique/etched satin working finish preferred. Micarta and hardwoods for strength. **Prices:** $150 to $700. **Remarks:** Part-time maker and full-time knife lover. First knife sold in 2004. **Mark:** B. Goode with NC separated by a feather.

GOODPASTURE, TOM
13432 Farrington Road, Ashland, VA 23005 **Contact:** 804-752-8363, rtg007@aol.com, goodpastureknives.com
Specialties: Working/using straight knives of his own design, or customer specs. File knives and primative reproductions. **Patterns:** Hunters, bowies, small double-edge daggers, kitchen, custom miniatures and camp/utility. **Technical:** Stock removal, D-2, 0-1, 12C27, 420 HC, 52100. Forged blades of W-2, 1084, and 1095. Flat grinds only. **Prices:** $60 - $300. **Remarks:** Part-time maker, first knife sold at Blade Show 2005. Lifetime guarantee and sharpening. **Mark:** Early mark were initials RTG, current **mark:** Goodpasture.

GORDON, LARRY B
23555 Newell Cir W, Farmington Hills, MI 48336 **Contact:** 248-477-5483, lbgordon1@aol.com
Specialties: Folders, small fixed blades. New design rotating scale release automatic. **Patterns:** Rotating handle locker. Ambidextrous fire (R&L) **Prices:** $450 minimum. **Remarks:** High line materials preferred. **Mark:** Gordon.

GORENFLO, JAMES T (JT)
9145 Sullivan Rd, Baton Rouge, LA 70818 **Contact:** 225-261-5868
Specialties: Traditional working and using straight knives of his design. **Patterns:** bowies, hunters and utility/camp knives. **Technical:** Forges 5160, 1095, 52100 and his own damascus. **Prices:** Start at $200. **Remarks:** Part-time maker, first knife sold in 1992. **Mark:** Last name or initials, J.S. on reverse.

GOSHOVSKYY, VASYL
BL.4, C. San Jaime 65, Torreblanca 12596, Castellon de la Plana, SPAIN **Contact:** +34-664-838-882, baz_knife@mail.ru, goshovskyy-knives.com
Specialties: Presentation and working fixed-blade knives. **Patterns:** R.W. Loveless-pattern knives, primarily hunters and skinners. **Technical:** Stock-removal method. Prefers natural materials for handle scales. Uses primarily RWL-34, CPM-154, N690 or similar blade steel. **Remarks:** Full-time maker.

custom knifemakers

GOSSMAN, SCOTT
PO Box 41, Whiteford, MD 21160 **Contact:** 443-617-2444, scogos@peoplepc.com, gossmanknives.com
Specialties: Heavy duty knives for big-game hunting and survival. **Patterns:** Modified clip-point/spear-point blades, bowies, hunters and bushcraft. **Technical:** Grinds A2, O1, CPM-154, CPM-3V, S7, flat/convex grinds and convex micro-bevel edges. **Prices:** $65 to $500. **Remarks:** Full-time maker doing business as Gossman Knives. **Mark:** Gossman and steel type.

GOTTAGE, DANTE
43227 Brooks Dr, Clinton Twp., MI 48038-5323 **Contact:** 586-286-7275
Specialties: Working knives of his design or to customer specs. **Patterns:** Large and small skinners, fighters, bowies and fillet knives. **Technical:** Grinds O1, 440C and 154CM and ATS-34. **Prices:** $150 to $600. **Remarks:** Part-time maker, first knife sold in 1975. **Mark:** Full name in script letters.

GOTTAGE, JUDY
43227 Brooks Dr, Clinton Twp., MI 48038-5323 **Contact:** 810-343-4662, jgottage@remaxmetropolitan.com
Specialties: Custom folders of her design or to customer specs. **Patterns:** Interframes or integral. **Technical:** Stock removal. **Prices:** $300 to $3000. **Remarks:** Full-time maker, first knife sold in 1980. **Mark:** Full name, maker in script.

GOTTSCHALK, GREGORY J
12 First St. (Ft. Pitt), Carnegie, PA 15106 **Contact:** 412-279-6692
Specialties: Fancy working straight knives and folders to customer specs. **Patterns:** Hunters to tantos, locking folders to minis. **Technical:** Grinds 440C, 154CM, ATS-34. Now making own damascus. Most knives have mirror finishes. **Prices:** Start at $150. **Remarks:** Part-time maker, first knife sold in 1977. **Mark:** Full name in crescent.

GOUKER, GARY B
PO Box 955, Sitka, AK 99835 **Contact:** 907-747-3476
Specialties: Hunting knives for hard use. **Patterns:** Skinners, semi-skinners, and such. **Technical:** Likes natural materials, inlays, stainless steel. **Prices:** Moderate. **Remarks:** New Alaskan maker. **Mark:** Name.

GRAHAM, GORDON
3145 CR 4008, New Boston, TX 75570 **Contact:** 903-293-2610, grahamknives.com
Prices: $325 to $850. **Mark:** Graham.

GRAHAM, LEVI
6296 W. 3rd St., Greeley, CO 80634 **Contact:** 970-371-0477, lgknives@hotmail.com, levigrahamknives.com
Specialties: Forged frontier/period/Western knives. **Patterns:** Hunters, patch knives, skinners, camp, belt and bowies. **Technical:** Forges high-carbon steels and some stock removal in 1095, 1084, 5160, L6, 80CRV2 and 52100. Handle materials include antler, bone, ivory, horn, hardwoods, Micarta and G-10. Rawhide-covered, vegetable-tanned sheaths decorated with deer fringe, quill work for a band or medicine wheel, beads, cones, horse hair, etc. Custom orders welcome. **Prices:** $300 and up. **Remarks:** Member of ABS and PKA. **Mark:** "lg" stamped in lower case letters.

GRANGER, PAUL J
704 13th Ct. SW, Largo, FL 33770-4471 **Contact:** 727-953-3249, grangerknives@live.com, http://palehorsefighters.blogspot.com
Specialties: Working straight knives of his own design and a few folders. **Patterns:** 2.75" to 4" work knives, tactical knives and bowies from 5"-9." **Technical:** Grinds CPM154-CM, ATS-34 and forges 52100 and 1084. Offers filework. **Prices:** $95 to $500. **Remarks:** Part-time maker since 1997. Sold first knife in 1997. Doing business as Granger Knives and Pale Horse Fighters. Member of ABS and Florida Knifemakers Association. **Mark:** "Granger" or "Palehorse Fighters."

GRANGETTE, ALAIN
7, Erenas, 23210 Azat-Chatenet, FRANCE **Contact:** 05-55-81-32-64, alain.grangette@gmail.com, alaingrangette.com
Specialties: Art knives and folders with precise, complex folding mechanisms and tight fits and finishes. **Patterns:** Art folders, fixed blades and cutlery. **Technical:** Uses Pantograph and includes mirror finishing, engraving and contemporary materials. Every knife realized is a unique piece, and every blade, mechanism, screw and all other parts are handmade.

GRAVELINE, PASCAL AND ISABELLE
38 Rue de Kerbrezillic, Moelan-sur-Mer, FRANCE 29350 **Contact:** 33 2 98 39 73 33, atelier.graveline@wanadoo.fr, graveline-couteliers.com
Specialties: French replicas from the 17th, 18th and 19th centuries. **Patterns:** Traditional folders and multi-blade pocket knives, traveling knives, fruit knives and fork sets, puzzle knives and friend's knives, rivet less knives. **Technical:** Grind 12C27, ATS-34, damascus and carbon steel. **Prices:** $500 to $5000. **Remarks:** Full-time makers, first knife sold in 1992. **Mark:** Last name over head of ram.

GRAVES, DAN
4887 Dixie Garden Loop, Shreveport, LA 71105 **Contact:** 318-865-8166, theknifemaker.com
Specialties: Traditional forged blades and damascus. **Patterns:** bowies (D guard also), fighters, hunters, large and small daggers. **Remarks:** Full-time maker. **Mark:** Initials with circle around them.

GRAY, BOB
8206 N Lucia Court, Spokane, WA 99208 **Contact:** 509-468-3924
Specialties: Straight working knives of his own design or to customer specs. **Patterns:**

Hunter, fillet and carving knives. **Technical:** Forges 5160, L6 and some 52100, grinds 440C. **Prices:** $100 to $600. **Remarks:** Part-time knifemaker, first knife sold in 1991. Doing business as Hi-Land Knives. **Mark:** HI-L.

GRAY, DANIEL
GRAY KNIVES, POB 718, Brownville, ME 04414 **Contact:** 207-965-2191, mail@grayknives.com, grayknives.com
Specialties: Straight knives, fantasy, folders, automatics and traditional of his own design. **Patterns:** Automatics, fighters, hunters. **Technical:** Grinds O1, 154CM and D2. **Prices:** From $155 to $750. **Remarks:** Full-time maker, first knife sold in 1974. **Mark:** Gray Knives.

GRAY, ROBB
6026 46th Ave. SW, Seattle, WA 98136 **Contact:** 206-280-7622, robb.gray@graycloud-designs.com, graycloud-designs.com
Specialties: Hunting, fishing and leather-workers' knives, along with daggers and utility ranch knives. **Technical:** Stock-removal maker using 440C, CPM-S30V, CPM-154, CPM-12C27, CPM-13C26 and CPM-19C27 stainless steels. Also engraves knives in Sheridan, single point and Western bright cut styles. Owner of "Resinwood," a certified wood fiber product sold to knifemaker supply companies for handle material. **Remarks:** Full-time artist/maker, first knife made in 2009. **Mark:** A rain cloud with name "Graycloud" next to it, surrounded by an oval.

GRAYMAN, MIKE
GRAYMAN KNIVES, Postal Annex, 1281 N State St , Ste A - 503 , San Jacinto, CA 92583-6313 **Contact:** info@graymanknives.com, graymanknives.com
Specialties: Single- and double-bevel fixed blades, and hard-use frame-lock folders. **Technical:** Hand grinds fixed blades using 1095 steel or 440 stainless with GunKote finishes, G-10 handles, Cordura sheaths and free personalized hand engraving on blade spines. Precision-machined folders include CPM 20CV and CPM S30V blade steels with titanium handles. **Prices:** $160 to $425. **Remarks:** Started making knives in 2004. **Mark:** "Grayman" hand engraved on the spine of each knife.

GRECO, JOHN
100 Mattie Jones Rd, Greensburg, KY 42743 **Contact:** 270-932-3335
Specialties: Folders. **Patterns:** Tactical, fighters, camp knives, short swords. **Technical:** Stock removal carbon steel. **Prices:** Affordable. **Remarks:** Full-time maker since 1979. First knife sold in 1979. **Mark:** GRECO

GREEN, BILL
6621 Eastview Dr, Sachse, TX 75048 **Contact:** 972-463-3147
Specialties: High-art and working straight knives and folders of his design and to customer specs. **Patterns:** bowies, hunters, kitchen knives and locking folders. **Technical:** Grinds ATS-34, D2 and 440V. Hand-tooled custom sheaths. **Prices:** $70 to $350, some to $750. **Remarks:** Part-time maker, first knife sold in 1990. **Mark:** Last name.

GREEN, WILLIAM (BILL)
46 Warren Rd, View Bank, VIC, AUSTRALIA 3084, (fax) 03-9459-1529
Specialties: Traditional high-tech straight knives and folders. **Patterns:** Japanese-influenced designs, hunters, bowies, folders and miniatures. **Technical:** Forges O1, D2 and his own damascus. Offers lost wax castings for bolsters and pommels. Likes natural handle materials, gems, silver and gold. **Prices:** $400 to $750, some to $1200. **Remarks:** Full-time maker. **Mark:** Initials.

GREENAWAY, DON
3325 Dinsmore Tr, Fayetteville, AR 72704 **Contact:** 501-521-0323
Specialties: Liner locks and bowies. **Prices:** $150 to $1500. **Remarks:** 20 years experience. **Mark:** Greenaway over Fayetteville, Ark.

GREENE, CHRIS
707 Cherry Lane, Shelby, NC 28150 **Contact:** 704-434-5620

GREENE, DAVID
570 Malcom Rd, Covington, GA 30209 **Contact:** 770-784-0657
Specialties: Straight working using knives. **Patterns:** Hunters. **Technical:** Forges mosaic and twist damascus. Prefers stag and desert ironwood for handle material.

GREENE, STEVE
DUNN KNIVES INC, PO Box 307 1449 Nocatee St., Intercession City, FL 33848 **Contact:** 800-245-6483, s.greene@earthlink.net, dunnknives.com
Specialties: Skinning & fillet knives. **Patterns:** Skinners, drop points, clip points and fillets. **Technical:** CPM-S30V powdered metal steel manufactured by Niagara Specialty Metals. **Prices:** $100 to $350. **Mark:** Dunn by Greene and year. **Remarks:** Full-time knifemaker. First knife sold in 1972. Each knife is handcrafted and includes holster-grade leather sheath.

GREENFIELD, G O
2605 15th St #310, Everett, WA 98201 **Contact:** 425-232-6011, garyg1946@yahoo.com
Specialties: High-tech and working straight knives and folders of his design. **Patterns:** Boots, daggers, hunters and one-of-a-kinds. **Technical:** Grinds ATS-34, D2, 440C and T-440V. Makes sheaths for each knife. **Prices:** $100 to $800, some to $10,000. **Remarks:** Part-time maker, first knife sold in 1978. **Mark:** Springfield®, serial number.

GREGORY, MATTHEW M.
74 Tarn Tr., Glenwood, NY 14069 **Contact:** 716-863-1215, mgregoryknives@yahoo.com, mgregoryknives.com
Patterns: Wide variation of styles, as I make what I like to make. bowies, fighters, Neo-American/Japanese-inspired blades, occasionally kitchen knives. **Technical:** Forging and stock removal, using forging steels such as 1084, 1095, W2 and CruForgeV, as well as

high-alloy steels like CPM-3V and CPM-S110V. Hamon (blade temper line) development and polishing. **Prices:** $350 and up. **Remarks:** Part-time maker since 2005. **Mark:** M. Gregory.

GREGORY, MICHAEL
211 Calhoun Rd, Belton, SC 29627 **Contact:** 864-338-8898, gregom.123@charter.net

Specialties: Interframe folding knives, working hunters and period pieces. Hand rubbed finish, engraving by maker. **Patterns:** Hunters, bowies, daggers and folding knives. **Technical:** Grinds ATS-34 and other makers' damascus. **Prices:** $200 and up. **Remarks:** Full-time maker, first knife sold in 1980. **Mark:** Name, city in logo.

GREINER, RICHARD
1073 E County Rd 32, Green Springs, OH 44836 **Contact:** 419-483-4613, rgreiner7295@yahoo.com

Specialties: High-carbon steels, edge hardened. **Patterns:** Most. **Technical:** Hand forged. **Prices:** $125 and up. **Remarks:** Have made knives for 30 years. **Mark:** Maple leaf.

GREISS, JOCKL
Herrenwald 15, Schenkenzell, GERMANY 77773 **Contact:** +49 7836 95 71 69 or +49 7836 95 55 76, jocklgreiss@yahoo.com

Specialties: Classic and working using straight knives of his design. **Patterns:** bowies, daggers and hunters. **Technical:** Uses only Jerry Rados damascus. All knives are one-of-a-kind made by hand, no machines are used. **Prices:** $700 to $2000, some to $3000. **Remarks:** Full-time maker, first knife sold in 1984. **Mark:** An "X" with a long vertical line through it.

GREY, PIET
PO Box 363, Naboomspruit, LP, SOUTH AFRICA 0560 **Contact:** 014-743-3613

Specialties: Fancy working and using straight knives of his design. **Patterns:** Fighters, hunters and utility/camp knives. **Technical:** Grinds ATS-34 and AEB-L, forges and grinds damascus. Solder less fitting of guards. Engraves and scrimshaws. **Prices:** $125 to $750, some to $1500. **Remarks:** Part-time maker, first knife sold in 1970. **Mark:** Last name.

GRIFFIN, JOHN
26101 Pine Shadows, Hockley, TX 77447 **Contact:** 281-414-7111, griff6363@yahoo.com, griffinknives.us

Specialties: Push button automatics. **Patterns:** All patterns, including custom-designed pieces. **Technical:** Stainless and damascus blade steels with differing textured designs on stainless steel bolsters. **Prices:** Start at $800. **Remarks:** Guaranteed for life, very durable and unique designs.

GRIFFIN JR., HOWARD A
14299 SW 31st Ct, Davie, FL 33330 **Contact:** 954-474-5406, mgriffin18@aol.com

Specialties: Working straight knives and folders. **Patterns:** Hunters, bowies, locking folders with his own push-button lock design. **Technical:** Grinds 440C. **Prices:** $100 to $200, some to $500. **Remarks:** Part-time maker, first knife sold in 1983. **Mark:** Initials.

GRIMES, MARK
PO BOX 1293, Bedford, TX 76095 **Contact:** 817-320-7274, ticktock107@gmail.com

Specialties: Qs. **Patterns:** Hunters, fighters, bowies. **Technical:** Custom hand forged 1084 steel blades full and hidden tang, heat treating, sheathes. **Prices:** $150-$400. **Remarks:** Part-time maker, first knife sold in 2009. **Mark:** Last name.

GRIZZARD, JIM
3626 Gunnels Ln., Oxford, AL 36203 **Contact:** 256-403-1232, grizzardforgiven@aol.com

Specialties: Hand carved art knives inspired by sole authorship. **Patterns:** Fixedblades, folders, and swords. **Technical:** Carving handles, artgrinding, forged and stock removal. **Prices:** Vary. **Remarks:** Uses knives mostly as a ministry to bless others. **Mark:** FOR HIS GLORY CUSTOM KNIVES OR j grizzard in a grizzly bear.

GROSPITCH, ERNIE
18440 Amityville Dr, Orlando, FL 32820 **Contact:** 407-568-5438, shrpknife@aol.com, erniesknives.com

Specialties: bowies, hunting, fishing, kitchen, lockback folders, leather craft and knifemaker logo stenciling/blue lightning stencil. **Patterns:** My design or customer's. **Technical:** Stock removal using most available steels. **Prices:** Vary. **Remarks:** Full-time maker, sold first knife in 1990. Blue Lightning stencils. **Mark:** Etched name over Thunderbird image.

GROSS, W W
109 Dylan Scott Dr, Archdale, NC 27263-3858

Specialties: Working knives. **Patterns:** Hunters, boots, fighters. **Technical:** Grinds. **Prices:** Moderate. **Remarks:** Full-time maker. **Mark:** Name.

GROSSMAN, STEWART
24 Water St #419, Clinton, MA 01510 **Contact:** 508-365-2291, 800-mysword

Specialties: Miniatures and full-size knives and swords. **Patterns:** One-of-a-kind miniatures—jewelry, replicas—and wire-wrapped figures. Full-size art, fantasy and combat knives, daggers and modular systems. **Technical:** Forges and grinds most metals and damascus. Uses gems, crystals, electronics and motorized mechanisms. **Prices:** $20 to $300, some to $4500 and higher. **Remarks:** Full-time maker, first knife sold in 1985. **Mark:** G1.

GROVES, GARY
P.O. Box 101, Canvas, WV 26662, ggroves51@gmail.com

Specialties: Fixed blades and hidden-tang knives. **Patterns:** Hunters, skinners and bowies. **Technical:** Stock-removal method using ATS 34 and 154CM steels. Handles are mainly natural materials such as bone, horn, stag and wood, with filework on just about all knives. Every knife comes with a made-to-fit sheath. **Prices:** $350 to $1,200.

Remarks: Full-time knifemaker, first knife sold in 2007. **Mark:** Last name over an anvil and a capital G in the middle of the anvil.

GRUSSENMEYER, PAUL G
310 Kresson Rd, Cherry Hill, NJ 08034 **Contact:** 856-428-1088, pgrussentne@comcast.net, pgcarvings.com

Specialties: Assembling fancy and fantasy straight knives with his own carved handles. **Patterns:** bowies, daggers, folders, swords, hunters and miniatures. **Technical:** Uses forged steel and damascus, stock removal and knapped obsidian blades. **Prices:** $250 to $4000. **Remarks:** Spare-time maker, first knife sold in 1991. **Mark:** First and last initial hooked together on handle.

GUARNERA, ANTHONY R
42034 Quail Creek Dr, Quartzhill, CA 93536 **Contact:** 661-722-4032

Patterns: Hunters, camp, bowies, kitchen, fighter knives. **Technical:** Forged and stock removal. **Prices:** $100 and up.

GUINN, TERRY
13026 Hwy 6 South, Eastland, TX 76448 **Contact:** 254-629-8603, terryguinn.com

Specialties: Working fixed blades and balisongs. **Patterns:** Almost all types of folding and fixed blades, from patterns and "one of a kind". **Technical:** Stock removal all types of blade steel with preference for air hardening steel. Does own heat treating, all knives Rockwell tested in shop. **Prices:** $200 to $2,000. **Remarks:** Part time maker since 1982, sold first knife 1990. **Mark:** Full name with cross in the middle.

GUNTER, BRAD
13 Imnaha Rd., Tijeras, NM 87059 **Contact:** 505-281-8080

GUNTHER, EDDIE
11 Nedlands Pl Burswood, Auckland, NEW ZEALAND 2013 **Contact:** 006492722373, eddit.gunther49@gmail.com

Specialties: Drop point hunters, boot, bowies. All mirror finished. **Technical:** Grinds D2, 440C, 12c27. **Prices:** $250 to $800. **Remarks:** Part-time maker, first knife sold in 1986. **Mark:** Name, city, country.

H

HAAS, RANDY
HHH Knives, 3875 Vandyke Rd., Marlette, MI 48453 **Contact:** 989-635-7059, hhhcustomknives.com

Specialties: Handmade custom kitchen and culinary knives, hunters, fighters, folders and art knives. **Technical:** damascus maker and sales. **Remarks:** Full-time maker for 10 years. **Mark:** Three H's with a knife behind the HHH.

HACKNEY, DANA A.
787 Mountain Meadows Rd., Naples, ID 83847-5044 **Contact:** 719-481-3940, Cell: 719-651-5634, danahackneyknives@gmail.com and dshackney@Q.com

Specialties: Hunters, bowies and everyday carry knives, and some kitchen cutlery. **Technical:** ABS journeyman smith who forges 1080 series, 5160, 52100, 01, W2 and his own damascus. Uses CPM-154 mostly for stainless knives. **Prices:** $150 and up. **Remarks:** Sole ownership knives and sheaths. Full-time maker as of July 2012. Sold first knife in 2005. ABS, MKA and PKA member. **Mark:** Last name, HACKNEY on left-side ricasso.

HAGEN, DOC
POB 58, 702 5th St. SE, Pelican Rapids, MN 56572 **Contact:** 218-863-8503, dochagen@gmail.com, dochagencustomknives.com

Specialties: Folders. Autos:bolster release-dual action. Slipjoint folders**Patterns:** Defense-related straight knives, wide variety of folders. **Technical:** Dual action release, bolster release autos. **Prices:** $300 to $800, some to $3000. **Remarks:** Full-time maker, first knife sold in 1975. Makes his own damascus. **Mark:** DOC HAGEN in shield, knife, banner logo, or DOC.

HAGGERTY, GEORGE S
PO Box 88, Jacksonville, VT 05342 **Contact:** 802-368-7437, swewater@sover.net

Specialties: Working straight knives and folders. **Patterns:** Hunters, claws, camp and fishing knives, locking folders and backpackers. **Technical:** Forges and grinds W2, 440C and 154CM. **Prices:** $85 to $300. **Remarks:** Part-time maker, first knife sold in 1981. **Mark:** Initials or last name.

HAGUE, GEOFF
Unit 5, Project Workshops, Lains Farm, Quarley, Hampshire, UNITED KINGDOM SP11 8PX **Contact:** (+44) 01672-870212, (fax) (+44) 01672 870212, geoff@hagueknives.com, hagueknives.com

Specialties: Fixed blade and folding knives. **Patterns:** Back lock, locking liner, slip joint, and friction folders. **Technical:** Grinds D2, RWL-34 and damascus. Mainly natural handle materials. **Prices:** $500 to $2,000. **Remarks:** Full-time maker. **Mark:** Last name.

HAINES, JEFF
Jeff Haines Custom Knives, W3678 Bay View Rd., Mayville, WI 53050 **Contact:** 920-387-0212, knifeguy95@gmail.com

Patterns: Hunters, skinners, camp knives, customer designs welcome. **Technical:** Forges 1095, 5160, and damascus, grinds A2. **Prices:** $100 and up. **Remarks:** Part-time maker since 1995. **Mark:** Last name.

HALE, LLOYD
7593 Beech Hill Rd., Pulaski, TN 38478 **Contact:** 931-424-5846, lloydahale@gmail.com

Specialties: Museum-grade, one-of-a-kind daggers, folders and sub-hilt fighting knives. **Remarks:** Full-time maker for 44+ years. Spent 20+ years creating a one-of-a-kind knife collection for Owsley Brown Frazier of Louisville, KY. I don't accept orders anymore.

HALFRICH, JERRY
340 Briarwood, San Marcos, TX 78666 **Contact:** 512-353-2582, jerryhalfrich@grandecom.net, halfrichknives.com

Specialties: Working knives and specialty utility knives for the professional and serious hunter. Uses proven designs in both straight and folding knives. Pays close attention to fit and finish. Art knives on special request. **Patterns:** Hunters, skinners, and lockback, LinerLock and slip-joint folders. **Technical:** Grinds both flat and hollow D2, Damasteel and CPM 154, makes high precision folders. **Prices:** $450 to $1,500. **Remarks:** Full-time maker since 2000. DBA Halfrich Custom Knives. **Mark:** HALFRICH.

HALL, JEFF
2753 E. Broadway Rd. Suite 101-300 Mesa, AZ 85204 **Contact:** 562-594-4740, info@nemesis-knives.com, nemisis-knives.com

Specialties: Collectible and working folders and fixed blades of his design. **Technical:** Grinds CPM-S35VN, CPM-154, and various makers' damascus. **Patterns:** Fighters, gentleman's, hunters and utility knives. **Prices:** $100 and up. **Remarks:** Full-time maker. First knife sold 1998. **Mark:** Last name.

HALL, KEN
606 Stevenson Cove Rd., Waynesville, NC 28785 **Contact:** 828-627-2135, khall@hallenergyconsulting.com, kenhallknives.com

Specialties: Standard and one-of-a-kind fixed-blade knives with leather sheaths. **Patterns:** Hunters, bowies, fighters, chef's knives and tantos. **Technical:** Forges high-carbon steel, flat grinds. **Prices:** $300 to $1,500. **Remarks:** Part-time maker, first knives sold in 2010. **Mark:** Etched "Ken Hall" or "KHall JS."

HALL, SCOTT M.
5 Hickory Hts., Geneseo, IL 61254 **Contact:** 309-945-2184, smhall@theinter.com, hallcustomknives.com

Specialties: Fixed-blade, hollow-ground working knives of his own design and to customer specs. **Patterns:** Designs catering to soldiers and outdoorsmen, including variations of hunters, bowies, fighters and occasionally fillet and kitchen knives. **Technical:** Usually grinds CPM S30V and 154CM, but uses other steels upon request. Handle materials include G-10, Micarta, stag, horn and exotic woods. Most knives are offered with hand-tooled and stitched leather sheaths or Spec Ops sheaths. **Prices:** $150 to $350+. **Remarks:** Part-time maker, first knife sold in 2000. **Mark:** Last name.

HAMLET JR., JOHNNY
300 Billington, Clute, TX 77531 **Contact:** 979-265-6929, nifeman@swbell.net, hamlets-handmade-knives.com

Specialties: Working straight knives and folders. **Patterns:** Hunters, fighters, fillet and kitchen knives, locking folders. Likes upswept knives and trailing-points. **Technical:** Grinds 440C, D2, ATS-34. Makes sheaths. **Prices:** $125 and up. **Remarks:** Full-time maker, sold first knife in 1988. **Mark:** Hamlet's Handmade in script.

HAMMOND, HANK
189 Springlake Dr, Leesburg, GA 31763 **Contact:** 229-434-1295, godogs57@bellsouth.net

Specialties: Traditional hunting and utility knives of his design. Will also design and produce knives to customer's specifications. **Patterns:** Straight or sheath knives, hunters skinners as well as bowies and fighters. **Technical:** Grinds (hollow and flat grinds) CPM 154CM, ATS-34. Also uses damascus and forges 52100. Offers filework on blades. Handle materials include all exotic woods, red stag, sambar stag, deer, elk, oosic, bone, fossil ivory, Micarta, etc. All knives come with sheath handmade for that individual knife. **Prices:** $100 up to $500. **Remarks:** Part-time maker. Sold first knife in 1981. Doing business as Double H Knives. **Mark:** "HH" inside 8 point deer rack.

HAMMOND, JIM
104 Owens Parkway, Ste. M, Birmingham, AL 35244 **Contact:** 256-651-1376, jim@jimhammondknives.com, jimhammondknives.com

Specialties: High-tech fighters and folders. **Patterns:** Proven-design fighters. **Technical:** Grinds 440C, 440V, S30V and other specialty steels. **Prices:** $385 to $1200, some to $9200. **Remarks:** Full-time maker, first knife sold in 1977. Designer for Columbia River Knife and Tool. **Mark:** Full name, city, state in shield logo.

HAMMOND, RAY
Hammond Knives, LLC, 3750 Quail Creek Dr., Buford, GA 30519 **Contact:** 678-300-2883, rayhammond01@yahoo.com, biggamehuntingblades.com

Specialties: Fixed blades, primarily hunting knives, utility knives and bowies. **Technical:** Stock removal and forged blades, including 5160, 1095, CPM-154 and damascus blade steels. **Prices:** Start at $300. **Remarks:** Part-time maker, first knife built in 2008. **Mark:** Capital letters RH surrounded by a broken circle, pierced by a knife silhouette, atop the circle is my name, and below the circle the words "custom knives." Will soon alter this to simply my last name.

HAND, BILL
PO Box 717, 1103 W. 7th St., Spearman, TX 79081 **Contact:** 806-659-2967, (fax) 806-659-5139, klinker43@yahoo.com

Specialties: Traditional working and using straight knives and folders of his design or to customer specs. **Patterns:** Hunters, bowies, folders and fighters. **Technical:** Forges 5160, 52100 and damascus. **Prices:** Start at $150. **Remarks:** Part-time maker, Journeyman Smith. Current delivery time 12 to 16 months. **Mark:** Stylized initials.

HANKALA, JUKKA
Tuhkurintie 225, 39580 Riitiala, FINLAND **Contact:** +358-400-684-625, jukka@hankala.com, hankala.com

Specialties: Traditional puukkos and maker's own knife models. **Patterns:** Maker's own puukko models, hunters, folders and ART-knives. **Technical:** Forges Silversteel, Bohler K510, Damasteel stainless damascus and RWL-34 blade steels, as well as his own 15N20-and-1.2842 damascus, mosaic damascus and color damascus. **Prices:** Start at $300. **Remarks:** Full-time maker since 1985. **Mark:** J. Hankala.

HANSEN, LONNIE
PO Box 4956, Spanaway, WA 98387 **Contact:** 253-847-4632, lonniehansen@msn.com, lchansen.com

Specialties: Working straight knives of his design. **Patterns:** Tomahawks, tantos, hunters, fillet. **Technical:** Forges 1086, 52100, grinds 440V, BG-42. **Prices:** Starting at $300. **Remarks:** Part-time maker since 1989. **Mark:** First initial and last name. Also first and last initial.

HANSEN, ROBERT W
405 357th Ave. NE, Cambridge, MN 55008 **Contact:** 763-689-3242

Specialties: Working straight knives, folders and integrals. **Patterns:** From hunters to minis, camp knives to miniatures, folding lockers and slip-joints in original styles. **Technical:** Grinds O1, 440C and 154CM, likes filework. **Prices:** $100 to $450, some to $600. **Remarks:** Part-time maker, first knife sold in 1983. **Mark:** Fish w/h inside surrounded by Bob Hansen maker.

HANSON, KYLE S.
POB 12, Success, MO 65570 **Contact:** 573-674-3045, khansonknives@gmail.com, https://kylehansonknives.wordpress.com/

Specialties: W2 fixed blades with striking hamons and one-of-a-kind, handforged damascus, as well as damascus bolsters and guards on many knives. **Patterns:** Utility knives, hunters, fighters, bowies and the occasional tactical piece. Fixed blades only, with full or hidden tangs. **Technical:** Forges his own damascus, though he can't help dig into his father, Don Hanson III's, stash once in a while, and is particularly fond of intricate hamons on W2 blades. Also fond of walrus ivory, mother-of-pearl, curly koa and desert ironwood handles. **Remarks:** Full-time maker, first knife sold in 2012. Learned everything he knows from his father and couldn't ask for a better teacher in the world of custom knives. **Mark:** KYLE HANSON.

HANSON III, DON L.
Sunfish Forge, PO Box 13, Success, MO 65570-0013 **Contact:** 573-674-3045, sunfishforge.com, donhansonknives.com

Specialties: One-of-a-kind damascus folders, slip joints and forged fixed blades. **Patterns:** Small, fancy pocket knives, large folding fighters and bowies. **Technical:** Forges own pattern welded damascus, file work and carving also carbon steel blades with hamons. **Prices:** $800 and up. **Remarks:** Full-time maker, first knife sold in 1984. ABS mastersmith. **Mark:** Sunfish.

HARA, KOJI
292-2 Osugi, Seki-City, Gifu, JAPAN 501-3922 **Contact:** 0575-24-7569, (fax) 0575-24-7569, info@knifehousehara.com, knifehousehara.com

Specialties: High-tech and working straight knives of his design, some folders. **Patterns:** Hunters, locking folders and utility/camp knives. **Technical:** Grinds Cowry X, Cowry Y and ATS-34. Prefers high mirror polish, pearl handle inlay. **Prices:** $400 to $2500. **Remarks:** Full-time maker, first knife sold in 1980. Doing business as Knife House "Hara." **Mark:** First initial, last name in fish.

HARDING, CHAD
12365 Richland Ln, Solsberry, IN 47459, hardingknives@yahoo.com, hardingknives.net

Specialties: Hunters and camp knives, occasional fighters or bowies. No folders. **Technical:** Hand forge 90% of work. Prefer 10XX steels and tool steels. Makes own damascus and cable and chainsaw chain damascus. 100% sole authorship on knives and sheaths. Mostly natural handle material, prefer wood and stag. **Prices:** $150 to $1,000. **Remarks:** Part-time maker, member of ABS. First knife sold in 2005. **Mark:** Last name.

HARDING, JACOB
POB 10451, Fairbanks, AK 99710 **Contact:** 907-347-2961, harding-jake@hotmail.com, etsy.com/shop/hardingjm9, Facebook at Walking Stick Arts

Specialties: Blacksmith making handforged blades, including hunting and camp knives, black powder patch knives and collector pieces. **Technical:** Forges high-carbon 5160 steel, and likes to use recycled materials whenever possible, including leaf springs, files, railroad spikes, ammo casings for brass work and handle parts. **Prices:** $80 to $500. **Mark:** Harding, and location: ALASKA.

HARDY, DOUGLAS E
114 Cypress Rd, Franklin, GA 30217 **Contact:** 706-675-6305

HARDY, SCOTT
639 Myrtle Ave, Placerville, CA 95667 **Contact:** 530-622-5780, innercite.com/~shardy

Specialties: Traditional working and using straight knives of his design. **Patterns:** Most anything with an edge. **Technical:** Forges carbon steels. Japanese stone polish. Offers mirror finish, differentially tempers. **Prices:** $100 to $1000. **Remarks:** Part-time maker, first knife sold in 1982. **Mark:** First initial, last name and Handmade with bird logo.

HARKINS, J A
PO Box 218, Conner, MT 59827 **Contact:** 406-821-1060, kutter@customknives.net, customknives.net

Specialties: OTFs. **Patterns:** OTFs, Automatics, Folders. **Technical:** Grinds ATS-34. Engraves, offers gem work. **Prices:** $1500 and up. **Remarks:** Celebrating 20th year as full-time maker. **Mark:** First and middle initials, last name.

HARLEY, RICHARD

609 Navaho Trl., Bristol, VA 24201 **Contact:** 423-878-5368, cell: 423-408-5720 **Specialties:** Hunting knives, bowies, friction folders, one-of-a-kind. **Technical:** Forges 1084, S160, 52100, Lg. **Prices:** $150 to $1000. **Mark:** Pine tree with name.

HARM, PAUL W

818 N. Young Rd, Attica, MI 48412 **Contact:** 810-724-5582, harm@blclinks.net **Specialties:** Early American working knives. **Patterns:** Hunters, skinners, patch knives, fighters, folders. **Technical:** Forges and grinds 1084, O1, 52100 and own damascus. **Prices:** $75 to $1000. **Remarks:** First knife sold in 1990. **Mark:** Connected initials.

HARNER III, "BUTCH" LLOYD R.

745 Kindig Rd., Littlestown, PA 17340, butch@harnerknives.com, harnerknives.com **Specialties:** Kitchen knives and straight razors. **Technical:** CPM-3V, CPM-154 and various Carpenter powdered steel alloys. **Remarks:** Full-time maker since 2007. **Mark:** L.R. Harner (2005-Sept. 2012) and Harner III (after Oct. 2012)

HARRINGTON, ROGER

P.O. Box 157, Battle, East Sussex, ENGLAND TN 33 3 DD **Contact:** 0854-838-7062, info@bisonbushcraft.co.uk, bisonbushcraft.co.uk **Specialties:** Working straight knives to his or customer's designs, flat saber Scandinavia-style grinds on full tang knives, also hollow and convex grinds. **Technical:** Grinds O1, D2, damascus. **Prices:** $200 to $800. **Remarks:** First knife made by hand in 1997 whilst traveling around the world. **Mark:** Bison with bison written under.

HARRIS, CASS

19855 Fraiser Hill Ln, Bluemont, VA 20135 **Contact:** 540-554-8774, tdogforge.com **Prices:** $160 to $500.

HARRIS, JAY

991 Johnson St, Redwood City, CA 94061 **Contact:** 415-366-6077 **Specialties:** Traditional high-tech straight knives and folders of his design. **Patterns:** Daggers, fighters and locking folders. **Technical:** Uses 440C, ATS-34 and CPM. **Prices:** $250 to $850. **Remarks:** Spare-time maker, first knife sold in 1980.

HARRIS, JOHN

PO Box 2466, Quartzsite, AZ 85346 **Contact:** 951-653-2755, johnharrisknives@yahoo.com, johnharrisknives.com **Specialties:** Hunters, daggers, bowies, bird and trout, period pieces, damascus and carbon steel knives, forged and stock removal. **Prices:** $200 to $1000.

HARRISON, BRIAN

BFH KNIVES, 2359 E Swede Rd, Cedarville, MI 49719 **Contact:** 906-430-0720, bfh_knives@yahoo.com **Specialties:** High grade fixed blade knives. **Patterns:** Many sizes & variety of patterns from small pocket carries to large combat and camp knives. Mirror and bead blast finishes. All handles of high grade materials from ivory to highly figured stabilized woods to stag, deer & moose horn and Micarta. Hand sewn fancy sheaths for pocket or belt. **Technical:** Flat & hollow grinds usually CPM154 but some O1, L6 and stellite 6K. **Prices:** $150 to $1200. **Remarks:** Full-time maker, sole authorship. Made first knife in 1980, sold first knife in 1999. Received much knowledge from the following makers: George Young, Eric Erickson, Webster Wood, Ed Kalfayan who are all generous men. **Mark:** Engraved blade outline w/ BFH Knives over the top edge, signature across middle & Cedarville, MI underneath.

HARRISON, JIM (SEAMUS)

721 Fairington View Dr, St. Louis, MO 63129 **Contact:** 314-791-6350, jrh@seamusknives.com, seamusknives.com **Specialties:** "Crossover" folders, liner-locks and frame-locks. **Patterns:** Uber, Author, Skyy Folders, Ryan, Landon, Connor and flipper folders. **Technical:** Uses CPM S30V and 154, Stellite 6k and stainless damascus by Norris, Thomas, Nichols and Damasteel. **Prices:** Folders $550 to $1,400. **Remarks:** Full-time maker since 2008, maker since 1999. **Mark:** Seamus

HARSEY, WILLIAM H

82710 N. Howe Ln, Creswell, OR 97426 **Contact:** 541-510-8707, billharsey@gmail.com **Specialties:** High-tech kitchen and outdoor knives. **Patterns:** Folding hunters, trout and bird folders, straight hunters, camp knives and axes. **Technical:** Grinds, etches. **Prices:** $125 to $300, some to $1500. Folders start at $350. **Remarks:** Full-time maker, first knife sold in 1979. **Mark:** Full name, state, U.S.A.

HART, BILL

647 Cedar Dr, Pasadena, MD 21122 **Contact:** 410-255-4981 **Specialties:** Fur-trade era working straight knives and folders. **Patterns:** Springback folders, skinners, bowies and patch knives. **Technical:** Forges and stock removes 1095 and 5160 wire damascus. **Prices:** $100 to $600. **Remarks:** Part-time maker, first knife sold in 1986. **Mark:** Name.

HARTMAN, ARLAN (LANNY)

6102 S Hamlin Cir, Baldwin, MI 49304 **Contact:** 231-745-4029 **Specialties:** Working straight knives and folders. **Patterns:** Drop-point hunters, coil spring lockers, slip-joints. **Technical:** Flat-grinds D2, 440C and ATS-34. **Prices:** $300 to $2000. **Remarks:** Part-time maker, first knife sold in 1982. **Mark:** Last name.

HARTMAN, TIM

3812 Pedroncelli Rd NW, Albuquerque, NM 87107 **Contact:** 505-385-6924, tbonz1@comcast.net **Specialties:** Exotic wood scales, sambar stag, filework, hunters. **Patterns:** Fixed blade hunters, skinners, utility and hiking. **Technical:** 154CM, Ats-34 and D2. Mirror finish and contoured scales. **Prices:** Start at $200-$450. **Remarks:** Started making knives in 2004.

Mark: 3 lines Ti Hartman, Maker, Albuquerque NM

HARVEY, KEVIN

HEAVIN FORGE, PO Box 768, Belfast, MP, SOUTH AFRICA 1100 **Contact:** 27-13-253-0914, info@heavinforge.co.za heavinforge.co.za **Specialties:** Large knives of presentation quality and creative art knives. **Patterns:** Fixed blades of bowie, dagger and fighter-styles, occasionally folders and swords. **Technical:** Stock removal of stainless and forging of carbon steel and own damascus. Indigenous African handle materials preferred. Own engraving Often collaborate with wife, Heather (ABS MS) under the logo "Heavin." **Prices:** $500 to $5000 average $1500. **Remarks:** Full-time maker and knifemaking instructor. Master bladesmith with ABS. First knife sold in 1984. **Mark:** First name and surname, oval with "M S" in the middle.

HARVEY, MAX

6 Winchester Way, Leeming, Perth, Western Australia 6149, AUSTRALIA **Contact:** 61 (8) 93101103 or 61-478-633-356, mcharveyknives@outlook.com, http://mcharveycustomknives.com/wordpress/?page_id=84 **Specialties:** Fixed-blade knives of all styles. **Patterns:** Camp knives, skinners, bowies, daggers and high-end art knives. **Technical:** Stock-removal using ATS-34, 154CM, 440C and damascus. Do all my own faceting of gem stones in the high-end knives. **Prices:** $250 to $5,000. **Remarks:** Full-time maker, first knife sold in 1981, and founding member of the Australian Knife Makers Guild. **Mark:** First and middle initials, and surname (M C Harvey).

HARVEY, MEL

P.O. Box 176, Nenana, AK 99760 **Contact:** 907-832-5660, tinker1mh@gmail.com **Specialties:** Fixed blade knives for hunting and fishing. **Patterns:** Hunters, skinners. **Technical:** Stock removal on ATS-34, 440C, O1, 1095, damascus blades using 1095 and 15N20. **Prices:** Starting at $350. **Remarks:** ABS member, attended Bill Moran School, 50+ knives sold since 2007. **Mark:** Mel Harvey over serial number over Nenana, AK.

HASLINGER, THOMAS

6460 Woodland Dr., British Columbia V1B 3G7, CANADA **Contact:** 778-212-6300, haslinger-knives.com, haslinger-culinary.com **Specialties:** One-of-a-kind using, working and art knives HCK signature sweeping grind lines. Maker of New Generation and Evolution Chef series. Differential heat treated stainless steel. **Patterns:** Likes to work with customers on design. **Technical:** Grinds various specialty alloys, including damascus, High end satin finish. Prefers natural handle materials e.g. ancient ivory stag, pearl, abalone, stone and exotic woods. Does inlay work with stone, some sterling silver, niobium and gold wire work. Custom sheaths using matching woods or hand stitched with unique leather. Offers engraving. **Prices:** $300 and up. **Remarks:** Full-time maker, first knife sold in 1994. Doing business as Haslinger Custom Knives. **Mark:** Two marks used, high end work uses stylized initials, other uses elk antler with Thomas Haslinger, Canada, handcrafted above.

HAWES, CHUCK

HAWES FORGE, PO Box 176, Weldon, IL 61882 **Contact:** 217-736-2479 **Specialties:** 95 percent of all work in own damascus. **Patterns:** Slip-joints liner locks, hunters, bowie's, swords, anything in between. **Technical:** Forges everything, uses all high-carbon steels, no stainless. **Prices:** $150 to $4000. **Remarks:** Like to do custom orders, his style or yours. Sells damascus. Full-time maker since 1995. **Mark:** Small football shape. Chuck Hawes maker Weldon, IL.

HAWK, GRANT AND GAVIN

Box 401, Idaho City, ID 83631 **Contact:** 208-392-4911, blademaker25@msn.com, hawkknifedesigns.com, @hawkknives on Instagram **Specialties:** Grant and Gavin Hawk make custom knives, mid-tech knives and have had designs with Kershaw, CRKT, Boker, Buck, Camillus, Chris Reeve Knives, Mantis Knives, Millit Knives and Quartermaster. Specialize in folders with innovative locking systems, such as their new Deadlock OTF, the first OTF (out the front auto) with zero blade play. **Technical:** Grind 204P, Elmax, CPM S35VN, CPM 530V, ATS-34, BG-42 and XHP, and use titanium and carbon fiber folder parts. **Prices:** $450 and up. **Remarks:** Full-time makers. **Mark:** G&G Hawk, Hawk Designs.

HAWKINS, BUDDY

PO Box 5969, Texarkana, TX 75505-5969 **Contact:** 903-838-7917, buddyhawkins@cableone.net

HAWKINS JR., CHARLES R.

2764 Eunice, San Angelo, TX 76901 **Contact:** 325-947-7875, chawk12354@aol.com, hawkcustomknives.com **Specialties:** Custom knives, fixed blades, railroad spike knives and rasp file knives. **Technical:** Stock removal and some forging, using 1095 and 440C steel. **Prices:** $135 and up. **Remarks:** Part-time maker, first knife sold in 2008. **Mark:** Full name, city and state.

HAWLEY, TROY G.

THAWLEY KNIVES, 226 CR 2036, Ivanhoe, TX 75447 **Contact:** 903-664-4568, thawley123@gmail.com **Specialties:** Hunting and fishing knives, kitchen cutlery, tacticals, fighters, tactical machetes and art knives of his own design. **Technical:** Stock removal method of blade making primarily working with 440C, CPM 154 and damascus, with other steels upon request. Forges high-carbon steels, such as 5160 spring steel, to create one-of-a-kind bowies, sabers and hunting knives. **Prices:** Start at $180 and up. **Remarks:** First knife sold in 2014. Member of the Texas Knifemakers Guild. **Mark:** "T."

HAYES, WALLY

9960, 9th Concession, RR#1, Essex, ON, CANADA N8M-2X5 **Contact:** 226-787-4289, hayesknives@hayesknives.com, hayesknives.com **Specialties:** Classic and fancy straight knives and folders. **Patterns:** Daggers, bowies, fighters, tantos. **Technical:** Forges own damascus and O1, engraves. **Prices:** $150 to $14,000. **Mark:** Last name, M.S. and serial number.

HAYNES, JERRY
260 Forest Meadow Dr, Gunter, TX 75058 **Contact:** 903-433-1424, jhaynes@arrow-head.com, arrow-head.com
Specialties: Working straight knives and folders of his design, also historical blades. **Patterns:** Hunters, skinners, carving knives, fighters, renaissance daggers, locking folders and kitchen knives. **Technical:** Grinds ATS-34, CPM, Stellite 6K, D2 and acquired damascus. Prefers exotic handle materials. Has B.A. in design. Studied with R. Buckminster Fuller. **Prices:** $200 to $1200. **Remarks:** Part-time maker. First knife sold in 1953. **Mark:** Arrowhead and last name.

HAYS, MARK
HAYS HANDMADE KNIVES, 1008 Kavanagh Dr., Austin, TX 78748 **Contact:** 512-292-4410, markhays@austin.rr.com
Specialties: Working straight knives and folders. Patterns inspired by Randall and Stone. **Patterns:** bowies, hunters and slip-joint folders. **Technical:** 440C stock removal. Repairs and restores Stone knives. **Prices:** Start at $200. **Remarks:** Part-time maker, brochure available, with Stone knives 1974-1983, 1990-1991. **Mark:** First initial, last name, state and serial number.

HAZE, JEFF
JEFF HAZE CUSTOM KNIVES, 1703 E. 168th St. N, Skiatook, OK 74070 **Contact:** 918-896-1205, jeffhaze@rocketmail.com, facebook.com/jeffhazecustoms
Specialties: Bushcraft, hunting and everyday carry (EDC) knives. **Technical:** Scandi, saber and flat grinds using the stock-removal method of blade making. Uses 1084 high-carbon and 80CrV2 steels. **Prices:** $100 to $350. **Remarks:** Full-time maker, first knife made in 2013. **Mark:** HAZE.

HEADRICK, GARY
122 Wilson Blvd, Juan Les Pins, FRANCE 06160 **Contact:** 033 610282885, headrick-gary@wanadoo.fr, http://garyheadrick.free.fr
Specialties: Hi-tech folders with natural furnishings. Back lock & back spring. **Patterns:** damascus and mokumes. **Technical:** Forges damascus using all steel (no nickel). All frames are titanium, and has a new tactical flipper folder model. **Prices:** $500 to $2,000. **Remarks:** Full-time maker for last eight years, active maker for the past 18 years. German Guild-French Federation, 10 years active, member of the ABS and Italian Corporation. **Mark:** HEADRICK on ricosso is new marking.

HEANEY, JOHN D
9 Lefe Court, Haines City, FL 33844 **Contact:** 863-422-5823, jdh199@msn.com, heaneyknives.com
Specialties: Forged 5160, O1 and damascus. Prefers using natural handle material such as bone, stag and oosic. Plans on using some of the various ivories on future knives. **Prices:** $250 and up. **Remarks:** ABS member. Received journeyman smith stamp in June. **Mark:** Heaney JS.

HEARD, TOM
Turning Point Knives, 2240 Westwood Dr., Waldorf, MD 20601 **Contact:** 301-843-8626, cell: 301-752-1944, turningpointknives@comcast.net
Specialties: Gent's working/using LinerLocks, automatics and flipper folders of his design. **Patterns:** Fixed blades of varying styles, folders and neck knives. **Technical:** Flat grinds 1095, O1, damascus and 154CM. Offers acid-etched blade embellishments, scrimshaw and hand-tooled custom leather sheaths. Does own heat-treating. **Prices:** $150 to $1300. **Remarks:** Full-time maker since retiring, first knife sold in 2012. **Mark:** TH over last name or last name only.

HEATH, WILLIAM
PO Box 131, Bondville, IL 61815 **Contact:** 217-863-2576
Specialties: Classic and working straight knives, folders. **Patterns:** Hunters and bowies LinerLock® folders. **Technical:** Grinds ATS-34, 440C, 154CM, damascus, handle materials Micarta, woods to exotic materials snake skins cobra, rattle snake, African flower snake. Does own heat treating. **Prices:** $75 to $300 some $1000. **Remarks:** Full-time maker. First knife sold in 1979. **Mark:** W. D. HEATH.

HEBEISEN, JEFF
310 19th Ave N, Hopkins, MN 55343 **Contact:** 952-935-4506, jhebeisen@peoplepc.com
Specialties: One of a kind fixed blade of any size up to 16". **Patterns:** Miniature, Hunters, Skinners, Daggers, bowies, Fighters and Neck knives. **Technical:** Stock removal using CPM-154, D2, 440C. Handle mterial varies depending on intended use, mostly natural materials such as bone, horn, antler, and wood. Filework on many. Heavy duty sheaths made to fit. **Prices:** From $100 to $750. **Remarks:** Full-time maker. First knife sold in 2007. **Mark:** Started new mark in 2012: J. Hebeisen, Hopkins, MN. Older **mark:** arched name over buffalo skull.

HEDGES, DEE
192 Carradine Rd., Bedfordale, WA, AUSTRALIA 6112, dark_woods_forge@yahoo.com.au, darkwoodsforge.com
Patterns: Makes any and all patterns and style of blades from working blades to swords to Japanese inspired. Favors exotic and artistic variations and unique one-off pieces. **Technical:** Forges all blades from a range of steels, favoring 1084, W2, 52100, 5160 and damascus steels she makes from a 1084/15n20 mix. **Prices:** Start at $200. **Remarks:** Full-time bladesmith and jeweller. Started making blades professionally in 1999, earning my Journeyman Smith rating in 2010. **Mark:** "Dark Woods" atop an ivy leaf, with "Forge" underneath.

HEDLUND, ANDERS
Samstad 400, Brastad, SWEDEN 45491 **Contact:** 46-523-139 48, anderskniv@passagen.se, http://hem.passagen.se/anderskniv
Specialties: Fancy high-end collectible folders, high-end collectible Nordic hunters with leather carvings on the sheath. Carvings combine traditional designs with own designs. **Patterns:** Own designs. **Technical:** Grinds most steels, but prefers mosaic damascus and RWL-34. Prefers mother-of-pearl, mammoth, and mosaic steel for folders. Prefers desert ironwood, mammoth, stabilized arctic birch, willow burl, and damascus steel or RWL-34 for stick tang knives. **Prices:** Starting at $750 for stick tang knives and staring at $1500 for folders. **Remarks:** Part-time maker, first knife sold in 1988. Nordic champion (five countries) several times and Swedish champion 20 times in different classes. **Mark:** Stylized initials or last name.

HEDRICK, DON
131 Beechwood Hills, Newport News, VA 23608 **Contact:** 757-877-8100, donaldhedrick@cox.net, donhedrickknives.com
Specialties: Miniature Randall replicas. **Patterns:** Hunters, boots, bowies and miniatures. **Technical:** Grinds 440C and commercial damascus. Also makes micro-mini Randall replicas. **Prices:** $150 to $550, some to $1200. **Remarks:** Part-time maker, first knife sold in 1982. **Mark:** First initial, last name in oval logo.

HEETER, TODD S.
9569 Polo Place N., Mobile, AL 36695 **Contact:** 251-490-5107, toddheeter78@yahoo.com, heeterknifeworks.com
Specialties: Complete range of handforged knives, one-of-a-kind custom pieces. **Patterns:** Military-style frame-lock folders, neck knives, railroad spike folders. **Technical:** Handforged blades, including 1095 and D2, stainless steel, Alabama damascus, doing one-sided chisel grinds and all ranges of flat grinds. Specializes in war-torn look, hand-hammered copper, pattern etching, antique copper and brass handle scales. **Prices:** $150 to $950. **Remarks:** Part-time maker, full-time fabricator and machinist, tool and die maker, first knife sold in 2009. **Mark:** Stamped first initial, middle initial and full last name, logo: HK with a dagger crossing letters.

HEGE, JOHN B.
P.O. Box 316, Danbury, NC 27106 **Contact:** 336-593-8324, jbhege@embarqmail.com, jbhegecustomknives.com
Specialties: Period-style knives and traditional bowies, utility hunters and fancy pieces. **Technical:** Forges larger pieces and often uses stock removal for knives 6 inches and smaller. **Remarks:** ABS journeyman smith since 2013.

HEGWALD, J L
1106 Charles, Humboldt, KS 66748 **Contact:** 316-473-3523
Specialties: Working straight knives, some fancy. **Patterns:** Makes bowies, miniatures. **Technical:** Forges or grinds O1, L6, 440C, mixes materials in handles. **Prices:** $35 to $200, some higher. **Remarks:** Part-time maker, first knife sold in 1983. **Mark:** First and middle initials.

HEHN, RICHARD KARL
Lehnmuehler Str 1, Dorrebach, GERMANY 55444 **Contact:** 06724 3152
Specialties: High-tech, full integral working knives. **Patterns:** Hunters, fighters and daggers. **Technical:** Grinds CPM T-440V, CPM T-420V, forges his own stainless damascus. **Prices:** $1000 to $10,000. **Remarks:** Full-time maker, first knife sold in 1963. **Mark:** Runic last initial in logo.

HEIMDALE, J E
7749 E 28 CT, Tulsa, OK 74129 **Contact:** 918-640-0784, heimdale@sbcglobal.net
Specialties: Art knives **Patterns:** bowies, daggers **Technical:** Makes allcomponents and handles - exotic woods and sheaths. Uses damascus blades by other Blademakers, notably R.W. Wilson. **Prices:** $300 and up. **Remarks:** Part-time maker. First knife sold in 1999. **Marks:** JEHCO

HEINZ, JOHN
611 Cafferty Rd, Upper Black Eddy, PA 18972 **Contact:** 610-847-8535, herugrim.com
Specialties: Historical pieces / copies. **Technical:** Makes his own steel. **Prices:** $150 to $800. **Mark:** "H."

HEITLER, HENRY
8106 N Albany, Tampa, FL 33604 **Contact:** 813-933-1645
Specialties: Traditional working and using straight knives of his design and to customer specs. **Patterns:** Fighters, hunters, utility/camp knives and fillet knives. **Technical:** Flat-grinds ATS-34, offers tapered tangs. **Prices:** $135 to $450, some to $600. **Remarks:** Part-time maker, first knife sold in 1990. **Mark:** First initial, last name, city, state circling double H's.

HELSCHER, JOHN W
2645 Highway 1, Washington, IA 52353 **Contact:** 319-653-7310

HELTON, ROY
HELTON KNIVES, 2941 Comstock St., San Diego, CA 92111 **Contact:** 858-277-5024

HEMPERLEY, GLEN
13322 Country Run Rd, Willis, TX 77318 **Contact:** 936-228-5048, hemperley.com
Specialties: Specializes in hunting knives, does fixed and folding knives.

HENDRICKS, SAMUEL J
2162 Van Buren Rd, Maurertown, VA 22644 **Contact:** 703-436-3305
Specialties: Integral hunters and skinners of thin design. **Patterns:** Boots, hunters and locking folders. **Technical:** Grinds ATS-34, 440C and D2. Integral liners and bolsters of N-S and 7075 T6 aircraft aluminum. Does leatherwork. **Prices:** $50 to $250, some to

$500. **Remarks:** Full-time maker, first knife sold in 1992. **Mark:** First and middle initials, last name, city and state in football-style logo.

HENDRICKSON, E JAY
Hendrickson Knives. 180 Lake Meade Drive, East Berlin, PA 17316 **Contact:** 301-305-8385, (fax) 301-663-6923, ejayhendrickson@comcast.net
 Specialties: Specializes in silver wire inlay. **Patterns:** bowies, Kukri's, camp, hunters, and fighters. **Technical:** Forges 06, 1084, 5160, 52100, D2, L6 and W2, makes damascus. Moran-styles on order. **Prices:** $400 to $8,000. **Remarks:** Full-time maker, first knife made in 1972, first knife sold in 1974. **Mark:** Last name, M.S.

HENDRICKSON, SHAWN
2327 Kaetzel Rd, Knoxville, MD 21758 **Contact:** 301-432-4306
 Specialties: Hunting knives. **Patterns:** Clip points, drop points and trailing point hunters. **Technical:** Forges 5160, 1084 and L6. **Prices:** $175 to $400.

HENDRIX, JERRY
HENDRIX CUSTOM KNIVES, 17 Skyland Dr. Ext., Clinton, SC 29325 **Contact:** 864-833-2659
 Specialties: Traditional working straight knives of all designs. **Patterns:** Hunters, utility, boot, bird and fishing. **Technical:** Grinds ATS-34 and 440C. **Prices:** $85 to $275. **Remarks:** Full-time maker. Hand stitched, waxed leather sheaths. **Mark:** Full name in shape of knife.

HENDRIX, WAYNE
9636 Burton's Ferry Hwy, Allendale, SC 29810 **Contact:** 803-584-3825, (fax) 803-584-3825, whendrixknives@gmail.com hendrixknives.com
 Specialties: Working/using knives of his design. **Patterns:** Hunters and fillet knives. **Technical:** Grinds ATS-34, D2 and 440C. **Prices:** $100 and up. **Remarks:** Full-time maker, first knife sold in 1985. **Mark:** Last name.

HENNINGSSON, MICHAEL
Klingkarrsvagen 8, 430 83 Vrango (Gothenburg), SWEDEN **Contact:** +46 76 626 06 51, michael.henningsson@gmail.com, henningssonknives.com
 Specialties: Handmade folding knives, mostly tactical linerlocks and framelocks. **Patterns:** Own design in both engravings and knife models. **Technical:** All kinds of stee, such as damascus, but prefer clean RWL-43. Tweaking a lot with hand engraving and therefore likes clean steel mostly. Work a lot with inlays of various materials. **Prices:** Starting at $1200 and up, depending on decoration and engravings. **Remarks:** Part-time maker, first knife sold in 2010. **Mark:** Hand engraved name or a Viking sail with initials in runes

HENSHAW, CRAIG
CDH Knives 1141 Put in Bay Road RR4, Huntsville, Ontario, P1H 2j6 Canada **Contact:** 416-428-7835, craig@cdhknives.com, www.CDHknives.com
 Patterns: Chef's knives.

HENSLEY, WAYNE
PO Box 904, Conyers, GA 30012 **Contact:** 770-483-8938, rebwayhe@bellsouth.net
 Specialties: Period pieces and fancy working knives. **Patterns:** Boots to bowies, locking folders to miniatures. Large variety of straight knives. **Technical:** Grinds ATS-34, 440C, D2 and commercial damascus. **Prices:** $175 and up. **Remarks:** Full-time maker, first knife sold in 1974. **Mark:** Hensley USA.

HERBST, GAWIE
PO Box 59158, Karenpark, Akasia, GT, SOUTH AFRICA 0118 **Contact:** +27 72 060 3687, (fax) +27 12 549 1876, gawie@herbst.co.za herbst.co.za
 Specialties: Hunters, Utility knives, Art knives and Liner lock folders.

HERBST, PETER
Komotauer Strasse 26, Lauf a.d. Pegn., GERMANY 91207 **Contact:** 09123-13315, (fax) 09123-13379
 Specialties: Working/using knives and folders of his design. **Patterns:** Hunters, fighters and daggers, interframe and integral. **Technical:** Grinds CPM-T-440V, UHB-Elmax, ATS-34 and stainless damascus. **Prices:** $300 to $3000, some to $8000. **Remarks:** Full-time maker, first knife sold in 1981. **Mark:** First initial, last name.

HERBST, THINUS
PO Box 59158, Karenpark, Akasia, GT, SOUTH AFRICA 0118 **Contact:** +27 82 254 8016, thinus@herbst.co.za, herbst.co.za
 Specialties: Plain and fancy working straight knives of own design and liner lock folders. **Patterns:** Hunters, utility knives, art knives, and liner lock folders. **Technical:** Prefer exotic materials for handles. Most knives embellished with file work, carving and scrimshaw. **Prices:** $200 to $2000. **Remarks:** Full-time maker, member of the Knifemakers Guild of South Africa.

HERMAN, TIM
517 E. 126 Terrace, Olathe, KS 66061-2731 **Contact:** 913-839-1924, HermanKnives@comcast.net
 Specialties: Investment-grade folders of his design, interframes and bolster frames. **Patterns:** Interframes and new designs in carved stainless. **Technical:** Grinds ATS-34 and damasteel damascus. Engraves and gold inlays with pearl, jade, lapis and Australian opal. **Prices:** $1500 to $20,000 and up. **Remarks:** Full-time maker, first knife sold in 1978. Inventor of full-color bulino engraving since 1993. **Mark:** Etched signature.

HERNDON, WM R "BILL"
32520 Michigan St, Acton, CA 93510 **Contact:** 661-269-5860, bherndons1@roadrunner.com
 Specialties: Straight knives, plain and fancy. **Technical:** Carbon steel (white and blued),

damascus, stainless steels. **Prices:** Start at $175. **Remarks:** Full-time maker, first knife sold in 1972. American Bladesmith Society journeyman smith. **Mark:** Signature and/or helm logo.

HERRING, MORRIS
Box 85 721 W Line St, Dyer, AR 72935 **Contact:** 501-997-8861, morrish@ipa.com

HETHCOAT, DON
Box 1764, Clovis, NM 88101 **Contact:** 575-762-5721, dhethcoat@plateautel.net, donhethcoat.com
 Specialties: Liner locks, lock backs and multi-blade folder patterns. **Patterns:** Hunters, bowies. **Technical:** Grinds stainless, forges damascus. **Prices:** Moderate to upscale. **Remarks:** Full-time maker, first knife sold in 1969. **Mark:** Last name on all.

HEWITT, RONALD "COTTON"
P.O. Box 326, Adel, GA 31620 **Contact:** 229-896-6366 or 229-237-4378, gobbler12@msn.com, hewittknives.com
 Specialties: LinerLock folders and assisted flippers. **Technical:** Grinds CPM 154, CPM S35VN, CPM 3V and 52100 blade steels. Assisted flippers all have thrust bearings. **Prices:** $350 and up. **Remarks:** Full-time maker, first knife sold in 1975. **Mark:** Last name.

HIBBEN, DARYL
PO Box 172, LaGrange, KY 40031-0172 **Contact:** 502-222-0983, dhibben1@bellsouth.net
 Specialties: Working straight knives, some fancy to customer specs. **Patterns:** Hunters, fighters, bowies, short sword, art and fantasy. **Technical:** Grinds 440C, ATS-34, 154CM, damascus, prefers hollow-grinds. **Prices:** $275 and up. **Remarks:** Full-time maker, first knife sold in 1979. Retired, part time. **Mark:** Etched full name in script.

HIBBEN, GIL
PO Box 13, LaGrange, KY 40031 **Contact:** 502-222-1397, (fax) 502-222-2676, gil@hibbenknives.com hibbenknives.com
 Specialties: Working knives and fantasy pieces to customer specs. **Patterns:** Full range of straight knives, including swords, axes and miniatures, some locking folders. **Technical:** Grinds ATS-34, 440C and D2. **Prices:** $300 to $2000, some to $10,000. **Remarks:** Full-time maker, first knife sold in 1957. Maker and designer of Rambo III knife, made swords for movie Marked for Death and throwing knife for movie Under Siege, made belt buckle knife and knives for movie Perfect Weapon, made knives featured in movie Star Trek the Next Generation, Star Trek Nemesis. 1990 inductee Cutlery Hall of Fame, designer for United Cutlery. Official klingon armourer for Star Trek. Knives also for movies of the Expendables and the Expendables sequel. Over 37 movies and TV productions. Past president of the Knifemakers' Guild. Celebrating 59 years since first knife sold. **Mark:** Hibben Knives. City and state, or signature.

HIBBEN, WESTLEY G
14101 Sunview Dr, Anchorage, AK 99515
 Specialties: Working straight knives of his design or to customer specs. **Patterns:** Hunters, fighters, daggers, combat knives and some fantasy pieces. **Technical:** Grinds 440C mostly. Filework available. **Prices:** $200 to $400, some to $3000. **Remarks:** Part-time maker, first knife sold in 1988. **Mark:** Signature.

HICKS, GARY
341 CR 275, Tuscola, TX 79562 **Contact:** 325-554-9762
Hielscher, Guy
PO Box 992, 6550 Otoe Rd., Alliance, NE 69301 **Contact:** 308-762-4318, g-hielsc@bbcwb.net ghknives.com
 Specialties: Working damascus fixed blade knives. **Patterns:** Hunters, fighters, capers, skinners, bowie, drop point. **Technical:** Forges own damascus using 1018 and 0-1 tool steels. **Prices:** $285 and up. **Remarks:** Member of PKA. Part-time maker, sold first knife in 1988. **Mark:** Arrowhead with GH inside.

HIGH, TOM
5474 S 1128 Rd, Alamosa, CO 81101 **Contact:** 719-589-2108, rockymountainscrimshaw.com
 Specialties: Hunters, some fancy. **Patterns:** Drop-points in several shapes, some semi-skinners. Knives designed by and for top outfitters and guides. **Technical:** Grinds ATS-34, likes hollow-grinds, mirror finishes, prefers scrimable handles. **Prices:** $300 to $8000.. **Remarks:** Full-time maker, first knife sold in 1965. Limited edition wildlife series knives. **Mark:** Initials connected, arrow through last name.

HILL, RICK
20 Nassau, Maryville, IL 62062-5618 **Contact:** 618-288-4370
 Specialties: Working knives and period pieces to customer specs. **Patterns:** Hunters, locking folders, fighters and daggers. **Technical:** Grinds D2, 440C and 154CM, forges his own damascus. **Prices:** $75 to $500, some to $3000. **Remarks:** Part-time maker, first knife sold in 1983. **Mark:** Full name in hill shape logo.

HILL, STEVE E
217 Twin Lake Tr., Spring Branch, TX 78070 **Contact:** 830-624-6258 (cell) or 830-885-6108 (home), kingpirateboy2@juno.com or kingpirateboy2@gvtc.com, stevehillknives.com
 Specialties: Fancy manual and automatic LinerLock folders, small fixed blades and classic bowie knives. **Patterns:** Classic to cool folding and fixed blade designs. **Technical:** Grinds damascus fabricated in the U.S.A. and occasional high-carbon 1095, etc. Prefers natural handle materials, and offers elaborate filework, carving and inlays. **Prices:** $250 to $6,000, some higher. **Remarks:** Knifemaker to rock stars, blues dudes, movie celebrities and other nice folks in all walks of life. Full-time maker, first knife sold in 1978. **Mark:** S. Hill Spring Branch Texas inscribed on inside of folder handle spine and on blade spine of fixed blade knives.

HILLMAN, CHARLES
225 Waldoboro Rd, Friendship, ME 04547 **Contact:** 207-832-4634
Specialties: Working knives of his own or custom design. Heavy Scagel influence. **Patterns:** Hunters, fishing, camp and general utility. Occasional folders. **Technical:** Grinds D2 and 440C. File work, blade and handle carving, engraving. Natural handle materials-antler, bone, leather, wood, horn. Sheaths made to order. **Prices:** $60 to $500. **Remarks:** Part-time maker, first knife sold 1986. **Mark:** Last name in oak leaf.

HINDERER, RICK
5373 Columbus Rd., Shreve, OH 44676 **Contact:** 330-317-2964, rhind64@earthlink. net, rickhindererknives.com
Specialties: Working tactical knives, and some one-of-a kind. **Patterns:** Makes his own. **Technical:** Grinds Duratech 20 CV and CPM S30V. **Prices:** $150 to $4000. **Remarks:** Full-time maker doing business as Rick Hinderer Knives, first knife sold in 1988. **Mark:** R. Hinderer.

HINDMARCH, GARTH
PO Box 135, Carlyle, SK, CANADA S0C 0R0 **Contact:** 306-453-2568
Specialties: Working and fancy straight knives, bowies. **Patterns:** Hunters, skinners, bowies. **Technical:** Grinds 440C, ATS 34, some damascus. **Prices:** $250 to $1,100. **Remarks:** Part-time maker, first knife sold 1994. All knives satin finished. Does filework, offers engraving, stabilized wood, giraffe bone, some Micarta. **Mark:** First initial, last name, city, province.

HINK III, LES
1599 Aptos Lane, Stockton, CA 95206 **Contact:** 209-547-1292
Specialties: Working straight knives and traditional folders in standard patterns or to customer specs. **Patterns:** Hunting and utility/camp knives, others on request. **Technical:** Grinds carbon and stainless steels. **Prices:** $80 to $200, some higher. **Remarks:** Part-time maker, first knife sold in 1980. **Mark:** Last name, or last name 3.

HINMAN, THEODORE
186 Petty Plain Road, Greenfield, MA 01301 **Contact:** 413-773-0448, armenemargosian@verizon.net
Specialties: Tomahawks and axes. Offers classes in bladesmithing and toolmaking.

HINSON AND SON, R
2419 Edgewood Rd, Columbus, GA 31906 **Contact:** 706-327-6801
Specialties: Working straight knives and folders. **Patterns:** Locking folders, liner locks, combat knives and swords. **Technical:** Grinds 440C and commercial damascus. **Prices:** $200 to $450, some to $1500. **Remarks:** Part-time maker, first knife sold in 1983. Son Bob is co-worker. **Mark:** HINSON, city and state.

HINTZ, GERALD M
5402 Sahara Ct, Helena, MT 59602 **Contact:** 406-458-5412
Specialties: Fancy, high-art, working/using knives of his design. **Patterns:** bowies, hunters, daggers, fish fillet and utility/camp knives. **Technical:** Forges ATS-34, 440C and D2. Animal art in horn handles or in the blade. **Prices:** $75 to $400, some to $1000. **Remarks:** Part-time maker, first knife sold in 1980. Doing business as Big Joe's Custom Knives. Will take custom orders. **Mark:** F.S. or W.S. with first and middle initials and last name.

HIRAYAMA, HARUMI
4-5-13 Kitamachi, Warabi City, Saitama, JAPAN 335-0001 **Contact:** 048-443-2248, (fax) 048-443-2248, swanbird3@gmail.com, ne.jp/asahi/harumi/knives
Specialties: High-tech working knives of her design. **Patterns:** Locking folders, interframes, straight gents and slip-joints. **Technical:** Grinds 440C or equivalent, uses natural handle materials and gold. **Prices:** Start at $2500. **Remarks:** Part-time maker, first knife sold in 1985. **Mark:** First initial, last name.

HIROTO, FUJIHARA
2-34-7 Koioosako, Nishi-ku, Hiroshima, JAPAN **Contact:** 082-271-8389, fjhr8363@ crest.ocn.ne.jp

HOBART, GENE
100 Shedd Rd, Windsor, NY 13865 **Contact:** 607-655-1345

HOCKENSMITH, DAN
104 North Country Rd 23, Berthoud, CO 80513 **Contact:** 970-231-6506, blademan@ skybeam.com, dhockensmithknives.com
Specialties: Traditional working and using straight knives of his design. **Patterns:** Hunters, bowies, folders and utility/camp knives. **Technical:** Uses his damascus, 5160, carbon steel, 52100 steel and 1084 steel. Hand forged. **Prices:** $250 to $1500. **Remarks:** Part-time maker, first knife sold in 1987. **Mark:** Last name or stylized "D" with H inside.

HODGE III, JOHN
422 S 15th St, Palatka, FL 32177 **Contact:** 904-328-3897
Specialties: Fancy straight knives and folders. **Patterns:** Various. **Technical:** Pattern-welded damascus—"Southern-style." **Prices:** To $1000. **Remarks:** Part-time maker, first knife sold in 1981. **Mark:** JH3 logo.

HOEL, STEVE
PO Box 283, Pine, AZ 85544-0283 **Contact:** 928-476-6523
Specialties: Investor-class folders, straight knives and period pieces of his design. **Patterns:** Folding interframes lockers and slip-joints, straight bowies, boots and daggers. **Technical:** Grinds 154CM, ATS-34 and commercial damascus. **Prices:** $600 to $1200, some to $7500. **Remarks:** Full-time maker. **Mark:** Initial logo with name and address.

HOFER, LOUIS
BOX 125, Rose Prairie, BC, CANADA V0C 2H0 **Contact:** 250-827-3999, anvil_ needles@hotmail.cq, anvilandneedles.com

Specialties: damascus knives, working knives, fixed blade bowies, daggers. **Patterns:** Hunting, skinning, custom. **Technical:** Wild damascus, random damascus. **Prices:** $450 and up. **Remarks:** Part-time maker since 1995. **Mark:** Logo of initials.

HOFFMAN, JAY
Hoffman Haus + Heraldic Device, 911 W Superior St., Munising, MI 49862 **Contact:** 906-387-3440, hoffmanhaus1@yahoo.com, hoffmanhausknives.com
Technical: Scrimshaw, metal carving, own casting of hilts and pommels, etc. Most if not all leather work for sheaths. **Remarks:** Has been making knives for 50 + years. Professionally since 1991. **Mark:** Early knives marked "Hoffman Haus" and year. Now marks "Hoffman Haus Knives" on the blades. Starting in 2010 uses heraldic device. Will build to your specs. Lag time 1-2 months.

HOFFMAN, JESS
W7089 Curt Black Rd., Shawano, WI 54166 **Contact:** 715-584-2466, mooseyard@ gmail.com, jhoffmanknives.com
Specialties: Working fixed blades. **Technical:** Stock removal of carbon, stainless and damascus steels. Handles range from paper Micarta to exotic hardwoods. **Prices:** Start at $75. **Remarks:** Part-time knifemaker. **Mark:** Ancestral lower-case "h" and/or J. Hoffman.

HOFFMAN, KEVIN L
28 Hopeland Dr, Savannah, GA 31419 **Contact:** 912-920-3579, (fax) 912-920-3579, kevh052475@aol.com, KLHoffman.com
Specialties: Distinctive folders and fixed blades. **Patterns:** Titanium frame lock folders. **Technical:** Sculpted guards and fittings cast in sterling silver and 14k gold. Grinds ATS-34, CPM S30V damascus. Makes kydex sheaths for his fixed blade working knives. **Prices:** $400 and up. **Remarks:** Full-time maker since 1981. **Mark:** KLH.

HOFFMAN, LIAM
POB 1584, Newland, NC 28657 **Contact:** 828-260-4593, liam@ hoffmanblacksmithing.com, hoffmanblacksmithing.com
Specialties: Handforged one-off knives and axes. **Technical:** Full-tang knives and integral knives out of high-carbon steel or damascus, generally preferring to use wood handles. Also utilitarian-type working axes. **Prices:** $170 to $400 (axes) and $400 to $1,500 (knives). **Remarks:** Full-time 19-year-old maker who made his first knife at 13 years old, a bladesmith by trade. Axes are some of the finest in the world, in comparison with known smiths Autine, John Neeman and Gansfors bruk, working axes with functionality over aesthetics in mind, and quality over quantity. Nearly all knives are one of a kind, preferring to make integral knives. Everything made in the U.S.A. **Mark:** Knife touch mark is a Japanese hammer with "Hoffman" underneath, and the axe touch mark reads NC, LH, USA.

HOGAN, THOMAS R
2802 S. Heritage Ave, Boise, ID 83709 **Contact:** 208-362-7848

HOGSTROM, ANDERS T
Kärrmarksvägen 4, 37277 Backaryd, SWEDEN **Contact:** 46 702 674 574, info@ andershogstrom.com, andershogstrom.com
Specialties: Short and long daggers, fighters and swords For select pieces makes wooden display stands. **Patterns:** Daggers, fighters, short knives and swords and an occasional sword. **Technical:** Grinds 1050 High Carbon, damascus and stainless, forges own Damasus on occasion, fossil ivories. Does clay tempering and uses exotic hardwoods. **Prices:** Start at $850. **Marks:** Last name in maker's own signature.

HOKE, THOMAS M
3103 Smith Ln, LaGrange, KY 40031 **Contact:** 502-222-0350
Specialties: Working/using knives, straight knives. Own designs and customer specs. **Patterns:** Daggers, bowies, hunters, fighters, short swords. **Technical:** Grind 440C, damascus and ATS-34. Filework on all knives. Tooling on sheaths (custom fit on all knives). Any handle material, mostly exotic. **Prices:** $100 to $700, some to $1500. **Remarks:** Full-time maker, first knife sold in 1986. **Mark:** Dragon on banner which says T.M. Hoke.

HOLBROOK, H L
PO Box 483, Sandy Hook, KY 41171 **Contact:** Cell: 606-794-1497, hhknives@mrtc. com
Specialties: Traditional working using straight knives of his design, to customer specs and in standard patterns. Stabilized wood. **Patterns:** Hunters, mild tacticals and neck knives with kydex sheaths. **Technical:** Grinds CPM154CM, 154CM. Blades have hand-rubbed satin finish. Uses exotic woods, stag, G-10 and Micarta. Hand-sewn sheath with each straight knife. **Prices:** $165 to $485. **Remarks:** Part-time maker, first knife sold in 1983. Doing business as Holbrook Knives. **Mark:** Name, city, state.

HOLDER, D'ALTON
D'Holder Custom Knives. 226 West Blue Wash Road, New River, AZ 85087 **Contact:** 928-684-2025, (fax) 623-878-3964, dholderknives@commspeed.net, dholder.com
Specialties: Deluxe working knives and high-art hunters. **Patterns:** Drop-point hunters, fighters, bowies. **Technical:** Grinds ATS-34, uses amber and other materials in combination on stick tangs. **Prices:** $400 to $1000, some to $2000. **Remarks:** Full-time maker, first knife sold in 1966. **Mark:** D'HOLDER, city and state.

HOLLOWAY, PAUL
714 Burksdale Rd, Norfolk, VA 23518 **Contact:** 757-547-6025, houdini969@yahoo. com
Specialties: Working straight knives and folders to customer specs. **Patterns:** Lockers, fighters and boots, push knives, from swords to miniatures. **Technical:** Grinds A2, D2, 154CM, 440C and ATS-34. **Prices:** $210 to $1,200, some to $1,500, higher. **Remarks:** Retired, first knife sold in 1981. USN 28 years, deputy sheriff 16 years. **Mark:** Name and city in logo.

HOOK, BOB

3247 Wyatt Rd, North Pole, AK 99705 **Contact:** 907-488-8886, grayling@alaska.net, alaskaknifeandforge.com

Specialties: Forged carbon steel. damascus blades. **Patterns:** Pronghorns, bowies, drop point hunters and knives for the kitchen. **Technical:** 5160, 52100, carbon steel and 1084 and 15N20 pattern welded steel blades are hand forged. Heat treated and ground by maker. Handles are natural materials from Alaska. I favor sole authorship of each piece. **Prices:** $300-$1000. **Remarks:** Journeyman smith with ABS. I have attended the Bill Moran School of Bladesmithing. Knife maker since 2000. **Mark:** Hook.

HORN, DES

PO Box 322, Onrusrivier, WC, SOUTH AFRICA 7201 **Contact:** 27283161795, (fax) +27866280824, deshorn@usa.net

Specialties: Folding knives. **Patterns:** Ball release side lock mechanism and interframe automatics. **Technical:** Prefers working in totally stainless materials. **Prices:** $800 to $7500. **Remarks:** Full-time maker. Enjoys working in gold, titanium, meteorite, pearl and mammoth. **Mark:** Des Horn.

HORNE, GRACE

The Old Public Convenience, 469 Fulwood Road, Sheffield, UNITED KINGDOM S10 3QA, gracehorne@hotmail.co.uk gracehorn.co.uk

Specialties: Knives of own design, mainly slip-joint folders. **Technical:** Grinds RWL34, Damasteel and own damascus for blades. Scale materials vary from traditional (coral, wood, precious metals, etc) to unusual (wool, fabric, felt, etc), **Prices:** $500 - $1500 **Remarks:** Part-time maker. **Mark:** 'gH' and 'Sheffield'.

HORRIGAN, JOHN

433 C.R. 200 D, Burnet, TX 78611 **Contact:** 512-756-7545 or 512-636-6562, jhorrigan@yahoo.com eliteknives.com

Specialties: High-end custom knives. **Prices:** $450 - $12,500. **Remarks:** Part-time maker. Obtained Mastersmith stamp 2005. First knife made in 1982. **Mark:** Horrigan M.S.

HORTON, SCOT

PO Box 451, Buhl, ID 83316 **Contact:** 208-543-4222

Specialties: Traditional working stiff knives and folders. **Patterns:** Hunters, skinners, utility, hatchets and show knives. **Technical:** Grinds ATS-34 and D-2 tool steel. **Prices:** $400 to $2500. **Remarks:** First knife sold in 1990. **Mark:** Full name in arch underlined with arrow, city, state.

HOSSOM, JERRY

3585 Schilling Ridge, Peachtree Corners, GA 30096 **Contact:** 770-713-6219, jerry@hossom.com, hossom.com

Specialties: Working straight knives of his own design. **Patterns:** Fighters, combat knives, modern bowies and daggers, modern swords, concealment knives for military and LE uses. **Technical:** Grinds 154CM, S30V, CPM-3V, CPM-154 and stainless damascus. Uses natural and synthetic handle materials. **Prices:** $350-1500, some higher. **Remarks:** Full-time maker since 1997. First knife sold in 1983. **Mark:** J. Hossom. Previous mark: First initial and last name, includes city and state since 2002.

HOSTETLER, LARRY

10626 Pine Needle Dr., Fort Pierce, FL 34945 **Contact:** 772-370-2682, hossknives@bellsouth.net Hoss-knives.com

Specialties: EDC working knives and custom collector knives. Utilizing own designs and customer designed creations. Maker uses a wide variety of exotic materials. **Patterns:** bowies, hunters and folders. **Technical:** Stock removal, grinds ATS-34, carbon and stainless damascus, embellishes most pieces with file work. **Prices:** $500 - $2000. Some custom orders higher. **Remarks:** Motto: "EDC doesn't have to be ugly." First knife made in 2001, full-time maker, voting member in the Knife Maker's Guild. Doing business as Hoss Knives, LLC. **Mark:** "Hoss" etched into blade with a turn of the century fused bomb in place of the "O" in Hoss.

HOSTETTER, WALLY

P.O. Box 404, San Mateo, FL 32187 **Contact:** 386-649-0731, shiningmoon_13@yahoo.com, shiningmoon13.com

Specialties: Japanese swords and pole arms, and all their mountings from different time periods, other sword styles. **Technical:** Hand forges 1075 on up to 1095 steels, some with vanadium alloys. **Prices:** $1,200 to $6,500. **Remarks:** Full-time maker, first sword was a katana in 1999. **Mark:** Signature on tang in Japanese kanji is Wally San.

HOUSE, CAMERON

2001 Delaney Rd Se, Salem, OR 97306 **Contact:** 503-585-3286, chouse357@aol.com

Specialties: Working straight knives. **Patterns:** Hunters, bowies, fighters. **Technical:** Grinds ATS-34, 530V, 154CM. **Remarks:** Part-time maker, first knife sold in 1993. **Prices:** $150 and up. **Mark:** HOUSE.

HOUSE, GARY

2851 Pierce Rd, Ephrata, WA 98823 **Contact:** 509-754-3272, spindry101@aol.com

Specialties: bowies, hunters, daggers and some swords. **Patterns:** Unlimited, SW Indian designs, geometric patterns, bowies, hunters and daggers. **Technical:** Mosaic damascus bar stock, forged blades, using 1084, 15N20 and some nickel. Forged company logos and customer designs in mosaic damascus. **Prices:** $500 & up. **Remarks:** Some of the finest and most unique patterns available. ABS master smith. **Marks:** Initials GTH, G hanging T, H.

HOWARD, DURVYN M.

4220 McLain St S, Hokes Bluff, AL 35903 **Contact:** 256-504-1853

Specialties: Collectible upscale folders, one-of-a-kind, gentlemen's folders. Unique mechanisms and multiple patents. **Patterns:** Conceptual designs, each unique and different. **Technical:** Uses natural and exotic materials and precious metals. **Prices:** $7,500 to $35,000. **Remarks:** Full-time maker, 52 years experience. **Mark:** Howard.

HOWE, TORI

30020 N Stampede Rd, Athol, ID 83801 **Contact:** 208-449-1509, wapiti@knifescales.com, knifescales.com

Specialties: Custom knives, knife scales & damascus blades. **Remarks:** Carry James Luman polymer clay knife scales.

HOWELL, JASON G

1112 Sycamore, Lake Jackson, TX 77566 **Contact:** 979-297-9454, tinyknives@yahoo.com, howellbladesmith.com

Specialties: Fixed blades and LinerLock® folders. Makes own damascus. **Patterns:** Clip and drop point. **Prices:** $150 to $750. **Remarks:** Likes making Mosaic damascus out of the ordinary stuff. Member of TX Knifemakers and Collectors Association, apprentice in ABS, working towards Journeyman Stamp. **Mark:** Name, city, state.

HOWELL, KEITH A.

67 Hidden Oaks Dr., Oxford, AL 36203 **Contact:** 256-283-3269, keith@howellcutlery.com, howellcutlery.com

Specialties: Working straight knives and folders of his design or to customer specs. **Patterns:** Hunters, utility pieces, neck knives, everyday carry knives and friction folders. **Technical:** Grinds damascus, 1095 and 154CM. **Prices:** $100 to $250. **Remarks:** Part-time maker, first knife sold in 2007. **Mark:** Last name.

HOWELL, LEN

550 Lee Rd 169, Opelika, AL 36804 **Contact:** 334-749-1942

Specialties: Traditional and working knives of his design and to customer specs. **Patterns:** Buckskinner, hunters and utility/camp knives. **Technical:** Forges cable damascus, 1085 and 5160, makes own damascus. **Mark:** Engraved last name.

HOWELL, TED

1294 Wilson Rd, Wetumpka, AL 36092 **Contact:** 205-569-2281, (fax) 205-569-1764

Specialties: Working/using straight knives and folders of his design, period pieces. **Patterns:** bowies, fighters, hunters. **Technical:** Forges 5160, 1085 and cable. Offers light engraving and scrimshaw, filework. **Prices:** $75 to $250, some to $450. **Remarks:** Part-time maker, first knife sold in 1991. Doing business as Howell Co. **Mark:** Last name, Slapout AL.

HOY, KEN

54744 Pinchot Dr, North Fork, CA 93643 **Contact:** 209-877-7805

HRISOULAS, JIM

SALAMANDER ARMOURY, 284-C Lake Mead Pkwy #157, Henderson, NV 89105 **Contact:** 702-566-8551, atar.com

Specialties: Working straight knives, period pieces. **Patterns:** Swords, daggers and sgian dubhs. **Technical:** Double-edged differential heat treating. **Prices:** $85 to $175, some to $600 and higher. **Remarks:** Full-time maker, first knife sold in 1973. Author of The Complete Bladesmith, The Pattern Welded Blade and The Master Bladesmith. Doing business as Salamander Armory. **Mark:** 8R logo and sword and salamander.

HUCKABEE, DALE

254 Hwy 260, Maylene, AL 35114 **Contact:** 205-664-2544, huckabeeknives@hotmail.com, http://dalehuckabeeknives.weebly.com

Specialties: Fixed-blade knives and tomahawks of his design. **Technical:** Steel used: 5160, 1084, and damascus. **Prices:** $225 and up, depending on materials used. **Remarks:** Hand forged. Journeyman Smith. Part-time maker. **Mark:** Stamped Huckabee J.S.

HUCKS, JERRY

KNIVES BY HUCKS, 1807 Perch Road, Moncks Corner, SC 29461 **Contact:** 843-761-6481, (fax) Cell: 843-708-1649, knivesbyhucks@gmail.com

Specialties: Drop points, bowies and oyster knives. **Patterns:** To customer specs or maker's own design. **Technical:** CPM-154, ATS-34, 5160, 15N20, D2 and 1095 mostly for damascus billets. **Prices:** $200 and up. **Remarks:** Full-time maker, retired as a machinist in 1990. Makes sheaths sewn by hand with some carving. Will custom make to order or by sketch. Will also make a miniature bowie on request. Thirty years making knives. **Mark:** Robin Hood hat with Moncks Corner under.

HUDSON, C ROBBIN

116 Hansonville Rd., Rochester, NH 03839 **Contact:** 603-786-9944, bladesmith8@gmail.com

Specialties: High-art working knives. **Patterns:** Hunters, bowies, fighters and kitchen knives. **Technical:** Forges W2, nickel steel, pure nickel steel, composite and mosaic damascus, makes knives one-at-a-time. **Prices:** 500 to $1200, some to $5000. **Remarks:** Full-time maker, first knife sold in 1970. **Mark:** Last name and MS.

HUDSON, ROBERT

3802 Black Cricket Ct, Humble, TX 77396 **Contact:** 713-454-7207

Specialties: Working straight knives of his design. **Patterns:** bowies, hunters, skinners, fighters and utility knives. **Technical:** Grinds D2, 440C, 154CM and commercial damascus. **Prices:** $85 to $350, some to $1500. **Remarks:** Part-time maker, first knife sold in 1980. **Mark:** Full name, handmade, city and state.

HUGHES, DAN

301 Grandview Bluff Rd, Spencer, TN 38585 **Contact:** 931-946-3044

Specialties: Working straight knives to customer specs. **Patterns:** Hunters, fighters, fillet knives. **Technical:** Grinds 440C and ATS-34. **Prices:** $55 to $175, some to $300. **Remarks:** Part-time maker, first knife sold in 1984. **Mark:** Initials.

HUGHES, DARYLE
10979 Leonard, Nunica, MI 49448 **Contact:** 616-837-6623, hughes.builders@verizon.net
Specialties: Working knives. **Patterns:** Buckskinners, hunters, camp knives, kitchen and fishing knives. **Technical:** Forges and grinds 52100 and damascus. **Prices:** $125 to $1000. **Remarks:** Part-time maker, first knife sold in 1979. **Mark:** Name and city in logo.

HUGHES, ED
280 1/2 Holly Lane, Grand Junction, CO 81503 **Contact:** 970-243-8547, edhughes26@msn.com
Specialties: Working and art folders. **Patterns:** Buys damascus. **Technical:** Grinds stainless steels. Engraves. **Prices:** $300 and up. **Remarks:** Full-time maker, first knife sold in 1978. **Mark:** Name or initials.

HUGHES, LAWRENCE
207 W Crestway, Plainview, TX 79072 **Contact:** 806-293-5406
Specialties: Working and display knives. **Patterns:** bowies, daggers, hunters, buckskinners. **Technical:** Grinds D2, 440C and 154CM. **Prices:** $125 to $300, some to $2000. **Remarks:** Full-time maker, first knife sold in 1979. **Mark:** Name with buffalo skull in center.

HUGHES, TONY
Tony Hughes Forged Blades, 7536 Trail North Dr., Littleton, CO 80125 **Contact:** 303-941-1092, tonhug@msn.com
Specialties: Fixed blades, bowies/fighters and hunters of maker's own damascus steel. **Technical:** Forges damascus and mosaic-damascus blades. Fittings are 416 stainless steel, 1095-and-nickel damascus, 1080-and-15N20 damascus or silicon bronze. Prefers ivory, desert ironwood, blackwood, ebony and other burls. **Prices:** $450 and up. **Remarks:** Full-time ABS journeyman smith forging knives for 20 years. **Mark:** Tony Hughes and JS on the other side.

HULETT, STEVE
115 Yellowstone Ave, West Yellowstone, MT 59758-0131 **Contact:** 406-646-4116, blade1231@msn.com, seldomseenknives.com
Specialties: Classic, working/using knives, straight knives, folders. Your design, custom specs. **Patterns:** Utility/camp knives, hunters, and LinerLock folders, lock back pocket knives. **Technical:** Grinds 440C stainless steel, O1 Carbon, 1095. Shop is retail and knife shop, people watch their knives being made. We do everything in house: "all but smelt the ore, or tan the hide." **Prices:** Strarting $250 to $7000. **Remarks:** Full-time maker, first knife sold in 1994. **Mark:** Seldom seen knives/West Yellowstone Montana.

HULSEY, HOYT
379 Shiloh, Attalla, AL 35954 **Contact:** 256-538-6765
Specialties: Traditional working straight knives and folders of his design. **Patterns:** Hunters and utility/camp knives. **Technical:** Grinds 440C, ATS-34, O1 and A2. **Prices:** $75 to $250. **Remarks:** Part-time maker, first knife sold in 1989. **Mark:** Hoyt Hulsey Attalla AL.

HUMENICK, ROY
PO Box 55, Rescue, CA 95672, rhknives@gmail.com, humenick.com
Specialties: Traditional multiblades and tactical slipjoints. **Patterns:** Original folder and fixed blade designs, also traditional patterns. **Technical:** Grinds premium steels and damascus. **Prices:** $350 and up, some to $1500. **Remarks:** First knife sold in 1984. **Mark:** Last name in ARC.

HUMPHREY, LON
4 Western Ave., Newark, OH 43055 **Contact:** 740-644-1137, lonhumphrey@gmail.com
Specialties: Hunters, tacticals, and bowie knives. **Prices:** I make knives that start in the $150 range and go up to $1000 for a large bowie. **Remarks:** Has been blacksmithing since age 13 and progressed to the forged blade.

HUMPHREYS, JOEL
90 Boots Rd, Lake Placid, FL 33852 **Contact:** 863-773-0439
Specialties: Traditional working/using straight knives and folders of his design and in standard patterns. **Patterns:** Hunters, folders and utility/camp knives. **Technical:** Grinds ATS-34, D2, 440C. All knives have tapered tangs, mitered bolster/handle joints, handles of horn or bone fitted sheaths. **Prices:** $135 to $225, some to $350. **Remarks:** Part-time maker, first knife sold in 1990. Doing business as Sovereign Knives. **Mark:** First name or "H" pierced by arrow.

HUNT, RAYMON E.
3H's KNIVES, LLC, 600 Milam Ct., Irving, TX 75038 **Contact:** 214-507-0896, (fax) 972-887-9931, 3hsknives.com
Specialties: Forged and stock removal for both using and collector-grade knives. **Patterns:** Kitchen cutlery, bowies, daggers, hunters, tactical, utility, slip joints and straight razors. **Technical:** Steels include 5160, 1075, 1084, 1095, O1, CPM 154, CTS XHP and damascus. Heat treating in-house using oven and torch edge hardening. Uses his own damascus of 1095 and 15N20 and purchases damascus. Engraving and gold inlay by Steve Dunn, filework, peined and polished pins of sterling silver and gold, fire and niter bluing. **Remarks:** American Bladesmith Society, apprentice. **Mark:** 3Hs on left side of blade near the grind line.

HUNTER, HYRUM
285 N 300 W, PO Box 179, Aurora, UT 84620 **Contact:** 435-529-7244
Specialties: Working straight knives of his design or to customer specs. **Patterns:** Drop and clip, fighters dagger, some folders. **Technical:** Forged from two-piece damascus. **Prices:** Prices are adjusted according to size, complexity and material used. **Remarks:** Will consider any design you have. Part-time maker, first knife sold in 1990. **Mark:** Initials encircled with first initial and last name and city, then state. Some patterns are numbered.

HUNTER, RICHARD D
7230 NW 200th Ter, Alachua, FL 32615 **Contact:** 386-462-3150
Specialties: Traditional working/using knives of his design or customer suggestions, filework. **Patterns:** Folders of various types, bowies, hunters, daggers. **Technical:** Traditional blacksmith, hand forges high-carbon steel (5160, 1084, 52100) and makes own damascus, grinds 440C and ATS-34. **Prices:** $200 and up. **Remarks:** Part-time maker, first knife sold in 1992. **Mark:** Last name in capital letters.

HURST, JEFF
PO Box 247, Rutledge, TN 37861 **Contact:** 865-828-5729, jhurst@esper.com
Specialties: Working straight knives and folders of his design. **Patterns:** Tomahawks, hunters, boots, folders and fighters. **Technical:** Forges W2, O1 and his own damascus. Makes mokume. **Prices:** $250 to $600. **Remarks:** Full-time maker, first knife sold in 1984. Doing business as Buzzard's Knob Forge. **Mark:** Last name, partnered knives are marked with Newman L. Smith, handle artisan, and SH in script.

HURTADO, DAN
2301 Chester Ct., Tallahassee, FL 32312 **Contact:** 850-566-0500, danhurtado@comcast.net, facebook.com/MaranathaForge/
Technical: Forges high-carbon and tool steels. Pattern-welded, cable, san mai and mono-steel blades. **Patterns:** Small to medium-sized hunters with leather sheaths. **Prices:** Most from $100 to $500. **Remarks:** Part-time maker since 2010. **Mark:** Interlocking DH touchmark.

HUSE, JAMES D. II
P.O. Box 1753, Buda, TX 78610 **Contact:** 512-296-9888, huseknives@gmail.com, huseknives.com
Specialties: Texas-legal carry knives, hunters and utility knives, and large camp knives and bowies on request. **Patterns:** Clip points, drop points, Puma-style trailing points and fighter styles. **Technical:** Makes most knives using the stock-removal method of blade making with A2 tool steel, hardening and tempering it to 60-61 HRC on the Rockwell Hardness Scale. Does forge some knives, and when forging, uses 1084, 52100, 1095 and 15N20 damascus, as well as CruForge V. **Prices:** $150 to $700. **Remarks:** Part-time maker, first knife made in 2001. Member of Texas Knifemakers' Guild (secretary) and American Bladesmith Society (apprentice).

HUSIAK, MYRON
PO Box 238, Altona, VIC, AUSTRALIA 3018 **Contact:** 03-315-6752
Specialties: Straight knives and folders of his design or to customer specs. **Patterns:** Hunters, fighters, lock-back folders, skinners and boots. **Technical:** Forges and grinds his own damascus, 440C and ATS-34. **Prices:** $200 to $900. **Remarks:** Part-time maker, first knife sold in 1974. **Mark:** First initial, last name in logo and serial number.

HUTCHESON, JOHN
SURSUM KNIFE WORKS, 1237 Brown's Ferry Rd., Chattanooga, TN 37419 **Contact:** 423-667-6193, sursum5071@aol.com, sursumknife.com
Specialties: Straight working knives, hunters. **Patterns:** Customer designs, hunting, speciality working knives. **Technical:** Grinds D2, S7, O1 and 5160, ATS-34 on request. **Prices:** $100 to $300, some to $600. **Remarks:** First knife sold 1985, also produces a mid-tech line. Doing business as Sursum Knife Works. **Mark:** Family crest boar's head over 3 arrows.

HUTCHINSON, ALAN
315 Scenic Hill Road, Conway, AR 72034 **Contact:** 501-470-9653, hutchinsonblades@yahoo.com
Specialties: Hunters, bowies, fighters, combat/survival knives. **Patterns:** Traditional edged weapons and tomahawks, custom patterns. **Technical:** Forges 10 series, 5160, L6, O1, CruForge V, damascus and his own patterns. **Prices:** $250 and up. **Remarks:** Prefers natural handle materials, part-time maker. **Mark:** Last name.

HYTOVICK, JOE "HY"
14872 SW 111th St, Dunnellon, FL 34432 **Contact:** 352-489-5336, (fax) 352-489-3732, hyclassknives@aol.com
Specialties: Straight, folder and miniature. **Technical:** Blades from Wootz, damascus and Alloy steel. **Prices:** To $5000. **Mark:** HY.

I

IKOMA, FLAVIO
R Manoel Rainho Teixeira 108, Presidente Prudente, SP, BRAZIL 19031-220 **Contact:** 0182-22-0115, fikoma@itelesonica.com.br
Specialties: Tactical fixed blade knives, LinerLock® folders and balisongs. **Patterns:** Utility and defense tactical knives built with hi-tech materials. **Technical:** Grinds S30V and Damasteel. **Prices:** $500 to $1000. **Mark:** Ikoma hand made beside Samurai

IMBODEN II, HOWARD L.
620 Deauville Dr, Dayton, OH 45429 **Contact:** 513-439-1536
Specialties: One-of-a-kind hunting, flint, steel and art knives. **Technical:** Forges and grinds stainless, high-carbon and damascus. Uses obsidian, cast sterling silver, 14K and 18K gold guards. Carves ivory animals and more. **Prices:** $65 to $25,000. **Remarks:** Full-time maker, first knife sold in 1986. Doing business as Hill Originals. **Mark:** First and last initials, II.

IMEL, BILLY MACE
1616 Bundy Ave, New Castle, IN 47362 **Contact:** 765-529-1651
Specialties: High-art working knives, period pieces and personal cutlery. **Patterns:** Daggers, fighters, hunters, locking folders and slip-joints with interframes. **Technical:** Grinds D2, 440C and 154CM. **Prices:** $300 to $2000, some to $6000. **Remarks:** Part-

time maker, first knife sold in 1973. **Mark:** Name in monogram.

IOANNIS-MINAS, FILIPPOU
Krinis 5 - Nea Smyrni 171 22 Athens, GREECE 171 22 **Contact:** (1) 210-9352093, kamami53@yahoo.gr

IRIE, MICHAEL L
MIKE IRIE HANDCRAFT, 1606 Auburn Dr., Colorado Springs, CO 80909 **Contact:** 719-572-5330, mikeirie@aol.com
Specialties: Working fixed blade knives and handcrafted blades for the do-it-yourselfer. **Patterns:** Twenty standard designs along with custom. **Technical:** Blades are ATS-34, BG-43, 440C with some outside damascus. **Prices:** Fixed blades $95 and up, blade work $45 and up. **Remarks:** Formerly dba Wood, Irie and Co. with Barry Wood. Full-time maker since 1991. **Mark:** Name.

ISAO, OHBUCHI
702-1 Nouso, Yame-City, Fukuoka, JAPAN **Contact:** 0943-23-4439, 5d.biglobe. ne.jp/~ohisao/

ISHIHARA, HANK
86-18 Motomachi, Sakura City, Chiba, JAPAN **Contact:** 043-485-3208, (fax) 043-485-3208
Specialties: Fantasy working straight knives and folders of his design. **Patterns:** Boots, bowies, daggers, fighters, hunters, fishing, locking folders and utility camp knives. **Technical:** Grinds ATS-34, 440C, D2, 440V, CV-134, COS25 and damascus. Engraves. **Prices:** $250 to $1000, some to $10,000. **Remarks:** Full-time maker, first knife sold in 1987. **Mark:** HANK.

J

JACKS, JIM
344 S. Hollenbeck Ave, Covina, CA 91723-2513 **Contact:** 626-331-5665
Specialties: Working straight knives in standard patterns. **Patterns:** bowies, hunters, fighters, fishing and camp knives, miniatures. **Technical:** Grinds Stellite 6K, 440C and ATS-34. **Prices:** Start at $100. **Remarks:** Spare-time maker, first knife sold in 1980. **Mark:** Initials in diamond logo.

JACKSON, CHARLTON R
6811 Leyland Dr, San Antonio, TX 78239 **Contact:** 210-601-5112

JACKSON, DAVID
214 Oleander Ave, Lemoore, CA 93245 **Contact:** 559-925-8247, jnbcrea@lemoorenet. com
Specialties: Forged steel. **Patterns:** Hunters, camp knives and bowies. **Prices:** $300 and up. **Mark:** G.D. Jackson - Maker - Lemoore CA.

JACKSON, LARAMIE
POB 442, Claysprings, AZ 85923 **Contact:** 480-747-3804, ljacksonknives@yahoo. com
Specialties: Traditional hunting and working knives and folders, chef's knives. **Patterns:** bowies, fighters, hunters, daggers and skinners. **Technical:** Grinds AEBL, 440C, CPM D2, CPM 154, Elmax, W2, O1, 52100, 5160, 1095, damascus and whatever customer wants. Offers sheaths. **Prices:** $100-$2500+. **Remarks:** Full-time maker, first knife sold in 2010. **Mark:** First initial and last name.

JACQUES, ALEX
350 Kinsley Ave. Providence, RI 02903 **Contact:** 617-771-4441, customrazors@ gmail.com, alexjacquesdesigns.com
Specialties: One-of-a-kind, heirloom quality straight razors, custom jewelry, functional art. **Technical:** damascus, O1, CPM154, and various other high-carbon and stainless steels. **Prices:** $450 and up. **Remarks:** First knife sold in 2008. **Mark:** Jack-O-Lantern logo with "A. Jacques" underneath.

JAKSIK JR., MICHAEL
427 Marschall Creek Rd, Fredericksburg, TX 78624 **Contact:** 830-997-1119
Mark: MJ or M. Jaksik.

JANGTANONG, SUCHAT
10901 W. Cave Blvd., Dripping Springs, TX 78620 **Contact:** 512-264-1501, shakeallpoints@yahoo.com, mrdamascusknives.com
Specialties: One-of-a-kind handmade art knives, carving pearl and titanium. **Patterns:** Folders (lock back and LinerLock), some fixed blades and butterfly knives. **Technical:** Grinds ATS-34 and damascus steels. **Prices:** $500 to $3,000. **Remarks:** Third-generation, began making knives in 1982, full-time maker who lives in Uthai Thani Province of Thailand. **Mark:** Name (Suchat) on blade.

JANSEN VAN VUUREN, LUDWIG
311 Brighton Rd., Waldronville 9018, Dunedin, NEW ZEALAND **Contact:** 64-3-7421012, ludwig@nzhandmadeknives.co.nz, nzhandmadeknives.co.nz
Specialties: Fixed-blade knives of his design or custom specifications. **Patterns:** Hunting, fishing, bird-and-trout and chef's knives. **Technical:** Stock-removal maker, Elmax, Sandvik 12C27 and other blade steels on request. Handle material includes Micarta, antler and a wide selection of woods. **Prices:** Starting at $250. **Remarks:** Part-time maker since 2008. **Mark:** L J van Vuuren.

JARVIS, PAUL M
30 Chalk St, Cambridge, MA 02139 **Contact:** 617-547-4355 or 617-661-3015
Specialties: High-art knives and period pieces of his design. **Patterns:** Japanese and Mid-Eastern knives. **Technical:** Grinds Myer damascus, ATS-34, D2 and O1. Specializes in height-relief Japanese-style carving. Works with silver, gold and gems. **Prices:** $200 to

$17,000. **Remarks:** Part-time maker, first knife sold in 1978.

JEAN, GERRY
25B Cliffside Dr, Manchester, CT 06040 **Contact:** 860-649-6449
Specialties: Historic replicas. **Patterns:** Survival and camp knives. **Technical:** Grinds A2, 440C and 154CM. Handle slabs applied in unique tongue-and-groove method. **Prices:** $125 to $250, some to $1000. **Remarks:** Spare-time maker, first knife sold in 1973. **Mark:** Initials and serial number.

JEFFRIES, MIKE
1015 Highland Ave., Louisville, KY 40204 **Contact:** 502-592-4240, 2birdsmetalworks@gmail.com, Facebook.com/2BirdsMetalWorks, Instagram @2BirdsMetalworks
Specialties: Handmade custom knives, mostly drop-point and wharncliffe-style blades. **Patterns:** Outdoor, camping, hiking, hunting and bushcraft knives. **Technical:** Stock removal of high-carbon and tool steels, as well as damascus. Prefers stabilized wood and synthetic handles, the latter including G-10, carbon fiber and Thunderstorm Kevlar. **Prices:** $150 to $800. **Remarks:** Three years making knives, two years full time. **Mark:** MJK.

JEFFRIES, ROBERT W
Route 2 Box 227, Red House, WV 25168 **Contact:** 304-586-9780, wvknifeman@ hotmail.com, jeffrieskniveswv.tripod.com
Specialties: Hunters, bowies, daggers, lockback folders and LinerLock push buttons. **Patterns:** Skinning types, drop points, typical working hunters, folders one-of-a-kind. **Technical:** Grinds all types of steel. Makes his own damascus. **Prices:** $125 to $600. Private collector pieces to $3000. **Remarks:** Starting engraving. Custom folders of his design. Part-time maker since 1988. **Mark:** Name etched or on plate pinned to blade.

JENKINS, MITCH
194 East 500 South, Manti, Utah 84642 **Contact:** 435-813-2532, mitch.jenkins@ gmail.com, MitchJenkinsKnives.com
Specialties: Hunters, working knives. **Patterns:** Johnson and Loveless Style. Drop points, skinners and semi-skinners, Capers and utilities. **Technical:** 154CM and ATS-34. Experimenting with S30V and love working with damascus on occasion. **Prices:** $150 and up. **Remarks:** Slowly transitioning to full-time maker, first knife made in 2008. **Mark:** Jenkins Manti, Utah and M. Jenkins, Utah.

JENSEN, DENNIS
6420 Evergreen Ave., Wisconsin Rapids, WI 54494 **Contact:** 715-325-5029, djensenknives@solarus.net
Specialties: One-of-a-kind fixed-blade hunters, fillet, EDC and Scandinavian puukkos. Maker's and customer's designs. **Technical:** Stock removal method of blade making using ATS-34, CPM-154, A2, 1084, O1 and commercial damascus. Natural handle materials, Micarta, G-10 and Kirinite. **Prices:** $150 to $350. **Remarks:** Makes own sheaths, including wood-lined Scandinavian sheaths. Part-time maker. **Mark:** D Jensen or DJ.

JENSEN, ELI
525 Shalimar Dr., Prescott, AZ 86303 **Contact:** 928-606-0373, ej89@nau.edu
Specialties: Fixed blades, mostly small and mid-size drop-points. **Technical:** Stock-removal method of blade making, preferring interesting natural materials, including burls, roots and uncommon species. **Prices:** $400 and up. **Remarks:** Part-time maker, first knife made in 2010. **Mark:** First and last name in cursive.

JENSEN, JOHN LEWIS
JENSEN KNIVES, 146 W. Bellevue Dr. #7, Pasadena, CA 91105 **Contact:** 626-773-0296, john@jensenknives.com, jensenknives.com
Specialties: Designer and fabricator of modern, original one-of-a-kind, hand crafted, custom ornamental edged weaponry. Combines skill, precision, distinction and the finest materials, geared toward the discriminating art collector. **Patterns:** Folding knives and fixed blades, daggers, fighters and swords. **Technical:** High embellishment, BFA 96 Rhode Island School of Design: jewelry and metalsmithing. Grinds carbon and stainless, and carbon/stainless damascus. Works with custom made damascus to his specs. Uses gold, silver, gemstones, pearl, titanium, fossil mastodon and walrus ivories. Carving, file work, soldering, deep etches damascus, engraving, layers, bevels, blood grooves. Also forges his own damascus. **Prices:** Start at $10,000. **Remarks:** Available on a first come basis and via commission based on his designs. **Mark:** Maltese cross/butterfly shield.

JOBIN, JACQUES
46 St Dominique, Levis, QC, CANADA G6V 2M7 **Contact:** 418-833-0283, (fax) 418-833-8378
Specialties: Fancy and working straight knives and folders, miniatures. **Patterns:** Minis, fantasy knives, fighters and some hunters. **Technical:** ATS-34, some damascus and titanium. Likes native snake wood. Heat-treats. **Prices:** Start at $250. **Remarks:** Full-time maker, first knife sold in 1986. **Mark:** Signature on blade.

JOEHNK, BERND
Posadowskystrasse 22, Kiel, GERMANY 24148 **Contact:** 0431-7297705, (fax) 0431-7297705
Specialties: One-of-a-kind fancy/embellished and traditional straight knives of his design and from customer drawing. **Patterns:** Daggers, fighters, hunters and letter openers. **Technical:** Grinds and file 440C, ATS-34, powder metal orgical, commercial damascus and various stainless and corrosion-resistant steels. **Prices:** Upscale. **Remarks:** Likes filework. Leather sheaths. Offers engraving. Part-time maker, first knife sold in1990. Doing business as metal design kiel. All knives made by hand. **Mark:** From 2005 full name and city, with certificate.

custom knifemakers

JOHANNING CUSTOM KNIVES, TOM

1735 Apex Rd, Sarasota, FL 34240 9386 **Contact:** 941-371-2104, (fax) 941-378-9427, survivalknives.com

Specialties: Survival knives. **Prices:** $375 to $775.

JOHANSSON, ANDERS

Konstvartarevagen 9, Grangesberg, SWEDEN 77240 **Contact:** 46 240 23204, (fax) +46 21 358778, scrimart.u.se

Specialties: Scandinavian traditional and modern straight knives. **Patterns:** Hunters, fighters and fantasy knives. **Technical:** Grinds stainless steel and makes own damascus. Prefers water buffalo and mammoth for handle material. **Prices:** Start at $100. **Remarks:** Spare-time maker, first knife sold in 1994. Works together with scrimshander Viveca Sahlin. **Mark:** Stylized initials.

JOHNSON, C E GENE

1240 Coan Street, Chesterton, IN 46304 **Contact:** 219-787-8324, ddjlady55@aol.com

Specialties: Lock-back folders and springers of his design or to customer specs. **Patterns:** Hunters, bowies, survival lock-back folders. **Technical:** Grinds D2, 440C, A18, O1, damascus, likes filework. **Prices:** $100 to $2000. **Remarks:** Full-time maker, first knife sold in 1975. **Mark:** Gene.

JOHNSON, DAVID A

1791 Defeated Creek Rd, Pleasant Shade, TN 37145 **Contact:** 615-774-3596, artsmith@mwsi.net

JOHNSON, GORDON A.

981 New Hope Rd, Choudrant, LA 71227 **Contact:** 318-768-2613

Specialties: Using straight knives and folders of my design, or customers. Offering filework and hand stitched sheaths. **Patterns:** Hunters, bowies, folders and miniatures. **Technical:** Forges 5160, 1084, 52100 and my own damascus. Some stock removal on working knives and miniatures. **Prices:** Mid range. **Remarks:** First knife sold in 1990. ABS apprentice smith. **Mark:** Interlocking initials G.J. or G. A. J.

JOHNSON, JERRY

PO Box 491, Spring City, Utah 84662 **Contact:** 435-851-3604 or 435-462-3688, sanpetesilver.com

Specialties: Hunter, fighters, camp. **Patterns:** Multiple. **Prices:** $225 - $3000. **Mark:** Jerry E. Johnson Spring City, UT in several fonts.

JOHNSON, JERRY L

29847 260th St, Worthington, MN 56187 **Contact:** 507-376-9253, Cell: 507-370-3523, doctorj55@yahoo.com

Specialties: Straight knives, hunters, bowies, and fighting knives. **Patterns:** Drop points, trailing points, bowies, and some favorite Loveless patterns. **Technical:** Grinds ATS 34, 440C, S30V, forges own damascus, mirror finish, satin finish, file work and engraving done by self. **Prices:** $250 to $1500. **Remarks:** Part-time maker since 1991, member of knifemakers guild since 2009. **Mark:** Name over a sheep head or elk head with custom knives under the head.

JOHNSON, JOHN R

PO Box 246, New Buffalo, PA 17069 **Contact:** 717-834-6265, jrj@jrjknives.com, jrjknives.com

Specialties: Working hunting and tactical fixed blade sheath knives. **Patterns:** Hunters, tacticals, bowies, daggers, neck knives and primitives. **Technical:** Flat, convex and hollow grinds. ATS-34, CPM154CM, L6, O1, D2, 5160, 1095 and damascus. **Prices:** $60 to $700. **Remarks:** Full-time maker, first knife sold in 1996. Doing business as JRJ Knives. Custom sheath made by maker for every knife, **Mark:** Initials connected.

JOHNSON, JOHN R

5535 Bob Smith Ave, Plant City, FL 33565 **Contact:** 813-986-4478, rottyjohn@msn.com

Specialties: Hand forged and stock removal. **Technical:** High tech. Folders. **Mark:** J.R. Johnson Plant City, FL.

JOHNSON, KEITH R.

9179 Beltrami Line Rd. SW, Bemidji, MN 56601 **Contact:** 218-368-7482, keith@greatriverforge.com, greatriverforge.com

Specialties: Slip-joint and lockback folders. **Patterns:** Mostly traditional patterns but with customer preferences, some of maker's own patterns. **Technical:** Mainly uses CTS XHP, sometimes other high-quality stainless steels, Damasteel. Variety of handle materials, including bone, mammoth ivory, Micarta, G-10 and carbon fiber. **Remarks:** Full-time maker, first knife sold in 1986. **Mark:** K.R. JOHNSON (arched) over BEMIDJI.

JOHNSON, MIKE

38200 Main Rd, Orient, NY 11957 **Contact:** 631-323-3509, mjohnsoncustomknives@hotmail.com

Specialties: Large bowie knives and cutters, fighters and working knives to customer specs. **Technical:** Forges 5160, O1. **Prices:** $325 to $1200. **Remarks:** Full-time bladesmith. **Mark:** Johnson.

JOHNSON, R B

Box 11, Clearwater, MN 55320 **Contact:** 320-558-6128, (fax) 320-558-6128, rb@rbjohnsonknives.com, rbjohnsonknives.com

Specialties: Liner locks with titanium, mosaic damascus. **Patterns:** LinerLock® folders, skeleton hunters, frontier bowies. **Technical:** damascus, mosaic damascus, A-2, O1, 1095. **Prices:** $200 and up. **Remarks:** Full-time maker since 1973. Not accepting orders. **Mark:** R B Johnson (signature).

JOHNSON, RANDY

2575 E Canal Dr, Turlock, CA 95380 **Contact:** 209-632-5401

Specialties: Folders. **Patterns:** Locking folders. **Technical:** Grinds damascus. **Prices:** $200 to $400. **Remarks:** Spare-time maker, first knife sold in 1989. Doing business as Puedo Knifeworks. **Mark:** PUEDO.

JOHNSON, RICHARD

W165 N10196 Wagon Trail, Germantown, WI 53022 **Contact:** 262-251-5772, rlj@execpc.com, execpc.com/~rlj/index.html

Specialties: Custom knives and knife repair.

JOHNSON, RYAN M

3103 Excelsior Ave., Signal Mountain, TN 37377 **Contact:** 866-779-6922, contact@rmjtactical.com, rmjforge.com rmjtactical.com

Specialties: Historical and Tactical Tomahawks. Some period knives and folders. **Technical:** Forges a variety of steels including own damascus. **Prices:** $500 - $1200 **Remarks:** Full-time maker began forging in 1986. **Mark:** Sledge-hammer with halo.

JOHNSON, STEVEN R

202 E 200 N, PO Box 5, Manti, UT 84642 **Contact:** 435-835-7941, srj@mail.manti.com, srjknives.com

Specialties: Investor-class working knives. **Patterns:** Hunters, fighters, boots. **Technical:** Grinds CPM-154CM and CTS-XHP. **Prices:** $1,500 to $20,000. Engraved knives up to $50,000. **Remarks:** Full-time maker, first knife sold in 1972. Also see SR Johnson forum on knifenetwork.com. **Mark:** Registered trademark, including name, city, state, and optional signature mark.

JOHNSON, TIMOTHY A.

Worcester, MA, tim@blackstoneknife.com

Specialties: Custom kitchen knives. **Technical:** Stock removal of stainless, high carbon, san mai and damascus blade steels. **Prices:** $250 to $800. **Remarks:** Part-time maker, first knife made around 1994. **Mark:** Stylized initials TAJ.

JOHNSON, TOMMY

144 Poole Rd., Troy, NC 27371 **Contact:** 910-975-1817, tommy@tjohnsonknives.com tjohnsonknives.com

Specialties: Straight knives for hunting, fishing, utility, and linerlock and slip joint folders since 1982.

JOHNSON, WM. C. "BILL"

225 Fairfield Pike, Enon, OH 45323 **Contact:** 937-864-7802, wjohnson64@woh.RR.com

Patterns: From hunters to art knives as well as custom canes, some with blades. **Technical:** Stock removal method utilizing 440C, ATS34, 154CPM, and custom damascus. **Prices:** $175 to over $2500, depending on design, materials, and embellishments. **Remarks:** Full-time maker. First knife made in 1978. Member of the Knifemakers Guild since 1982. **Mark:** Crescent shaped WM. C. "BILL" JOHNSON, SPRING HILL FL. (previous mark used ENON OHIO) Also uses an engraved or electro signature on some art knives and on damascus blades.

JOHNSTON, DR. ROBT

PO Box 9887 1 Lomb Mem Dr, Rochester, NY 14623

JOKERST, CHARLES

9312 Spaulding, Omaha, NE 68134 **Contact:** 402-571-2536

Specialties: Working knives in standard patterns. **Patterns:** Hunters, fighters and pocketknives. **Technical:** Grinds 440C, ATS-34. **Prices:** $90 to $170. **Remarks:** Spare-time maker, first knife sold in 1984. **Mark:** Early work marked RCJ, current work marked with last name and city.

JONAS, ZACHARY

204 Village Rd., Wilmot, NH 03287 **Contact:** 603-877-0128, zack@jonasblade.com, jonasblade.com

Specialties: Custom high-carbon damascus, sporting knives, kitchen knives and art knives. Always interested in adding to the repertoire. **Patterns:** Kitchen and bowie knives, hunters, daggers, push daggers, tantos, boot knives, all custom. **Technical:** Forges all damascus blades, works with high-carbon steels to suit the client's individual tastes and needs. **Remarks:** Full-time maker, ABS journeyman smith trained by ABS master smith J.D. Smith, juried member of League of New Hampshire Craftsmen. **Mark:** Sytlized "Z" symbol on one side, "JS" on other, either stamped, engraved or etched.

JONES, BARRY M AND PHILLIP G

221 North Ave, Danville, VA 24540 **Contact:** 804-793-5282

Specialties: Working and using straight knives and folders of their design and to customer specs, combat and self-defense knives. **Patterns:** bowies, fighters, daggers, swords, hunters and LinerLock® folders. **Technical:** Grinds 440C, ATS-34 and D2, flat-grinds only. All blades hand polished. **Prices:** $100 to $1000, some higher. **Remarks:** Part-time makers, first knife sold in 1989. **Mark:** Jones Knives, city, state.

JONES, ENOCH

7278 Moss Ln, Warrenton, VA 20187 **Contact:** 540-341-0292

Specialties: Fancy working straight knives. **Patterns:** Hunters, fighters, boots and bowies. **Technical:** Forges and grinds O1, W2, 440C and damascus. **Prices:** $100 to $350, some to $1000. **Remarks:** Part-time maker, first knife sold in 1982. **Mark:** First name.

JONES, JACK P.

17670 Hwy. 2 East, Ripley, MS 38663 **Contact:** 662-837-3882, jacjones@ripleycable.net

Specialties: Working knives in classic design. **Patterns:** Hunters, fighters, and bowies.

Technical: Grinds D2, A2, CPM-154, CTS-XHP and ATS-34. **Prices:** $200 and up. **Remarks:** Full-time maker since retirement in 2005, first knife sold in 1976. **Mark:** J.P. Jones, Ripley, MS.

JONES, ROGER MUDBONE
GREENMAN WORKSHOP, 320 Prussia Rd, Waverly, OH 45690 **Contact:** 740-739-4562, greenmanworkshop@yahoo.com
Specialties: Working in cutlery to suit working woodsman and fine collector. **Patterns:** bowies, hunters, folders, hatchets in both period and modern style, scale miniatures a specialty. **Technical:** All cutlery hand forged to shape with traditional methods, multiple quench and draws, limited damascus production hand carves wildlife and historic themes in stag/antler/ivory, full line of functional and high art leather. All work sole authorship. **Prices:** $50 to $5000 **Remarks:** Full-time maker/first knife sold in 1979. **Mark:** Stamped R. Jones hand made or hand engraved sig. W/bowie knife mark.

JORGENSEN, CARSON
1805 W Hwy 116, Mt Pleasant, UT 84647, tcjorgensenknife@gmail.com, tcjknives.com
Specialties: Stock removal, Loveless Johnson and young styles. **Prices:** Most $100 to $800.

K

K B S, KNIVES
RSD 181, North Castlemaine, VIC, AUSTRALIA 3450 **Contact:** 0011 61 3 54 705864
Specialties: Historically inspired bowies, and restoration of fixed and folding knives. **Patterns:** bowies and folders. **Technical:** Flat and hollow grinds, filework. **Prices:** $500 and up. **Remarks:** First knife sold in 1983, foundation member of Australian Knife Guild. **Mark:** Initials and address within Southern cross.

KACZOR, TOM
375 Wharncliffe Rd N, Upper London, ON, CANADA N6G 1E4 **Contact:** 519-645-7640

KAGAWA, KOICHI
1556 Horiyamashita, Hatano-Shi, Kanagawa, JAPAN
Specialties: Fancy high-tech straight knives and folders to customer specs. **Patterns:** Hunters, locking folders and slip-joints. **Technical:** Uses 440C and ATS-34. **Prices:** $500 to $2000, some to $20,000. **Remarks:** Part-time maker, first knife sold in 1986. **Mark:** First initial, last name-YOKOHAMA.

KAIN, CHARLES
KAIN DESIGNS, 1736 E. Maynard Dr., Indianapolis, IN 46227 **Contact:** 317-781-9549, (fax) 317-781-8521, charles@kaincustomknives.com, kaincustomknives.com
Specialties: Unique damascus art folders. **Patterns:** Any. **Technical:** Specialized & patented mechanisms. **Remarks:** Unique knife & knife mechanism design. **Mark:** Kain and Signet stamp for unique pieces.

KANKI, IWAO
691-2 Tenjincho, Ono-City, Hyogo, JAPAN 675-1316 **Contact:** 07948-3-2555, chiyozurusadahide.jp
Specialties: Plane, knife. **Prices:** Not determined yet. **Remarks:** Masters of traditional crafts designated by the Minister of International Trade and Industry (Japan). **Mark:** Chiyozuru Sadahide.

KANSEI, MATSUNO
109-8 Uenomachi, Nishikaiden, Gifu, JAPAN 501-1168 **Contact:** 81-58-234-8643
Specialties: Folders of original design. **Patterns:** LinerLock® folder. **Technical:** Grinds VG-10, damascus. **Prices:** $350 to $2000. **Remarks:** Full-time maker. First knife sold in 1993. **Mark:** Name.

KANTER, MICHAEL
ADAM MICHAEL KNIVES, 14550 West Honey Ln., New Berlin, WI 53151 **Contact:** 262-860-1136, mike@adammichaelknives.com, adammichaelknives.com
Specialties: Fixed blades and folders. **Patterns:** Drop point hunters, bowies and fighters. **Technical:** Jerry Rados damascus, BG42, CPM, S60V and S30V. **Prices:** $375 and up. Remarks: Ivory, mammoth ivory, stabilized woods, and pearl handles. **Mark:** Engraved Adam Michael.

KARP, BOB
PO Box 47304, Phoenix, AZ 85068 **Contact:** 602 870-1234, (fax) 602-331-0283
Remarks: Bob Karp "Master of the Blade."

KATO, SHINICHI
Rainbow Amalke 402, Moriyama-ku Nagoya, Aichi, JAPAN 463-0002 **Contact:** 81-52-736-6032, skato-402@u0l.gate01.com
Specialties: Flat grind and hand finish. **Patterns:** bowie, fighter. Hunting and folding knives. **Technical:** Hand forged,flat grind. **Prices:** $100 to $2000. **Remarks:** Part-time maker. **Mark:** Name.

KATSUMARO, SHISHIDO
2-6-11 Kamiseno, Aki-ku, Hiroshima, JAPAN **Contact:** 090-3634-9054, (fax) 082-227-4438, shishido@d8.dion.ne.jp

KAUFFMAN, DAVE
158 Jackson Creek Rd., Clancy, MT 59634 **Contact:** 406-431-8435
Specialties: Field grade and exhibition grade hunting knives and ultra light folders. **Patterns:** Fighters, bowies and drop-point hunters. **Technical:** S30V and SS damascus. **Prices:** $155 to $1200. **Remarks:** Full-time maker, first knife sold in 1989. On the cover of Knives '94. **Mark:** First and last name, city and state.

KAY, J WALLACE
332 Slab Bridge Rd, Liberty, SC 29657

KAZSUK, DAVID
1015 Sunny Ridge Dr., Lake Havasu City, AZ 86406-7963 **Contact:** 951-216-0883 (cell, text only), ddkaz@hotmail.com
Specialties: Hand-forged damascus. **Prices:** $250+. **Mark:** Last name.

KEARNEY, JAROD
1505 Parkersburg Turnpike, Swoope, VA 24479, jarodkearney@gmail.com jarodkearney.com
Patterns: bowies, skinners, hunters, Japanese blades, Sgian Dubhs

KEESLAR, JOSEPH F
391 Radio Rd, Almo, KY 42020 **Contact:** 270-753-7919, (fax) 270-753-7919, suzjoe.kees@gmail.com
Specialties: Classic and contemporary bowies, combat, hunters, daggers and folders. **Patterns:** Decorative filework, engraving and custom leather sheaths available. **Technical:** Forges 5160, 52100 and his own damascus steel. **Prices:** $300 to $3000. **Remarks:** Full-time maker, first knife sold in 1976. ABS Master Smith, and 50 years as a bladesmith (1962-2012). **Mark:** First and middle initials, last name in hammer, knife and anvil logo, M.S.

KEESLAR, STEVEN C
115 Lane 216 Hamilton Lake, Hamilton, IN 46742 **Contact:** 260-488-3161, sskeeslar@hotmail.com
Specialties: Traditional working/using straight knives of his design and to customer specs. **Patterns:** bowies, hunters, utility/camp knives. **Technical:** Forges 5160, files 52100 damascus. **Prices:** $100 to $600, some to $1500. **Remarks:** Part-time maker, first knife sold in 1976. ABS member. **Mark:** Fox head in flames over Steven C. Keeslar.

KEETON, WILLIAM L
6095 Rehobeth Rd SE, Laconia, IN 47135-9550 **Contact:** 812-969-2836, wlkeeton@hughes.net, keetoncustomknives.com
Specialties: Plain and fancy working knives. **Patterns:** Hunters and fighters, locking folders and slip-joints. Names patterns after Kentucky Derby winners. **Technical:** Grinds any of the popular alloy steels. **Prices:** $250 to $8,000. **Remarks:** Full-time maker, first knife sold in 1971. **Mark:** Logo of key.

KEHIAYAN, ALFREDO
Cuzco 1455 Ing., Maschwitz, Buenos Aires, ARGENTINA B1623GXU **Contact:** 540-348-4442212, (fax) 54-077-75-4493-5359, alfredo@kehiayan.com.ar, kehiayan.com.ar
Specialties: Functional straight knives. **Patterns:** Utility knives, skinners, hunters and boots. **Technical:** Forges and grinds SAE 52.100, SAE 6180, SAE 9260, SAE 5160, 440C and ATS-34, titanium with nitride. All blades mirror-polished, makes leather sheath and wood cases. **Prices:** From $350 up. **Remarks:** Full-time maker, first knife sold in 1983. Some knives are satin finish (utility knives). **Mark:** Name.

KEISUKE, GOTOH
105 Cosumo-City Otozu 202, Oita-city, Oita, JAPAN **Contact:** 097-523-0750, k-u-an@ki.rim.or.jp

KEITH, GREG
Keith Knives 536 Montague Rd, Montague Gold Mines, Nova Scotia, Canada **Contact:** 902-464-4604, keithknives.com, Instagram: Keithknives, Facebook: Greg Keith
Remarks: ABS journeyman smith.

KELLER, BILL
12211 Las Nubes, San Antonio, TX 78233 **Contact:** 210-653-6609
Specialties: Primarily folders, some fixed blades. **Patterns:** Autos, liner locks and hunters. **Technical:** Grinds stainless and damascus. **Prices:** $400 to $1000, some to $4000. **Remarks:** Part-time maker, first knife sold 1995. **Mark:** Last name inside outline of Alamo.

KELLEY, GARY
17485 SW Pheasant Lane, Aloha, OR 97006 **Contact:** 503-649-7867, garykelley@theblademaker.com, theblademaker.com
Specialties: Primitive knives and blades. **Patterns:** Fur trade era rifleman's knives, tomahawks, and hunting knives. **Technical:** Hand-forges and precision investment casts. **Prices:** $35 to $125. **Remarks:** Family business. Doing business as The Blademaker. **Mark:** Fir tree logo.

KELLY, DAVE
865 S. Shenandoah St., Los Angeles, CA 90035 **Contact:** 310-657-7121, dakcon@sbcglobal.net
Specialties: Collector and user one-of-a-kind (his design) fixed blades, liner lock folders, and leather sheaths. **Patterns:** Utility and hunting fixed blade knives with hand-sewn leather sheaths, Gentleman liner lock folders. **Technical:** Grinds carbon steels, hollow, convex, and flat. Offers clay differentially hardened blades, etched and polished. Uses Sambar stag, mammoth ivory, and high-grade burl woods. Hand-sewn leather sheaths for fixed blades and leather pouch sheaths for folders. **Prices:** $250 to $750, some higher. **Remarks:** Full-time maker, first knife made in 2003. **Mark:** First initial, last name with large K.

KELLY, STEVEN
11407 Spotted Fawn Ln., Bigfork, MT 59911 **Contact:** 406-212-2195, steve@skknives.com, skknives.com
Specialties: Tactical-style folders. **Technical:** damascus from 1084 or 1080 and 15n20.

custom knifemakers

52100.

KELSEY, NATE
Edge Alaska. 3867 N. Forestwood Dr., Palmer, AK 99645 **Contact:** 907-360-4469, edgealaska@me.com, edgealaska.com
Specialties: Functional hard use blades. Made for use in Alaska using stabilized wood or fossil ivory. **Patterns:** bowies, hunters, skinners and neck knives. **Technical:** Stock removal Carpenter XHP, 154CM for extreme use. Forges own damascus and 52100. **Prices:** $250 to $5,000. **Remarks:** Maker since 1990, member ABS. **Mark:** EDGE ALASKA or last name and Palmer AK.

KELSO, JIM
577 Collar Hill Rd, Worcester, VT 05682 **Contact:** 802-229-4254, (fax) 802-229-0595, kelsomaker@gmail.com, jimkelso.com
Specialties: Fancy high-art straight knives and folders that mix Eastern and Western influences. Only uses own designs. **Patterns:** Daggers, swords and locking folders. **Technical:** Works with top bladesmiths. **Prices:** $15,000 to $60,000. **Remarks:** Full-time maker, first knife sold in 1980. **Mark:** Stylized initials.

KEMP, LAWRENCE
8503 Water Tower Rd, Ooltewah, TN 37363 **Contact:** 423-344-2357, larry@kempknives.com kempknives.com
Specialties: bowies, hunters and working knives. **Patterns:** bowies, camp knives, hunters and skinners. **Technical:** Forges carbon steel, and his own damascus. **Prices:** $250 to $1500. **Remarks:** Part-time maker, first knife sold in 1991. ABS Journeyman Smith since 2006. **Mark:** L.A. Kemp.

KENNEDY JR., BILL
PO Box 850431, Yukon, OK 73085 **Contact:** 405-354-9150, bkfish1@gmail.com, billkennedyjrknives.com
Specialties: Working straight knives and folders. **Patterns:** Hunters, minis, fishing, and pocket knives. **Technical:** Grinds D2, 440C, ATS-34, BG42. **Prices:** $110 and up. **Remarks:** Part-time maker, first knife sold in 1980. **Mark:** Last name and year made.

KERANEN, PAUL
4122 S. E. Shiloh Ct., Tacumseh, KS 66542 **Contact:** 785-220-2141, pk6269@yahoo.com
Specialties: Specializes in Japanese style knives and swords. Most clay tempered with hamon. **Patterns:** Does bowies, fighters and hunters. **Technical:** Forges and grinds carbons steel only. Make my own damascus. **Prices:** $75 to $800. **Mark:** Keranen arched over anvil.

KEYES, DAN
6688 King St, Chino, CA 91710 **Contact:** 909-628-8329

KEYES, GEOFF P.
13027 Odell Rd NE, Duvall, WA 98019 **Contact:** 425-844-0758, 5ef@polarisfarm.com, 5elementsforge.com
Specialties: Working grade fixed blades, 19th century style gents knives. **Patterns:** Fixed blades, your design or mine. **Technical:** Hnad-forged 5160, 1084, and own damascus. **Prices:** $200 and up. **Remarks:** Geoff Keyes DBA 5 Elements Forge, ABS Journeyman Smith. **Mark:** Early mark KEYES etched in script. New mark as of 2009: pressed GPKeyes.

KHALSA, JOT SINGH
368 Village St, Millis, MA 02054 **Contact:** 508-376-8162, (fax) 508-532-0517, jotkhalsa@comcast.net, khalsakirpans.com, lifeknives.com, and thekhalsaraj.com
Specialties: Liner locks, one-of-a-kind daggers, swords, and kirpans (Sikh daggers) all original designs. **Technical:** Forges own damascus, uses others high quality damascus including stainless, and grinds stainless steels. Uses natural handle materials frequently unusual minerals. Pieces are frequently engraved and more recently carved. **Prices:** Start at $700.

KHARLAMOV, YURI
Oboronnay 46, Tula, RUSSIA 300007
Specialties: Classic, fancy and traditional knives of his design. **Patterns:** Daggers and hunters. **Technical:** Forges only damascus with nickel. Uses natural handle materials, engraves on metal, carves on nut-tree, silver and pearl inlays. **Prices:** $600 to $2380, some to $4000. **Remarks:** Full-time maker, first knife sold in 1988. **Mark:** Initials.

KI, SHIVA
5222 Ritterman Ave, Baton Rouge, LA 70805 **Contact:** 225-356-7274, shivakicustomknives@netzero.net, shivakicustomknives.com
Specialties: Working straight knives and folders. **Patterns:** Emphasis on personal defense knives, martial arts weapons. **Technical:** Forges and grinds, makes own damascus, prefers natural handle materials. **Prices:** $550 to $10,000. **Remarks:** Full-time maker, first knife sold in 1981. **Mark:** Name with logo.

KIEFER, TONY
112 Chateaugay Dr, Pataskala, OH 43062 **Contact:** 740-927-6910
Specialties: Traditional working and using straight knives in standard patterns. **Patterns:** bowies, fighters and hunters. **Technical:** Grinds 440C and D2, forges D2. Flat-grinds bowies, hollow-grinds drop-point and trailing-point hunters. **Prices:** $110 to $300, some to $200. **Remarks:** Spare-time maker, first knife sold in 1988. **Mark:** Last name.

KILBY, KEITH
1902 29th St, Cody, WY 82414 **Contact:** 307-587-2732
Specialties: Works with all designs. **Patterns:** Mostly bowies, camp knives and hunters of his design. **Technical:** Forges 52100, 5160, 1095, damascus and mosaic damascus. **Prices:** $250 to $3500. **Remarks:** Part-time maker, first knife sold in 1974. Doing business as Foxwood Forge. **Mark:** Name.

KILEY, MIKE AND JANDY
ROCKING K KNIVES, 1325 Florida, Chino Valley, AZ 86323 **Contact:** 928-910-2647
Specialties: Period knives for cowboy action shooters and mountain men. **Patterns:** bowies, drop-point hunters, skinners, sheepsfoot blades and spear points. **Technical:** Steels are 1095, 0-1, damascus and others upon request. Handles include all types of wood, with cocobolo, ironwood, rosewood, maple and bacote being favorites as well as buffalo horn, stag, elk antler, mammoth ivory, giraffe boon, sheep horn and camel bone. **Prices:** $100 to $500 depending on style and materials. Hand-tooled leather sheaths by Jan and Mike. **Mark:** Stylized K on one side, Kiley on the other.

KILPATRICK, CHRISTIAN A
6925 Mitchell Ct, Citrus Hieghts, CA 95610 **Contact:** 916-729-0733, crimsonkil@gmail.com, crimsonknives.com
Specialties: All forged weapons (no firearms) from ancient to modern. All blades produced are first and foremost useable tools, and secondly but no less importantly, artistic expressions. **Patterns:** Hunters, bowies, daggers, swords, axes, spears, boot knives, bird knives, ethnic blades and historical reproductions. Customer designs welcome. **Technical:** Forges and grinds, makes own damascus. Does file work. **Prices:** $125 to $3200. **Remarks:** 26 year part time maker. First knife sold in 2002.

KILROY, KYLE
POB 24655, Knoxville, TN 37933 **Contact:** 843-729-5141, kylekilroy@yahoo.com, kylekilroy.com
Specialties: Traditional forged knives in a mixture of traditional and modern materials. Professional chemical engineering background in polymers allows the exclusive use of many unique handle materials. **Patterns:** bowie/fighting knife patterns, hunting knives, chef's knives and modern bearing flipper folders. **Technical:** Forges D2, 1090, 1095 and several other carbon steels depending on application. Forges own damascus and can produce stainless blades via stock removal. **Prices:** $80 and up. **Remarks:** Professional engineer, first knife sold in 1996. **Mark:** Name above Charleston SC, with earlier stamp being "Chicora Gun Works" in three lines.

KIMBERLEY, RICHARD L.
86-B Arroyo Hondo Rd, Santa Fe, NM 87508 **Contact:** 505-820-2727
Specialties: Fixed-blade and period knives. **Technical:** O1, 52100, 9260 steels. **Remarks:** Member ABS. Marketed under "Kimberleys of Santa Fe." **Mark:** "By D. KIMBERLEY SANTA FE NM."

KIMSEY, KEVIN
198 Cass White Rd. NW, Cartersville, GA 30121 **Contact:** 770-387-0779 and 770-655-8879
Specialties: Tactical fixed blades and folders. **Patterns:** Fighters, folders, hunters and utility knives. **Technical:** Grinds 440C, ATS-34 and D2 carbon. **Prices:** $100 to $400, some to $600. **Remarks:** Three-time Blade magazine award winner, knifemaker since 1983. **Mark:** Rafter and stylized KK.

KING, BILL
14830 Shaw Rd, Tampa, FL 33625 **Contact:** 813-961-3455, billkingknives@yahoo.com
Specialties: Folders, lockbacks, liner locks, automatics and stud openers. **Patterns:** Wide varieties, folders. **Technical:** ATS-34 and some damascus, single and double grinds. Offers filework and jewel embellishment, nickel-silver damascus and mokume bolsters. **Prices:** $150 to $475, some to $850. **Remarks:** Full-time maker, first knife sold in 1976. All titanium fitting on liner-locks, screw or rivet construction on lock-backs. **Mark:** Last name in crown.

KING, FRED
430 Grassdale Rd, Cartersville, GA 30120 **Contact:** 770-382-8478, fking83264@aol.com
Specialties: Fancy and embellished working straight knives and folders. **Patterns:** Hunters, bowies and fighters. **Technical:** Grinds ATS-34 and D2: forges 5160 and damascus. Offers filework. **Prices:** $100 to $3500. **Remarks:** Spare-time maker, first knife sold in 1984. **Mark:** Kings Edge.

KING JR., HARVEY G
32170 Hwy K4, Alta Vista, KS 66834 **Contact:** 785-499-5207, harveykingknives.com
Specialties: Traditional working and using straight knives of his design and to customer specs. **Patterns:** Hunters, bowies and fillet knives. **Technical:** Grinds O1, A2 and D2. Prefers natural handle materials, offers leatherwork. **Prices:** Start at $150. **Remarks:** Full-time maker, first knife sold in 1988. **Mark:** Name, city, state, and serial number.

KINKER, MIKE
8755 E County Rd 50 N, Greensburg, IN 47240 **Contact:** 812-663-5277, kinkercustomknives@gmail.com
Specialties: Working/using knives, straight knives. Starting to make folders. Your design. **Patterns:** Boots, daggers, hunters, skinners, hatchets. **Technical:** Grind 440C and ATS-34, others if required. damascus, dovetail bolsters, jeweled blade. **Prices:** $125 to 375, some to $1000. **Remarks:** Part-time maker, first knife sold in 1991. Doing business as Kinker Custom Knives. **Mark:** Kinker

KINNIKIN, TODD
EUREKA FORGE, 7 Capper Dr., Pacific, MO 63069-3603 **Contact:** 314-938-6248
Specialties: Mosaic damascus. **Patterns:** Hunters, fighters, folders and automatics. **Technical:** Forges own mosaic damascus with tool steel damascus edge. Prefers natural, fossil and artifact handle materials. **Prices:** $1200 to $2400. **Remarks:** Full-time maker, first knife sold in 1994. **Mark:** Initials connected.

KIRK, RAY

Raker Knives and Steel. PO Box 1445, Tahlequah, OK 74465 **Contact:** 918-207-8076, ray@rakerknives.com, rakerknives.com
Specialties: Folders, skinners fighters, and bowies. **Patterns:** Neck knives and small hunters and skinners. Full and hidden-tang integrals from 52100 round bar. **Technical:** Forges all knives from 52100 and own damascus. **Prices:** $65 to $3000. **Remarks:** Started forging in 1989, makes own damascus. **Mark:** Stamped "Raker" on blade.

KIRKES, BILL

235 Oaklawn Cir., Little Rock, AR 72206 **Contact:** 501-551-0135, bill@kirkesknives.com, kirkesknives.com
Specialties: Handforged fixed blades. **Technical:** High-carbon 5160 and 1084 blade steels. Will build to customer's specs, prefers to use natural handle material. **Remarks:** ABS Journeyman smith. **Mark:** Kirkes.

KISLINGER, MILOS

KISLINGER KNIVES, Dobronin 314 58812, CZECH REPUBLIC **Contact:** +420724570451, kislinger.milos@centrum.cz, http://kislingerknives.blogspot.cz, Facebook.com/KislingerKnives
Specialties: Fine folders, daggers, automatic knives, flipper folders and bowies. **Technical:** Forges own damascus steel, and uses ivory, pearl and more luxurious handle materials. **Prices:** $400 and up. **Remarks:** Knifemaker and blacksmith since 2005, with first knife made eight years ago.

KISTNER, DEE

107 Whitecrest Dr., Crossville, TN 38571 **Contact:** 931-200-1233, dkknives@gmail.com, kistnerknives.com
Specialties: Working knives. **Patterns:** Everyday carry, hunting and outdoor knives, military knives. **Technical:** Flat grinds 1075 steel, differentially heat treated. **Prices:** $100 and up. **Remarks:** Full-time maker, sole authorship. **Mark:** KISTNER.

KITSMILLER, JERRY

67277 Las Vegas Dr, Montrose, CO 81401 **Contact:** 970-249-4290
Specialties: Working straight knives in standard patterns. **Patterns:** Hunters, boots. **Technical:** Grinds ATS-34 and 440C only. **Prices:** $75 to $200, some to $300. **Remarks:** Spare-time maker, first knife sold in 1984. **Mark:** JandS Knives.

KLAASEE, TINUS

PO Box 10221, George, WC, SOUTH AFRICA 6530
Specialties: Hunters, skinners and utility knives. **Patterns:** Uses own designs and client specs. **Technical:** N690 stainless steel 440C damascus. **Prices:** $700 and up. **Remarks:** Use only indigenous materials. Hardwood, horns and ivory. Makes his own sheaths and boxes. **Mark:** Initials and sur name over warthog.

KLEIN, KEVIN

129 Cedar St., Apt. 2, Boston, MA 02119 **Contact:** 609-937-8949, kevin.a.klein779@gmail.com
Specialties: Forged damascus blades using 15N20 and 1084. **Remarks:** Full-time maker, first knife made in 2012. Apprentice to J.D. Smith starting in 2012. **Mark:** KAK? or ?, depending on piece.

KLEIN, KIERAN

2436 Stonewall Rd. NE, Check, VA 24072 **Contact:** 540-651-2454, hammerdownkjk@gmail.com, hammerdownforge.com
Specialties: Large chopping blades as well as camping and EDC (everyday carry) styles. **Patterns:** Custom khukuri styles, drop points, sheepsfoot, etc. **Technical:** Stock removal method of blade making using 80CrV2, 52100, 1075, W2 and CPM 3V blade steels, and high-quality stabilized burl wood, carbon fiber, G-10 and Micarta handles. **Prices:** $125 to $1,200. **Remarks:** Full-time maker since 2013, first knife made in 2012. **Mark:** Mountain range profile over HDF initials with Virginia, USA under that.

KNAPP, MARK

Mark Knapp Custom Knives, 1971 Fox Ave, Fairbanks, AK 99701 **Contact:** 907-452-7477, info@markknappcustomknives.com, markknappcustomknives.com
Specialties: Mosaic handles of exotic natural materials from Alaska and around the world. Folders, fixed blades, full and hidden tangs. **Patterns:** Folders, hunters, skinners, and camp knives. **Technical:** Forges own damascus, uses both forging and stock removal with ATS-34, 154CM, stainless damascus, carbon steel and carbon damascus. **Prices:** $800-$3000. **Remarks:** Full time maker, sold first knife in 2000. **Mark:** Mark Knapp Custom Knives Fairbanks, AK.

KNAPTON, CHRIS C.

76 Summerland Dr., Henderson, Aukland, NEW ZEALAND **Contact:** 09-835-3598, knaptch76@gmail.com, knappoknives.com
Specialties: Working and fancy straight and folding knives of his own design. **Patterns:** Tactical, utility, hunting fixed and folding knives. **Technical:** Predominate knife steels are Elmax, CPM-154 and D2. All blades made via the stock removal method. **Prices:** $120 - $500. **Remarks:** Part-time maker. **Mark:** Stylized letter K, country name and Haast eagle.

KNICKMEYER, HANK

6300 Crosscreek, Cedar Hill, MO 63016 **Contact:** 636-285-3210
Specialties: Complex mosaic damascus constructions. **Patterns:** Fixed blades, swords, folders and automatics. **Technical:** Mosaic damascus with all tool steel damascus edges. **Prices:** $500 to $2000, some $3000 and higher. **Remarks:** Part-time maker, first knife sold in 1989. Doing business as Dutch Creek Forge and Foundry. **Mark:** Initials connected.

KNICKMEYER, KURT

6344 Crosscreek, Cedar Hill, MO 63016 **Contact:** 314-274-0481

KNIGHT, JASON

110 Paradise Pond Ln, Harleyville, SC 29448 **Contact:** 843-452-1163, jasonknightknives.com
Specialties: bowies. **Patterns:** bowies and anything from history or his own design. **Technical:** 1084, 5160, O1, 52102, damascus/forged blades. **Prices:** $200 and up. **Remarks:** Bladesmith. **Mark:** KNIGHT.

KNIPSCHIELD, TERRY

808 12th Ave NE, Rochester, MN 55906 **Contact:** 507-288-7829, terry@knipknives.com, knipknives.com
Specialties: Folders and fixed blades and leather working knives. **Patterns:** Variations of traditional patterns and his own new designs. **Technical:** Stock removal. Grinds CPM-154CM, ATS-34, stainless damascus, 01. **Prices:** $60 to $1200 and higher for upscale folders. **Mark:** Etchd logo on blade, KNIP with shield image.

KNOTT, STEVE

KNOTT KNIVES, 203 Wild Rose, Guyton, GA 31312 **Contact:** 912-536-7651, knottknives@yahoo.com, Facebook: Knott Knives/Steve Knott
Technical: Uses ATS-34/440C and some commercial damascus, single and double grinds with mirror or satin finishes. **Patterns:** Hunters, boot knives, bowies, and tantos, slip joint, LinerLock and lock-back folders. Uses a wide variety of handle materials to include ironwood, coca-bola and colored stabilized wood, also horn, bone and ivory upon customer request. **Remarks:** First knife sold in 1991. Part-time maker.

KNOWLES, SHAWN

750 Townsbury Rd, Great Meadows, NJ 07838 **Contact:** 973-670-3307, skcustomknives@gmail.com, shawnknowlescustomknives.com

KNOX, JEFF

KNOX KNIFE, Baldwin, MO **Contact:** knox@knoxknife.com, www.knoxknife.com
Patterns: Fixed blades, fantasy **Remarks:** Part-time maker

KOHLS, JERRY

N4725 Oak Rd, Princeton, WI 54968 **Contact:** 920-295-3648
Specialties: Working knives and period pieces. **Patterns:** Hunters-boots and bowies, your designs or his. **Technical:** Grinds, ATS-34 440c 154CM and 1095 and commercial damascus. **Remarks:** Part-time maker. **Mark:** Last name.

KOJETIN, W

20 Bapaume Rd Delville, Germiston, GT, SOUTH AFRICA 1401 **Contact:** 27118733305/mobile 27836256208
Specialties: High-art and working straight knives of all designs. **Patterns:** Daggers, hunters and his own Man hunter bowie. **Technical:** Grinds D2 and ATS-34, forges and grinds 440B/C. Offers "wrap-around" pava and abalone handles, scrolled wood or ivory, stacked filework and setting of faceted semi-precious stones. **Prices:** $185 to $600, some to $11,000. **Remarks:** Spare-time maker, first knife sold in 1962. **Mark:** Billy K.

KOLENKO, VLADIMIR

505 Newell Dr., Huntingdon Valley, PA 19006 **Contact:** 617-501-8366, kolenkv@yahoo.com, kolenko.com
Specialties: Daggers and fighters. **Patterns:** Art knives. **Technical:** Typically uses custom mosaic damascus blades forged by various bladesmiths and commercial damascus makers. **Prices:** $1,000 to $2,500. **Remarks:** Making jewelry and fashioning knives have been longstanding hobbies, so the maker combined them and says he enjoys the whole process, not just the end product. He guesses that makes the difference between a hobby and business.

KOLITZ, ROBERT

W9342 Canary Rd, Beaver Dam, WI 53916 **Contact:** 920-887-1287
Specialties: Working straight knives to customer specs. **Patterns:** bowies, hunters, bird and trout knives, boots. **Technical:** Grinds O1, 440C, commercial damascus. **Prices:** $50 to $100, some to $500. **Remarks:** Spare-time maker, first knife sold in 1979. **Mark:** Last initial.

KOMMER, RUSS

4609 35th Ave N, Fargo, ND 58102 **Contact:** 701-281-1826, russkommer@yahoo.com russkommerknives.com
Specialties: Working straight knives with the outdoorsman in mind. **Patterns:** Hunters, semi-skinners, fighters, folders and utility knives, art knives. **Technical:** Hollow-grinds ATS-34, 440C and 440V. **Prices:** $125 to $850, some to $3000. **Remarks:** Full-time maker, first knife sold in 1995. **Mark:** Bear paw—full name, city and state or full name and state.

KOPP, TODD M

PO Box 3474, Apache Jct., AZ 85217 **Contact:** 480-983-6143, tmkopp@msn.com
Specialties: Classic and traditional straight knives. Fluted handled daggers. **Patterns:** bowies, boots, daggers, fighters, hunters, swords and folders. **Technical:** Grinds 5160, 440C, ATS-34. All damascus steels, or customers choice. Some engraving and filework. **Prices:** $200 to $1200, some to $4000. **Remarks:** Part-time maker, first knife sold in 1989. **Mark:** Last name in Old English, some others name, city and state.

KOSTER, DANIEL

KOSTER KNIVES, 1711 Beverly Ct., Bentonville, AR 72712 **Contact:** 479-366-7794, dan@kosterknives.com, kosterknives.com
Patterns: Bushcraft, survival, outdoor and utility knives. **Technical:** Stock-removal method of blade making, using CPM 3V steel. **Prices:** $150 to $300. **Remarks:** Full-time knifemaker in business since 2005. **Mark:** "K" in a circle, negative shape.

KOSTER, STEVEN C

16261 Gentry Ln, Huntington Beach, CA 92647 **Contact:** 714-907-7250, kosterknives@verizon.net kosterhandforgedknives.com

Specialties: Walking sticks, hand axes, tomahawks, damascus. **Patterns:** Ladder, twists, round horn. **Technical:** Use 5160, 52100, 1084, 1095 steels. Ladder, twists, **Prices:** $200 to $1000. **Remarks:** Wood and leather sheaths with silver furniture. ABS Journeyman 2003. California knifemakers member. **Mark:** Koster squeezed between lines.

KOVACIK, ROBERT
Zavadska 122, Tomasovce 98401, SLOVAKIA **Contact:** Mobil: 00421907644800, kovacikart@gmail.com robertkovacik.com
Specialties: Engraved hunting knives, guns engraved, Knifemakers. **Technical:** Fixed blades, folder knives, miniatures. **Prices:** $350 to $10,000 U.S. **Mark:** R.

KOVAR, EUGENE
2626 W 98th St., Evergreen Park, IL 60642 **Contact:** 708-636-3724/708-790-4115, baldemaster333@aol.com
Specialties: One-of-a-kind miniature knives only. **Patterns:** Fancy to fantasy miniature knives, knife pendants and tie tacks. **Technical:** Files and grinds nails, nickel-silver and sterling silver. **Prices:** $5 to $35, some to $100. **Mark:** GK.

KOYAMA, CAPTAIN BUNSHICHI
3-23 Shirako-cho, Nakamura-ku, Nagoya, Aichi, JAPAN City 453-0817 **Contact:** 052-461-7070, (fax) 052-461-7070
Specialties: Innovative folding knife. **Patterns:** General purpose one hand. **Technical:** Grinds ATS-34 and damascus. **Prices:** $400 to $900, some to $1500. **Remarks:** Part-time maker, first knife sold in 1994. **Mark:** Captain B. Koyama and the shoulder straps of CAPTAIN.

KRAFT, STEVE
408 NE 11th St, Abilene, KS 67410 **Contact:** 785-263-1411
Specialties: Folders, lockbacks, scale release auto, push button auto. **Patterns:** Hunters, boot knives and fighters. **Technical:** Grinds ATS-34, damascus, uses titanium, pearl, ivory etc. **Prices:** $500 to $2500. **Remarks:** Part-time maker, first knife sold in 1984. **Mark:** Kraft.

KRAMMES, JEREMY
138 W. Penn St., Schuylkill Haven, PA 17972 **Contact:** 570-617-5753, blade@jkknives.com, jkknives.com
Specialties: Working folders and collectible art knives. **Technical:** Stock removal, hollow grinding, carving and engraving. **Prices:** $550+ for working knives, and $1,000+ for art knives. **Remarks:** Part-time maker, first knife sold in 2004. **Mark:** Stylized JK on blade.

KRAPP, DENNY
1826 Windsor Oak Dr, Apopka, FL 32703 **Contact:** 407-880-7115
Specialties: Fantasy and working straight knives of his design. **Patterns:** Hunters, fighters and utility/camp knives. **Technical:** Grinds ATS-34 and 440C. **Prices:** $85 to $300, some to $800. **Remarks:** Spare-time maker, first knife sold in 1988. **Mark:** Last name.

KRAUSE, JIM
3272 Hwy H, Farmington, MO 63640 **Contact:** 573-756-7388 or 573-701-7047, james_krause@sbcglobal.net
Specialties: Folders, fixed blades and neck knives. **Patterns:** New pattern for each knife. **Technical:** CPM steels or high-carbon steel on request. **Prices:** $125 and up for neck knives, $250 and up for fixed blades and $250 to $1,000 for folders and damascus pieces. **Remarks:** Full-time maker, first knife made in 2000. Makes one knife at a time with the best materials the maker can find. **Mark:** Krause Handmade with Christian fish.

KREGER, THOMAS
1996 Dry Branch Rd., Lugoff, SC 29078 **Contact:** 803-438-4221, tdkreger@bellsouth.net
Specialties: South Carolina/George Herron style working/using knives. Customer designs considered. **Patterns:** Hunters, skinners, fillet, liner lock folders, kitchen, and camp knives. **Technical:** Hollow and flat grinds of ATS-34, CPM154CM, and 5160. **Prices:** $100 and up. **Remarks:** Full-time maker. President of the South Carolina Association of Knifemakers 2002-2006, and current president since 2013. **Mark:** TDKreger.

KREH, LEFTY
210 Wichersham Way, "Cockeysville", MD 21030

KREIBICH, DONALD L.
1638 Commonwealth Circle, Reno, NV 89503 **Contact:** 775-746-0533, dmkreno@sbcglobal.net
Specialties: Working straight knives in standard patterns. **Patterns:** bowies, boots and daggers, camp and fishing knives. **Technical:** Grinds 440C, 154CM and ATS-34, likes integrals. **Prices:** $100 to $200, some to $500. **Remarks:** Part-time maker, first knife sold in 1980. **Mark:** First and middle initials, last name.

KREIN, TOM
P.O. Box 994, 337 E. Main St., Gentry, AR 72734 **Contact:** 479-233-0508, kreinknives@gmail.com, kreinknives.net
Specialties: LinerLock folders and fixed blades designed to be carried and used. **Technical:** Stock removal using D2, A2, CPM 3V, CPM 154, CPM M4, Stellite 6K and damascus, and makes his own sheaths. **Prices:** $250 to $500 and up. **Remarks:** Full-time maker, first knife made in 1993. **Mark:** Last name and the year the knife was made in the shape of a circle, with a bulldog in the middle.

KRESSLER, D F
Mittelweg 31 i, D-28832 Achim, GERMANY 28832 **Contact:** +49 (0) 42 02/76-5742, (fax) +49 (0) 42 02/7657 41, info@kresslerknives.com, kresslerknives.com
Specialties: High-tech integral and interframe knives. **Patterns:** Hunters, fighters, daggers. **Technical:** Grinds new state-of-the-art steels, prefers natural handle materials.

Prices: Upscale. **Mark:** Name in logo.

KUBASEK, JOHN A
74 Northhampton St, Easthampton, MA 01027 **Contact:** 413-527-7917, jaknife01@yahoo.com
Specialties: Left- and right-handed LinerLock® folders of his design or to customer specs. Also new knives made with Ripcord patent. **Patterns:** Fighters, tantos, drop points, survival knives, neck knives and belt buckle knives. **Technical:** Grinds 154CM, S30 and damascus. **Prices:** $395 to $1500. **Remarks:** Part-time maker, first knife sold in 1985. **Mark:** Name and address etched.

KULIS, DAVID S.
10741 S. Albany Ave., Chicago, IL 60655, windycitywoodworks@hotmail.com
Patterns: Folding LinerLocks, frame locks, straight hunters, fighters and kitchen knives. **Technical:** Stock removal method of making blades with hollow grinds and using CPM S30V, CPM 154, O1 and damascus steels. Handle materials include everything from stabilized wood to carbon fiber. **Prices:** $150 to $1,000. **Remarks:** Part-time maker, first knife sold in 2015. **Mark:** Stylized "DK" etched into blade.

KURT, DAVID
POB 1377, Molalla, OR 97038 **Contact:** 503-871-5420, dkurtknives@aol.com, dkurtknives.com
Specialties: Fixed blades. **Patterns:** Tactical, utility, kitchen and hunting knives. **Technical:** Stock removal method of blade making using primarily 154CM steel or to customers' preferences. **Remarks:** Full-time maker. **Mark:** Bear skull with maker's full name.

L

LAINSON, TONY
114 Park Ave, Council Bluffs, IA 51503 **Contact:** 712-322-5222
Specialties: Working straight knives, liner locking folders. **Technical:** Grinds 154CM, ATS-34, 440C buys damascus. Handle materials include Micarta, carbon fiber G-10 ivory pearl and bone. **Prices:** $95 to $600. **Remarks:** Part-time maker, first knife sold in 1987. **Mark:** Name and state.

LAIRSON SR., JERRY
H C 68 Box 970, Ringold, OK 74754 **Contact:** 580-876-3426, bladesmt@brightok.net, lairson-custom-knives.net
Specialties: damascus collector grade knives & high performance field grade hunters & cutting competition knives. **Patterns:** damascus, random, raindrop, ladder, twist and others. **Technical:** All knives hammer forged. Mar Tempering **Prices:** Field grade knives $300. Collector grade $400 & up. **Mark:** Lairson. **Remarks:** Makes any style knife but prefer fighters and hunters. ABS Mastersmith, AKA member, KGA member. Cutting competition competitor.

LAKE, RON
3360 Bendix Ave, Eugene, OR 97401 **Contact:** 541-484-2683
Specialties: High-tech working knives, inventor of the modern interframe folder. **Patterns:** Hunters, boots, etc., locking folders. **Technical:** Grinds 154CM and ATS-34. Patented interframe with special lock release tab. **Prices:** $2200 to $3000, some higher. **Remarks:** Full-time maker, first knife sold in 1966. **Mark:** Last name.

LALA, PAULO RICARDO P AND LALA, ROBERTO P.
R Daniel Martins 636, Presidente Prudente, SP, BRAZIL 19031-260 **Contact:** 0182-210125, korthknives@terra.com.br, ikbsknifetech.com
Specialties: Straight knives and folders of all designs to customer specs. **Patterns:** bowies, daggers fighters, hunters and utility knives. **Technical:** Grinds and forges D6, 440C, high-carbon steels and damascus. **Prices:** $60 to $400, some higher. **Remarks:** Full-time makers, first knife sold in 1991. All stainless steel blades are ultra sub-zero quenched. **Mark:** Sword carved on top of anvil under KORTH.

LAMB, CURTIS J
3336 Louisiana Ter, Ottawa, KS 66067-8996 **Contact:** 785-242-6657

LAMBERT, KIRBY
2131 Edgar St, Regina, SK, CANADA S4N 3K8, kirby@lambertknives.com, lambertknives.com
Specialties: Tactical/utility folders. Tactical/utility Japanese style fixed blades. **Prices:** $200 to $1500 U.S. **Remarks:** Full-time maker since 2002. **Mark:** Black widow spider and last name Lambert.

LAMEY, ROBERT M
15800 Lamey Dr, Biloxi, MS 39532 **Contact:** 228-396-9066, (fax) 228-396-9022, rmlamey@ametro.net, lameyknives.com
Specialties: bowies, fighters, hard use knives. **Patterns:** bowies, fighters, hunters and camp knives. **Technical:** Forged and stock removal. **Prices:** $125 to $350. **Remarks:** Lifetime reconditioning, will build to customer designs, specializing in hard use, affordable knives. **Mark:** LAMEY.

LAMOTHE, JORDAN
1317 County Rte. 31, Granville, NY 12832 **Contact:** 518-368-5147, jordanlamotheblades@gmail.com, jordanlamothe.com
Specialties: Forged working knives and collectors' pieces. **Patterns:** Anything from chef's knives to swords. **Technical:** Forges carbon steels and makes damascus; also does leather sheath work. **Prices:** $150 and up. **Remarks:** Full-time maker, ABS Journeyman Smith since 2018, first knife sold in 2014. **Mark:** Stamped JL.

LANCASTER, C G
No 2 Schoonwinkel St, Parys, Free State, SOUTH AFRICA **Contact:** 0568112090

Specialties: High-tech working and using knives of his design and to customer specs. **Patterns:** Hunters, locking folders and utility/camp knives. **Technical:** Grinds Sandvik 12C27, 440C and D2. Offers anodized titanium bolsters. **Prices:** $450 to $750, some to $1500. **Remarks:** Part-time maker, first knife sold in 1990. **Mark:** Etched logo.

LANCE, BILL
12820 E. Scott Rd., Palmer, AK 99645-8863 **Contact:** 907-694-1487, lanceknives.com

Specialties: Ulu sets and working straight knives, limited issue sets. **Patterns:** Several ulu patterns, drop-point skinners. **Technical:** Uses ATS-34 and AEBL, ivory, horn and high-class wood handles. **Prices:** $145 to $500, art sets to $7,500. **Remarks:** First knife sold in 1981. **Mark:** Last name over a lance.

LANCE, DAN
889 Pamela Kay Ln., Weatherford, TX 76088 **Contact:** 940-682-5381, dan@danlanceknives.com, danlanceknives.com

Specialties: High-end locking folders of maker's own designs. **Patterns:** Locking folders, fighters, skinners, hunting and camp knives. **Technical:** Stock removal using stainless damascus, CPM 154 and PSF-27 primarily. Performs own heat treating. Handle materials consist of mammoth ivory, stag, exotic woods, Kirinite, carbon fiber and various bones and horns. **Prices:** $250 to $1,250, some higher. **Remarks:** Full-time maker, first knife made and sold in 2014. Member of the ABS and Knifemakers' Guild. **Mark:** Dan Lance over a lance with a broken shaft.

LANCE, LUCAS
3600 N. Charley, Wasilla, AK 99654 **Contact:** 907-357-0349, lucas@lanceknives.com, lanceknives.com

Specialties: Working with materials native to Alaska such as fossilized ivory, bone, musk ox bone, sheep horn, moose antler, all combined with exotic materials from around the world. **Patterns:** Fully functional knives of my own design. **Technical:** Mainly stock removal, flat grinds in ATS-34, 440C, 5160 and various makes of American-made damascus. **Prices:** $165 to $850. **Remarks:** Second-generation knifemaker who grew up and trained in father, Bill Lance's, shop. First knife designed and made in 1994. **Mark:** Last name over a lance.

LANDERS, JOHN
758 Welcome Rd, Newnan, GA 30263 **Contact:** 404-253-5719

Specialties: High-art working straight knives and folders of his design. **Patterns:** Hunters, fighters and slip-joint folders. **Technical:** Grinds 440C, ATS-34, 154CM and commercial damascus. **Prices:** $85 to $250, some to $500. **Remarks:** Part-time maker, first knife sold in 1989. **Mark:** Last name.

LANDIS, DAVID E. SR.
4544 County Rd. 29, Galion, OH 44833 **Contact:** 419-946-3145, del@redbird.net

Specialties: damascus knives in ladder, twist, double-twist and "W's" patterns. Makes leather sheaths and forges his own damascus. **Prices:** $250 to $500. **Remarks:** Retiree who says knifemaking keeps him learning with new challenges and meeting a lot of great people. **Mark:** DEL.

LANG, DAVID
6153 Cumulus Circle, Kearns, UT 84118 **Contact:** 801-809-1241, dknifeguy@msn.com

Specialties: Art knives, metal sheaths, push daggers, fighting knives, hunting knives, camp knives, skinning knives, pocketknives, utility knives and three-finger knives. **Patterns:** Prefers to work with own patterns, but will consider other designs. **Technical:** Flat grinds, hollow grinds, hand carving on the blades and handles, and gold and silver casting. **Remarks:** Will work from his designs or to customer specifications. Has been making knives for over 20 years and has learned from some of the best. **Prices:** $250 to $3,000, with most work ranging from $750 to $1,500. **Mark:** Dlang over UTAH.

LANGLEY, GARY
10800 Frankie Ln., Dumas, TX 79029, gll@gllangley.com, gllangley.com

Specialties: Fixed blades, hunting knives, bowies and daggers. **Technical:** Practices stock-removal method of blade making using CPM-154, and has the steel professionally heat treated. Most blades have tapered tangs and dovetailed bolsters, a few frame handles. **Remarks:** Built first knife in 1977 and has retired from full-time job and spends more time building knives. Current Board member of the Texas Knifemakers Guild. Also a wildlife photographer.

LANGLEY, GENE H
1022 N. Price Rd, Florence, SC 29506 **Contact:** 843-669-3150

Specialties: Working knives in standard patterns. **Patterns:** Hunters, boots, fighters, locking folders and slip-joints. **Technical:** Grinds 440C, 154CM and ATS-34. **Prices:** $125 to $450, some to $1000. **Remarks:** Part-time maker, first knife sold in 1979. **Mark:** Name.

LANGLEY, MICK
1015 Centre Crescent, Qualicum Beach, BC, CANADA V9K 2G6 **Contact:** 250-752-4261

Specialties: Period pieces and working knives. **Patterns:** bowies, push daggers, fighters, boots. Some folding lockers. **Technical:** Forges 5160, 1084, W2 and his own damascus. **Prices:** $250 to $2500, some to $4500. **Remarks:** Full-time maker, first knife sold in 1977. **Mark:** Langley with M.S. (for ABS Master Smith)

LANKTON, SCOTT
8065 Jackson Rd. R-11, Ann Arbor, MI 48103 **Contact:** 313-426-3735

Specialties: Pattern welded swords, krisses and Viking period pieces. **Patterns:** One-of-a-kind. **Technical:** Forges W2, L6 nickel and other steels. **Prices:** $600 to $12,000. **Remarks:** Part-time bladesmith, full-time smith, first knife sold in 1976. **Mark:** Last name logo.

LAPEN, CHARLES
Box 529, W. Brookfield, MA 01585

Specialties: Chef's knives for the culinary artist. **Patterns:** Camp knives, Japanese-style swords and wood working tools, hunters. **Technical:** Forges 1075, car spring and his own damascus. Favors narrow and Japanese tangs. **Prices:** $200 to $400, some to $2000. **Remarks:** Part-time maker, first knife sold in 1972. **Mark:** Last name.

LAPLANTE, BRETT
4545 CR412, McKinney, TX 75071 **Contact:** 972-838-9191, blap007@aol.com

Specialties: Working straight knives and folders to customer specs. **Patterns:** Survival knives, bowies, skinners, hunters. **Technical:** Grinds D2 and 440C. Heat-treats. **Prices:** $200 to $800. **Remarks:** Part-time maker, first knife sold in 1987. **Mark:** Last name in Canadian maple leaf logo.

LARGIN, KEN
KELGIN Knifemakers Co-Op, 2001 S. State Rd. 1, Connersville, IN 47331 **Contact:** 765-969-5012, kelginfinecutlery@gmail.com, kelgin.com

Specialties: Retired from general knifemaking. Only take limited orders in meteorite damascus or solid meteorite blades. **Patterns:** Any. **Technical:** Stock removal or forged. **Prices:** $500 & up. **Remarks:** Travels the U.S. full time teaching hands-on "History Of Cutting Tools" to Scouts and any interested group. Participants flint knap, forge and keep three tools they make! **Mark:** K.C. Largin (Kelgin mark retired in 2004).

LARK, DAVID
6641 Schneider Rd., Kingsley, MI 49649 **Contact:** 231-342-1076, dblark58@yahoo.com

Specialties: Traditional straight knives, art knives, folders. **Patterns:** All types. **Technical:** Grinds all types of knife making steel and makes damascus. **Prices:** $600 and up. **Remarks:** Full-time maker, custom riflemaker, and engraver. **Mark:** Lark in script and DBL on engraving.

LAROCHE, JEAN-MARC
16 rue Alexandre Dumas, 78160 Marly le Roi, FRANCE **Contact:** +33 1 39 16 16 58, infojmlaroche@orange.fr, jmlaroche.com

Specialties: Fantasy pieces to customer specs. **Patterns:** Straight knives and folding knives. **Technical:** Stainless or damascus blade steels. **Prices:** $800 to $4,000, some to $10,000. **Remarks:** Full-time sculptor, full-time knifemaker for 12 years from 1992 to 2004. Awards won include BLADEhandmade "Best In Show" Award in 1997 and "Best Fantasy Knife" at the 1998 BLADE Show West. Artistic design knives are influenced by fantasy movies and comics with handles in bronze, silver or resin, including animal skulls, bones and natural stones. Collaborations with Gil Hibben and Roger Bergh. Recently created a knife capable of mechanical movement: "The Living Knife" with a blade by Bergh. **Mark:** Logo, + name sometimes.

LARSON, RICHARD
549 E Hawkeye Ave, Turlock, CA 95380 **Contact:** 209-668-1615, lebatardknives@aol.com

Specialties: Sound working knives, lightweight folders, practical tactical knives. **Patterns:** Hunters, trout and bird knives, fish fillet knives, bowies, tactical sheath knives, one- and two-blade folders. **Technical:** Grinds ATS-34, A2, D2, CPM 3V and commercial. damascus, forges and grinds 52100, O1 and 1095. Machines folder frames from aircraft aluminum. **Prices:** $40 to $650. **Remarks:** Full-time maker, first knife sold in 1974. Charter member Gulf Coast Custom Knifemakers. Voting member Knifemakers' Guild. Member of the 100%er Group. **Mark:** Stamped last name or etched logo of last name, city, and state.

LARSTEIN, FRANCINE
Francine Etched Knives, Watsonville, CA 95076 **Contact:** 800-557-1525, 831-426-6046 www.francineetchedknives.com, francine@francineetchedknives.com

Specialties: Etching for customers and other knifemakers. **Patterns:** Kitchen cutlery, fixed blade sheaths, folding pocket knives. **Technical:** Boye Dendritic Steel and Boye Dendritic Cobalt.

LARY, ED
951 Rangeline Rd., Mosinee, WI 54455 **Contact:** 715-630-6202, laryblades@hotmail.com

Specialties: Upscale hunters and art knives with display presentations. **Patterns:** Hunters, period pieces. **Technical:** Grinds all steels, heat treats, fancy filework and engraving. **Prices:** Upscale. **Remarks:** Full-time maker since 1974. **Mark:** Hand engraved "Ed Lary" in script.

LAURENT, KERMIT
1812 Acadia Dr, LaPlace, LA 70068 **Contact:** 504-652-5629

Specialties: Traditional and working straight knives and folders of his design. **Patterns:** bowies, hunters, utilities and folders. **Technical:** Forges own damascus, plus uses most tool steels and stainless. Specializes in altering cable patterns. Uses stabilized handle materials, especially select exotic woods. **Prices:** $100 to $2500, some to $50,000. **Remarks:** Full-time maker, first knife sold in 1982. Doing business as Kermit's Knife Works. Favorite material is meteorite damascus. **Mark:** First name.

LAURENT, VERONIQUE
Avenue du Capricorne, 53, 1200 Brussels, BELGIUM **Contact:** 0032 477 48 66 73, whatsonthebench@gmail.com

Specialties: Fixed blades and friction folders. **Patterns:** bowies, camp knives, "ladies knives" and maker's own designs. **Technical:** Makes own san mai steel with the edges in blue paper steel and the sides in pure nickel and O2, called "Nickwich," meaning nickel in a sandwich. Makes own damascus, numerical milling embellishment, inlays and sheaths.

custom knifemakers

Prices: Start at $350. **Remarks:** Part-time knifemaker since 2005 and ABS journeyman smith since 2013.

LAWRENCE, ALTON
201 W Stillwell, De Queen, AR 71832 **Contact:** 870-642-7643, (fax) 870-642-4023, uncle21@riversidemachine.net, riversidemachine.net
Specialties: Classic straight knives and folders to customer specs. **Patterns:** bowies, hunters, folders and utility/camp knives. **Technical:** Forges 5160, 1095, 1084, damascus and railroad spikes. **Prices:** Start at $100. **Remarks:** Part-time maker, first knife sold in 1988. **Mark:** Last name inside fish symbol.

LAY, L J
602 Mimosa Dr, Burkburnett, TX 76354 **Contact:** 940-569-1329
Specialties: Working straight knives in standard patterns, some period pieces. **Patterns:** Drop-point hunters, bowies and fighters. **Technical:** Grinds ATS-34 to mirror finish, likes Micarta handles. **Prices:** Moderate. **Remarks:** Full-time maker, first knife sold in 1985. **Mark:** Name or name with ram head and city or stamp L J Lay.

LAY, R J (BOB)
333 Dutch Lake Road, Clearwater, BC, Canada V0E1N2 **Contact:** 250-674-2124, rjlay@telus.net
Specialties: Traditional-styled, fancy straight knifes of his design. Specializing in hunters. **Patterns:** bowies, fighters and hunters. **Technical:** Grinds high-performance stainless and tool steels. Uses exotic handle and spacer material. File cut, prefers narrow tang. Sheaths available. **Prices:** $200 to $500, some to $5000. **Remarks:** Full-time maker, first knife sold in 1976. Doing business as Lay's Custom Knives. **Mark:** Signature acid etched.

LEAVITT JR., EARL F
Pleasant Cove Rd Box 306, E. Boothbay, ME 04544 **Contact:** 207-633-3210
Specialties: 1500-1870 working straight knives and fighters, pole arms. **Patterns:** Historically significant knives, classic/modern custom designs. **Technical:** Flat-grinds O1, heat-treats. Filework available. **Prices:** $90 to $350, some to $1000. **Remarks:** Full-time maker, first knife sold in 1981. Doing business as Old Colony Manufactory. **Mark:** Initials in oval.

LEBATARD, PAUL M
14700 Old River Rd, Vancleave, MS 39565 **Contact:** 228-826-4137, (fax) Cell phone: 228-238-7461, lebatardknives@aol.com
Specialties: Sound working hunting and fillet knives, folding knives, practical tactical knives. **Patterns:** Hunters, trout and bird knives, fish fillet knives, kitchen knives, bowies, tactical sheath knives,one- and two-blade folders. **Technical:** Grinds ATS-34, D-2, CPM 3-V, CPM-154CM, and commercial damascus, forges and grinds 1095, O1, and 52100. **Prices:** $75 to $850, some to $1,200. **Remarks:** Full-time maker, first knife made in 1974. Charter member Gulf Coast Custom Knifemakers, Voting member Knifemaker's Guild. **Mark:** Stamped last name, or etched logo of last name, city, and state. **Other:** All knives are serial numbered and registered in the name of the original purchaser.

LEBER, HEINZ
Box 446, Hudson's Hope, BC, CANADA V0C 1V0 **Contact:** 250-783-5304
Specialties: Working straight knives of his design. **Patterns:** 20 models, from capers to bowies. **Technical:** Hollow-grinds D2 and M2 steel, mirror-finishes and full tang only. Likes moose, elk, stone sheep for handles. **Prices:** $175 to $1000. **Remarks:** Full-time maker, first knife sold in 1975. **Mark:** Initials connected.

LEBLANC, GARY E
1403 Fairview Ln., Little Falls, MN 56345 **Contact:** 320-232-0245, butternutcove@hotmail.com
Specialties: Hunting and fishing, some kitchen knives and the Air Assault tactical knife. Does own leather and Kydex work. **Patterns:** Stock removal. **Technical:** Mostly ATS34 for spec knives--orders, whatever the customer desires. **Prices:** Full range: $85 for parring knife, up $4000 plus fro collector grade hunter and fillet set. **Remarks:** First knife in 1998. **Mark:** Circular with star in center and LEBLANC on upper curve and KNIFEWORKS on lower curve.

LECK, DAL
Box 1054, Hayden, CO 81639 **Contact:** 970-276-3663
Specialties: Classic, traditional and working knives of his design and in standard patterns, period pieces. **Patterns:** Boots, daggers, fighters, hunters and push daggers. **Technical:** Forges O1 and 5160, makes his own damascus. **Prices:** $175 to $700, some to $1500. **Remarks:** Part-time maker, first knife sold in 1990. Doing business as The Moonlight Smithy. **Mark:** Stamped: hammer and anvil with initials.

LEE, ETHAN
9350 Highway 941, Gonzales, LA 70737 **Contact:** 573-682-4364, eleecustomknives@gmail.com, Facebook page ELEE Knives, Instagram @eleecustomknives.com
Specialties: Practical, usable, quality-crafted custom knives. **Technical:** Primarily damascus and hand-forged high-carbon steel, as well as 440C or 154CM stainless. **Prices:** $250-$1000. **Remarks:** Part-time knifemaker, first knife made in 2007. **Mark:** ELEE.

LEE, RANDY
PO Box 1873, St. Johns, AZ 85936 **Contact:** 928-337-2594, randylee.knives@yahoo.com, randyleeknives.com
Specialties: Traditional working and using straight knives of his design. **Patterns:** bowies, fighters, hunters, daggers. **Technical:** Grinds ATS-34, 440C damascus, and 154CPM. Offers sheaths. **Prices:** $325 to $2500. **Remarks:** Full-time maker, first knife sold in 1979. **Mark:** Full name, city, state.

LEEPER, DAN
10344 Carney Dr. SE, Olympia, WA 98501 **Contact:** 360-250-2130, leeperd@ymail.com, leeperknives.com
Specialties: Hunters, fighters, bowies and chef's knives. **Technical:** Forges 52100, W2, 1084 and 5160 blade steels. Stock removal using CPM 154 stainless and other modern alloy steels. Does own heat treating and leather work. **Prices:** Start at $200. **Remarks:** ABS member. **Mark:** Dan Leeper Olympia WA.

LELAND, STEVE
2300 Sir Francis Drake Blvd, Fairfax, CA 94930-1118 **Contact:** 415-457-0318, stephenleland@comcast.net
Specialties: Traditional and working straight knives and folders of his design. **Patterns:** Hunters, fighters, bowies, chefs. **Technical:** Grinds O1, ATS-34 and 440C. Does own heat treat. Makes nickel silver sheaths. **Prices:** $150 to $750, some to $1500. **Remarks:** Part-time maker, first knife sold in 1987. Doing business as Leland Handmade Knives. **Mark:** Last name.

LEMAIRE, RYAN M.
14045 Leon Rd., Abbeville, LA 70510 **Contact:** 337-893-1937, ryanlemaire@yahoo.com
Specialties: All styles. Enjoys early American and frontier styles. Also, office desk sets for hunters and fishermen. **Patterns:** Hunters, camp knives, miniatures and period styles. **Technical:** Stock removal, carbon steel, stainless steel and damascus. Some forging of guards. Leather and wooden sheaths. **Prices:** Vary. **Remarks:** Member of American Bladesmith Society and Louisiana Craft Guild. **Mark:** First name, city and state in oval.

LEMCKE, JIM L
10649 Haddington Ste 180, Houston, TX 77043 **Contact:** 888-461-8632, (fax) 713-461-8221, jimll@hal-pc.org, texasknife.com
Specialties: Large supply of custom ground and factory finished blades, knife kits, leather sheaths, in-house heat treating and cryogenic tempering, exotic handle material (wood, ivory, oosik, horn, stabilized woods), machines and supplies for knifemaking, polishing and finishing supplies, heat treat ovens, etching equipment, bar, sheet and rod material (brass, stainless steel, nickel silver), titanium sheet material. Catalog. $4.

LEMELIN, STEPHANIE
3495 Olivier St., Brossard, CANADA J4Y 2J9 **Contact:** 514-462-1322, stephlemelin@hotmail.com
Specialties: Art knives, mostly ornate. **Patterns:** Knives with sculptured or carved handles. Straight knives and folders. **Technical:** Grinds 440C, CPM 154 and ATS-34, all knives hand filed and flat ground. **Remarks:** Part-time maker, jeweler and knifemaker, first knife sold in 2013. **Mark:** Lemelin.

LEMOINE, DAVID C
239 County Rd. 637, Mountain Home, AR 72653 **Contact:** 870-656-4730, dlemoine@davidlemoineknives.com, davidlemoineknives.com
Specialties: Superior edge geometry on high performance custom classic and tactical straight blades and liner lock folders. **Patterns:** Hunters, skinners, bird and trout, fillet, camp, tactical, and military knives. Some miniatures. **Technical:** Flat and hollow grinds, CPMS90V, CPMS35V, CPMS30V, D2, A2, O1, 440C, ATS34, 154cm,Damasteel, Chad Nichols, Devin Thomas, and Robert Eggerling damascus. Hidden and full tapered tangs, ultra-smooth folding mechanisms. File work, will use most all handle materials, does own professional in-house heat treatment and Rockwell testing. Hot blueing. **Prices:** $250 and up. **Remarks:** Part-time maker, giving and selling knives since 1986. Each patron receives a NIV Sportsman's Field Bible. **Mark:** Name, city and state in full oval with cross in the center. Reverse image on other side. The cross never changes.

LENNON, DALE
459 County Rd 1554, Alba, TX 75410 **Contact:** 903-765-2392, devildaddy1@netzero.net
Specialties: Working / using knives. **Patterns:** Hunters, fighters and bowies. **Technical:** Grinds high carbon steel, ATS-34, forges some. **Prices:** Starts at $120. **Remarks:** Part-time maker, first knife sold in 2000. **Mark:** Last name.

LEONARD, RANDY JOE
188 Newton Rd, Sarepta, LA 71071 **Contact:** 318-994-2712

LEONE, NICK
9 Georgetown Dr, Pontoon Beach, IL 62040 **Contact:** 618-792-0734, nickleone@sbcglobal.net
Specialties: 18th century period straight knives. **Patterns:** Fighters, daggers, bowies. Besides period pieces makes modern designs. **Technical:** Forges 5160, W2, O1, 1098, 52100 and his own damascus. **Prices:** $100 to $1000, some to $3500. **Remarks:** Full-time maker, first knife sold in 1987. Doing business as Anvil Head Forge. **Mark:** AHF, Leone, NL

LERCH, MATTHEW
N88 W23462 North Lisbon Rd, Sussex, WI 53089 **Contact:** 262-246-6362, lerchcustomknives.com
Specialties: Folders and folders with special mechanisms. **Patterns:** Interframe and integral folders, lock backs, assisted openers, side locks, button locks and liner locks. **Technical:** Grinds ATS-34, 1095, 440 and damascus. Offers filework and embellished bolsters. **Prices:** $900 and up. **Remarks:** Full-time maker, first knife made in 1986. **Mark:** Last name.

LESSWING, KEVIN
29A East 34th St, Bayonne, NJ 07002 **Contact:** 551-221-1841, klesswing@excite.com
Specialties: Traditonal working and using straight knives of his design or to customer specs. A few folders. Makes own leather sheaths. **Patterns:** Hunters, daggers, bowies, bird and trout. **Technical:** Forges high carbon and tool steels, makes own damascus, grinds CPM154CM, Damasteel, and other stainless steels. Does own heat treating. **Remarks:** Voting member of Knifemakers Guild, part-time maker. **Mark:** KL on early

knives, LESSWING on Current knives.

LEU, POHAN
PO BOX 15423, Rio Rancho, NM 87174 **Contact:** 949-300-6412, pohanleu@hotmail.com leucustom.com
Specialties: Japanese influenced fixed blades made to your custom specifications. Knives and swords. A2 tool steel, Stock Removal. **Prices:** $180 and up. **Remarks:** Full-time, first knife sold in 2003. **Mark:** LEU or PL.

LEVENGOOD, BILL
15011 Otto Rd, Tampa, FL 33624 **Contact:** 813-961-5688, bill.levengood@verison.net, levengoodknives.com
Specialties: Working straight knives and folders. **Patterns:** Hunters, bowies, folders and collector pieces. **Technical:** Grinds ATS-34, S-30V, CPM-154 and damascus. **Prices:** $175 to $1500. **Remarks:** Full time maker, first knife sold in 1983. **Mark:** Last name, city, state.

LEVIN, JACK
201 Brighton 1st Road, Suite 3R, Brooklyn, NY 11235 **Contact:** 718-415-7911, jacklevin1@yahoo.com
Specialties: Folders with mechanisms.

LEVINE, BOB
101 Westwood Dr, Tullahoma, TN 37388 **Contact:** 931-454-9943, levineknives@msn.com
Specialties: Working left- and right-handed LinerLock® folders. **Patterns:** Hunters and folders. **Technical:** Grinds ATS-34, 440C, D2, O1 and some damascus, hollow and some flat grinds. Uses fossil ivory, Micarta and exotic woods. Provides custom leather sheath with each fixed knife. **Prices:** Starting at $135. **Remarks:** Full-time maker, first knife sold in 1974. Voting member Knifemakers Guild, German Messermaher Guild. **Mark:** Name and logo.

LEWIS, BILL
PO Box 63, Riverside, IA 52327 **Contact:** 319-461-1609, kalewis52@exede.net
Specialties: Folders of all kinds including those made from one-piece of white tail antler with or without the crown. **Patterns:** Hunters, folding hunters, fillet, bowies, push daggers, etc. **Prices:** $20 to $200. **Remarks:** Full-time maker, first knife sold in 1978. **Mark:** W.E.L.

LEWIS, MIKE
94134 Covey Ln., Coquille, OR 97423-6736 **Contact:** 386-753-0936, mikeswords@outlook.com
Specialties: Traditional straight knives. **Patterns:** Swords and daggers. **Technical:** Grinds 440C, ATS-34 and 5160. Frequently uses cast bronze and cast nickel guards and pommels. **Prices:** $100 to $750. **Remarks:** Part-time maker, first knife sold in 1988. **Mark:** Mike Lewis.

LEWIS, TOM R
1613 Standpipe Rd, Carlsbad, NM 88220 **Contact:** 575-885-3616, lewisknives@gmail.com
Specialties: Traditional working straight knives. **Patterns:** Outdoor knives, hunting knives and bowies. **Technical:** Grinds ATS-34 and CPM-154, forges 5168, W2, 1084 and O1. Makes wire, pattern welded and chainsaw damascus. **Prices:** $140 to $1500. **Remarks:** Full-time maker, first knife sold in 1980. Doing business as TR Lewis Handmade Knives. **Mark:** Lewis family crest.

LICATA, STEVEN
LICATA CUSTOM KNIVES, 146 Wilson St. 1st Floor, Boonton, NJ 07005 **Contact:** (973) 615-3227, kniveslicata@aol.com, licataknives.com
Specialties: Fantasy swords and knives. One-of-a-kind sculptures in steel. **Prices:** $200 to $25,000.

LIEBENBERG, ANDRE
8 Hilma Rd, Bordeaux, Randburg, GT, SOUTH AFRICA 2196 **Contact:** 011-787-2303
Specialties: High-art straight knives of his design. **Patterns:** Daggers, fighters and swords. **Technical:** Grinds 440C and 12C27. **Prices:** $250 to $500, some $4000 and higher. Giraffe bone handles with semi-precious stones. **Remarks:** Spare-time maker, first knife sold in 1990. **Mark:** Initials.

LIEGEY, KENNETH R
288 Carney Dr, Millwood, WV 25262 **Contact:** 304-273-9545
Specialties: Traditional working/using straight knives of his design and to customer specs. **Patterns:** Hunters, utility/camp knives, miniatures. **Technical:** Grinds 440C. **Prices:** $125 and up. **Remarks:** Spare-time maker, first knife sold in 1977. **Mark:** First and middle initials, last name.

LIGHTFOOT, GREG
RR #2, Kitscoty, AB, CANADA T0B 2P0 **Contact:** 780-846-2812, 780-800-1061, Pitbull@lightfootknives.com, lightfootknives.com
Specialties: Stainless steel and damascus. **Patterns:** Boots, fighters and locking folders. **Technical:** Grinds BG-42, 440C, D2, CPM steels, Stellite 6K. Offers engraving. **Prices:** $500 to $2000. **Remarks:** Full-time maker, first knife sold in 1988. Doing business as Lightfoot Knives. **Mark:** Shark with Lightfoot Knives below.

LIN, MARCUS
Mailboxes, etc. Avenida de Mijas, 14 (P-203), Fuengirola 29640, Malaga Province, Spain **Contact:** +1 (310) 720-4368, marcuslin7@gmail.com, linknives.com, Instagram @linknives
Specialties: All types of cutlery, both forged and stock removal, specializing in the Loveless tradition. **Patterns:** Actual patterns direct from the Loveless Shop. Mentored by both Bob Loveless and Jim Merritt. Maker's own designs on special request. **Technical:** Main blade material is RWL-34. Uses carbon and other stainless steels as well. Stellite 6K also available. **Prices:** $350 to several thousand depending on work involved. **Remarks:** Full time maker, first knife was made in 2004. **Mark:** Main logo is "Marcus Lin, maker, Loveless Design."

LINKLATER, STEVE
8 Cossar Dr, Aurora, ON, CANADA L4G 3N8 **Contact:** 905-727-8929, knifman@sympatico.ca
Specialties: Traditional working/using straight knives and folders of his design. **Patterns:** Fighters, hunters and locking folders. **Technical:** Grinds ATS-34, 440V and D2. **Prices:** $125 to $350, some to $600. **Remarks:** Part-time maker, first knife sold in 1987. Doing business as Links Knives. **Mark:** LINKS.

LISCH, DAVID K
16948 Longmire Rd., Yelm, WA 98597 **Contact:** 206-919-5431, davidlisch.com
Specialties: One-of-a-kind collectibles, straight knives and custom kitchen knives of own design and to customer specs. **Patterns:** Hunters, bowies and fighters. **Technical:** Forges all his own damascus under 360-pound air hammer. Forges and chisels wrought iron, pure iron, and bronze butt caps. **Prices:** Starting at $1,000. **Remarks:** Full-time blacksmith, part-time bladesmith. **Mark:** D. Lisch M.S.

LISTER JR., WELDON E
116 Juniper Ln, Boerne, TX 78006 **Contact:** 210-269-0102, wlister@grtc.com, weldonlister.com
Specialties: One-of-a-kind fancy and embellished folders. **Patterns:** Locking and slip-joint folders. **Technical:** Commercial damascus and O1. All knives embellished. Engraves, inlays, carves and scrimshaws. **Prices:** Upscale. **Remarks:** Spare-time maker, first knife sold in 1991. **Mark:** Last name.

LITTLE, GARY M
94716 Conklin Meadows Ln, PO Box 156, Broadbent, OR 97414 **Contact:** 503-572-2656
Specialties: Fancy working knives. **Patterns:** Hunters, tantos, bowies, axes and buckskinners, locking folders and interframes. **Technical:** Forges and grinds O1, L6m, 1095, and 15N20, makes his own damascus, bronze fittings. **Prices:** $120 to $1500. **Remarks:** Full-time maker, first knife sold in 1979. Doing business as Conklin Meadows Forge. **Mark:** Name, city and state.

LITTLE, LARRY
1A Cranberry Ln, Spencer, MA 01562 **Contact:** 508-885-2301, littcran@aol.com
Specialties: Working straight knives of his design or to customer specs. Likes Scagel-style. **Patterns:** Hunters, fighters, bowies, folders. **Technical:** Grinds and forges L6, O1, 5160, 1095, 1080. Prefers natural handle material especially antler. Uses nickel silver. Makes own heavy duty leather sheath. **Prices:** Start at $125. **Remarks:** Part-time maker. First knife sold in 1985. Offers knife repairs. **Mark:** Little on one side, LL brand on the other.

LIVESAY, NEWT
3306 S. Dogwood St, Siloam Springs, AR 72761 **Contact:** 479-549-3356, (fax) 479-549-3357, newt@newtlivesay.com, newtlivesay.com
Specialties: Combat utility knives, hunting knives, titanium knives, swords, axes, KYDWX sheaths for knives and pistols, custom orders.

LIVINGSTON, ROBERT C
PO Box 6, Murphy, NC 28906 **Contact:** 704-837-4155
Specialties: Art letter openers to working straight knives. **Patterns:** Minis to machetes. **Technical:** Forges and grinds most steels. **Prices:** Start at $20. **Remarks:** Full-time maker, first knife sold in 1988. Doing business as Mystik Knifeworks. **Mark:** MYSTIK.

LOCKETT, LOWELL C.
LC Lockett. 344 Spring Hill Dr., Canton, GA 30115 **Contact:** 770-846-8114, lcl1932@gmail.com
Technical: Forges 5160, 1095 and other blade steels, and uses desert ironwood, ivory and other handle materials. **Prices:** $150 to $1,500. **Remarks:** ABS journeyman smith.

LOCKETT, STERLING
527 E Amherst Dr, Burbank, CA 91504 **Contact:** 818-846-5799
Specialties: Working straight knives and folders to customer specs. **Patterns:** Hunters and fighters. **Technical:** Grinds. **Prices:** Moderate. **Remarks:** Spare-time maker. **Mark:** Name, city with hearts.

LOERCHNER, WOLFGANG
WOLFE FINE KNIVES, PO Box 255, Bayfield, ON, CANADA N0M 1G0 **Contact:** 519-565-2196
Specialties: Traditional straight knives, mostly ornate. **Patterns:** Small swords, daggers and stilettos, locking folders and miniatures. **Technical:** Grinds D2, 440C and 154CM, all knives hand-filed and flat-ground. **Prices:** Vary. **Remarks:** Full-time maker, first knife sold in 1983. Doing business as Wolfe Fine Knives. **Mark:** WOLFE.

LOGAN, IRON JOHN
4260 Covert, Leslie, MI 49251, ironjohnlogan@gmail.com, ironjohnlogan.com
Patterns: Hunting, camping, outdoor sheath knives, folding knives, axes, tomahawks, historical knives. swords, working chef's knives, and woodwork and leather work knives. **Technical:** Forges low-alloy steels, wrought iron, bloom and hearth materials, or high-alloy steel as the job insists. Makes own damascus and San Mai seel, modern materials and stainlesses. Vegetable-tanned leather sheaths, and American hardwood handles like hickory, walnut and cherry. **Prices:** $200 to $2,000. **Remarks:** Full-time bladesmith, first knife made in 1998. **Mark:** Two horizontal lines crossed by one vertical line and an angle off the bottom to creat a "J."

custom knifemakers

LONEWOLF, J AGUIRRE
481 Hwy 105, Demorest, GA 30535 **Contact:** 706-754-4660, (fax) 706-754-8470, lonewolfandsons@windstream.net, knivesbylonewolf.com eagleswinggallery.com
Specialties: High-art working and using straight knives of his design. **Patterns:** bowies, hunters, utility/camp knives and fine steel blades. **Technical:** Forges damascus and high-carbon steel. Most knives have hand-carved moose antler handles. **Prices:** $55 to $500, some to $2000. **Remarks:** Full-time maker, first knife sold in 1980. Doing business as Lonewolf and Sons LLC. **Mark:** Signature. Previous: Stamp.

LONG, GLENN A
10090 SW 186th Ave, Dunnellon, FL 34432 **Contact:** 352-489-4272, galong99@att.net
Specialties: Classic working and using straight knives of his design and to customer specs. **Patterns:** Hunters, bowies, utility. **Technical:** Grinds 440C D2 and 440V. **Prices:** $85 to $300, some to $800. **Remarks:** Part-time maker, first knife sold in 1990. **Mark:** Last name inside diamond.

LONGWORTH, DAVE
1200 Red Oak Ridge, Felicity, OH 45120 **Contact:** 513-876-2372
Specialties: High-tech working knives. **Patterns:** Locking folders, hunters, fighters and elaborate daggers. **Technical:** Grinds O1, ATS-34, 440C, buys damascus. **Prices:** $125 to $600, some higher. **Remarks:** Part-time maker, first knife sold in 1980. **Mark:** Last name.

LOOS, HENRY C
210 Ingraham, New Hyde Park, NY 11040 **Contact:** 516-354-1943, hcloos@optonline.net
Specialties: Miniature fancy knives and period pieces of his design. **Patterns:** bowies, daggers and swords. **Technical:** Grinds O1 and 440C. Uses sterling, 18K, rubies and emeralds. All knives come with handmade hardwood cases. **Prices:** $90 to $195, some to $250. **Remarks:** Spare-time maker, first knife sold in 1990. **Mark:** Script last initial.

LOUKIDES, DAVID E
76 Crescent Circle, Cheshire, CT 06410 **Contact:** 203-271-3023, Loussharp1@sbcglobal.net, prayerknives.com
Specialties: Hand forged working blades and collectible pieces. **Patterns:** Chef knives, bowies, and hunting knives. . **Technical:** Uses 1084, 1095, 5160, W2, O1 and 1084-and-15N20 damascus. **Prices:** Normally $200 to $1,000. **Remarks:** part-time maker, Journeyman Bladesmith, Full-time Journeyman Toolmaker. **Mark:** Loukides JS.

LOVE, ED
19443 Mill Oak, San Antonio, TX 78258 **Contact:** 210-497-1021, (fax) 210-497-1021, annaedlove@sbcglobal.net
Specialties: Hunting, working knives and some art pieces. **Technical:** Grinds ATS-34, and 440C. **Prices:** $150 and up. **Remarks:** Part-time maker. First knife sold in 1980. **Mark:** Name in a weeping heart.

LOVESTRAND, SCHUYLER
1136 19th St SW, Vero Beach, FL 32962 **Contact:** 772-778-0282, (fax) 772-466-1126, lovestranded@aol.com
Specialties: Fancy working straight knives of his design and to customer specs, unusual fossil ivories. **Patterns:** Hunters, fighters, bowies and fishing knives. **Technical:** Grinds stainless steel. **Prices:** $550 to $2,500. **Remarks:** Part-time maker, first knife sold in 1982. **Mark:** Name in logo.

LOVETT, MICHAEL
PO Box 121, Mound, TX 76558 **Contact:** 254-865-9956, michaellovett@embarqmail.com
Specialties: The Loveless Connection Knives as per R.W. Loveless-Jim Merritt. **Patterns:** All Loveless Patterns and Original Lovett Patterns. **Technical:** Complicated double grinds and premium fit and finish. **Prices:** $1000 and up. **Remarks:** High degree of fit and finish - Authorized collection by R. W. Loveless **Mark:** Loveless Authorized football or double nude.

LOZIER, DON
5394 SE 168th Ave, Ocklawaha, FL 32179 **Contact:** 352-625-3576
Specialties: Tactical folders, collaborative art pieces and sole authorship fixed blades. **Patterns:** Various. **Technical:** Grinds CPM 154, 440C and stainless damascus. **Prices:** $350 to $15,000. **Remarks:** Full-time maker and dealer. **Mark:** Name or DLFF.

LUCHAK, BOB
15705 Woodforest Blvd, Channelview, TX 77530 **Contact:** 281-452-1779
Specialties: Presentation knives, start of The Survivor series. **Patterns:** Skinners, bowies, camp axes, steak knife sets and fillet knives. **Technical:** Grinds 440C. Offers electronic etching, filework. **Prices:** $50 to $1500. **Remarks:** Full-time maker, first knife sold in 1983. Doing business as Teddybear Knives. **Mark:** Full name, city and state with Teddybear logo.

LUCHINI, BOB
1220 Dana Ave, Palo Alto, CA 94301 **Contact:** 650-321-8095, rwluchin@bechtel.com

LUCKETT, BILL
108 Amantes Ln, Weatherford, TX 76088 **Contact:** 817-320-1568, luckettknives@gmail.com billluckettcustomknives.com
Specialties: Uniquely patterned robust straight knives. **Patterns:** Fighters, bowies, hunters. **Technical:** 154CM stainless.**Prices:** $550 to $1500. **Remarks:** Part-time maker, first knife sold in 1975. Knifemakers Guild Member. **Mark:** Last name over bowie logo.

LUDWIG, RICHARD O
57-63 65 St, Maspeth, NY 11378 **Contact:** 718-497-5969
Specialties: Traditional working/using knives. **Patterns:** Boots, hunters and utility/camp knives folders. **Technical:** Grinds 440C, ATS-34 and BG42. File work on guards and handles, silver spacers. Offers scrimshaw. **Prices:** $325 to $400, some to $2000. **Remarks:** Full-time maker. **Mark:** Stamped first initial, last name, state.

LUI, RONALD M
4042 Harding Ave, Honolulu, HI 96816 **Contact:** 808-734-7746
Specialties: Working straight knives and folders in standard patterns. **Patterns:** Hunters, boots and liner locks. **Technical:** Grinds 440C and ATS-34. **Prices:** $100 to $700. **Remarks:** Spare-time maker, first knife sold in 1988. **Mark:** Initials connected.

LUNDSTROM, JAN-AKE
Mastmostigen 8, Dals-Langed, SWEDEN 66010 **Contact:** 0531-40270
Specialties: Viking swords, axes and knives in cooperation with handle makers. **Patterns:** All traditional-styles, especially swords and inlaid blades. **Technical:** Forges his own damascus and laminated steel. **Prices:** $200 to $1000. **Remarks:** Full-time maker, first knife sold in 1985, collaborates with museums. **Mark:** Runic.

LUNDSTROM, TORBJORN (TOBBE)
Knivmakaren i Åre. Norrskenet 4, Are, SWEDEN 83013, 9lundstrm@telia.com, http://tobbeiare.se/site/
Specialties: Hunters and collectible knives. **Patterns:** Nordic-style hunters and art knives with unique materials such as mammoth and fossil walrus ivory. **Technical:** Uses forged blades by other makers, particularly Mattias Styrefors who mostly uses 15N20 and 20C steels and is a mosaic blacksmith. **Remarks:** First knife made in 1986.

LUNN, GAIL
Gassville, AR 72635 **Contact:** 870-471-0131, gail@lunnknives.com, lunnknives.com
Specialties: Fancy folders and double action autos, some straight blades. **Patterns:** One-of-a-kind, all types. **Technical:** Stock removal, hand made. **Prices:** $300 and up. **Remarks:** Fancy file work, exotic materials, inlays, stone etc. **Mark:** Name in script.

LUNN, LARRY A
434 CR 1422, Mountain Home, AR 72653 **Contact:** 870-424-2662, larry@lunnknives.com, lunnknives.com
Specialties: Fancy folders and double action autos, some straight blades. **Patterns:** All types, his own designs. **Technical:** Stock removal, commercial damascus. **Prices:** $125 and up. **Remarks:** File work inlays and exotic materials. **Mark:** Name in script.

LUPOLE, JAMIE G
KUMA KNIVES, 285 Main St., Kirkwood, NY 13795 **Contact:** 607-775-9368, jlupole@stny.rr.com
Specialties: One-off working and collector grade fixed blades, ethnic-styled blades. **Patterns:** Fighters, bowies, tacticals, hunters, camp, utility, personal carry knives, some swords. **Technical:** Forges and grinds 10XX series and other high-carbon steels, grinds ATS-34 and 440C, will use just about every handle material available. Almost every aspect done in-house. **Prices:** $125 to $800 and up. **Remarks:** Part-time maker since 1999. **Mark:** "KUMA" etched and hot stamped, or name, city, state etched, or "Daiguma saku" in kanji.

LURQUIN, SAMUEL
Hameau Du Bois, Hoyaux 10, 7133 Buvrinnes Belgique, Binches, BELGIUM **Contact:** 0032-478-349-051, knifespirit@hotmail.com, samuel-lurquin.com
Specialties: Forged bowies, fighters, hunters and working knives. **Technical:** Uses, but is not limited to, W1, W2 and L6 blade steels, creates own pattern-welded steel. Commonly uses wood, walrus ivory, mammoth ivory and stag for handles. **Prices:** $500 and up. **Remarks:** Full-time maker beginning in 2014, ABS master smith as of 2015.

LUTZ, GREG
127 Crescent Rd, Greenwood, SC 29646 **Contact:** 864-229-7340
Specialties: Working and using knives and period pieces of his design and to customer specs. **Patterns:** Fighters, hunters and swords. **Technical:** Forges 1095 and O1, grinds ATS-34. Differentially heat-treats forged blades, uses cryogenic treatment on ATS-34. **Prices:** $50 to $350, some to $1200. **Remarks:** Part-time maker, first knife sold in 1986. Doing business as Scorpion Forge. **Mark:** First initial, last name.

LYLE III, ERNEST L
LYLE KNIVES, PO Box 1755, Chiefland, FL 32644 **Contact:** 352-490-6693, ernestlyle@msn.com
Specialties: Fancy period pieces, one-of-a-kind and limited editions. **Patterns:** Arabian/Persian influenced fighters, military knives, bowies and Roman short swords, several styles of hunters. **Technical:** Grinds 440C, D2 and 154 CM. Engraves. **Prices:** $200 - $7500. **Remarks:** Full-time maker, first knife sold in 1972. **Mark:** Lyle Knives over Chiefland, Fla.

LYNCH, TAD
140 Timberline Dr., Beebe, AR 72012 **Contact:** 501-626-1647, lynchknives@yahoo.com, lynchknives.com
Specialties: Forged fixed blades. **Patterns:** bowies, choppers, fighters, hunters. **Technical:** Hand-forged W-2, 1084, 1095 clay quenched 52100, 5160. **Prices:** Starting at $250. **Remarks:** Part-time maker, also offers custom leather work via wife Amy Lynch. **Mark:** T.D. Lynch over anvil.

LYNN, ARTHUR
29 Camino San Cristobal, Galisteo, NM 87540 **Contact:** 505-466-3541, amyandarthur@aol.com
Specialties: Handforged damascus knives. **Patterns:** Folders, hunters, bowies, fighters, kitchen. **Technical:** Forges own damascus. **Prices:** Moderate.

LYONS, WILLIAM R. (BILL)
7287 Ave. 354, Palisade, NE 69040 **Contact:** 970-219-1600, wrlyons@lyonsknives.com, lyonsknives.com

244 DIRECTORY

KNIVES 2021

Specialties: Scrimshaw, ivory inlay, silver wire inlay, hand-carved wood handles and leather handles. **Patterns:** Fighters, bowies, camp knives, integrals, and Moran and Scagel styles. **Technical:** Heat treating to very precise levels, makes own damascus and forges O1, O6, W2, 5160, 1084, 1095, 15N20 and L6. **Prices:** $250 to $3,000. **Remarks:** Full-time maker, member of ABS since 1990. Antique reproductions, all natural handle material, leather sheaths. **Mark:** LYONS.

M

MACCAUGHTRY, SCOTT F.
Fullerton Forge, 1824 Sorrel St, Camarillo, CA 93010 **Contact:** 805-750-2137, smack308@hotmail.com
Specialties: Fixed blades and folders. **Technical:** Forges 5160, 52100, W2 and his own damascus using 1084 and 15N20 steels. **Prices:** $275 and up. **Remarks:** ABS journeyman smith. **Mark:** S. MacCaughtry in script, and J.S. on the back side.

MACDONALD, DAVID
2824 Hwy 47, Los Lunas, NM 87031 **Contact:** 505-866-5866

MACKIE, JOHN
13653 Lanning, Whittier, CA 90605 **Contact:** 562-945-6104
Specialties: Forged. **Patterns:** bowie and camp knives. **Technical:** Attended ABS Bladesmith School. **Prices:** $75 to $500. **Mark:** Oval JOHN MACKIE over FORGED with an anvil and thistle in the middle.

MACKRILL, STEPHEN
PO Box 1580, Pinegowrie, Johannesburg, GT, SOUTH AFRICA 2123 **Contact:** 087 808 3968, 27 82 850 7046 (cell), 27-11-474-7139 (fax), info@mackrill.co.za, mackrill.co.za
Specialties: Art fancy, historical, collectors and corporate gifts cutlery. **Patterns:** Fighters, hunters, camp, custom lock back and LinerLock® folders. **Technical:** N690, 12C27, ATS-34, silver and gold inlay on handles, wooden and silver sheaths. **Prices:** $330 and upwards. **Remarks:** First knife sold in 1978. Full time maker since 1991. Doing business as Mackrill Custom Knives. All knives handmade by the maker. **Mark:** Mackrill fish with country of origin.

MADRULLI, MME JOELLE
Residence Ste Catherine B1, Salon De Provence, FRANCE 13330

MAESTRI, PETER A
S11251 Fairview Rd, Spring Green, WI 53588 **Contact:** 608-546-4481
Specialties: Working straight knives in standard patterns. **Patterns:** Camp and fishing knives, utility green-river-styled. **Technical:** Grinds 440C, 154CM and 440A. **Prices:** $15 to $45, some to $150. **Remarks:** Full-time maker, first knife sold in 1981. Provides professional cutler service to professional cutters. **Mark:** CARISOLO, MAESTRI BROS., or signature.

MAGEE, JIM
741 S. Ohio St., Salina, KS 67401 **Contact:** 785-820-6928, jimmagee@cox.net
Specialties: Working and fancy folding knives. **Patterns:** Liner locking folders, favorite is his Persian. **Technical:** Grinds ATS-34, Devin Thomas & Eggerling damascus, titanium. Liners Prefer mother-of-pearl handles. **Prices:** Start at $225 to $1200. **Remarks:** Part-time maker, first knife sold in 2001. Purveyor since 1982. Past president of the Professional Knifemakers Association **Mark:** Last name.

MAGRUDER, JASON
Cromulent Knife Co. Kent, Washington 98031 **Contact:** 719-210-1579, CromulentKnifeCo@Gmail.com, CromulentKnifeCo.com
Specialties: Unique and innovative designs made to be used hard and appreciated down to the finest detail. Mid-tech through full customs combining modern production methods with hand craftsmanship using the best available materials. **Patterns:** Fancy neck knives, lightweight flipper folders, mid-sized working knives. **Technical:** CNC machined handles and inlays from titanium, carbon fiber, micarta, mother of pearl, and exotic woods. Flat ground CPM3v, S35vn, AEB-L, M390 and stainless damascus blades. **Prices:** $150 and up. **Remarks:** Full-time maker. First knife sold in 2000. **Mark:** Angry robot engraved on knives made using CNC. Last name only on fully handmade knives.

MAHOMEDY, A R
PO Box 76280, Marble Ray, KZN, SOUTH AFRICA 4035 **Contact:** +27 31 577 1451, arm-koknives@mweb.co.za, arm-koknives.co.za
Specialties: Daggers and elegant folders of own design finished with finest exotic materials currently available. **Technical:** Via stock removal, grinds Damasteel, damascus and the famous hardenable stainless steels. **Prices:** U.S. $650 and up. **Remarks:** Part-time maker. First knife sold in 1995. Voting member knifemakers guild of SA, FEGA member starting out Engraving. **Mark:** Initials A R M crowned with a "Minaret."

MAHOMEDY, HUMAYD A.R.
PO BOX 76280, Marble Ray, KZN, SOUTH AFRICA 4035 **Contact:** +27 31 577 1451, arm-koknives@mweb.co.za
Specialties: Tactical folding and fixed blade knives. **Patterns:** Fighters, utilities, tacticals, folders and fixed blades, daggers, modern interpretation of bowies. **Technical:** Stock-removal knives of Bohler N690, Bohler K110, Bohler K460, Sandvik 12C27, Sandvik RWL 34. Handle materials used are G10, Micarta, Cape Buffalo horn, Water Buffalo horn, Kudu horn, Gemsbok horn, Giraffe bone, Elephant ivory, Mammoth ivory, Arizona desert ironwood, stabilised and dyed burls. **Prices:** $250 - $1000. **Remarks:** First knife sold in 2002. Full-time knifemaker since 2002. First person of color making knives full-time in South Africa. Doing business as HARM EDGED TOOLS. **Mark:** HARM and arrow over EDGED TOOLS.

MAIENKNECHT, STANLEY
38648 S R 800, Sardis, OH 43946

MAINES, JAY
SUNRISE RIVER CUSTOM KNIVES, 5584 266th St., Wyoming, MN 55092 **Contact:** 651-462-5301, jaymaines@fronternet.net, sunrisecustomknives.com
Specialties: Heavy duty working, classic and traditional fixed blades. Some high-tech and fancy embellished knives available. **Patterns:** Hunters, including wild boar hunting knives and spears, skinners, fillet knives, bowies tantos, boot daggers, barbecue implements and cutlery sets. **Technical:** Hollow ground, stock removal blades of 440C, ATS-34 and CPM S-90V. Prefers natural handle materials, exotic hard woods, and stag, rams and buffalo horns. Offers dovetailed bolsters in brass, stainless steel and nickel silver. Custom sheaths from matching wood or hand-stitched from heavy duty water buffalo hide. **Prices:** Moderate to up-scale. **Remarks:** Part-time maker, first knife sold in 1992. Doing business as Sunrise River Custom Knives. Offers fixed blade knife repair and handle conversions, and custom leather sheaths. **Mark:** Full name under a Rising Sun logo.

MAINOLFI, DR. RICCARDO
Via Pastiniello, 6-84017, Positano (SA), ITALY **Contact:** +39 3338128775 OR +39 3493586416, riccardomainolfi@gmail.com, mainolfiknife.com, Instagram @ riccardomainolfi, Facebook @ Riccardo Mainolfi
Specialties: Handmade hunting and tactical knives, as well as art knives and collaborative pieces with famous engravers. **Technical:** Stock removal method of blade making using RWL-34, CPM 154 and CPM S30V, CPM S35V and damascus steel. Heat treats own blades in furnace with electronically controlled temperature. Uses AISI 416 and AISI 304 for bolsters and pins. **Patterns:** Hunters, fighters, boots. **Prices:** $200 and up. **Remarks:** Part-time maker, first knife sold in 2004. **Mark:** Stylized blade in which is written the maker's name, with the beautiful city in which he resides.

MAISEY, ALAN
PO Box 197, Vincentia, NSW, AUSTRALIA 2540 **Contact:** 2-4443 7829, tosanaji@excite.com
Specialties: Daggers, especially krisses, period pieces. **Technical:** Offers knives and finished blades in damascus and nickel damascus. **Prices:** $75 to $2000, some higher. **Remarks:** Part-time maker, provides complete restoration service for krisses. Trained by a Japanese Kris smith. **Mark:** None, triangle in a box, or three peaks.

MAJORS, CHARLIE
1911 King Richards Ct, Montgomery, TX 77316 **Contact:** 713-826-3135, charliemajors@sbcglobal.net
Specialties: Fixed-blade hunters and slip-joint and lock-back folders. **Technical:** Practices stock removal method, preferring CPM154 steel and natural handle materials such as ironwood, stag, and mammoth ivory. Also takes customer requests. Does own heat treating and cryogenic quenching. **Remarks:** First knife made in 1980.

MAKOTO, KUNITOMO
3-3-18 Imazu-cho, Fukuyama-city, Hiroshima, JAPAN **Contact:** 084-933-5874, kunitomo@po.iijnet.or.jp

MALABY, RAYMOND J
835 Calhoun Ave, Juneau, AK 99801 **Contact:** 907-586-6981, (fax) 907-523-8031, malaby@gci.net
Specialties: Straight working knives. **Patterns:** Hunters, skiners, bowies, and camp knives. **Technical:** Hand forged 1084, 5160, O1 and grinds ATS-34 stainless. **Prices:** $195 to $400. **Remarks:** First knife sold in 1994. **Mark:** First initial, last name, city, and state.

MALLOY, JOE
1039 Schwabe St, Freeland, PA 18224 **Contact:** 570-436-6416, jdmalloy@msn.com
Specialties: Working straight knives of his own design or to customers' specs. **Patterns:** Full-tang hunters, bird & trout knives, neck knives, folders (plain or fancy), fighters, camp knives, khukuris and tomahawks. DEA specs. Each knife comes with a custom leather or Kydex sheath. **Technical:** Hollow or flat grinds CPM 154, D2, A2, 440C and damascus. Titanium on fancy folders with multi-color anodizing and filework. **Prices:** $200 to $1,800. **Remarks:** Part-time maker, first knife sold in 1982. Voting member of the Knifemakers' Guild since 1990. **Mark:** First and middle initials and last name, city and state.

MANARO, SAL
10 Peri Ave., Holbrook, NY 11741 **Contact:** 631-737-1180, maker@manaroknives.com
Specialties: Tactical folders, bolstered titanium LinerLocks, handmade folders, and fixed blades with hand-checkered components. **Technical:** Compound grinds, hidden fasteners and welded components, with blade steels including CPM-154, damascus, Stellite, D2, S30V and O-1 by the stock-removal method of blade making. **Prices:** $500 and up. **Remarks:** Part-time maker, made first knife in 2001. **Mark:** Last name with arrowhead underline.

MANDT, JOE
3735 Overlook Dr. NE, St. Petersburg, FL 33703 **Contact:** 813-244-3816, jmforge@mac.com
Specialties: Forged bowies, camp knives, hunters, skinners, fighters, boot knives, military style field knives. **Technical:** Forges plain carbon steel and high carbon tool steels, including W2, 1084, 5160, O1, 9260, 15N20, cable damascus, pattern welded damascus, flat and convex grinds. Prefers natural handle materials, hand-rubbed finishes, and stainless low carbon steel, damascus and wright iron fittings. Does own heat treat. **Prices:** $150 to $750. **Remarks:** Part-time maker, first knife sold in 206. **Mark:** "MANDT".

custom knifemakers

MANEKER, KENNETH
RR 2, Galiano Island, BC, CANADA V0N 1P0 **Contact:** 604-539-2084
Specialties: Working straight knives, period pieces. **Patterns:** Camp knives and hunters, French chef knives. **Technical:** Grinds 440C, 154CM and Vascowear. **Prices:** $50 to $200, some to $300. **Remarks:** Part-time maker, first knife sold in 1981. Doing business as Water Mountain Knives. **Mark:** Japanese Kanji of initials, plus glyph.

MANLEY, DAVID W
3270 Six Mile Hwy, Central, SC 29630 **Contact:** 864-654-1125, dmanleyknives@bellsouth.net
Specialties: Working straight knives of his design or to custom specs. **Patterns:** Hunters, boot and fighters. **Technical:** Grinds 440C and ATS-34. **Prices:** $80 to $400. **Remarks:** Part-time maker, first knife sold in 1994. **Mark:** First initial, last name, year and serial number.

MANN, MICHAEL L
IDAHO KNIFE WORKS, PO Box 144, Spirit Lake, ID 83869 **Contact:** 509 994-9394, idahoknifeworks.com
Specialties: Good working blades, historical reproductions, modern or custom designs. **Patterns:** Cowboy bowies, mountain man period blades, old-style folders, designer and maker of "The Cliff Knife," hunting and fillet knives. **Technical:** Forges 5160 high-carbon steel blades. Stock removal of 15N20. **Prices:** $200 to $730. **Remarks:** Made first knife in 1965. Full-time making knives as Idaho Knife Works since 1989. Functional as well as collectible. Each knife is truly unique! **Mark:** Four mountain peaks are his initials MM.

MANN, TIM
BLADEWORKS, PO Box 1196, Honokaa, HI 96727 **Contact:** 808-775-0949, (fax) 808-775-0949, birdman@shaka.com
Specialties: Hand-forged knives and swords. **Patterns:** bowies, tantos, pesh kabz, daggers. **Technical:** Use 5160, 1050, 1075, 1095 and ATS-34 steels, cable damascus. **Prices:** $200 to $800. **Remarks:** Just learning to forge damascus. **Mark:** None yet.

MARAGNI, DAN
RD 1 Box 106, Georgetown, NY 13072 **Contact:** 315-662-7490
Specialties: Heavy-duty working knives, some investor class. **Patterns:** Hunters, fighters and camp knives, some Scottish types. **Technical:** Forges W2 and his own damascus, toughness and edge-holding a high priority. **Prices:** $125 to $500, some to $1000. **Remarks:** Full-time maker, first knife sold in 1975. **Mark:** Celtic initials in circle.

MARCHAND, RICK
Wildertools, 69 Maple Ave., POB 1635, Lunenburg, Nova Scotia, CANADA B0J 2C0 **Contact:** 226-783-8771, rickmarchand@wildertools.com, wildertools.com
Specialties: Specializing in multicultural, period stylized blades and accoutrements. **Technical:** Hand forged from 1070/84/95, L6 and 52100 steel. **Prices:** $175 - $1,500. **Remarks:** Maker since 2007. ABS apprentice smith. **Mark:** Tang stamp: "MARCHAND" along with two Japanese-style characters resembling "W" and "M."

MARINGER, TOM
2692 Powell St., Springdale, AR 72764, maringer@arkansas.net, shirepost.com/cutlery.
Specialties: Working straight and curved blades with stainless steel furniture and wire-wrapped handles. **Patterns:** Subhilts, daggers, boots, swords. **Technical:** Grinds D-2, A-2, ATS-34. May be safely disassembled by the owner via pommel screw or pegged construction. **Prices:** $2000 to $3000, some to $20,000. **Remarks:** Former full-time maker, now part-time. First knife sold in 1975. **Mark:** Full name, year, and serial number etched on tang under handle.

MARKLEY, KEN
7651 Cabin Creek Lane, Sparta, IL 62286 **Contact:** 618-443-5284
Specialties: Traditional working and using knives of his design and to customer specs. **Patterns:** Fighters, hunters and utility/camp knives. **Technical:** Forges 5160, 1095 and L6, makes his own damascus, does file work. **Prices:** $150 to $800, some to $2000. **Remarks:** Part-time maker, first knife sold in 1991. Doing business as Cabin Creek Forge. **Mark:** Last name, JS.

MARLOWE, CHARLES
10822 Poppleton Ave, Omaha, NE 68144 **Contact:** 402-933-5065, cmarlowe1@cox.net, marloweknives.com
Specialties: Folding knives and balisong. **Patterns:** Tactical pattern folders. **Technical:** Grind ATS-34, S30V, CPM154, 154CM, Damasteel, others on request. Forges/grinds 1095 on occasion. **Prices:** Start at $450. **Remarks:** First knife sold in 1993. Full-time since 1999. **Mark:** Turtle logo with Marlowe above, year below.

MARLOWE, DONALD
2554 Oakland Rd, Dover, PA 17315 **Contact:** 717-764-6055
Specialties: Working straight knives in standard patterns. **Patterns:** bowies, fighters, boots and utility knives. **Technical:** Grinds D2 and 440C. Integral design hunter models. **Prices:** $130 to $850. **Remarks:** Spare-time maker, first knife sold in 1977. **Mark:** Last name.

MARSH, JEREMY
6169 3 Mile NE, Ada, MI 49301 **Contact:** 616-889-1945, steelbean@hotmail.com, marshcustomknives.com
Specialties: Locking liner folders, dressed-up gents knives, tactical knives, and dress tacticals. **Technical:** CPM S30V stainless and damascus blade steels using the stock-removal method of bladesmithing. **Prices:** $450 to $1500. **Remarks:** Self-taught, part-time knifemaker, first knife sold in 2004. **Mark:** Maker's last name and large, stylized M.

MARSHALL, REX
1115 State Rte. 380, Wilmington, OH 45177 **Contact:** 937-604-8430, rexmarshall@hotmail.com, rexmarshallcustomknives.com
Specialties: Handforged fixed-blade traditional hunters, bowies and fighters. **Technical:** Forges and stock removal, using 5160, 1080, 1095 and 52100 high carbon steels, with stainless steels on request. Will custom build to customer's specifications. **Prices:** $125 and up. **Remarks:** Offers custom plain and lined sheaths, decorative filework. First knife made in 2011. **Mark:** Rex Marshall over eagle.

MARTIN, CORY
4249 Taylor Harbor #7, Racine, WI 53403 **Contact:** 262-352-5392, info@corymartinimaging.com, corymartinimaging.com, Facebook: Cory Martin Imaging, Instagram: corymartinimaging
Specialties: Unique high-tech folders using a wide variety of materials. CNC skills used to create inlays, textures and patterns. **Technical:** Forges own damascus as well as his own unique "reverse san mai damascus." **Prices:** Moderate. **Remarks:** Part-time maker and son of Peter Martin, Cory is establishing his own unique style with creative designs and unmatched fit and finish. **Mark:** "CMD" and "C. Martin."

MARTIN, GENE
PO Box 396, Williams, OR 97544 **Contact:** 541-846-6755, bladesmith@customknife.com
Specialties: Straight knives and folders. **Patterns:** Fighters, hunters, skinners, boot knives, spring back and lock back folders. **Technical:** Grinds ATS34, 154CM, S30V, S35V, O-1, D2, 1095, 8670. Forges, makes own damascus. Scrimshaws. **Prices:** $250 to $2500. **Remarks:** Full-time maker, first knife sold in 1993. Doing business as Provision Forge. **Mark:** Name, TGBTG or name with Latin inscription. Previous: Name and/or crossed staff and sword.

MARTIN, HAL W
781 Hwy 95, Morrilton, AR 72110 **Contact:** 501-354-1682, hal.martin@sbcglobal.net
Specialties: Hunters, bowies and fighters. **Prices:** $250 and up. **Mark:** MARTIN.

MARTIN, HERB
2500 Starwood Dr, Richmond, VA 23229 **Contact:** 804-747-1675, hamjlm@hotmail.com
Specialties: Working straight knives. **Patterns:** Skinners, hunters and utility. **Technical:** Hollow grinds ATS-34, and Micarta handles. **Prices:** $125 to $200. **Remarks:** Part-time Maker. First knife sold in 2001. **Mark:** HA MARTIN.

MARTIN, MICHAEL W
Box 572, Jefferson St, Beckville, TX 75631 **Contact:** 903-678-2161
Specialties: Classic working/using straight knives of his design and in standard patterns. **Patterns:** Hunters. **Technical:** Grinds ATS-34, 440C, O1 and A2. Bead blasted, Parkerized, high polish and satin finishes. Sheaths are handmade. Also hand forges cable damascus. **Prices:** $185 to $280 some higher. **Remarks:** Part-time maker, first knife sold in 1995. Doing business as Michael W. Martin Knives. **Mark:** Name and city, state in arch.

MARTIN, PETER
28220 N. Lake Dr, Waterford, WI 53185 **Contact:** 262-706-3076, petermartinknives.com
Specialties: Fancy, fantasy and working straight knives and folders of his design and in standard patterns. **Patterns:** bowies, fighters, hunters, locking folders and liner locks. **Technical:** Forges own Mosaic damascus, powdered steel and his own damascus. Prefers natural handle material, offers file work and carved handles. **Prices:** Moderate. **Remarks:** Full-time maker, first knife sold in 1988. Doing business as Martin Custom Products. **Mark:** Martin Knives.

MARTIN, RANDALL J
51 Bramblewood St, Bridgewater, MA 02324 **Contact:** 508-279-0682
Specialties: High tech folding and fixed blade tactical knives employing the latest blade steels and exotic materials. Employs a unique combination of 3d-CNC machining and hand work on both blades and handles. All knives are designed for hard use. Clean, radical grinds and ergonomic handles are hallmarks of RJ's work, as is his reputation for producing "Scary Sharp" knives. **Technical:** Grinds CPM30V, CPM 3V, CPM154CM, A2 and stainless damascus. Other CPM alloys used on request. Performs all heat treating and cryogenic processing in-house. **Remarks:** Full-time maker since 2001 and materials engineer. Former helicopter designer. First knife sold in 1976.

MARTIN, TONY
PO Box 10, Arcadia, MO 63621 **Contact:** 573-546-2254, arcadian@charter.net, arcadianforge.com
Specialties: Specializes in historical designs, esp. puukko, skean dhu. **Remarks:** Premium quality blades, exotic wood handles, unmatched fit and finish. **Mark:** AF.

MARTIN, JOHN ALEXANDER
821 N Grand Ave, Okmulgee, OK 74447 **Contact:** 918-758-1099, jam@jamblades.com, jamblades.com
Specialties: Inlaid and engraved handles. **Patterns:** bowies, fighters, hunters and traditional patterns. Swords, fixed blade knives, folders and axes. **Technical:** Forges 5160, 1084, 10XX, O1, L6 and his own damascus. **Prices:** Start at $300. **Remarks:** Part-time maker. **Mark:** Two initials with last name and MS or 5 pointed star.

MARZITELLI, PETER
19929 35A Ave, Langley, BC, CANADA V3A 2R1 **Contact:** 604-532-8899, info@marzknives.com, marzknives.com
Specialties: Specializes in unique functional knife shapes and designs using natural and synthetic handle materials. **Patterns:** Fixed blades: hunting, tactical, utility and art knives. **Technical:** Grinds 154CM, CPM steels, damascus and more. **Prices:** $220 to $1000 (average $375). **Remarks:** Full-time maker, first knife sold in 1984. **Mark:** Stylized logo reads "Marz."

MASON, BILL
9306 S.E. Venns St., Hobe Sound, FL 33455 **Contact:** 772-545-3649
Specialties: Combat knives, some folders. **Patterns:** Fighters to match knife types in book Cold Steel. **Technical:** Grinds O1, 440C and ATS-34. **Prices:** $115 to $250, some to $350. **Remarks:** Spare-time maker, first knife sold in 1979. **Mark:** Initials connected.

MASSEY, AL
26 Lake Drive, Mount Uniacke, NS, CANADA B0N 1Z0 **Contact:** 902-866-4754, armjan@eastlink.ca
Specialties: Working knives and period pieces. **Patterns:** Swords and daggers of Celtic to medieval design, bowies. **Technical:** Forges 5160, 1084 and 1095. Makes own damascus. **Prices:** $200 to $500, damascus $300-$1000. **Remarks:** Part-time maker, first blade sold in 1988. **Mark:** Initials and JS on Ricasso.

MASSEY, ROGER
4928 Union Rd, Texarkana, AR 71854 **Contact:** 870-779-1018, rmassey668@aol.com
Specialties: Traditional and working straight knives and folders of his design and to customer specs. **Patterns:** bowies, hunters, daggers and utility knives. **Technical:** Forges 1084 and 52100, makes his own damascus. Offers filework and silver wire inlay in handles. **Prices:** $200 to $1500, some to $2500. **Remarks:** Part-time maker, first knife sold in 1991. **Mark:** Last name, M.S.

MASSEY, RON
61638 El Reposo St., Joshua Tree, CA 92252 **Contact:** 760-366-9239 after 5 p.m., (fax) 763-366-4620
Specialties: Classic, traditional, fancy/embellished, high art, period pieces, working/using knives, straight knives, folders, and automatics. Your design, customer specs, about 175 standard patterns. **Patterns:** Automatics, hunters and fighters. All folders are side-locking folders. Unless requested as lock books slip joint he specializes or custom designs. **Technical:** ATS-34, 440C, D-2 upon request. Engraving, filework, scrimshaw, most of the exotic handle materials. All aspects are performed by him: inlay work in pearls or stone, handmade Pem' work. **Prices:** $110 to $2500, some to $6000. **Remarks:** Part-time maker, first knife sold in 1976.

MATA, LEONARD
3583 Arruza St, San Diego, CA 92154 **Contact:** 619-690-6935

MATHEWS, CHARLIE AND HARRY
TWIN BLADES, 121 Mt Pisgah Church Rd., Statesboro, GA 30458 **Contact:** 912-865-9098, twinblades@bulloch.net, twinxblades.com
Specialties: Working straight knives, carved stag handles. **Patterns:** Hunters, fighters, bowies and period pieces. **Technical:** Grinds D2, CPM S30V, CPM 3V, ATS-34 and commercial damascus, handmade sheaths some with exotic leather, filework. **Prices:** Starting at $200. **Remarks:** Twin brothers making knives full-time under the label of Twin Blades. Charter members Georgia Custom Knifemakers Guild. Members of The Knifemakers Guild. Charlie is secretary/treasurer of the Knifemakers' Guild. **Mark:** Twin Blades over crossed knives, reverse side steel type.

MATSUNO, KANSEI
109-8 Uenomachi, Nishikaiden, Gifu-City, JAPAN 501-1168 **Contact:** 81 58 234 8643

MATSUOKA, SCOT
94-415 Ukalialii Place, Mililani, HI 96789 **Contact:** 808-625-6658, (fax) 808-625-6658, scottym@hawaii.rr.com, matsuokaknives.com
Specialties: Folders, fixed blades with custom hand-stitched sheaths. **Patterns:** Gentleman's knives, hunters, tactical folders. **Technical:** CPM 154CM, 440C, 154, BG42, bolsters, file work, and engraving. **Prices:** Starting price $350. **Remarks:** Part-time maker, first knife sold in 2002. **Mark:** Logo, name and state.

MATSUSAKI, TAKESHI
MATSUSAKI KNIVES, 151 Ono-Cho, Sasebo-shi, Nagasaki, JAPAN **Contact:** 0956-47-2938, (fax) 0956-47-2938
Specialties: Working and collector grade front look and slip joint. **Patterns:** Sheffierd type folders. **Technical:** Grinds ATS-34 k-120. **Prices:** $250 to $1000, some to $8000. **Remarks:** Part-time maker, first knife sold in 1990. **Mark:** Name and initials.

MAXEN, MICK
2 Huggins Welham Green, Hatfield, Herts, UNITED KINGDOM AL97LR **Contact:** 01707 261213, mmaxen@aol.com
Specialties: damascus and Mosaic. **Patterns:** Medieval-style daggers and bowies. **Technical:** Forges CS75 and 15N20 / nickel damascus. **Mark:** Last name with axe above.

MAXWELL, DON
1484 Celeste Ave, Clovis, CA 93611 **Contact:** 559-299-2197, maxwellknives@aol.com, maxwellknives.com
Specialties: Fancy folding knives and fixed blades of his design. **Patterns:** Hunters, fighters, utility/camp knives, LinerLock® folders, flippers and fantasy knives. **Technical:** Grinds 440C, ATS-34, D2, CPM 154, and commercial damascus. **Prices:** $250 to $1000, some to $2500. **Remarks:** Full-time maker, first knife sold in 1987. **Mark:** Last name only or Maxwell MAX-TAC.

MAY, CHARLES
10024 McDonald Rd., Aberdeen, MS 39730 **Contact:** 662-369-0404, charlesmayknives@yahoo.com, charlesmayknives.blademakers.com
Specialties: Fixed-blade sheath knives. **Patterns:** Hunters and fillet knives. **Technical:** Scandinavian-ground D2 and S30V blades, black micarta and wood handles, nickel steel pins with maker's own pocket carry or belt-loop pouches. **Prices:** $215 to $495. **Mark:** "Charles May Knives" and a knife in a circle.

MAYNARD, LARRY JOE
PO Box 493, Crab Orchard, WV 25827
Specialties: Fancy and fantasy straight knives. **Patterns:** Big knives, a bowie with a full false edge, fighting knives. **Technical:** Grinds standard steels. **Prices:** $350 to $500, some to $1000. **Remarks:** Full-time maker, first knife sold in 1986. **Mark:** Middle and last initials.

MAYNARD, WILLIAM N.
2677 John Smith Rd, Fayetteville, NC 28306 **Contact:** 910-425-1615
Specialties: Traditional and working straight knives of all designs. **Patterns:** Combat, bowies, fighters, hunters and utility knives. **Technical:** Grinds 440C, ATS-34 and commercial damascus. Offers fancy filework, handmade sheaths. **Prices:** $100 to $300, some to $750. **Remarks:** Full-time maker, first knife sold in 1988. **Mark:** Last name.

MAYO JR., HOMER
18036 Three Rivers Rd., Biloxi, MS 39532 **Contact:** 228-326-8298
Specialties: Traditional working straight knives, folders and tactical. **Patterns:** Hunters, fighters, tactical, bird, bowies, fish fillet knives and lightweight folders. **Technical:** Grinds 440C, ATS-34, D-2, damascus, forges and grinds 52100 and custom makes sheaths. **Prices:** $100 to $1000. **Remarks:** Part-time maker **Mark:** All knives are serial number and registered in the name of the original purchaser, stamped last name or etched.

MAYO JR., TOM
67 412 Alahaka St, Waialua, HI 96791 **Contact:** 808-637-6560, mayot001@hawaii.rr.com, mayoknives.com
Specialties: Framelocks/tactical knives. **Patterns:** Combat knives, hunters, bowies and folders. **Technical:** Titanium/stellite/S30V. **Prices:** $500 to $1000. **Remarks:** Full-time maker, first knife sold in 1982. **Mark:** Volcano logo with name and state.

MAYVILLE, OSCAR L
2130 E. County Rd 910S, Marengo, IN 47140 **Contact:** 812-338-4159
Specialties: Working straight knives, period pieces. **Patterns:** Kitchen cutlery, bowies, camp knives and hunters. **Technical:** Grinds A2, O1 and 440C. **Prices:** $50 to $350, some to $500. **Remarks:** Full-time maker, first knife sold in 1984. **Mark:** Initials over knife logo.

MCABEE, WILLIAM
27275 Norton Grade, Colfax, CA 95713 **Contact:** 530-389-8163
Specialties: Working/using knives. **Patterns:** Fighters, bowies, Hunters. **Technical:** Grinds ATS-34. **Prices:** $75 to $200, some to $350. **Remarks:** Part-time maker, first knife sold in 1990. **Mark:** Stylized WM stamped.

MCCALLEN JR., HOWARD H
110 Anchor Dr, So Seaside Park, NJ 08752

MCCARLEY, JOHN
4165 Harney Rd, Taneytown, MD 21787
Specialties: Working straight knives, period pieces. **Patterns:** Hunters, bowies, camp knives, miniatures, throwing knives. **Technical:** Forges W2, O1 and his own damascus. **Prices:** $150 to $300, some to $1000. **Remarks:** Part-time maker, first knife sold in 1977. **Mark:** Initials in script.

MCCARTY, HARRY
1479 Indian Ridge Rd, Blaine, TN 37709, harrymccarty1757@att.net
Specialties: Period pieces. **Patterns:** Trade knives, bowies, 18th and 19th century folders and hunting swords. **Technical:** Forges and grinds high-carbon steel. **Prices:** $75 to $1300. **Remarks:** Full-time maker, first knife sold in 1977. Doing business as Indian Ridge Forge. **Mark:** Stylized initials inside a shamrock.

MCCLURE, JERRY
3052 Isim Rd, Norman, OK 73026 **Contact:** 405-321-3614, jerry@jmcclureknives.net, jmcclureknives.net
Specialties: Gentleman's folder, linerlock with my jeweled pivot system of eight rubies, forged one-of-a-kind damascus bowies, and a line of hunting/camp knives. **Patterns:** Folders, bowie, and hunting/camp **Technical:** Forges own damascus, also uses Damasteel and does own heat treating. **Prices:** $500 to $3,000 and up **Remarks:** Full-time maker, made first knife in 1965. **Mark:** J.MCCLURE

MCCLURE, MICHAEL
803 17th Ave, Menlo Park, CA 94025 **Contact:** 650-323-2596, mikesknives@att.net, customknivesbymike.com
Specialties: Working/using straight knives of his design and to customer specs. **Patterns:** bowies, hunters, skinners, utility/camp, tantos, fillets and boot knives. **Technical:** Forges high-carbon and damascus, also grinds stainless, all grades. **Prices:** Start at $300. **Remarks:** Part-time maker, first knife sold in 1991. ABS Journeyman Smith. **Mark:** Mike McClure.

MCCONNELL, DAVID
North Woods Forge Kaklkaska, MI **Contact:** 989-858-6344, northwoodsforge@yahoo.com, www.northwoodsforge.com
Specialties: Colonial period knives and accoutrements.

MCCONNELL JR., LOYD A
309 County Road 144-B, Marble Falls, TX 78654 **Contact:** 830-596-3488, ccknives@ccknives.com, ccknives.com
Specialties: Working straight knives and folders, some fancy. **Patterns:** Hunters, boots, bowies, locking folders and slip-joints. **Technical:** Grinds CPM Steels, ATS-34 and BG-42 and commercial damascus. **Prices:** $450 to $10,000. **Remarks:** Full-time maker, first knife sold in 1975. Doing business as Cactus Custom Knives. Markets product knives under name: Lone Star Knives. **Mark:** Name, city and state in cactus logo.

MCCORNOCK, CRAIG
McC MTN OUTFITTERS, PO Box 162, Willow, NY 12495 **Contact:** 845-679-9758, mccmtn@aol.com, mccmtn.com
   Specialties: Carry, utility, hunters, defense knives and functional swords. **Patterns:** Drop points, hawkbills, tantos, waklzashis, katanas **Technical:** Stock removal, forged and damascus (yes, he still "knaps" flint and obsidian points and blades). **Prices:** $200 to $2000. **Mark:** McC.

MCCOUN, DYLAN
McCoun Tomahawks 14206 Pine Drive, DeWitt, VA 23840 **Contact:** 804-892-1668, mccountomahawks@gmail.com, Facebook: Dylan McCoun, Instagram: mccoun_bladesmith
   Specialties: Combat tomahawks. **Remarks:** Full-time maker.

MCCOUN, MARK
McCoun Tomahawks. 14212 Pine Dr, DeWitt, VA 23840 **Contact:** 804-469-7631, mccounandsons@live.com
   Specialties: Specializing in hand forged combat tomahawks. **Patterns:** Locking liners, integrals, tomahawks. **Technical:** 'Hawk steel is 4140 and knife steel is 1095. **Prices:** $200 to $700. **Remarks:** Part-time maker, first knife sold in 1989. **Mark:** Name, city and state.

MCCRACKIN, KEVIN
3720 Hess Rd, House Springs, MO 63051 **Contact:** 636-677-6066

MCCRACKIN AND SON, V J
3720 Hess Rd, House Springs, MO 63051 **Contact:** 636-677-6066
   Specialties: Working straight knives in standard patterns. **Patterns:** Hunters, bowies and camp knives. **Technical:** Forges L6, 5160, his own damascus, cable damascus. **Prices:** $125 to $700, some to $1500. **Remarks:** Part-time maker, first knife sold in 1983. Son Kevin helps make the knives. **Mark:** Last name, M.S.

MCCULLOUGH, JERRY
274 West Pettibone Rd, Georgiana, AL 36033 **Contact:** 334-382-7644, ke4er@alaweb.com
   Specialties: Standard patterns or custom designs. **Technical:** Forge and grind scrap-tool and damascus steels. Use natural handle materials and turquoise trim on some. Filework on others. **Prices:** $65 to $250 and up. **Remarks:** Part-time maker. **Mark:** Initials (JM) combined.

MCDONALD, RICH
5010 Carmel Rd., Hillboro, OH 45133 **Contact:** 937-466-2071, rmclongknives@aol.com, longknivesandleather.com
   Specialties: Traditional working/using and art knives of his design. **Patterns:** bowies, hunters, folders, primitives and tomahawks. **Technical:** Forges 5160, 1084, 1095, 52100 and his own damascus. Fancy filework. **Prices:** $200 to $1500. **Remarks:** Full-time maker, first knife sold in 1994. **Mark:** First and last initials connected.

MCDONALD, ROBERT J
14730 61 Court N, Loxahatchee, FL 33470 **Contact:** 561-790-1470
   Specialties: Traditional working straight knives to customer specs. **Patterns:** Fighters, swords and folders. **Technical:** Grinds 440C, ATS-34 and forges own damascus. **Prices:** $150 to $1000. **Remarks:** Part-time maker, first knife sold in 1988. **Mark:** Electro-etched name.

MCDONALD, W.J. "JERRY"
7173 Wickshire Cove E, Germantown, TN 38138 **Contact:** 901-756-9924, wjmcdonaldknives@msn.com, mcdonaldknives.com
   Specialties: Classic and working/using straight knives of his design and in standard patterns. **Patterns:** bowies, hunters kitchen and traditional spring back pocket knives. **Technical:** Grinds ATS-34, 154CM, D2, 440V, BG42 and 440C. **Prices:** $125 to $1000. **Remarks:** Full-time maker, first knife sold in 1989. **Mark:** First and middle initials, last name, maker, city and state. Some of his knives are stamped McDonald in script.

MCFALL, KEN
PO Box 458, Lakeside, AZ 85929 **Contact:** 928-537-2026, (fax) 928-537-8066, knives@citlink.net
   Specialties: Fancy working straight knives and some folders. **Patterns:** Daggers, boots, tantos, bowies, some miniatures. **Technical:** Grinds D2, ATS-34 and 440C. Forges his own damascus. **Prices:** $200 to $1200. **Remarks:** Part-time maker, first knife sold in 1984. **Mark:** Name, city and state.

MCFARLIN, ERIC E
PO Box 2188, Kodiak, AK 99615 **Contact:** 907-486-4799, e2mc@reagan.com
   Specialties: Working knives of his design. **Patterns:** bowies, skinners, camp knives and hunters. **Technical:** Flat and convex grinds 440C, A2 and AEB-L. **Prices:** Start at $350. **Remarks:** Part-time maker, first knife sold in 1989. **Mark:** Name and city and Old Goat logo.

MCFARLIN, J W
3331 Pocohantas Dr, Lake Havasu City, AZ 86404 **Contact:** 928-453-7612, (fax) 928-453-7612, aztheedge@NPGcable.com
   Technical: Flat grinds, D2, ATS-34, 440C, Thomas and Peterson damascus. **Remarks:** From working knives to investment. Customer designs always welcome. 100 percent handmade. Made first knife in 1972. **Prices:** $150 to $3000. **Mark:** Hand written in the blade.

MCGHEE, E. SCOTT
7136 Lisbon Rd., Clarkton, NC 28433 **Contact:** 910-448-2224, guineahogforge@gmail.com, guineahogforge.com
   Specialties: Hunting knives, kitchen blades, presentation blades, tactical knives and sword canes. **Technical:** Forge and stock removal, all flat-ground blades, including 1080-and-15N20 damascus, 1084, O1 and W2. **Prices:** $200 to $3,500. **Remarks:** Full-

time maker, first knife sold in 2009. Currently an ABS journeyman smith. **Mark:** E. Scott McGhee (large print) above Guinea Hog Forge (small print).

MCGILL, JOHN
PO Box 302, Blairsville, GA 30512 **Contact:** 404-745-4686
   Specialties: Working knives. **Patterns:** Traditional patterns, camp knives. **Technical:** Forges L6 and 9260, makes damascus. **Prices:** $50 to $250, some to $500. **Remarks:** Full-time maker, first knife sold in 1982. **Mark:** XYLO.

MCGOWAN, FRANK E
12629 Howard Lodge Rd., Sykesville, MD 21784 **Contact:** 443-745-2611, lizmcgowan31@gmail.com
   Specialties: Fancy working knives and folders to customer specs. **Patterns:** Survivor knives, fighters, fishing knives, folders and hunters. **Technical:** Grinds and forges O1, 440C, 5160, ATS-34, 52100, or customer choice. **Prices:** $100 to $1000, some more. **Remarks:** Full-time maker, first knife sold in 1986. **Mark:** Last name.

MCGRATH, PATRICK T
8343 Kenyon Ave, Westchester, CA 90045 **Contact:** 310-338-8764, hidinginLA@excite.com

MCGRODER, PATRICK J
5725 Chapin Rd, Madison, OH 44057 **Contact:** 216-298-3405, (fax) 216-298-3405
   Specialties: Traditional working/using knives of his design. **Patterns:** bowies, hunters and utility/camp knives. **Technical:** Grinds ATS-34, D2 and customer requests. Does reverse etching, heat-treats, prefers natural handle materials, custom made sheath with each knife. **Prices:** $125 to $250. **Remarks:** Part-time maker. **Mark:** First and middle initials, last name, maker, city and state.

MCGUANE IV, THOMAS F
410 South 3rd Ave, Bozeman, MT 59715 **Contact:** 406-586-0248, thomasmcguane.com
   Specialties: Multi metal inlaid knives of handmade steel. **Patterns:** Lock back and LinerLock® folders, fancy straight knives. **Technical:** 1084/1SN20 damascus and Mosaic steel by maker. **Prices:** $1000 and up. **Mark:** Surname or name and city, state.

MCINTYRE, SHAWN
71 Leura Grove, Hawthornm, E VIC, AUSTRALIA 3123 **Contact:** 61 3 9813 2049/Cell 61 412 041 062, macpower@netspace.net.au, mcintyreknives.com
   Specialties: damascus & CS fixed blades and art knives. **Patterns:** bowies, hunters, fighters, kukris, integrals. **Technical:** Forges, makes own damascus including pattern weld, mosaic, and composite multi-bars form O1 & 15N20 Also uses 1084, W2, and 52100. **Prices:** $275 to $2000. **Remarks:** Full-time maker since 1999. **Mark:** Mcintyre in script.

MCKEE, NEIL
674 Porter Hill Rd., Stevensville, MT 59870 **Contact:** 406-777-3507, mckeenh@wildblue.net
   Specialties: Early American. **Patterns:** Nessmuk, DeWeese, French folders, art pieces. **Technical:** Engraver. **Prices:** $150 to $1000. **Mark:** Oval with initials.

MCKENZIE, DAVID BRIAN
2311 B Ida Rd, Campbell River, BC, CANADA V9W-4V7

MCKIERNAN, STAN
11751 300th St, Lamoni, IA 50140 **Contact:** 641-784-6873/641-781-0368, slmck@hotmailc.om
   Specialties: Self-sheathed knives and miniatures. **Patterns:** Daggers, ethnic designs and individual styles. **Technical:** Grinds damascus and 440C. **Prices:** $200 to $500, some to $1500. **Mark:** "River's Bend" inside two concentric circles.

MCLUIN, TOM
36 Fourth St, Dracut, MA 01826 **Contact:** 978-957-4899, tmcluin@comcast.net
   Specialties: Working straight knives and folders of his design. **Patterns:** Boots, hunters and folders. **Technical:** Grinds ATS-34, 440C, O1 and damascus, makes his own mokume. **Prices:** $100 to $400, some to $700. **Remarks:** Part-time maker, first knife sold in 1991. **Mark:** Last name.

MCLURKIN, ANDREW
2112 Windy Woods Dr, Raleigh, NC 27607 **Contact:** 919-834-4693, mclurkincustomknives.com
   Specialties: Collector grade folders, working folders, fixed blades, and miniatures. Knives made to order and to his design. **Patterns:** Locking liner and lock back folders, hunter, working and tactical designs. **Technical:** Using patterned damascus, Mosaic damascus, ATS-34, BG-42, and CPM steels. Prefers natural handle materials such as pearl, ancient ivory and stabilized wood. Also using synthetic materials such as carbon fiber, titanium, and G10. **Prices:** $250 and up. **Mark:** Last name. Mark is often on inside of folders.

MCNEES, JONATHAN
15203 Starboard Pl, Northport, AL 35475 **Contact:** 205-391-8383, jmackusmc@yahoo.com, mcneescustomknives.com
   Specialties: Tactical, outdoors, utility. **Technical:** Stock removal method utilizing carbon and stainless steels to include 1095, cpm154, A2, cpms35v. **Remarks:** Part-time maker, first knife made in 2007. **Mark:** Jmcnees

MCRAE, J MICHAEL
6100 Lake Rd, Mint Hill, NC 28227 **Contact:** 704-545-2929, scotia@carolina.rr.com, scotiametalwork.com
   Specialties: Scottish dirks, sgian dubhs, broadswords. **Patterns:** Traditional blade styles with traditional and slightly non-traditional handle treatments. **Technical:** Forges 5160 and his own damascus. Prefers stag and exotic hardwoods for handles, many intricately

carved. **Prices:** Starting at $125, some to $3500. **Remarks:** Journeyman Smith in ABS, member of ABANA. Full-time maker, first knife sold in 1982. Doing business as Scotia Metalwork. **Mark:** Last name underlined with a claymore.

MCWILLIAMS, SEAN
PO Box 1685, Carbondale, CO 81623 **Contact:** 970-618-0198, info@ seanmcwilliamsforge.com, seanmcwilliamsforge.com
Specialties: Tactical, survival and working knives in Kydex-and-nylon sheaths. **Patterns:** Fighters, bowies, hunters and sports knives, period pieces, swords, martial arts blades and some folders, including Panama Folder linerlocks. **Technical:** Forges only CPM T440V, CPM S90V and CPM S35VN. **Prices:** $230 to $2,500. **Remarks:** Full-time maker, first knife sold in 1972. **Mark:** Stylized bear paw.

MEERDINK, KURT
248 Yulan Barryville Rd., Barryville, NY 12719-5305 **Contact:** 845-557-0783
Specialties: Working straight knives. **Patterns:** Hunters, bowies, tactical and neck knives. **Technical:** Grinds ATS-34, 440C, D2, damascus. **Prices:** $95 to $1100. **Remarks:** Full-time maker, first knife sold in 1994. **Mark:** Meerdink Maker, Rio NY.

MEERS, ANDREW
1100 S Normal Ave., Allyn Bldg MC 4301, Carbondale, IL 62901 **Contact:** 774-217-3574, namsuechool@gmail.com
Specialties: Pattern welded blades, in the New England style. **Patterns:** Can do open or closed welding and fancies middle eastern style blades. **Technical:** 1095, 1084, 15n20, 5160, w1, w2 steels **Remarks:** Part-time maker attending graduate school at SIUC, looking to become full-time in the future as well as earn ABS Journeyman status. **Mark:** Korean character for south.

MEIER, DARYL
75 Forge Rd, Carbondale, IL 62903 **Contact:** 618-549-3234, meiersteel.com
Specialties: One-of-a-kind knives and swords. **Patterns:** Collaborates on blades. **Technical:** Forges his own damascus, W1 and A203E, 440C, 431, nickel 200 and clad steel. **Prices:** $500 and up. **Remarks:** Full-time smith and researcher since 1974, first knife sold in 1974. **Mark:** Name.

MELIN, GORDON C
14207 Coolbank Dr, La Mirada, CA 90638 **Contact:** 562-946-5753

MELOY, SEAN
7148 Rosemary Lane, Lemon Grove, CA 91945-2105 **Contact:** 619-465-7173
Specialties: Traditional working straight knives of his design. **Patterns:** bowies, fighters and utility/camp knives. **Technical:** Grinds 440C, ATS-34 and D2. **Prices:** $125 to $300. **Remarks:** Part-time maker, first knife sold in 1985. **Mark:** Broz Knives.

MENEFEE, RICKY BOB
2440 County Road 1322, Blanchard, OK 73010, rmenefee@pldi.net, menefeeknives.com
Specialties: Working straight knives and pocket knives. **Patterns:** Hunters, fighters, minis & bowies. **Technical:** Grinds 154CM, A2 and CPM S90V. **Prices:** $200 to $2,000. **Remarks:** Part-time maker, first knife sold in 1996. Member of KGA of Oklahoma, also Knifemakers Guild. **Mark:** Menefee made or Menefee stamped in blade.

MENSCH, LARRY C
Larry's Knife Shop, 578 Madison Ave, Milton, PA 17847 **Contact:** 570-742-9554
Specialties: Custom orders. **Patterns:** bowies, daggers, hunters, tantos, short swords and miniatures. **Technical:** Grinds ATS-34, stainless steel damascus, blade grinds hollow, flat and slack. Filework, bending guards and fluting handles with finger grooves. **Prices:** $200 and up. **Remarks:** Full-time maker, first knife sold in 1993. Doing business as Larry's Knife Shop. **Mark:** Connected capital "L" and small "m" in script.

MERCER, MIKE
149 N. Waynesville Rd, Lebanon, OH 45036 **Contact:** 513-932-2837, mmercer08445@roadrunner.com
Specialties: Miniatures and autos. **Patterns:** All folder patterns. **Technical:** Diamonds and gold, one-of-a-kind, damascus, O1, stainless steel blades. **Prices:** $500 to $5000. **Remarks:** Carved wax - lost wax casting. **Mark:** Stamp - Mercer.

MERCHANT, TED
7 Old Garrett Ct, White Hall, MD 21161 **Contact:** 410-343-0380
Specialties: Traditional and classic working knives. **Patterns:** bowies, hunters, camp knives, fighters, daggers and skinners. **Technical:** Forges W2 and 5160, makes own damascus. Makes handles with wood, stag, horn, silver and gem stone inlay, fancy filework. **Prices:** $125 to $600, some to $1500. **Remarks:** Full-time maker, first knife sold in 1985. **Mark:** Last name.

MEROLA, JIM
6648 Ridge Blvd., Brooklyn, NY 11220 **Contact:** 347-342-6923, jimolds@earthlink.net, jimmerola.com
Specialties: Folders and fixed blades, including antique bowie reproductions, all in stainless steel and damascus. **Technical:** Stock removal method of blade making, using the finest steels and handle materials. **Prices:** $400 to $1,500. **Remarks:** Part-time maker since 1998.

MERZ III, ROBERT L
1447 Winding Canyon, Katy, TX 77493 **Contact:** 281-391-2897, bobmerz@ consolidated.net, merzknives.com
Specialties: Folders. **Prices:** $400 to $2,000. **Remarks:** Full-time maker, first knife sold in 1974. **Mark:** MERZ.

MESENBOURG, NICK
2545 Upper 64th Ct. E, Inver Grove Heights, MN 55076 **Contact:** 651-457-2753 or

651-775-7505, mesenbourg_nicholas@hotmail.com, ndmknives.com
Specialties: Working straight knives of his design or to customer specs, also sport-themed knives. **Patterns:** Hunters, skinners, bowies, fighters, utility and fillet knives. **Technical:** Grinds 440C stainless steel and commercial damascus. **Prices:** $175-$450, special knives higher. **Remarks:** Part-time maker, first knife sold in 2008. **Mark:** Encircled N D M capital letters.

MESHEJIAN, MARDI
5 Bisbee Court 109 PMB 230, Santa Fe, NM 87508 **Contact:** 505-310-7441, toothandnail13@yahoo.com
Specialties: One-of-a-kind art knives, folders and kitchen knives. **Patterns:** Swords, daggers, folders and other weapons. **Technical:** Forged steel damascus and titanium damascus. **Prices:** $300 to $5000 some to $7000. **Mark:** Stamped stylized "M."

METHENY, H A "WHITEY"
7750 Waterford Dr, Spotsylvania, VA 22551 **Contact:** 540842-1440, (fax) 540-582-3095, hametheny@aol.com, methenyknives.com
Specialties: Working and using straight knives of his design and to customer specs. **Patterns:** Hunters and kitchen knives. **Technical:** Grinds 440C and ATS-34. Offers filework, tooled custom sheaths. **Prices:** $350 to $450. **Remarks:** Spare-time maker, first knife sold in 1990. **Mark:** Initials/full name football logo.

METSALA, ANTHONY
30557 103rd St. NW, Princeton, MN 55371 **Contact:** 763-389-2628, acmetsala@ izoom.net, metsalacustomknives.com
Specialties: Sole authorship one-off mosaic damascus liner locking folders, sales of makers finished one-off mosaic damascus blades. **Patterns:** Except for a couple EDC folding knives, maker does not use patterns. **Technical:** Forges own mosaic damascus carbon blade and bolster material. All stainless steel blades are heat treated by Paul Bos. **Prices:** $250 to $1500. **Remarks:** Full-time knifemaker and damascus steel maker, first knife sold in 2005. **Mark:** A.C. Metsala or Metsala.

METZ, GREG T
c/o Yellow Pine Bar HC 83, BOX 8080, Cascade, ID 83611 **Contact:** 208-382-4336, metzenterprise@yahoo.com
Specialties: Hunting and utility knives. **Prices:** $350 and up. **Remarks:** Natural handle materials, hand forged blades, 1084 and 1095. **Mark:** METZ (last name).

MEYER, CHRISTOPHER J
737 Shenipsit Lake Rd, Tolland, CT 06084 **Contact:** 860-875-1826, shenipsitforge. cjm@gmail.com
Specialties: Handforged tool steels. **Technical:** Forges tool steels, grinds stainless. **Remarks:** Spare-time maker, sold first knife in 2003. **Mark:** Name and/or "Shenipsit Forge."

MICHINAKA, TOSHIAKI
I-679 Koyamacho-nishi, Tottori-shi, Tottori, JAPAN 680-0947 **Contact:** 0857-28-5911
Specialties: Art miniature knives. **Patterns:** bowies, hunters, fishing, camp knives & miniatures. **Technical:** Grinds ATS-34 and 440C. **Prices:** $300 to $900 some higher. **Remarks:** Part-time maker. First knife sold in 1982. **Mark:** First initial, last name.

MICKLEY, TRACY
42112 Kerns Dr, North Mankato, MN 56003 **Contact:** 507-947-3760, tracy@ mickleyknives.com, mickleyknives.com
Specialties: Working and collectable straight knives using mammoth ivory or burl woods, LinerLock® folders. **Patterns:** Custom and classic hunters, utility, fighters and bowies. **Technical:** Grinding 154-CM, BG-42 forging O1 and 52100. **Prices:** Starting at $325 **Remarks:** Part-time since 1999. **Mark:** Last name.

MIDGLEY, BEN
PO Box 577, Wister, OK 74966 **Contact:** 918-655-6701, mauricemidgley@ windstream.net
Specialties: Multi-blade folders, slip-joints, some lock-backs and hunters. File work, engraving and scrimshaw. **Patterns:** Reproduce old patterns, trappers, muskrats, stockman, whittlers, lockbacks an hunters. **Technical:** Grinds ATS-34, 440C, 12-C-27, CPM-154, some carbon steel, and commercial damascus. **Prices:** $385 to $1875. **Remarks:** Full-time maker, first knife sold in 2002. **Mark:** Name, city, and state stamped on blade.

MIKOLAJCZYK, GLEN
4650 W. 7 Mile Rd., Caledonia, WI 53108 **Contact:** 414-791-0424, (fax) 262-835-9697, glenmikol@aol.com customtomahawk.com
Specialties: Pipe hawks, fancy folders, bowies, long blades, hunting knives, all of his own design. **Technical:** Sole-author, forges own damascus and powdered steel. Works with ivory, bone, tortoise, horn and antlers, tiger maple, pearl for handle materials. Designs and does intricate file work and custom sheaths. Enjoys exotic handle materials. **Prices:** Moderate. **Remarks:** Founded Weg Von Wennig Forge in 2003, first knife sold in 2004. Also, designs and builds mini-forges. Will build upon request. International sales accepted. **Mark:** Tomahawk and name.

MILES JR., C R "IRON DOCTOR"
1541 Porter Crossroad, Lugoff, SC 29078 **Contact:** 803-600-9397
Specialties: Traditional working straight knives of his design or made to custom specs. **Patterns:** Hunters, fighters, utility camp knives and hatches. **Technical:** Grinds O1, D2, ATS-34, 440C, 1095, and 154 CPM. Forges 18th century style cutlery of high carbon steels. Also forges and grinds old files and farrier's rasps to make knives. Custom leather sheaths. **Prices:** $100 and up. **Remarks:** Part-time maker, first knife sold in 1997. **Mark:**

custom knifemakers

Iron doctor plus name and serial number.

MILITANO, TOM
CUSTOM KNIVES, 77 Jason Rd., Jacksonville, AL 36265-6655 **Contact:** 256-435-7132, jeffkin57@aol.com
Specialties: Fixed blade, one-of-a-kind knives. **Patterns:** bowies, fighters, hunters and tactical knives. **Technical:** Grinds 440C, CPM 154CM, A2, and damascus. Hollow grinds, flat grinds, and decorative filework. **Prices:** $150 plus. **Remarks:** Part-time maker. Sold first knives in the mid-to-late 1980s. **Mark:** Name engraved in ricasso area - type of steel on reverse side.

MILLARD, FRED G
27627 Kopezyk Ln., Richland Center, WI 53581 **Contact:** 608-647-5376
Specialties: Working/using straight knives of his design or to customer specs. **Patterns:** bowies, hunters, utility/camp knives, kitchen/steak knives. **Technical:** Grinds ATS-34, O1, D2 and 440C. Makes sheaths. **Prices:** $110 to $300. **Remarks:** Full-time maker, first knife sold in 1993. Doing business as Millard Knives. **Mark:** Mallard duck in flight with serial number.

MILLER, CHELSEA GRACE
80 Ainslie St., Brooklyn, NY 11211 **Contact:** 917-623-7804, chelsea@chelseamillerknives.com, chelseamillerknives.com
Specialties: Selection of rustic cheese knives and kitchen knives. **Technical:** Uses recycled tool steel, such as mechanic's files, wood files and rasps. Forges cheese and smaller kitchen knives, using stock removal to preserve the rasp pattern on large kitchen knives. All the wood for handles is collected from the maker's family farm in Vermont, including spalted maple, apple and walnut. **Prices:** $200 to $500. **Remarks:** Full-time maker, first knife made in 2011. Maker often examines that first knife and admires its simplicity, though it lacks functionality, and uses it as inspiration to remain as imaginative as possible.

MILLER, HANFORD J
1751 Mountain Ranch Rd., Lakespur, CO 80118 **Contact:** 719-999-2551, hanford.miller@gmail.com
Specialties: Working knives in Moran styles, bowie, period pieces, Cinquedea. **Patterns:** Daggers, bowies, working knives. **Technical:** All work forged: W2, 1095, 5160 and damascus. ABS methods, offers fine silver repousse, scabboard mountings and wire inlay, oak presentation cases. **Prices:** $400 to $1000, some to $3000 and up. **Remarks:** Full-time maker, first knife sold in 1968. **Mark:** Initials or name within bowie logo.

MILLER, JAMES P
9024 Goeller Rd, RR 2, Box 28, Fairbank, IA 50629 **Contact:** 319-635-2294, damascusknives.biz
Specialties: All tool steel damascus, working knives and period pieces. **Patterns:** Hunters, bowies, camp knives and daggers. **Technical:** Forges and grinds 1095, 52100, 440C and his own damascus. **Prices:** $175 to $500, some to $1500. **Remarks:** Full-time maker, first knife sold in 1970. **Mark:** First and middle initials, last name with knife logo.

MILLER, LEVI
7960 N. 450 West, Howe, IN 46746 **Contact:** 260-562-2724, lmcustomknives@gmail.com, Facebook.com/Lmknives
Specialties: Traditional knives. **Patterns:** Slip joints, hunters, camp knives and hoof knives. **Technical:** Forges 52100 and 80CrV2. **Prices:** $200 and up. **Remarks:** Part-time maker, first knife sold in 2009. ABS journeyman smith. **Mark:** LRMiller Howe IN JS.

MILLER, M A
11625 Community Center Dr, Unit #1531, Northglenn, CO 80233 **Contact:** 303-280-3816
Specialties: Using knives for hunting. 3-1/2"-4" Loveless drop-point. Made to customer specs. **Patterns:** Skinners and camp knives. **Technical:** Grinds 440C, D2, O1 and ATS-34 damascus miniatures. **Prices:** $225 to $350, miniatures $75 to $150. **Remarks:** Part-time maker, first knife sold in 1988. **Mark:** Last name stamped in block letters or first and middle initials, last name, maker, city and state with triangles on either side etched.

MILLER, MICHAEL
3030 E Calle Cedral, Kingman, AZ 86401 **Contact:** 928-757-1359, mike@mmilleroriginals.com
Specialties: Hunters, bowies, and skinners with exotic burl wood, stag, ivory and gemstone handles. **Patterns:** High carbon steel knives. **Technical:** High carbon and nickel alloy damascus and high carbon and meteorite damascus. Also mosaic damascus. **Prices:** $235 to $4500. **Remarks:** Full-time maker since 2002, first knife sold 2000, doing business as M Miller Originals. **Mark:** First initial and last name with 'handmade' underneath.

MILLER, MICHAEL E
910146 S. 3500 Rd., Chandler, OK 74834 **Contact:** 918-377-2411, mimiller1@cotc.net
Specialties: Traditional working/using knives of his design. **Patterns:** bowies, hunters and kitchen knives. **Technical:** Grinds ATS-34, CPM 440V, forges damascus and cable damascus and 52100. Prefers scrimshaw, fancy pins, basket weave and embellished sheaths. **Prices:** $130 to $500. **Remarks:** Part-time maker, first knife sold in 1984. Doing business as Miller Custom Knives. Member of Knife Group Of Oklahoma. **Mark:** First and middle initials, last name, maker.

MILLER, NATE
Sportsman's Edge, 1075 Old Steese Hwy N, Fairbanks, AK 99712 **Contact:** 907-460-4718, sportsmansedge@gci.net alaskasportsmansedge.com
Specialties: Fixed blade knives for hunting, fishing, kitchen and collector pieces. **Patterns:** Hunters, skinners, utility, tactical, fishing, camp knives-your pattern or mine. **Technical:** Stock removal maker, ATS-34, 154CM, 440C, D2, 1095, other steels on request. Handle material includes micarta, horn, antler, fossilized ivory and bone, wide selection of woods. **Prices:** $225-$800. **Remarks:** Full time maker since 2002. **Mark:** Nate Miller, Fairbanks, AK.

MILLER, RICK
516 Kanaul Rd, Rockwood, PA 15557 **Contact:** 814-926-2059
Specialties: Working/using straight knives of his design and in standard patterns. **Patterns:** bowies, daggers, hunters and friction folders. **Technical:** Grinds L6. Forges 5160, L6 and damascus. Patterns for damascus are random, twist, rose or ladder. **Prices:** $75 to $250, some to $400. **Remarks:** Part-time maker, first knife sold in 1982. **Mark:** Script stamp "R.D.M."

MILLER, RONALD T
12922 127th Ave N, Largo, FL 34644 **Contact:** 813-595-0378 (after 5 p.m.)
Specialties: Working straight knives in standard patterns. **Patterns:** Combat knives, camp knives, kitchen cutlery, fillet knives, locking folders and butterflies. **Technical:** Grinds D2, 440C and ATS-34, offers brass inlays and scrimshaw. **Prices:** $45 to $325, some to $750. **Remarks:** Part-time maker, first knife sold in 1984. **Mark:** Name, city and state in palm tree logo.

MILLER, STEVE
1376 Pine St., Clearwater, FL 33756 **Contact:** 727-461-4180, millknives@aol.com, millerknives.com
Patterns: bowies, hunters, skinners, folders. **Technical:** Primarily uses CPM 154, 440C, ATS-34, CPM S30V, damascus and Sandvik stainless steels. Exotic hardwoods, bone, horn, antler, ivory, synthetics. All leather work and sheaths made by me and handstitched. **Remarks:** Have been making custom knives for sale since 1990. Part-time maker, hope to go full time in about five and a half years (after retirement from full-time job). **Mark:** Last name inside a pentagram.

MILLER, TERRY
P.O. Box 262, Healy, AK 99743 **Contact:** 907-683-1239, terry@denalidomehome.com
Specialties: Alaskan ulus with wood or horn. **Remarks:** New to knifemaking (7 years).

MILLER, WILLIAM (BILL)
21937 Holiday Ln., Warsaw, MO 65355 **Contact:** 660-723-1866, wmknives@hotmail.com
Specialties: Uses own handforged high-carbon damascus for bowies, daggers, push daggers and hunters. **Patterns:** All different styles. **Prices:** $250 to $3,000. **Remarks:** Uses exotic hardwood, stag, fossil ivory and fossil bone as handle materials. **Mark:** "W" over "M" in an oval.

MILLS, LOUIS G
9450 Waters Rd, Ann Arbor, MI 48103 **Contact:** 734-668-1839
Specialties: High-art Japanese-style period pieces. **Patterns:** Traditional tantos, daggers and swords. **Technical:** Makes steel from iron, makes his own damascus by traditional Japanese techniques. **Prices:** $900 to $2000, some to $8000. **Remarks:** Spare-time maker. **Mark:** Yasutomo in Japanese Kanji.

MILLS, MICHAEL
151 Blackwell Rd, Colonial Beach, VA 22443-5054 **Contact:** 804-224-0265
Specialties: Working knives, hunters, skinners, utility and bowies. **Technical:** Forge 5160 differential heat-treats. **Prices:** $300 and up. **Remarks:** Part-time maker, ABS Journeyman. **Mark:** Last name in script.

MINCHEW, RYAN
2101 Evans Ln., Midland, TX 79705 **Contact:** (432) 301-0603, ryan@minchewknives.com, minchewknives.com
Specialties: Hunters and folders. **Patterns:** Standard hunters and bird-and-trout knives. **Prices:** $150 to $500. **Mark:** Minchew.

MINNICK, JIM & JOYCE
144 North 7th St, Middletown, IN 47356 **Contact:** 765-354-4108, jmjknives@aol.com, minnickknives.com
Specialties: Lever-lock folding art knives, liner-locks. **Patterns:** Stilettos, Persian and one-of-a-kind folders. **Technical:** Grinds and carves damascus, stainless, and high-carbon. **Prices:** $950 to $7000. **Remarks:** Part-time maker, first knife sold in 1976. Husband and wife team. **Mark:** Minnick and JMJ.

MIRABILE, DAVID
PO BOX 20417, Juneau, AK 99802 **Contact:** 907-321-1103, dmirabile02@gmail.com, mirabileknives.com
Specialties: Elegant edged weapons and hard use Alaskan knives. **Patterns:** Fighters, personal carry knives, special studies of the Tlinget dagger. **Technical:** Uses W-2, 1080, 15n20, 1095, 5160, and his own damascus, and stainless/high carbon San Mai.

MITCHELL, ALAN
133 Standard Dr., Blairgowrie, Randburg, Gauteng, SOUTH AFRICA **Contact:** +27(83) 501 0944, alspostbox@hotmail.com, Facebook.com/mitchellhandmade
Specialties: Forged working and using knives. **Patterns:** Hunters, utility knives and bowies. **Technical:** Forges high-carbon steels with flat and hollow grinds and hamons (temper lines). **Prices:** $100 to $1,000. **Remarks:** Member of Knife Makers Guild of South Africa. **Mark:** Mitchell.

MITCHELL, JAMES A
PO Box 4646, Columbus, GA 31904 **Contact:** 404-322-8582
Specialties: Fancy working knives. **Patterns:** Hunters, fighters, bowies and locking folders. **Technical:** Grinds D2, 440C and commercial damascus. **Prices:** $100 to $400, some to $900. **Remarks:** Part-time maker, first knife sold in 1976. Sells knives in sets.

MITCHELL, MAX DEAN AND BEN

3803 VFW Rd, Leesville, LA 71440 **Contact:** 318-239-6416
Specialties: Hatchet and knife sets with folder and belt and holster all match. **Patterns:** Hunters, 200 L6 steel. **Technical:** L6 steel, soft back, hand edge. **Prices:** $300 to $500. **Remarks:** Part-time makers, first knife sold in 1965. Custom orders only, no stock. **Mark:** First names.

MITCHELL, WM DEAN

260 FM 2578 Bldg 7, Apt 27, TERRELL, TX 75160 **Contact:** 469-652-5456, wmdeanmitchell@gmail.com
Specialties: Functional and collectable cutlery. **Patterns:** Personal and collector's designs. **Technical:** Forges own damascus and carbon steels. **Prices:** Determined by the buyer. **Remarks:** Gentleman knifemaker. ABS Master Smith 1994. **Mark:** Full name with anvil and MS. Early knives have initals only, or initials with JS.

MITSUYUKI, ROSS

PO Box 29577, Honolulu, HI 96820 **Contact:** 808-778-5907, (fax) 808-671-3335, r.p.mitsuyuki@gmail.com, picturetrail.com/homepage/mrbing
Specialties: Working straight knives and folders/engraving titanium & 416 S.S. **Patterns:** Hunting, fighters, utility knives and boot knives. **Technical:** 440C, BG42, ATS-34, S30V, CPM154, and damascus. **Prices:** $150 and up. **Remarks:** Spare-time maker, first knife sold in 1998. **Mark:** (Honu) Hawaiian sea turtle.

MIVILLE-DESCHENES, ALAIN

1952 Charles A Parent, Quebec, CANADA G2B 4B2 **Contact:** 418-845-0950, (fax) 418-845-0950, amd@miville-deschenes.com, miville-deschenes.com
Specialties: Working knives of his design or to customer specs and art knives. **Patterns:** bowies, skinner, hunter, utility, camp knives, fighters, art knives. **Technical:** Grinds ATS-34, CPMS30V, O-1, D2, and sometime forge carbon steel. **Prices:** $250 to $700, some higher. **Remarks:** Part-time maker, first knife sold in 2001. **Mark:** Logo (small hand) and initials (AMD).

MOELLER, HARALD

#17-493 Pioneer Crescent, Parksville, BC, CANADA V9P 1V2 **Contact:** 250-248-0391, moeknif@shaw.ca, collectiblecustomknives.com
Specialties: Collector grade San Fransisco Dagger, small fighters, Fantasy Axes, bowies, Survival Knives. Special design award winning liner lock folders, Viper throwing knives. **Technical:** Steels - 440-C, ATS34, damascus, etc. Materials: mammoth, Abalone, MOP, Black Water Buffalo, 14K Gold, rubies, diamonds, etc. **Prices:** Throwing knives - $80 to $350, Fighters - $400 to $600, Axe - $3200, Folders - $600 to $3400, Dagger - Up to $9,000 **Remarks:** Now part time maker, first knife sold in 1979. member Southern California Blades, Member Oregon Knife Collectors Assoc. **Mark:** Moeller

MOEN, JERRY

4478 Spring Valley Rd., Dallas, TX 75244 **Contact:** 972-839-1609, jmoen@moencustomknives.com, moencustomknives.com
Specialties: Hunting, pocket knives, fighters tactical, and exotic. **Prices:** $500 to $5,000.

MOIZIS, STAN

8213 109B St., Delta, British Columbia (BC), CANADA V4C 4G9 **Contact:** 604-597-8929, moizis@telus.net
Specialties: Automatic and spring-assist folding knives and soon to come out-the-fronts. **Patterns:** Well-made carry knives with some upper-end materials available for steel and handles. All patterns are freehand, and thus each knife is unique. Marks: "SM" on blade with date and place of manufacture on inside of spacer. On knives with professionally out-of-house machined parts, mark is "BRNO BORN."

MOJZIS, JULIUS

B S Timravy 6, 98511 Halic, SLOVAKIA, julius.mojzis@gmail.com, juliusmojzis.com
Specialties: Art Knives. **Prices:** USD 2000. **Mark:** MOJZIS.

MONCUS, MICHAEL STEVEN

1803 US 19 N, Smithville, GA 31787 **Contact:** 912-846-2408

MONTANO, GUS A

P.O. Box 501264, San Diego, CA 92150 **Contact:** 619-273-5357
Specialties: Traditional working/using straight knives of his design. **Patterns:** Boots, bowies and fighters. **Technical:** Grinds 1095 and 5160, grinds and forges cable. Double or triple hardened and triple drawn, hand-rubbed finish. Prefers natural handle materials. **Prices:** $200 to $400, some to $600. **Remarks:** Spare-time maker, first knife sold in 1997. **Mark:** First initial and last name.

MONTEIRO, VICTOR

31 Rue D'Opprebais, Maleves Ste Marie, BELGIUM 1360 **Contact:** 010 88 0441, victor.monteiro@skynet.be
Specialties: Working and fancy straight knives, folders and integrals of his design. **Patterns:** Fighters, hunters and kitchen knives. **Technical:** Grinds ATS-34, 440C, D2, Damasteel and other commercial damascus, embellishment, filework and domed pins. **Prices:** $300 to $1000, some higher. **Remarks:** Part-time maker, first knife sold in 1989. **Mark:** Logo with initials connected.

MONTELL, TY

PO BOX 1312, Thatcher, AZ 85552 **Contact:** 575-538-1610, (fax) Cell: 575-313-4373, tymontell54@gmail.com
Specialties: Automatics, slip-joint folders, hunting and miniatures. **Technical:** Stock removal. Steel of choice is CPM-154, Devin Thomas damascus. **Prices:** $250 and up. **Remarks:** First knife made in 1980 **Mark:** Tang stamp - Montell.

MONTENEGRO, FACUNDO

777 Jorge L. Borges St., Merlo (5881) San Luis, ARGENTINA **Contact:** 005492664759472, faca32@yahoo.com.ar, montenegroknives.com.ar
Specialties: bowies, hunters, gaucho knives and integrals. **Technical:** Forges own damascus and O1, specializing in Turkish and mosaic damascus on gaucho knives and hunting swords. **Prices:** $400 and up, with most pieces around $850 to $2,000. **Remarks:** First ABS journeyman smith from Argentina, and considered one of the best knifemakers of Argentina. **Mark:** Montenegro JS.

MONTGOMERY, STEPHEN R.

4621 Crescent Rd., Madison, WI 53711 **Contact:** 608-658-2623, smontgomery2211@gmail.com
Specialties: Modern, karambits, fantasy, Viking. **Patterns:** Small hunters of the maker's design. **Technical:** Using high end steels, crv80. **Prices:** $65 to $300. **Remarks:** Uses what he makes, as he is a hunter, archer and armored combat fighter. **Mark:** sm.

MOONEY, MIKE

19432 E. Cloud Rd., Queen Creek, AZ 85142 **Contact:** 480-244-7768, mikemoonblades@gmail.com, moonblades.com
Specialties: Hand-crafted high-performing straight knives of his or customer's design. **Patterns:** bowies, fighters, hunting, camp and kitchen users or collectible. **Technical:** Flat-grind, hand-rubbed finish. S30V, CPM 154, damascus, any steel. **Prices:** $300 to $3000. **Remarks:** Doing business as moonblades.com. Commissions are welcome. **Mark:** M. Mooney followed by crescent moon.

MOORE, DAVY

Moyriesk, Quin, Co Clare, IRELAND **Contact:** 353 (0)65 6825975, davy@mooreireland.com, mooreireland.com
Specialties: Traditional and Celtic outdoor hunting and utility knives. **Patterns:** Traditional hunters and skinners, Celtic pattern hunting knives, Bushcrafting, fishing, utility/camp knives. **Technical:** Stock removal knives 01, D2, RWL 34, ATS 34, CPM 154, Damasteel (various). **Prices:** 250-1700 Euros. **Remarks:** Full-time maker, first knife sold in 2004. **Mark:** Three stars over rampant lion / MOORE over Ireland.

MOORE, EDDIE WILLIAM "PITT"

Fiery Pitt Forge 1256 County Road 226, LaFayette, AL 36862 **Contact:** 334-755-6013, fierypittforge@outlook.com
Patterns: Kitchen cutlery and sheaths. **Remarks:** Veteran owned and operated.

MOORE, JAMES B

1707 N Gillis, Ft. Stockton, TX 79735 **Contact:** 915-336-2113
Specialties: Classic working straight knives and folders of his design. **Patterns:** Hunters, bowies, daggers, fighters, boots, utility/camp knives, locking folders and slip-joint folders. **Technical:** Grinds 440C, ATS-34, D2, L6, CPM and commercial damascus. **Prices:** $85 to $700, exceptional knives to $1500. **Remarks:** Full-time maker, first knife sold in 1972. **Mark:** Name, city and state.

MOORE, JON P

304 South N Rd, Aurora, NE 68818 **Contact:** 402-849-2616, sharpdecisionknives.com
Specialties: Working and fancy straight knives using antler, exotic bone, wood and Micarta. Will use customers' antlers on request. **Patterns:** Hunters, skinners, camp and bowies. **Technical:** Hand-forged high carbon steel. Makes his own damascus. **Prices:** Start at $125. **Remarks:** Full-time maker, sold first knife in 2003. Does on-location knife forging demonstrations. **Mark:** Sword through anvil with name.

MOORE, MARVE

HC 89 Box 393, Willow, AK 99688 **Contact:** 907-232-0478, marvemoore@aol.com
Specialties: Fixed blades forged and stock removal. **Patterns:** Hunter, skinners, fighter, short swords. **Technical:** 100 percent of his work is done by hand. **Prices:** $100 to $500. **Remarks:** Also makes his own sheaths. **Mark:** -MM-.

MOORE, MICHAEL ROBERT

70 Beauliew St, Lowell, MA 01850 **Contact:** 978-479-0589, (fax) 978-441-1819

MOORE, TED

340 E Willow St, Elizabethtown, PA 17022 **Contact:** 717-367-3939, tedmoore@tedmooreknives.com, tedmooreknives.com
Specialties: damascus folders, cigar cutters, high art. **Patterns:** Slip joints, linerlock, cigar cutters. **Technical:** Grinds damascus and stainless steels. **Prices:** $250 and up. **Remarks:** Part-time maker, first knife sold 1993. **Mark:** Moore U.S.A.

MORALES, RAMON

LP-114, Managua, NICARAGUA **Contact:** 011-505-824-8950, nicaraguabladesmith@gmail.com
Specialties: Forges knives and enjoys making brut de forge pieces. **Patterns:** Choppers, bowies and hunters. **Technical:** Does all his own blade heat treating in house and makes his own damascus. **Remarks:** Only ABS journeyman smith in Central America. **Mark:** Initials "RM" inside the outline of Nicaragua.

MORETT, DONALD

116 Woodcrest Dr, Lancaster, PA 17602-1300 **Contact:** 717-746-4888

MORGAN, JEFF

9200 Arnaz Way, Santee, CA 92071 **Contact:** 619-448-8430
Specialties: Early American style knives. **Patterns:** Hunters, bowies, etc. **Technical:** Carbon steel and carbon steel damascus. **Prices:** $60 to $400

MORGAN, TOM

14689 Ellett Rd, Beloit, OH 44609 **Contact:** 330-537-2023

custom knifemakers

Specialties: Working straight knives and period pieces. **Patterns:** Hunters, boots and presentation tomahawks. **Technical:** Grinds O1, 440C and 154CM. **Prices:** Knives, $65 to $200, tomahawks, $100 to $325. **Remarks:** Full-time maker, first knife sold in 1977. **Mark:** Last name and type of steel used.

MORMAN, KELLY
Lubbock, TX **Contact:** 806-777-8964, ksmorman@outlook.com, blockstockblade.com
Specialties: Working fixed blades and folders. **Patterns:** bowies, hunters. **Technical:** D2. **Remarks:** Also makes custom cartridge boxes.

MORO, CORRADO
Via Omegna, 22 - Rivoli 10098, Torino, ITALY **Contact:** +39 3472451255, info@moroknives.com, moroknives.com
Specialties: High-end folders of his own design and to customer specs, unique locking and pivoting systems. **Patterns:** Inspired by nature and technology. **Technical:** Uses ATS 34, 916 and 904L blade steels, and titanium, carbon-lip inlays, precious metals and diamonds. **Prices:** $3,500 to $11,000 and above. **Remarks:** Full-time maker, first knife sold in 2011. **Mark:** MORO on blade.

MORRIS, C H
1590 Old Salem Rd, Frisco City, AL 36445 **Contact:** 334-575-7425
Specialties: LinerLock® folders. **Patterns:** Interframe liner locks. **Technical:** Grinds 440C and ATS-34. **Prices:** Start at $350. **Remarks:** Full-time maker, first knife sold in 1973. Doing business as Custom Knives. **Mark:** First and middle initials, last name.

MORRIS, ERIC
306 Ewart Ave, Beckley, WV 25801 **Contact:** 304-255-3951

MORRIS, MICHAEL S.
609 S. Main St., Yale, MI 48097 **Contact:** 810-887-7817, michaelmorrisknives@gmail.com
Specialties: Hunting and Tactical fixed blade knives of his design made from files. **Technical:** All knives hollow ground on 16" wheel. Hand stitches his own sheaths also. **Prices:** From $60 to $350 with most in the $90 to $125 range. **Remarks:** Machinist since 1980, made his first knife in 1984, sold his first knife in 2004. Now full-time maker. **Mark:** Last name with date of manufacture.

MOSES, STEVEN
1610 W Hemlock Way, Santa Ana, CA 92704

MOSIER, DAVID
1725 Millburn Ave., Independence, MO 64056 **Contact:** 816-796-3479, dmknives@aol.com dmknives.com
Specialties: Tactical folders and fixed blades. **Patterns:** Fighters and concealment blades. **Technical:** Uses S35VN, CPM 154, S30V, 154CM, ATS-34, 440C, A2, D2, Stainless damascus, and Damasteel. Fixed blades come with Kydex sheaths made by maker. **Prices:** $150 to $1000. **Remarks:** Full-time maker, business name is DM Knives. **Mark:** David Mosier Knives encircling sun.

MOULTON, DUSTY
135 Hillview Lane, Loudon, TN 37774 **Contact:** 865-408-9779, moultonknives.com
Specialties: Fancy and working straight knives. **Patterns:** Hunters, fighters, fantasy and miniatures. **Technical:** Grinds ATS-34 and damascus. **Prices:** $300 to $2000. **Remarks:** Full-time maker, first knife sold in 1991. Now doing engraving on own knives as well as other makers. **Mark:** Last name.

MOYER, RUSS
1266 RD 425 So, Havre, MT 59501 **Contact:** 406-395-4423
Specialties: Working knives to customer specs. **Patterns:** Hunters, bowies and survival knives. **Technical:** Forges W2 & 5160. **Prices:** $150 to $350. **Remarks:** Part-time maker, first knife sold in 1976. **Mark:** Initials in logo.

MULKEY, GARY
533 Breckenridge Rd, Branson, MO 65616 **Contact:** 417-335-0123, gary@mulkeyknives.com, mulkeyknives.com
Specialties: Sole authorship damascus and high-carbon steel hunters, bowies and fighters. **Patterns:** Fixed blades (hunters, bowies, and fighters). **Prices:** $450 and up. **Remarks:** Full-time maker since 1997. **Mark:** MUL above skeleton key.

MULLER, JODY
3359 S. 225th Rd., Goodson, MO 65663 **Contact:** 417-752-3260, mullerforge2@hotmail.com, mullerforge.com
Specialties: Hand engraving, carving and inlays, fancy folders and oriental styles. **Patterns:** One-of-a-kind fixed blades and folders in all styles. **Technical:** Forges own damascus and high carbon steel. **Prices:** $300 and up. **Remarks:** Full-time knifemaker, does hand engraving, carving and inlay. All work done by maker. **Mark:** Muller

MUNJAS, BOB
600 Beebe Rd., Waterford, OH 45786 **Contact:** 740-336-5538, hairofthebear.com
Specialties: damascus and carbon steel sheath knives. **Patterns:** Hunters and neck knives. **Technical:** My own damascus, 5160, 1095, 1984, L6, and W2. Forge and stock removal. Does own heat treating and makes own sheaths. **Prices:** $100 to $500. **Remarks:** Part-time maker. **Mark:** Moon Munjas.

MURA, DENIS
Via Pesciule 15 56021, Cascina (Pi), ITALY **Contact:** +39 3388365277, zeb1d@libero.it, denismura.com
Specialties: Straight knives. **Patterns:** Hunters, bowies, camp knives and everyday carry (EDC) knives. **Technical:** Grinds A2, D2, W2, 440C, RWL 34, CPM 154, Sleipner, Niolox, 1095, 1084, 1070, C145SC, Becut, damascus and san mai steels. **Prices:** Start at $250.

Remarks: Full-time maker, first knife made in 2006. **Mark:** MD.

MURSKI, RAY
12129 Captiva Ct, Reston, VA 22091-1204 **Contact:** 703-264-1102, rmurski@gmail.com
Specialties: Fancy working/using folders of his design. **Patterns:** Hunters, slip-joint folders and utility/camp knives. **Technical:** Grinds CPM 154 **Prices:** $125 to $500. **Remarks:** Spare-time maker, first knife sold in 1996. **Mark:** Engraved name with serial number under name.

MUTZ, JEFF
8210 Rancheria Dr. Unit 7, Rancho Cucamonga, CA 91730 **Contact:** 909-559-7129, jmutzknives@hotmail.com, jmutzknives.com
Specialties: Traditional working/using fixed blade and slip-jointed knives of own design and customer specs. **Patterns:** Hunters, skinners, and folders. **Technical:** Forges and grinds all steels Offers scrimshaw. **Prices:** $225 to $800. **Remarks:** Full-time maker, first knife sold in 1998. **Mark:** First initial, last name over "maker."

MYERS, PAUL
644 Maurice St, Wood River, IL 62095 **Contact:** 618-258-1707
Specialties: Fancy working straight knives and folders. **Patterns:** Full range of folders, straight hunters and bowies, tie tacks, knife and fork sets. **Technical:** Grinds D2, 440C, ATS-34 and 154CM. **Prices:** $100 to $350, some to $3000. **Remarks:** Full-time maker, first knife sold in 1974. **Mark:** Initials with setting sun on front, name and number on back.

MYERS, STEVE
1045 Marshall St., Carlinville, IL 62626-1048 **Contact:** 217-416-0800, myersknives@ymail.com
Specialties: Working straight knives and integrals. **Patterns:** Camp knives, hunters, skinners, bowies, and boot knives. **Technical:** Forges own damascus and high carbon steels. **Prices:** $250 to $1,000. **Remarks:** Full-time maker, first knife sold in 1985. **Mark:** Last name in logo.

N

NADEAU, BRIAN
SHARPBYDESIGN LLC, 8 Sand Hill Rd., Stanhope, NJ 07874 **Contact:** 862-258-0792, nadeau@sharpbydesign.com, sharpbydesign.com
Specialties: High-quality tactical fixed blades and folders, collector and working blades. All blades and sheaths of maker's own design. Designs, writes programs and machines all components on CNC equipment, nothing water jet, everything hand finished. **Technical:** Works with new CPM steels, but loves to get an order for a W2 blade with a nice hamon or temper line. **Prices:** $100 and up. **Remarks:** Part-time maker. **Mark:** Name in script, or initials "BN" skewed on top of one another.

NARASADA, MAMORU
9115-8 Nakaminowa, Minowa-machi, Kamiina-gun, NAGANO, JAPAN 399-4601 **Contact:** 81-265-79-3960, (fax) 81-265-79-3960
Specialties: Utility working straight knife. **Patterns:** Hunting, fishing, and camping knife. **Technical:** Grind and forges / ATS34, VG10, 440C, CRM07. **Prices:** $150 to $500, some higher. **Remarks:** First knife sold in 2003. **Mark:** M.NARASADA with initial logo.

NATEN, GREG
1804 Shamrock Way, Bakersfield, CA 93304-3921
Specialties: Fancy and working/using folders of his design. **Patterns:** Fighters, hunters and locking folders. **Technical:** Grinds 440C, ATS-34 and CPM440V. Heat-treats, prefers desert ironwood, stag and mother-of-pearl. Designs and sews leather sheaths for straight knives. **Prices:** $175 to $600, some to $950. **Remarks:** Spare-time maker, first knife sold in 1992. **Mark:** Last name above battle-ax, handmade.

NAUDE, LOUIS
P.O. Box 1103, Okahandja, Namibia, AFRICA 7560 **Contact:** +264 (0)81-38-36-285, info@louisnaude.co.za louisnaude.co.za
Specialties: Folders, Hunters, Custom.. **Patterns:** See website. **Technical:** Stock removal, African materials. **Prices:** See website. **Remarks:** Still the tool! **Mark:** Louis Naude Knives with family crest.

NAZZ, THEO "ROCK"
159 2nd Ave., Apt. 12, New York, NY 10003 **Contact:** 917-532-7291, theorocknazz@gmail.com, theorocknazz.com
Specialties: Knives, daggers and swords with 3-D-printed cast metal components that increase the ability to grip while offering extensive customization. **Technical:** Monosteel bades are CruForgeV, 80CrV2 and W2, san mai is typically one of the aforementioned steels with a stainless, pattern-welded or wrought iron shell. Pattern-welded blades are 1080, W2, 80CrV2 and/or 15N20 for the cutting edge, and wrought iron, pure nickel, stainless and/or 15N20 for the shell/spine if applicable. Does own heat treat to form a variety of hamons (temper lines). **Prices:** $400 to $1,500, or $1,000 to $8,000 for swords. **Remarks:** Part-time maker since 2007. **Mark:** "N" fileworked on the spine, or "N" incorporated in a 3-D printed metal component.

NEALY, BUD
125 Raccoon Way, Stroudsburg, PA 18360 **Contact:** 570-402-1018, (fax) 570-402-1018, bnealy@ptd.net, budnealyknifemaker.com
Specialties: Original design concealment knives with designer multi-concealment sheath system. **Patterns:** Fixed Blades and Folders **Technical:** Grinds CPM 154, XHP, and damascus. **Prices:** $200 to $2500. **Remarks:** Full-time maker, first knife sold in 1980. **Mark:** Name, city, state or signature.

NEASE, WILLIAM
2336 Front Rd., LaSalle, ON, CANADA Canada N9J 2C4, wnease@hotmail.com

unsubtleblades.com
Specialties: Hatchets, choppers, and Japanese-influenced designs. **Technical:** Stock removal. Works A-2, D-2, S-7, O-1, powder stainless alloys, composite laminate blades with steel edges. **Prices:** $125 to $2200. **Remarks:** Part-time maker since 1994. **Mark:** Initials W.M.N. engraved in cursive on exposed tangs or on the spine of blades.

NEDVED, DAN
206 Park Dr, Kalispell, MT 59901, bushido2222@yahoo.com
Specialties: Slip joint folders, liner locks, straight knives. **Patterns:** Mostly traditional or modern blend with traditional lines. **Technical:** Grinds ATS-34, 440C, 1095 and uses other makers damascus. **Prices:** $95 and up. Mostly in the $150 to $200 range. **Remarks:** Part-time maker, averages 2 a month. **Mark:** Dan Nedved or Nedved with serial # on opposite side.

NEELY, GREG
5419 Pine St, Bellaire, TX 77401 **Contact:** 713-991-2677, gtneely64@comcast.net
Specialties: Traditional patterns and his own patterns for work and/or collecting. **Patterns:** Hunters, bowies and utility/camp knives. **Technical:** Forges own damascus, 1084, 5160 and some tool steels. Differentially tempers. **Prices:** $225 to $5000. **Remarks:** Part-time maker, first knife sold in 1987. **Mark:** Last name or interlocked initials, MS.

NEELY, JONATHAN
JAECO KNIVES, 2401 N. Beech Ln., Greensboro, NC 27455 **Contact:** 336-540-4925, jaecoknives@gmail.com, jaecoknives.com
Specialties: Fixed-blade hunters, EDC (everyday carry) and utility-style knives. **Technical:** Stock removal maker using 1084 steel. **Prices:** Start at $25 to $30 per inch. **Remarks:** Part-time maker and full-time stay-at-home dad who feels confident he will be making knives for the rest of his life, first knife made in 2014. **Mark:** "Jaeco" (Jon and Erin's Company) with a mountain range logo.

NEILSON, J
187 Cistern Ln., Towanda, PA 18848 **Contact:** 570-721-0470, mountainhollow.net
Specialties: Working and collectable fixed blade knives. **Patterns:** Hunter/fighters, bowies, neck knives and daggers. **Technical:** Multiple high-carbon steels as well as maker's own damascus. **Prices:** $100 to $7,500. **Remarks:** ABS Master Smith, full-time maker, judge on History Channel's "Forged In Fire" program, doing business as Neilson's Mountain Hollow. Each knife comes with a sheath. **Mark:** J. Neilson MS.

NELL, CHAD
2424 E. 2070 S, St. George, UT 84790 **Contact:** 435-229-6442, chad@nellknives.com, nellknives.com
Specialties: Frame-lock folders and fixed blades. **Patterns:** Templar, ESG, Hybrid and Loveless patterns. **Technical:** Grinds CPM-154, ATS-34. **Prices:** Starting at $300. **Remarks:** Full-time maker since Sep 2011, First knife made in May 2010. **Mark:** C. Nell Utah, USA or C. Nell Kona, Hawaii.

NELSON, KEN
2712 17th St., Racine, WI 53405 **Contact:** 262-456-7519 or 262-664-5293, ken@ironwolfonline.com ironwolfonline.com
Specialties: Working straight knives, period pieces. **Patterns:** Utility, hunters, dirks, daggers, throwers, hawks, axes, swords, pole arms and blade blanks as well. **Technical:** Forges 5160, 52100, W2, 10xx, L6, carbon steels and own damascus. Does his own heat treating. **Prices:** $50 to $350, some to $3000. **Remarks:** Part-time maker. First knife sold in 1995. Doing business as Iron Wolf Forge. **Mark:** Stylized wolf paw print.

NETO JR.,, NELSON AND DE CARVALHO, HENRIQUE M.
R. Joao Margarido No 20-V, Braganca Paulista, SP, BRAZIL 12900-000 **Contact:** 011-7843-6889, (fax) 011-7843-6889
Specialties: Straight knives and folders. **Patterns:** bowies, katanas, jambyias and others. **Technical:** Forges high-carbon steels. **Prices:** $70 to $3000. **Remarks:** Full-time makers, first knife sold in 1990. **Mark:** HandN.

NEVLING, MARK
BURR OAK KNIVES, 3567 N. M52, Owosso, MI 48867 **Contact:** 989-472-3167, burroakknives@aol.com, burroakknives.com
Specialties: Tactical folders using stainless over high-carbon San Mai. **Patterns:** Hunters, fighters, bowies, folders and small executive knives. **Technical:** Convex grinds, forges, uses only high-carbon and damascus. **Prices:** $200 to $4,000. **Remarks:** Full-time maker, first knife sold 1988. Apprentice damascus smith to George Werth and Doug Ponzio.

NEWBERRY, ALLEN
Lowell, AR 72745 **Contact:** 479-530-6439, newberry@newberryknives.com newberryknives.com
Specialties: Fixed blades, both forged and stock removal, often with hamons and silver wire inlay. **Patterns:** Traditional patterns as well as newer designs inspired by historical and international blades. **Technical:** Uses 1095, W2, 5160, 1084, 154-CM and damascus. **Prices:** $200 and up. **Remarks:** ABS journeyman smith and "Forged In Fire" champion. He also enjoys teaching Bladesmithing. **Mark:** Newberry J.S. with a capital N for forged pieces and newberry with a lower case n for stock removal pieces.

NEWCOMB, CORBIN
628 Woodland Ave, Moberly, MO 65270 **Contact:** 660-263-4639
Specialties: Working straight knives and folders, period pieces. **Patterns:** Hunters, axes, bowies, folders, buckskinned blades and boots. **Technical:** Hollow-grinds D2, 440C and 154CM, prefers natural handle materials. Makes own damascus, offers cable damascus. **Prices:** $100 to $500. **Remarks:** Full-time maker, first knife sold in 1982. Doing business as Corbin Knives. **Mark:** First name and serial number.

NEWHALL, TOM
3602 E 42nd Stravenue, Tucson, AZ 85713 **Contact:** 520-721-0562, gggaz@aol.com

NEWTON, LARRY
1758 Pronghorn Ct, Jacksonville, FL 32225 **Contact:** 904-537-2066, lnewton1@comcast.net, larrynewtonknives.com
Specialties: Traditional and slender high-grade gentlemen's automatic folders, locking liner type tactical, and working straight knives. **Patterns:** Front release locking folders, interframes, hunters, and skinners. **Technical:** Grinds damascus, ATS-34, 440C and D2. **Prices:** Folders start at $350, straights start at $150. **Remarks:** Retired teacher. Full-time maker. First knife sold in 1989. Won Best Folder for 2008 - Blade Magazine.**Mark:** Last name.

NEWTON, RON
223 Ridge Ln, London, AR 72847 **Contact:** 479-293-3001, rnewton@centurylink.net
Specialties: All types of folders and fixed blades. Blackpowder gun knife combos. **Patterns:** Traditional slip joint, multi-blade patterns, antique bowie repros. **Technical:** Forges traditional and mosaid damascus. Performs engraving and gold inlay. **Prices:** $500 and up. **Remarks:** Creates hidden mechanisms in assisted opening folders. **Mark:** NEWTON M.S. in a western invitation font."

NGUYEN, MIKE
213 Fawn Ct., Pittsburgh, PA 15239 **Contact:** 949-812-2749, mike12_nguyen@yahoo.com, Instagram.com: mike12_nguyen
Patterns: Folders, flipper folders and fixed blades. **Technical:** Stock-removal maker using no smart-controlled machines, sole authorship, in-house heat-treating and custom one-off designs. Uses all types of stainless steels such as CPM 154, CTS-XHP, CPM S90V, as well as high-carbon and damascus. Any materials available, such as carbon fiber, Micarta, copper, zirconium and titanium. **Prices:** $850 to $1,300 and up. **Remarks:** Part-time maker working on one knife at a time. Does not have bookings, but rather holds a lotto for the next build spot at the end of his current build. **Mark:** "M" with extended horizontal lines at end, but maker never puts mark on the blade or anywhere visible.

NICHOLS, CALVIN
710 Colleton Rd., Raleigh, NC 27610 **Contact:** 919-523-4841, calvin.nichols@nicholsknives.com, nicholsknives.com
Specialties: Flame-colored high carbon damascus. **Patterns:** Fixed blades or folders, bowies and daggers. **Technical:** Stock removal. **Prices:** Start at $200. **Remarks:** Full-time maker, 22 years experience, own heat treating, 2012 Best Custom and High Art winner, National and North Carolina Knifemakers Guild member. **Mark:** First, last name--city, state.

NICHOLS, CHAD
1125 Cr 185, Blue Springs, MS 38828 **Contact:** 662-538-5966, chadn28@hotmail.com, chadnicholsdamascus.com
Specialties: Gents folders and everyday tactical/utility style knives and fixed hunters. **Technical:** Makes own stainless damascus, mosaic damascus, and high carbon damascus. **Prices:** $450 - $1000. **Mark:** Name and Blue Springs.

NICHOLSON, R. KENT
16502 Garfield Ave., Monkton, MD 21111 **Contact:** 410-323-6925
Specialties: Large using knives. **Patterns:** bowies and camp knives in the Moran-style. **Technical:** Forges W2, 9260, 5160, makes damascus. **Prices:** $150 to $995. **Remarks:** Part-time maker, first knife sold in 1984. **Mark:** Name.

NIELSON, JEFF V
1060 S Jones Rd, Monroe, UT 84754 **Contact:** 435-527-4242, jvn1u205@hotmail.com
Specialties: Classic knives of his design and to customer specs. **Patterns:** Fighters, hunters, miniatures. **Technical:** Grinds 440C stainless and damascus. **Prices:** $100 to $1200. **Remarks:** Part-time maker, first knife sold in 1991. **Mark:** Name, location.

NIEMUTH, TROY
3143 North Ave, Sheboygan, WI 53083 **Contact:** 414-452-2927
Specialties: Period pieces and working/using straight knives of his design and to customer specs. **Patterns:** Hunters and utility/camp knives. **Technical:** Grinds 440C, 1095 and A2. **Prices:** $85 to $350, some to $500. **Remarks:** Full-time maker, first knife sold in 1995. **Mark:** Etched last name.

NILSSON, JONNY WALKER
Akkavare 16, 93391 Arvidsjaur, SWEDEN **Contact:** +46 702144207, 0960.13048@telia.com, jwnknives.com
Specialties: High-end collectible Nordic hunters, engraved reindeer antler. World class freehand engravings. Matching engraved sheaths in leather, bone and Arctic wood with inlays. Combines traditional techniques and design with his own innovations. Master Bladesmith who specializes in forging mosaic damascus. Sells unique mosaic damascus bar stock to folder makers. **Patterns:** Own designs and traditional Sami designs. **Technical:** Mosaic damascus of UHB 20 C 15N20 with pure nickel, hardness HRC 58-60. **Prices:** $1500 to $6000. **Remarks:** Full-time maker since 1988. Nordic Champion (5 countries) numerous times, 50 first prizes in Scandinavian shows. Yearly award in his name in Nordic Championship. Knives inspired by 10,000 year old indigenous Sami culture. **Mark:** JN on sheath, handle, custom wood box. JWN on blade.

NIRO, FRANK
1948 Gloaming Dr, Kamloops, B.C., CANADA V1S1P8 **Contact:** 250-372-8332, niro@telus.net
Specialties: Liner locking folding knives in his designs in what might be called standard patterns. **Technical:** Enjoys grinding mosaic damascus with pure nickel of the make up for blades that are often double ground, as well as meteorite for bolsters which are then etched and heat colored. Uses 416 stainless for spacers with inlays of natural materials, gem stones with also file work. Liners are made from titanium are most often fully file

worked and anodized. Only uses natural materials particularly mammoth ivory for scales. **Prices:** $500 to $1500 **Remarks:** Full time maker. Has been selling knives for over thirty years. **Mark:** Last name on the inside of the spacer.

NISHIUCHI, MELVIN S

6121 Forest Park Dr, Las Vegas, NV 89156 **Contact:** 702-501-3724, msnknives@yahoo.com

Specialties: Collectable quality using/working knives. **Patterns:** Locking liner folders, fighters, hunters and fancy personal knives. **Technical:** Grinds ATS-34 and Devin Thomas damascus, prefers semi-precious stone and exotic natural handle materials. **Prices:** $375 to $2000. **Remarks:** full-time maker, first knife sold in 1985. **Mark:** Circle with a line above it.

NOAKE, BRETT

Noake Custom Knives 1822 Katlyn Ln, Spring, TX 77386 **Contact:** 832-573-3061, www.noakecustomknives.com, facebook.com/noakecustomknives, Instagram: @noakecustomknives

Patterns: Heirloom-quality hunters, fighters, camp knives and kitchen cutlery **Technical:** Damascus and san mai forged in-house.

NOLEN, STEVE

3325 Teton, Longmont, CO 80504-6251 **Contact:** 720-334-1801, stevenolen1@msn.com, nolenknives.org

Specialties: Working knives and hunters. **Patterns:** Wide variety of straight knives and neck knives. **Technical:** Grinds D2, ATS-34 and 440C. Offers filework and makes exotic handles. **Prices:** $75 to $1,000, some higher. **Remarks:** Part-time maker, third generation, and still has quite a few of R.D. Nolen's collection. **Mark:** NK in oval logo and NOLEN-Steve Nolen knives have hardness and steel engraved by logo.

NOLTE, BARBIE

10801 Gram B Cir., Lowell, AR 72745 **Contact:** 479-283-2095, barbie.b@gmail.com

Specialties: Collector-grade high art knives. **Technical:** Hollow grinds high-carbon, mosaic-damascus blades. Limited supply. **Prices:** Start at $600. All prices include handmade exotic leather sheaths. **Mark:** B Bell and B Nolte.

NOLTE, STEVE

10801 Gram B Cir., Lowell, AR 72745 **Contact:** 479-629-1676, snolte@alertalarmsys.com, snolteknives.com

Specialties: Fancy hunters and skinners, a few fighters, some collector-grade, high-art knives. One-of-a-kind mosaic handle creations including exotic stone work. **Technical:** Mostly high-carbon damascus, some stainless damascus with very few straight stainless blades. Hollow grinds. **Prices:** Start at $400. All prices include handmade sheaths, mostly exotic leathers. **Mark:** S.Nolte.

NOOT, ALEXANDER

LX Blades Staringstraat 236, 5343GM, Oss, The Netherlands **Contact:** +31628757048, xemergency@gmail.com, Instagram: @lx_emergency

Specialties: Custom knives and sheaths, rehandles and regrinds.

NORDELL, INGEMAR

Skarp Œvagen 5, F Šrila, SWEDEN 82041 **Contact:** 0651-23347, ingi@ingemarnordell.se, ingemarnordell.se

Specialties: Classic working and using straight knives. **Patterns:** Hunters, bowies and fighters. **Technical:** Forges and grinds ATS-34, D2 and Sandvik. **Prices:** $300 to $3,000. **Remarks:** Part-time maker, first knife sold in 1985. **Mark:** Initials or name.

NOREN, DOUGLAS E

14676 Boom Rd, Springlake, MI 49456 **Contact:** 616-842-4247, gnoren@icsworldmail.com

Specialties: Hand forged blades, custom built and made to order. Hand filework, carving and casting. Stag and stacked handles. Replicas of Scagel and Joseph Rogers pieces, as well as American bowies. Hand-tooled custom made sheaths. **Technical:** Master smith, 5160, 52100 and 1084 steel. **Prices:** $400 and up. **Remarks:** Sole authorship, works in all mediums, ABS Mastersmith, all knives come with a custom hand-tooled sheath. Enjoys the challenge and meeting people.

NORFLEET, ROSS W

4110 N Courthouse Rd, Providence Forge, VA 23140-3420 **Contact:** 804-966-2596, rossknife@aol.com

Specialties: Classic, traditional and working/using knives of his design or in standard patterns. **Patterns:** Hunters and folders. **Technical:** Hollow-grinds 440C and ATS-34. **Prices:** $150 to $550. **Remarks:** Part-time maker, first knife sold in 1992. **Mark:** Last name.

NORTON, DON

95N Wilkison Ave, Port Townsend, WA 98368-2534 **Contact:** 306-385-1978

Specialties: Fancy and plain straight knives. **Patterns:** Hunters, small bowies, tantos, boot knives, fillets. **Technical:** Prefers 440C, Micarta, exotic woods and other natural handle materials. Hollow-grinds all knives except fillet knives. **Prices:** $185 to $2800, average is $200. **Remarks:** Full-time maker, first knife sold in 1980. **Mark:** Full name, Hsi Shuai, city, state.

NOVINC, KEVIN

Novinc Knives 2869 Wimbledon Drive, Gastonia, NC 28056 **Contact:** 704-747-2288, www.NovincKnives.com

Specialties: Stock removal, full-tang working knives. **Patterns:** Outdoors. **Technical:** Carbon, stainless, and damascus steel. **Remarks:** Full-time maker. NC Custom Knifemakers Guild and The Knifemakers' Guild.

NOWACKI, STEPHEN R.

167 King Georges Ave, Regents Park, Southampton, Hampshire, ENGLAND SO154LD **Contact:** 023 81 785 630 or 079 29 737 872, forgesmith9@gmail.com, whitetigerknives.com

Specialties: Hand-forged, bowies, daggers, tactical blades, hunters and mountain-man style folders. **Technical:** Hitachi white paper steel and stainless carbon San Mai. Heat treats and uses natural handle materials. **Prices:** $200 - $1500. **Remarks:** Full-time maker. First knife sold in 2000. Doing business as White Tiger Knives. **Mark:** Stylized W T.

NOWLAND, RICK

3677 E Bonnie Rd, Waltonville, IL 62894 **Contact:** 618-279-3170, ricknowland@frontiernet.net

Specialties: Slip joint folders in traditional patterns. **Patterns:** Trapper, whittler, sowbelly, toothpick and copperhead. **Technical:** Uses ATS-34, bolsters and liners have integral construction. **Prices:** $225 to $1000. **Remarks:** Part-time maker. **Mark:** Last name.

NUCKELS, STEPHEN J

1105 Potomac Ave, Hagerstown, MD 21742 **Contact:** 301-739-1287, sgnucks@myactv.net

Specialties: Traditional using/working/everyday carry knives and small neck knives. **Patterns:** Hunters, bowies, Drop and trailing point knives, frontier styles. **Technical:** Hammer forges carbon steels, stock removal. Modest silver wire inlay and file work. Sheath work. **Remarks:** Spare-time maker forging under Potomac Forge, first knife made in 2008. Member W.F. Moran Jr. Foundation, American Bladesmith Society. **Mark:** Initials.

NUNN, GREGORY

HC64 Box 2107, Castle Valley, UT 84532 **Contact:** 435-259-8607

Specialties: High-art working and using knives of his design, new edition knife with handle made from anatomized dinosaur bone, first ever made. **Patterns:** Flaked stone knives. **Technical:** Uses gem-quality agates, jaspers and obsidians for blades. **Prices:** $250 to $2300. **Remarks:** Full-time maker, first knife sold in 1989. **Mark:** Name, knife and edition numbers, year made.

NYLUND, ERIK

Kyrontie 31, 65320 Vaasa, FINLAND **Contact:** +358456349392, erik.nylund@pp2.inet.fi, personal.inet.fi/koti/erik.nylund/

Specialties: Art knives. **Patterns:** Art knives, hunters and leuku knives. **Technical:** Forges Silversteel and 52100, and grinds RWL-34, Damasteel and 13C26. **Prices:** Start at $250. **Remarks:** Part-time maker. **Mark:** Erik Nylund, or earlier knives marked EN.

O

OATES, LEE

Bear Claw Knives. PO BOX 214, Bethpage, TN 37022 **Contact:** 281-838-0480 or 281-838-0468, bearoates89@comcast.net, bearclawknives.com

Specialties: Friction folders, period correct replicas, traditional, working and primitive knives of my design or to customer specs. **Patterns:** bowies, teflon-coated fighters, daggers, hunters, fillet and kitchen cutlery. **Technical:** Heat treating service for other makers. Teaches blacksmithing/bladesmithing classes. Forges carbon, 440C, D2, and makes own damascus, stock removal on SS and kitchen cutlery, Teflon coatings available on custom hunters/fighters, makes own sheaths. **Prices:** $150 to $2500. **Remarks:** Full-time maker and heat treater since 1996. First knife sold in 1988. **Mark:** Harmony (yin/yang) symbol with two bear tracks inside all forged blades, etched "Commanche Cutlery" on SS kitchen cutlery.

O'BRIEN, MIKE J.

3807 War Bow, San Antonio, TX 78238 **Contact:** 210-256-0673, obrien8700@att.net

Specialties: Quality straight knives of his design. **Patterns:** Mostly daggers (safe queens), some hunters. **Technical:** Grinds 440c, ATS-34, and CPM-154. Emphasis on clean workmanship and solid design. Likes hand-rubbed blades and fittings, exotic woods. **Prices:** $300 to $700 and up. **Remarks:** Part-time maker, made first knife in 1988. **Mark:** O'BRIEN in semi-circle.

OCHS, CHARLES F

124 Emerald Lane, Largo, FL 33771 **Contact:** 727-536-3827, (fax) 727-536-3827, charlesox@oxforge.com, ochsworx.com

Specialties: Working knives, period pieces. **Patterns:** Hunters, fighters, bowies, buck skinners and folders. **Technical:** Forges 52100, 5160 and his own damascus. **Prices:** $150 to $1800, some to $2500. **Remarks:** Full-time maker, first knife sold in 1978. **Mark:** OX Forge.

OCHS, ERIC

PO BOX 1311, Sherwood, OR 97140 **Contact:** 503-925-9790, (fax) 503-925-9790, eric@ochs.com ochssherworx.com

Specialties: Tactical folders and flippers, as well as fixed blades for tactical, hunting and camping. **Patterns:** Tactical liner- and frame-lock folders with texture in various synthetic and natural materials. **Technical:** Focus on powder metals, including CPM-S30V, Elmax, CPM-154, CPM-3V and CPM-S35VN, as well as damascus steels. Flat, hollow, compound and Loveless-style grinds. **Prices:** $300 - $2,500. **Remarks:** Full-time maker, made first knife in 2008 and started selling knives in mid-2009. **Mark:** The words "Ochs Sherworx" separated by an eight point compass insignia was used through 2013. Beginning in January 2014, "Ochs Worx" separated by navigation star compass insignia.

ODOM JR., VICTOR L.

PO Box 572, North, SC 29112 **Contact:** 803-247-2749, cell 803-608-0829, vlodom3@tds.net, odomforge.com

Specialties: Forged knives and tomahawks, stock removal knives. **Patterns:** Hunters, bowies, George Herron patterns, and folders. **Technical:** Use 1095, 5160, 52100 high carbon and alloy steels, ATS-34, and 154 CM. **Prices:** Straight knives $60 and up. Folders $250 and up. **Remarks:** Student of Mr. George Herron. SCAK.ORG. **Mark:** Steel stamp "ODOM" and etched "Odom Forge North, SC" plus year.

OELOFSE, TINUS
P.O. Box 33879, Glenstantia, Pretoria, SOUTH AFRICA 0100 **Contact:** +27-82-3225090, tinusoelofseknives@gmail.com
Specialties: Top-class folders, mainly LinerLocks, and practical fixed blades. **Technical:** Using damascus, mostly Damasteel, and blade billets. Mammoth ivory, mammoth tooth, mother-of-pearl, gold and black-lip-pearl handles for folders. Giraffe bone, warthog ivory, horn and African hardwoods for hunters. Deep relief engraving, mostly leaf and scroll, and daughter Mariscke's scrimshaw. Likes to work on themed knives and special projects. Hand-stitched sheaths by Kitty. **Prices:** $350 to $1,500. **Mark:** Tinus Oelofse in an oval logo with a dagger outline used for the "T."

OGDEN, BILL
OGDEN KNIVES, PO Box 52, Avis
AVIS, PA 17721 **Contact:** 570-974-9114
Specialties: One-of-a-kind, liner-lock folders, hunters, skinners, minis. **Technical:** Grinds ATS-34, 440-C, D2, 52100, damascus, natural and unnatural handle materials, hand-stitched custom sheaths. **Prices:** $50 and up. **Remarks:** Part-time maker since 1992. Marks: Last name or "OK" stamp (Ogden Knives).

OGLETREE JR., BEN R
2815 Israel Rd., Livingston, TX 77351 **Contact:** 409-327-8315
Specialties: Working/using straight knives of his design. **Patterns:** Hunters, kitchen and utility/camp knives. **Technical:** Grinds ATS-34, W1 and 1075, heat-treats. **Prices:** $200 to $400. **Remarks:** Part-time maker, first knife sold in 1955. **Mark:** Last name, city and state in oval with a tree on either side.

O'HARE, SEAN
1831 Rte. 776, Grand Manan, NB, CANADA E5G 2H9 **Contact:** 506-662-8524, sean@oharecustomknives.com, oharecustomknives.com
Specialties: Fixed blade hunters and folders. **Patterns:** Fixed and folding knives, daily carry to collectible art. **Technical:** Stock removal, flat ground. **Prices:** $250 USD to $2,000 USD. **Remarks:** Strives to balance aesthetics, functionality and durability. **Mark:** O'Hare.

OHLEMANN, BOB
RANGERMADE KNIVES **Contact:** 832-549-7218, ohlemannr@hotmail.com, rangermadeknives.com, Facebook.com/rangermadeknives
Specialties: Texas-based maker of custom LinerLocks and fixed blades. **Technical:** Forges and stock removal working primarily in W2, CPM 154 and damascus, with other materials including zirconium, meteorite, Timascus, stag, mammoth ivory and precious metals and gems. **Prices:** Fixed blades start at $350 and folders start at $700. **Remarks:** Full-time maker who has been making knives since 2014.

OLIVE, MICHAEL E
6388 Angora Mt Rd, Leslie, AR 72645 **Contact:** 870-363-4668
Specialties: Fixed blades. **Patterns:** bowies, camp knives, fighters and hunters. **Technical:** Forged blades of 1084, W2, 5160, damascus of 1084, and1572. **Prices:** $250 and up. **Remarks:** Received J.S. stamp in 2005. **Mark:** Olive.

OLIVER, TODD D
OLIVER CUSTOM BLADES, 7430 Beckle Rd., Cheyenne, WY 82009 **Contact:** 307-274-6454, tdblues7@aol.com
Specialties: damascus hunters and daggers. High-carbon as well. **Patterns:** Ladder, twist random. **Technical:** Sole author of all his blades. **Prices:** $350 and up. **Remarks:** Learned bladesmithing from Jim Batson at the ABS school and damascus from Billy Merritt in Indiana. **Mark:** T.D. Oliver Spencer IN. Two crossed swords and a battle ax.

OLSON, DARROLD E
PO Box 1182, McMinnville, OR 97128 **Contact:** 541-285-1412
Specialties: Straight knives and folders of his design and to customer specs. **Patterns:** Hunters, liner locks and slip joints. **Technical:** Grinds ATS-34, 154CM and 440C. Uses anodized titanium, sheaths wet-molded. **Prices:** $125 to $550 and up. **Remarks:** Part-time maker, first knife sold in 1989. **Mark:** Name, type of steel and year.

OLSON, JOE
2008 4th Ave., #8, Great Falls, MT 59405 **Contact:** 406-735-4404, olsonhandmade@hotmail.com, olsonhandmade.com
Specialties: Theme based art knives specializing in mosaic damascus autos, folders, and straight knives, all sole authorship. **Patterns:** Mas. **Technical:** Foix. **Prices:** $300 to $5000 with most in the $3500 range. **Remarks:** Full-time maker for 15 years. **Mark:** Folders marked OLSON relief carved into back bar. Carbon steel straight knives stamped OLSON, forged hunters also stamped JS on reverse side.

OLSON, ROD
Box 373, Nanton, AB, CANADA T0L 1R0 **Contact:** 403-646-5838, rod.olson@hotmail.com
Patterns: Button lock folders. **Technical:** Grinds RWL 34 blade steel, titanium frames. **Prices:** Mid range. **Remarks:** Part-time maker, first knife sold in 1979. **Mark:** Last name.

OLSZEWSKI, STEPHEN
1820 Harkney Hill Rd, Coventry, RI 02816 **Contact:** 401-397-4774, blade5377@yahoo.com, olszewskiknives.com
Specialties: Lock back, liner locks, automatics (art knives). **Patterns:** One-of-a-kind art knives specializing in figurals. **Technical:** damascus steel, titanium file worked liners,

fossil ivory and pearl. Double actions. **Prices:** $400 to $20,000. **Remarks:** Will custom build to your specifications. Quality work with guarantee. **Mark:** SCO inside fish symbol. Also "Olszewski."

O'MACHEARLEY, MICHAEL
129 Lawnview Dr., Wilmington, OH 45177 **Contact:** 937-728-2818, omachearleycustomknives@yahoo.com
Specialties: Forged and Stock removal, hunters, skinners, bowies, plain to fancy. **Technical:** ATS-34 and 5160, forges own damascus. **Prices:** $180-$1000 and up. **Remarks:** Full-time maker, first knife made in 1999. **Mark:** Last name and shamrock.

O'MALLEY, DANIEL
4338 Evanston Ave N, Seattle, WA 98103 **Contact:** 206-261-1735
Specialties: Custom chef's knives. **Remarks:** Making knives since 1997.

ONION, KENNETH J
47-501 Hui Kelu St, Kaneohe, HI 96744 **Contact:** 808-239-1300, shopjunky@aol.com, kenonionknives.com
Specialties: Folders featuring speed safe as well as other invention gadgets. **Patterns:** Hybrid, art, fighter, utility. **Technical:** S30V, CPM 154V, Cowry Y, SQ-2 and damascus. **Prices:** $500 to $20,000. **Remarks:** Full-time maker, designer and inventor. First knife sold in 1991. **Mark:** Name and state.

O'QUINN, W. LEE
2654 Watson St., Elgin, SC 29045 **Contact:** 803-438-8322, wleeoquinn@bellsouth.net, creativeknifeworks.com
Specialties: Hunters, utility, working, tactical and neck knives. **Technical:** Grinds ATS-34, CPM-154, 5160, D2, 1095 and damascus steels. **Prices:** Start at $100. **Remarks:** Member of South Carolina Association of Knifemakers. **Mark:** O'Quinn.

ORFORD, BEN
Nethergreen Farm, Ridgeway Cross, Malvern, Worcestershire, ENGLAND WR13 5JS **Contact:** 44 01886 880410, benorford.com
Specialties: Working knives for woodcraft and the outdoorsman, made to his own designs. **Patterns:** Mostly flat Scandinavian grinds, full and partial tang. Also makes specialist woodcraft tools and hook knives. Custom leather sheaths by Lois, his wife. **Technical:** Grinds and forges O1, EN9, EN43, EN45 plus recycled steels. Heat treats. **Prices:** $25 - $650. **Remarks:** Full-time maker, first knife made in 1997. **Mark:** Celtic knot with name underneath.

ORTON, RICH
1218 Cary Ave.r., Wilmington, CA 90744 **Contact:** 310-549-2990, rorton2@ca.rr.com
Specialties: Straight knives only. **Patterns:** Fighters, hunters, skinners. **Technical:** Grinds ATS-34. Heat treats by Paul Bos.**Prices:** $100 to $1000. **Remarks:** Full-time maker, first knife sold in 1992. Doing business as Orton Knife Works. **Mark:** Rich Orton/Maker/Wilmington, CA./Orton Knifeworks.

OSBORNE, DONALD H
5840 N McCall, Clovis, CA 93611 **Contact:** 559-250-7701, oforge@sbcglobal.net
Specialties: Traditional working using straight knives and folder of his design. **Patterns:** Working straight knives, bowies, hunters, camp knives and folders. **Technical:** Forges carbon steels and makes damascus. Grinds ATS-34, 154CM, and 440C. **Prices:** $150 and up. **Remarks:** Part-time maker. **Mark:** Last name logo and J.S.

OTT, FRED
1257 Rancho Durango Rd, Durango, CO 81303 **Contact:** 970-375-9669, fredsknives@wildblue.net
Patterns: bowies, hunters tantos and daggers. **Technical:** Forges 1086M, W2 and damascus. **Prices:** $250 to $2,000. **Remarks:** Full-time maker. **Mark:** Last name.

OTT, TED
154 Elgin Woods Ln., Elgin, TX 78621 **Contact:** 512-413-2243, tedottknives@aol.com
Specialties: Fixed blades, chef knives, butcher knives, bowies, fillet and hunting knives. **Technical:** Use mainly CPM powder steel, also ATS-34 and D-2. **Prices:** $250 - $1000, depending on embellishments, including scrimshaw and engraving. **Remarks:** Part-time maker, sold first knife in 1993. Won world cutting competition title in 2010 and 2012, along with the Bladesports championship. **Mark:** Ott Knives Elgin Texas.

OUYE, KEITH
PO Box 25307, Honolulu, HI 96825 **Contact:** 808-395-7000, keith@keithouyeknives.com, keithouyeknives.com
Specialties: Folders with 1/8 blades and titanium handles. **Patterns:** Tactical design with liner lock and flipper. **Technical:** Blades are stainless steel ATS 34, CPM154 and S30V. Titanium liners (.071) and scales 3/16 pivots and stop pin, titanium pocket clip. Heat treat by Paul Bos.**Prices:** $495 to $995, with engraved knives starting at $1,200. **Remarks:** Engraving done by C.J. Cal, Bruce Shaw, Lisa Tomlin and Tom Ferry. Retired, so basically a full time knifemaker. Sold first fixed blade in 2004 and first folder in 2005. **Mark:** Ouye/Hawaii with steel type on back side **Other:** Selected by Blade Magazine (March 2006 issue) as one of five makers to watch in 2006.

OVERALL, JASON
111 Golfside Cir., Sanford, FL 32773 **Contact:** 407-883-5800, Larevo@gmail.com, larevoknives.com, Instagram: larevoknives
Specialties: High-grade tactical and dress tactical folders and fixed blades. **Technical:** Stock removal method of blade making with various stainless steels and stainless damascus, and uses titanium, zirconium, Timascus, Mokuti, Mokume and other high-performance alloys. Manmade and natural handle materials used, and offers custom-designed pocket clips. **Prices:** $650 and up, depending on materials and details. **Mark:** Combined L and K.

custom knifemakers

OVEREYNDER, T.R.
1800 S. Davis Dr, Arlington, TX 76013 **Contact:** 817-277-4812, troverreynder@gmail.com or tom@overeynderknives.com, overeynderknives.com
Specialties: Highly finished collector-grade knives. Multi-blades. **Patterns:** Fighters, bowies, daggers, locking folders, 70 percent collector-grade multi blade slip joints, 25 percent interframe, 5 percent fixed blade **Technical:** Grinds CPM-D2, CPM-S60V, CPM-S30V, CPM-154, CPM-M4, BG-42, CTS-XHP, PSF27, RWL-34 and vendor supplied damascus. Has been making titanium-frame folders since 1977. **Prices:** $800 to $2,500, some to $9,000. **Remarks:** Full-time maker, first knife sold in 1977. Doing business as TRO Knives. AKI and ABS member. **Mark:** T.R. OVEREYNDER KNIVES, city and state.

OWEN, DAVID J.A.
30 New Forest Rd., Forest Town, Johannesburg, SOUTH AFRICA **Contact:** +27-11-486-1086, cell: +27-82-990-7178, djaowen25@gmail.com
Specialties: Steak knife sets, carving sets, bird-and-trout knives, top-end hunting knives, LinerLock folders. **Patterns:** Variety of knives and techniques. **Technical:** Stock-removal method, freehand hollow and flat grinds, exotic handle materials such as African hardwoods, giraffe bone, hippo tooth and warthog tusk. **Prices:** $150 and up. **Remarks:** Full-time maker since 1993. **Mark:** Two knives back-to-back with words "Owen" and "original" acid etched above and below the knives.

OWENS, DONALD
2274 Lucille Ln, Melbourne, FL 32935 **Contact:** 321-254-9765

OWENS, JOHN
P.O. Box 455, Buena Vista, CO 81211 **Contact:** 719-207-0067
Specialties: Hunters. **Prices:** $225 to $425 some to $700. **Remarks:** Spare-time maker. **Mark:** Last name.

OWNBY, JOHN C
708 Morningside Tr., Murphy, TX 75094-4365 **Contact:** 972-442-7352, john@johnownby.com, johnownby.com
Specialties: Hunters, utility/camp knives. **Patterns:** Hunters, locking folders and utility/camp knives. **Technical:** 440C, D2 and ATS-34. All blades are flat ground. Prefers natural materials for handles—exotic woods, horn and antler. **Prices:** $150 to $350, some to $500. **Remarks:** Part-time maker, first knife sold in 1993. Doing business as John C. Ownby Handmade Knives. **Mark:** Name, city, state.

OYSTER, LOWELL R
543 Grant Rd, Corinth, ME 04427 **Contact:** 207-884-8663
Specialties: Traditional and original designed multi-blade slip-joint folders. **Patterns:** Hunters, minis, camp and fishing knives. **Technical:** Grinds O1, heat-treats. **Prices:** $55 to $450, some to $750. **Remarks:** Full-time maker, first knife sold in 1981. **Mark:** A scallop shell.

P

PACKARD, RONNIE
301 White St., Bonham, TX 75418 **Contact:** 903-227-3131, packardknives@gmail.com, packardknives.com
Specialties: bowies, folders (lockback, slip joint, frame lock, hobo knives) and hunters of all sizes. **Technical:** Grinds 440C, ATS-34, D2 and stainless damascus. Makes own sheaths, does heat treating and sub-zero quenching in shop. **Prices:** $160 to $2,000. **Remarks:** Part-time maker, first knife sold in 1975. **Mark:** Last name over year.

PADILLA, GARY
336 36th Street #371 Bellingham, Washington 98225 **Contact:** 360-756-7573, gkpadilla@yahoo.com
Specialties: Unique knives of all designs and uses. **Patterns:** Hunters, kitchen knives, utility/camp knives and obsidian ceremonial knives. **Technical:** Grinds 440C, ATS-34 and damascus, with limited flintknapped obsidian. **Prices:** Discounted from $50 to $200 generally. **Remarks:** Retired part-time maker, first knife sold in 1977. **Mark:** Stylized name.

PAGE, LARRY
1200 Mackey Scott Rd, Aiken, SC 29801-7620 **Contact:** 803-648-0001
Specialties: Working knives of his design. **Patterns:** Hunters, boots and fighters. **Technical:** Grinds ATS-34. **Prices:** Start at $85. **Remarks:** Part-time maker, first knife sold in 1983. **Mark:** Name, city and state in oval.

PAGE, REGINALD
6587 Groveland Hill Rd, Groveland, NY 14462 **Contact:** 716-243-1643
Specialties: High-art straight knives and one-of-a-kind folders of his design. **Patterns:** Hunters, locking folders and slip-joint folders. **Technical:** Forges O1, 5160 and his own damascus. Prefers natural handle materials but will work with Micarta. **Remarks:** Spare-time maker, first knife sold in 1985. **Mark:** First initial, last name.

PAINTER, TONY
87 Fireweed Dr, Whitehorse, YT, CANADA Y1A 5T8 **Contact:** 867-633-3323, yukonjimmies@gmail.com, tonypainterdesigns.com
Specialties: One-of-a-kind using knives, some fancy, fixed and folders. **Patterns:** No fixed patterns. **Technical:** Grinds ATS-34, D2, O1, S30V, damascus satin finish. Prefers to use exotic woods and other natural materials. Micarta and G10 on working knives. **Prices:** Starting at $200. **Remarks:** Full-time knifemaker and carver. First knife sold in 1996. **Mark:** Two stamps used: initials TP in a circle and painter.

PALIKKO, J-T
B30 B1, Suomenlinna, 00190 Helsinki, FINLAND **Contact:** +358-400-699687, jt@kp-art.fi, art-helsinki.com
Specialties: One-of-a-kind knives and swords. **Patterns:** Own puukko models, hunters,

integral & semi-integral knives, swords & other historical weapons and friction folders. **Technical:** Forges 52100 & other carbon steels, Damasteel stainless damascus & RWL-34, makes own damascus steel, makes carvings on walrus ivory and antler. **Prices:** Starting at $250. **Remarks:** Full-time maker, first knife sold in 1989. **Mark:** JT

PALM, RIK
10901 Scripps Ranch Blvd, San Diego, CA 92131 **Contact:** 858-530-0407, rikpalm@knifesmith.com, knifesmith.com
Specialties: Sole authorship of one-of-a-kind unique art pieces, working/using knives and sheaths. **Patterns:** Carved nature themed knives, camp, hunters, friction folders, tomahawks, and small special pocket knives. **Technical:** Makes own damascus, forges 5160H, 1084, 1095, W2, O1. Does his own heat treating including clay hardening. **Prices:** $80 and up. **Remarks:** American Bladesmith Society Journeyman Smith. First blade sold in 2000. **Mark:** Stamped, hand signed, etched last name signature.

PALMER, TAYLOR
TAYLOR-MADE SCENIC KNIVES INC., 1607 E. 450 S, Blanding, UT 84511 **Contact:** 435-678-2523, taylormadewoodeu@citlink.net
Specialties: Bronze carvings inside of blade area. **Prices:** $250 and up. **Mark:** Taylor Palmer Utah.

PANAK, PAUL S
6103 Leon Rd., Andover, OH 44003 **Contact:** 330-442-2724, burn@burnknives.com, burnknives.com
Specialties: Italian-styled knives. DA OTF's, Italian style stilettos. **Patterns:** Vintage-styled Italians, fighting folders and high art gothic-styles all with various mechanisms. **Technical:** Grinds ATS-34, 154 CM, 440C and damascus. **Prices:** $800 to $3000. **Remarks:** Full-time maker, first knife sold in 1998. **Mark:** "Burn."

PANCHENKO, SERGE
5927 El Sol Way, Citrus Heights, CA 95621 **Contact:** 916-588-8821, serge@sergeknives.com sergeknives.com
Specialties: Unique art knives using natural materials, copper and carbon steel for a rustic look. **Patterns:** Art knives, tactical folders, Japanese- and relic-style knives. **Technical:** Forges carbon steel, grinds carbon and stainless steels. **Prices:** $100 to $800. **Remarks:** Part-time maker, first knife sold in 2008. **Mark:** SERGE

PARDUE, JOE
PO Box 569, Hillister, TX 77624 **Contact:** 409-429-7074, (fax) 409-429-5657, joepardue@hughes.net, melpardueknives.com/Joeparudueknives/index.htm

PARDUE, MELVIN M
4461 Jerkins Rd., Repton, AL 36475 **Contact:** 251-248-2686, mpardue@frontiernet.net, pardueknives.com
Specialties: Folders, collectable, combat, utility and tactical. **Patterns:** Lockback, liner lock, push button, all blade and handle patterns. **Technical:** Grinds 154CM, 440C, 12C27. Forges mokume and damascus. Uses titanium. **Prices:** $400 to $1600. **Remarks:** Full-time maker, Guild member, ABS member, AFC member. First knife made in 1957, first knife sold professionally in 1974. **Mark:** Mel Pardue.

PARKER, CLIFF
6350 Tulip Dr, Zephyrhills, FL 33544 **Contact:** 813-973-1682, cooldamascus@aol.com, cliffparkerknives.com
Specialties: damascus gent knives. **Patterns:** Locking liners, some straight knives. **Technical:** Mostly use 1095, 1084, 15N20, 203E and powdered steel. **Prices:** $700 to $2100. **Remarks:** Making own damascus and specializing in mosaics, first knife sold in 1996. Full-time beginning in 2000. **Mark:** CP.

PARKER, J E
11 Domenica Cir, Clarion, PA 16214 **Contact:** 814-226-4837, jimparkerknives@hotmail.com, jimparkerknives.com
Specialties: Fancy/embellished, traditional and working straight knives of his design and to customer specs. Engraving and scrimshaw by the best in the business. **Patterns:** bowies, hunters and LinerLock® folders. **Technical:** Grinds 440C, 440V, ATS-34 and nickel damascus. Prefers mastodon, oosik, amber and malachite handle material. **Prices:** $75 to $5200. **Remarks:** Full-time maker, first knife sold in 1991. List under art shows as Jim Parker Custom Knives. **Mark:** J E Parker and Clarion PA stamped or etched in blade.

PARKER, ROBERT NELSON
1527 E Fourth St, Royal Oak, MI 48067 **Contact:** 248-709-8622, rnparkerknives@gmail.com, classicknifedesign.com
Specialties: Traditional working and using straight knives of his design. **Patterns:** Chutes, subhilts, hunters, and fighters. **Technical:** Grinds CPM-154, CPM-D2, BG-42 and ATS-34, no forging, hollow and flat grinds, full and hidden tangs. Hand-stitched leather sheaths. **Prices:** $400 to $2,000, some to $3,000. **Remarks:** Full-time maker, first knife sold in 1986. I do forge sometimes. **Mark:** Full name.

PARKINSON, MATTHEW
DRAGON'S BREATH FORGE, 10 Swiss Ln., Wolcott, CT 06716 **Contact:** 203-879-1786, swordmatt@yahoo.com and info@fallinghammerproductions.com, dragonsbreathforge.com
Specialties: Knives, swords and axes from the 7th-19th centuries, as well as kitchen knives. **Technical:** Forges blades in a number of steels, including 1084, W1, 80CrV2, L6 and his own damascus in 1095/15N20 and 8670/1095. Specializes in the low-layer, multi-bar Viking style of pattern welding. **Prices:** Knives start at $200 and swords at $1,000. **Remarks:** First knife made in 1990, "Forged In Fire" champion, winning the first aired episode (katana making) on History Channel. **Mark:** Connected MP in a shield, and in the past used simply a connected MP. Viking-era blades are marked with the runes for M&P.

PARKS, BLANE C
15908 Crest Dr, Woodbridge, VA 22191 **Contact:** 703-221-4680
Specialties: Knives of his design. **Patterns:** Boots, bowies, daggers, fighters, hunters, kitchen knives, locking and slip-joint folders, utility/camp knives, letter openers and friction folders. **Technical:** Grinds ATS-34, 440C, D2 and other carbon steels. Offers filework, silver wire inlay and wooden sheaths. **Prices:** Start at $250 to $650, some to $1000. **Remarks:** Part-time maker, first knife sold in 1993. Doing business as B.C. Parks Knives. **Mark:** First and middle initials, last name.

PARKS, JOHN
3539 Galilee Church Rd, Jefferson, GA 30549 **Contact:** 706-367-4916
Specialties: Traditional working and using straight knives of his design. **Patterns:** Hunters, integral bolsters, and personal knives. **Technical:** Forges 1095 and 5168. **Prices:** $275 to $600, some to $800. **Remarks:** Part-time maker, first knife sold in 1989. **Mark:** Initials.

PARLER, THOMAS O
11 Franklin St, Charleston, SC 29401 **Contact:** 803-723-9433

PARRISH, ROBERT
271 Allman Hill Rd, Weaverville, NC 28787 **Contact:** 828-645-2864
Specialties: Heavy-duty working knives of his design or to customer specs. **Patterns:** Survival and duty knives, hunters and fighters. **Technical:** Grinds 440C, D2, O1 and commercial damascus. **Prices:** $200 to $300, some to $6000. **Remarks:** Part-time maker, first knife sold in 1970. **Mark:** Initials connected, sometimes with city and state.

PARRISH III, GORDON A
940 Lakloey Dr, North Pole, AK 99705 **Contact:** 907-488-0357, ga-parrish@gci.net
Specialties: Classic and high-art straight knives of his design and to customer specs, working and using knives. **Patterns:** bowies and hunters. **Technical:** Grinds tool steel and ATS-34. Uses mostly Alaskan handle materials. **Prices:** Starting at $300. **Remarks:** Spare-time maker, first knife sold in 1980. **Mark:** Last name, FBKS. ALASKA

PARSONS, LARRY
539 S. Pleasant View Dr., Mustang, OK 73064 **Contact:** 405-376-9408, l.j.parsons@sbcglobal.net, parsonssaddleshop.com
Specialties: Variety of sheaths from plain leather, geometric stamped, also inlays of various types. **Prices:** Starting at $35 and up

PARSONS, PETE
5905 High Country Dr., Helena, MT 59602 **Contact:** 406-202-0181, Parsons14@MT.net, ParsonsMontanaKnives.com
Specialties: Forged utility blades in straight steel or damascus (will grind stainless on customer request). Folding knives of my own design. **Patterns:** Hunters, fighters, bowies, hikers, camp knives, everyday carry folders, tactical folders, gentleman's folders. Some customer designed pieces. **Technical:** Forges carbon steel, grinds carbon steel and some stainless. Forges own damascus. **Mark:** Left side of blade PARSONS stamp or Parsons Helena, MT etch.

PARTRIDGE, JERRY D.
P.O. Box 977, DeFuniak Springs, FL 32435 **Contact:** 850-520-4873, jerry@partridgeknives.com, partridgeknives.com
Specialties: Fancy and working straight knives and straight razors of his designs. **Patterns:** Hunters, skinners, fighters, chef's knives, straight razors, neck knives, and miniatures. **Technical:** Grinds 440C, ATS-34, carbon damascus, and stainless damascus. **Prices:** $250 and up, depending on materials used. **Remarks:** Part-time maker, first knife sold in 2007. **Mark:** Partridge Knives logo on the blade, Partridge or Partridge Knives engraved in script.

PASSMORE, JIMMY D
316 SE Elm, Hoxie, AR 72433 **Contact:** 870-886-1922

PATRICK, BOB
12642 24A Ave, S. Surrey, BC, CANADA V4A 8H9 **Contact:** 604-538-6214, (fax) 604-888-2683, bob@knivesonnet.com, knivesonnet.com
Specialties: Maker's designs only, No orders. **Patterns:** bowies, hunters, daggers, throwing knives. **Technical:** D2, 5160, damascus. **Prices:** Good value. **Remarks:** Full-time maker, first knife sold in 1987. Doing business as Crescent Knife Works. **Mark:** Logo with name and province or Crescent Knife Works.

PATRICK, CHUCK
4650 Pine Log Rd., Brasstown, NC 28902 **Contact:** 828-837-7627, chuckandpeggypatrick@gmail.com chuckandpeggypatrick.com
Specialties: Period pieces. **Patterns:** Hunters, daggers, tomahawks, pre-Civil War folders. **Technical:** Forges hardware, his own cable and damascus, available in fancy pattern and mosaic. **Prices:** $150 to $1000, some higher. **Remarks:** Full-time maker. **Mark:** Hand-engraved name or flying owl.

PATRICK, PEGGY
4650 Pine Log Rd., Brasstown, NC 28902 **Contact:** 828-837-7627, chuckandpeggypatrick@gmail.com chuckandpeggypatrick.com
Specialties: Authentic period and Indian sheaths, braintan, rawhide, beads and quill work. **Technical:** Does own braintan, rawhide, uses only natural dyes for quills, old color beads.

PATRICK, WILLARD C
PO Box 5716, Helena, MT 59604 **Contact:** 406-458-6552, wilamar@mt.net
Specialties: Working straight knives and one-of-a-kind art knives of his design or to customer specs. **Patterns:** Hunters, bowies, fish, patch and kitchen knives. **Technical:** Grinds ATS-34, 1095, O1, A2 and damascus. **Prices:** $100 to $2000. **Remarks:** Full-time maker, first knife

sold in 1989. Doing business as Wil-A-Mar Cutlery. **Mark:** Shield with last name and a dagger.

PATTAY, RUDY
8739 N. Zurich Way, Citrus Springs, FL 34434 **Contact:** 516-318-4538, dolphin51@att.net, pattayknives.com
Specialties: Fancy and working straight knives of his design. **Patterns:** bowies, hunters, utility/camp knives, drop point, skinners. **Technical:** Hollow-grinds ATS-34, 440C, O1. Offers commercial damascus, stainless steel soldered guards, fabricates guard and butt cap on lathe and milling machine. Heat-treats. Prefers synthetic handle materials. Offers hand-sewn sheaths. **Prices:** $100 to $350, some to $500. **Remarks:** Full-time maker, first knife sold in 1990. **Mark:** First initial, last name in sorcerer logo.

PATTERSON, PAT
Box 246, Barksdale, TX 78828 **Contact:** 830-234-3586, pat@pattersonknives.com
Specialties: Traditional fixed blades and LinerLock folders. **Patterns:** Hunters and folders. **Technical:** Grinds 440C, ATS-34, D2, O1 and damascus. **Prices:** $250 to $1000. **Remarks:** Full-time maker. First knife sold in 1991. **Mark:** Name and city.

PATTON, DICK AND ROB
6803 View Ln, Nampa, ID 83687 **Contact:** 208-468-4123, grpatton@pattonknives.com, pattonknives.com
Specialties: Custom damascus, hand forged, fighting knives, bowie and tactical. **Patterns:** Mini bowie, Merlin Fighter, Mandrita Fighting bowie. **Prices:** $100 to $2000.

PATTON, PHILLIP
PO BOX 113, Yoder, IN 46798, phillip@pattonblades.com pattonblades.com
Specialties: Tactical fixed blades, including fighting, camp, and general utility blades. Also makes bowies and daggers. Known for leaf and recurve blade shapes. **Technical:** Forges carbon, stainless, and high alloy tool steels. Makes own damascus using 1084/15n20 or O1/L6. Makes own carbon/stainless laminated blades. For handle materials, prefers high end woods and sythetics. Uses 416 ss and bronze for fittings. **Prices:** $175 - $1000 for knives, $750 and up for swords. **Remarks:** Full-time maker since 2005. Two-year backlog. ABS member. **Mark:** "Phillip Patton" with Phillip above Patton.

PAULO, FERNANDES R
Raposo Tavares No 213, Lencois Paulista, SP, BRAZIL 18680 **Contact:** 014-263-4281
Specialties: An apprentice of Jose Alberto Paschoarelli, his designs are heavily based on the later designs. **Technical:** Grinds tool steels and stainless steels. Part-time knifemaker. **Prices:** Start from $100. **Mark:** P.R.F.

PAWLOWSKI, JOHN R
19380 High Bluff Ln., Barhamsville, VA 23011 **Contact:** 757-870-4284 or 804-843-2223, (fax) 757-223-5935, bigjohnknives@yahoo.com, bigjohnknives.com
Specialties: Traditional working and using straight knives and folders. **Patterns:** Hunters, bowies, fighters and camp knives. **Technical:** Stock removal, grinds 440C, ATS-34, 154CM and buys damascus. **Prices:** $400 and up. **Remarks:** Part-time maker, first knife sold in 1983, Knifemaker Guild Member. **Mark:** Big John, Virginia.

PAYNE, TRAVIS
T-BONE'S CUSTOM CREATIONS, 1588 CR 2655, Telephone, TX 75488 **Contact:** 903-640-6484, tbone7599@yahoo.com, tbonescustomcreations.com
Specialties: Full-time maker of fixed blades, specializing in a unique style of castration knives, but also hunting and everyday carry (EDC's). **Technical:** Prefers 440C, PSF27, CPM 154 and Damasteel blade steels. **Prices:** $200 to $1,000. **Remarks:** Full-time maker since 1993.

PEAGLER, RUSS
PO Box 1314, Moncks Corner, SC 29461 **Contact:** 803-761-1008 or 843-312-7371, rpeagler1@homesc.com or rfpeagler1@gmail.com
Specialties: Traditional working straight knives of his design and to customer specs. **Patterns:** Hunters, fighters, boots. **Technical:** Hollow-grinds 440C, ATS-34 and O1. Uses 0-1, 440-C, ATS-34, D-2, damascus. Forges own damascus. Prefers bone handles. **Prices:** From $125. **Remarks:** Started making knives in 1983. **Mark:** PEAGLER. Previous: initials.

PEARCE, LOGAN
1013 Dogtown Rd, De Queen, AR 71832 **Contact:** 580-212-0995, night_everclear@hotmail.com, pearceknives.com
Specialties: Edged weapons, art knives, stright working knives. **Patterns:** bowie, hunters, tomahawks, fantasy, utility, daggers, and slip-joint. **Technical:** Fprges 1080, L6, 5160, 440C, steel cable, and his own damascus. **Prices:** $35 to $500. **Remarks:** Full-time maker, first knife sold in 1992. Doing business as Pearce Knives **Mark:** Name

PEASE, W D
657 Cassidy Pike, Ewing, KY 41039 **Contact:** 606-845-0387, wdpeaseknives.com
Specialties: Display-quality working folders. **Patterns:** Fighters, tantos and boots, locking folders and interframes. **Technical:** Grinds ATS-34 and commercial damascus, has own side-release lock system. **Prices:** $500 to $1000, some to $3000. **Remarks:** Full-time maker, first knife sold in 1970. **Mark:** First and middle initials, last name and state. W. D. Pease Kentucky.

PEDERSEN, OLE
23404 W. Lake Kayak Dr., Monroe, WA 98272 **Contact:** 425-931-5750, ole@pedersenknives.com, pedersenknives.com
Specialties: Fixed blades of own design. **Patterns:** Hunters, working and utility knives. **Technical:** Stock removal, hollow grinds CPM 154 and stainless steel, 416 stainless fittings, makes own custom sheaths. Handles are mostly stabilized burl wood, some G-10. Heat treats and tempers own knives. **Prices:** $275 to $500. **Remarks:** Full-time

maker, sold first knife in 2012. **Mark:** Ole Pedersen - Maker.

PEELE, BRYAN
219 Ferry St, PO Box 1363, Thompson Falls, MT 59873 **Contact:** 406-827-4633, banana_peele@yahoo.com
Specialties: Fancy working and using knives of his design. **Patterns:** Hunters, bowies and fighters. **Technical:** Grinds 440C, ATS-34, D2, O1 and commercial damascus. **Prices:** $110 to $300, some to $900. **Remarks:** Part-time maker, first knife sold in 1985. **Mark:** The Elk Rack, full name, city, state.

PELLEGRIN, MIKE
MP3 Knives, 107 White St., Troy, IL 62294-1126 **Contact:** 618-667-6777, P3knives.com
Specialties: Lockback folders with stone inlays, and one-of-a-kind art knives with stainless steel or damascus handles. **Technical:** Stock-removal method of blade making using 440C, Damasteel or high-carbon damascus blades. **Prices:** $800 and up. **Remarks:** Making knives since 2000. **Mark:** MP (combined) 3.

PENNINGTON, C A
163 Kainga Rd, Kainga Christchurch, NEW ZEALAND 8009 **Contact:** 03-3237292, capennington@xtra.co.nz
Specialties: Classic working and collectors knives. Folders a specialty. **Patterns:** Classical styling for hunters and collectors. **Technical:** Forges his own all tool steel damascus. Grinds D2 when requested. **Prices:** $240 to $2000. **Remarks:** Full-time maker, first knife sold in 1988. Color brochure $3. **Mark:** Name, country.

PEPIOT, STEPHAN
73 Cornwall Blvd, Winnipeg, MB, CANADA R3J-1E9 **Contact:** 204-888-1499
Specialties: Working straight knives in standard patterns. **Patterns:** Hunters and camp knives. **Technical:** Grinds 440C and industrial hack-saw blades. **Prices:** $75 to $125. **Remarks:** Spare-time maker, first knife sold in 1982. Not currently taking orders. **Mark:** PEP.

PERRY, CHRIS
1654 W. Birch, Fresno, CA 93711 **Contact:** 559-246-7446, chris.perry4@comcast.net
Specialties: Traditional working/using straight knives of his design. **Patterns:** Boots, hunters and utility/camp knives. **Technical:** Grinds ATS-34, damascus, 416ss fittings, silver and gold fittings, hand-rubbed finishes. **Prices:** Starting at $250. **Remarks:** Part-time maker, first knife sold in 1995. **Mark:** Name above city and state.

PERRY, JIM
Hope Star PO Box 648, Hope, AR 71801, jenn@comfabinc.com

PERRY, JOHN
9 South Harrell Rd, Mayflower, AR 72106 **Contact:** 501-470-3043, jpknives@cyberback.com
Specialties: Investment grade and working folders, Antique bowies and slip joints. **Patterns:** Front and rear lock folders, liner locks, hunters and bowies. **Technical:** Grinds CPM440V, D2 and making own damascus. Offers filework. **Prices:** $375 to $1200, some to $3500. **Remarks:** Part-time maker, first knife sold in 1991. Doing business as Perry Custom Knives. **Mark:** Initials or last name in high relief set in a diamond shape.

PERRY, JOHNNY
PO Box 35, Inman, SC 29349 **Contact:** 864-431-6390, perr3838@bellsouth.net
Mark: High Ridge Forge.

PERSSON, CONNY
PL 588, Loos, SWEDEN 82050 **Contact:** +46 657 10305, (fax) +46 657 413 435, connyknives@swipnet.se, connyknives.com
Specialties: Mosaic damascus. **Patterns:** Mosaic damascus. **Technical:** Straight knives and folders. **Prices:** $1000 and up. **Mark:** C. Persson.

PETEAN, FRANCISCO AND MAURICIO
R. Dr. Carlos de Carvalho Rosa 52, Birigui, SP, BRAZIL 16200-000 **Contact:** 0186-424786
Specialties: Classic knives to customer specs. **Patterns:** bowies, boots, fighters, hunters and utility knives. **Technical:** Grinds D6, 440C and high-carbon steels. Prefers natural handle material. **Prices:** $70 to $500. **Remarks:** Full-time maker, first knife sold in 1985. **Mark:** Last name, hand made.

PETERS, DANIEL
Woodlawn, TN 37191 **Contact:** 360-451-9386, dan@danpeterscustomknives.com, danpeterscustomknives.com
Specialties: Angry Ginger (Kukri style), hunters, skinners, tactical and combat knives. **Patterns:** Drop points, daggers, folders, hunters, skinners, Kukri style and fillet knives. **Technical:** CPM S35VN, CPM 3V, CPM 154. **Prices:** $75 for bottle openers, and $175 and up on all others. **Remarks:** Part-time maker, full-time military. Member of The Knifemakers' Guild. **Mark:** Peters USA etched or engraved with crossed knives.

PETERSEN, DAN L
10610 SW 81st, Auburn, KS 66402 **Contact:** 785-220-8043, dan@petersenknives.com, petersenknives.com
Specialties: Period pieces and forged integral hilts on hunters and fighters. Vitreous enameling on guards and buttcaps. **Patterns:** Texas-style bowies, boots and hunters in high-carbon and damascus steel. **Technical:** Precision heat treatments. Bainite blades with mantensite cores. **Prices:** $800 to $10,000. **Remarks:** First knife sold in 1978. ABS Master Smith. **Mark:** Stylized initials.

PETERSON, CHRIS
Box 143, 2175 W Rockyford, Salina, UT 84654 **Contact:** 435-529-7194
Specialties: Working straight knives of his design. **Patterns:** Large fighters, boots, hunters and some display pieces. **Technical:** Forges O1 and meteor. Makes and sells his own damascus. Engraves, scrimshaws and inlays. **Prices:** $150 to $600, some to $1500. **Remarks:** Full-time maker, first knife sold in 1986. **Mark:** A drop in a circle with a line through it.

PETERSON, LLOYD (PETE) C
64 Halbrook Rd, Clinton, AR 72031 **Contact:** 501-893-0000, wmblade@cyberback.com
Specialties: Miniatures and mosaic folders. **Prices:** $250 and up. **Remarks:** Lead time is 6-8 months. **Mark:** Pete.

PFANENSTIEL, DAN
1824 Lafayette Ave, Modesto, CA 95355 **Contact:** 209-602-6714, dpfan@sbcglobal.net
Specialties: Japanese tanto, swords. One-of-a-kind knives. **Technical:** Forges simple carbon steels, some damascus. **Prices:** Start at $200. **Mark:** Stylized chiseled kanji.

PHILIPPE, D A
3024 Stepping Stone Path, The Villages, FL 32163 **Contact:** 352-633-9676, dave.philippe@yahoo.com
Specialties: Traditional working straight knives. **Patterns:** Hunters, trout and bird, camp knives etc. **Technical:** Grinds ATS-34, 440C, A-2, damascus, flat and hollow ground. Exotic woods and antler handles. Brass, nickel silver and stainless components. **Prices:** $125 to $800. **Remarks:** Full-time maker, first knife sold in 1984. **Mark:** First initial, last name.

PHILLIPS, ALISTAIR
Amaroo, ACT, AUSTRALIA 2914, alistair.phillips@knives.mutantdiscovery.com, http://knives.mutantdiscovery.com
Specialties: Slipjoint folders, forged or stock removal fixed blades. **Patterns:** Single blade slipjoints, smaller neck knives, and hunters. **Technical:** Flat grnds O1, ATS-34, and forged 1055. **Prices:** $80 to $400. **Remarks:** Part-time maker, first knife made in 2005. **Mark:** Stamped signature.

PHILLIPS, DENNIS
16411 West Bennet Rd, Independence, LA 70443 **Contact:** 985-878-8275
Specialties: Specializes in fixed blade military combat tacticals.

PHILLIPS, DONAVON
905 Line Prairie Rd., Morton, MS 39117 **Contact:** 662-907-0322, bigdknives@gmail.com
Specialties: Flat ground, tapered tang working/using knives. **Patterns:** Hunters, Capers, Fillet, EDC, Field/Camp/Survival, Competition Cutters. Will work with customers on custom designs or changes to own designs. **Technical:** Stock removal maker using CPM-M4, CPM-154, and other air-hardening steels. Will use 5160 or 52100 on larger knives. G-10 or rubber standard, will use natural material if requested including armadillo. Kydex sheath is standard, outsourced leather available.†Heat treat is done by maker. **Prices:** $100 - $1000 **Remarks:** Part-time/hobbyist maker. First knife made in 2004, first sold 2007. **Mark:** Mark is etched, first and last name forming apex of triangle, city and state at the base, D in center.

PICA, DANIEL
SCREECH OWL KNIVES, 109 Olde Farm Rd., Pittsboro, NC 27312 **Contact:** 919-542-2335, screechowlknives@gmail.com, screechowlknives.com
Specialties: Outdoor/sportsman's blades and tactical/EDC knives, also folders, excelling in fit and finish, and making each knife an heirloom tool to be passed down from generation to generation. **Patterns:** Wharncliffe blades, small EDC/neck knives, Bushcrafter, bird & trout knives, skinners and two sizes of fillet knives for large- and medium-sized fish. **Technical:** Stock removal maker using mainly CPM 154, O1 and CPM 3V steels, all work done by hand, in-house heat-treating and sheath work. **Prices:** $200 to $1,000-plus. **Remarks:** Full-time maker as of January 2015, first knife made in 2013. **Mark:** Side profile of an owl head looking down the blade of the knife.

PICKENS, SELBERT
2295 Roxalana Rd, Dunbar, WV 25064 **Contact:** 304-744-4048
Specialties: Using knives. **Patterns:** Standard sporting knives. **Technical:** Stainless steels, stock removal method. **Prices:** Moderate. **Remarks:** Part-time maker. **Mark:** Name.

PICKETT, TERRELL
66 Pickett Ln, Lumberton, MS 39455 **Contact:** 601-794-6125, pickettfence66@bellsouth.net
Specialties: Fix blades, camp knives, bowies, hunters, & skinners. Forge and stock removal and some firework. **Technical:** 5160, 1095, 52100, 440C and ATS-34. **Prices:** Range from $150 to $550. **Mark:** Logo on stock removal T.W. Pickett and on forged knives Terrell Pickett's Forge.

PIENAAR, CONRAD
19A Milner Rd, Bloemfontein, Free State, SOUTH AFRICA 9300 **Contact:** 027 514364180, (fax) 027 514364180
Specialties: Fancy working and using straight knives and folders of his design, to customer specs and standard patterns. **Patterns:** Hunters, locking folders, cleavers, kitchen and utility/camp knives. **Technical:** Grinds 12C27, D2 and ATS-34. Uses some damascus. Embellishments, scrimshaws, inlays gold. Knives come with wooden box and custom-made leather sheath. **Prices:** $300 to $1000. **Remarks:** Part-time maker, first

PIERCE, HAROLD L
106 Lyndon Lane, Louisville, KY 40222 **Contact:** 502-429-5136
Specialties: Working straight knives, some fancy. **Patterns:** Big fighters and bowies. **Technical:** Grinds D2, 440C, 154CM, likes sub-hilts. **Prices:** $150 to $450, some to $1200. **Remarks:** Full-time maker, first knife sold in 1982. **Mark:** Last name with knife through the last initial.

PIERCE, RANDALL
903 Wyndam, Arlington, TX 76017 **Contact:** 817-468-0138

PIERGALLINI, DANIEL E
4011 N. Forbes Rd, Plant City, FL 33565 **Contact:** 813-754-3908 or 813-967-1471, coolnifedad@wildblue.net, piergalliniknives.com
Specialties: Traditional and fancy straight knives and folders of his design or to customer's specs. **Patterns:** Hunters, fighters, skinners, working and camp knives. **Technical:** Grinds 440C, O1, D2, ATS-34, some damascus, forges his own mokume. Uses natural handle material. **Prices:** $450 to $800, some to $1800. **Remarks:** Full-time maker, sold first knife in 1994. **Mark:** Last name, city, state or last name in script.

PIESNER, DEAN
1786 Sawmill Rd, Conestogo, ON, CANADA N0B 1N0 **Contact:** 519-664-3648, dean47@rogers.com
Specialties: Classic and period pieces of his design and to customer specs. **Patterns:** bowies, skinners, fighters and swords. **Technical:** Forges 5160, 52100, steel damascus and nickel-steel damascus. Makes own mokume gane with copper, brass and nickel silver. Silver wire inlays in wood. **Prices:** Start at $150. **Remarks:** Full-time maker, first knife sold in 1990. **Mark:** First initial, last name, JS.

PITMAN, DAVID
PO Drawer 2566, Williston, ND 58802 **Contact:** 701-572-3325

PITT, DAVID F
Anderson, CA 96007 **Contact:** 530-357-2393, handcannons@tds.net, bearpawcustoms.blademakers.com
Specialties: Fixed blade, hunters and hatchets. Flat ground mirror finish. **Patterns:** Hatchets with gut hook, small gut hooks, guards, bolsters or guard less. **Technical:** Grinds A2, 440C, 154CM, ATS-34, D2. **Prices:** $150 to $1,000. **Remarks:** All work done in-house including heat treat, and all knives come with hand-stitched, wet-fromed sheaths. **Mark:** Bear paw with David F. Pitt Maker.

PLOPPERT, TOM
1407 2nd Ave. SW, Cullman, AL 35055 **Contact:** 256-962-4251, tomploppert3@bellsouth.net
Specialties: Highly finished single- to multiple-blade slip-joint folders in standard and traditional patterns, some lockbacks. **Technical:** Hollow grinds CPM-154, 440V, damascus and other steels upon customer request. Uses elephant ivory, mammoth ivory, bone and pearl. **Mark:** Last name stamped on main blade.

PLUNKETT, RICHARD
29 Kirk Rd, West Cornwall, CT 06796 **Contact:** 860-672-3419, Toll free: 888-KNIVES-8
Specialties: Traditional, fancy folders and straight knives of his design. **Patterns:** Slip-joint folders and small straight knives. **Technical:** Grinds O1 and stainless steel. Offers many different file patterns. **Prices:** $150 to $450. **Remarks:** Full-time maker, first knife sold in 1994. **Mark:** Signature and date under handle scales.

PODMAJERSKY, DIETRICH
9219 15th Ave NE, Seattle, WA 98115 **Contact:** 206-552-0763, podforge@gmail.com, podforge.com
Specialties: Straight and folding knives that use fine engraving and materials to create technically intricate, artistic visions. **Technical:** Stainless and carbon steel blades, with titanium and precious metal fittings, including Japanese ornamental alloys. **Prices:** $500 and up.

POIRIER, RICK
1149 Sheridan Rd., McKees Mills, New Brunswick E4V 2W7, CANADA **Contact:** 506-525-2818, ripknives@gmail.com, ripcustomknives.com
Specialties: Working straight knives of his design or to customer specs, hunters, fighters, bowies, utility, camp, tantos and short swords. **Technical:** Forges own damascus and cable damascus using 1084, 15N20, O1 and mild steel. Forges/grinds mostly O1 and W2. Varied handle materials inlcude G-10, Micarta, wood, bone, horn and Japanese cord wrap. **Prices:** $200 and up. **Remarks:** Full-time maker, apprenticed under ABS master smith Wally Hayes, first knife sold in 1998. **Marks:** R P (pre. 2007), RIP (2007 on), also etches gravestone RIP.

POLING, JIM
25907 440th AV NW, Alvarado MN, 56710 **Contact:** 701-739-8243, jim@irontraditions.com **Specialties:** Fancy and working straight knives **Patterns:** Bowies, hunters, fighters, working blades **Technical:** Forged blades of 5160, 1075, 1080, 1084, 1095, 15N20 and own Damascus; Fitting of mild, non-Ferris, Damascus metals; Handles of wood, stag and synthetics **Remarks:** First knife sold in 1984. **Mark:** J.P.Poling

POLK, CLIFTON
4625 Webber Creek Rd, Van Buren, AR 72956 **Contact:** 479-474-3828, cliffpolkknives1@aol.com, polkknives.com
Specialties: Fancy working folders. **Patterns:** One blades spring backs in five sizes, LinerLock®, automatics, double blades spring back folder with standard drop & clip blade or bird knife with drop and vent hook or cowboy's knives with drop and hoof pick and straight knives. **Technical:** Uses D2 & ATS-34. Makes all own damascus using 1084, 1095, O1, 15N20, 5160. Using all kinds of exotic woods. Stag, pearls, ivory, mastodon ivory and other bone and horns. **Prices:** $200 to $3000. **Remarks:** Retired fire fighter, made knives since 1974. **Mark:** Polk.

POLK, RUSTY
5900 Wildwood Dr, Van Buren, AR 72956 **Contact:** 870-688-3009, polkknives@yahoo.com, facebook.com/polkknives
Specialties: Skinners, hunters, bowies, fighters and forging working knives fancy damascus, daggers, boot knives, survival knives, and folders. **Patterns:** Drop point, and forge to shape. **Technical:** ATS-34, 440C, damascus, D2, 51/60, 1084, 15N20, does all his forging. **Prices:** $200 to $2000. **Mark:** R. Polk

POLLOCK, WALLACE J
806 Russet Valley Dr., Cedar Park, TX 78613 **Contact:** 512-918-0528, jarlsdad@gmail.com, pollacknives.com
Specialties: Using knives, skinner, hunter, fighting, camp knives. **Patterns:** Use his own patterns or yours. Traditional hunters, daggers, fighters, camp knives. **Technical:** Grinds ATS-34, D-2, BG-42, makes own damascus, D-2, O-1, ATS-34, prefer D-2, handles exotic wood, horn, bone, ivory. **Remarks:** Full-time maker, sold first knife 1973. **Prices:** $250 to $2500. **Mark:** Last name, maker, city/state.

POLZIEN, DON
1912 Inler Suite-L, Lubbock, TX 79407 **Contact:** 806-791-0766, blindinglightknives.net
Specialties: Traditional Japanese-style blades, restores antique Japanese swords, scabbards and fittings. **Patterns:** Hunters, fighters, one-of-a-kind art knives. **Technical:** 1045-1050 carbon steels, 440C, D2, ATS-34, standard and cable damascus. **Prices:** $150 to $2500. **Remarks:** Full-time maker. First knife sold in 1990. **Mark:** Oriental characters inside square border.

PONZIO, DOUG
10219 W State Rd 81, Beloit, WI 53511 **Contact:** 608-313-3223, prfgdoug@gmail.com, dougponzio.com
Specialties: Mosaic damascus, stainless damascus. **Mark:** P.F.

POOLE, MARVIN O
PO Box 552, Commerce, GA 30529 **Contact:** 803-225-5970
Specialties: Traditional working/using straight knives and folders of his design and in standard patterns. **Patterns:** bowies, fighters, hunters, locking folders, bird and trout knives. **Technical:** Grinds 440C, D2, ATS-34. **Prices:** $50 to $150, some to $750. **Remarks:** Part-time maker, first knife sold in 1980. **Mark:** First initial, last name, year, serial number.

POTIER, TIMOTHY F
PO Box 711, Oberlin, LA 70655 **Contact:** 337-639-2229, tpotier@hotmail.com
Specialties: Classic working and using straight knives to customer specs, some collectible. **Patterns:** Hunters, bowies, utility/camp knives and belt axes. **Technical:** Forges carbon steel and his own damascus, offers filework. **Prices:** $300 to $1800, some to $4000. **Remarks:** Part-time maker, first knife sold in 1981. **Mark:** Last name, MS.

POTTER, BILLY
6323 Hyland Dr., Dublin, OH 43017 **Contact:** 614-589-8324, potterknives@yahoo.com, potterknives.com
Specialties: Working straight knives, his design or to customers patterns. **Patterns:** bowie, fighters, utilities, skinners, hunters, folding lock blade, miniatures and tomahawks. **Technical:** Grinds and forges, carbon steel, L6, O-1, 1095, 5160, 1084 and 52000. Grinds 440C stainless. Forges own damascus. Handles: prefers exotic hardwood, curly and birdseye maples. Bone, ivory, antler, pearl and horn. Some scrimshaw. **Prices:** Start at $100 up to $800. **Remarks:** Part-time maker, first knife sold 1996. **Mark:** First and last name (maker).

POWELL, ROBERT CLARK
PO Box 321, 93 Gose Rd., Smarr, GA 31086 **Contact:** 478-994-5418
Specialties: Composite bar damascus blades. **Patterns:** Art knives, hunters, combat, tomahawks. **Patterns:** Hand forges all blades. **Prices:** $300 and up. **Remarks:** ABS Journeyman Smith. **Mark:** Powell.

POWERS, WALTER R.
PO BOX 82, Lolita, TX 77971 **Contact:** 361-874-4230, carlyn@laward.net, waltscustomknives.blademakers.com
Specialties: Skinners and hunters. **Technical:** Uses mainly CPM D2, CPM 154, CPM S35VN and 52100, but will occasionally use 3V. Stock removal. **Prices:** $160 - $225. **Remarks:** Part-time maker, first knife made in 2002. **Mark:** WP

PRATER, MIKE
PRATER AND COMPANY, 81 Sanford Ln., Flintstone, GA 30725 **Contact:** 706-820-7300, cmprater@aol.com, pratercustoms.com
Specialties: Customizing factory knives. **Patterns:** Buck knives, case knives, hen and rooster knives. **Technical:** Manufacture of mica pearl. **Prices:** Varied. **Remarks:** First knife sold in 1980. **Mark:** Mica pearl.

PRESSBURGER, RAMON
59 Driftway Rd, Howell, NJ 07731 **Contact:** 732-363-0816
Specialties: BG-42. Only knifemaker in U.S.A. that has complete line of affordable hunting knives made from BG-42. **Patterns:** All types hunting styles. **Technical:** Uses all steels, main steels are D-2 and BG-42. **Prices:** $75 to $500. **Remarks:** Full-time maker, has been making hunting knives for 30 years. Makes knives to your patterning. **Mark:** NA.

PRESTI, MATT
5280 Middleburg Rd, Union Bridge, MD 21791 **Contact:** 410-775-1520, Cell: 240-357-3592
Specialties: Hunters and chef's knives, fighters, bowies, and period pieces.**Technical:** Forges 5160, 52100, 1095, 1080, W2, and O1 steels as well as his own damascus. Does own heat treating and makes sheaths. Prefers natural handle materials, particularly antler and curly maple. **Prices:** $150 and up. **Remarks:** Part-time knifemaker who made his first knife in 2001. **Mark:** MCP.

PRICE, DARRELL MORRIS
92 Union, Plymouth, Devon, ENGLAND PL1 3EZ **Contact:** 0752 223546
Specialties: Traditional Japanese knives, bowies and high-art knives. **Technical:** Nickel damascus and mokume. **Prices:** $1000 to $4000. **Remarks:** Part-time maker, first knife sold in 1990. **Mark:** Initials and Japanese name—Kuni Shigae.

PRICE, TIMMY
PO Box 906, Blairsville, GA 30514 **Contact:** 706-745-5111

PRIDGEN JR., LARRY
PO Box 127, Davis, OK 73030 **Contact:** 229-457-6522, pridgencustomknives@gmail.com pridgencustomknives.com
Specialties: Custom folders. **Patterns:** bowie, fighter, skinner, trout, liner lock, and custom orders. **Technical:** I do stock removal and use carbon and stainless damascus and stainless steel. **Prices:** $300 and up. **Remarks:** Each knife comes with a hand-crafted custom sheath and life-time guarantee. **Mark:** Distinctive logo that looks like a brand with LP and a circle around it.

PRIMOS, TERRY
932 Francis Dr, Shreveport, LA 71118 **Contact:** 318-686-6625, tprimos@sport.rr.com or terry@primosknives.com, primosknives.com
Specialties: Traditional forged straight knives. **Patterns:** Hunters, bowies, camp knives, and fighters. **Technical:** Forges primarily 1084 and 5160, also forges damascus. **Prices:** $250 to $600. **Remarks:** Full-time maker, first knife sold in 1993. **Mark:** Last name.

PRINSLOO, THEUNS
PO Box 2263, Bethlehem, Free State, SOUTH AFRICA 9700 **Contact:** 27824663885, theunsmes@yahoo.com, theunsprinsloo.co.za
Specialties: Handmade folders and fixed blades. **Technical:** Own damascus and mokume. I try to avoid CNC work, laser cutting and machining as much as possible. **Prices:** $650 and up. **Mark:** Handwritten name with bushman rock art and mountain scene.

PRITCHARD, RON
613 Crawford Ave, Dixon, IL 61021 **Contact:** 815-284-6005
Specialties: Plain and fancy working knives. **Patterns:** Variety of straight knives, locking folders, interframes and miniatures. **Technical:** Grinds 440C, 154CM and commercial damascus. **Prices:** $100 to $200, some to $1500. **Remarks:** Part-time maker, first knife sold in 1979. **Mark:** Name and city.

PROVENZANO, JOSEPH D
39043 Dutch Lane, Ponchatoula, LA 70454 **Contact:** 225-615-4846, gespro61@gmail.com
Specialties: Working straight knives and folders in standard patterns. **Patterns:** Hunters, bowies, folders, camp and fishing knives. **Technical:** Grinds ATS-34, 440C, 154CM, CPM-S60V, CPM-S90V, CPM-3V and damascus. Hollow-grinds hunters. **Prices:** $125 to $300, some to $1,000. **Remarks:** Part-time maker, first knife sold in 1980. **Mark:** Joe-Pro.

PROVOST, J.C.
1634 Lakeview Dr., Laurel, MS 39440 **Contact:** 601-498-1143, jcprovost2@gmail.com, jcprovost.com
Specialties: Classic working straight knives and folders. **Patterns:** Hunters, skinners, bowies, daggers, fighters, fillet knives, chef's and steak knives, folders and customs. **Technical:** Grinds 440C, CPM-154 and commercial damascus. **Prices:** $175 and up. **Remarks:** Part-time maker, first knife made in 1979. Taught by R.W. Wilson. **Mark:** Name, city and state.

PRUYN, PETER
Brothersville Custom Knives, 110 Reel La., Grants Pass, OR 97527 **Contact:** 631-793-9052, (fax) 541-479-1889, brothersvilleknife@gmail.com, brothersvilleknife.com
Specialties: Chef knives and fighters in damascus and san mai, as well as stainless steels. **Patterns:** Fixed-blade knives of all styles, some folding models. **Technical:** damascus, high-carbon and stainless steels, does own heat treating, san mai. **Prices:** $200 to $2,000, with a discount to active and retired military personnel. **Remarks:** Full-time maker, first knife sold in 2009. **Mark:** Anvil with "Brothersville" crested above.

PUDDU, SALVATORE
Via Lago Bunnari #12, 09045 Quartu Sant 'Elena, (Cagliari) Sardinia, ITALY **Contact:** 0039-070-892208, salvatore.puddu@tin.it
Specialties: Custom knives. **Remarks:** Full-time maker.

PULIS, VLADIMIR
CSA 230-95, 96701 Kremnica, SLOVAKIA **Contact:** 00421 903 340076, vpulis@gmail.com, vpulis.host.sk
Specialties: Fancy and high-art straight knives of his design. **Patterns:** Daggers and hunters. **Technical:** Forges damascus steel. All work done by hand. **Prices:** $250 to $3000, some to $10,000. **Remarks:** Full-time maker, first knife sold in 1990. **Mark:** Initials in sixtagon.

PURSLEY, AARON
8885 Coal Mine Rd, Big Sandy, MT 59520 **Contact:** 406-378-3200
Specialties: Fancy working knives. **Patterns:** Locking folders, straight hunters and daggers, personal wedding knives and letter openers. **Technical:** Grinds O1 and 440C, engraves. **Prices:** $900 to $2500. **Remarks:** Full-time maker, first knife sold in 1975. **Mark:** Initials connected with year.

PURVIS, BOB AND ELLEN
2416 N Loretta Dr, Tucson, AZ 85716 **Contact:** 520-795-8290, repknives2@cox.net
Specialties: Hunter, skinners, bowies, using knives, gentlemen folders and collectible knives. **Technical:** Grinds ATS-34, 440C, damascus, Dama steel, heat-treats and cryogenically quenches. We do gold-plating, salt bluing, scrimshawing, filework and fashion handmade leather sheaths. Materials used for handles include exotic woods, mammoth ivory, mother-of-pearl, G-10 and Micarta. **Prices:** $165 to $800. **Remarks:** Knifemaker since retirement in 1984. Selling them since 1993. **Mark:** Script or print R.E. Purvis ~ Tucson, AZ or last name only.

Q

QUAKENBUSH, THOMAS C
2426 Butler Rd, Ft Wayne, IN 46808 **Contact:** 219-483-0749

QUARTON, BARR
PO Box 4335, McCall, ID 83638 **Contact:** 208-634-3641
Specialties: Plain and fancy working knives, period pieces. **Patterns:** Hunters, tantos and swords. **Technical:** Forges and grinds 154CM, ATS-34 and his own damascus. **Prices:** $180 to $450, some to $4500. **Remarks:** Part-time maker, first knife sold in 1978. Doing business as Barr Custom Knives. **Mark:** First name with bear logo.

QUESENBERRY, MIKE
110 Evergreen Cricle, Blairsden, CA 96103 **Contact:** 775-233-1527, quesenberryknives@gmail.com, quesenberryknives.com
Specialties: Hunters, daggers, bowies and integrals. **Technical:** Forges 52100 and W2. Makes own damascus. Will use stainless on customer requests. Does own heat-treating and own leather work. **Prices:** Starting at $400. **Remarks:** Part-time maker. ABS member since 2006. ABS master bladesmith. **Mark:** Last name.

R

RABUCK, JASON
W3080 Hay Lake Road, Springbrook, WI 54875 **Contact:** 715-766-8220, sales@rabuckhandmadeknives.com, rabuckhandmadeknives.com
Patterns: Hunters, skinners, camp knives, fighters, survival/tactical, neck knives, kitchen knives. Include whitetail antler, maple, walnut, as well as stabilized woods and micarta. **Technical:** Flat grinds 1095, 5160, and 0-1 carbon steels. Blades are finished with a hand-rubbed satin blade finish. Hand stitched leather sheaths specifically fit to each knife. Boot clips, swivel sheaths, and leg ties include some of the available sheath options. **Prices:** $140 - $560. **Remarks:** Also knife restoration (handle replacement, etc.) Custom and replacement sheath work available for any knife. **Mark:** "RABUCK" over a horseshoe

RACHLIN, LESLIE S
412 Rustic Ave., Elmira, NY 14905 **Contact:** 607-733-6889, lrachlin@stry.rr.com
Specialties: Classic and working kitchen knives, carving sets and outdoors knives. **Technical:** Grinds 440C or cryogenically heat-treated A2. **Prices:** $65 to $1,400. **Remarks:** Spare-time maker, first knife sold in 1989. Doing business as Tinkermade Knives. **Mark:** LSR

RADER, MICHAEL
23706 7th Ave. SE, Ste. D, Bothell, WA 98021, michael@raderblade.com, raderblade.com
Specialties: Swords, kitchen knives, integrals. **Patterns:** Non traditional designs. Inspired by various cultures. **Technical:** damascus is made with 1084 and 15N-20, forged blades in 52100, W2 and 1084.**Prices:** $350 - $5,000 **Remarks:** ABS Journeyman Smith **Mark:** ABS Mastersmith Mark "Rader" on one side, "M.S." on other

RADOS, JERRY F
134 Willie Nell Rd., Columbia, KY 42728 **Contact:** 606-303-3334, jerry@radosknives.com radosknives.com
Specialties: Deluxe period pieces. **Patterns:** Hunters, fighters, locking folders, daggers and camp knives. **Technical:** Forges and grinds his own damascus which he sells commercially, makes pattern-welded Turkish damascus. **Prices:** Start at $900. **Remarks:** Full-time maker, first knife sold in 1981. **Mark:** Last name.

RAFN, DAN C.
Norholmvej 46, 7400 Herning, DENMARK, contact@dcrknives.com dcrknives.com
Specialties: One of a kind collector art knives of own design. **Patterns:** Mostly fantasy style fighters and daggers. But also swords, hunters, and folders. **Technical:** Grinds RWL-34, sleipner steel, damasteel, and hand forges damascus. **Prices:** Start at $500. **Remarks:** Part-time maker since 2003. **Mark:** Rafn. or DCR. or logo.

RAGSDALE, JAMES D
160 Clear Creek Valley Tr., Ellijay, GA 30536 **Contact:** 706-636-3180, jimmarrags@etcmail.com
Specialties: Fancy and embellished working knives of his design or to customer specs. **Patterns:** Hunters, folders and fighters. **Technical:** Grinds 440C, ATS-34 and A2. Uses some damascus **Prices:** $150 and up. **Remarks:** Full-time maker, first knife sold in 1984. **Mark:** Fish symbol with name above, town below.

RAINVILLE, RICHARD
126 Cockle Hill Rd, Salem, CT 06420 **Contact:** 860-859-2776, w1jo@comcast.net
Specialties: Traditional working straight knives. **Patterns:** Outdoor knives, including

fishing knives. **Technical:** L6, 400C, ATS-34. **Prices:** $100 to $800. **Remarks:** Full-time maker, first knife sold in 1982. **Mark:** Name, city, state in oval logo.

RALEY, R. WAYNE
825 Poplar Acres Rd, Collierville, TN 38017 **Contact:** 901-853-2026

RALPH, DARREL
DDR CUSTOM KNIVES, 12034 S. Profit Row, Forney, TX 75126 **Contact:** 469-728-7242, ddr@darrelralph.com, darrelralph.com
Specialties: Tactical and tactical dress folders and fixed blades. **Patterns:** Daggers, fighters and swords. **Technical:** High tech. Forges his own damascus, nickel and high-carbon. Uses mokume and damascus, mosaics and special patterns. Engraves and heat treats. Prefers pearl, ivory and abalone handle material, uses stones and jewels. **Prices:** $600 to $30,000. **Remarks:** Full-time maker, first knife sold in 1987. Doing business as Briar Knives. **Mark:** DDR.

RAMONDETTI, SERGIO
VIA MARCONI N 24, CHIUSA DI PESIO (CN), ITALY 12013 **Contact:** 0171 734490, (fax) 0171 734490, info@ramon-knives.com ramon-knives.com
Specialties: Folders and straight knives of his design. **Patterns:** Utility, hunters and skinners. **Technical:** Grinds RWL-34 and damascus. **Prices:** $500 to $2000. **Remarks:** Part-time maker, first knife sold in 1999. **Mark:** Logo (S.Ramon) with last name.

RAMOS, STEVEN
2466 Countryside Ln., West Jordan, UT 84084 **Contact:** 801-913-1696, srknives88@gmail.com, stevenramosknives.com
Specialties: Mirror finishes, complex filework, tapered tangs, genuine polished gemstone handles, all original and unique blade designs. **Patterns:** Fixed, full-tang hunters/utility, fighters, modified bowies, daggers, cooking and chef's knives, personalized wedding cake knives and art pieces. **Technical:** Stock removal, predominantly using CPM 154 stainless steel, but also 440C, D2, 154CM and others. Mostly polished gemstone handles, but also Micarta, G-10 and various woods. Sheaths and custom display stands with commemorative engravings also available. **Prices:** $400 to $3,000. **Remarks:** Full-time maker. **Mark:** Signature "Steven Ramos" laser etched on blade.

RAMSEY, RICHARD A
8525 Trout Farm Rd, Neosho, MO 64850 **Contact:** 417-592-1494, ramseyknives@gmail.com, ramseyknives.net
Specialties: Drop point hunters. **Patterns:** Various damascus. **Prices:** $125 to $1500. **Mark:** RR double R also last name-RAMSEY.

RANDALL, PATRICK
Patrick Knives, 160 Mesa Ave., Newbury Park, CA 91320 **Contact:** 805-390-5501, pat@patrickknives.com, patrickknives.com
Specialties: Chef's and kitchen knives, bowies, hunters and utility folding knives. **Technical:** Preferred materials include 440C, 154CM, CPM-3V, 1084, 1095 and ATS-34. Handle materials include stabilized wood, Micarta, stag and jigged bone. **Prices:** $125 to $225. **Remarks:** Part-time maker since 2005.

RANDALL, STEVE
3438 Oak Ridge Cir., LIncolnton, NC 28092 **Contact:** 704-472-4957, steve@ksrblades.com, ksrblades.com
Specialties: One of a kind pieces and fancy fixed blades. **Patterns:** Bowies, daggers, some hunters. **Technical:** Forged high carbon steel blades. Mostly damascus with some high carbon steels. **Prices:** $400 and up. **Remarks:** Part-time maker, first knife sold in 2009. Earned Master Smith Rating 2016. Doing business as Knives by Steve Randall or KSR Blades. **Mark:** KS Randall on left side, MS on right side.

RANDALL JR., JAMES W
11606 Keith Hall Rd, Keithville, LA 71047 **Contact:** 318-925-6480, (fax) 318-925-1709, jw@jwrandall.com, jwrandall.com
Specialties: Collectible and functional knives. **Patterns:** bowies, hunters, daggers, swords, folders and combat knives. **Technical:** Forges 5160, 1084, O1 and his damascus. **Prices:** $400 to $8000. **Remarks:** Part-time. First knife sold in 1998. **Mark:** JW Randall, MS.

RANDALL MADE KNIVES
4857 South Orange Blossom Trail, Orlando, FL 32839 **Contact:** 407-855-8075, (fax) 407-855-9054, randallknives.com
Specialties: Working straight knives. **Patterns:** Hunters, fighters and bowies. **Technical:** Forges and grinds O1 and 440B. **Prices:** $170 to $550, some to $450. **Remarks:** Full-time maker, first knife sold in 1937. **Mark:** Randall made, city and state in scimitar logo.

RANDOW, RALPH
7 E. Chateau Estates Dr., Greenbrier, AR 72058 **Contact:** 318-729-3368, randow3368@gmail.com

RANKL, CHRISTIAN
Possenhofenerstr 33, Munchen, GERMANY 81476 **Contact:** 0049 01 71 3 66 26 79, (fax) 0049 8975967265, german-knife.com/german-knifemakers-guild.html
Specialties: Tail-lock knives. **Patterns:** Fighters, hunters and locking folders. **Technical:** Grinds ATS-34, D2, CPM1440V, RWL 34 also stainless damascus. **Prices:** $450 to $950, some to $2000. **Remarks:** Part-time maker, first knife sold in 1989. **Mark:** Electrochemical etching on blade.

RAPP, STEVEN J
8033 US Hwy 25-70, Marshall, NC 28753 **Contact:** 828-649-1092
Specialties: Gold quartz, mosaic handles. **Patterns:** Daggers, bowies, fighters and San Francisco knives. **Technical:** Hollow- and flat-grinds 440C and damascus. **Prices:** Start at $500. **Remarks:** Full-time maker, flrst knife sold in 1981. **Mark:** Name and state.

RAPPAZZO, RICHARD
142 Dunsbach Ferry Rd, Cohoes, NY 12047 **Contact:** 518-783-6843
Specialties: damascus locking folders and straight knives. **Patterns:** Folders, dirks, fighters and tantos in original and traditional designs. **Technical:** Hand-forges all blades, specializes in damascus, uses only natural handle materials. **Prices:** $400 to $1500. **Remarks:** Part-time maker, first knife sold in 1985. **Mark:** Name, date, serial number.

RARDON, A D
1589 SE Price Dr, Polo, MO 64671 **Contact:** 660-354-2330
Specialties: Folders, miniatures. **Patterns:** Hunters, buck skinners, bowies, miniatures and daggers. **Technical:** Grinds O1, D2, 440C and ATS-34. **Prices:** $150 to $2000, some higher. **Remarks:** Full-time maker, first knife sold in 1954. **Mark:** Fox logo.

RARDON, ARCHIE F
1589 SE Price Dr, Polo, MO 64671 **Contact:** 660-354-2330
Specialties: Working knives. **Patterns:** Hunters, bowies and miniatures. **Technical:** Grinds O1, D2, 440C, ATS-34, cable and damascus. **Prices:** $50 to $500. **Remarks:** Part-time maker. **Mark:** Boar hog.

RASSENTI, PETER
218 Tasse, St-Eustache, Quebec J7P 4C2, CANADA **Contact:** 450-598-6250, guireandgimble@hotmail.com
Specialties: Tactical mono-frame folding knives.

RAY, ALAN W
1287 FM 1280 E, Lovelady, TX 75851, awray@rayzblades.com, rayzblades.com
Specialties: Working straight knives of his design. **Patterns:** Hunters. **Technical:** Forges 01, L6 and 5160 for straight knives. **Prices:** $200 to $1000. **Remarks:** Full-time maker, first knife sold in 1979. **Mark:** Stylized initials.

RAYMOND, MICHAEL
4000 Weber Rd., Malabar, FL 32950 **Contact:** 321-300-5515, michael@michaelraymondknives.com, michaelraymondknives.com
Specialties: Integral folding knives with bushings and washer pivot construction. All parts made in-house. **Technical:** Uses Bohler M390, Crucible 20CV and Uddeholm Elmax steels. **Prices:** $1,200+. **Remarks:** Full-time maker, first folder made in late 2011, graduate of machinist school and apprentice tool & die maker.

REBELLO, INDIAN GEORGE
358 Elm St, New Bedford, MA 02740-3837 **Contact:** 508-999-7090, indgeo@juno.com, indiangeorgesknives.com
Specialties: One-of-a-kind fighters and bowies. **Patterns:** To customer's specs, hunters and utilities. **Technical:** Forges his own damascus, 5160, 52100, 1084, 1095, cable and O1. Grinds S30V, ATS-34, 154CM, 440C, D2 and A2. **Prices:** Starting at $250. **Remarks:** Full-time maker, first knife sold in 1991. Doing business as Indian George's Knives. Founding father and President of the Southern New England Knife-Makers Guild. Member of the N.C.C.A. **Mark:** Indian George's Knives.

RED, VERNON
2020 Benton Cove, Conway, AR 72034 **Contact:** 501-450-7284, knivesvr@conwaycorp.net
Specialties: Lock-blade folders, as well as fixed-blade knives of maker's own design or customer's. **Patterns:** Hunters, fighters, bowies, folders. **Technical:** Hollow grind, flat grind, stock removal and forged blades. Uses 440C, D-2, A-2, ATS-34, 1084, 1095, and damascus. **Prices:** fixed blades $175 and up, lock blade folders $225 and up **Remarks:** Made first knife in 1982, first folder in 1992. Member of (AKA) Arkansas Knives Association. **Mark:** Last name RED

REDD, BILL
2647 West 133rd Circle, Broomfield, Colorado 80020 **Contact:** 303-469-9803, unlimited_design@msn.com
Prices: Contact maker. **Remarks:** Full-time custom maker, member of PKA and RMBC (Rocky Mountain Blade Collectors). **Mark:** Redd Knives, Bill Redd.

REDDIEX, BILL
27 Galway Ave, Palmerston North, NEW ZEALAND **Contact:** 06-357-0383, (fax) 06-358-2910
Specialties: Collector-grade working straight knives. **Patterns:** Traditional-style bowies and drop-point hunters. **Technical:** Grinds 440C, D2 and O1, offers variety of grinds and finishes. **Prices:** $130 to $750. **Remarks:** Full-time maker, first knife sold in 1980. **Mark:** Last name around kiwi bird logo.

REEVES, J.R.
5181 South State Line, Texarkana, AR 71854 **Contact:** 870-773-5777, jos123@netscape.com
Specialties: Working straight knives of my design or customer design if a good flow. **Patterns:** Hunters, fighters, bowies, camp, bird, and trout knives. **Technical:** Forges and grinds 5160, 1084, 15n20, L6, 52100 and some damascus. Also some stock removal 440C, 01, D2, and 154 CM steels. I offer flat or hollow grinds. Natural handle material to include Sambar stag, desert Ironwood, sheep horn, other stabilized exotic woods and ivory. Custom filework offered. **Prices:** $200 - $1500. **Remarks:** Full-time maker, first knife sold in 1985. **Mark:** JR Reeves.

REGEL, JEAN-LOUIS
les ichards, Saint Leger de Fougeret, FRANCE 58120 **Contact:** 0033-66-621-6185, jregel2@hotmail.com
Specialties: bowies, camp knives, swords and folders. **Technical:** Forges own Wootz steel by hand, and damascus and high-carbon blade steels. **Remarks:** American Bladesmith Society journeyman smith. **Mark:** Jean-louis on right side of blade.

REGGIO JR., SIDNEY J
PO Box 851, Sun, LA 70463 **Contact:** 985-886-1397
Specialties: Miniature classic and fancy straight knives of his design or in standard patterns. **Patterns:** Fighters, hunters and utility/camp knives. **Technical:** Grinds 440C, ATS-34 and commercial damascus. Engraves, scrimshaws, offers filework. Hollow grinds most blades. Prefers natural handle material. Offers handmade sheaths. **Prices:** $85 to $250, some to $500. **Remarks:** Part-time maker, first knife sold in 1988. Doing business as Sterling Workshop. **Mark:** Initials.

REID, JIM
6425 Cranbrook St. NE, Albuquerque, NM 87111, jhrabq7@Q.com
Specialties: Fixed-blade knives.**Patterns:** Hunting, neck, and cowboy bowies. **Technical:** A2, D2, and damascus, stock removal. **Prices:** $125 to $300. **Mark:** Jim Reid over New Mexico zia sign.

RENFER, MASON
4521 N. 35th St., Phoenix, AZ 85018 **Contact:** 602-791-7879, info@renferknives.com
Specialties: Fixed blades (utility, tactical and kitchen) and folding knives (utility and tactical). **Technical:** Stock-removal method of blade making, and prefers using stainless steels, particularly CPM-154 and AEB-L. **Prices:** $175-$700. **Remarks:** Part-time maker since 2015. **Mark:** Uses either a hand stamp or an etched mark, depending on the model. Maker's mark is either last name "Renfer" or an "M" with a backwards "R" inside it.

RENNER, TERRY
TR Blades, Inc., 707 13th Ave. Cir. W, Palmetto, FL 34221 **Contact:** 941-729-3226, 941-545-6320, terrylmusic@gmail.com trblades.com
Specialties: High art folders and straight-blades, specialty locking mechanisms. Designer of the Neckolas knife by CRKT. Deep-relief carving.**Technical:** Prefer CPM154, S30V, 1095 carbon, damascus by Rob Thomas, Delbert Ealey, Bertie Reitveld, Todd Fischer, Joel Davis. Does own heat treating. **Remarks:** Full-time maker as of 2005. Formerly in bicylce manufacturing business, with patents for tooling and fixtures. President of the Florida Knifemaker's Association since 2009. **Mark:** TR* stylized

REPKE, MIKE
4191 N. Euclid Ave., Bay City, MI 48706 **Contact:** 517-684-3111
Specialties: Traditional working and using straight knives of his design or to customer specs, classic knives, display knives. **Patterns:** Hunters, bowies, skinners, fighters boots, axes and swords. **Technical:** Grind 440C. Offer variety of handle materials. **Prices:** $99 to $1500. **Remarks:** Full-time makers. Doing business as Black Forest Blades. **Mark:** Knife logo.

REVERDY, NICOLE AND PIERRE
5 Rue de L'egalite', Romans, FRANCE 26100 **Contact:** 334 75 05 10 15, reverdy.com
Specialties: Art knives, legend pieces. Pierre and Nicole, his wife, are creating knives of art with combination of enamel on pure silver (Nicole) and poetic damascus (Pierre) such as the "La dague a la licorne." **Patterns:** Daggers, folding knives damascus and enamel, bowies, hunters and other large patterns. **Technical:** Forges his damascus and "poetic damascus", where animals such as unicorns, stags, dragons or star crystals appear, works with his own EDM machine to create any kind of pattern inside the steel with his own touch. **Prices:** $2000 and up. **Remarks:** Full-time maker since 1989, first knife sold in 1986. Nicole (wife) collaborates with enamels. **Mark:** Reverdy.

REVISHVILI, ZAZA
2102 Linden Ave, Madison, WI 53704 **Contact:** 608-243-7927
Specialties: Fancy/embellished and high-art straight knives and folders of his design. **Patterns:** Daggers, swords and locking folders. **Technical:** Uses damascus, silver filigree, silver inlay in wood, enameling. **Prices:** $1000 to $9000, some to $15,000. **Remarks:** Full-time maker, first knife sold in 1987. **Mark:** Initials, city.

REXFORD, TODD
4531 W. Hwy. 24, Florissant, CO 80816 **Contact:** 719-492-2282, rexfordknives@gmail.com, rexfordknives.com
Specialties: Dress tactical and tactical folders and fixed blades. **Technical:** I work in stainless steels, stainless damascus, titanium, Stellite and other high performance alloys. All machining and part engineering is done in house.

REXROAT, KIRK
12 Crow Ln., Banner, WY 82832 **Contact:** 307-689-5430, rexroatknives@gmail.com, rexroatknives.com
Specialties: Using and collectible straight knives and folders of his design or to customer specs. **Patterns:** bowies, hunters, folders. **Technical:** Forges damascus patterns, mosaic and 52100. Does own engraving. **Prices:** $400 and up. **Remarks:** Part-time maker, master smith in the ABS, first knife sold in 1984. Doing business as Rexroat Knives. Designs and builds prototypes for Al Mar Knives. **Mark:** Last name.

REYNOLDS, DAVE
1404 Indian Creek, Harrisville, WV 26362 **Contact:** 304-643-2889, wvreynolds@zoomintevnet.net
Specialties: Working straight knives of his design. **Patterns:** bowies, kitchen and utility knives. **Technical:** Grinds and forges L6, 1095 and 440C. Heat-treats. **Prices:** $50 to $85, some to $175. **Remarks:** Full-time maker, first knife sold in 1980. Doing business as Terra-Gladius Knives. **Mark:** Mark on special orders only, serial number on all knives.

REYNOLDS, JOHN C
#2 Andover HC77, Gillette, WY 82716 **Contact:** 307-682-6076
Specialties: Working knives, some fancy. **Patterns:** Hunters, bowies, tomahawks and buck skinners, some folders. **Technical:** Grinds D2, ATS-34, 440C and forges own damascus and knives. Scrimshaws. **Prices:** $200 to $3000. **Remarks:** Spare-time maker, first knife sold in 1969. **Mark:** On ground blades JC Reynolds Gillette, WY, on forged blades, initials make the mark-JCR.

RHEA, LIN
413 Grant 291020, Prattsville, AR 72129 **Contact:** 870-942-6419, lwrhea@rheaknives.com, rheaknives.com
Specialties: Traditional and early American styled bowies in high carbon steel or damascus. **Patterns:** bowies, hunters and fighters. **Technical:** Filework wire inlay. Sole authorship of construction, damascus and embellishment. **Prices:** $280 to $1500. **Remarks:** Serious part-time maker and rated as a Master Smith in the ABS.

RHO, MARCELO ADRIAN
Primera Junta 589, Junin, Buenos Aires, ARGENTINA CP 6000 **Contact:** +54-236-15-4670686, info@cuchillosrho.com.ar, cuchillosrho.com.ar
Specialties: Classic and fancy straight knives of his design. **Patterns:** bowies, fighters and hunters. **Technical:** Grinds 420C, 440C, 1084, 5160, 52100, L6 and W1. Offers semi-precious stones on handles, acid etching on blades and blade engraving. **Prices:** $120 to $600, collector's pieces up to $3,000. **Remarks:** Business originally started with Nestor Lorenzo Rhó, who passed away in 2015. Son Marcelo now runs the business. Info listed here is for Nestor. Full-time maker, first knife sold in 1975. **Mark:** Name.

RIBONI, CLAUDIO
Via L Da Vinci, Truccazzano (MI), ITALY **Contact:** 02 95309010, riboni-knives.com

RICARDO ROMANO, BERNARDES
Ruai Coronel Rennò 1261, Itajuba MG, BRAZIL 37500 **Contact:** 0055-2135-622-5896
Specialties: Hunters, fighters, bowies. **Technical:** Grinds blades of stainless and tools steels. **Patterns:** Hunters. **Prices:** $100 to $700. **Mark:** Romano.

RICHARD, RAYMOND
31047 SE Jackson Rd., Gresham, OR 97080 **Contact:** 503-663-1219, rayskee13@hotmail.com, hawknknives.com
Specialties: Hand-forged knives, tomahawks, axes, and spearheads, all one-of-a-kind. **Prices:** $200 and up, some to $3000. **Remarks:** Full-time maker since 1994. **Mark:** Name on spine of blades.

RICHARDS, CHUCK
7243 Maple Tree Lane SE, Salem, OR 97317 **Contact:** 503-569-5549, woodchuckforge@gmail.com, acrichardscustomknives.com
Specialties: Fixed blade damascus. One-of-a-kind. **Patterns:** Hunters, fighters. **Prices:** $300 to $1,500+ **Remarks:** Likes to work with customers on a truly custom knife. **Mark:** A.C. Richards J.S. or ACR J.S.

RICHARDS, RALPH (BUD)
6413 Beech St, Bauxite, AR 72011 **Contact:** 501-602-5367, DoubleR042@aol.com, ralphrichardscustomknives.com
Specialties: Forges 55160, 1084, and 15N20 for damascus. S30V, 440C, and others. Wood, mammoth, giraffe and mother of pearl handles.

RICHARDSON, PERCY
7000 Hwy 69 South, Lufkin, TX 75901 **Contact:** 936-288-1690 or 936-634-1690, richardsonknives@yahoo.com, americasfightingshipsknives.com or richardsonhandmadeknives.com
Specialties: Knives forged from steel off old ships. **Patterns:** Slip joints, lockbacks, hunters, bowies, mostly knives forged from steel from old Navy ships. **Prices:** $300 to $2,000. **Remarks:** Five-year project of ships knives, 2014 until 2019. **Mark:** Richardson over five-point star and Lone Star USA.

RICHARDSON III, PERCY (RICH)
1508 Atkinson Dr., Lufkin, TX 75901 **Contact:** 318-455-5309 or 936-634-1690, prichardson100@yahoo.com, facebook.com/PRichKnives
Specialties: Straight knives of others' damascus, laser etching, some stabilized woods. **Patterns:** Hunters, skinners, small bowies and fighters. **Technical:** Stock removal, hollow grinds using CPM 154, ATS 34, 440C and damascus blade steels. **Prices:** $150 to $600. **Remarks:** Full-time maker, first knife made in 1995. **Mark:** Rich with year after on backbone of blade.

RICHARDSON JR., PERCY
1508 Atkinson Dr., Lufkin, TX 75901 **Contact:** 936-288-1690, Percy@Richardsonhandmadeknives.com, Richardsonhandmadeknives.com
Specialties: Working straight knives and folders. **Patterns:** Hunters, skinners, bowies, fighters and folders. **Technical:** Mostly grinds CPM-154. **Prices:** $175 - $750 some bowies to $1200. **Remarks:** Full-time maker, first knife sold in 1990. Doing business as Richardsons Handmade Knives. **Mark:** Texas star with last name across it.

RICHERSON, RON
P.O. Box 51, Greenburg, KY 42743 **Contact:** 270-405-0491, (fax) 270-932-5601, RRicherson1@windstream.net
Specialties: Collectible and functional fixed blades, locking liners, and autos of his design. **Technical:** Grinds ATS-34, S30V, S60V, CPM-154, D2, 440, high carbon steel, and his and others' damascus. Prefers natural materials for handles and does both stock removal and forged work, some with embellishments. **Prices:** $250 to $850, some higher. **Remarks:** Full-time maker. Member American Bladesmith Society. Made first knife in September 2006, sold first knife in December 2006. **Mark:** Name in oval with city and state. Also name in center of oval Green River Custom Knives.

RICKE, DAVE
1209 Adams St, West Bend, WI 53090 **Contact:** 262-334-5739
Specialties: Working knives, period pieces. **Patterns:** Hunters, boots, bowies, locking folders and slip joints. **Technical:** Grinds ATS-34, A2, 440C and 154CM. **Prices:** $145 and up. **Remarks:** Full-time maker, first knife sold in 1976. **Mark:** Last name.

RICKS, KURT J.
Darkhammer Forge, 29 N. Center, Trenton, UT 84338 **Contact:** 435-563-3471, kopsh@hotmail.com, http://darkhammerworks.tripod.com
Specialties: Fixed blade working knives of all designs and to customer specs. **Patterns:** Fighters, daggers, hunters, swords, axes, and spears. **Technical:** Uses a coal fired forge. Forges high carbon, tool and spring steels. Does own heat treat on forge. Prefers natural handle materials. Leather sheaths available. **Prices:** Start at $50 plus shipping. **Remarks:** A knife should be functional first and pretty second. Part-time maker, first knife sold in 1994. **Mark:** Initials.

RIDER, DAVID M
PO Box 5946, Eugene, OR 97405-0911 **Contact:** 541-343-8747

RIDGE, TIM
SWAMP FOX KNIVES, 1282 W. Creston Rd., Crossville, TN 38571 **Contact:** 931-484-0216, swampfoxknives@frontiernet.net, swampfoxknives.com
Specialties: Handforged historical American knives circa 1700 to 1865, colonial through Civil War eras. **Technical:** Forges 1095, 5160, 1084 and 1075 high-carbon steels. **Prices:** $135 to $2,000, depending on style and size of knife. **Remarks:** Full-time maker for 17 years. **Mark:** Patented running fox with TR in the body.

RIDLEY, ROB
RR1, Sundre, AB, CANADA T0M 1X0 **Contact:** 405-556-1113, rob@rangeroriginal.com, rangeroriginal.com, knifemaker.ca
Specialties: The knives I make are mainly fixed blades, though I'm exploring the complex world of folders. **Technical:** I favour high-end stainless alloys and exotic handle materials because a knife should provide both cutting ability and bragging rights. **Remarks:** I made my first knife in 1998 and still use that blade today. I've gone from full time, to part time, to hobby maker, but I still treasure time in the shop or spent with other enthusiasts. Operates Canadian Knifemakers Supply

RIEPE, RICHARD A
17604 E 296 St, Harrisonville, MO 64701

RIETVELD, BERTIE
PO Box 53, Magaliesburg, GT, SOUTH AFRICA 1791 **Contact:** 2783 232 8766, bertie@rietveldknives.com, rietveldknives.com
Specialties: Art daggers, Bolster lock folders, Persian designs, embraces elegant designs. **Patterns:** Mostly one-of-a-kind. **Technical:** Sole authorship, work only in own damascus, gold inlay, blued stainless fittings. **Prices:** $500 - $8,000 **Remarks:** First knife made in 1979. Annual shows attended: ECCKS, Blade Show, Milan Show, South African Guild Show. **Marks:** Logo is elephant in half circle with name, enclosed in Stanhope lens

RIGGI, NICK
470 Wheaton Ave, Bayville NJ 08721 **Contact:** 609-847-6269, Nriggi@comcast.net
Specialties: One-offs and customs. **Patterns:** Kitchen, EDC and outdoor blades. **Technical:** Variety of handle materials and stainless steels available.

RIGNEY JR., WILLIE
191 Colson Dr, Bronston, KY 42518 **Contact:** 606-679-4227
Specialties: High-tech period pieces and fancy working knives. **Patterns:** Fighters, boots, daggers and push knives. **Technical:** Grinds 440C and 154CM, buys damascus. Most knives are embellished. **Prices:** $150 to $1500, some to $10,000. **Remarks:** Full-time maker, first knife sold in 1978. **Mark:** First initial, last name.

RINKES, SIEGFRIED
Am Sportpl 2, Markterlbach, GERMANY 91459

RITCHIE, ADAM
Koi Knifeworks, 10925 Sheridan Ave. S, Bloomington, MN 55431 **Contact:** 651-503-2818, adamkara2@earthlink.net
Specialties: Japanese-influenced fixed blades. **Patterns:** Small utility knives to larger hunter/tactical pieces, Kwaikens, tantos and Kiridashis. **Technical:** Flat and convex grinds O1 tool steel and 1095, differentially heat treated to 58-60 Rockwell hardness. **Prices:** $150-$1,000. **Remarks:** Part-time maker, full-time firefighter/EMT/FEO. **Mark:** Koi Knifeworks in circle around Kanji or Koi.

RIZZI, RUSSELL J
37 March Rd, Ashfield, MA 01330 **Contact:** 413-625-2842
Specialties: Fancy working and using straight knives and folders of his design or to customer specs. **Patterns:** Hunters, locking folders and fighters. **Technical:** Grinds 440C, D2 and commercial damascus. **Prices:** $150 to $750, some to $2500. **Remarks:** Part-time maker, first knife sold in 1990. **Mark:** Last name, Ashfield, MA.

ROBBINS, BILL
2160 E. Fry Blvd., Ste. C5, Sierra Vista, AZ 85635-2794, billrknifemaker@aol.com
Specialties: Plain and fancy working straight knives. Makes to his designs and most anything you can draw. **Patterns:** Hunting knives, utility knives, and bowies. **Technical:** Grinds ATS-34, 440C, tool steel, high carbon, buys damascus. **Prices:** $70 to $450. **Remarks:** Part-time maker, first knife sold in 2001. **Mark:** Last name or desert scene with name.

ROBBINS, HOWARD P
1310 E. 310th Rd., Flemington, MO 65650 **Contact:** 417-282-5055, ARobb1407@aol.com

Specialties: High-tech working knives with clean designs, some fancy. **Patterns:** Folders, hunters and camp knives. **Technical:** Grinds 440C. Heat-treats, likes mirror finishes. Offers leatherwork. **Prices:** $100 to $500, some to $1000. **Remarks:** Full-time maker, first knife sold in 1982. **Mark:** Name, city and state.

ROBBINS, LANDON
2370 State Hwy. U, Crane, MO 65633 **Contact:** 417-207-4290, lwrobbins71@gmail.com
Specialties: Fixed blades using high-carbon damascus. **Patterns:** Hunters, bowies and fighters. **Technical:** Hand-forged, flat-ground 1084, 1074, 5160, 52100 and maker's own damascus. **Prices:** $300 and up. **Remarks:** Part-time maker, ABS journeyman smith. **Mark:** Robbins with an arrow under name.

ROBERT, ULYSSE
176 Chemin du Pinacle, Frelighsburg, QC, J0J 1C0 Canada **Contact:** contact.u.robert@gmail.com, Facebook/Instagram: @ulysserobertknives

ROBERTS, CHUCK
PO Box 7174, Golden, CO 80403 **Contact:** 303-642-2388, chuck@crobertsart.com, crobertsart.com
Specialties: Price daggers, large bowies, hand-rubbed satin finish. **Patterns:** bowies and California knives. **Technical:** Grinds 440C, 5160 and ATS-34. Handles made of stag, ivory or mother-of-pearl. **Prices:** $1250. **Remarks:** Full-time maker. Company name is C. Roberts - Art that emulates the past. **Mark:** Last initial or last name.

ROBERTS, JACK
10811 Sagebluff Dr, Houston, TX 77089 **Contact:** 281-481-1784, jroberts59@houston.rr.com
Specialties: Hunting knives and folders, offers scrimshaw by wife Barbara. **Patterns:** Drop point hunters and LinerLock® folders. **Technical:** Grinds 440-C, offers file work, texturing, natural handle materials and Micarta. **Prices:** $200 to $800 some higher. **Remarks:** Part-time maker, sold first knife in 1965. **Mark:** Name, city, state.

ROBERTS, T. C. (TERRY)
142131 Lake Forest Heights Rd., Siloam Springs, AR 72761 **Contact:** 479-373-6502, carolcroberts@cox.net
Specialties: Working straight knives and folders of the maker's original design. **Patterns:** bowies, daggers, fighters, locking folders, slip joints to include multiblades and whittlers. **Technical:** Grinds all types of carbon and stainless steels and commercially available damascus. Works in stone and casts in bronze and silver. Some inlays and engraving. **Prices:** $250 - $3500. **Remarks:** Full-time maker, sold first knife in 1983. **Mark:** Stamp is oval with initials inside.

ROBERTSON, LEO D
3728 Pleasant Lake Dr, Indianapolis, IN 46227 **Contact:** 317-882-9899, ldr52@juno.com
Specialties: Hunting and folders. **Patterns:** Hunting, bowie, utility, folders and kitchen. **Technical:** Uses ATS-34, 154CM, 440C, 1095, D2 and damascus steels. **Prices:** Fixed knives $200 to $600, folders $500 to $800, bowies $600 to $1200. **Remarks:** Handles made with stag, wildwoods, laminates, mother-of-pearl. Made first knife in 1990. Member of American Bladesmith Society. **Mark:** Logo with full name in oval around logo.

ROBINSON, CALVIN
5501 Twin Creek Circle, Pace, FL 32571 **Contact:** 850 572 1504, calvin@calvinrobinsonknives.com, CalvinRobinsonKnives.com
Specialties: Working knives of my own design. **Patterns:** Hunters, fishing, folding and kitchen and purse knives. **Technical:** Now using 14C28N stainless blade steel, as well as 12C27, 13C26 and D2. **Prices:** $180 to $2500. **Remarks:** Full-time maker. Knifemakers' Guild Board of Directors. **Mark:** Robinson.

ROBINSON, CHUCK
SEA ROBIN FORGE, 1423 Third Ave., Picayune, MS 39466 **Contact:** 601-798-0060, robi5515@bellsouth.net
Specialties: Deluxe period pieces and working / using knives of his design and to customer specs. **Patterns:** bowies, fighters, hunters, utility knives and original designs. **Technical:** Forges own damascus, 52100, O1, W2, L6, A2 and 1070 thru 1095. **Prices:** Start at $250. **Remarks:** First knife 1958. **Mark:** Fish logo, anchor and initials C.R.

ROBINSON III, REX R
10531 Poe St, Leesburg, FL 34788 **Contact:** 352-787-4587
Specialties: One-of-a-kind high-art automatics of his design. **Patterns:** Automatics, liner locks and lock back folders. **Technical:** Uses tool steel and stainless damascus and mokume, flat grinds. Hand carves folders. **Prices:** $1800 to $7500. **Remarks:** First knife sold in 1988. **Mark:** First name inside oval.

ROCHFORD, MICHAEL R
PO Box 577, Dresser, WI 54009 **Contact:** 715-755-3520, mrrochford@centurytel.net
Specialties: Working straight knives and folders. Classic bowies and Moran traditional. **Patterns:** bowies, fighters, hunters: slip-joint, locking and liner locking folders. **Technical:** Grinds ATS-34, 440C, 154CM and D-2, forges W2, 5160, and his own damascus. Offers metal and metal and leather sheaths. Filework and wire inlay. **Prices:** $150 to $1000, some to $2000. **Remarks:** Part-time maker, first knife sold in 1984. **Mark:** Name.

RODDENBERRY, CHARLES
SUWANNEE RIVER KNIFE, 160 Elm St. NE, Live Oak, FL 32064 **Contact:** 386-362-5641, suwanneeknife@yahoo.com, Facebook: Suwanee River Knife & Jewelry
Patterns: Small three-finger fixed blades, friction folders and miniatures. **Technical:** Uses forging and stock removal methods of blademaking, with preferred steels currently being 1095, L6, 52100 and D2. **Prices:** $50 to $500. **Remarks:** Full-time knifemaker

since 2012, first knife made in 2000 under the tutoring of Paul Martrildonno, with further training by Billy Brown. **Mark:** Simple skull face hot stamped.

RODDY, ROY "TIM"
7640 Hub-Bedford Rd., Hubbard, OH 44425 **Contact:** 330-770-5921, pfr2rtr@hotmail.com
> **Specialties:** Any type of knife a customer wants, large knives, small knives and anything in between. **Patterns:** Hunters, fighters, martial arts knives, hide-outs, neck knives, throwing darts and locking-liner folders. Leather or Kydex sheaths with exotic-skin inlays. **Technical:** 440C, D2, ATS-34 or damascus blade steels. **Remarks:** Started making knives 25 years ago. **Mark:** Railroad sign (circle with an X inside and an R on either side of the X).

RODEBAUGH, JAMES L
P.O. Box 404, Carpenter, WY 82054 **Contact:** 307-649-2394, jlrodebaugh@gmail.com

RODEWALD, GARY
447 Grouse Ct, Hamilton, MT 59840 **Contact:** 406-363-2192
> **Specialties:** bowies of his design as inspired from historical pieces. **Patterns:** Hunters, bowies and camp/combat. Forges 5160 1084 and his own damascus of 1084, 15N20, field grade hunters AT-34-440C, 440V, and BG42. **Prices:** $200 to $1500. **Remarks:** Sole author on knives, sheaths done by saddle maker. **Mark:** Rodewald.

RODKEY, DAN
18336 Ozark Dr, Hudson, FL 34667 **Contact:** 727-863-8264
> **Specialties:** Traditional straight knives of his design and in standard patterns. **Patterns:** Boots, fighters and hunters. **Technical:** Grinds 440C, D2 and ATS-34. **Prices:** Start at $200. **Remarks:** Full-time maker, first knife sold in 1985. Doing business as Rodkey Knives. **Mark:** Etched logo on blade.

ROEDER, DAVID
426 E. 9th Pl., Kennewick, WA 99336, d.roeder1980@yahoo.com
> **Specialties:** Fixed blade field and exposition grade knives. **Patterns:** Favorite styles are bowie and hunter. **Technical:** Forges primarily 5160 and 52100. Makes own damascus. **Prices:** Start at $150. **Remarks:** Made first knife in September, 1996. **Mark:** Maker's mark is a D and R with the R resting at a 45-degree angle to the lower right of the D.

ROGERS, RAY
PO Box 126, Wauconda, WA 98859 **Contact:** 509-486-8069, knives @rayrogers.com, rayrogers.com
> **Specialties:** LinerLock® folders. Asian and European professional chef's knives. **Patterns:** Rayzor folders, chef's knives and cleavers of his own and traditional designs, drop point hunters and fillet knives. **Technical:** Stock removal S30V, 440, 1095, O1 damascus and other steels. Does all own heat treating, clay tempering, some forging G-10, Micarta, carbon fiber on folders, stabilized burl woods on fixed blades. **Prices:** $300 to $700. **Remarks:** Knives are made one-at-a-time to the customer's order. Happy to consider customizing knife designs to suit your preferences and sometimes create entirely new knives when necessary. As a full-time knifemaker is willing to spend as much time as it takes (usually through email) discussing the options and refining details of a knife's design to insure that you get the knife you really want.

ROGERS, RICHARD
PO Box 769, Magdalena, NM 87825 **Contact:** 575-838-7237, r.s.rogersknives@gmail.com, richardrogersknives.com
> **Specialties:** Folders. **Patterns:** Modern slip joints, LinerLocks and frame-locks. **Prices:** $300 and up. **Mark:** Last name.

ROGHMANS, MARK
607 Virginia Ave, LaGrange, GA 30240 **Contact:** 706-885-1273
> **Specialties:** Classic and traditional knives of his design. **Patterns:** bowies, daggers and fighters. **Technical:** Grinds ATS-34, D2 and 440C. **Prices:** $250 to $500. **Remarks:** Part-time maker, first knife sold in 1984. Doing business as LaGrange Knife. **Mark:** Last name and/or LaGrange Knife.

ROHDE, DANIEL S.
25692 County Rd. 9, Winona, MN 55987 **Contact:** 507-312-6664, rohdeedge@gmail.com, rohdeedge.com
> **Specialties:** High performance fixed blades, chef's knives and slip-joint folders. **Patterns:** Loveless- and Fowler-style hunters, SharkTail and other hunting, EDC and chef's knives. **Technical:** Highly thermal cycled and forged 52100 and 1095, and AEB-L for a stainless steel. **Prices:** $100 to $400, some to $1,200, with the typical EDC knife going for about $185. **Remarks:** HEPK apprentice smith, part-time maker, and consistent, repeatable performance is the goal. **Mark:** Electro-etched last name (typically).

ROHN, FRED
7675 W Happy Hill Rd, Coeur d'Alene, ID 83814 **Contact:** 208-667-0774
> **Specialties:** Hunters, boot knives, custom patterns. **Patterns:** Drop points, double edge, etc. **Technical:** Grinds 440 or 154CM. **Prices:** $85 and up. **Remarks:** Part-time maker. **Mark:** Logo on blade, serial numbered.

ROLLERT, STEVE
PO Box 65, Keensburg, CO 80643-0065 **Contact:** 303-732-4858, steve@doveknives.com, doveknives.com
> **Specialties:** Highly finished working knives. **Patterns:** Variety of straight knives, locking folders and slip-joints. **Technical:** Forges and grinds W2, 1095, ATS-34 and his pattern-welded, cable damascus and nickel damascus. **Prices:** $300 to $1000, some to $3000. **Remarks:** Full-time maker, first knife sold in 1980. Doing business as Dove Knives. **Mark:** Last name in script.

ROMEIS, GORDON
1521 Coconut Dr., Fort Myers, FL 33901 **Contact:** 239-940-5060, gordonromeis@gmail.com, Romeisknives.com
> **Specialties:** Smaller using knives. **Patterns:** I have a number of standard designs that include both full tapered tangs and narrow tang knives. Custom designs are welcome. Many different types. No folders. **Technical:** Standard steel is 440C. Also uses Alabama damascus steel. **Prices:** Start at $165. **Remarks:** I am a part-time maker however I do try to keep waiting times to a minimum. **Mark:** Either my name, city, and state or simply ROMEIS depending on the knife.

RONZIO, N. JACK
PO Box 248, Fruita, CO 81521 **Contact:** 970-858-0921

ROOSEVELT, RUSSELL
448 County Road 400 N, Albion IL 62806-4753 **Contact:** 618-445-3226 or 618-302-7272, rroosevelt02@gmail.com
> **Specialties:** Using straight knives of his design and to customers' specs. **Patterns:** Hunters, utility and camp knives. **Technical:** Forges 1084 and high-carbon damascus. **Prices:** $250 to $1,200. **Remarks:** Part-time maker, first knife sold in 1999. **Mark:** Full name left side, ABS JS stamp right side.

ROOT, GARY
644 East 14th St, Erie, PA 16503 **Contact:** 814-459-0196
> **Specialties:** damascus bowies with hand carved eagles, hawks and snakes for handles. Few folders made. **Patterns:** Daggers, fighters, hunter/field knives. **Technical:** Using handforged damascus from Ray Bybar Jr (M.S.) and Robert Eggerling. Grinds D2, 440C, 1095 and 5160. Some 5160 is hand forged. **Prices:** $80 to $300 some to $1000. **Remarks:** Full time maker, first knife sold in 1976. **Mark:** Name over Erie, PA.

ROSE, BOB
PO BOX 126, Wagontown, PA 19376 **Contact:** 484-883-3925, bobmedit8@comcast.net bobroseknives.com
> **Patterns:** bowies, fighters, drop point hunters, daggers, bird and trout, camp, and other fixed blade styles. **Technical:** Mostly using 1095 and damascus steel, desert ironwood and other top-of-the-line exotic woods as well as mammoth tooth. **Prices:** $49 - $300. **Remarks:** Been making and selling knives since 2004. "Knife Making is a meditation technique for me."

ROSE, DEREK W
14 Willow Wood Rd, Gallipolis, OH 45631 **Contact:** 740-446-4627

ROSE II, DOUN T.
Ltc US Special Operations Command (ret.), 1795/96 W Sharon Rd SW, Fife Lake, MI 49633 **Contact:** 231-645-1369, rosecutlery@gmail.com, rosecutlery.com
> **Specialties:** Straight working, collector and presentation knives to a high level of fit and finish. Design in collaboration with customer. **Patterns:** Field knives, Scagel, bowies, tactical, period pieces, axes and tomahawks, fishing and hunting spears and fine kitchen cutlery. **Technical:** Forged and billet ground, high carbon and stainless steel appropriate to end use. Steel from leading industry sources. Some period pieces from recovered stock. Makes own damascus (to include multi-bar and mosaic) and mokume gane. **Remarks:** Full-time maker, ABS since 2000, William Scagel Memorial Scholarship 2002, Bill Moran School of Blade Smithing 2003, apprentice under Master Blacksmith Dan Nickels at Black Rock Forge current. Working at Crooked Pine Forge. **Mark:** Last name ROSE in block letters with five petal "wild rose" in place of O. Doing business as Rose Cutlery.

ROSENBAUGH, RON
2806 Stonegate Dr, Crystal Lake, IL 60012 **Contact:** 815-477-9233 or 815-345-1633, ron@rosenbaughknives.com, rosenbaughknives.com
> **Specialties:** Fancy and plain working knives using own designs, collaborations, and traditional patterns. **Patterns:** Bird, trout, boots, hunters, fighters, some bowies. **Technical:** Grinds high alloy stainless, tool steels, and damascus, forges 1084,5160, 52100, carbon and spring steels. **Prices:** $150 to $1000. **Remarks:** Full-time maker, first knife sold in 2004. **Mark:** Last name, logo, city.

ROSS, STEPHEN
534 Remington Dr, Evanston, WY 82930 **Contact:** 307-799-7653
> **Specialties:** One-of-a-kind collector-grade classic and contemporary straight knives and folders of his design and to customer specs, some fantasy pieces. **Patterns:** Combat and survival knives, hunters, boots and folders. **Technical:** Grinds stainless and tool steels. Engraves, scrimshaws. Makes leather sheaths. **Prices:** $160 to $3000. **Remarks:** Part-time maker, first knife sold in 1971. **Mark:** Last name in modified Roman, sometimes in script.

ROSS, TIM
3239 Oliver Rd, Thunder Bay, ON, CANADA P7G 1S9 **Contact:** 807-627-5086, rosscustomknives@gmail.com
> **Specialties:** Fixed blades, natural handle material. **Patterns:** Hunting, fishing, bowies, fighters. **Technical:** 52100 series bearing steel, circular saw blade steel, 440c stainless, 5160, natural handle materials. **Prices:** $150 to $750 some higher. **Remarks:** Forges and stock removal. Teaching classes on bladesmithing. Supplier of some materials and equipment. **Mark:** Ross Custom Knives.

ROSSDEUTSCHER, ROBERT N
133 S Vail Ave, Arlington Heights, IL 60005 **Contact:** 847-577-0404, rnrknives.com
> **Specialties:** Frontier-style and historically inspired knives. **Patterns:** Trade knives, bowies, camp knives and hunting knives, tomahawks and lances. **Technical:** Most knives are hand forged, a few are stock removal. **Prices:** $135 to $1500. **Remarks:** Journeyman Smith of the American Bladesmith Society. **Mark:** Back-to-back "R's", one upside down and backwards, one right side up and forward in an oval. Sometimes with name, town

and state, depending on knife style.

ROTELLA, RICHARD A

643 75th St., Niagara Falls, NY 14304, richarpo@roadrunner.com
Specialties: Highly finished working knives of his own design, as well as some Loveless-style designs. **Patterns:** Hunters, fishing, small game, utility, fighters and boot knives. **Technical:** Grinds ATS-34, 154CM, CPM 154 and 440C. **Prices:** $150 to $600. **Remarks:** Part-time maker, first knife sold in 1977. Sells completed knives only and does not take orders, makes about 70 knives a year. **Mark:** Name and city.

ROVATTI, ANDREA

AR Knives Verona, Italy **Contact:** 393385974666, www.arknives.com

ROUGEAU, DERICK

1465 Cloud Peak Dr., Sparks, NV 89436 **Contact:** 775-232-6167, derick@rougeauknives.com, rougeauknives.com
Specialties: A wide range of original designs from practical to tactical and traditional. **Patterns:** bowies, hunters, fighters, bushcraft blades, tantos, machetes, chef's knives, tomahawks, hatchets, swords, neck and tool knives. Also makes assorted accessories and other cool items. **Technical:** Using stock-removal process. Flat and hollow grinds using a wide range of steels from damascus to 1080, 1095, 5160, 6150, O1, D2, ATS 34, CPM 154 and other CPM stainless steels. Does own heat treating, leather work and Kydex, and uses synthetic materials, stabilized woods and antler. **Prices:** $250 to $650 or more. **Remarks:** Part-time maker, full-time artist/designer. **Mark:** "DR" logo in front of "ROUGEAU."

ROULIN, CHARLES

113 B Rt. de Soral, Geneva, SWITZERLAND 1233 **Contact:** 022-757-4479, (fax) 079-218-9754, charles.roulin@bluewin.ch, coutelier-roulin.com
Specialties: Fancy high-art straight knives and folders of his design. **Patterns:** bowies, locking folders, slip-joint folders and miniatures. **Technical:** Grinds 440C, ATS-34 and D2. Engraves, carves nature scenes and detailed animals in steel, ivory, on handles and blades. **Prices:** $500 to $3000, some to Euro: 14,600. **Remarks:** Full-time maker, first knife sold in 1988. **Mark:** Symbol of fish with name or name engraved.

ROUSH, SCOTT

Big Rock Forge, 30955 Hove Ln., Washburn, WI 54891 **Contact:** 715-682-2844, scott@bigrockforge.com, bigrockforge.com
Specialties: Forged blades representing a diversity of styles from trasditional hunters, fighters, camp knives, and EDC's to artistic pieces of cultural and historical inspiration with an emphasis in unique materials. **Technical:** Forges Aldo 1084, W2, low MN 1075, stainless/high carbon san mai, wrought iron/high carbon san mai, damascus. **Prices:** $85 to $1000 **Remarks:** Full-time maker, first knife sold in 2010. **Mark:** Stamped initials (SAR) set in a diamond.

ROWE, FRED

BETHEL RIDGE FORGE, 3199 Roberts Rd, Amesville, OH 45711 **Contact:** 866-325-2164, fred_rowe@bethelridgeforge.com, bethelridgeforge.com
Specialties: damascus and carbon steel sheath knIves. **Patterns:** bowies, hunters, fillet small kokris. **Technical:** His own damascus, 52100, O1, L6, 1095 carbon steels, mosaics. **Prices:** $200 to $2000. **Remarks:** All blades are clay hardened. **Mark:** Bethel Ridge Forge.

ROYER, KYLE

9021 State Hwy. M, Clever, MO 65631 **Contact:** 417-247-5572, royerknifeworks@live.com, kyleroyerknives.com
Specialties: All fixed knives, giant bowies, art daggers and folders. **Technical:** Complex mosaic damascus, gold inlay, engraving, details and design. **Prices:** $5000 to $100000. **Remarks:** Sole-authorship, full-time ABS master smith and artist. **Mark:** K~ROYER~MS.

ROZAS, CLARK D

1436 W "G" St, Wilmington, CA 90744 **Contact:** 310-518-0488
Specialties: Hand forged blades. **Patterns:** Pig stickers, toad stabbers, whackers, choppers. **Technical:** damascus, 52100, 1095, 1084, 5160. **Prices:** $200 to $600. **Remarks:** A.B.S. member, part-time maker since 1995. **Mark:** Name over dagger.

RUA, GARY

400 Snell St., Apt. 2, Fall River, MA 02721 **Contact:** 508-677-2664
Specialties: Working straight knives of his design. 1800 to 1900 century standard patterns. **Patterns:** bowies, hunters, fighters, and patch knives. **Technical:** Forges and grinds. damascus, 5160, 1095, old files. Uses only natural handle material. **Prices:** $350 - $2000. **Remarks:** Part-time maker. (Harvest Moon Forge) **Mark:** Last name.

RUANA KNIFE WORKS

Box 520, Bonner, MT 59823 **Contact:** 406-258-5368, (fax) 406-258-2895, info@ruanaknives.com, ruanaknives.com
Specialties: Working knives and period pieces. **Patterns:** Variety of straight knives. **Technical:** Forges 5160 chrome alloy for bowies and 1095. **Prices:** $300 and up. **Remarks:** Full-time maker, first knife sold in 1938. For free catalog email regular mailing address to info@ruanaknives.com **Mark:** Name.

RUCKER, THOMAS

30222 Mesa Valley Dr., Spring, TX 77386 **Contact:** 832-216-8122, admin@knivesbythomas.com knivesbythomas.com
Specialties: Personal design and custom design. Hunting, tactical, folding knives, and cutlery. **Technical:** Design and grind ATS34, D2, O1, damascus, and VG10. **Prices:** $150 - $5,000. **Remarks:** Full-time maker and custom scrimshaw and engraving done by wife, Debi Rucker. First knife done in 1969, first design sold in 1975 **Mark:** Etched logo and signature.

RUIZ, JERELL A.

Volundr Forge San Antonio, TX **Contact:** www.volundrforge.com, Facebook: Volundr Forge, Instagram: volundr_forge
Specialties: Hand-forged ironwork and custom knives. **Remarks:** Lone Star Member of the Texas Knifemakers Guild and a member of Balcones Forge: Central Texas Blacksmiths.

RUPERT, BOB

301 Harshaville Rd, Clinton, PA 15026 **Contact:** 724-573-4569, rbrupert@aol.com
Specialties: Wrought period pieces with natural elements. **Patterns:** Elegant straight blades, friction folders. **Technical:** Forges colonial 7, 1095, 5160, diffuse mokume-gane and damascus. **Prices:** $150 to $1500, some higher. **Remarks:** Part-time maker, first knife sold in 1980. Evening hours studio since 1980. Likes simplicity that disassembles. **Mark:** R etched in Old English.

RUPLE, WILLIAM H

201 Brian Dr., Pleasanton, TX 78064 **Contact:** 830-569-0007, bknives@devtex.net
Specialties: Multi-blade folders, slip joints, some lock backs. **Patterns:** Like to reproduce old patterns. Offers filework and engraving. **Technical:** Grinds CPM-154 and other carbon and stainless steel and commercial damascus. **Prices:** $950 to $2500. **Remarks:** Full-time maker, first knife sold in 1988. **Mark:** Ruple.

RUSNAK, JOSEF

Breclavska 6, 323 00 Plzen, CZECH REPUBLIC **Contact:** 00420721329442, rusnak.josef@centrum.cz, http://knife.guaneru.cz
Specialties: Highly artistically designed knives. **Patterns:** Straight knives and folders. Collaboration with Buddy Weston. **Technical:** Engraving in high-quality steel and organic materials (mammoth tusk, giraffe bone, mother-of-pearl, bone), miniature sculpting, casting (Au, Ag, bronze). **Prices:** $1,000 and up. **Remarks:** Part-time maker, first knife sold in 1994. **Mark:** Signature.

RUSS, RON

5351 NE 160th Ave, Williston, FL 32696 **Contact:** 352-528-2603, RussRs@aol.com
Specialties: damascus and mokume. **Patterns:** Ladder, rain drop and butterfly. **Technical:** Most knives, including damascus, are forged from 52100-E. **Prices:** $65 to $2500. **Mark:** Russ.

RUSSELL, MICK

4 Rossini Rd, Pari Park, Port Elizabeth, EC, SOUTH AFRICA 6070
Specialties: Art knives. **Patterns:** Working and collectible bird, trout and hunting knives, defense knives and folders. **Technical:** Grinds D2, 440C, ATS-34 and damascus. Offers mirror or satin finishes. **Prices:** Start at $100. **Remarks:** Full-time maker, first knife sold in 1986. **Mark:** Stylized rhino incorporating initials.

RUSSELL, TOM

6500 New Liberty Rd, Jacksonville, AL 36265 **Contact:** 205-492-7866
Specialties: Straight working knives of his design or to customer specs. **Patterns:** Hunters, folders, fighters, skinners, bowies and utility knives. **Technical:** Grinds D2, 440C and ATS-34, offers filework. **Prices:** $75 to $225. **Remarks:** Part-time maker, first knife sold in 1987. Full-time tool and die maker. **Mark:** Last name with tulip stamp.

RUTH, MICHAEL G

3101 New Boston Rd, Texarkana, TX 75501 **Contact:** 903-832-7166/cell:903-277-3663, (fax) 903-832-4710, mike@ruthknives.com, ruthknives.com
Specialties: Hunters, bowies & fighters. damascus & carbon steel. **Prices:** $375 & up. **Mark:** Last name.

RUTH, JR., MICHAEL

5716 Wilshire Dr., Texarkana, TX 75503 **Contact:** 903-293-2663, michael@ruthlesscustomknives.com, ruthlesscustomknives.com
Specialties: Custom hand-forged blades, utilizing high carbon and damascus steels. **Patterns:** bowies, hunters and fighters ranging from field to presentation-grade pieces. **Technical:** Steels include 5160, 1084, 15n20, W-2, 1095, and O-1. Handle materials include a variety of premium hardwoods, stag, assorted ivories and micarta. **Mark:** 8-pointed star with capital "R" in center.

RUUSUVUORI, ANSSI

Verkkotie 38, Piikkio, FINLAND 21500 **Contact:** 358-50-520 8057, anssi.ruusuvuori@akukon.fi, arknives.suntuubi.com
Specialties: Traditional and modern puukko knives and hunters. Sole author except for damascus steel. **Technical:** Forges mostly 1080 steel and grinds RWL-34. **Prices:** $200 to $500, some to $1200. **Remarks:** Part-time maker. **Mark:** A inside a circle (stamped)

RYBAR JR., RAYMOND B

2328 S. Sunset Dr., Camp Verde, AZ 86322 **Contact:** 928-567-6372
Specialties: Straight knives or folders with customers name, logo, etc. in mosaic pattern. **Patterns:** Common patterns plus mosaics of all types. **Technical:** Forges own damascus. Primary forging of self smelted steel - smelting classes. **Prices:** $200 to $1200, Bible blades to $10,000. **Remarks:** Master Smith (A.B.S.) Primary focus toward Biblicaly themed blades **Mark:** Rybar or stone church forge or Rev. 1:3 or R.B.R. between diamonds.

RYDBOM, JEFF

PO Box 548, Annandale, MN 55302 **Contact:** 320-274-9639, jry1890@hotmail.com
Specialties: Ring knives. **Patterns:** Hunters, fighters, bowie and camp knives. **Technical:** Straight grinds O1, A2, 1566 and 5150 steels. **Prices:** $150 to $1000. **Remarks:** No pinning of guards or pommels. All silver brazed. **Mark:** Capital "C" with J R inside.

RYUICHI, KUKI

504-7 Tokorozawa-Shinmachi, Tokorozawa-city, Saitama, JAPAN **Contact:** 042-943-3451

RZEWNICKI, GERALD
8833 S Massbach Rd, Elizabeth, IL 61028-9714 **Contact:** 815-598-3239

S

SAINDON, R BILL
233 Rand Pond Rd, Goshen, NH 03752 **Contact:** 603-843-7840, dayskier71@aol.com
Specialties: Collector-quality folders of his design or to customer specs. **Patterns:** Latch release, LinerLock® and lockback folders. **Technical:** Offers limited amount of own damascus, also uses Damas makers steel. Prefers natural handle material, gold and gems. **Prices:** $500 to $4000. **Remarks:** Full-time maker, first knife sold in 1981. Doing business as Daynia Forge. **Mark:** Sun logo or engraved surname.

SAKMAR, MIKE
4337 E. Grand River Ave. #113, Howell, MI 48843 **Contact:** 517-546-6388, (fax) 517-546-6399, sakmarent@yahoo.com, sakmarenterprises.com
Specialties: Mokume in various patterns and alloy combinations. **Patterns:** bowies, fighters, hunters and integrals. **Technical:** Grinds ATS-34, damascus and high-carbon tool steels. Uses mostly natural handle materials—elephant ivory, walrus ivory, stag, wildwood, oosic, etc. Makes mokume for resale. **Prices:** $250 to $2500, some to $4000. **Remarks:** Part-time maker, first knife sold in 1990. Supplier of mokume. **Mark:** Last name.

SALLEY, JOHN D
3965 Frederick-Ginghamsburg Rd., Tipp City, OH 45371 **Contact:** 937-698-4588, (fax) 937-698-4131
Specialties: Fancy working knives and art pieces. **Patterns:** Hunters, fighters, daggers and some swords. **Technical:** Grinds ATS-34, 12C27 and W2, buys damascus. **Prices:** $85 to $1000, some to $6000. **Remarks:** Part-time maker, first knife sold in 1979. **Mark:** First initial, last name.

SALTER, GREGG
Salter Fine Cutlery, POB 384571, Waikoloa, HI 96738-4571 **Contact:** 808-883-0128, SalterFineCutlery@gmail.com, SalterFineCutlery.com
Specialties: Knife sets. Made-to-order cutlery, custom display boxes and stands. Chef knife sets, steak knife sets, carving sets, individual chef knives and collectible knives. Work in collaboration with several individual bladesmiths who create blades to our own designs and specifications. **Technical:** Variety of steels used including SG2, R2, Gingami3, and SRS13, VG-10 stainless steels. OU-31, YSS White Paper Shirogami, and YSS Aogami Blue Paper carbon steels. damascus patterns, hammered and laser-etched patterns. **Prices:** Range widely, from approximately $300 to $15000. **Remarks:** Full-time business making a range of products based around knives, including custom display boxes for other knifemakers. **Mark:** Hawaiian koa tree with crossed chef's knives and crown outline.

SAMPSON, LYNN
381 Deakins Rd, Jonesborough, TN 37659 **Contact:** 423-348-8373
Specialties: Highly finished working knives, mostly folders. **Patterns:** Locking folders, slip-joints, interframes and two-blades. **Technical:** Grinds D2, 440C and ATS-34, offers extensive filework. **Prices:** Start at $300. **Remarks:** Full-time maker, first knife sold in 1982. **Mark:** Name and city in logo.

SANDBERG, RONALD B
24784 Shadowwood Ln, Brownstown, MI 48134-9560 **Contact:** 734-671-6866, msc2009@comcast.net
Specialties: Good looking and functional hunting knives, filework, mixing of handle materials. **Patterns:** hunters, skinners, daggers, bowies, fillets, kitchen. **Prices:** $120 and up. **Remarks:** Full lifetime workmanship guarantee. **Mark:** R.B. SANDBERG

SANDERS, BILL
335 Bauer Ave, PO Box 957, Mancos, CO 81328 **Contact:** 970-533-7223, (fax) 970-533-7390, billsand@frontier.net, billsandershandmadeknives.com
Specialties: Survival knives, working straight knives, some fancy and some fantasy, of his design. **Patterns:** Hunters, boots, utility knives, using belt knives. **Technical:** Grinds 440C, ATS-34 and commercial damascus. Provides wide variety of handle materials. **Prices:** $170 to $800. **Remarks:** Full-time maker. Formerly of Timberline Knives. **Mark:** Name, city and state.

SANDOW, BRENT EDWARD
50 O'Halloran Road, Howick, Auckland, NEW ZEALAND 2014 **Contact:** 64 9 537 4166, knifebug@vodafone.co.nz, brentsandowknives.com
Specialties: Tactical fixed blades, hunting, camp, bowie. **Technical:** All blades made by stock removal method. **Prices:** From US $200 upward. **Mark:** Name etched or engraved.

SANDS, SCOTT
2 Lindis Ln, New Brighton, Christchurch 9, NEW ZEALAND
Specialties: Classic working and fantasy swords. **Patterns:** Fantasy, medieval, celtic, viking, katana, some daggers. **Technical:** Forges own damascus, 1080 and L6, 5160 and L6, O1 and L6. All hand-polished, does own heat-treating, forges non-damascus on request. **Prices:** $1500 to $15,000+. **Remarks:** Full-time maker, first blade sold in 1996. **Mark:** Stylized Moon.

SANFORD, DICK
151 London Ln., Chehalis, WA 98532 **Contact:** 360-748-2128, richardsanfo364@centurytel.net
Remarks: Ten years experience hand forging knives

SANGSTER, JOE
POB 312, Vienna, GA 31092 **Contact:** 229-322-3407, ssangster@sowega.net, sangsterknives.com
Specialties Gent's LinerLock folders with filework. **Patterns:** Traditional LinerLock folders, hunters, skinners and kitchen knives. **Technical:** Grinds ATS-34, CPM 134, 440C and commercial damascus. Handle materials of mammoth ivory, mammoth tooth, pearl, oosic, coral and exotic burl woods. **Prices:** $250 to $500, some up to $1,200. **Remarks:** Full-time maker, first knife sold in 2003. **Mark:** name or name, city and state.

SANTA, LADISLAV "LASKY"
Stara Voda 264/10, 97637 Hrochot, SLOVAKIA **Contact:** +421-907-825-2-77, lasky@lasky.sk, lasky.sk
Specialties: damascus hunters, daggers and swords. **Patterns:** Various damascus patterns. **Prices:** $300 to $6,000 U.S. **Mark:** L or Lasky.

SANTIAGO, ABUD
Av Gaona 3676 PB, Buenos Aires, ARGENTINA 1416 **Contact:** 5411 4612 8396, info@phi-sabud.com, phi-sabud.com/blades.html

SANTINI, TOM
101 Clayside Dr, Pikeville, NC 27863 **Contact:** 586-354-0245, tomsantiniknives@hotmail.com, tomsantiniknives.com
Specialties: working/using straight knives, tactical, and some slipjoints **Technical:** Grinds ATS-34, S-90-V, D2, and damascus. I handstitch my leather sheaths. **Prices:** $150 - $500. **Remarks:** Full-time maker, first knife sold in 2004. **Mark:** Full name.

SARGANIS, PAUL
2215 Upper Applegate Rd, Jacksonville, OR 97530 **Contact:** 541-899-2831, paulsarganis@hotmail.com, sarganis.50megs.com
Specialties: Hunters, folders, bowies. **Technical:** Forges 5160, 1084. Grinds ATS-34 and 440C. **Prices:** $120 to $500. **Remarks:** Spare-time maker, first knife sold in 1987. **Mark:** Last name.

SASS, GARY N
815 W Ridge Ave, Sharpsville, PA 16150 **Contact:** 724-866-6165, gnsass@yahoo.com
Specialties: Working straight knives of his design or to customer specifications. **Patterns:** Hunters, fighters, utility knives, push daggers. **Technical:** Grinds 440C, ATS-34 and damascus. Uses exotic wood, buffalo horn, warthog tusk and semi-precious stones. **Prices:** $50 to $250, some higher. **Remarks:** Part-time maker. First knife sold in 2003. **Mark:** Initials G.S. formed into a diamond shape or last name.

SATTERFIELD, SCOTT
Satterfield Knives, NY **Contact:** 914-260-7085, Scott@satterfieldknives.com
Patterns: Hunting and culinary knives.

SAVIANO, JAMES
124 Wallis St., Douglas, MA 01516 **Contact:** 508-476-7644, jimsaviano@gmail.com
Specialties: Straight knives. **Patterns:** Hunters, bowies, fighters, daggers, short swords. **Technical:** Hand-forged high-carbon and my own damascus steel. **Prices:** Starting at $300. **Remarks:** ABS mastersmith, maker since 2000, sole authorship. **Mark:** Last name or stylized JPS initials.

SAWBY, SCOTT
480 Snowberry Ln, Sandpoint, ID 83864 **Contact:** 208-263-4253, scotmar3@gmail.com, sawbycustomknives.com
Specialties: Folders, working and fancy. **Patterns:** Locking folders, patent locking systems and interframes. **Technical:** Grinds D2, 440C, CPM154, ATS-34, S30V, and damascus. **Prices:** $700 to $3000. **Remarks:** Full-time maker, first knife sold in 1974. **Mark:** Last name, city and state.

SALYERS, BILLY
Yellow Rose Forge 280 Honeysuckle Ct, Rutherfordton, NC 28139 **Contact:** 828-289-6884, www.yellowroseforge.com
Specialties: Knives and also decorative ironwork.

SCARROW, WIL
c/o Scarrow's Custom Stuff, PO Box 1036, Gold Hill, OR 97525-1036 **Contact:** 541-855-1236, willsknife@gmail.com
Specialties: Carving knives and tools, and some mini wood lathe tools. **Patterns:** Carving, fishing, hunting, skinning, utility, swords and bowies. **Technical:** Forges and grinds: A2, W1, O1, 5160 and 1095. Offers some filework. **Prices:** $45 and up. **Remarks:** Spare-time maker, first knife made/sold in 1983. One month turnaround on orders. Doing business as Scarrow's Custom Stuff (Gold Hill, OR, USA). Carving knives available at Raven Dog Enterprises. Contact at Ravedog@aol.com. **Mark:** SC with arrow and year made.

SCHALLER, ANTHONY BRETT
5609 Flint Ct. NW, Albuquerque, NM 87120 **Contact:** 505-899-0155, brett@schallerknives.com, schallerknives.com
Specialties: Straight knives and locking-liner folders of his design and in standard patterns. **Patterns:** Boots, fighters, utility knives and folders. **Technical:** Grinds CPM154, S30V, and stainless damascus. Offers filework, hand-rubbed finishes and full and narrow tangs. Prefers stabilized wood, Micarta, and G-10 for handle materials. **Prices:** $135 to $600. **Remarks:** Part-time maker, first knife sold in 1990. **Mark:** A.B. Schaller - Albuquerque NM - handmade.

SCHEID, MAGGIE
124 Van Stallen St, Rochester, NY 14621-3557
Specialties: Simple working straight knives. **Patterns:** Kitchen and utility knives, some

miniatures. **Technical:** Forges 5160 high-carbon steel. **Prices:** $100 to $200. **Remarks:** Part-time maker, first knife sold in 1986. **Mark:** Full name.

SCHEMPP, ED
PO Box 1181, Ephrata, WA 98823 **Contact:** 509-754-2963, (fax) 509-754-3212, edschempp@yahoo.com
Specialties: Mosaic damascus and unique folder designs. **Patterns:** Primarily folders. **Technical:** Grinds CPM440V, forges many patterns of mosaic using powdered steel. **Prices:** $100 to $400, some to $2000. **Remarks:** Part-time maker, first knife sold in 1991. Doing business as Ed Schempp Knives. **Mark:** Ed Schempp Knives over five heads of wheat, city and state.

SCHEMPP, MARTIN
PO Box 1181, 5430 Baird Springs Rd NW, Ephrata, WA 98823 **Contact:** 509-754-2963, (fax) 509-754-3212
Specialties: Fantasy and traditional straight knives of his design, to customer specs and in standard patterns, Paleolithic-styles. **Patterns:** Fighters and Paleolithic designs. **Technical:** Uses opal, Mexican rainbow and obsidian. Offers scrimshaw. **Prices:** $15 to $100, some to $250. **Remarks:** Spare-time maker, first knife sold in 1995. **Mark:** Initials and date.

SCHEURER, ALFREDO E FAES
Av Rincon de los Arcos 104, Col Bosque Res del Sur, Distrito Federal, MEXICO 16010 **Contact:** 5676 47 63
Specialties: Fancy and fantasy knives of his design. **Patterns:** Daggers. **Technical:** Grinds stainless steel, casts and grinds silver. Sets stones in silver. **Prices:** $2000 to $3000. **Remarks:** Spare-time maker, first knife sold in 1989. **Mark:** Symbol.

SCHIPPNICK, JIM
PO Box 326, Sanborn, NY 14132 **Contact:** 716-731-3715, ragnar@ragweedforge.com, ragweedforge.com
Specialties: Nordic, early American, rustic. **Mark:** Runic R. **Remarks:** Also imports Nordic knives from Norway, Sweden and Finland.

SCHLUETER, DAVID
2172 Cedar Gate Rd., Madison Heights, VA 24572 **Contact:** 434-384-8642, drschlueter@hotmail.com
Specialties: Japanese-style swords. **Patterns:** Larger blades. O-tanto to Tachi, with focus on less common shapes. **Technical:** Forges and grinds carbon steels, heat-treats and polishes own blades, makes all fittings, does own mounting and finishing. **Prices:** Start at $3000. **Remarks:** Sells fully mounted pieces only, doing business as Odd Frog Forge. **Mark:** Full name and date.

SCHMITZ, RAYMOND E
PO Box 1787, Valley Center, CA 92082 **Contact:** 760-749-4318

SCHNEIDER, CRAIG M
Schneider Custom Knives 5380 N Amity Rd, Claremont, IL 62421 **Contact:** 217-377-5715, rafetownslam@gmail.com, www.grindhaus.org, Instagram: @schneidercustoms, Facebook: Schneider Metalworks
Patterns: Bowies, tactical, hunters and bushcraft. **Technical:** Forged and stock removal high carbon steels. **Prices:** $150 to $3,500. **Remarks:** Part-time maker, first knife sold in 1985. All knives come with a sheath. **Mark:** Stylized initials with Schneider Claremont IL.

SCHOEMAN, CORRIE
Box 28596, Danhof, Free State, SOUTH AFRICA 9310 **Contact:** 027 51 4363528 Cell: 027 82-3750789, corries@intekom.co.za
Specialties: High-tech folders of his design or to customer's specs. **Patterns:** Linerlock folders and automatics. **Technical:** ATS-34, damascus or stainless damascus with titanium frames, prefers exotic materials for handles. **Prices:** $650 to $2000. **Remarks:** Full-time maker, first knife sold in 1984. All folders come with filed liners and back and jeweled inserts. **Mark:** Logo in knife shape engraved on inside of back bar.

SCHOENFELD, MATTHEW A
RR #1, Galiano Island, BC, CANADA V0N 1P0 **Contact:** 250-539-2806
Specialties: Working knives of his design. **Patterns:** Kitchen cutlery, camp knives, hunters. **Technical:** Grinds 440C. **Prices:** $85 to $500. **Remarks:** Part-time maker, first knife sold in 1978. **Mark:** Signature, Galiano Is. B.C., and date.

SCHOENINGH, MIKE
49850 Miller Rd, North Powder, OR 97867 **Contact:** 541-856-3239

SCHOLL, TIM
1389 Langdon Rd, Angier, NC 27501 **Contact:** 910-897-2051, tschollknives@live.com, timschollcustomknives.com
Specialties: Fancy and working/using straight knives and folders of his design and to customer specs. **Patterns:** bowies, hunters, tomahawks, daggers & fantasy knives. **Technical:** Forges high carbon and tool steel makes damascus, grinds ATS-34 and D2 on request. **Prices:** $150 to $6000. **Remarks:** Part-time maker, first knife sold in 1990. Doing business as Tim Scholl Custom Knives. Member North Carolina Custom Knifemakers Guild. American Bladesmith Society journeyman smith. **Mark:** S pierced by arrow.

SCHORSCH, KENDALL
693 Deer Trail Dr., Jourdanton, TX 78026 **Contact:** 830-770-0205, schorschknives@gmail.com, schorschknives.com
Specialties: Slip-joint folders and straight blades. **Patterns:** Single- and double-blade trappers and straight hunting knives, all with or without filework. **Technical:** Grinds CPM 154, ATS-34, D2 and damascus. **Prices:** $350 to $750 and up. **Remarks:** Full-time maker, first knife sold in 2010. **Mark:** Stamped SCHORSCH on the tang or Schorsch Knives

etched in a circle with an Arrow "S" in the center.

SCHOW, LYLE
2103 Ann Ave., Harrisonville, MO 64701 **Contact:** 816-738-9849, rocktips17@yahoo.com, LDknives.com
Specialties: bowies, hunters, skinners, camp knives and some folders. **Technical:** Forges hunters and big knives, and practices stock-removal method of blade making on small blades. Uses high-carbon steels such as 1075, 1080, 1084, 1095 and W2, makes his own damascus and stainless/high-carbon San Mai steel. **Prices:** $110 to $2,000. **Remarks:** Part-time maker, started making knives in 2009. **Mark:** Maker's initials LDS configured together in the center, with LYLE D. in an arch on the top and SCHOW in an upward arch on the bottom.

SCHRADER, ROBERT
55532 Gross De, Bend, OR 97707 **Contact:** 541-598-7301
Specialties: Hunting, utility, bowie. **Patterns:** Fixed blade. **Prices:** $150 to $600.

SCHRAP, ROBERT G
CUSTOM LEATHER KNIFE SHEATH CO., 7024 W Wells St, Wauwatosa, WI 53213-3717 **Contact:** 414-771-6472 or 414-379-6819, (fax) 414-479-9765, knifesheaths@aol.com, customsheaths.com
Specialties: Leather knife sheaths. **Prices:** $38 to $150. **Mark:** Schrap in oval.

SCHREINER, TERRY
4310 W. Beech St., Duncan, OK 73533 **Contact:** 580-255-4880, Rhino969@hotmail.com
Specialties Hunters, bird-and-trout knives, handforged, one-of-a-kind bowies. **Patterns:** Hunters and bird-and-trout knives. **Technical:** Stainless damascus, Damasteel, hand-forged carbon damascus and RWL stainless steels, with handle materials mostly natural, including stag, mastodon ivory, horn and wood. **Prices:** $350 to $1,500. **Remarks:** Part-time maker. **Mark:** TerryJack Knives, TSchreiner with interlocking T&S.

SCHROEN, KARL
4042 Bones Rd, Sebastopol, CA 95472 **Contact:** 707-823-4057, schroenknives.com
Specialties: Using knives made to fit. **Patterns:** Sgian dubhs, carving sets, wood-carving knives, fishing knives, kitchen knives and new cleaver design. **Technical:** Forges D2, CPM S30V and 204P. **Prices:** $150 to $6000. **Remarks:** Full-time maker, first knife sold in 1968. Author of The Hand Forged Knife. **Mark:** Last name.

SCHUCHMANN, RICK
1251 Wilson Dunham Hill Rd., New Richmond, OH 45157 **Contact:** 513-553-4316
Specialties: Replicas of antique and out-of-production Scagels and Randalls, primarily miniatures. **Patterns:** All sheath knives, mostly miniatures, hunting and fighting knives, some daggers and hatchets. **Technical:** Stock removal, 440C and O1 steel. Most knives are flat ground, some convex. **Prices:** $175 to $600 and custom to $4000. **Remarks:** Part-time maker, sold first knife in 1997. Knives on display in the Randall Museum. Sheaths are made exclusively at Sullivan's Holster Shop, Tampa, FL **Mark:** SCAR.

SCHUETTE, CHARLES
9115 Silver Maple Rd, Glen St Mary, FL 32040 **Contact:** 443-254-7011, cwsknife66@gmail.com
Patterns: Hunters, fighters, daggers, bowies utility knives, culinary and kitchen knives, folders and other self-defense "sharp and pointy" Items. **Technical:** Forged high carbon 1084, 1095, 01, 52100, w2. Own forged damascus and mosaic steel of 15n20 and 1084. Stock removal in stainless steels 440c, damasteel, and cpm 154cm. All types of natural and synthetic handle materials. **Prices:** $300 to $1700. **Remarks:** Part-time retired maker with over 40 years experience. Goes by Chuck. **Mark:** After 2000: football-shaped logo with CWS in the center, C. W. Schuette above and town and state below. Prior to 2000: CWS with the W shaped as a crown.

SCHUTTE, NEILL
01 Moffet St., Fichardt Park, Bloemfontein, SOUTH AFRICA 9301 **Contact:** +27(0) 82 787 3429, neill@schutteknives.co.za, schutteknives.co.za
Specialties: Bob Loveless-style knives, George Herron fighters, custom designs and designs/requests from clients. **Technical:** Mainly stock removal of Bohler N690, RWL-34 and ATS-34, if available, blade steels. Uses the materials clients request. **Prices:** $450 to $1,250. **Remarks:** Full-time maker, first knife made at 10 years old, seriously started knifemaking in 2008. **Mark:** Kneeling archer/bowman (maker's surname, Schutte, directly translates to archer or bowman.)

SCHWARTZ, AARON
4745 B Asdee Ln., Woodbridge, VA 22192 **Contact:** 908-256-3869, big_hammer_forge@yahoo.com, bighammerforge.com
Specialties Fantasy custom designs and one-off custom pieces to order. **Technical:** Stock-removal method of blade making. **Remarks:** Made first knife around eight years ago.

SCHWARZER, LORA SUE
119 Shoreside Trail, Crescent City FL 32112 **Contact:** 904-608-5259, auntielora57@yahoo.com
Specialties: Scagel style knives. **Patterns:** Hunters and miniatures **Technical:** Forges 1084 and damascus. **Prices:** Start at $400. **Remarks:** Part-time maker, first knife sold in 1997. Journeyman Bladesmith, American Bladesmith Society. Now working with Steve Schwarzer on some projects.**Mark:** Full name - JS on reverse side.

SCHWARZER, STEPHEN
POB 6, Crescent City, FL 32112 **Contact:** 904-307-0872, schwarzeranvil@gmail.com, steveschwarzer.com
Specialties: Mosaic damascus and picture mosaic in folding knives. All Japanese blades are finished working with Wally Hostetter considered the top Japanese lacquer specialist

in the U.S.A. Also produces a line of carbon steel skinning knives at $300. **Patterns:** Folders, axes and buckskinner knives. **Technical:** Specializes in picture mosaic damascus and powder metal mosaic work. Sole authorship, all work including carving done in-house. Most knives have file work and carving. Hand carved steel and precious metal guards. **Prices:** $1500 to $5000, some higher, carbon steel and primitive knives much less. **Remarks:** Full-time maker, first knife sold in 1976, considered by many to be one of the top mosaic damascus specialists in the world. Mosaic Master level work. I am now working with Lora Schwarzer on some projects. **Mark:** Schwarzer + anvil.

SCIMIO, BILL
4554 Creek Side Ln., Spruce Creek, PA 16683 **Contact:** 814-632-3751, sprucecreekforge@gmail.com sprucecreekforge.com
Specialties: Hand-forged primitive-style knives with curly maple, antler, bone and osage handles.

SCORDIA, PAOLO
Via Terralba 144, Torrimpietra, Roma, ITALY 00050 **Contact:** 06-61697231, paolo.scordia@uni.net, scordia-knives.com
Specialties: Working, fantasy knives, Italian traditional folders and fixed blades of own design. **Patterns:** Any. **Technical:** Forge mosaic damascus, forge blades, welds own mokume and grinds ATS-34, etc. use hardwoods and Micarta for handles, brass and nickel-silver for fittings. Makes sheaths. **Prices:** $200 to $2000, some to $4000. **Remarks:** Part-time maker, first knife sold in 1988. **Mark:** Sun and moon logo and ititials.

SCROGGS, JAMES A
108 Murray Hill Dr, Warrensburg, MO 64093 **Contact:** 660-747-2568, jscroggsknives@gmail.com
Specialties: Straight knives, prefers light weight. **Patterns:** Hunters, hideouts, and fighters. **Technical:** Grinds CPM-154 stainless plus experiments in steel. Prefers handles of walnut in English, bastonge, American black. Also uses myrtle, maple, Osage orange. **Prices:** $200 to $1000. **Remarks:** 1st knife sold in 1985. Full-time maker. Won "Best Hunter Award" at Branson Hammer-In & Knife Show for 2012 and 2014. **Mark:** SCROGGS in block or script.

SCULLEY, PETER E
340 Sunset Dr, Rising Fawn, GA 30738 **Contact:** 706-398-0169

SEATON, DAVID D
1028 South Bishop Ave, #237, Rolla, MO 65401 **Contact:** 573-465-3193, aokcustomknives@gmail.com
Specialties: Gentleman's and Lady's folders. **Patterns:** Liner lock folders of own design and to customer specs, lock backs, slip joints, some stright knives, tactical folders, skinners, fighters, and utility knives. **Technical:** Grinds ATS 34, O1, 1095, 154CM, CPM154, commercial damascus. Blades are mostly flat ground, some hollow ground. Does own heat treating, tempering, and Nitre Bluing. Prefers natural handle materials such as ivory, mother of pearl, bone, and exotic woods, some use of G10 and micarta on hard use knives. Use gem stones, gold, silver on upscale knives, offers some carving, filework, and engrving. **Prices:** $150 to $600 avg, some to $1500 and up depending on materials and embellishments. **Remarks:** First knife sold in 2002, part-time maker, doing business at AOK Custom Knives. **Mark:** full or last name engraved on blade.

SEIB, STEVE
7914 Old State Road, Evansville, IN 47710 **Contact:** 812-867-2231, sseib@insightbb.com
Specialties: Working straight knives. Pattern: Skinners, hunters, bowies and camp knives. **Technical:** Forges high-carbon and makes own damascus. **Remarks:** Part-time maker. ABS member. **Mark:** Last name.

SELBY, BRIAN
Selby Knives 834 Glasgow Court, Lincoln, CA 95648 **Contact:** (209) 352-2281, selbyknives.com, selbydesign@sbcglobal.net
Specialties: Mid-tech. **Pattern:** Outdoor knives. **Remarks:** Started making knives in 2012.

SELF, ERNIE
950 O'Neill Ranch Rd, Dripping Springs, TX 78620-9760 **Contact:** 512-940-7134, ernieself@yahoo.com
Specialties: Traditional and working straight knives and folders of his design and in standard patterns. **Patterns:** Hunters, locking folders and slip-joints. **Technical:** Grinds 440C, D2, 440V, ATS-34 and damascus. Offers fancy filework. **Prices:** $250 to $1000, some to $2500. **Remarks:** Full-time maker, first knife sold in 1982. Also customizes Buck 110's and 112's folding hunters. **Mark:** In oval shape - Ernie Self Maker Dripping Springs TX.

SELLEVOLD, HARALD
PO Box 4134, Sandviken S Kleivesmau:2, Bergen, NORWAY N5835 **Contact:** 47 55-310682, haraldsellevold@gmail.com, knivmakeren.com
Specialties: Norwegian-styles, collaborates with other Norse craftsmen. **Patterns:** Distinctive ferrules and other mild modifications of traditional patterns, bowies and friction folders. **Technical:** Buys damascus blades, blacksmiths his own blades. Semi-gemstones used in handles, gemstone inlay. **Prices:** $350 to $2000. **Remarks:** Full-time maker, first knife sold in 1980. **Mark:** Name and country in logo.

SELZAM, FRANK
Martin Reinhard Str 23, Bad Koenigshofen, GERMANY 97631 **Contact:** 09761-5980, frankselzam.de
Specialties: Hunters, working knives to customers specs, hand tooled and stitched leather sheaths large stock of wood and German stag horn. **Patterns:** Mostly own design. **Technical:** Forged blades, own damascus, also stock removal stainless. **Prices:** $250 to

$1500. **Remarks:** First knife sold in 1978. **Mark:** Last name stamped.

SENTZ, MARK C
4084 Baptist Rd, Taneytown, MD 21787 **Contact:** 410-756-2018
Specialties: Fancy straight working knives of his design. **Patterns:** Hunters, fighters, folders and utility/camp knives. **Technical:** Forges 1085, 1095, 5160, 5155 and his damascus. Most knives come with wood-lined leather sheath or wooden presentation sheath. **Prices:** Start at $275. **Remarks:** Full-time maker, first knife sold in 1989. Doing business as M. Charles Sentz Gunsmithing, Inc. **Mark:** Last name.

SERAFEN, STEVEN E
24 Genesee St, New Berlin, NY 13411 **Contact:** 607-847-6903
Specialties: Traditional working/using straight knives of his design and to customer specs. **Patterns:** bowies, fighters, hunters. **Technical:** Grinds ATS-34, 440C, high-carbon steel. **Prices:** $175 to $600, some to $1200. **Remarks:** Part-time maker, first knife sold in 1990. **Mark:** First and middle initial, last name in script.

SEVECEK, PAVEL
Lhota u Konice 7, BRODEK U KONICE, 79845 CZECH REPUBLIC **Contact:** 00420 603 545333, seva.noze@seznam.cz, sevaknives.cz
Specialties Production of handforged mosaic damascus knives, all including the plastic engravings and sheaths of his own exclusive work. **Prices:** $800 and up. **Remarks:** First knife sold in 2001. **Mark:** Logo SP in blade.

SEVEY CUSTOM KNIFE
94595 Chandler Rd, Gold Beach, OR 97444 **Contact:** 541-247-2649, sevey@charter.net, seveyknives.com
Specialties: Fixed blade hunters. **Patterns:** Drop point, trailing paint, clip paint, full tang, hidden tang. **Technical:** D-2, and ATS-34 blades, stock removal. Heat treatment by Paul Bos. **Prices:** $225 and up depending on overall length and grip material. **Mark:** Sevey Custom Knife.

SEWARD, BEN
471 Dogwood Ln., Austin, AR 72007 **Contact:** 501-416-1543, sewardsteel@gmail.com, bensewardknives.com
Specialties: Forged blades, mostly bowies and fighters. **Technical:** Forges high-carbon steels such as 1075 and W2. **Remarks:** First knife made in 2005, ABS journeyman smith and member Arkansas Knifemakers Association.

SFREDDO, RODRIGO MENEZES
Rua 7 De Setembro 66 Centro, Nova Petropolis, RS, BRAZIL 95150-000 **Contact:** 011-55-54-303-303-90, r.sfreddoknives@gmail.com, sbccutelaria.org.br
Specialties: Integrals, bowies, hunters, dirks & swords. **Patterns:** Forges his own damascus and 52100 steel. **Technical:** Specialized in integral knives and damascus. **Prices:** From $350 and up. Most around $750 to $1000. **Remarks:** Considered by many to be the Brazil's best bladesmith. ABS SBC Member. **Mark:** S. Sfreddo on the left side of the blade.

SHADLEY, EUGENE W
209 NW 17th Street, Grand Rapids, MN 55744 **Contact:** 218-398-3772, call first, geneshadley@gmail.com
Specialties: Gold frames are available on some models. **Patterns:** Whittlers, stockman, sowbelly, congress, trapper, autos, small EDC. **Technical:** Grinds ATS-34, 416 frames. **Prices:** Starts at $600, some models up to $15,000. **Remarks:** Full-time maker, first knife sold in 1985. Doing business as Shadley Knives. **Mark:** Last name.

SHADMOT, BOAZ
MOSHAV PARAN D N, Arava, ISRAEL 86835, srb@arava.co.il

SHARON, DANIEL
Ozark Wood And Steel Co. 10790 Meadowlark Ln. Gravette, AR 72736 **Contact:** 479-855-7499
Patterns: Knives, swords and hatchets.

SHARP, CHRIS
Chris Sharp Knives/Oxford Forge 13500 County Road 103, Oxford, FL 34484 17485 **Contact:** 352-266-3365, CSharpKnives@OxfordForge.com
Specialties: Fixed blades. **Patterns:** Original and real Loveless pattern utilities, hunters and fighters. **Technical:** Stock removal, tool steel and stainless steel, hollow grind, machine finish, full polish, various handle materials. **Prices:** $300 to $1,500. **Remarks:** Part-time maker, first knife sold in 2011. **Mark:** "Sharpwerks" on original designs, "D. Sharp" on Loveless designs.

SHARP, DAVID
17485 Adobe St., Hesperia, CA 92345 **Contact:** 520-370-1899, sharpwerks@gmail.com or david@sharpwerks.com, sharpwerks.com
Specialties: Fixed blades. **Patterns:** Original and real Loveless pattern utilities, hunters and fighters. **Technical:** Stock removal, tool steel and stainless steel, hollow grind, machine finish, full polish, various handle materials. **Prices:** $300 to $1,500. **Remarks:** Part-time maker, first knife sold in 2011. **Mark:** "Sharpwerks" on original designs, "D. Sharp" on Loveless designs.

SHARRIGAN, MUDD
111 Bradford Rd, Wiscasset, ME 04578-4457 **Contact:** 207-882-9820, (fax) 207-882-9835
Specialties: Custom designs, repair straight knives, custom leather sheaths. **Patterns:** Daggers, fighters, hunters, crooked knives and seamen working knives, traditional Scandinavian-styles. **Technical:** Forges 1095, 5160, and W2. **Prices:** $50 to $325, some to $1200. **Remarks:** Full-time maker, first knife sold in 1982. **Mark:** Swallow tail carving. Mudd engraved.

SHEEHY, THOMAS J
4131 NE 24th Ave, Portland, OR 97211-6411 **Contact:** 503-493-2843
Specialties: Hunting knives and ulus. **Patterns:** Own or customer designs. **Technical:** 1095/O1 and ATS-34 steel. **Prices:** $35 to $200. **Remarks:** Do own heat treating, forged or ground blades. **Mark:** Name.

SHEELY, "BUTCH" FOREST
15784 Custar Rd., Grand Rapids, OH 43522 **Contact:** 419-308-3471, sheelyblades@gmail.com
Specialties: Traditional bowies and pipe tomahawks. **Patterns:** bowies, hunters, integrals, dirks, axes and hawks. **Technical:** Forges 5160, 52100, 1084, 1095, and damascus.**Prices:** $150 to $1500,**Remarks:** Full-time bladesmith part-time blacksmith, first knife sold in 1982. ABS Journeysmith, sole author of all knives and hawks including hand sewn leather sheaths, doing business as Beaver Creek Forge. **Mark:** First and last name above Bladesmith.

SHEETS, STEVEN WILLIAM
6 Stonehouse Rd, Mendham, NJ 07945 **Contact:** 201-543-5882

SHEWMAKER, BOB
Shewmaker Custom Knives 7022 CR 662, Farmersville, TX 75442 **Contact:** 214-478-2751, rjshewmaker@gmail.com, Facebook: Shewmaker Custom Knives
Patterns: Fixed blade hunting knives with leather sheaths. Slip joint folders and lockbacks with one or two blades, with or without file work. **Technical:** Stock removal method. Steels used are ATS 34, 154CPM, stainless Damascus, and carbon Damascus. Giraffe bone, Mammoth ivory, stagg, stagg bone, cow bone, desert ironwood, pearl, and exotic woods. **Prices:** $350 to $1,000 depending on style and materials. **Remarks:** Maker since 2001. **Mark:** SHEWMAKER stamped on blades.

SHIFFER, STEVE
PO Box 471, Leakesville, MS 39451 **Contact:** 601-394-4425, aiifish2@yahoo.com, choctawplantationforge.com
Specialties: bowies, fighters, hard use knives. **Patterns:** Fighters, hunters, combat/utility knives. Walker pattern LinerLock® folders. Allen pattern scale and bolster release autos. **Technical:** Most work forged, stainless stock removal. Makes own damascus. O1 and 5160 most used also 1084, 440c, 154cm, s30v. **Prices:** $125 to $1000. **Remarks:** First knife sold in 2000, all heat treatment done by maker. Doing business as Choctaw Plantation Forge. **Mark:** Hot mark sunrise over creek.

SHIGENO, MAMORU
2-12-3 Hirosehigashi, Sayama-shi, Saitama, 350-1320, JAPAN, shigeno-knife@tbc.t-com.ne.jp, http://www2.tbb.t-com.ne.jp/shigeno-knife/
Specialties: Fixed blades. **Patterns:** Hunters, boot knives, fighters, including most Loveless patterns, bowies and others. **Technical:** Stock removal of ATS-34. **Prices:** $700 to $3,000 and up. **Remarks:** Full-time maker, first knife sold in 2003. **Mark:** SHIGENO (last name).

SHINOSKY, ANDY
3117 Meanderwood Dr, Canfield, OH 44406 **Contact:** 330-702-0299, andrew@shinosky.com, shinosky.com
Specialties: Collectable folders and interframes. **Patterns:** Drop point, spear point, trailing point, daggers. **Technical:** Grinds ATS-34 and damascus Prefers natural handle materials. Most knives are engraved by Andy himself. **Prices:** Start at $800. **Remarks:** Part-time maker/engraver. First knife sold in 1992. **Mark:** Name.

SHINOZAKI, AKIO
24-10 Jyouseigaoka 2-chome, Munakata-city, Fukuoka-ken, JAPAN 811-3404 **Contact:** 81-940-32-6768, shinozakiknife4152@ab.auone-net.jp
Specialties: One-of-a-kind straight knives and locking folders. **Patterns:** Hunters, skinners, bowies and utility knives of maker's own design and to customer's specifications. **Technical:** Stock removal method of blade making using ATS-34, CPM S30V, CV134 and SPG2 steels, mirror polishes. Handle materials are stag, exotic woods, Micarta and mammoth ivory. **Prices:** $350 to $800, with bowies and fighters starting at $1,200 and up. **Remarks:** Full-time maker, first knife sold in 1987. **Mark:** Akio S or Akio Shinozaki.

SHIPLEY, STEVEN A
800 Campbell Rd Ste 137, Richardson, TX 75081 **Contact:** 972-644-7981, (fax) 972-644-7985, steve@shipleysphotography.com
Specialties: Hunters, skinners and traditional straight knives. **Technical:** Hand grinds ATS-34, 440C and damascus steels. Each knife is custom sheathed by his son, Dan. **Prices:** $175 to $2000. **Remarks:** Part-time maker, like smooth lines and unusual handle materials. **Mark:** S A Shipley

SHOEMAKER, CARROLL
380 Yellowtown Rd, Northup, OH 45658 **Contact:** 740-446-6695
Specialties: Working/using straight knives of his design. **Patterns:** Hunters, utility/camp and early American backwoodsmen knives. **Technical:** Grinds ATS-34, forges old files, O1 and 1095. Uses some damascus, offers scrimshaw and engraving. **Prices:** $100 to $175, some to $350. **Remarks:** Spare-time maker, first knife sold in 1977. **Mark:** Name and city or connected initials.

SHOEMAKER, SCOTT
316 S Main St, Miamisburg, OH 45342 **Contact:** 513-859-1935
Specialties: Twisted, wire-wrapped handles on swords, fighters and fantasy blades, new line of seven models with quick-draw, multi-carry Kydex sheaths. **Patterns:** bowies, boots and one-of-a-kinds in his design or to customer specs. **Technical:** Grinds A6 and ATS-34, buys damascus. Hand satin finish is standard. **Prices:** $100 to $1500, swords to $8000. **Remarks:** Part-time maker, first knife sold in 1984. **Mark:** Angel wings with last initial, or last name.

SHOGER, MARK O
POB 778, Kalama, WA 98625 **Contact:** 503-816-8615, mosdds@msn.com
Specialties: Working and using straight knives and folders of his design, fancy and embellished knives. **Patterns:** Hunters, bowies, daggers and folders. **Technical:** Forges O1, W2, 1084, 5160, 52100 and 1084/15n20 pattern weld. **Remarks:** Spare-time maker. **Mark:** Last name "Shoger" or stamped last initial over anvil.

SHROPSHIRE, SHAWN
PO Box 453, Piedmont, OK 73078 **Contact:** 405-833-5239, shawn@sdsknifeworks.com, sdsknifeworks.com
Specialties: Working straight knives and frontier style period pieces. **Patterns:** bowies, hunters, skinners, fighters, patch/neck knives.**Technical:** Grinds D2, 154CM and some damascus, forges 1084, 5160.**Prices:** Starting at $125. **Remarks:** Part-time maker, first knife sold in 1997. Doing business at SDS Knifeworks. **Mark:** Etched "SDS Knifeworks - Oklahoma" in an oval or "SDS" tang stamp.

SHULL, JAMES
5146 N US 231 W, Rensselaer, IN 47978 **Contact:** 219-866-0436, nbjs@netnitco.net shullhandforgedknives.com
Specialties: Working knives of hunting, fillet, bowie patterns. **Technical:** Forges or uses 1095, 5160, 52100 & O1. **Prices:** $100 to $300. **Remarks:** DBA Shull Handforged Knives. **Mark:** Last name in arc.

SIBERT, SHANE
PO BOX 241, Gladstone, OR 97027 **Contact:** 503-650-2082, shane.sibert@comcast.net sibertknives.com
Specialties: Innovative knives designed for hostile environments, lightweight hiking and backpacking knives for outdoorsman and adventurers, progressive fixed blade combat and fighting knives. One-of-a-kind knives of various configurations. Titanium frame lock folders. **Patterns:** Modern configurations of utility/camp knives, bowies, modified spear points, daggers, tantos, recurves, clip points and spine serrations. **Technical:** Stock removal. Specializes in CPM S30V, CPM S35VN, CPM D2, CPM 3V, stainless damascus. Micarta, G-10, stabilized wood and titanium. **Prices:** $200 - $1000, some pieces $1500 and up. **Remarks:** Full-time maker, first knife sold in 1994. **Mark:** Stamped "SIBERT" and occasionally uses electro-etch with oval around last name.

SIBRIAN, AARON
4308 Dean Dr, Ventura, CA 93003 **Contact:** 805-642-6950
Specialties: Tough working knives of his design and in standard patterns. **Patterns:** Makes a "Viper utility"—a kukri derivative and a variety of straight using knives. **Technical:** Grinds 440C and ATS-34. Offers traditional Japanese blades, soft backs, hard edges, temper lines. **Prices:** $60 to $100, some to $250. **Remarks:** Spare-time maker, first knife sold in 1989. **Mark:** Initials in diagonal line.

SIMMONS, H R
1100 Bay City Rd, Aurora, NC 27806 **Contact:** 252-916-2241
Specialties: Working/using straight knives of his design. **Patterns:** Fighters, hunters and utility/camp knives. **Technical:** Forges and grinds damascus and L6, grinds ATS-34. **Prices:** $150 and up. **Remarks:** Part-time maker, first knife sold in 1987. Doing business as HRS Custom Knives, Royal Forge and Trading Company. **Mark:** HRS.

SIMONELLA, GIANLUIGI
Via Battiferri 33, Maniago, ITALY 33085 **Contact:** 01139-427-730350
Specialties: Traditional and classic folding and working/using knives of his design and to customer specs. **Patterns:** bowies, fighters, hunters, utility/camp knives. **Technical:** Forges ATS-34, D2, 440C. **Prices:** $250 to $400, some to $1000. **Remarks:** Full-time maker, first knife sold in 1988. **Mark:** Wilson.

SINCLAIR, J E
520 Francis Rd, Pittsburgh, PA 15239 **Contact:** 412-793-5778
Specialties: Fancy hunters and fighters, liner locking folders. **Patterns:** Fighters, hunters and folders. **Technical:** Flat-grinds and hollow grind, prefers hand rubbed satin finish. Uses natural handle materials. **Prices:** $185 to $800. **Remarks:** Part-time maker, first knife sold in 1995. **Mark:** First and middle initials, last name and maker.

SIROIS, DARRIN
Tactical Combat Tools, 6182 Lake Trail Dr., Fayetteville, NC 28304 **Contact:** 910-730-0536, knives@tctknives.com, tctknives.com
Specialties: Tactical fighters, hunters and camp knives. **Technical:** Stock removal method of blade making, using D2 and 154CM steels. Entire process, including heat treat, done in-house. **Prices:** $80 to $750. **Remarks:** Part-time maker, first knife sold in 2008. **Mark:** Letters TCT surrounded by a triangle, or "Delta Tactical Combat Tools."

SISKA, JIM
48 South Maple St, Westfield, MA 01085 **Contact:** 413-642-3059, siskaknives@comcast.net
Specialties: Traditional working straight knives, no folders. **Patterns:** Hunters, fighters, bowies and one-of-a-kinds, folders. **Technical:** Grinds D2, A2, 154CM and ATS-34, buys damascus and forges some blades. Likes exotic woods. **Prices:** $300 to $400. **Remarks:** Part-time. **Mark:** Siska in Old English, or for forged blades, a hammer over maker's name.

SJOSTRAND, KEVIN
1541 S Cain St, Visalia, CA 93292 **Contact:** 559-625-5254
Specialties: Traditional and working/using straight knives and folders of his design or to customer specs. **Patterns:** Fixed blade hunters, bowies, utility/camp knives. **Technical:** Grinds ATS-34, 440C and 1095. Prefers high polished blades and full tang. Natural and stabilized hardwoods, Micarta and stag handle material. **Prices:** $250 to $400. **Remarks:** Part-time maker, first knife sold in 1992. **Mark:** SJOSTRAND

SKIFF, STEVEN

SKIFF MADE BLADES, PO Box 537, Broadalbin, NY 12025 **Contact:** 518-883-4875, skiffmadeblades @hotmail.com, skiffmadeblades.com

Specialties: Custom using/collector grade straight blades and LinerLock® folders of maker's design or customer specifications. **Patterns:** Hunters, utility/camp knives, tactical/fancy art folders. **Prices:** Straight blades $225 and up. Folders $450 and up. **Technical:** Stock removal hollow ground ATS-34, 154 CM, S30V, and tool steel. damascus-Devon Thomas, Robert Eggerling, Mike Norris and Delbert Ealy. Nickel silver and stainless in-house heat treating. Handle materials: man made and natural woods (stablilized). Horn shells sheaths for straight blades, sews own leather and uses sheaths by "Tree-Stump Leather." **Remarks:** First knife sold 1997. Started making folders in 2000. **Mark:** SKIFF on blade of straight blades and in inside of backspacer on folders.

SLEE, FRED

9 John St, Morganville, NJ 07751 **Contact:** 732-591-9047

Specialties: Working straight knives, some fancy, to customer specs. **Patterns:** Hunters, fighters, fancy daggers and folders. **Technical:** Grinds D2, 440C and ATS-34. **Prices:** $285 to $1100. **Remarks:** Part-time maker, first knife sold in 1980. **Mark:** Letter "S" in Old English.

SLOAN, DAVID

PO BOX 83, Diller, NE 68342 **Contact:** 402-793-5755, sigp22045@hotmail.com

Specialties: Hunters, choppers and fighters. **Technical:** Forged blades of W2, 1084 and damascus. **Prices:** Start at $225. **Remarks:** Part-time maker, made first knife in 2002, received JS stamp 2010. **Mark:** Sloan JS.

SLOAN, SHANE

4226 FM 61, Newcastle, TX 76372 **Contact:** 940-846-3290

Specialties: Collector-grade straight knives and folders. **Patterns:** Uses stainless damascus, ATS-34 and 12C27. bowies, lockers, slip-joints, fancy folders, fighters and period pieces. **Technical:** Grinds D2 and ATS-34. Uses hand-rubbed satin finish. Prefers rare natural handle materials. **Prices:** $250 to $6500. **Remarks:** Full-time maker, first knife sold in 1985. **Mark:** Name and city.

SLOBODIAN, SCOTT

PO Box 1498, San Andreas, CA 95249 **Contact:** 209-286-1980, (fax) 209-286-1982, info@slobodianswords.com, slobodianswords.com

Specialties: Japanese-style knives and swords, period pieces, fantasy pieces and miniatures. **Patterns:** Small kweikens, tantos, wakazashis, katanas, traditional samurai swords. **Technical:** Flat-grinds 1050, commercial damascus. **Prices:** Prices start at $1500. **Remarks:** Full-time maker, first knife sold in 1987. **Mark:** Blade signed in Japanese characters and various scripts.

SMALE, CHARLES J

509 Grove Ave, Waukegan, IL 60085 **Contact:** 847-244-8013

SMALL, ED

Rt 1 Box 178-A, Keyser, WV 26726 **Contact:** 304-298-4254, coldanvil@gmail.com

Specialties: Working knives of his design, period pieces. **Patterns:** Hunters, daggers, buckskinners and camp knives, likes one-of-a-kinds, very primative bowies. **Technical:** Forges and grinds W2, L6 and his own damascus. **Prices:** $150 to $1500. **Remarks:** Full-time maker, first knife sold in 1978. **Mark:** Script initials connected.

SMART, STEVE

907 Park Row Cir, McKinney, TX 75070-3847 **Contact:** 214-882-0441, (fax) 972-548-7151

Specialties: Working/using straight knives and folders of his design, to customer specs and in standard patterns. **Patterns:** bowies, hunters, kitchen knives, locking folders, utility/camp, fishing and bird knives. **Technical:** Grinds ATS-34, D2, 440C and O1. Prefers mirror polish or satin finish, hollow-grinds all blades. All knives come with sheath. Offers some filework. **Prices:** $95 to $225, some to $500. **Remarks:** Spare-time maker, first knife sold in 1983. **Mark:** Name, Custom, city and state in oval.

SMIT, GLENN

627 Cindy Ct, Aberdeen, MD 21001 **Contact:** 410-272-2959, wolfsknives@comcast.net, facebook.com/Wolf'sKnives

Specialties: Working and using straight and folding knives of his design or to customer specs. Customizes and repairs all types of cutlery. Exclusive maker of Dave Murphy Style knives. **Patterns:** Hunters, bowies, daggers, fighters, utility/camp, folders, kitchen knives and miniatures, Murphy combat, C.H.A.I.K., Little 88 and Tiny 90-styles. **Technical:** Grinds 440C, ATS-34, O1, A2 also grinds 6AL4V titanium allox for blades. Reforges commercial damascus and makes cast aluminum handles. **Prices:** Miniatures start at $50, full-size knives start at $100. **Remarks:** Spare-time maker, first knife sold in 1986. Doing business as Wolf's Knives. **Mark:** G.P. SMIT, with year on reverse side, Wolf's Knives-Murphy's way with date.

SMITH, CHRIS

POB 351, Burgin, KY 40310 **Contact:** 859-948-1505, fireman6152000@yahoo.com, Facebook page CS&Sons

Technical: Forged blades. Stock removal method of blade making using mainly simple carbon steels like 1080, 1084, 5160 and some damascus. **Prices:** $150 to $1000. **Remarks:** Part-time maker since June of 2014. **Mark:** Maker's initials in his own cursive script, the same way he has signed his work since he was in art class in elementary school.

SMITH, DEBBIE & JERRY

Knives Unplugged 1950 CR 5120, Willow Springs, MO 65793 **Contact:** 417-252-7463, knivesunplugged@gmail.com, www.knivesunplugged.com, Facebook & Instagram: @knivesunplugged

Specialties: Leather working, denim and burlap micarta, hybrid honeycomb, and stabilized exotic wood handle materials. **Technical:** CPM 154, D2 and A2 **Patterns:** Fixed blades. **Remarks:** Powered by solar, all handmade. Formerly JW Smith & Sons Custom Knives. **Mark:** Jerry W Smith USA.

SMITH, J.D.

Hammersmith Knives, 22 Ledge St., Melrose, MA 02176 **Contact:** 857-492-5324, mamboslave@yahoo.com

Specialties: Fighters, bowies, Persian, locking folders and swords. **Patterns:** bowies, fighters and locking folders. **Technical:** Forges and grinds D2, his damascus, O1, 52100 etc. and wootz-pattern hammer steel. **Prices:** $500 to $2000, some to $5000. **Remarks:** Full-time maker, first knife sold in 1987. Doing business as Hammersmith. **Mark:** Last initial alone or in cartouche.

SMITH, J.B.

21 Copeland Rd., Perkinston, MS 39573 **Contact:** 228-380-1851

Specialties: Traditional working knives for the hunter and fisherman. **Patterns:** Hunters, bowies, and fishing knives, copies of 1800 period knives. **Technical:** Grinds ATS-34, 440C. **Prices:** $100 to $800. **Remarks:** Full-time maker, first knife sold in 1972. **Mark:** J.B. Smith MAKER PERKINSTON, MS.

SMITH, JOHN M

3450 E Beguelin Rd, Centralia, IL 62801 **Contact:** 618-249-6444, jknife@frontiernet.net

Specialties: Folders. **Patterns:** Folders. **Prices:** $250 to $2500. **Remarks:** First knife sold in 1980. Not taking orders at this time on fixed blade knives. Part-time maker. **Mark:** Etched signature or logo.

SMITH, JOHN W

1322 Cow Branch Rd, West Liberty, KY 41472 **Contact:** 606-743-3599, jwsknive@mrtc.com, jwsmithknives.com

Specialties: Fancy and working locking folders of his design or to customer specs. **Patterns:** Interframes, traditional and daggers. **Technical:** Grinds 530V and his own damascus. Offers gold inlay, engraving with gold inlay, hand-fitted mosaic pearl inlay and filework. Prefers hand-rubbed finish. Pearl and ivory available. **Prices:** Utility pieces $375 to $650. Art knives $1200 to $10,000. **Remarks:** Full-time maker. **Mark:** Initials engraved inside diamond.

SMITH, JOSH

Box 753, Frenchtown, MT 59834 **Contact:** 406-626-5775, joshsmithknives@gmail.com, joshsmithknives.com

Specialties: Mosaic, damascus, LinerLock folders, automatics, bowies, fighters, etc. **Patterns:** All kinds. **Technical:** Advanced Mosaic and damascus. **Prices:** $1200 and up. **Remarks:** A.B.S. Master Smith. **Mark:** Josh Smith with last two digits of the current year.

SMITH, LACY

PO BOX 188, Jacksonville, AL 36265 **Contact:** 256-310-4619, sales@smith-knives.com, smith-knives.com

Specialties: All styles of fixed-blade knives. **Technical:** Stock removal method of blade making. **Prices:** $100 and up. **Mark:** Circle with three dots and three S's on inside.

SMITH, LENARD C

PO Box D68, Valley Cottage, NY 10989 **Contact:** 914-268-7359

SMITH, MICHAEL J

P.O. Box 4075, Clearwater, FL 33758 **Contact:** 813-431-3790, smithknife@hotmail.com, instagram.com/michaelsmithcustoms/

Specialties: Tactical folders, everyday carry to presentation grade. **Patterns:** High-tech patterns of his own design, flippers, linerlocks, framelocks, autos. Fixed blade fighters and daggers. **Technical:** Hollow grinds CPM154, damascus, stainless damascus. Uses titanium, titanium damascus, carbon fiber, G10, micarta, ivory, pearl and other select natural handle materials. Very fine, hand-rubbed satin finished blades. **Prices:** $1000 to $5000. **Remarks:** Full-time maker, Started in 1987. **Mark:** M Smith, M J Smith, Michael Smith, Michael J Smith

SMITH, NEWMAN L.

865 Glades Rd Shop #3, Gatlinburg, TN 37738 **Contact:** 423-436-3322, thesmithshop@aol.com, thesmithsshop.com

Specialties: Collector-grade and working knives. **Patterns:** Hunters, slip-joint and lock-back folders, some miniatures. **Technical:** Grinds O1 and ATS-34, makes fancy sheaths. **Prices:** $165 to $750, some to $1000. **Remarks:** Full-time maker, first knife sold in 1984. Partners part-time to handle damascus blades by Jeff Hurst, marks these with SH connected. **Mark:** First and middle initials, last name.

SMITH, RALPH L

525 Groce Meadow Rd, Taylors, SC 29687 **Contact:** 864-444-0819, ralph_smith1@charter.net, smithhandcraftedknives.com

Specialties: Working knives: straight and folding knives. Hunters, skinners, fighters, bird, boot, bowie and kitchen knives. **Technical:** Concave Grind D2, ATS 34, 440C, steel hand finish or polished. **Prices:** $125 to $350 for standard models. **Remarks:** First knife sold in 1976. KMG member since 1981. SCAK founding member and past president. **Mark:** SMITH handcrafted knives in SC state outline.

SMITH, RAYMOND L

217 Red Chalk Rd, Erin, NY 14838 **Contact:** 607-795-5257, Bladesmith@wildblue.net, theanvilsedge.com

Specialties: Working/using straight knives and folders to customer specs and in standard patterns, period pieces. **Patterns:** bowies, hunters, slip joints. **Technical:** Forges 5160, 52100, 1018, 15N20, 1084, ATS 34. damascus and wire cable damascus. Filework. **Prices:** $125 to $1500, estimates for custom orders. **Remarks:** Full-time maker, first knife sold in 1991. ABS Master Smith. Doing business as The Anvils Edge. **Mark:** Ellipse with RL Smith, Erin NY MS in center.

SMITH, RICK
BEAR BONE KNIVES, 1843 W Evans Creek Rd., Rogue River, OR 97537 **Contact:** 541-582-4144, BearBoneSmith@msn.com, bearbone.com
Specialties: Classic, historical style bowie knives, hunting knives and various contemporary knife styles. **Technical:** Blades are either forged or made by stock removal method depending on steel used. Forge weld various damascus patterns. Does own heat treating and tempering using digital even heat kiln. Stainless blades are sent out for cryogenic "freeze treat." Preferred steels are O1, tool, 5160, 1095, 1084, ATS-34, 154CM, 440C and various high carbon damascus. **Prices:** $350 to $1500. Custom leather sheaths available for knives. **Remarks:** Serial numbers no longer put on knives. Official business name is "Bear Bone Knives." **Mark:** Early maker's mark was "Bear Bone" over capital letters "RS" with downward arrow between letters and "Hand Made" underneath letters. Mark on small knives is 3/8 circle containing "RS" with downward arrow between letters. Current mark since 2003 is "R Bear Bone Smith" arching over image of coffin bowie knife with two shooting stars and "Rogue River, Oregon" underneath.

SMITH, SHAWN
2644 Gibson Ave, Clouis, CA 93611 **Contact:** 559-323-6234, kslc@sbcglobal.net
Specialties: Working and fancy straight knives. **Patterns:** Hunting, trout, fighters, skinners. **Technical:** Hollow grinds ATS-34, 154CM, A-2. **Prices:** $150.00 and up. **Remarks:** Part time maker. **Mark:** Shawn Smith handmade.

SMITH, STUART
Smith Hand Forged Knives, 32 Elbon Rd., Blairgowrie, Gauteng, SOUTH AFRICA 2123 **Contact:** +27 84 248 1324, samuraistu@forgedknives.co.za, forgedknives. co.za
Specialties: Hand-forged bowie knives and puukos in high-carbon steel and maker's own damascus. **Patterns:** bowies, puukos, daggers, hunters, fighters, skinners and swords. **Technical:** Forges 5160, 1070, 52100 and SilverSteel, and maker's own damascus from 5160 and Bohler K600 nickel tool steel. Fitted guards and threaded pommels. Own heat treating. Wood and bronze carving. Own sheaths and custom sheaths. **Prices:** $150 to $1,500. **Remarks:** Full-time maker since 2004, first knife sold in 2000. **Mark:** Stamped outline of an anvil with SMITH underneath on right side of knife. For 2014, anvil and surname with 10Yrs.

SMOCK, TIMOTHY E
1105 N Sherwood Dr, Marion, IN 46952 **Contact:** 765-664-0123

SNODY, MIKE
108 E 6th Street, Walsenburg, CO 81089 **Contact:** 719 717 6813, snodyknives@ yahoo.com
Specialties: High performance straight knives in traditional and Japanese-styles. **Patterns:** Skinners, hunters, tactical, Kwaiken and tantos. **Technical:** Grinds BG42, ATS-34, 440C and A2. Offers full or tapered tangs, upgraded handle materials such as fossil ivory, coral and exotic woods. Traditional diamond wrap over stingray on Japanese-style knives. Sheaths available in leather or Kydex. **Prices:** $100 to $1000. **Remarks:** Part-time maker, first knife sold in 1999. **Mark:** Name over knife maker.

SNOW, BILL
4824 18th Ave, Columbus, GA 31904 **Contact:** 706-576-4390, tipikw@knology.net
Specialties: Traditional working/using straight knives and folders of his design and to customer specs. Offers engraving and scrimshaw. **Patterns:** bowies, fighters, hunters and folders. **Technical:** Grinds ATS-34, 440V, 440C, 420V, CPM350, BG42, A2, D2, 5160, 52100 and O1, forges if needed. Cryogenically quenches all steels, inlaid handles, some integrals, leather or Kydex sheaths. **Prices:** $125 to $700, some to $3500. **Remarks:** Now also have 530V, 10V and 3V steels in use. Full-time maker, first knife sold in 1958. Doing business as Tipi Knife works. **Mark:** Old English scroll "S" inside a tipi.

SOAPER, MAX H.
2375 Zion Rd, Henderson, KY 42420 **Contact:** 270-827-8143
Specialties: Primitive Longhunter knives, scalpers, camp knives, cowboy bowies, neck knives, working knives, period pieces from the 18th century. **Technical:** Forges 5160, 1084, 1095, all blades differentially heat treated. **Prices:** $80 to $800. **Remarks:** Part-time maker since 1989. **Mark:** Initials in script.

SOILEAU, DAMON
POB 7292, Kingsport, TN 37664 **Contact:** 423-297-4665, oiseaumetalarts@gmail. com, oiseaumetalarts.etsy.com
Specialties: Natural and exotic materials, slip-joint folders, fixed blades, hidden tang and full tang, hand engraving. **Patterns:** Slip-joint folders, hunters, skinners and art knives. **Technical:** Stock removal of damascus, forges W2, O1 and 1084. **Prices:** $150 to $2,000. **Remarks:** Full-time maker and hand engraver. **Mark:** Hand engraved last name on spine of blade, or inside back spring of folders.

SONNTAG, DOUGLAS W
902 N 39th St, Nixa, MO 65714 **Contact:** 417-693-1640, dougsonntag@gmail.com
Specialties: Working knives, art knives. **Patterns:** Hunters, boots, straight working knives, bowies, some folders, camp/axe sets. **Technical:** Grinds D2, ATS-34, forges own damascus, does own heat treating. **Prices:** $225 and up. **Remarks:** Full-time maker, first knife sold in 1986. **Mark:** Etched name in arch.

SONNTAG, JACOB D
14148 Trisha Dr., St. Robert, MO 65584 **Contact:** 573-336-4082, Jake0372@live. com
Specialties: Working knives, some art knives. **Patterns:** Hunters, bowies, and

tomahawks. **Technical:** Grinds D2, ATS34 and damascus. Forges some damascus and tomahawks, does own heat treating. **Prices:** $200 and up. **Remarks:** Part-time maker, first knife sold in 2010. **Mark:** Etched name or stamped

SONNTAG, KRISTOPHER D
902 N 39th St, Nixa, MO 65714 **Contact:** 417-838-8327, kriss@buildit.us
Specialties: Working fixed blades, hunters, skinners, using knives. **Patterns:** Hunters, bowies, skinners. **Technical:** Grinds D2, ATS 34, damascus. Makes some damascus, does own heat treating. **Prices:** $200 and up. **Remarks:** Part-time maker, first knife sold in 2010. **Mark:** Etched name or stamped

SONTHEIMER, G DOUGLAS
14821 Dufief Mill Rd., Gaithersburg, MD 20878 **Contact:** 301-948-5227
Specialties: Fixed blade knives. **Patterns:** Whitetail deer, backpackers, camp, claws, fillet, fighters. **Technical:** Hollow Grinds. **Prices:** $500 and up. **Remarks:** Spare-time maker, first knife sold in 1976. **Mark:** LORD.

SORNBERGER, JIM
25126 Overland Dr, Volcano, CA 95689 **Contact:** 209-295-7819, sierrajs@volcano. net
Specialties: Master engraver making classic San Francisco-style knives. Collectible straight knives. **Patterns:** Fighters, daggers, bowies, miniatures, hunters, custom canes and LinerLock folders. **Technical:** Grinds 440C, 154CM and ATS-34, engraves, carves and embellishes. **Prices:** $500 to $35,000 in gold with gold quartz inlays. **Remarks:** Full-time maker, first knife sold in 1970. Master engraver. **Mark:** First initial, last name, city and state.

SOUTHER, MICHAEL
MSCustomknives 905 E Violet Ave., Coeur D' Alene, ID 83815 **Contact:** 208-651-8075, www.etsy.com/shop/MSCustomKnives
Patterns: Hunting, belt knives, bowies, daggers. **Technical:** Stock removal primarily D2, 5160, 52100. Other steels available on order. Makes own sheaths and scabbards. Exotic wood or Micarta handles.

SOWELL, BILL
100 Loraine Forest Ct, Macon, GA 31210 **Contact:** 478- 994-9863, billsowell@ reynoldscable.net
Specialties: Antique reproduction bowies, forging bowies, hunters, fighters, and most others. Also folders. **Technical:** Makes own damascus, using 1084/15N20, also making own designs in powder metals, forges 5160-1095-1084, and other carbon steels, grinds ATS-34. **Prices:** Starting at $150 and up. **Remarks:** Part-time maker. Sold first knife in 1998. Does own leather work. ABS Master Smith. **Mark:** Iron Horse Forge - Sowell - MS.

SPAKE, JEREMY
6128 N. Concord Ave., Portland, OR 97217-4735, jeremy@spakeknife.com, spakeknife.com, instagram.com/jspake
Specialties: Handmade hidden-tang fixed blade knives. **Patterns:** Utility, hunting and Nordic-influenced knives, kitchen cutlery and others as the occasion arises. **Technical:** Concentration on forged three-layer laminated blades with high-carbon steel cores, damascus, and high-carbon mono-steel blades. Stock removal on occasion. For handles, prefers a variety of stabilized woods and premium natural materials. **Prices:** $550 and up. **Remarks:** Part-time maker. First knife sold in 2012. American Bladesmith Society member. **Mark:** Last name etched or stamped in Gotham typeface.

SPARKS, BERNARD
PO Box 73, Dingle, ID 83233 **Contact:** 208-847-1883, dogknifeii@juno.com, sparksknives.com
Specialties: Maker engraved, working and art knives. Straight knives and folders of his own design. **Patterns:** Locking inner-frame folders, hunters, fighters, one-of-a-kind art knives. **Technical:** Grinds 530V steel, 440-C, 154CM, ATS-34, D-2 and forges by special order, triple temper, cryogenic soak. Mirror or hand finish. New Liquid metal steel. **Prices:** $300 to $2000. **Remarks:** Full-time maker, first knife sold in 1967. **Mark:** Last name over state with a knife logo on each end of name. Prior 1980, stamp of last name.

SPICKLER, GREGORY NOBLE
5614 Mose Cir, Sharpsburg, MD 21782 **Contact:** 301-432-2746

SPINALE, RICHARD
4021 Canterbury Ct, Lorain, OH 44053 **Contact:** 440-282-1565
Specialties: High-art working knives of his design. **Patterns:** Hunters, fighters, daggers and locking folders. **Technical:** Grinds 440C, ATS-34 and 07, engraves. Offers gold bolsters and other deluxe treatments. **Prices:** $300 to $1000, some to $3000. **Remarks:** Spare-time maker, first knife sold in 1976. **Mark:** Name, address, year and model number.

SPIVEY, JEFFERSON
9244 W Wilshire, Yukon, OK 73099 **Contact:** 405-371-9304, jspivey5@cox.net
Specialties: The Saber tooth: a combination hatchet, saw and knife. **Patterns:** Built for the wilderness, all are one-of-a-kind. **Technical:** Flat-grind blade chromemoly steel. The saw tooth spine curves with a row of biangular teeth. **Prices:** Start at $310. **Remarks:** First knife sold in 1977. As of September 2006 Spivey, knives have resumed production of the Sabertooth knife (one-word trademark). **Mark:** Name and serial number.

SPRAGG, WAYNE E
252 Oregon Ave, Lovell, WY 82431 **Contact:** 307-548-7212
Specialties: Working straight knives, some fancy. **Patterns:** Folders. **Technical:** Forges carbon steel and makes damascus. **Prices:** $200 and up. **Remarks:** All stainless heat-treated by Paul Bos. Carbon steel in shop heat treat. **Mark:** Last name front side w/s initials on reverse side.

SPROKHOLT, ROB

Burgerweg 5, Gatherwood, NETHERLANDS 1754 KB Burgerbrug **Contact:** 0031 6 51230225, (fax) 0031 84 2238446, info@gatherwood.nl, gatherwood.nl
Specialties: One-of-a-kind knives. Top materials collector grade, made to use. **Patterns:** Outdoor knives (hunting, sailing, hiking), bowies, man's surviving companions MSC, big tantos, folding knives. **Technical:** Handles mostly stabilized or oiled wood, ivory, Micarta, carbon fibre, G10. Stiff knives are full tang. Characteristic one row of massive silver pins or tubes. Folding knives have a LinerLock® with titanium or damascus powdersteel liner thumb can have any stone you like. Stock removal grinder: flat or convex. Steel 440-C, RWL-34, ATS-34, PM damascener steel. **Prices:** Start at 320 euro. **Remarks:** Writer of the first Dutch knifemaking book, supply shop for knife enthusiastic. First knife sold in 2000. **Mark:** Gatherwood in an eclipse etched blade or stamped in an intarsia of silver in the spine.

SQUIRE, JACK

350 W. 7th St., McMinnville, OR 97182-5509 **Contact:** 503-472-7290

ST. AMOUR, MURRAY

2066 Lapasse Rd., Beachburg, Ontario, CANADA K0J 1C0 **Contact:** 613-587-4194, knives@nrtco.net, st-amourknives.com
Specialties: Hunters, fish knives, outdoor knives, bowies and some collectors' pieces. **Technical:** Steels include CPM S30V, CPM S90V, CPM 154, 154CM and ATS 34. **Remarks:** Full-time maker, first knife sold in 1992. **Mark:** St. Amour over Canada or small print st. amour.

ST. CLAIR, THOMAS K

12608 Fingerboard Rd, Monrovia, MD 21770 **Contact:** 301-482-0264

STAFFORD, RICHARD

104 Marcia Ct, Warner Robins, GA 31088 **Contact:** 912-923-6372, (fax) Cell: 478-508-5821, rnrstafford@cox.net
Specialties: High-tech straight knives and some folders. **Patterns:** Hunters in several patterns, fighters, boots, camp knives, combat knives and period pieces. **Technical:** Grinds ATS-34 and 440C. Machine satin finish offered. **Prices:** Starting at $150. **Remarks:** Part-time maker, first knife sold in 1983. **Mark:** R. W. STAFFORD GEORGIA.

STAHL, KIM

STAHLSTEELKNIVES St. Louis, MO **Contact:** 929-324-1206, www.kimstahldesigns. com, kim.stahl@gmail.com
Patterns: Fixed blades. **Remarks:** First female on the History Channel's *Forged in Fire.*

STAINTHORP, GUY

4 Fisher St, Brindley Ford, Stroke-on-Trent, ENGLAND ST8 7QJ **Contact:** 07946 469 888, guystainthorp@hotmail.com, stainthorpknives.co.uk/index.html
Specialties: Tactical and outdoors knives to his own design. **Patterns:** Hunting, survival and occasionally folding knives. **Technical:** Grinds RWL-34, O1, S30V, Damasteel. Micarta, G10 and stabilised wood/bone for handles. **Prices:** $200 - $1000. **Remarks:** Full-time knifemaker. **Mark:** Squared stylised GS over "Stainthorp".

STALCUP, EDDIE

PO Box 2200, Gallup, NM 87305 **Contact:** 505-863-3107, sharon.stalcup@gmail.com
Specialties: Working and fancy hunters, bird and trout. Special custom orders. **Patterns:** Drop point hunters, locking liner and multi blade folders. **Technical:** ATS-34, 154 CM, 440C, CPM 154 and S30V. **Prices:** $150 to $1500. **Remarks:** Scrimshaw, exotic handle material, wet formed sheaths. Membership Arizona Knife Collectors Association. Southern California blades collectors & professional knife makers assoc. **Mark:** E.F. Stalcup, Gallup, NM.

STANCER, CHUCK

62 Hidden Ranch Rd NW, Calgary, AB, CANADA T3A 5S5 **Contact:** 403-295-7370, stancerc@telusplanet.net
Specialties: Traditional and working straight knives. **Patterns:** bowies, hunters and utility knives. **Technical:** Forges and grinds most steels. **Prices:** $175 and up. **Remarks:** Part-time maker. **Mark:** Last name.

STANFORD, PERRY

405N Walnut #9, Broken Arrow, OK 74012 **Contact:** 918-251-7983 or 866-305-5690, stanfordoutdoors@valornet, stanfordoutdoors.homestead.com
Specialties: Drop point, hunting and skinning knives, handmade sheaths. **Patterns:** Stright, hunting and skinners. **Technical:** Grinds 440C, ATS-34 and damascus. **Prices:** $65 to $275. **Remarks:** Part-time maker, first knife sold in 2007. Knifemaker supplier, manufacturer of paper sharpening systems. Doing business as Stanford Outdoors. **Mark:** Company name and nickname.

STANLEY, JOHN

604 Elm St, Crossett, AR 71635 **Contact:** 970-304-3005
Specialties: Hand forged fixed blades with engraving and carving. **Patterns:** Scottish dirks, skeans and fantasy blades. **Technical:** Forge high-carbon steel, own damascus. Prices $70 to $500. **Remarks:** All work is sole authorship. Offers engraving and carving services on other knives and handles. **Mark:** Varies.

STAPLETON, WILLIAM E

BUFFALO 'B' FORGE, 5425 Country Ln, Merritt Island, FL 32953
Specialties: Classic and traditional knives of his design and customer spec. **Patterns:** Hunters and using knives. **Technical:** Forges, O1 and L6 damascus, cable damascus and 5160, stock removal on request. **Prices:** $150 to $1000. **Remarks:** Part-time maker, first knife sold 1990. Doing business as Buffalo "B" Forge. **Mark:** Anvil with S initial in center of anvil.

STATES, JOSHUA C

43905 N 16th St, New River, AZ 85087 **Contact:** 623-826-3809, dosgatosforge.com
Specialties: Design and fabrication of forged working and art knives from O1 and my own damascus. Stock removal from 440C and CM154 upon request. Folders from 440C, CM154 and damascus. Flat and Hollow grinds. Knives made to customer specs and/or design. **Patterns:** bowies, hunters, daggers, chef knives, and exotic shapes. **Technical:** damascus is 1095, 1084, O1 and 15N20. Carved or file-worked fittings from various metals including my own mokume gane and damascus. **Prices:** $250 and up. **Remarks:** Part-time maker with waiting list. First knife sold in 2006. **Mark:** Initials JCS in small oval, or States in italisized script. Unmarked knives come with certificate of authorship.

STECK, VAN R

260 W Dogwood Ave, Orange City, FL 32763 **Contact:** 407-416-1723, van@ thudknives.com
Specialties: Specializing in double-edged grinds. Free-hand grinds: folders, spears, bowies, swords and miniatures. **Patterns:** Tomahawks with a crane for the spike, tactical merged with nature. **Technical:** Hamon lines, folder lock of own design, the arm-lock! **Prices:** $50 - $1500. **Remarks:** Builds knives designed by Laci Szabo or builds to customer design. Studied with Reese Weiland on folders and automatics. **Mark:** GEISHA holding a sword with initials and THUD KNIVES in a circle.

STEGALL, KEITH

701 Outlet View Dr, Wasilla, AK 99654 **Contact:** 907-376-0703, kas5200@yahoo.com
Specialties: Traditional working straight knives. **Patterns:** Most patterns. **Technical:** Grinds 440C and 154CM. **Prices:** $100 to $300. **Remarks:** Spare-time maker, first knife sold in 1987. **Mark:** Name and state with anchor.

STEGNER, WILBUR G

9242 173rd Ave SW, Rochester, WA 98579 **Contact:** 360-273-0937, wilbur@wgsk. net, wgsk.net
Specialties: Working/using straight knives and folders of his design. **Patterns:** Hunters and locking folders. **Technical:** Makes his own damascus steel. **Prices:** $100 to $1000, some to $5000. **Remarks:** Full-time maker, first knife sold in 1979. Google search key words-"STEGNER KNIVES." Best folder awards NWKC 2009, 2010 and 2011. **Mark:** First and middle initials, last name in bar over shield logo.

STEIER, DAVID

Steier Custom Knives. 7722 Zenith Way, Louisville, KY 40219 **Contact:** 502-969-8409, umag300@aol.com, steierknives.com
Specialties: Folding LinerLocks, bowies, slip joints, lockbacks, and straight hunters. **Technical:** Stock removal blades of 440C, ATS-34, and damascus from outside sources like Robert Eggerling and Mike Norris. **Prices:** $150 for straight hunters to $1400 for fully decked-out folders. **Remarks:** First knife sold in 1979. **Mark:** Last name STEIER.

STEIGER, MONTE L

Box 186, Genesee, ID 83832 **Contact:** 208-285-1769, montesharon@genesee-id. com
Specialties: Traditional working/using straight knives of all designs. **Patterns:** Hunters, utility/camp knives, fillet and chefs. Carving sets and steak knives. **Technical:** Grinds 1095, O1, 440C, ATS-34. Handles of stacked leather, natural wood, Micarta or pakkawood. Each knife comes with right- or left-handed sheath. **Prices:** $110 to $600. **Remarks:** Spare-time maker, first knife sold in 1988. Retired librarian **Mark:** First initial, last name, city and state.

STEIGERWALT, KEN

507 Savagehill Rd, Orangeville, PA 17859 **Contact:** 570-683-5156, steigerwaltknives. com
Specialties: Elaborate carving and inlays, primarily in Art Deco design. **Patterns:** Folders, button locks and rear locks. **Technical:** Uses CPM 154, CPM S35V, RWL-34 and damascus steels. **Prices:** $500 to $10,000. **Remarks:** Full-time maker, first knife sold in 1981. **Mark:** Kasteigerwalt

STEINAU, JURGEN

Julius-Hart Strasse 44, Berlin, GERMANY 01162 **Contact:** 372-6452512, (fax) 372-645-2512
Specialties: Fantasy and high-art straight knives of his design. **Patterns:** Boots, daggers and switch-blade folders. **Technical:** Grinds 440B, 2379 and X90 Cr.Mo.V. 78. **Prices:** $1500 to $2500, some to $3500. **Remarks:** Full-time maker, first knife sold in 1984. **Mark:** Symbol, plus year, month day and serial number.

STEINBERG, AL

5244 Duenas, Laguna Woods, CA 92653 **Contact:** 949-951-2889, lagknife@fea.net
Specialties: Fancy working straight knives to customer specs. **Patterns:** Hunters, bowies, fishing, camp knives, push knives and high end kitchen knives. **Technical:** Grinds O1, 440C and 154CM. **Prices:** $60 to $2500. **Remarks:** Full-time maker, first knife sold in 1972. **Mark:** Signature, city and state.

STEINBRECHER, MARK W

1122 92nd Place, Pleasant Prairie, WI 53158-4939
Specialties: Working and fancy folders. **Patterns:** Daggers, pocket knives, fighters and gents of his own design or to customer specs. **Technical:** Hollow grinds ATS-34, O1 other makers damascus. Uses natural handle materials: stag, ivories, mother-of-pearl. File work and some inlays. **Prices:** $500 to $1200, some to $2500. **Remarks:** Part-time maker, first folder sold in 1989. **Mark:** Name etched or handwritten on ATS-34, stamped on damascus.

STEINGASS, T.K.

334 Silver Lake Rd., Bucksport, ME 04416 **Contact:** 304-268-1161, tksteingass@

frontier.com, steingassknives.com

Specialties: Loveless style hunters and fighters and sole authorship knives: Man Knife, Silent Hunter, and Silent Fighter. Harpoon Grind Camp Knife and Harpoon Grind Man Hunter. **Technical:** Stock removal, use CPM 154, S3V and occasionally 1095 or O1 for camp choppers.**Prices:** $200 to $500. **Remarks:** Part-time maker, first knife made in 2010. **Mark:** STEINGASS.

STEKETEE, CRAIG A
871 NE US Hwy 60, Billings, MO 65610 **Contact:** 417-744-2770, stekknives04@yahoo.com

Specialties: Classic and working straight knives and swords of his design. **Patterns:** bowies, hunters, and Japanese-style swords. **Technical:** Forges his own damascus, bronze, silver and damascus fittings, offers filework. Prefers exotic and natural handle materials. **Prices:** $200 to $4000. **Remarks:** Full-time maker. **Mark:** STEK.

STEPHAN, DANIEL
2201 S Miller Rd, Valrico, FL 33594 **Contact:** 727-580-8617, knifemaker@verizon.net

Specialties: Art knives, one-of-a-kind.

STERLING, MURRAY
693 Round Peak Church Rd, Mount Airy, NC 27030 **Contact:** 336-352-5110, (fax) (fax) 336-352-5105, sterck@surry.net, sterlingcustomknives.com

Specialties: Single and dual blade folders. Interframes and integral dovetail frames. **Technical:** Grinds ATS-34 or damascus by Mike Norris and/or Devin Thomas. **Prices:** $400 to $1,200. **Remarks:** Full-time maker, first knife sold in 1991. **Mark:** Last name stamped.

STERLING, THOMAS J
ART KNIVES BY, POB 1621, Coupeville, WA 98239 **Contact:** 360-678-9269, (fax) 360-678-9269, netsuke@comcast.net, sterlingsculptures.com

Specialties: Since 2003, Tom Sterling has created one-of-a-kind, ultra-quality art knives, jewelry and assorted doodads using high-quality precious and semi-precious materials, steel, titanium, shibuichi and shakudo. His work is often influenced by the traditions of Japanese netsuke and a unique fusion of cultures and styles. Tom's highly sought-after engraving skills reflect stylistically integrated choices of materials and contrasting inlays for a unique presentation style. **Prices:** $300 to $14,000. **Remarks:** Limited output ensures highest quality artwork and exceptional levels of craftsmanship. **Mark:** TJSterling.

STEYN, PETER
PO Box 76, Welkom, Freestate, SOUTH AFRICA 9460 **Contact:** 27573522015, 27573523566 (fax), petersteynknives.com, email:info@petersteynknives.com

Specialties: Fixed blade knives of own design. Folding knives of own design. Friction folders, slip joints and lockbacks. **Patterns:** Fixed blades: hunters and skinners. Folding knives: friction folders, slip joints and lockbacks. **Technical:** Steels Bohler N690 and Damascus. Blades are bead-blasted in plain or patterned finish. Ceramic wash also available in satin or antiqued finish. Grind style is COVEX, concave on the obverse, and convex on the reverse. Works with a wide variety of handle materials, prefers exotic woods and synthetics. **Prices:** $150 to $650. **Remarks:** Full-time maker, first knife sold 2005, member of South African Guild. **Mark:** Letter 'S' in shape of pyramid with full name above and 'Handcrafted' below.

STICE, DOUGLAS W
PO Box 12815, Wichita, KS 67277 **Contact:** 316-295-6855, doug@sticecraft.com, sticecraft.com

Specialties: Working fixed blade knives of own design. **Patterns:** Tacticals, hunters, skinners,utility, and camp knives. **Technical:** Grinds CPM154CM, 154CM, CPM3V, damascus, uses 18" contact grinds where wheel for hollow grinds, also flat. **Prices:** $100 to $750. **Remarks:** Full-time maker, first professional knife made in 2009. All knives have serial numbers and include certificate of authenticity. **Mark:** Stylized "Stice" stamp.

STIDHAM, DANIEL
3106 Mill Cr. Rd., Gallipolis, Ohio 45631 **Contact:** 740-446-1673, danstidham@yahoo.com

Specialties: Fixed blades, folders, bowies and hunters. **Technical:** 440C, Alabama damascus, 1095 with filework. **Prices:** Start at $150. **Remarks:** Has made fixed blades since 1961, folders since 1986. Also sells various knife brands.**Mark:** Stidham Knives Gallipolis, Ohio 45631.

STIMPS, JASON M
374 S Shaffer St, Orange, CA 92866 **Contact:** 714-744-5866

STIPES, DWIGHT
2651 SW Buena Vista Dr, Palm City, FL 34990 **Contact:** 772-597-0550, dwightstipes@adelphia.net

Specialties: Traditional and working straight knives in standard patterns. **Patterns:** Boots, bowies, daggers, hunters and fighters. **Technical:** Grinds 440C, D2 and D3 tool steel. Handles of natural materials, animal, bone or horn. **Prices:** $75 to $150. **Remarks:** Full-time maker, first knife sold in 1972. **Mark:** Stipes.

STOKES, ED
22614 Cardinal Dr, Hockley, TX 77447 **Contact:** 713-351-1319

Specialties: Working straight knives and folders of all designs. **Patterns:** Boots, bowies, daggers, fighters, hunters and miniatures. **Technical:** Grinds ATS-34, 440C and D2. Offers decorative butt caps, tapered spacers on handles and finger grooves, nickel-silver inlays, handmade sheaths. **Prices:** $185 to $290, some to $350. **Remarks:** Full-time maker, first knife sold in 1973. **Mark:** First and last name, Custom Knives with Apache logo.

STONE, JERRY
PO Box 1027, Lytle, TX 78052 **Contact:** 830-709-3042

Specialties: Traditional working and using folders of his design and to customer specs,

fancy knives. **Patterns:** Fighters, hunters, locking folders and slip joints. Also make automatics. **Technical:** Grinds 440C and ATS-34. Offers filework. **Prices:** $175 to $1000. **Remarks:** Full-time maker, first knife sold in 1973. **Mark:** Name over Texas star/town and state underneath.

STORCH, ED
RR 4, Mannville, AB, CANADA T0B 2W0 **Contact:** 780-763-2214, storchknives@gmail.com, storchknives.com

Specialties: Working knives, fancy fighting knives, kitchen cutlery and art knives. Knifemaking classes. **Patterns:** Working patterns, bowies and folders. **Technical:** Forges his own damascus. Grinds ATS-34. Builds friction folders. Salt heat treating. **Prices:** $100 to $3,000 (U.S.). **Remarks:** Full-time maker, first knife sold in 1984. Classes taught in stock-removal, and damascus and sword making. **Mark:** Last name.

STORMER, BOB
34354 Hwy E, Dixon, MO 65459 **Contact:** 636-734-2693, bs34354@gmail.com

Specialties: Straight knives, using and collector grade. **Patterns:** bowies, skinners, hunters, camp knives. **Technical:** Forges 5160, 1095. **Prices:** $200 to $500. **Remarks:** Part-time maker, ABS Journeyman Smith 2001. **Mark:** Setting sun/fall trees/initials, or lightning bolt.

STOUT, CHARLES
RT3 178 Stout Rd, Gillham, AR 71841 **Contact:** 870-386-5521

STOUT, JOHNNY
1205 Forest Trail, New Braunfels, TX 78132 **Contact:** 830-606-4067, johnny@stoutknives.com, stoutknives.com, Facebook-Johnny Stout, Instagram-Stout Handmade Knives

Specialties: Folders, some fixed blades. Working knives, some fancy. **Patterns:** Hunters, automatics, LinerLocks and slip joints. **Technical:** Grinds stainless and carbon steels, forges some damascus. **Prices:** $450 to $895, some to $6,500. **Remarks:** Full-time maker, first knife sold in 1983. Hosts semi-annual Guadalupe Forge Hammer-in and Knifemakers Rendezvous. **Mark:** Name and city in logo.

STRAIGHT, KENNETH J
11311 103 Lane N, Largo, FL 33773 **Contact:** 813-397-9817

STRANDE, POUL
Soster Svenstrup Byvej 16, Viby Sj., Dastrup, DENMARK 4130 **Contact:** 46 19 43 05, (fax) 46 19 53 19, poulstrande.com

Specialties: Classic fantasy working knives, Damasceret blade, Nikkel Damasceret blade, Lamineret: Lamineret blade with Nikkel. **Patterns:** bowies, daggers, fighters, hunters and swords. **Technical:** Uses carbon steel and 15C20 steel. **Prices:** NA. **Remarks:** Full-time maker, first knife sold in 1985. **Mark:** First and last initials.

STRAUB, SALEM F.
324 Cobey Creek Rd., Tonasket, WA 98855 **Contact:** 509-486-2627, vorpalforge@hotmail.com prometheanknives.com

Specialties: Elegant working knives, fixed blade hunters, utility, skinning knives, liner locks. Makes own horsehide sheaths. **Patterns:** A wide range of syles, everything from the gentleman's pocket to the working kitchen, integrals, bowies, folders, check out my website to see some of my work for ideas. **Technical:** Forges several carbon steels, 52100, W1, etc. Grinds stainless and makes/uses own damascus, cable, san mai, stadard patterns. Likes clay quenching, hamons, hand rubbed finishes. Flat, hollow, or convex grinds. Prefers synthetic handle materials. Hidden and full tapered tangs. **Prices:** $150 - $600, some higher. **Remarks:** Full-time maker. Doing what it takes to make your knife ordering and buying experience positive and enjoyable, striving to exceed expectations. All knives backed by lifetime guarantee. **Mark:** "Straub" stamp or "Promethean Knives" etched. Some older pieces stamped "Vorpal" though no longer using this mark. **Other:** Feel free to call or e-mail anytime. I love to talk knives.

STRICKLAND, DALE
1440 E Thompson View, Monroe, UT 84754 **Contact:** 435-896-8362

Specialties: Traditional and working straight knives and folders of his design and to customer specs. **Patterns:** Hunters, folders, miniatures and utility knives. **Technical:** Grinds damascus and 440C. **Prices:** $120 to $350, some to $500. **Remarks:** Part-time maker, first knife sold in 1991. **Mark:** Oval stamp of name, Maker.

STRIDER, MICK
STRIDER KNIVES, 565 Country Club Dr., Escondido, CA 92029 **Contact:** 760-471-8275, (fax) 503-218-7069, striderguys@striderknives.com, striderknives.com

STRONG, SCOTT
1599 Beaver Valley Rd, Beavercreek, OH 45434 **Contact:** 937-426-9290

Specialties: Working knives, some deluxe. **Patterns:** Hunters, fighters, survival and military-style knives, art knives. **Technical:** Forges and grinds O1, A2, D2, 440C and ATS-34. Uses no solder, most knives disassemble. **Prices:** $75 to $450, some to $1500. **Remarks:** Spare-time maker, first knife sold in 1983. **Mark:** Strong Knives.

STROYAN, ERIC
Box 218, Dalton, PA 18414 **Contact:** 717-563-2603

Specialties: Classic and working/using straight knives and folders of his design. **Patterns:** Hunters, locking folders, slip-joints. **Technical:** Forges damascus, grinds ATS-34, D2. **Prices:** $200 to $600, some to $2000. **Remarks:** Part-time maker, first knife sold in 1968. **Mark:** Signature or initials stamp.

STUART, MASON
24 Beech Street, Mansfield, MA 02048 **Contact:** 508-339-8236, smasonknives@verizon.net, smasonknives.com, Facebook.com/S. Mason Custom Knives

Specialties: Hand forged and stock removal. Alter, horn, wood and pearl handles. Sheath hand tooled and sewn. **Patterns:** bowies, hunters, fighters and neck knives. **Technical:**

custom knifemakers

Forges and grinds. damascus, 5160, 1095, 1084, old files. Uses only natural handle material. **Prices:** $350 - 2,000. **Remarks:** Part-time maker. **Mark:** First initial and last name.

STUART, STEVE
Box 168, Gores Landing, ON, CANADA K0K 2E0 **Contact:** 905-440-6910, stevestuart@xplornet.com
Specialties: Straight knives. **Patterns:** Tantos, fighters, skinners, file and rasp knives. **Technical:** Uses 440C, CPM154, CPMS30V, Micarta and natural handle materials. **Prices:** $60 to $400. **Remarks:** Part-time maker. **Mark:** SS.

STUCKY, DANIEL
37924 Shenandoah Loop, Springfield, OR 97478 **Contact:** 541-747-6496, stuckyj1@msn.com, stuckyknives.com
Specialties: Tactical, fancy and everyday carry folders, fixed-blade hunting knives, trout, bird and fillet knives. **Technical:** Stock removal maker. Steels include but are not limited to damascus, CPM 154, CPM S30V, CPM S35VN, 154CM and ATS-34. **Prices:** Start at $300 and can go to thousands, depending on materials used. **Remarks:** Full-time maker, first knife sold in 1999. **Mark:** Name over city and state.

STYREFORS, MATTIAS
Unbyn 23, Boden, SWEDEN 96193, infor@styrefors.com
Specialties: damascus and mosaic damascus. Fixed blade Nordic hunters, folders and swords. **Technical:** Forges, shapes and grinds damascus and mosaic damascus from mostly UHB 15N20 and 20C with contrasts in nickel and 15N20. Hardness HR 58. **Prices:** $800 to $3000. **Remarks:** Full-time maker since 1999. International reputation for high end damascus blades. Uses stabilized Arctic birch and willow burl, horn, fossils, exotic materials, and scrimshaw by Viveca Sahlin for knife handles. Hand tools and hand stitches leather sheaths in cow raw hide. Works in well equipped former military forgery in northern Sweden. **Mark:** MS.

SUEDMEIER, HARLAN
762 N 60th Rd, Nebraska City, NE 68410 **Contact:** 402-873-4372
Patterns: Straight knives. **Technical:** Forging hi carbon damascus. **Prices:** Starting at $175. **Mark:** First initials & last name.

SUGIHARA, KEIDOH
4-16-1 Kamori-Cho, Kishiwada City, Osaka, JAPAN F596-0042, (fax) 0724-44-2677
Specialties: High-tech working straight knives and folders of his design. **Patterns:** bowies, hunters, fighters, fishing, boots, some pocket knives and liner-lock folders. **Technical:** Grinds ATS-34, COS-25, buys damascus and high-carbon steels. Prices $60 to $4000. **Remarks:** Full-time maker, first knife sold in 1980. **Mark:** Initial logo with fish design.

SUGIYAMA, EDDY K
2361 Nagayu, Naoirimachi Naoirigun, Oita, JAPAN **Contact:** 0974-75-2050
Specialties: One-of-a-kind, exotic-style knives. **Patterns:** Working, utility and miniatures. **Technical:** CT rind, ATS-34 and D2. **Prices:** $400 to $1200. **Remarks:** Full-time maker. **Mark:** Name or cedar mark.

SUMMERS, ARTHUR L
1310 Hess Rd, Concord, NC 28025 **Contact:** 704-787-9275 Cell: 704-305-0735, arthursummers88@hotmail.com
Specialties: Drop points, clip points, straight blades. **Patterns:** Hunters, bowies and personal knives. **Technical:** Grinds ATS-34, CPM-D2, CPM-154 and damascus. **Prices:** $250 to $1000. **Remarks:** Full-time maker, first knife sold in 1988. **Mark:** Serial number is the date.

SUMMERS, DAN
2675 NY Rt. 11, Whitney Pt., NY 13862 **Contact:** 607-692-2391, dansumm11@gmail.com
Specialties: Period knives and tomahawks. **Technical:** All hand forging. **Prices:** Most $100 to $400.

SUMMERS, DENNIS K
827 E. Cecil St, Springfield, OH 45503 **Contact:** 513-324-0624
Specialties: Working/using knives. **Patterns:** Fighters and personal knives. **Technical:** Grinds 440C, A2 and D2. Makes drop and clip point. **Prices:** $75 to $200. **Remarks:** Part-time maker, first knife sold in 1995. **Mark:** First and middle initials, last name, serial number.

SUNDERLAND, RICHARD
Av Infraganti 23, Col Lazaro Cardenas, Puerto Escondido, OA, MEXICO 71980 **Contact:** 011 52 94 582 1451, sunamerica@prodigy.net.mx7
Specialties: Personal and hunting knives with carved handles in oosic and ivory. **Patterns:** Hunters, bowies, daggers, camp and personal knives. **Technical:** Grinds 440C, ATS-34 and O1. Handle materials of rosewoods, fossil mammoth ivory and oosic. **Prices:** $150 to $1000. **Remarks:** Part-time maker, first knife sold in 1983. Doing business as Sun Knife Co. **Mark:** SUN.

SURLS, W. ALLEN
W.A. SURLS KNIVES, 3889 Duncan Ives Dr., Buford, GA 30519 **Contact:** 678-897-1624, wasknives@gmail.com
Patterns: Bushcraft knives, traditional fixed blades, Loveless patterns, skinners and gent's knives. **Technical:** Stock removal method of blade making with occasional forging, using CPM 154, A2 and O1 steels. **Prices:** $150 to $1,200. **Remarks:** Full-time maker, first blade ground in May of 2013. Owner and operator of W.A. Surls Knives, and vice president of Fiddleback Forge Inc. **Mark:** Current mark is "W.A. Surls," with early production pieces marked "WAS."

SUTTON, S RUSSELL
4900 Cypress Shores Dr, New Bern, NC 28562 **Contact:** 252-637-3963, srsutton@suddenlink.net, suttoncustomknives.com

Specialties: Straight knives and folders to customer specs and in standard patterns. **Patterns:** Boots, hunters, interframes, slip joints and locking liners. **Technical:** Grinds ATS-34, 440C and stainless damascus. **Prices:** $220 to $2000. **Remarks:** Full-time maker, first knife sold in 1992. Provides relief engraving on bolsters and guards. **Mark:** Etched last name.

SWARZ-BURT, PETER T.
FALLING HAMMER PRODUCTIONS, LLC, 10 Swiss Ln., Wolcott, CT 06716 **Contact:** 203-879-1786, dragonsbreathforge@gmail.com, fallinghammerproductions.com or dragonsbreathforge.com
Specialties: Makes own Wootz and other crucible steels, specializing in unusual blade shapes with a focus on Indian and Middle Eastern weapons, historical reproductions from all regions. **Patterns:** Designs focus on utility and comfort. **Technical:** Uses 5160, L6, 10xx, and his own Wootz and damascus steels. Forges closely to shape. **Prices:** $150 to $2,000 (knives) and $500 to $5,000 (swords). **Remarks:** Full-time blacksmith and bladesmith, first knife made in 1992. **Mark:** PTSB combined to look like a snake twined around a sword on one side of ricasso, and the Dragon's Breath Forge symbol that looks like a talon on the other side.

SWEARINGEN, KURT
22 Calvary Rd., Cedar Crest, NM 87008 **Contact:** 575-613-0500, kurt@swearingenknife.com, swearingenknife.com
Specialties: Traditional hunting and camp knives, as well as slip-joint and lockback folders of classic design with an emphasis on utility. Hand-carved and tooled sheaths accompany each knife. **Patterns:** Loveless-style hunters, Scagel folders, as well as original designs. **Technical:** Grinds CPM 154 for all standard hunting models and D2 for all folders. Smiths W2 for forged hunters, and 5160 or 1084 for camp knives. **Prices:** Standard models in CPM 154 start at $320, including a custom sheath. **Remarks:** Serious part-time maker and ABS journeyman smith, I personally test each knife in my shop and in the field during hunting season (hunters) and in my work as a forester (camp knives).

SWEAZA, DENNIS
4052 Hwy 321 E, Austin, AR 72007 **Contact:** 501-941-1886, knives4den@aol.com

SWENSON, LUKE
SWENSON KNIVES, 1667 Brushy Creek Dr., Lakehills, TX 78063 **Contact:** 210-722-3227, luke@swensonknives.com, swensonknives.com
Specialties: Small hunting knives, concentrating on traditional multi-blade slip joints. **Technical:** Stock-removal method of blade making. Flat grinds A2 tool steel for fixed blades, and hollow grinds CPM 154 for slip-joint folders. Credits Bill Ruple for mentoring him in the making slip joints. **Prices:** $275 to $675. **Remarks:** Part-time maker/full-time firefighter, first knife made in 2003. Starting to do some traditional lockback patterns also. **Mark:** Name and city where maker lives.

SWYHART, ART
509 Main St, PO Box 267, Klickitat, WA 98628 **Contact:** 509-369-3451, swyhart@gorge.net, knifeoutlet.com/swyhart.htm
Specialties: Traditional working and using knives of his design. **Patterns:** bowies, hunters and utility/camp knives. **Technical:** Forges 52100, 5160 and damascus 1084 mixed with either 15N20 or 0186. Blades differentially heat-treated with visible temper line. **Prices:** $75 to $250, some to $350. **Remarks:** Part-time maker, first knife sold in 1983. **Mark:** First name, last initial in script.

SYLVESTER, DAVID
465 Sweede Rd., Compton, QC, CANADA J0B 1L0 **Contact:** 819-837-0304, david@swedevilleforge.com, swedevilleforge.com
Patterns: I hand forge all my knives and I like to make hunters and integrals and some bowies and fighters. I work with W2, 1084, 1095, and my damascus. **Prices:** $200 - $1500. **Remarks:** Part-time maker. ABS Journeyman Smith. **Mark:** D.Sylvester

SYMONDS, ALBERTO E
Rambla M Gandhi 485, Apt 901, Montevideo, URUGUAY 11300 **Contact:** 011 598 27103201, (fax) 011 598 2 7103201, albertosymonds@hotmail.com
Specialties: All kinds including puukos, nice sheaths, leather and wood. **Prices:** $300 to $2200. **Mark:** AESH and current year.

SYSLO, CHUCK
3418 South 116 Ave, Omaha, NE 68144 **Contact:** 402-333-0647, ciscoknives@cox.net
Specialties: Hunters, working knives, daggers and misc. **Patterns:** Hunters, daggers and survival knives, locking folders. **Technical:** Flat-grinds D2, 440C and 154CM, hand polishes only. **Prices:** $250 to $1,000, some to $3,000. **Remarks:** Part-time maker, first knife sold in 1978. Uses many natural materials. Making some knives, mainly retired from knifemaking. **Mark:** CISCO in logo.

SZCZERBIAK, MACIEJ
Crusader Forge Knives, PO Box 2181, St. George, UT 84771 **Contact:** 435-574-2193, crusaderforge@yahoo.com, crusaderforge.com
Patterns: Drop-point, spear-point and tanto fixed blades and tactical folders. **Technical:** Stock removal using CPM-S30V and D2 steels. Knives designed with the technical operator in mind, and maintain an amazing balance in the user's hand. **Prices:** $300 to $2,500. **Remarks:** First knife made in 1999.

SZILASKI, JOSEPH
School of Knifemaking, 52 Woods Dr., Pine Plains, NY 12567 **Contact:** 518-398-0309, joe@szilaski.com, szilaski.com
Specialties: Straight knives, folders and tomahawks of his design, to customer specs and in standard patterns. Many pieces are one-of-a-kind. Offers knifemaking classes for all levels in 4,000-square-foot shop. Courses are in forging, grinding, damascus,

tomahawk engraving and carving. **Patterns:** bowies, daggers, fighters, hunters, art knives and early American styles. **Technical:** Forges A2, D2, O1 and damascus. **Prices:** $450 to $4,000, some to $10,000. **Remarks:** Full-time maker, first knife sold in 1990. ABS master smith. **Mark:** Snake logo.

T

TABER, DAVID E.
51 E. 4th St., Ste. 300, Winona, MN 55987 **Contact:** 507-450-1918, dtaber@qwestoffice.net
Specialties: Traditional slip joints, primarily using and working knives. **Technical:** Blades are hollow ground on a 20" wheel, ATS-34 and some damascus steel. **Remarks:** Full-time orthodontist, part-time maker, first knife made in January 2011. **Mark:** dr.t.

TABOR, TIM
18925 Crooked Lane, Lutz, FL 33548 **Contact:** 813-948-6141, taborknives.com
Specialties: Fancy folders, damascus bowies and hunters. **Patterns:** My own design folders & customer requests. **Technical:** ATS-34, hand forged damascus, 1084, 15N20 mosaic damascus, 1095, 5160 high carbon blades, flat grind, file work & jewel embellishments. **Prices:** $175 to $1500. **Remarks:** Part-time maker, sold first knife in 2003. **Mark:** Last name.

TAKACH, ANDREW
1390 Fallen Timber Rd., Elizabeth, PA 15037 **Contact:** 724-691-2271, a-takach@takachforge.com, takachforge.com
Specialties: One-of-a-kind fixed blade working knives (own design or customer's). Mostly all fileworked. **Patterns:** Hunters, skinners, caping, fighters, and designs of own style. **Technical:** Forges mostly 5160, 1090, 01, an down pattern welded damascus, nickle damascus, and cable and various chain damascus. Also do some San Mai. **Prices:** $100 to $350, some over $550. **Remarks:** Doing business as Takach Forge. First knife sold in 2004. **Mark:** Takach (stamped).

TALLY, GRANT
26961 James Ave, Flat Rock, MI 48134 **Contact:** 313-414-1618
Specialties: Straight knives and folders of his design. **Patterns:** bowies, daggers, fighters. **Technical:** Grinds ATS-34, 440C and D2. Offers filework. **Prices:** $250 to $1000. **Remarks:** Part-time maker, first knife sold in 1985. Doing business as Tally Knives. **Mark:** Tally (last name).

TAMATSU, KUNIHIKO
5344 Sukumo, Sukumo City, Kochi-ken, JAPAN 788-0000 **Contact:** 0880-63-3455, ktamatsu@mb.gallery.ne.jp, knife.tamatu.net
Specialties: Loveless-style fighters, sub-hilt fighters and hunting knives. **Technical:** Mirror-finished ATS-34, BG-42 and CPM-S30V blades. **Prices:** $400 to $2,500. **Remarks:** Part-time maker, making knives for eight years. **Mark:** Electrical etching of "K. Tamatsu."

TAMBOLI, MICHAEL
12447 N 49 Ave, Glendale, AZ 85304 **Contact:** 602-978-4308, mnbtamboli@gmail.com
Specialties: Miniatures, some full size. **Patterns:** Miniature hunting knives to fantasy art knives. **Technical:** Grinds ATS-34 & damascus. **Prices:** $75 to $500, some to $2000. **Remarks:** Full time maker, first knife sold in 1978. **Mark:** Initials, last name, last name city and state, MT Custom Knives or Mike Tamboli in Japanese script.

TASMAN, KERLEY
9 Avignon Retreat, Pt Kennedy, WA, AUSTRALIA 6172 **Contact:** 61 8 9593 0554, (fax) 61 8 9593 0554, taskerley@optusnet.com.au
Specialties: Knife/harness/sheath systems for elite military personnel and body guards. **Patterns:** Utility/tactical knives, hunters small game and presentation grade knives. **Technical:** ATS-34 and 440C, damascus, flat and hollow grids. **Prices:** $200 to $1800 U.S. **Remarks:** Will take presentation grade commissions. Multi award winning maker and custom jeweler. **Mark:** Maker's initials.

TAYLOR, BILLY
10 Temple Rd, Petal, MS 39465 **Contact:** 601-544-0041
Specialties: Straight knives of his design. **Patterns:** bowies, skinners, hunters and utility knives. **Technical:** Flat-grinds 440C, ATS-34 and 154CM. **Prices:** $60 to $300. **Remarks:** Part-time maker, first knife sold in 1991. **Mark:** Full name, city and state.

TAYLOR, C. GRAY
560 Poteat Ln, Fall Branch, TN 37656 **Contact:** 423-348-8304 or 423-765-6434, graysknives@aol.com, cgraytaylor.com
Specialties: Traditonal multi-blade lobster folders, also art display bowies and daggers. **Patterns:** Orange Blossom, sleeveboard and gunstocks. **Technical:** Grinds. **Prices:** Upscale. **Remarks:** Full-time maker, first knife sold in 1975. **Mark:** Name, city and state.

TAYLOR, SHANE
42 Broken Bow Ln, Miles City, MT 59301 **Contact:** 406-234-7175, shane@taylorknives.com, taylorknives.com
Specialties: One-of-a-kind fancy damascus straight knives and folders. **Patterns:** bowies, folders and fighters. **Technical:** Forges own mosaic and pattern welded damascus. **Prices:** $450 and up. **Remarks:** ABS Master Smith, full-time maker, first knife sold in 1982. **Mark:** First name.

TEDFORD, STEVEN J.
14238 Telephone Rd., Colborne, ON, CANADA K0K 1S0 **Contact:** 613-689-7569, firebornswords@yahoo.com, steventedfordknives.com
Specialties: Handmade custom fixed blades, specialty outdoors knives. **Patterns:** Swept Survival bowie, large, medium and small-size field-dressing/hunting knives, drop-point

skinners, and world-class fillet knives. **Technical:** Exclusively using ATS-34 stainless steel, Japanese-inspired, free-hand ground, zero-point edge blade design. **Prices:** All knives are sold wholesale directly from the shop starting at $150 to $500+. **Remarks:** Tedford Knives, Function is beauty. Every knife is unconditionally guaranteed for life.

TENDICK, BEN
BRT Bladeworks. 1645 Horn Ln, Eugene, OR 97404 **Contact:** 541-912-1280, bentendick@gmail.com, brtbladeworks.com
Specialties: Japanese fusion blades, chef's knives, tactical. **Technical:** Preferred steel is CPM 3V. **Prices:** $130 to $700. **Remarks:** Full-time, has been making knives since early 90's but started seriously making knives in 2010. In business at BRT Bladeworks. **Mark:** Initials (BRT) with B backwards and T between the B and R, and also use last name.

TERRILL, STEPHEN
16357 Goat Ranch Rd, Springville, CA 93265 **Contact:** 559-920-2722, steve@slterrillknives.com, slterrillknives.com
Specialties: Deluxe working straight knives and folders. **Patterns:** Fighters, tantos, boots, locking folders and axes, traditional oriental patterns. **Technical:** Forged and stock removal of 1095, 5160, damascus, stock removal ATS-34. **Prices:** $400 and up. **Remarks:** Full-time maker, semi-retired, first knife sold in 1972. **Mark:** Name, name-city-state.

TERZUOLA, ROBERT
10121 Eagle Rock NE, Albuquerque, NM 87122 **Contact:** 505-856-7077, terzuola@earthlink.net
Specialties: Working folders of his design, period pieces. **Patterns:** High-tech utility, defense and gentleman's folders. **Technical:** Grinds CPM154 and damascus. Offers titanium, carbon fiber and G10 composite for side-lock folders and tactical folders. **Prices:** $1,200 to $3,000. **Remarks:** Full-time maker, first knife sold in 1980. **Mark:** Mayan dragon head, name.

TESARIK, RICHARD
Pisecnik 87, 614 00 Brno, Czech Republic **Contact:** 00420-602-834-726, rtesarik@gmail.com, tesarikknives.com
Specialties: Handmade art knives. **Patterns:** Daggers, hunters and LinerLock or back-lock folders. **Technical:** Grinds RWL-34, N690 and stainless or high-carbon damascus. Carves on blade, handle and other parts. I prefer fossil material and exotic wood, don't use synthetic material. **Prices:** $600 to $2,000. **Remarks:** Part-time maker, full-time hobby, first knife sold in 2009. **Mark:** TR.

THAYER, DANNY O
8908S 100W, Romney, IN 47981 **Contact:** 765-538-3105, dot61h@juno.com, thayerknives.com, Instagram @thayer_knives
Specialties: Hunters, fighters, bowies. **Technical:** Forges carbon steels and his own pattern welded steels. **Prices:** $350 to $5000.

THEVENOT, JEAN-PAUL
16 Rue De La Prefecture, Dijon, FRANCE 21000
Specialties: Traditional European knives and daggers. **Patterns:** Hunters, utility-camp knives, daggers, historical or modern style. **Technical:** Forges own damascus, 5160, 1084. **Remarks:** Part-time maker. ABS Master Smith. **Mark:** Interlocked initials in square.

THIE, BRIAN
13250 150th St, Burlington, IA 52601 **Contact:** 319-850-2188, thieknives@gmail.com, mepotelco.net/web/tknives
Specialties: Working using knives from basic to fancy. **Patterns:** Hunters, fighters, camp and folders. **Technical:** Forges blades and own damascus. **Prices:** $250 and up. **Remarks:** ABS Journeyman Smith, part-time maker. Sole author of blades including forging, heat treat, engraving and sheath making. **Mark:** Last name hand engraved into the blade, JS stamped into blade.

THILL, JIM
9325 Bear Run Trl., Missoula, MT 59803 **Contact:** 406-251-5475, bearrunmt@hotmail.com
Specialties: Traditional and working/using knives of his design. **Patterns:** Fighters, hunters and utility/camp knives. **Technical:** Grinds D2 and ATS-34, forges 10-95-85, 52100, 5160, 10 series, reg. damascus-mosaic. Offers hand cut sheaths with rawhide lace. **Prices:** $145 to $350, some to $1250. **Remarks:** Full-time maker, first knife sold in 1962. **Mark:** Running bear in triangle.

THOMAS, BOB
Sunset Forge, 3502 Bay Rd., Ferndale, WA 98248 **Contact:** 360-201-0160, (fax) 360-366-5723, sunsetforge@rockisland.com

THOMAS, DAVID E
8502 Hwy 91, Lillian, AL 36549 **Contact:** 251-961-7574, redbluff@gulftel.com
Specialties: bowies and hunters. **Technical:** Hand forged blades in 5160, 1095 and own damascus. **Prices:** $400 and up. **Mark:** Stylized DT, maker's last name, serial number.

THOMAS, DEVIN
PO Box 568, Panaca, NV 89042 **Contact:** 775-728-4363, hoss@devinthomas.com, devinthomas.com
Specialties: Traditional straight knives and folders in standard patterns. **Patterns:** bowies, fighters, hunters. **Technical:** Forges stainless damascus, nickel and 1095. Uses, makes and sells mokume with brass, copper and nickel-silver. **Prices:** $300 to $1200. **Remarks:** Full-time maker, first knife sold in 1979. **Mark:** First and last name, city and state with anvil, or first name only.

THOMAS, KIM
PO Box 531, Seville, OH 44273 **Contact:** 330-769-9906
Specialties: Fancy and traditional straight knives of his design and to customer specs,

custom knifemakers

period pieces. **Patterns:** Boots, daggers, fighters, swords. **Technical:** Forges own damascus from 5160, 1010 and nickel. **Prices:** $135 to $1500, some to $3000. **Remarks:** Part-time maker, first knife sold in 1986. Doing business as Thomas Iron Works. **Mark:** KT.

THOMAS, ROCKY
1716 Waterside Blvd, Moncks Corner, SC 29461 **Contact:** 843-761-7761
Specialties: Traditional working knives in standard patterns. **Patterns:** Hunters and utility/camp knives. **Technical:** ATS-34 and commercial damascus. **Prices:** $130 to $350. **Remarks:** Spare-time maker, first knife sold in 1986. **Mark:** First name in script and/or block.

THOMPSON, KENNETH
4887 Glenwhite Dr, Duluth, GA 30136 **Contact:** 770-446-6730
Specialties: Traditional working and using knives of his design. **Patterns:** Hunters, bowies and utility/camp knives. **Technical:** Forges 5168, O1, 1095 and 52100. **Prices:** $75 to $1500, some to $2500. **Remarks:** Part-time maker, first knife sold in 1990. **Mark:** P/W, or name, P/W, city and state.

THOMPSON, LEON
3400 S.W. Dilley Rd., Forest Grove, OR 97116 **Contact:** 503-357-2573, lsthomp@msn.com
Specialties: Working knives. **Patterns:** Locking folders, slip-joints and liner locks. **Technical:** Grinds ATS-34, D2 and 440C. **Prices:** $450 to $1000. **Remarks:** Full-time maker, first knife sold in 1976. **Mark:** First and middle initials, last name, city and state.

THOMPSON, LLOYD
PO Box 1664, Pagosa Springs, CO 81147 **Contact:** 970-264-5837
Specialties: Working and collectible straight knives and folders of his design. **Patterns:** Straight blades, lock back folders and slip joint folders. **Technical:** Hollow-grinds ATS-34, D2 and O1. Uses sambar stag and exotic woods. **Prices:** $150 to upscale. **Remarks:** Full-time maker, first knife sold in 1985. Doing business as Trapper Creek Knife Co. **Remarks:** Offers three-day knife-making classes. **Mark:** Name.

THOMPSON, TOMMY
4015 NE Hassalo, Portland, OR 97232-2607 **Contact:** 503-235-5762
Specialties: Fancy and working knives, mostly liner-lock folders. **Patterns:** Fighters, hunters and liner locks. **Technical:** Grinds D2, ATS-34, CPM440V and T15. Handles are either hardwood inlaid with wood banding and stone or shell, or made of agate, jasper, petrified woods, etc. **Prices:** $75 to $500, some to $1000. **Remarks:** Part-time maker, first knife sold in 1987. Doing business as Stone Birds. Knife making temporarily stopped due to family obligations. **Mark:** First and last name, city and state.

THOMSEN, LOYD W
25241 Renegade Pass, Custer, SD 57730 **Contact:** 605-673-2787, loydt@yahoo.com, horseheadcreekknives.com
Specialties: High-art and traditional working/using straight knives and presentation pieces of his design and to customer specs, period pieces. Hand carved animals in crown of stag on handles and carved display stands. **Patterns:** bowies, hunters, daggers and utility/camp knives. **Technical:** Forges and grinds 1095HC, 1084, L6, 15N20, 440C stainless steel, nickel 200, special restoration process on period pieces. Makes sheaths. Uses natural materials for handles. **Prices:** $350 to $1000. **Remarks:** Full-time maker, first knife sold in 1995. Doing business as Horsehead Creek Knives. **Mark:** Initials and last name over a horse's head.

THORBURN, ANDRE E.
P.O. Box 1748, Bela Bela, Warmbaths, LP, SOUTH AFRICA 0480 **Contact:** 27-82-650-1441, (fax) 27-86-750-2765, andrethorburn@gmail.com, thorburnknives.co.za
Specialties: Working and fancy folders of own design to customer specs. **Technical:** Uses RWL-34, Damasteel, CPM steels, Bohler N690, and carbon and stainless damascus. **Prices:** Starting at $350. **Remarks:** Full-time maker since 1996, first knife sold in 1990. Member of South African, Italian, and German guilds. **Mark:** Initials and name in a double circle.

THOUROT, MICHAEL W
T-814 Co Rd 11, Napoleon, OH 43545 **Contact:** 419-533-6832, (fax) 419-533-3516, mike2row@henry-net.com, safariknives.com
Specialties: Working straight knives to customer specs. Designed two-handled skinning ax and limited edition engraved knife and art print set. **Patterns:** Fishing and fillet knives, bowies, tantos and hunters. **Technical:** Grinds O1, D2, 440C and damascus. **Prices:** $200 to $5000. **Remarks:** Part-time maker, first knife sold in 1968. **Mark:** Initials.

THUESEN, ED
21211 Knolle Rd, Damon, TX 77430 **Contact:** 979-553-1211, (fax) 979-553-1211
Specialties: Working straight knives. **Patterns:** Hunters, fighters and survival knives. **Technical:** Grinds D2, 440C, ATS-34 and Vascowear. **Prices:** $150 to $275, some to $600. **Remarks:** Part-time maker, first knife sold in 1979. Runs knifemaker supply business. **Mark:** Last name in script.

TIENSVOLD, ALAN L
PO Box 355, 3277 U.S. Hwy. 20, Rushville, NE 69360 **Contact:** 308-360-0613, tiensvoldknives@gpcom.net
Specialties: Working knives, tomahawks and period pieces, high end damascus knives. **Patterns:** Random, ladder, twist and many more. **Technical:** Hand forged blades, forges own damascus. **Prices:** Working knives start at $300. **Remarks:** Received Journeyman rating with the ABS in 2002. Does own engraving and fine work. **Mark:** Tiensvold hand made U.S.A. on left side, JS on right.

TIENSVOLD, JASON
PO Box 795, Rushville, NE 69360 **Contact:** 308-360-2217, jasontiensvoldknives@yahoo.com

Specialties: Working and using straight knives of his design, period pieces. Gentlemen folders, art folders. Single action automatics. **Patterns:** Hunters, skinners, bowies, fighters, daggers, liner locks. **Technical:** Forges own damascus using 15N20 and 1084, 1095, nickel, custom file work. **Prices:** $200 to $4000. **Remarks:** Full-time maker, first knife sold in 1994, doing business under Tiensvold Custom Knives. **Mark:** J. Tiensvold on left side, MS on right.

TIGHE, BRIAN
12-111 Fourth Ave, Suite 376 Ridley Square, St. Catharines, ON, CANADA L2S 3P5 **Contact:** 905-892-2734, tigheknives.com
Specialties: Folding knives, bearing pivots. High tech tactical folders. **Patterns:** Boots, daggers and locking. **Technical:** BG-42, RWL-34, Damasteel, 154CM, S30V, CPM 440V and CPM 420V. Prefers natural handle material inlay, hand finishes. **Prices:** $450 to $4000. **Remarks:** Full-time maker, first knife sold in 1989. **Mark:** Etched signature.

TILL, CALVIN E AND RUTH
1010 Maple St., Lot 4, Chadron, NE 69337-6967 **Contact:** 308-430-2231
Specialties: Straight knives, hunters, bowies, no folders **Patterns:** Training point, drop point hunters, bowies. **Technical:** ATS-34 sub zero quench RC59, 61. **Prices:** $700 to $1200. **Remarks:** Sells only the absolute best knives they can make. Manufactures every part in their knives. **Mark:** RC Till. The R is for Ruth, the C for Calvin.

TILTON, JOHN
24041 Hwy 383, Iowa, LA 70647 **Contact:** 337-582-6785, john@jetknives.com
Specialties: bowies, camp knives, skinners and folders. **Technical:** All forged blades. Makes own damascus. **Prices:** $150 and up. **Remarks:** ABS Journeyman Smith. **Mark:** Initials J.E.T.

TINDERA, GEORGE
BURNING RIVER FORGE, 751 Hadcock Rd, Brunswick, OH 44212-2648 **Contact:** 330-220-6212
Specialties: Straight knives, his designs. **Patterns:** Personal knives, classic bowies and fighters. **Technical:** Hand-forged high-carbon, his own cable and pattern welded damascus. **Prices:** $125 to $600. **Remarks:** Spare-time maker, sold first knife in 1995. Natural handle materials.

TINGLE, DENNIS P
19390 E Clinton Rd, Jackson, CA 95642 **Contact:** 209-223-4586, dtknives@earthlink.net
Specialties: Swords, fixed blades: small to medium, tomahawks. **Technical:** All blades forged. **Remarks:** ABS, JS. **Mark:** D. Tingle over JS.

TIPPETTS, COLTEN
4515 W. Long Meadow Dr., Hidden Springs, ID 83714 **Contact:** 208-473-1474, coltentippetts@gmail.com, ctknives.webs.com
Specialties: Fancy and working fixed blades and folders of his own design or to customer specifications. **Patterns:** Hunters and skinners, fighters, tactical blades and lockback folders. **Technical:** Grinds BG-42 and CPM S30V, and forges O1. **Prices:** $200 to $1,000. **Remarks:** Full-time maker, first knife sold in 1996. **Mark:** Fused initials.

TOBOLAK, LIBOR
NO COMPROMISE DESIGN, 635 N. Twin Oaks Valley Rd., Ste. 20, San Marcos, CA 92069 **Contact:** 201-668-9885, nocompromisedesign@gmail.com, nocompromisedesign.com, Facebook: No Compromise Design

TODD, RICHARD C
375th LN 46001, Chambersburg, IL 62323 **Contact:** 217-327-4380, ktodd45@yahoo.com
Specialties: Multi blade folders and silver sheaths. **Patterns:** Jewel setting and hand engraving. **Mark:** RT with letter R crossing the T or R Todd.

TOICH, NEVIO
Via Pisacane 9, Rettorgole di Caldogna, Vincenza, ITALY 36030 **Contact:** 0444-985065, (fax) 0444-301254
Specialties: Working/using straight knives of his design or to customer specs. **Patterns:** bowies, hunters, skinners and utility/camp knives. **Technical:** Grinds 440C, D2 and ATS-34. Hollow-grinds all blades and uses mirror polish. Offers hand-sewn sheaths. Uses wood and horn. **Prices:** $120 to $300, some to $450. **Remarks:** Spare-time maker, first knife sold in 1989. Doing business as Custom Toich. **Mark:** Initials and model number punched.

TOKAR, DANIEL
Box 1776, Shepherdstown, WV 25443
Specialties: Working knives, period pieces. **Patterns:** Hunters, camp knives, buckskinners, axes, swords and battle gear. **Technical:** Forges L6, 1095 and his damascus, makes mokume, Japanese alloys and bronze daggers, restores old edged weapons. **Prices:** $25 to $800, some to $3000. **Remarks:** Part-time maker, first knife sold in 1979. Doing business as The Willow Forge. **Mark:** Arrow over rune and date.

TOMBERLIN, BRION R
ANVIL TOP CUSTOM KNIVES, 825 W Timberdell, Norman, OK 73072 **Contact:** 405-202-6832, anviltopp@aol.com
Specialties: Handforged blades, working pieces, standard classic patterns, some swords and customer designs. **Patterns:** bowies, hunters, fighters, Persian and eastern-styles. Likes Japanese blades. **Technical:** Forges 1050, 1075, 1084, 1095, 5160, some forged stainless, also does some stock removal in stainless. Also makes own damascus. **Prices:** $350 to $4,000 or higher for swords and custom pieces. **Remarks:** Part-time maker, ABS master smith. Prefers natural handle materials, hand-rubbed finishes. Likes temper lines. **Mark:** BRION with MS.

TOMEY, KATHLEEN
146 Buford Pl, Macon, GA 31204 **Contact:** 478-746-8454, ktomey@tomeycustomknives.com, tomeycustomknives.com

Specialties: Working hunters, skinners, daily users in fixed blades, plain and embellished. Tactical neck and belt carry. Japanese influenced. bowies. **Technical:** Grinds O1, ATS-34, flat or hollow grind, filework, satin and mirror polish finishes. High quality leather sheaths with tooling. Kydex with tactical. **Prices:** $150 to $500. **Remarks:** Almost full-time maker. **Mark:** Last name in diamond.

TONER, ROGER
531 Lightfoot Pl, Pickering, ON, CANADA L1V 5Z8 **Contact:** 905-420-5555
Specialties: Exotic sword canes. **Patterns:** bowies, daggers and fighters. **Technical:** Grinds 440C, D2 and damascus. Scrimshaws and engraves. Silver cast pommels and guards in animal shapes, twisted silver wire inlays. Uses semi-precious stones. **Prices:** $200 to $2000, some to $3000. **Remarks:** Part-time maker, first knife sold in 1982. **Mark:** Last name.

TORRES, HENRY
2329 Moody Ave., Clovis, CA 93619 **Contact:** 559-297-9154, htknives.com
Specialties: Forged high-performance hunters and working knives, bowies, and fighters. **Technical:** 52100 and 5160 and makes own damascus. **Prices:** $350 to $3000. **Remarks:** Started forging in 2004. Has mastersmith with American Bladesmith Association.

TOSHIFUMI, KURAMOTO
3435 Higashioda, Asakura-gun, Fukuoka, JAPAN **Contact:** 0946-42-4470

TOWELL, DWIGHT L
2375 Towell Rd, Midvale, ID 83645 **Contact:** 208-355-2419
Specialties: Solid, elegant working knives, art knives, high quality hand engraving and gold inlay. **Patterns:** Hunters, bowies, daggers and folders. **Technical:** Grinds 154CM, ATS-34, 440C and other maker's damascus. **Prices:** Upscale. **Remarks:** Full-time maker. First knife sold in 1970. Member of AKI. **Mark:** Towell, sometimes hand engraved.

TOWNSEND, ALLEN MARK
6 Pine Trail, Texarkana, AR 71854 **Contact:** 870-772-8945

TOWNSLEY, RUSSELL
PO BOX 91, Floral, AR 72534-0091 **Contact:** 870-307-8069, circleTRMtownsley@yahoo.com
Specialties: Using knives of his own design. **Patterns:** Hunters, skinners, folders. **Technical:** Hollow grinds D2 and O1. Handle material - antler, tusk, bone, exotic woods. **Prices:** Prices start at $125. **Remarks:** Arkansas knifemakers association. Sold first knife in 2009. Doing business as Circle-T knives. **Mark:** Encircled T.

TRACE RINALDI CUSTOM BLADES
1470 Underpass Rd, Plummer, ID 83851, Trace@thrblades.com, thrblades.com
Technical: Grinds S30V, 3V, A2 and talonite fixed blades. **Prices:** $300-$1000. **Remarks:** Tactical and utility for the most part. **Mark:** Diamond with THR inside.

TRIBBLE, SKYLAR
Cold Handle Custom Knives, 1413 Alabama St., Leakesville, MS 39451 **Contact:** 601-394-3490, skylartribble@yahoo.com
Specialties: Fixed blades and friction folders. **Patterns:** Small to large and everything in between. **Technical:** Uses repurposed steel, carbon flat stock, stainless flat stock and damascus. Steels of all sorts, carbon is specialty. Does both stock removal and forging, saying its up to the customer. **Prices:** $85 to $800). **Remarks:** Part-time maker, full-time student, first knife made and sold in 2009 at the age of 13. **Mark:** C with H and K on the tail of the C (for Cold Handle Custom Knives).

TRINDLE, BARRY
1660 Ironwood Trail, Earlham, IA 50072-8611 **Contact:** 515-462-1237
Specialties: Engraved folders. **Patterns:** Mostly small folders, classical-styles and pocket knives. **Technical:** 440 only. Engraves. Handles of wood or mineral material. **Prices:** Start at $1000. **Mark:** Name on tang.

TRISLER, KENNETH W
6256 Federal 80, Rayville, LA 71269 **Contact:** 318-728-5541

TRITZ, JEAN-JOSE
Pinneberger Chaussee 48, Hamburg, GERMANY 22523 **Contact:** +49(40) 49 78 21, jeanjosetritz@aol.com, tritz-messer.com
Specialties: Scandinavian knives, Japanese kitchen knives, friction folders, swords. **Patterns:** Puukkos, Tollekniven, Hocho, friction folders, swords. **Technical:** Forges tool steels, carbon steels, 52100 damascus, mokume, San Maj. **Prices:** $200 to $2000, some higher. **Remarks:** Full-time maker, first knife sold in 1989. Does own leatherwork, prefers natural materials. Sole authorship. Speaks French, German, English, Norwegian. **Mark:** Initials in monogram.

TROUT, GEORGE H.
727 Champlin Rd, Wilmington, OH 45177 **Contact:** 937-382-2331, gandjtrout@msn.com
Specialties: Working knives, some fancy. **Patterns:** Hunters, drop points, bowies and fighters. **Technical:** Stock removal: ATS-34, 440C Forged: 5160, W2, 1095, O1 Full integrals: 440C, A2, O1. **Prices:** $150 and up. **Remarks:** Makes own sheaths and mosaic pins. Fileworks most knives. First knife 1985. **Mark:** "G. Trout Knives" engraved on blade. Previous mark: Etched name and state on stock removal, forged, stamped name and forged.

TRUJILLO, ALBERT M B
2035 Wasmer Cir, Bosque Farms, NM 87068 **Contact:** 505-869-0428, trujilloscutups@comcast.net
Specialties: Working/using straight knives of his design or to customer specs. **Patterns:** Hunters, skinners, fighters, working/using knives. File work offered. **Technical:** Grinds ATS-34, D2, 440C, S30V. Tapers tangs, all blades cryogenically treated. **Prices:** $75 to $500.

Remarks: Part-time maker, first knife sold in 1997. **Mark:** First and last name under logo.

TRUNCALI, PETE
966 Harmony Circle, Nevada, TX 75173 **Contact:** 214-763-7127, truncaliknives@yahoo.com, truncaliknives.com
Specialties: Lockback folders and automatics. Does business as Truncali Custom Knives.

TSCHAGER, REINHARD
S. Maddalena di Sotto 1a, Bolzano, ITALY 39100 **Contact:** 0471-975005, (fax) 0471-975005, reinhardtschager@virgilio.it
Specialties: Classic, high-art, collector-grade straight knives of his design. **Patterns:** Jewel knife, daggers, and hunters. **Technical:** Grinds ATS-34, D2 and damascus. Oval pins. Gold inlay. Offers engraving. **Prices:** $900 to $2000, some to $3000. **Remarks:** Spare-time maker, first knife sold in 1979. **Mark:** Gold inlay stamped with initials.

TUCH, ERIC
4145 NE Cully Blvd., Portland, OR 97218 **Contact:** 503-593-9160

TUCH, WILLIAM
4145 NE Cully Blvd., Portland, OR 97218 **Contact:** 503-504-1261, tuchknives@gmail.com, tuchknives.com
Specialties: Folding knives and daggers, mostly ornate. **Patterns:** One-of-a-kind locking knives, lockbacks, side locks, switchblades, miniatures and more. **Technical:** Flat and hollow grinds, ornate sculpture. All knives are hand filed and hand polished. Materials vary. **Prices:** $1,800 to $10,000 and up. **Remarks:** Full-time maker since 2004. **Mark:** TUCH.

TUOMINEN, PEKKA
Pohjois-Keiteleentie 20, Tossavanlahti, FINLAND 72930 **Contact:** 358405167853, puukkopekka@luukku.com, puukkopekka.com
Specialties: Puukko knives. **Patterns:** Puukkos, hunters, leukus, and folders. **Technical:** Forges silversteel, 1085, 52100, and makes own damascus 15N20 and 1095. Grinds RWL-34 and ATS-34. **Prices:** Starting at $300. **Remarks:** Full-time maker. **Mark:** PEKKA, earlier whole name.

TURECEK, JIM
12 Elliott Rd, Ansonia, CT 06401 **Contact:** 203-734-8406, jturecek@sbcglobal.net
Specialties: Exotic folders, art knives and some miniatures. **Patterns:** Trout and bird knives with split bamboo handles and one-of-a-kind folders. **Technical:** Grinds and forges stainless and carbon damascus. All knives are handmade using no computer-controlled machinery. **Prices:** $2,000 to $10,000. **Remarks:** Full-time maker, first knife sold in 1983. **Mark:** Last initial in script, or last name.

TURNBULL, RALPH A
14464 Linden Dr, Spring Hill, FL 34609 **Contact:** 352-688-7089, tbull2000@bellsouth.net, turnbullknives.com
Specialties: Fancy folders. **Patterns:** Primarily gents pocket knives. **Technical:** Wire EDM work on bolsters. **Prices:** $300 and up. **Remarks:** Full-time maker, first knife sold in 1973. **Mark:** Signature or initials.

TURNER, KEVIN
17 Hunt Ave, Montrose, NY 10548 **Contact:** 914-739-0535
Specialties: Working straight knives of his design and to customer specs, period pieces. **Patterns:** Daggers, fighters and utility knives. **Technical:** Forges 5160 and 52100. **Prices:** $90 to $500. **Remarks:** Part-time maker, first knife sold in 1991. **Mark:** Acid-etched signed last name and year.

TURNER, MIKE
3065 Cedar Flat Rd., Williams, OR 97544 **Contact:** 541-846-0204, mike@turnerknives.com turnerknives.com
Specialties: Forged and stock removed full tang, hidden and thru tang knives. **Patterns:** Hunters, fighters, bowies, boot knives, skinners and kitchen knives. **Technical:** I make my own damascus. **Prices:** $200 - $1,000. **Remarks:** Part-time maker, sold my first knife in 2008, doing business as Mike Turner Custom Knives. **Mark:** Name, City, & State.

TYRE, MICHAEL A
1219 Easy St, Wickenburg, AZ 85390 **Contact:** 928-684-9601/602-377-8432, mtyre86@gmail.com, miketyrecustomknives.com
Specialties: Quality folding knives, upscale gents folders, one-of-a-kind collectable models. **Patterns:** Working fixed blades for hunting, kitchen and fancy bowies. Forging my own damascus patterns. **Technical:** Grinds, prefers hand-rubbed satin finishes and uses natural handle materials. **Prices:** $250 to $1,300. **Remarks:** ABS journeyman smith.

TYSER, ROSS
1015 Hardee Court, Spartanburg, SC 29303 **Contact:** 864-585-7616
Specialties: Traditional working and using straight knives and folders of his design and in standard patterns. **Patterns:** bowies, hunters and slip-joint folders. **Technical:** Grinds 440C and commercial damascus. Mosaic pins, stone inlay. Does filework and scrimshaw. Offers engraving and cut-work and some inlay on sheaths. **Prices:** $45 to $125, some to $400. **Remarks:** Part-time maker, first knife sold in 1995. Doing business as RT Custom Knives. **Mark:** Stylized initials.

U

UCHIDA, CHIMATA
977-2 Oaza Naga Shisui Ki, Kumamoto, JAPAN 861-1204

UPTON, TOM
Little Rabbit Forge, 1414 Feast Pl., Rogers, AR 72758 **Contact:** 479-636-6755, upton-knives.com
Specialties: Working fixed blades. **Patterns:** Hunters, utility, fighters, bowies and small

hatchets. **Technical:** Forges 5160, 1084 and W2 blade steels, or stock removal using D2, 440C and 154CM. Performs own heat treat. **Prices:** $150 and up. **Remarks:** Part-time maker, first knife sold in 1977. Member of the Knife Group Association. **Mark:** Name (Small Rabbit logo), city and state, etched or stamped.

URBACH, SCOTT
Laughing Coyote Knives. 19135 E. Oxford Dr., Aurora, CO 80013 **Contact:** 303-882-1875, laughingcoyoteknives@gmail.com, facebook.com/laughingcoyoteknivescolorado
Specialties: Unique hard-use working knives. **Patterns:** Western, cowboy and traditional/historic bowies, fighters, mountain man styles, camp knives and hunters. **Technical:** Customer's choice of steel, from high-end carbon to custom damascus, including natural handle material, and custom leather or Kydex sheaths. Specializes in repurposing discarded steel from old saws, kitchen knives, auto parts, etc., as well as repairing damaged knives that would otherwise be discarded. **Prices:** $95 to $300+. **Remarks:** Part-time maker looking to transition to full time, first knife sold in 2014. **Mark:** Petroglyph coyote logo with Urbach (last name).

V

VAGNINO, MICHAEL
1415 W. Ashland Ave., Visalia, CA 93277 **Contact:** 559-636-0501, cell: 559-827-7802, mike@mvknives.com, mvknives.com
Specialties: Folders and straight knives, working and fancy. **Patterns:** Folders--locking liners, slip joints, lock backs, double and single action autos. Straight knives--hunters, bowies, camp and kitchen. **Technical:** Forges 52100, W2, 15N20 and 1084. Grinds stainless. Makes own damascus and does engraving. **Prices:** $300 to $4,000 and above. **Remarks:** Full-time maker, ABS Mastersmith. **Mark:** Logo, last name.

VAIL, DAVE
554 Sloop Point Rd, Hampstead, NC 28443 **Contact:** 910-270-4456
Specialties: Working/using straight knives of his own design or to the customer's specs. **Patterns:** Hunters/skinners, camp/utility, fillet, bowies. **Technical:** Grinds ATS-34, 440c, 154 CM and 1095 carbon steel. **Prices:** $90 to $450. **Remarks:** Part-time maker. Member of NC Custom Knifemakers Guild. **Mark:** Etched oval with "Dave Vail Hampstead NC" inside.

VALLOTTON, RAINY D
1295 Wolf Valley Dr, Umpqua, OR 97486 **Contact:** 541-459-0465
Specialties: Folders, one-handed openers and art pieces. **Patterns:** All patterns. **Technical:** Stock removal all steels, uses titanium liners and bolsters, uses all finishes. **Prices:** $350 to $3500. **Remarks:** Full-time maker. **Mark:** Name.

VALLOTTON, THOMAS
621 Fawn Ridge Dr, Oakland, OR 97462 **Contact:** 541-459-2216
Specialties: Custom autos. **Patterns:** Tactical, fancy. **Technical:** File work, uses damascus, uses Spectrum Metal. **Prices:** From $350 to $700. **Remarks:** Full-time maker. Maker of ProtŽgé 3 canoe. **Mark:** T and a V mingled.

VAN CLEVE, STEVE
Box 372, Sutton, AK 99674 **Contact:** 907-745-3038, (fax) 907-745-8770, sucents@mtaonline.net, alaskaknives.net

VAN DE BRUINHORST, JACCO
JVB Knives 496953 10th Line, Tavistock, Ontario N0B 2R0 Canada **Contact:** 519-441-7395, vdb.jacco@gmail.com, www.jvbknives.com
Patterns: Hunting knives.

VAN DE MANAKKER, THIJS
Koolweg 34, Holland, NETHERLANDS **Contact:** 0493539369, ehijsvandemanakker.com
Specialties: Classic high-art knives. **Patterns:** Swords, utility/camp knives and period pieces. **Technical:** Forges soft iron, carbon steel and Bloomery Iron. Makes own damascus, Bloomery Iron and patterns. **Prices:** $20 to $2000, some higher. **Remarks:** Full-time maker, first knife sold in 1969. **Mark:** Stylized "V."

VAN DEN BERG, NEELS
166 Van Heerdan St., Capital Park, Pretoria, Gauteng, SOUTH AFRICA **Contact:** +27(0)12-326-5649 or +27(0)83-451-3105, neels@blackdragonforge.com, blackdragonforge.com, facebook.com/neels.vandenberg
Specialties: Handforged damascus and high-carbon steel axes, hunters, swords and art knives. **Patterns:** All my own designs and customer collaborations, from axes, hunters, choppers, bowies, swords and folders to one-off tactical prototypes. **Technical:** Flat and hollow grinding. Handforges high-carbon steels and maker's own damascus. Also works in high-carbon stainless steels. **Prices:** $50 to $1,000. **Remarks:** Part-time maker, first knife sold in Oct. 2009. **Mark:** Stylized capital letter "N" resembling a three-tier mountain, normally hot stamped in forged blades.

VAN DEN ELSEN, GERT
Purcelldreef 83, Tilburg, NETHERLANDS 5012 AJ **Contact:** 013-4563200, gvdelsen@home.nl
Specialties: Fancy, working/using, miniatures and integral straight knives of the maker's design or to customer specs. **Patterns:** bowies, fighters, hunters and Japanese-style blades. **Technical:** Grinds ATS-34 and 440C, forges damascus. Offers filework, differentially tempered blades and some mokume-gane fittings. **Prices:** $350 to $1000, some to $4000. **Remarks:** Part-time maker, first knife sold in 1982. Doing business as G-E Knives. **Mark:** Initials GE in lozenge shape.

VAN DER WESTHUIZEN, PETER
PO Box 1698, Mossel Bay, SC, SOUTH AFRICA 6500 **Contact:** 27 446952388, pietvdw@telkomsa.net

Specialties: Working knives, folders, daggers and art knives. **Patterns:** Hunters, skinners, bird, trout and sidelock folders. **Technical:** Sandvik, 12627. damascus indigenous wood and ivory. **Prices:** From $450 to $5500. **Remarks:** First knife sold in 1987. Full-time since 1996. **Mark:** Initial & surname. Handmade RSA.

VAN DIJK, RICHARD
76 Stepney Ave Rd 2, Harwood Dunedin, NEW ZEALAND **Contact:** 0064-3-4780401, hoihoknives.com
Specialties: damascus, Fantasy knives, sgiandubhs, dirks, swords, and hunting knives. **Patterns:** Mostly one-offs, anything from bird and trout to swords, no folders. **Technical:** Forges mainly own damascus, some 5160, O1, 1095, L6. Prefers natural handle materials, over 40 years experience as goldsmith, handle fittings are often made from sterling silver and sometimes gold, manufactured to cap the handle, use gemstones if required. Makes own sheaths. **Prices:** $300 and up. **Remarks:** Full-time maker, first knife sold in 1980. Doing business as HOIHO KNIVES. **Mark:** Stylized initials RvD in triangle.

VAN EIZENGA, JERRY W
14281 Cleveland, Nunica, MI 49448 **Contact:** 616-638-2275
Specialties: Hand forged blades, Scagel patterns and other styles. **Patterns:** Camp, hunting, bird, trout, folders, axes, miniatures. **Technical:** 5160, 52100, 1084. **Prices:** Start at $250. **Remarks:** Part-time maker, sole author of knife and sheath. First knife made 1970s. ABS member who believes in the beauty of simplicity. **Mark:** J.S. stamp.

VAN ELDIK, FRANS
Ho Flaan 3, Loenen, NETHERLANDS 3632 BT **Contact:** 0031 294 233 095, (fax) 0031 294 233 095
Specialties: Fancy collector-grade straight knives and folders of his design. **Patterns:** Hunters, fighters, boots and folders. **Technical:** Forges and grinds D2, 154CM, ATS-34 and stainless damascus. **Prices:** Start at $450. **Remarks:** Spare-time maker, first knife sold in 1979. Knifemaker 30 years, 25 year member of Knifemakers Guild. **Mark:** Lion with name and Amsterdam.

VAN HEERDEN, ANDRE
P.O. Box 905-417, Garsfontein, Pretoria, GT, SOUTH AFRICA 0042 **Contact:** 27 82 566 6030, andrevh@iafrica.com, a2knives.com
Specialties: Tactical, tactical gent, working folders of his own design. **Technical:** Grinds M390, CTS-XHP, RWL34, and Damasteel. **Prices:** Starting at $695. **Remarks:** Part-time maker, collaborates with Andre Thorburn in A2 Knives. **Mark:** Initials and name in a double circle.

VAN REENEN, IAN
6003 Harvard St, Amarillo, TX 79109 **Contact:** 806-236-8333, ianvanreenen@suddenlink.net ianvanreenencustomknives.com
Specialties: Pocketknives and hunting knives. **Patterns:** Tactical pocketknives. **Technical:** 14C28N, 12C27 and ATS-34 blade steels. **Prices:** $600 to $1,500. **Remarks:** Specializing in tactical pocketknives. **Mark:** IVR with TEXAS underneath.

VAN RYSWYK, AAD
AVR KNIVES, Werf Van Pronk 8, Vlaardingen, NETHERLANDS 3134 HE **Contact:** +31 10 4742952, info@avrknives.com, avrknives.com
Specialties: High-art interframe folders of his design. **Patterns:** Hunters and locking folders. **Technical:** Uses semi-precious stones, mammoth ivory, iron wood, etc. **Prices:** $550 to $3800. **Remarks:** Full-time maker, first knife sold in 1993.

VANCE, DAVID
2646 Bays Bend Rd., West Liberty, KY 41472 **Contact:** 606-743-1465 and 606-362-8339, dtvance@mrtc.com, facebook.com/ddcutlery
Specialties: Custom hunting or collectible knives, folders and fixed blades, also unique bullet casing handle pins and filework. **Patterns:** Maker's design or made to customers' specifications. **Technical:** Uses stock removal method on 1095 steel. **Remarks:** Part-time maker, first knife made in 2006. **Mark:** Cursive D&D.

VANDERFORD, CARL G
2290 Knob Creek Rd, Columbia, TN 38401 **Contact:** 931-381-1488
Specialties: Traditional working straight knives and folders of his design. **Patterns:** Hunters, bowies and locking folders. **Technical:** Forges and grinds 440C, O1 and wire damascus. **Prices:** $60 to $125. **Remarks:** Part-time maker, first knife sold in 1987. **Mark:** Last name.

VANDERKOLFF, STEPHEN
5 Jonathan Crescent, Mildmay, ON, CANADA N0g 2JO **Contact:** 519-367-3401, steve@vanderkolffknives.com, vanderkolffknives.com
Specialties: Fixed blades from gent's pocketknives and drop hunters to full sized bowies and art knives. **Technical:** Primary blade steel 440C, Damasteel or custom made damascus. All heat treat done by maker and all blades hardness tested. Handle material: stag, stabilized woods or MOP. **Prices:** $150 to $1200. **Remarks:** Started making knives in 1998 and sold first knife in 2000. Winner of the best of show art knife 2005 Wolverine Knife Show.

VANDEVENTER, TERRY L
1915 Timberlake Pl., Byram, MS 39272 **Contact:** 601-371-7414, vandeventerterry@gmail.com, vandeventerknives.com
Specialties: Bowies, hunters, camp knives, friction folders. **Technical:** 1084, 1095, 15N20 and L6 steels. damascus and mokume. Natural handle materials. **Prices:** $1200 to $5000. **Remarks:** Sole author, makes everything here. First ABS MS from the state of Mississippi. **Mark:** Vandeventer (silhouette of snake underneath). MS on ricasso.

VANHOY, ED AND TANYA
24255 N Fork River Rd, Abingdon, VA 24210 **Contact:** 276-944-4885, vanhoyknives@centurylink.net

Specialties: Traditional and working/using straight knives and folders and innovative locking mechanisms. **Patterns:** Fighters, straight knives, folders, hunters, art knives and bowies. **Technical:** Grinds ATS-34 and carbon/stainless steel damascus, forges carbon and stainless damascus. Offers filework and engraving with hammer and chisel. **Prices:** $250 to $3000. **Remarks:** Full-time maker, first knife sold in 1977. Wife also engraves. Doing business as Van Hoy Custom Knives. **Mark:** Acid etched last name.

VARDAMAN, ROBERT
2406 Mimosa Lane, Hattiesburg, MS 39402 **Contact:** 601-268-3889, rvx222@gmail.com
Specialties: Working straight knives, mainly integrals, of his design or to customer specs. **Patterns:** Mainly integrals, bowies and hunters. **Technical:** Forges 52100, W2 and 1084. Filework. **Prices:** $250 to $1,000. **Remarks:** Part-time maker. First knife sold in 2004. **Mark:** Last name, last name with Mississippi state logo.

VASQUEZ, JOHNNY DAVID
1552 7th St, Wyandotte, MI 48192 **Contact:** 734-837-7733, trollhammerv@aol.com

VEIT, MICHAEL
3289 E Fifth Rd, LaSalle, IL 61301 **Contact:** 815-223-3538, whitebear@starband.net
Specialties: damascus folders. **Technical:** Engraver, sole author. **Prices:** $2500 to $6500. **Remarks:** Part-time maker, first knife sold in 1985. **Mark:** Name in script.

VELARDE, RICARDO
7240 N Greenfield Dr, Park City, UT 84098 **Contact:** 435-901-1773, velardeknives@mac.com velardeknives.com
Specialties: Investment grade integrals and interfrains. **Patterns:** Boots, fighters and hunters, hollow grind. **Technical:** BG on Integrals. **Prices:** $1450 to $5200. **Remarks:** First knife sold in 1992. **Mark:** First initial and last name.

VELICK, SAMMY
3457 Maplewood Ave, Los Angeles, CA 90066 **Contact:** 310-663-6170, metaltamer@gmail.com
Specialties: Working knives and art pieces. **Patterns:** Hunter, utility and fantasy. **Technical:** Stock removal and forges. **Prices:** $100 and up. **Mark:** Last name.

VENSILD, HENRIK
Gl Estrup, Randersvei 4, Auning, DENMARK 8963 **Contact:** +45 86 48 44 48
Specialties: Classic and traditional working and using knives of his design, Scandinavian influence. **Patterns:** Hunters and using knives. **Technical:** Forges damascus. Hand makes handles, sheaths and blades. **Prices:** $350 to $1000. **Remarks:** Part-time maker, first knife sold in 1967. **Mark:** Initials.

VERONIQUE, LAURENT
Avenue du Capricorne, 53, 1200 Bruxelles, BELGIUM **Contact:** 0032-477-48-66-73, whatsonthebench@gmail.com
Specialties: Fixed blades and friction folders. **Patterns:** bowies, camp knives, ladies' knives and maker's own designs. **Technical:** Maker's own San Mai steel with a Blue Paper Steel edge and pure-nickel-and-O1 outer layers, called "Nickwich" (nickel in sandwich), and damascus, numerical milling embellishments and inlays, and hand-fashioned sheaths. **Prices:** Start at $350. **Remarks:** Part-time maker since 2005, ABS journeyman smith since 2013.

VESTAL, CHARLES
26662 Shortsville Rd., Abingdon, VA 24210 **Contact:** 276-492-3262, charles@vestalknives.com, vestalknives.com
Specialties: Hunters and double ground fighters in traditional designs and own designs. **Technical:** Grinds CPM-154, ATS-134, 154-CM and other steels. **Prices:** $300 to $1000, some higher. **Remarks:** First knife sold in 1995.

VIALLON, HENRI
Les Belins, Thiers, FRANCE 63300 **Contact:** 04-73-80-24-03, (fax) 04 73-51-02-02
Specialties: Folders and complex damascus **Patterns:** His draws. **Technical:** Forge. **Prices:** $1000 to $5000. **Mark:** H. Viallon.

VICKERS, DAVID
11620 Kingford Dr., Montgomery, TX 77316 **Contact:** 936-537-4900, jdvickers@gmail.com
Specialties: Working/using blade knives especially for hunters. His design or to customer specs. **Patterns:** Hunters, skinners, camp/utility. **Technical:** Grinds ATS-34, 440C, and D-2. Uses stag, various woods, and micarta for handle material. Hand-stitched sheaths. **Remarks:** Full-time maker. **Prices:** $125 - $350. **Mark:** VICKERS

VILAR, RICARDO
Al. dos Jasmins 243, Mairipora, SP, BRAZIL 07600-000 **Contact:** +55 (15) 8133-0196, ricardovilar@gmail.com, rvilarknives.com.br
Specialties: Straight working knives to customer specs. **Patterns:** bowies, fighters and utility/camp knives. **Technical:** Grinds D6, ATS-34 and 440C stainless. **Prices:** $80 to $200. **Remarks:** Part-time maker, first knife sold in 1993. **Mark:** Percor over sword and circle.

VILAR, RICARDO AUGUSTO FERREIRA
Rua Alemada Dos Jasmins NO 243, Parque Petropolis, Mairipora, SP, BRAZIL 07600-000 **Contact:** 011-55-11-44-85-43-46, ricardovilar@ig.com.br.
Specialties: Traditional Brazilian-style working knives of the Sao Paulo state. **Patterns:** Fighters, hunters, utility, and camp knives, welcome customer design. Specialize in the "true" Brazilian camp knife "Soracabana." **Technical:** Forges only with sledge hammer to 100 percent shape in 5160 and 52100 and his own damascus steels. Makes own sheaths in the "true" traditional "Paulista"-style of the state of Sao Paulo. **Remarks:** Full-time maker. **Prices:** $250 to $600. Uses only natural handle materials. **Mark:** Special designed signature styled name R. Vilar.

VILLA, LUIZ
R. Com. Miguel Calfat 398, Itaim Bibi, SP, BRAZIL 04537-081 **Contact:** 011-8290649
Specialties: One-of-a-kind straight knives and jewel knives of all designs. **Patterns:** bowies, hunters, utility/camp knives and jewel knives. **Technical:** Grinds D6, damascus and 440C, forges 5160. Prefers natural handle material. **Prices:** $70 to $200. **Remarks:** Part-time maker, first knife sold in 1990. **Mark:** Last name and serial number.

VILPPOLA, MARKKU
Jaanintie 45, Turku, FINLAND 20540 **Contact:** +358 (0)50 566 1563, markku@mvforge.fi mvforge.fi
Specialties: All kinds of swords and knives. **Technical:** Forges silver steel, CO, 8%, nickel, 1095, A203E, etc. Mokume (sterling silver/brass/copper). Bronze casting (sand casting, lost-wax casting). **Prices:** Starting at $200.

VINING, BILL
12 Stephens Way, Gardner, MA 01440 **Contact:** 978 618-9970, billv@medawebs.com, medawebs.com
Specialties Liner locking folders. Slip joints & lockbacks. **Patterns:** Likes to make patterns of his own design. **Technical:** S30V, 440C, ATS-34. damascus from various makers. **Prices:** $450 and up. **Remarks:** Part-time maker. **Mark:** VINING or B. Vining.

VISTE, JAMES
EDGEWISE FORGE, 9745 Dequindre, Hamtramck, MI 48212 **Contact:** 313-587-8899, edgewiseforge@hotmail.com
Mark: EWF touch mark.

VISTNES, TOR
Svelgen, NORWAY N-6930 **Contact:** 047-57795572
Specialties: Traditional and working knives of his design. **Patterns:** Hunters and utility knives. **Technical:** Grinds Uddeholm Elmax. Handles made of rear burls of different Nordic stabilized woods. **Prices:** $300 to $1100. **Remarks:** Part-time maker, first knife sold in 1988. **Mark:** Etched name and deer head.

VITALE, MACE
925 Rt 80, Guilford, CT 06437 **Contact:** 203-457-5591, laurelrockforge.com
Specialties: Hand forged blades. **Patterns:** Hunters, utility, chef, bowies and fighters. **Technical:** W2, 1095, 1084, L6. Hand forged and finished. **Prices:** $100 to $1000. **Remarks:** American Bladesmith Society, Journeyman Smith. Full-time maker, first knife sold 2001. **Mark:** MACE.

VOGT, DONALD J
9007 Hogans Bend, Tampa, FL 33647 **Contact:** 813-973-3245, vogtknives@verizon.net
Specialties: Art knives, folders, automatics. **Technical:** Uses damascus steels for blade and bolsters, filework, hand carving on blade bolsters and handles. Other materials used: jewels, gold, mother-of-pearl, gold-lip pearl, black-lip pearl, ivory. **Prices:** $4,000 to $10,000. **Remarks:** Part-time maker, first knife sold in 1997. **Mark:** Last name.

VOGT, PATRIK
Kungsvagen 83, Halmstad, SWEDEN 30270 **Contact:** 46-35-30977
Specialties: Working straight knives. **Patterns:** bowies, hunters and fighters. **Technical:** Forges carbon steel and own damascus. **Prices:** From $100. **Remarks:** Not currently making knives. **Mark:** Initials or last name.

VOORHIES, LES
14511 Lk Mazaska Tr, Faribault, MN 55021 **Contact:** 507-332-0736, lesvor@msn.com, lesvoorhiesknives.com
Specialties: Steels. **Patterns:** Liner locks & autos. **Technical:** ATS-34 damascus. **Prices:** $250 to $1200. **Mark:** L. Voorhies.

VOSS, BEN
2212 Knox Rd. 1600 Rd. E, Victoria, IL 61485-9644 **Contact:** 309-879-2940
Specialties: Fancy working knives of his design. **Patterns:** bowies, fighters, hunters, boots and folders. **Technical:** Grinds 440C, ATS-34 and D2. **Prices:** $35 to $1200. **Remarks:** Part-time maker, first knife sold in 1986. **Mark:** Name, city and state.

VOTAW, DAVID P
305 S State St, Pioneer, OH 43554 **Contact:** 419-737-2774
Specialties: Working knives, period pieces. **Patterns:** Hunters, bowies, camp knives, buckskinners and tomahawks. **Technical:** Grinds O1 and D2. **Prices:** $100 to $200, some to $500. **Remarks:** Part-time maker, took over for the late W.K. Kneubuhler. Doing business as W-K Knives. **Mark:** WK with V inside anvil.

W

WACHOLZ, DOC
95 Anne Rd, Marble, NC 28905 **Contact:** 828-557-1543, killdrums@aol.com, rackforge.com
Specialties: Forged tactical knives and tomahawks. **Technical:** Use 52100 and 1084 high carbon steel, make own damascus, design and dew own sheaths. Grind up and down fashion on a 3" wheel. **Prices:** $300 to $800. **Remarks:** Part-time maker, started forging in 1999, with ABS master Charles Ochs.. **Mark:** Early knives stamped RACK, newer knives since 2005 stamped WACHOLZ.

WADA, YASUTAKA
2-6-22 Fujinokidai, Nara City, Nara, JAPAN 631-0044 **Contact:** 0742 46-0689
Specialties: Fancy and embellished one-of-a-kind straight knives of his design. **Patterns:** bowies, daggers and hunters. **Technical:** Grinds ATS-34. All knives hand-filed and flat grinds. **Prices:** $400 to $2500, some higher. **Remarks:** Part-time maker, first knife sold in 1990. **Mark:** Owl eyes with initial and last name underneath or last name.

custom knifemakers

WAGAMAN, JOHN K
107 E Railroad St, Selma, NC 27576 **Contact:** 919-965-9659, (fax) 919-965-9901
Specialties: Fancy working knives. **Patterns:** bowies, miniatures, hunters, fighters and boots. **Technical:** Grinds D2, 440C, 154CM and commercial damascus, inlays mother-of-pearl. **Prices:** $110 to $2000. **Remarks:** Part-time maker, first knife sold in 1975. **Mark:** Last name.

WAIDE, RUSTY
Triple C Knives, PO Box 499, Buffalo, MO 65622 **Contact:** 417-345-7231, (fax) 417-345-1911, wrrccc@yahoo.com
Specialties: Custom-designed hunting knives and cowboy working knives in high-carbon and damascus steels. **Prices:** $150 to $450. **Remarks:** Part-time maker, first knife sold in 2010. **Mark:** Triple C. Previous: Name.

WAITES, RICHARD L
PO Box 188, Broomfield, CO 80038 **Contact:** 303-324-2905, (fax) 303-465-9971, dickknives@aol.com
Specialties: Working fixed blade knives of all kinds including "paddle blade" skinners. Hand crafted sheaths, some upscale and unusual. **Technical:** Grinds 440C, damascus and D2. **Prices:** $100 to $500. **Remarks:** Part-time maker. First knife sold in 1998. Doing business as R.L. Waites Knives. **Mark:** Oval etch with first and middle initial and last name on top and city and state on bottom. Memberships, Professional Knifemakers Association and Rocky Mountain Blade Collectors Club.

WALKER, BILL
431 Walker Rd, Stevensville, MD 21666 **Contact:** 410-643-5041

WALKER, DON
2850 Halls Chapel Rd, Burnsville, NC 28714 **Contact:** 828-675-9716, dlwalkernc@gmail.com

WALKER, JIM
22 Walker Ln, Morrilton, AR 72110 **Contact:** 501-354-3175, jwalker46@att.net
Specialties: Period pieces and working/using knives of his design and to customer specs. **Patterns:** bowies, fighters, hunters, camp knives. **Technical:** Forges 5160, O1, L6, 52100, 1084, 1095. **Prices:** Start at $450. **Remarks:** Full-time maker, first knife sold in 1993. **Mark:** Three arrows with last name/MS.

WALKER, MICHAEL L
925-A Paseo del, Pueblo Sur Taos, NM 87571 **Contact:** 505-751-3409, (fax) 505-751-3417, metalwerkr@msn.com
Specialties: Innovative knife designs and locking systems, titanium and SS furniture and art. **Patterns:** Folders from utility grade to museum quality art, others upon request. **Technical:** State-of-the-art materials: titanium, stainless damascus, gold, etc. **Prices:** $3500 and above. **Remarks:** Designer/MetalCrafts, full-time professional knifemaker since 1980, four U.S. patents, invented LinerLock® and was awarded registered U.S. trademark no. 1,585,333. **Mark:** Early mark MW, Walker's Lockers by M.L. Walker, current M.L. Walker or Michael Walker.

WALL, GREG
4753 Michie Pebble Hill Rd., Michie, TN 38357 **Contact:** 662-415-2909, glwall36@hotmail.com, wallhandmadeknives.com
Specialties: Working straight knives. **Patterns:** Classic hollow-handle survival knives, Ek-style fighters, drop-point hunters and big 7's models. **Technical:** Stock removal method of blade making, convex and flat grinds, using O1 tool steels and 440C stainless steel. **Prices:** $295 to $395. **Remarks:** First knife made and sold in 1983.

WALLINGFORD JR., CHARLES W
9024 Old Union Rd, Union, KY 41091 **Contact:** 859-384-4141, cwknives.com
Specialties: 18th and 19th century styles, patch knives, rifleman knives. **Technical:** 1084 and 5160 forged blades. **Prices:** $125 to $300. **Mark:** CW.

WARD, CHUCK
PO Box 2272, 1010 E North St, Benton, AR 72018-2272 **Contact:** 501-778-4329, chuckbop@aol.com
Specialties: Traditional working and using straight knives and folders of his design. **Technical:** Grinds 440C, D2, A2, ATS-34 and O1, uses natural and composite handle materials. **Prices:** $90 to $400, some higher. **Remarks:** Part-time maker, first knife sold in 1990. **Mark:** First initial, last name.

WARD, KEN
1125 Lee Roze Ln, Grants Pass, OR 97527 **Contact:** 541-956-8864
Specialties: Working knives, some to customer specs. **Patterns:** Straight, axes, bowies, buckskinners and miniatures. **Technical:** Grinds ATS-34, damascus. **Prices:** $100 to $700. **Remarks:** Part-time maker, first knife sold in 1977. **Mark:** Name.

WARD, RON
PO BOX 21, Rose Hill, VA 24281 **Contact:** 276-445-4757
Specialties: Classic working and using straight knives, fantasy knives. **Patterns:** bowies, hunter, fighters, and utility/camp knives. **Technical:** Grinds 440C, 154CM, ATS-34, uses composite and natural handle materials. **Prices:** $50 to $750. **Remarks:** Part-time maker, first knife sold in 1992. Doing business as Ron Ward Blades. **Mark:** RON WARD BLADES.

WARD, TOM
204 Village Rd., Wilmot, NH 03287 **Contact:** 508-277-3190, tempestcraft@gmail.com, tempestcraft.com
Specialties: Axes and pattern welding, multi-billet twist constructions. Open to all commissions. **Technical:** Forges to shape, generally using 15N20, 1095 and 1084 blade steels. **Prices:** $400 for mono-steel hunting/camping knives to $3,000 and up on elaborate pieces. **Remarks:** Full-time maker, first knife made in 2008. **Mark:** An ornate T.

WARD, W C
817 Glenn St, Clinton, TN 37716 **Contact:** 615-457-3568
Specialties: Working straight knives, period pieces. **Patterns:** Hunters, bowies, swords and kitchen cutlery. **Technical:** Grinds O1. **Prices:** $85 to $150, some to $500. **Remarks:** Part-time maker, first knife sold in 1969. He styled the Tennessee Knife Maker. **Mark:** TKM.

WARDELL, MICK
20 Clovelly Rd, Bideford, N Devon, ENGLAND EX39 3BU, wardellknives@hotmail.co.uk wardellscustomknives.com
Specialties: Spring back folders and a few fixed blades. **Patterns:** Locking and slip-joint folders, bowies. **Technical:** Grinds stainless damascus and RWL34. Heat-treats. **Prices:** $300 to $2500. **Remarks:** Full-time maker, first knife sold in 1986. Takes limited Comissions. **Mark:** Wardell.

WARDEN, ROY A
275 Tanglewood Rd, Union, MO 63084 **Contact:** 314-583-8813, rwarden@yhti.net
Specialties: Complex mosaic designs of "EDM wired figures" and "stack up" patterns and "lazer cut" and "torch cut" and "sawed" patterns combined. **Patterns:** Mostly "all mosaic" folders, automatics, fixed blades. **Technical:** Mosaic damascus with all tool steel edges. **Prices:** $100 to $1000. **Remarks:** Part-time maker, first knife sold in 1987. **Mark:** WARDEN stamped or initials connected.

WARE, J.D.
Calle Laurel x 24 y 26 Cholul, Merida Yucatan 97305 MEXICO, jdware@jdwareknives.com, jdwareknives.com
Specialties: Coin knives, slip-joint folders, chef's knives and hunting/camping/fishing knives. **Technical:** Practices stock-removal and forging methods of blade making using O1, 440C and D2 blade steels. **Prices:** Start at $200. **Remarks:** Full-time maker, first knife made in 1976. **Mark:** Usually etched "JD Ware, Artesano, Merida Yucatan, Hecho a Mano, Mexico."

WARE, TOMMY
158 Idlewilde, Onalaska, TX 77360 **Contact:** 936-646-4649
Specialties: Traditional working and using straight knives, folders and automatics of his design and to customer specs. **Patterns:** Hunters, automatics and locking folders. **Technical:** Grinds ATS-34, 440C and D2. Offers engraving and scrimshaw. **Prices:** $425 to $650, some to $1500. **Remarks:** Full-time maker, first knife sold in 1990. Doing business as Wano Knives. **Mark:** Last name inside oval, business name above, city and state below, year on side.

WARREN, AL
1423 Sante Fe Circle, Roseville, CA 95678 **Contact:** 916-257-5904, al@warrenknives.com, warrenknives.com
Specialties: Working straight knives and folders, some fancy. **Patterns:** Hunters, bowies, fillets, lockback, folders & multi blade. **Technical:** grinds S90V, S35VN but primarily S30V **Prices:** $280 to $2,500. **Remarks:** Full-time maker, first knife sold in 1978. **Mark:** First and last initials, last name, USA, handmade

WARREN, ALAN AND CARROLL
6605 S.E. 69th Ave., Portland, OR 97206 **Contact:** 503-788-6863 or 503-926-3559, alanwarrenknives@yahoo.com
Specialties: Mostly one-of-a-kind straight knives, bird & trout knives, skinners, fighters, bowies, daggers, short swords and LinerLock folders (tactical and gent's). My designs or custom. **Technical:** Hair flat grinds 154CM, ATS-34, CPM-S30V, O1, 5160 and others. Uses just about all handle materials available. Makes custom-to-fit, hand-tooled and hand stitched leather sheaths, some with skin inlays or hard inlays to match knife handle materials such as G-10, Micarta, ironwood, ivory, stag, etc. **Prices:** $200 to $1,800, some to $3,595. **Remarks:** Full-time maker for nine years, first knife sold in 1998. **Mark:** Name, state, USA.

WARREN, DANIEL
571 Lovejoy Rd, Canton, NC 28716 **Contact:** 828-648-7351
Specialties: Using knives. **Patterns:** Drop point hunters. **Prices:** $200 to $500. **Mark:** Warren-Bethel NC.

WASHBURN, ARTHUR D
ADW CUSTOM KNIVES, 211 Hinman St / PO Box 625, Pioche, NV 89043 **Contact:** 775-962-5463, knifeman@lcturbonet.com, adwcustomknives.net
Specialties: Locking liner folders. **Patterns:** Slip joint folders (single and multiplied), lock-back folders, some fixed blades. Do own heat-treating, Rockwell test each blade. **Technical:** Carbon and stainless damascus, some 1084, 1095, AEBL, 12C27, S30V. **Prices:** $200 to $1000 and up. **Remarks:** Sold first knife in 1997. Part-time maker. **Mark:** ADW enclosed in an oval or ADW.

WASHBURN JR., ROBERT LEE
636 75th St., Tuscaloosa, AL 35405 **Contact:** 435-619-4432, (fax) 435-574-8554, rlwashburn@excite.com, washburnknives.net
Specialties: Hand-forged period, bowies, tactical, boot and hunters. **Patterns:** bowies, tantos, loot hunters, tactical and folders. **Prices:** $100 to $2500. **Remarks:** All hand forged. 52100 being his favorite steel. **Mark:** Washburn Knives W.

WATANABE, MELVIN
1297 Kika St., Kailua, HI 96734 **Contact:** 808-429-9403, meltod808@yahoo.com
Specialties: Fancy folding knives. Some hunters. **Patterns:** Liner-locks and hunters. **Technical:** Grinds ATS-34, stainless damascus. **Prices:** $350 and up. **Remarks:** Part-time maker, first knife sold in 1985. **Mark:** Name and state.

WATANABE, WAYNE
PO Box 3563, Montebello, CA 90640, wwknives@yahoo.com

Specialties: Straight knives in Japanese-styles. One-of-a-kind designs, welcomes customer designs. **Patterns:** Tantos to katanas, bowies. **Technical:** Flat grinds A2, O1 and ATS-34. Offers hand-rubbed finishes and wrapped handles. **Prices:** Start at $200. **Remarks:** Part-time maker. **Mark:** Name in characters with flower.

WATERS, GLENN
11 Shinakawa Machi, Hirosaki City, JAPAN 036 **Contact:** 0172-886741, watersglenn@hotmail.com, glennwaters.com
Specialties: One-of-a-kind collector-grade highly embellished art knives. Mostly folders with a few fixed blades and up-market tactical flippers. **Patterns:** Locking-liner folders and collectible flippers and fixed art knives. **Technical:** Grinds blades from Damasteel, VG-10, CowryX, ZDP-189, San Mai from ZDP-189 and VG-10, and Super Gold 2 powdered stainless by Takefu. Does own engraving, gold inlaying and stone setting, filework and carving. Gold and Japanese precious metal fabrication. Prefers exotic material, high karat gold, silver, Shyaku Dou, Shibu Ichi Gin, precious gemstones. **Prices:** Upscale. **Remarks:** Designs and makes one-of-a-kind highly embellished art knives, often with fully engraved handles and blades that tell a story. A jeweler by trade for 20 years before starting to make knives in 1993. First knife sold in 1994. **Mark:** On knives before 2010, Glenn Waters maker Japan or Glenn in Japanese. Knives since 2010 uses a new engraved logo that says Glenn in Japanese.

WATSON, BERT
9315 Meade St., Westminster, CO 80031 **Contact:** 303-587-3064, watsonbd21960@q.com
Specialties: Working/using straight knives of his design and to customer specs. **Patterns:** Hunters, utility/camp knives. **Technical:** Grinds O1, ATS-34, 440C, D2, A2 and others. **Prices:** $150 to $800. **Remarks:** Full-time maker. **Mark:** GTK and/or Bert.

WATSON, BILLY
440 Forge Rd, Deatsville, AL 36022 **Contact:** 334-365-1482, hilldweller44@att.net
Specialties: Working and using straight knives and folders of his design, period pieces. **Patterns:** Hunters, bowies and utility/camp knives. **Technical:** Forges and grinds his own damascus, 1095, 5160 and 52100. **Prices:** $40 to $1500. **Remarks:** Full-time maker, first knife sold in 1970. **Mark:** Last name.

WATSON, DANIEL
350 Jennifer Ln, Driftwood, TX 78619 **Contact:** 512-847-9679, info@angelsword.com, angelsword.com
Specialties: One-of-a-kind knives and swords. **Patterns:** Hunters, daggers, swords. **Technical:** Hand-purify and carbonize his own high-carbon steel, pattern-welded damascus, cable and carbon-induced crystalline damascus. Teehno-Wootz™ damascus steel, heat treats including cryogenic processing. European and Japanese tempering. **Prices:** $125 to $25,000. **Remarks:** Full-time maker, first knife sold in 1979. **Mark:** "Angel Sword" on forged pieces, "Bright Knight" for stock removal. Avatar on Techno-Wootz™ damascus. Bumon on traditional Japanese blades.

WATSON, PETER
66 Kielblock St, La Hoff, NW, SOUTH AFRICA 2570 **Contact:** 018-84942
Specialties: Traditional working and using straight knives and folders of his design. **Patterns:** Hunters, locking folders and utility/camp knives. **Technical:** Sandvik and 440C. **Prices:** $120 to $250, some to $1500. **Remarks:** Part-time maker, first knife sold in 1989. **Mark:** Buffalo head with name.

WATSON, TOM
1103 Brenau Terrace, Panama City, FL 32405 **Contact:** 850-785-9209, tom@tomwatsonknives.com, tomwatsonknives.com
Specialties: Utility/tactical LinerLocks and flipper folders. **Patterns:** Various patterns. **Technical:** Grinds D2 and CPM-154. **Prices:** $375 and up. **Remarks:** In business since 1978. **Mark:** Name and city.

WATTELET, MICHAEL A
4526 Maple Ridge Dr., Rhinelander, WI 54501 **Contact:** 715-282-2203, redtroll776@gmail.com
Specialties: Working and using straight knives of his design and to customer specs, fantasy knives. **Patterns:** Daggers, fighters and swords. **Technical:** Grinds 440C and L6, forges and grinds O1. Silversmith. **Prices:** $75 to $1000, some to $5000. **Remarks:** Full-time maker, first knife sold in 1966. Doing business as M and N Arts Ltd. **Mark:** First initial, last name.

WATTS, JOHNATHAN
9440 S. Hwy. 36, Gatesville, TX 76528 **Contact:** 254-223-9669
Specialties: Traditional folders. **Patterns:** One and two blade folders in various blade shapes. **Technical:** Grinds ATS-34 and damascus on request. **Prices:** $120 to $400. **Remarks:** Part-time maker, first knife sold in 1997. **Mark:** J Watts.

WATTS, RODNEY
Watts Custom Knives, 1100 Hwy. 71 S, Hot Springs, SD 57747 **Contact:** 605-890-0645, wattscustomknives@yahoo.com, wattscustomknives.com
Specialties: Fixed blades and some folders, most of maker's own designs, some Loveless and Johnson patterns. **Technical:** Stock remvoal method of blade making, using CPM 154 and ATS-34 steels. **Prices:** $450 to $1,100. **Remarks:** Part-time maker, first knife made in 2007. Won "Best New Maker" award at the 2011 BLADE Show. **Mark:** Watts over Custom Knives.

WEBSTER, BILL
58144 West Clear Lake Rd, Three Rivers, MI 49093 **Contact:** 269-244-2873, wswebster_5@msn.com, websterknifeworks.com
Specialties: Working and using straight knives, especially for hunters. His patterns are custom designed. **Patterns:** Hunters, skinners, camp knives, bowies and daggers. **Technical:** Hand-filed blades made of D2 steel only, unless other steel is requested. Preferred handle material is stabilized and exotic wood and stag. Sheaths are hand-sewn by Bill Dehn in Three Rivers, MI. **Prices:** $75 to $500. **Remarks:** Part-time maker, first knife sold in 1978. **Mark:** Originally WEB stamped on blade, at present, Webster Knifeworks Three Rivers, MI laser etched on blade.

WEEKS, RYAN
PO Box 1101, Bountiful, UT 84001 **Contact:** 801-755-6789, ryan@ryanwknives.com, ryanwknives.com
Specialties: Military and Law Enforcement applications as well as hunting and utility designs. **Patterns:** Fighters, bowies, hunters, and custom designs, I use man made as well as natural wood and exotic handle materials. **Technical:** Make via forge and stock removal methods, preferred steel includes high carbon, CPM154 CM and ATS34, damascus and San Mai. **Prices:** $160 to $750. **Remarks:** Part-time maker, Business name is "Ryan W. Knives." First knife sold in 2009. **Mark:** Encircled "Ryan" beneath the crossed "W" UTAH, USA.

WEEVER, JOHN
150 Valley View St., Glen Rose, TX 76043 **Contact:** 254-898-9595, john.weever@gmail.com, WeeverKnives.com
Specialties: Traditional hunters (fixed blade, slip joint, and lockback) and tactical. **Patterns:** See website. **Technical:** Types of steel: S30V, damascus or customer choice. Handles in mammoth ivory, oosic, horn, sambar, stag, etc. Sheaths in exotic leathers. **Prices:** $400 to $1200. **Remarks:** Stock removal maker full-time, began making knives in 1985. Member of knifemakers guild. **Mark:** Tang stamp: head of charging elephant with ears extended and WEEVER curved over the top.

WEHNER, RUDY
297 William Warren Rd, Collins, MS 39428 **Contact:** 601-765-4997
Specialties: Reproduction antique bowies and contemporary bowies in full and miniature. **Patterns:** Skinners, camp knives, fighters, axes and bowies. **Technical:** Grinds 440C, ATS-34, 154CM and damascus. **Prices:** $100 to $500, some to $850. **Remarks:** Full-time maker, first knife sold in 1975. **Mark:** Last name on bowies and antiques, full name, city and state on skinners.

WEILAND JR., J REESE
PO Box 2337, Riverview, FL 33568 **Contact:** 813-671-0661, RWPHIL413@verizon.net, reeseweilandknives.com
Specialties: Hawk bills, tactical to fancy folders. **Patterns:** Hunters, tantos, bowies, fantasy knives, spears and some swords. **Technical:** Grinds ATS-34, 154CM, 440C, D2, O1, A2, damascus. Titanium hardware on locking liners and button locks. **Prices:** $150 to $4000. **Remarks:** Full-time maker, first knife sold in 1978. Knifemakers Guild member since 1988.

WEINAND, GEROME M
14440 Harpers Bridge Rd, Missoula, MT 59808 **Contact:** 406-543-0845
Specialties: Working straight knives. **Patterns:** bowies, fishing and camp knives, large special hunters. **Technical:** Grinds O1, 440C, ATS-34, 1084, L6, also stainless damascus, Aebl and 304, makes all-tool steel damascus, Dendritic D2 from powdered steel. Heat-treats. **Prices:** $30 to $100, some to $500. **Remarks:** Full-time maker, first knife sold in 1982. **Mark:** Last name.

WEINSTOCK, ROBERT
PO Box 170028, San Francisco, CA 94117-0028 **Contact:** 415 731-5968, robertweinstock@att.net
Specialties: Folders, slip joins, lockbacks, autos. **Patterns:** Daggers, folders. **Technical:** Grinds A2, O1 and 440C. Chased and hand-carved blades and handles. Also using various damascus steels from other makers. **Prices:** $3000 to 7000. **Remarks:** Full-time maker, first knife sold in 1994. **Mark:** Last name carved in steel.

WEISS, CHARLES L
PO BOX 1037, Waddell, AZ 85355 **Contact:** 623-935-0924, weissknife@live.com
Specialties: High-art straight knives and folders, deluxe period pieces. **Patterns:** Daggers, fighters, boots, push knives and miniatures. **Technical:** Grinds 440C, 154CM and ATS-34. **Prices:** $300 to $1200, some to $2000. **Remarks:** Full-time maker, first knife sold in 1975. **Mark:** Name and city.

WELLING, RONALD L
15446 Lake Ave, Grand Haven, MI 49417 **Contact:** 616-846-2274
Specialties: Scagel knives of his design or to customer specs. **Patterns:** Hunters, camp knives, miniatures, bird, trout, folders, double edged, hatchets, skinners and some art pieces. **Technical:** Forges damascus 1084 and 1095. Antler, ivory and horn. **Prices:** $250 to $3000. **Remarks:** Full-time maker. ABS Journeyman maker. **Mark:** First initials and or name and last name. City and state. Various scagel kris (1or 2).

WELLING, WILLIAM
Up-armored Knives, 5437 Pinecliff Dr., West Valley, NY 14171 **Contact:** 716-942-6031, uparmored@frontier.net, up-armored.com
Specialties: Innovative tactical fixed blades each uniquely coated in a variety of Up-armored designed patterns and color schemes.Convexed edged bushcraft knives for the weekend camper, backpacker, or survivalist. Knives developed specifically for tactical operators. Leather- and synthetic-suede-lined Kydex sheaths. **Patterns:** Modern samples of time tested designs as well as contemporary developed cutting tools. **Technical:** Stock removal specializing in tested 1095CV and 5160 steels. **Prices:** $200 to $500. **Remarks:** Part-time maker, first knife sold in 2010. **Mark:** Skull rounded up by Up-Armored USA.

WERTH, GEORGE W
5223 Woodstock Rd, Poplar Grove, IL 61065 **Contact:** 815-544-4408
Specialties: Period pieces, some fancy. **Patterns:** Straight fighters, daggers and bowies.

Technical: Forges and grinds O1, 1095 and his damascus, including mosaic patterns. **Prices:** $200 to $650, some higher. **Remarks:** Full-time maker. Doing business as Fox Valley Forge. **Mark:** Name in logo or initials connected.

WESCOTT, CODY
5330 White Wing Rd, Las Cruces, NM 88012 **Contact:** 575-382-5008
Specialties: Fancy and presentation grade working knives. **Patterns:** Hunters, locking folders and bowies. **Technical:** Hollow-grinds D2 and ATS-34, all knives file worked. Offers some engraving. Makes sheaths. **Prices:** $110 to $500, some to $1200. **Remarks:** Full-time maker, first knife sold in 1982. **Mark:** First initial, last name.

WEST, CHARLES A
1315 S Pine St, Centralia, IL 62801 **Contact:** 618-532-2777
Specialties: Classic, fancy, high tech, period pieces, traditional and working/using straight knives and folders. **Patterns:** bowies, fighters and locking folders. **Technical:** Grinds ATS-34, O1 and damascus. Prefers hot blued finishes. **Prices:** $100 to $1000, some to $2000. **Remarks:** Full-time maker, first knife sold in 1963. Doing business as West Custom Knives. **Mark:** Name or name, city and state.

WEST, MICHAEL
Westknives Sandstræde 27, 9500 Hobro, DK Denmark **Contact:** +45 21 67 37 41, mw@westknives.com, westknives.com, instagram.com/westknives, facebook.com/westknives
Specialties: Art knives.

WESTBERG, LARRY
305 S Western Hills Dr, Algona, IA 50511 **Contact:** 515-368-1974, westberg@netamumail.com
Specialties: Traditional and working straight knives of his design and in standard patterns. **Patterns:** bowies, hunters, fillets and folders. **Technical:** Grinds 440C, D2 and 1095. Heat-treats. Uses natural handle materials. **Prices:** $85 to $600, some to $1000. **Remarks:** Part-time maker, first knife sold in 1987. **Mark:** Last name-town and state.

WETTEN, BOBBY
550 W. Caracas Ave., Hershey, PA 17033 **Contact:** 717-439-7686, bobwetten@gmail.com, https://bobbywett.wordpress.com
Patterns: Forged hunters, camp knives, bowies, fighters and tomahawks. Likes to make pieces that blend into nature. Now making folders. **Technical:** Forges 10xx, 5160 and W2 steels, occasionally doing stock removal pieces. Father-in-law Paul Wittle makes sheaths. **Prices:** $300 to $1,500. **Remarks:** First knife completed in 2006, ABS journeyman smith. **Mark:** BobbyWett (one word, no spaces).

WHEELER, GARY
351 Old Hwy 48, Clarksville, TN 37040 **Contact:** 931-552-3092, LR22SHTR@charter.net, Instagram @jsgarywheelerknives
Specialties: Working to high end fixed blades. **Patterns:** bowies, Hunters, combat knives, daggers and a few folders. **Technical:** Forges 5160, 1095, 52100 and his own damascus. **Prices:** $125 to $2000. **Remarks:** Full-time maker since 2001, first knife sold in 1985 collaborates/works at B&W Blade Works. ABS Journeyman Smith 2008. **Mark:** Stamped last name.

WHEELER, NICK
140 Studebaker Rd., Castle Rock, WA 98611 **Contact:** 360-967-2357, merckman99@yahoo.com
Specialties: bowies, integrals, fighters, hunters and daggers. **Technical:** Forges W2, W1, 1095, 52100 and 1084. Makes own damascus, from random pattern to complex mosaics. Also grinds stainless and other more modern alloys. Does own heat-treating and leather work. Also commissions leather work from Paul Long. **Prices:** Start at $250. **Remarks:** Full-time maker, ABS member since 2001. Journeyman bladesmith. **Mark:** Last name.

WHEELER, ROBERT
289 S Jefferson, Bradley, IL 60915 **Contact:** 815-932-5854, b2btaz@brmemc.net

WHIPPLE, WESLEY A
1002 Shoshoni St, Thermopolis, WY 82443 **Contact:** 307-921-2445, wildernessknife@yahoo.com
Specialties: Working straight knives, some fancy. **Patterns:** Hunters, bowies, camp knives, fighters. **Technical:** Forges high-carbon steels, damascus, offers relief carving and silver wire inlay and checkering. **Prices:** $300 to $1400, some higher. **Remarks:** Full-time maker, first knife sold in 1989. A.K.A. Wilderness Knife and Forge. **Mark:** Last name/JS.

WHITE, BRYCE
1415 W Col Glenn Rd, Little Rock, AR 72210 **Contact:** 501-821-2956
Specialties: Hunters, fighters, makes damascus, file work, handmade only. **Technical:** L6, 1075, 1095, O1 steels used most. **Patterns:** Will do any pattern or use his own. **Prices:** $200 to $300. Sold first knife in 1995. **Mark:** White.

WHITE, CALEB A.
502 W. River Rd. #88, Hooksett, NH 03106 **Contact:** 603-340-4716, caleb@calebwhiteknives.com, calebwhiteknives.com
Specialties: Hunters, tacticals, dress knives, daggers and utilitarian pieces. **Patterns:** Multiple. **Technical:** Mostly stock removal, preferring high-carbon steels. **Prices:** $275 to $4,100. **Remarks:** Full-time maker. **Mark:** Derivation of maker's last name, replacing the "T" with a symbol loosely based on the Templars' cross and shield.

WHITE, DALE
525 CR 212, Sweetwater, TX 79556 **Contact:** 325-798-4178, dalew@taylortel.net
Specialties: Working and using knives. **Patterns:** Hunters, skinners, utilities and bowies. **Technical:** Grinds 440C, offers file work, fancy pins and scrimshaw by Sherry Sellers. **Prices:** From $45 to $300. **Remarks:** Sold first knife in 1975. **Mark:** Full name, city and state.

WHITE, LOU
7385 Red Bud Rd NE, Ranger, GA 30734 **Contact:** 706-334-2273

WHITE, RICHARD T
359 Carver St, Grosse Pointe Farms, MI 48236 **Contact:** 313-881-4690

WHITE, RUSSELL D.
4 CR 8240, Rienzi, MS 38865 **Contact:** 662-416-3461, rwhite292@gmail.com, Facebook: Handmade Knives by Russell White
Patterns: Hunters, bowies and camp knives using natural handle materials and micarta. **Technical:** Forges 1084, 15N20, 52100, 5160, O1 and damascus. **Prices:** Start at $200. **Remarks:** Part-time maker, first knife sold in 2010. ABS journeyman smith, sole authorship knifemaker offering handmade leather sheaths if wanted. **Mark:** R. White, J.S. on ricasso.

WHITENECT, JODY
Halifax County, Elderbank, NS, CANADA B0N 1K0 **Contact:** 902-384-2511
Specialties: Fancy and embellished working/using straight knives of his design and to customer specs. **Patterns:** bowies, fighters and hunters. **Technical:** Forges 1095 and O1, forges and grinds ATS-34. Various filework on blades and bolsters. **Prices:** $200 to $400, some to $800. **Remarks:** Part-time maker, first knife sold in 1996. **Mark:** Longhorn stamp or engraved.

WHITESELL, J. DALE
P.O. Box 455, Stover, MO 65078 **Contact:** 573-569-0753, daleskniwes@yahoo.com, whitesell-knives.webs.com
Specialties: Fixed blade working knives,a nd some collector pieces. **Patterns:** Hunting and skinner knives, camp knives, and kitchen knives. **Technical:** Blades ground from O1, 1095, and 440C in hollow, flat and saber grinds. Wood, bone, deer antler, and G10 are basic handle materials. **Prices:** $100 to $450. **Remarks:** Part-time maker, first knife sold in 2003. Doing business as Dale's Knives. All knives have serial number to indicate steel (since June 2010).**Mark:** Whitesell on the left side of the blade.

WHITLEY, L WAYNE
1675 Carrow Rd, Chocowinity, NC 27817-9495 **Contact:** 252-946-5648

WHITLEY, WELDON G
4308 N Robin Ave, Odessa, TX 79764 **Contact:** 432-530-0448, (fax) 432-530-0448, wgwhitley@juno.com
Specialties: Working knives of his design or to customer specs. **Patterns:** Hunters, folders and various double-edged knives. **Technical:** Grinds 440C, 154CM and ATS-34. **Prices:** $150 to $1250. **Mark:** Name, address, road-runner logo.

WHITTAKER, ROBERT E
PO Box 204, Mill Creek, PA 17060
Specialties: Using straight knives. Has a line of knives for buckskinners. **Patterns:** Hunters, skinners and bowies. **Technical:** Grinds O1, A2 and D2. Offers filework. **Prices:** $35 to $100. **Remarks:** Part-time maker, first knife sold in 1980. **Mark:** Last initial or full initials.

WHITTAKER, WAYNE
167 Glendale Dr, Clarksville, GA 30523 **Contact:** 810-797-5315, lindorwayne@yahoo.com
Specialties: Liner locks and autos.**Patterns:** Folders. **Technical:** damascus, mammoth, ivory, and tooth. **Prices:** $500 to $1500. **Remarks:** Full-time maker. **Mark:** Inside of backbar.

WICK, JONATHAN P.
5541 E. Calle Narciso, Hereford, AZ 85615 **Contact:** 520-227-5228, vikingwick@aol.com
Specialties: Fixed blades, pocketknives, neck knives, hunters, bowies, fighters, Roman-style daggers with full tangs, stick tangs and some integrals, and leather-lined, textured copper sheaths. **Technical:** Forged blades and own damascus and mosaic damascus, along with shibuichi, mokume, lost wax casting. **Prices:** $250 - $1800 and up. **Remarks:** Full-time maker, ABS member, sold first knife in 2008. **Mark:** J P Wick, also on small blades a JP over a W.

WICKER, DONNIE R
2544 E 40th Ct, Panama City, FL 32405 **Contact:** 904-785-9158
Specialties: Traditional working and using straight knives of his design or to customer specs. **Patterns:** Hunters, fighters and slip-joint folders. **Technical:** Grinds 440C, ATS-34, D2 and 154CM. Heat-treats and does hardness testing. **Prices:** $90 to $200, some to $400. **Remarks:** Part-time maker, first knife sold in 1975. **Mark:** First and middle initials, last name.

WIGGINS, BILL
105 Kaolin Lane, Canton, NC 28716 **Contact:** 828-226-2551, wncbill@bellsouth.net wigginsknives.com
Specialties: Forged working knives. **Patterns:** Hunters, bowies, camp knives and utility knives of own design or will work with customer on design. **Technical:** Forges 1084 and 52100 as well as making own damascus. **Prices:** $250 - $1500. **Remarks:** Part-time maker. First knife sold in 1989. ABS board member. **Mark:** Wiggins

WILBURN, AARON
2521 Hilltop Dr., #364, Redding, CA 96002 **Contact:** 530-227-2827, wilburnforge.aw@gmail.com, wilburnforge.com
Patterns: Daggers, bowies, fighters, hunters and slip-joint folders. **Technical:** Forges own damascus and works with high-carbon steel. **Prices:** $500 to $5,000. **Remarks:** Full-time maker and ABS master smith. **Mark:** Wilburn Forge.

WILKINS, MITCHELL
15523 Rabon Chapel Rd, Montgomery, TX 77316 **Contact:** 936-588-2696, mwilkins@consolidated.net

WILLEY, WG
14210 Sugar Hill Rd, Greenwood, DE 19950 **Contact:** 302-349-4070, willeyknives.com
Specialties: Fancy working straight knives. **Patterns:** Small game knives, bowies and throwing knives. **Technical:** Grinds 440C and 154CM. **Prices:** $350 to $600, some to $1500. **Remarks:** Part-time maker, first knife sold in 1975. Owns retail store. **Mark:** Last name inside map logo.

WILLIAMS, JASON L
PO Box 67, Wyoming, RI 02898 **Contact:** 401-539-8353, (fax) 401-539-0252
Specialties: Fancy and high tech folders of his design, co-inventor of the Axis Lock. **Patterns:** Fighters, locking folders, automatics and fancy pocket knives. **Technical:** Forges damascus and other steels by request. Uses exotic handle materials and precious metals. Offers inlaid spines and gemstone thumb knobs. **Prices:** $1000 and up. **Remarks:** Full-time maker, first knife sold in 1989. **Mark:** First and last initials on pivot.

WILLIAMS, MICHAEL
333 Cherrybark Tr., Broken Bow, OK 74728 **Contact:** 580-420-3051, hforge@pine-net.com, williamscustomknives.com
Specialties: Functional, personalized, edged weaponry. Working and collectible art. **Patterns:** bowies, hunters, camp knives, daggers, others. **Technical:** Forges high carbon steel and own forged damascus. **Prices:** $500 - $12000. **Remarks:** Full-time ABS Master Smith. **Mark:** Williams MS.

WILLIAMS, ROBERT
15962 State Rt. 267, East Liverpool, OH 43920 **Contact:** 203-979-0803, wurdmeister@gmail.com, customstraightrazors.com
Specialties: Custom straight razors with a philosophy that form must follow function, so shaving performance drives designs and aesthetics. **Technical:** Stock removal and forging, working with 1095, O1 and damascus. Natural handle materials and synthetics, accommodating any and all design requests and can incorporate gold inlays, scrimshaw, hand engraving and jewel setting. All work done in maker's shop, sole-source maker shipping worldwide. **Remarks:** Full-time maker, first straight razor in 2005. **Mark:** Robert Williams - Handmade, USA with a hammer separating the two lines.

WILLIAMS, ROBERT
5722 Palisades Vw, New Braunfels, TX 78132 **Contact:** 210-620-3120, Instagram: @attellknives
Patterns: Kitchen knives.

WILLIAMS JR., RICHARD
1440 Nancy Circle, Morristown, TN 37814 **Contact:** 615-581-0059
Specialties: Working and using straight knives of his design or to customer specs. **Patterns:** Hunters, dirks and utility/camp knives. **Technical:** Forges 5160 and uses file steel. Hand-finish is standard, offers filework. **Prices:** $80 to $180, some to $250. **Remarks:** Spare-time maker, first knife sold in 1985. **Mark:** Last initial or full initials.

WILLIAMSON, TONY
Rt 3 Box 503, Siler City, NC 27344 **Contact:** 919-663-3551
Specialties: Flint knapping: knives made of obsidian flakes and flint with wood, antler or bone for handles. **Patterns:** Skinners, daggers and flake knives. **Technical:** Blades have width/thickness ratio of at least 4 to 1. Hafts with methods available to prehistoric man. **Prices:** $58 to $160. **Remarks:** Student of Errett Callahan. **Mark:** Initials and number code to identify year and number of knives made.

WILLIS, BILL
RT 7 Box 7549, Ava, MO 65608 **Contact:** 417-683-4326
Specialties: Forged blades, damascus and carbon steel. **Patterns:** Cable, random or ladder lamented. **Technical:** Professionally heat treated blades. **Prices:** $75 to $600. **Remarks:** Lifetime guarantee on all blades against breakage. All work done by maker, including leather work. **Mark:** WF.

WILLUMSEN, MIKKEL
Nyrnberggade 23, S Copenhagen, DENMARK 2300 **Contact:** 4531176333, mw@willumsen-cph.com wix.com/willumsen/urbantactical
Specialties: Folding knives, fixed blades, and balisongs. Also kitchen knives. **Patterns:** Primarily influenced by design that is function and quality based. Tactical style knives inspired by classical designs mixed with modern tactics. **Technical:** Uses CPM 154, RW 134, S30V, and carbon fiber titanium G10 for handles. **Prices:** Starting at $600.

WILSON, CURTIS M
PO Box 383, Burleson, TX 76097 **Contact:** 817-295-3732, cwknifeman2026@att.net, cwilsonknives.com
Specialties: Traditional working/using knives, fixed blade, folders, slip joint, LinerLock® and lock back knives. Art knives, presentation grade bowies, folder repair, heat treating services. Sub-zero quench. **Patterns:** Hunters, camp knives, military combat, single and multi-blade folders. Dr's knives large or small or custom design knives. **Technical:** Grinds ATS-34, 440C 52100, D2, S30V, CPM 154, mokume gane, engraves, scrimshaw, sheaths leather of kykex heat treating and file work. **Prices:** $150-750. **Remarks:** Part-time maker since 1984. Sold first knife in 1993. **Mark:** Curtis Wilson in ribbon or Curtis Wilson with hand made in a half moon.

WILSON, JAMES G
PO Box 4024, Estes Park, CO 80517 **Contact:** 303-586-3944
Specialties: Bronze Age knives, Medieval and Scottish-styles, tomahawks. **Patterns:** Bronze knives, daggers, swords, spears and battle axes, 12-inch steel Misericorde daggers, sgian dubhs, "his and her" skinners, bird and fish knives, capers, boots and daggers. **Technical:** Casts bronze, grinds D2, 440C and ATS-34. **Prices:** $49 to $400, some to $1300. **Remarks:** Part-time maker, first knife sold in 1975. **Mark:** WilsonHawk.

WILSON, MIKE
1416 McDonald Rd, Hayesville, NC 28904 **Contact:** 828-389-8145
Specialties: Fancy working and using straight knives of his design or to customer specs, folders. **Patterns:** Hunters, bowies, utility knives, gut hooks, skinners, fighters and miniatures. **Technical:** Hollow grinds 440C, 1095, D2, XHP and CPM-154. Mirror finishes are standard. Offers filework. **Prices:** $130 to $600. **Remarks:** Full-time maker, first knife sold in 1985. **Mark:** Last name.

WILSON, P.R. "REGAN"
805 Janvier Rd., Scott, LA 70583 **Contact:** 504-427-1293, pat71ss@cox.net, acadianawhitetailtaxidermy.com
Specialties: Traditional working knives. **Patterns:** Old-school working knives, trailing points, drop points, hunters, boots, etc. **Technical:** 440C, ATS-34 and 154CM steels, all hollow ground with mirror or satin finishes. **Prices:** Start at $175 with sheath. **Remarks:** Mentored by Jim Barbee, first knife sold in 1988, lessons and guidance offered in maker's shop. **Mark:** Name and location with "W" in center of football-shaped logo.

WILSON, RON
2639 Greenwood Ave, Morro Bay, CA 93442 **Contact:** 805-772-3381
Specialties: Classic and fantasy straight knives of his design. **Patterns:** Daggers, fighters, swords and axes, mostly all miniatures. **Technical:** Forges and grinds damascus and various tool steels, grinds meteorite. Uses gold, precious stones and exotic wood. **Prices:** Vary. **Remarks:** Part-time maker, first knives sold in 1995. **Mark:** Stamped first and last initials.

WILSON, RW
PO Box 2012, Weirton, WV 26062 **Contact:** 304-723-2771, rwknives@comcast.net or rwknives@hotmail.com, rwwilsonknives.com, Facebook: RW Wilson Knives
Specialties: Custom-made knives and tomahawks. **Patterns:** bowies, drop-point hunters, skinners, tomahawks and more. **Technical:** Grinds. **Prices:** $7 to $5,000. **Remarks:** First knife sold in 1966. Made tomahawks for the movie "Jeremiah Johnson." **Mark:** "RW Wilson" above a tomahawk and "Weirton WV" under tomahawk.

WILSON, STAN
8931 Pritcher Rd, Lithia, FL 33547 **Contact:** 727-461-1992, swilson@stanwilsonknives.com, stanwilsonknives.com
Specialties: Fancy folders and automatics of his own design. **Patterns:** Locking liner folders, single and dual action autos, daggers. **Technical:** Stock removal, uses damascus, stainless and high carbon steels, prefers ivory and pearl, damascus with blued finishes and filework. **Prices:** $400 and up. **Remarks:** Member of Knifemakers Guild and Florida Knifemakers Association. Full-time maker will do custom orders. **Mark:** Name in script.

WILSON, VIC
9130 Willow Branch Dr, Olive Branch, MS 38654 **Contact:** 901-591-6550, vdubjr55@earthlink.net, knivesbyvic.com
Specialties: Classic working and using knives and folders. **Patterns:** Hunters, boning, utility, camp, my patterns or customers. **Technical:** Grinds O1 and D2. Also does own heat treating. Offer file work and decorative liners on folders. Fabricate custom leather sheaths for all knives. **Prices:** $150 to $400. **Remarks:** Part-time maker, first knife sold in 1989. **Mark:** Etched V over W with oval circle around it, name, Memphis, TN

WINGO, GARY
240 Ogeechee, Ramona, OK 74061 **Contact:** 918-536-1067, wingg_2000@yahoo.com, geocities.com/wingg_2000/gary.html
Specialties: Folder specialist. Steel 440C, D2, others on request. Handle bone-stag, others on request. **Patterns:** Trapper three-blade stockman, four-blade congress, single- and two-blade barlows. **Prices:** 150 to $400. **Mark:** First knife sold 1994. Steer head with Wingo Knives or Straight line Wingo Knives.

WINGO, PERRY
22 55th St, Gulfport, MS 39507 **Contact:** 228-863-3193
Specialties: Traditional working straight knives. **Patterns:** Hunters, skinners, bowies and fishing knives. **Technical:** Grinds 440C. **Prices:** $75 to $1000. **Remarks:** Full-time maker, first knife sold in 1988. **Mark:** Last name.

WINKLER, DANIEL
PO Box 2166, Blowing Rock, NC 28605 **Contact:** 828-295-9156, danielwinkler@bellsouth.net, winklerknives.com
Specialties: Forged cutlery styled in the tradition of an era past as well as producing a custom-made stock removal line. **Patterns:** Fixed blades, friction folders, lock back folders, and axes/tomahawks. **Technical:** Forges, grinds, and heat treats carbon steels, specialty steels, and his own damascus steel. **Prices:** $350 to $4000+. **Remarks:** Full-time maker since 1988. Exclusively offers leatherwork by Karen Shook. ABS Master Smith, Knifemakers Guild voting member. **Mark:** Hand forged: Dwinkler, Stock removal: Winkler Knives

WINN, MARVIN
Maxcutter Custom Knives, 587 Winn Rd., Sunset, LA 70584 **Contact:** 214-471-7012, maxcutter03@yahoo.com maxcutterknives.com
Patterns: Hunting knives, some tactical and some miniatures. **Technical:** 1095, 5160, 154 CM, 12C27, CPM S30V, CPM 154, CTS-XHP and CTS-40CP blade steels, damascus or to customer's specs. Stock removal. **Prices:** $200 to $2,000. **Remarks:** Part-time maker. First knife made in 2002. **Mark:** Name and state.

WINN, TRAVIS A.
558 E 3065 S, Salt Lake City, UT 84106 **Contact:** 801-467-5957

custom knifemakers

Specialties: Fancy working knives and knives to customer specs. **Patterns:** Hunters, fighters, boots, bowies and fancy daggers, some miniatures, tantos and fantasy knives. **Technical:** Grinds D2 and 440C. Embellishes. **Prices:** $125 to $500, some higher. **Remarks:** Part-time maker, first knife sold in 1976. **Mark:** TRAV stylized.

WINSTON, DAVID
1671 Red Holly St, Starkville, MS 39759 **Contact:** 601-323-1028
Specialties: Fancy and traditional knives of his design and to customer specs. **Patterns:** bowies, daggers, hunters, boot knives and folders. **Technical:** Grinds 440C, ATS-34 and D2. Offers filework, heat-treats. **Prices:** $40 to $750, some higher. **Remarks:** Part-time maker, first knife sold in 1984. Offers lifetime sharpening for original owner. **Mark:** Last name.

WIRTZ, ACHIM
Mittelstrasse 58, Wuerselen, GERMANY 52146 **Contact:** 0049-2405-462-486, wootz@web.de
Specialties: Medieval, Scandinavian and Middle East-style knives. **Technical:** Forged blades only, damascus steel, Wootz, Mokume. **Prices:** Start at $200. **Remarks:** Part-time maker. First knife sold in 1997. **Mark:** Stylized initials.

WISE, DONALD
304 Bexhill Rd, St Leonardo-On-Sea, East Sussex, ENGLAND TN3 8AL
Specialties: Fancy and embellished working straight knives to customer specs. **Patterns:** Hunters, bowies and daggers. **Technical:** Grinds Sandvik 12C27, D2 D3 and O1. Scrimshaws. **Prices:** $110 to $300, some $500. **Remarks:** Full-time maker, first knife sold in 1983. **Mark:** KNIFECRAFT.

WITHERS, TIM
WITHERS KNIVES, 4625 N. Granada Ln., Linden, CA 95236, tim@withersknives.com, withersknives.com
Specialties: Loveless and original designs. **Patterns:** bowies, fighters, hunters, daggers and custom pieces. **Technical:** Stock removal method of blade making using ATS-34, 440C, 1095 and CPM 154 steels, and with hollow and flat grinds. Heat-treating includes sub-zero quenching done in-house. Every blade Rockwell Hardness tested. Uses Micarta, exotic wood, stag and mother-of-pearl handles, and each knife comes with a quality 8-9-ounce leather sheath, also made in-house. **Prices:** $350 to $1,100. **Remarks:** Part-time maker, first knife completed in 2011. **Mark:** TIM WITHERS over LINDEN, CA.

WOLF, BILL
4618 N 79th Ave, Phoenix, AZ 85033 **Contact:** 623-910-3147, bwcustomknives143@gmail.com, billwolfcustomknives.com
Specialties: Investment grade knives. **Patterns:** Own designs or customer's. **Technical:** Grinds stainless and all steels. **Prices:** $400 to ? **Remarks:** First knife made in 1988. **Mark:** WOLF

WOLF JR., WILLIAM LYNN
4006 Frank Rd, Lagrange, TX 78945 **Contact:** 409-247-4626

WOOD, ALAN
Greenfield Villa, Greenhead, Brampton, ENGLAND CA8 7HH, info@alanwoodknives.com, alanwoodknives.com
Specialties: High-tech working straight knives of his design. **Patterns:** Hunters, utility/camp and bushcraft knives. **Technical:** Grinds 12C27, RWL-34, stainless damascus and O1. Blades are cryogenic treated. **Prices:** $200 to $800, some to $1,200. **Remarks:** Full-time maker, first knife sold in 1979. Not currently taking orders. **Mark:** Full name with stag tree logo.

WOOD, OWEN DALE
6492 Garrison St, Arvada, CO 80004-3157 **Contact:** 303-456-2748, wood.owen@gmail.com, owenwoodknives.net
Specialties: Folding knives and daggers. **Patterns:** Own damascus, specialties in 456 composite blades. **Technical:** Materials: damascus stainless steel, exotic metals, gold, rare handle materials. **Prices:** $1000 to $9000. **Remarks:** Folding knives in art deco and art noveau themes. Full-time maker from 1981. **Mark:** OWEN WOOD.

WOOD, WEBSTER
22041 Shelton Trail, Atlanta, MI 49709 **Contact:** 989-785-2996, mainganikan@src-milp.com
Specialties: Works mainly in stainless, art knives, bowies, hunters and folders. **Remarks:** Full-time maker, first knife sold in 1980. Retired guild member. All engraving done by maker. **Mark:** Initials inside shield and name.

WORLEY, JOEL A., J.S.
PO BOX 64, Maplewood, OH 45340 **Contact:** 937-638-9518, jaworleyknives@gmail.com
Specialties: bowies, hunters, fighters, utility/camp knives also period style friction folders. **Patterns:** Classic styles, recurves, his design or customer specified. **Technical:** Most knives are fileworked and include a custom made leather sheath. Forges 5160, W2, Cru forge V, files own damascus of 1080 and 15N20. **Prices:** $250 and up. **Remarks:** Part-time maker. ABS journeyman smith. First knife sold in 2005. **Mark:** First name, middle initial and last name over a shark incorporating initials.

WRIGHT, KEVIN
671 Leland Valley Rd W, Quilcene, WA 98376-9517 **Contact:** 360-765-3589, kevinw@ptpc.com
Specialties: Fancy working or collector knives to customer specs. **Patterns:** Hunters, boots, buckskinners, miniatures. **Technical:** Forges and grinds L6, 1095, 440C and his own damascus. **Prices:** $75 to $500, some to $2000. **Remarks:** Part-time maker, first knife sold in 1978. **Mark:** Last initial in anvil.

WRIGHT, L.T.
130b Warren Ln., Wintersville, OH 43953 **Contact:** 740-317-1404, info@ltwrightknives.com, ltwrightknives.com
Specialties: Hunting, bushcraft and tactical knives. **Patterns:** Drop-point hunters, spear-point bushcraft and tactical. **Technical:** Grinds A2, D2 and O1. **Remarks:** Full-time maker.

WRIGHT, RICHARD S
PO Box 201, 111 Hilltop Dr, Carolina, RI 02812 **Contact:** 401-364-3579, rswswitchblades@hotmail.com, richardswright.com
Specialties: Bolster release switchblades, tactical automatics. **Patterns:** Folding fighters, gents pocket knives, one-of-a-kind high-grade automatics. **Technical:** Reforges and grinds various makers damascus. Uses a variety of tool steels. Uses natural handle material such as ivory and pearl, extensive file-work on most knives. **Prices:** $850 and up. **Remarks:** Full-time knifemaker with background as a gunsmith. Made first folder in 1991. **Mark:** RSW on blade, all folders are serial numbered.

WRIGHT, ROBERT A
21 Wiley Bottom Rd, Savannah, GA 31411 **Contact:** 912-777-7864, Cell: 912-656-9085, maker@robwrightknives.com, RobWrightKnives.com
Specialties: Hunting, skinning, fillet, fighting and tactical knives. **Patterns:** Custom designs by client and/or maker. **Technical:** All types of steel, including CPM-S30V, D2, 440C, O1 tool steel and damascus upon request, as well as exotic wood and other high-quality handle materials. **Prices:** $200 and up depending on cost of steel and other materials. **Remarks:** Full-time maker, member of The Knifemakers' Guild and Georgia Custom Knifemaker's Guild. **Mark:** Etched maple leaf with maker's name: R.A. Wright.

WRIGHT, TIMOTHY
PO Box 3746, Sedona, AZ 86340 **Contact:** 928-282-4180
Specialties: High-tech folders and working knives. **Patterns:** Interframe locking folders, non-inlaid folders, straight hunters and kitchen knives. **Technical:** Grinds BG-42, AEB-L, K190 and Cowry X, works with new steels. All folders can disassemble and are furnished with tools. **Prices:** $150 to $1800, some to $3000. **Remarks:** Full-time maker, first knife sold in 1975. **Mark:** Last name and type of steel used.

WUERTZ, TRAVIS
2487 E Hwy 287, Casa Grande, AZ 85222 **Contact:** 520-723-4432

WULF, DERRICK
Wilhelm-von-Miller Weg 28, 82467 Garmisch-Partenkirchen, Germany **Contact:** +49 0152 23177869, derrickwulf@gmail.com, wulfknives.com
Specialties: Makes predominantly forged fixed blade knives using carbon steels and his own damascus. **Mark:** "WULF".

WYATT, WILLIAM R
Box 237, Rainelle, WV 25962 **Contact:** 304-438-5494
Specialties: Classic and working knives of all designs. **Patterns:** Hunters and utility knives. **Technical:** Forges and grinds saw blades, files and rasps. Prefers stag handles. **Prices:** $45 to $95, some to $350. **Remarks:** Part-time maker, first knife sold in 1990. **Mark:** Last name in star with knife logo.

WYLIE, TOM
Peak Knives, 2 Maun Close, Sutton-In-Ashfield, Notts, England NG17 5JG, tom@peakknives.com
Specialties: Knives for adventure sports and hunting, mainly fixed blades. **Technical:** Damasteel or European stainless steel used predominantly, handle material to suit purpose, embellished as required. Work can either be all handmade or CNC machined. **Prices:** $450+. **Remarks:** Pro-Am maker. **Mark:** Ogram "tinne" in circle of life, sometimes with addition of maker's name.

Y

YASHINSKI, JOHN L
207 N Platt, PO Box 1284, Red Lodge, MT 59068 **Contact:** 406-446-3916
Specialties: Indian knife sheaths, beaded, tacked, painted rawhide sheaths, antiqued to look old, old beads and other parts, copies of originals. Write with color copies to be made. **Prices:** $100 to $600. Call to discuss price variations.

YELLE, JEREMY
Yelle's Cutlery & Custom Knives Sherbrooke, Quebec, Canada **Contact:** 819-238-5591, yellescutlery@gmail.com
Patterns: Hunting and kitchen knives. **Prices:** Starting at $150.

YESKOO, RICHARD C
76 Beekman Rd, Summit, NJ 07901

YONEYAMA, CHICCHI K.
5-19-8 Nishikicho, Tachikawa-City, Tokyo, JAPAN 190-0022 **Contact:** 081-1-9047449370, chicchi.ky1007@gmail.com, Web: https://sites.google.com/site/chicchiyoneyama/
Specialties: Folders, hollow ground, lockback and slip-joint folders with interframe handles. **Patterns:** Pocketknives, desk and daily-carry small folders. **Technical:** Stock-removal method on ATS-34, 440C, V10 and SG2/damascus blade steels. **Prices:** $300 to $1,000 and up. **Remarks:** Full-time maker, first knife sold in 1999. **Mark:** Saber tiger mark with logos/Chicchi K. Yoneyama.

YORK, DAVID C
York Knives, PO Box 3166, Chino Valley, AZ 86323 **Contact:** 928-636-1709, dmatj@msn.com
Specialties: Working straight knives and folders. **Patterns:** Prefers small hunters and skinners, locking folders. **Technical:** Grinds D2. **Prices:** $75 to $300, some to $600. **Remarks:** Full-time maker, first knife sold in 1975. **Mark:** Last name.

YOSHIHARA, YOSHINDO
8-17-11 Takasago Katsushi, Tokyo, JAPAN

YOSHIKAZU, KAMADA
540-3 Kaisaki Niuta-cho, Tokushima, JAPAN **Contact:** 0886-44-2319

YOSHIO, MAEDA
3-12-11 Chuo-cho tamashima, Kurashiki-city, Okayama, JAPAN **Contact:** 086-525-2375

YOUNG, BUD
Box 336, Port Hardy, BC, CANADA V0N 2P0 **Contact:** 250-949-6478
Specialties: Fixed blade, working knives, some fancy. **Patterns:** Drop-points to skinners. **Technical:** Hollow or flat grind, 5160, 440C, mostly ATS-34, satin finish. Using supplied damascus at times. **Prices:** $150 to $2000 CDN. **Remarks:** Spare-time maker, making knives since 1962, first knife sold in 1985. Not taking orders at this time, sell as produced. **Mark:** Name.

YOUNG, CLIFF
Fuente De La Cibeles No 5, Atascadero, San Miguel De Allende, GJ, MEXICO 37700 **Contact:** 011-52-415-2-57-11
Specialties: Working knives. **Patterns:** Hunters, fighters and fishing knives. **Technical:** Grinds all, offers D2, 440C and 154CM. **Prices:** Start at $250. **Remarks:** Part-time maker, first knife sold in 1980. **Mark:** Name.

YOUNG, GEORGE
713 Pinoak Dr, Kokomo, IN 46901 **Contact:** 765-457-8893
Specialties: Fancy/embellished and traditional straight knives and folders of his design and to customer specs. **Patterns:** Hunters, fillet/camp knives and locking folders. **Technical:** Grinds 440C, CPM440V, and stellite 6K. Fancy ivory, black pearl and stag for handles. Filework: all stellite construction (6K and 25 alloys). Offers engraving. **Prices:** $350 to $750, some $1500 to $3000. **Remarks:** Full-time maker, first knife sold in 1954. Doing business as Young's Knives. **Mark:** Last name integral inside bowie.

YOUNG, JOHN
483 E. 400 S, Ephraim, UT 84627 **Contact:** 435-340-1417 or 435-283-4555
Patterns: Fighters, hunters and bowies. **Technical:** Stainless steel blades, including ATS-34, 440C and CTS-40CP. **Prices:** $800 to $5,000. **Remarks:** Full-time maker since 2006, first knife sold in 1997. **Mark:** Name, city and state.

YOUNG, RAYMOND L
CUTLER/BLADESMITH, 2922 Hwy 188E, Mt. Ida, AR 71957 **Contact:** 870-867-3947
Specialties: Cutler-Bladesmith, sharpening service. **Patterns:** Hunter, skinners, fighters, no guard, no ricasso, chef tools. **Technical:** Edge tempered 1095, 516C, mosiac handles, water buffalo and exotic woods. **Prices:** $100 and up. **Remarks:** Federal contractor since 1995. Surgical steel sharpening. **Mark:** R.

YURCO, MICKEY
PO Box 712, Canfield, OH 44406 **Contact:** 330-533-4928, shorinki@aol.com
Specialties: Working straight knives. **Patterns:** Hunters, utility knives, bowies and fighters, push knives, claws and other hideouts. **Technical:** Grinds 440C, ATS-34 and 154CM, likes mirror and satin finishes. **Prices:** $20 to $500. **Remarks:** Part-time maker, first knife sold in 1983. **Mark:** Name, steel, serial number.

Z

ZAFEIRIADIS, KONSTANTINOS
Dionyson Street, Marathon Attiki, GREECE 19005 **Contact:** 011-30697724-5771 or 011-30697400-6245
Specialties: Fixed blades, one-of-a-kind swords with bronze fittings made using the lost wax method. **Patterns:** Ancient Greek, central Asian, Viking, bowies, hunting knives, fighters, daggers. **Technical:** Forges 5160, O1 and maker's own damascus. **Prices:** $1,100 and up. **Remarks:** Full-time maker, first knife sold in 2010. **Mark:** (backward K)ZK.

ZAHM, KURT
488 Rio Casa, Indialantic, FL 32903 **Contact:** 407-777-4860
Specialties: Working straight knives of his design or to customer specs. **Patterns:** Daggers, fancy fighters, bowies, hunters and utility knives. **Technical:** Grinds D2, 440C, likes filework. **Prices:** $75 to $1000. **Remarks:** Part-time maker, first knife sold in 1985. **Mark:** Last name.

ZAKABI, CARL S
PO Box 893161, Mililani Town, HI 96789-0161 **Contact:** 808-626-2181
Specialties: User-grade straight knives of his design, cord wrapped and bare steel handles exclusively. **Patterns:** Fighters, hunters and utility/camp knives. **Technical:** Grinds 440C and ATS-34. **Prices:** $90 to $400. **Remarks:** Spare-time maker, first knife sold in 1988. Doing business as Zakabi's Kniteworks LLC. **Mark:** Last name and state inside a Hawaiian sharktooth dagger.

ZAKHAROV, GLADISTON
Rua Pernambuca, 175-Rio Comprido (Long River), Jacaret-SP, BRAZIL 12302-070 **Contact:** 55 12 3958 4021, (fax) 55 12 3958 4103, arkhip@terra.com.br, arkhip.com.br
Specialties: Using straight knives of his design. **Patterns:** Hunters, kitchen, utility/camp and barbecue knives. **Technical:** Grinds his own "secret steel." **Prices:** $30 to $200. **Remarks:** Full-time maker. **Mark:** Arkhip Special Knives.

ZBORIL, TERRY
5320 CR 130, Caldwell, TX 77836 **Contact:** 979-535-4157, tzboril@tconline.net
Specialties: ABS Journeyman Smith.

ZEMBKO III, JOHN
140 Wilks Pond Rd, Berlin, CT 06037 **Contact:** 860-828-3503, johnzembko@hotmail.com
Specialties: Working knives of his design or to customer specs. **Patterns:** Likes to use stabilized high-figured woods. **Technical:** Grinds ATS-34, A2, D2, forges O1, 1095, grinds Damasteel. **Prices:** $50 to $400, some higher. **Remarks:** First knife sold in 1987. **Mark:** Name.

ZEMITIS, JOE
14 Currawong Rd, Cardiff Heights, NSW, AUSTRALIA 2285 **Contact:** +610249549907 or +614034599396, jjvzem@bigpond.com
Specialties: Traditional working straight knives. **Patterns:** Hunters, bowies, tantos, fighters and camp knives. **Technical:** Grinds O1, D2, W2 and 440C. Embellishes, offers engraving. **Prices:** $150 to $3000. **Remarks:** Full-time maker, first knife sold in 1983. **Mark:** First initial, last name and country, or last name.

ZERMENO, WILLIAM D.
9131 Glenshadow Dr, Houston, TX 77088 **Contact:** 281-726-2459, will@wdzknives.com wdzknives.com
Specialties: Tactical/utility folders and fixed blades. **Patterns:** Frame lock and liner lock folders the majority of which incorporate flippers and utility fixed blades. **Technical:** Grinds CPM 154, S30V, 3V and stainless damascus. **Prices:** $250 - $600. **Remarks:** Part-time maker, first knife sold in 2008. Doing business as wdzknives.com. **Mark:** WDZ over logo.

ZIEBA, MICHAEL
95 Commercial St., #4, Brooklyn, NY 11222 **Contact:** 347-335-9944, ziebametal@gmail.com, ziebaknives.com or brooklynknives.com
Specialties: High-end kitchen knives under maker's last name, ZIEBA, also tactical knives under HUSSAR name. **Technical:** Uses stainless steels: CPM S30V, CPM S35VN, CPM S60V, CPM D2 and AEB-L, and high-carbon steels: 52100 and Aogami #2. Forges carbon steel in his shop. **Remarks:** Full-time maker. Marks: Feather logo (kitchen knives only with 24k gold as a standard), ZIEBA (kitchen knives and folders) and "H" Hussar (tactical).

ZIMA, DOUGLAS
Blackbeard Education, Service and Tools, LLC 34 Pickford Dr. Lancaster, PA 17603 **Contact:** 717-399-3475, blkbrd_98@yahoo.com
Patterns: EDC and outdoor.

ZIMA, MICHAEL F
732 State St, Ft. Morgan, CO 80701 **Contact:** 970-867-6078, Web: http://zimaknives.com
Specialties: Working and collector quality straight knives and folders. **Patterns:** Hunters, lock backs, LinerLock®, slip joint and automatic folders. **Technical:** Grinds damascus, 440C, ATS-34 and 154CM. **Prices:** $200 and up. **Remarks:** Full-time maker, first knife sold in 1982. **Mark:** Last name.

ZIMMERMAN, NATHAN
416 S. Comanche Ln., Waukesha, WI 53188 **Contact:** 262-510-3563, zimknives@gmail.com, zimknives.com
Specialties: Custom high-end chef's knives. Large, elaborate fantasy weapons. **Patterns:** Unique matching sets of kitchen knives, as well as various hunters, fighters and utility knives. **Technical:** Thin-ground AEB-L chef's knives, forged 1084 knives with hamons (temper lines). Uses burls, Micartas, bone and horn. Favorite handle materials include ebony, African blackwood, bog oak and ironwood. **Prices:** Start at $200. **Remarks:** Full-time maker and knife sharpener, first knife sold in 2012. **Mark:** Hand-chiseled Z with dash. Signature on forged blades.

ZINKER, BRAD
BZ KNIVES, 1591 NW 17 St, Homestead, FL 33030 **Contact:** 305-216-0404, bzinker@gmail.com
Specialties: Fillets, folders and hunters. **Technical:** Uses ATS-34 and stainless damascus. **Prices:** $200 to $600. **Remarks:** Voting member of Knifemakers Guild and Florida Knifemakers Association. **Mark:** Offset connected initials BZ.

ZIRBES, RICHARD
Neustrasse 15, Niederkail, GERMANY 54526 **Contact:** 0049 6575 1371, r.zirbes@freenet.de zirbes-knives.com zirbes-messer.de
Specialties: Fancy embellished knives with engraving and self-made scrimshaw (scrimshaw made by maker). High-tech working knives and high-tech hunters, boots, fighters and folders. All knives made by hand. **Patterns:** Boots, fighters, folders, hunters. **Technical:** Uses only the best steels for blade material like CPM-T 440V, CPM-T 420V, ATS-34, D2, C440, stainless damascus or steel according to customer's desire. **Prices:** Working knives and hunters: $200 to $600. Fancy embellished knives with engraving and/or scrimshaw: $800 to $3000. **Remarks:** Part-time maker, first knife sold in 1991. Member of the German Knifemaker Guild. **Mark:** Zirbes or R. Zirbes.

ZOWADA, TIM
4509 E Bear River Rd, Boyne Falls, MI 49713 **Contact:** 231-838-4120, timzowada@gmail.com, tzknives.com
Specialties: Working knives and straight razors. **Technical:** Forges O1, L6, his own damascus and smelted steel "Michi-Gane". **Prices:** $200 to $2500, some to $5000. **Remarks:** Full-time maker, first knife sold in 1980. **Mark:** Gothic, lower case "TZ"

ZSCHERNY, MICHAEL
1840 Rock Island Dr, Ely, IA 52227 **Contact:** 319-321-5833, zschernyknives@aol.com
Specialties: Quality folders--slip joints and flipper folders. **Patterns:** Liner-lock and lock-back folders in titanium, working straight knives. **Technical:** Grinds ATS-34 and commercial damascus, prefers natural materials such as pearls and ivory. Uses Timascus, mokume, san mai and carbon fibers. **Prices:** Start at $600. **Remarks:** Full-time maker, first knife sold in 1978. **Mark:** Last name with image of a scorpion.

AK

Barlow, Jana Poirier	Anchorage
Brennan, Judson	Delta Junction
Breuer, Lonnie	Wasilla
Broome, Thomas A	Kenai
Chamberlin, John A	Anchorage
Cornwell, Jeffrey	Anchorage
Desrosiers, Adam	Petersburg
Desrosiers, Haley	Petersburg
Dufour, Arthur J	Anchorage
England, Virgil	Anchorage
Flint, Robert	Anchorage
Gouker, Gary B	Sitka
Harding, Jacob	Fairbanks
Harvey, Mel	Nenana
Hibben, Westley G	Anchorage
Hook, Bob	North Pole
Kelsey, Nate	Palmer
Knapp, Mark	Fairbanks
Lance, Bill	Palmer
Lance, Lucas	Wasilla
Malaby, Raymond J	Juneau
Mcfarlin, Eric E	Kodiak
Miller, Nate	Fairbanks
Miller, Terry	Healy
Mirabile, David	Juneau
Moore, Marve	Willow
Parrish Iii, Gordon A	North Pole
Stegall, Keith	Wasilla
Van Cleve, Steve	Sutton

AL

Alverson, Tim (R.V.)	Arab
Batson, James	Huntsville
Baxter, Dale	Trinity
Bell, Tony	Woodland
Brothers, Dennis L.	Oneonta
Coffman, Danny	Jacksonville
Conn Jr., C T	Attalla
Dark, Robert	Oxford
Deibert, Michael	Trussville
Durham, Kenneth	Cherokee
Elrod, Roger R	Enterprise
Gilbreath, Randall	Dora
Grizzard, Jim	Oxford
Hammond, Jim	Birmingham
Heeter, Todd S.	Mobile
Howard, Durvyn M.	Hokes Bluff
Howell, Keith A.	Oxford
Howell, Len	Opelika
Howell, Ted	Wetumpka
Huckabee, Dale	Maylene
Hulsey, Hoyt	Attalla
Mccullough, Jerry	Georgiana
Mcnees, Jonathan	Northport
Militano, Tom	Jacksonville
Moore, Eddie	LaFayette
Morris, C H	Frisco City
Pardue, Melvin M	Repton
Ploppert, Tom	Cullman
Russell, Tom	Jacksonville
Smith, Lacy	Jacksonville
Thomas, David E	Lillian
Washburn Jr., Robert Lee	Tuscaloosa
Watson, Billy	Deatsville

AR

Anders, David	Center Ridge
Ardwin, Corey	Bryant
Barker, Reggie	Taylor
Barnes Jr., Cecil C.	Center Ridge
Brown, Jim	Little Rock
Browning, Steven W	Benton
Bullard, Benoni	Bradford
Bullard, Tom	Flippin
Chambers, Ronny	Beebe
Cook, James R	Nashville
Copeland, Thom	Nashville
Cox, Larry	Murfreesboro
Crawford, Pat And Wes	West Memphis
Crotts, Dan	Elm Springs
Crowell, James L	Mtn. View
Dozier, Bob	Springdale
Duvall, Fred	Benton
Echols, Rodger	Nashville
Edge, Tommy	Cash
Ferguson, Lee	Hindsville
Fisk, Jerry	Nashville
Fitch, John S	Clinton
Fleming, Mark	Washington
Flournoy, Joe	El Dorado
Foster, Ronnie E	Morrilton
Foster, Timothy L	El Dorado
Frizzell, Ted	West Fork
Gadberry, Emmet	Hattieville
Greenaway, Don	Fayetteville
Herring, Morris	Dyer
Hutchinson, Alan	Conway
Kirkes, Bill	Little Rock
Koster, Daniel	Bentonville
Krein, Tom	Gentry
Lawrence, Alton	De Queen
Lemoine, David C	Mountain Home
Livesay, Newt	Siloam Springs
Lunn, Gail	Gassville
Lunn, Larry A	Mountain Home
Lynch, Tad	Beebe
Maringer, Tom	Springdale
Martin, Hal W	Morrilton
Massey, Roger	Texarkana
Newberry, Allen	Lowell
Newton, Ron	London
Nolte, Barbie	Lowell
Nolte, Steve	Lowell
Olive, Michael E	Leslie
Passmore, Jimmy D	Hoxie
Pearce, Logan	De Queen
Perry, Jim	Hope
Perry, John	Mayflower
Peterson, Lloyd (Pete) C	Clinton
Polk, Clifton	Van Buren
Polk, Rusty	Van Buren
Randow, Ralph	Greenbrier
Red, Vernon	Conway
Reeves, J.R.	Texarkana
Rhea, Lin	Prattsville
Richards, Ralph (Bud)	Bauxite
Roberts, T. C. (Terry)	Siloam Springs
Seward, Ben	Austin
Sharon, Daniel	Gravette
Stanley, John	Crossett
Stout, Charles	Gillham
Sweaza, Dennis	Austin
Townsend, Allen Mark	Texarkana
Townsley, Russell	Floral
Upton, Tom	Rogers
Walker, Jim	Morrilton
Ward, Chuck	Benton
White, Bryce	Little Rock
Young, Raymond L	Mt. Ida

AZ

Allan, Todd	Glendale
Ammons, David C	Tucson
Bennett, Glen C	Tucson
Birdwell, Ira Lee	Congress
Boye, David	Dolan Springs
Dawson, Barry	Prescott Valley
Dawson, Lynn	Prescott Valley
Deubel, Chester J.	Tucson
Dodd, Robert F	Camp Verde
Fuegen, Larry	Prescott
Genovese, Rick	Peeples Valley
Goo, Tai	Tucson
Hall, Jeff	Mesa
Harris, John	Quartzsite
Hoel, Steve	Pine
Holder, D'Alton	New River
Jackson, Laramie	Claysprings
Jensen, Eli	Prescott
Karp, Bob	Phoenix
Kazsuk, David	Lake Havasu City
Kiley, Mike And Jandy	Chino Valley
Kopp, Todd M	Apache Jct.
Lee, Randy	St. Johns
Mcfall, Ken	Lakeside
Mcfarlin, J W	Lake Havasu City
Miller, Michael	Kingman
Montell, Ty	Thatcher
Mooney, Mike	Queen Creek
Newhall, Tom	Tucson
Purvis, Bob And Ellen	Tucson
Robbins, Bill	Sierra Vista
Rybar Jr., Raymond B	Camp Verde
States, Joshua C	New River
Tamboli, Michael	Glendale
Tyre, Michael A	Wickenburg
Weiss, Charles L	Waddell
Wick, Jonathan P.	Hereford
Wolf, Bill	Phoenix
Wright, Timothy	Sedona
Wuertz, Travis	Casa Grande
York, David C	Chino Valley

CA

Abegg, Arnie	Huntington Beach
Adkins, Richard L	Mission Viejo
Andrade, Don Carlos	Los Osos
Athey, Steve	Riverside
Barnes, Roger	Bay Point
Barnes, Roger	Bay Point
Barron, Brian	San Mateo
Begg, Todd M.	Petaluma
Benson, Don	Escalon
Berger, Max A.	Carmichael
Bolduc, Gary	Corona
Bost, Roger E	Palos Verdes
Boyd, Francis	Berkeley
Breshears, Clint	Manhattan Beach
Brooks, Buzz	Los Angles
Brous, Jason	Buellton
Browne, Rick	Upland
Bruce, Richard L.	Yankee Hill
Butler, Bart	Ramona
Cabrera, Sergio B	Wilmington
Cantrell, Kitty D	Ramona
Caston, Darriel	Folsom
Caswell, Joe	Newbury
Clinco, Marcus	Venice
Coffey, Bill	Clovis
Coleman, John A	Citrus Heights
Colwell, Kevin	Cheshire
Connolly, James	Oroville
Cucchiara, Matt	Fresno
Davis, Charlie	Lakeside
De Maria Jr., Angelo	Carmel Valley
Dion, Greg	Oxnard
Dobratz, Eric	Laguna Hills
Doolittle, Mike	Novato
Driscoll, Mark	La Mesa
Dwyer, Duane	Escondido
Ellis, William Dean	Sanger
Emerson, Ernest R	Harbor City
English, Jim	Jamul
Ernest, Phil (Pj)	Whittier
Essegian, Richard	Fresno
Felix, Alexander	Torrance
Ferguson, Jim	Lakewood
Finney, Garett	Loomis
Forrest, Brian	Descanso
Fraley, D B	Dixon
Fred, Reed Wyle	Sacramento
Freeman, Matt	Fresno
Freer, Ralph	Seal Beach
Fulton, Mickey	Willows
Girtner, Joe	Brea
Grayman, Mike	San Jacinto
Guarnera, Anthony R	Quartzhill
Hardy, Scott	Placerville
Harris, Jay	Redwood City
Helton, Roy	San Diego
Herndon, Wm R "Bill"	Acton
Hink Iii, Les	Stockton
Hoy, Ken	North Fork
Humenick, Roy	Rescue
Jacks, Jim	Covina
Jackson, David	Lemoore
Jensen, John Lewis	Pasadena

Johnson, Randy — Turlock
Kelly, Dave — Los Angeles
Keyes, Dan — Chino
Kilpatrick, Christian A — Citrus Hieghts
Koster, Steven C — Huntington Beach
Larson, Richard — Turlock
Larstein, Francine — Watsonville
Leland, Steve — Fairfax
Lin, Marcus — Mission Viejo
Lockett, Sterling — Burbank
Luchini, Bob — Palo Alto
Maccaughtry, Scott F. — Camarillo
Mackie, John — Whittier
Massey, Ron — Joshua Tree
Mata, Leonard — San Diego
Maxwell, Don — Clovis
Mcabee, William — Colfax
Mcclure, Michael — Menlo Park
Mcgrath, Patrick T — Westchester
Melin, Gordon C — La Mirada
Meloy, Sean — Lemon Grove
Montano, Gus A — San Diego
Morgan, Jeff — Santee
Moses, Steven — Santa Ana
Mutz, Jeff — Rancho Cucamonga
Naten, Greg — Bakersfield
Orton, Rich — Wilmington
Osborne, Donald H — Clovis
Palm, Rik — San Diego
Panchenko, Serge — Citrus Heights
Perry, Chris — Fresno
Pfanenstiel, Dan — Modesto
Pitt, David F — Anderson
Quesenberry, Mike — Blairsden
Randall, Patrick — Newbury Park
Rozas, Clark D — Wilmington
Schmitz, Raymond E — Valley Center
Schroen, Karl — Sebastopol
Sclby, Brian — Lincoln
Sharp, David — Hesperia
Sibrian, Aaron — Ventura
Sjostrand, Kevin — Visalia
Slobodian, Scott — San Andreas
Smith, Shawn — Clouis
Sornberger, Jim — Volcano
Steinberg, Al — Laguna Woods
Stimps, Jason M — Orange
Strider, Mick — Escondido
Terrlll, Stephen — Springville
Tingle, Dennis P — Jackson
Tobolak, Libor — San Marcos
Torres, Henry — Clovis
Vagnino, Michael — Visalia
Velick, Sammy — Los Angeles
Warren, Al — Roseville
Watanabe, Wayne — Montebello
Weinstock, Robert — San Francisco
Wilburn, Aaron — Redding
Wilson, Ron — Morro Bay
Withers, Tim — Linden

CO

Anderson, Mel — Hotchkiss
Booco, Gordon — Hayden
Brock, Kenneth L — Allenspark
Burrows, Chuck — Durango
Corich, Vance — Morrison
Davis, Don — Loveland
Dennehy, John D — Greeley
Dill, Robert — Loveland
Fairly, Daniel — Bayfield
Fronefield, Daniel — Peyton
Graham, Levi — Greeley
High, Tom — Alamosa
Hockensmith, Dan — Berthoud
Hughes, Ed — Grand Junction
Hughes, Tony — Littleton
Irie, Michael L — Colorado Springs
Kitsmiller, Jerry — Montrose
Leck, Dal — Hayden
Mcwilliams, Sean — Carbondale
Miller, Hanford J — Lakespur
Miller, M A — Northglenn

Nolen, Steve — Longmont
Ott, Fred — Durango
Buena Vista
Rexford, Todd — Florissant
Roberts, Chuck — Golden
Rollert, Steve — Keenesburg
Ronzio, N. Jack — Fruita
Sanders, Bill — Mancos
Snody, Mike — Walsenburg
Thompson, Lloyd — Pagosa Springs
Urbach, Scott — Aurora
Waites, Richard L — Broomfield
Watson, Bert — Westminster
Wilson, James G — Estes Park
Wood, Owen Dale — Arvada
Zima, Michael F — Ft. Morgan
Redd, Bill — Broomfield

CT

Buebendorf, Robert E — Monroe
Chapo, William G — Wilton
Cross, Kevin — Portland
Framski, Walter P — Prospect
Jean, Gerry — Manchester
Loukides, David E — Cheshire
Meyer, Christopher J — Tolland
Parkinson, Matthew — Wolcott
Plunkett, Richard — West Cornwall
Rainville, Richard — Salem
Swarz-Burt, Peter T. — Wolcott
Turecek, Jim — Ansonia
Vitale, Mace — Guilford
Zembko lii, John — Berlin

DE

Willey, Wg — Greenwood

FL

Adams, Les — Cape Coral
Alexander,, Oleg, And Cossack Blades — Wellington
Anders, Jerome — Miramar
Angell, Jon — Hawthorne
Atkinson, Dick — Wausau
Barnes, Gary L. — Defuniak Springs
Barry lii, James J. — West Palm Beach
Beers, Ray — Lake Wales
Benjamin Jr., George — Kissimmee
Bosworth, Dean — Key Largo
Bradley, John — Pomona Park
Bray Jr., W Lowell — New Port Richey
Brown, Harold E — Arcadia
Butler, John — Havana
Clark, Jason — O'Brien
D'Andrea, John — Citrus Springs
Davis Jr., Jim — Zephyrhills
Dietzel, Bill — Middleburg
Dintruff, Chuck — Plant City
Dotson, Tracy — Baker
Ellerbe, W B — Geneva
Ellis, Willy B — Tarpon Springs
Enos lii, Thomas M — Orlando
Fowler, Charles R — Ft McCoy
Gallagher, Scott — Santa Rosa Beach
Gamble, Roger — Newberry
Gardner, Robert — West Palm Beach
Ghio, Paolo — Pensacola
Goers, Bruce — Lakeland
Granger, Paul J — Largo
Greene, Steve — Intercession City
Griffin Jr., Howard A — Davie
Grospitch, Ernie — Orlando
Heaney, John D — Haines City
Heitler, Henry — Tampa
Hodge lii, John — Palatka
Hostetler, Larry — Fort Pierce
Hostetter, Wally — San Mateo
Humphreys, Joel — Lake Placid
Hunter, Richard D — Alachua
Hytovick, Joe "Hy" — Dunnellon
Johanning Custom Knives, Tom — Sarasota
Johnson, John R — Plant City
King, Bill — Tampa
Krapp, Denny — Apopka

Levengood, Bill — Tampa
Long, Glenn A — Dunnellon
Lovestrand, Schuyler — Vero Beach
Lozier, Don — Ocklawaha
Lyle lii, Ernest L — Chiefland
Mandt, Joe — St. Petersburg
Mason, Bill — Hobe Sound
Mcdonald, Robert J — Loxahatchee
Miller, Ronald T — Largo
Miller, Steve — Clearwater
Newton, Larry — Jacksonville
Ochs, Charles F — Largo
Overall, Jason — Sanford
Owens, Donald — Melbourne
Parker, Cliff — Zephyrhills
Partridge, Jerry D. — DeFuniak Springs
Pattay, Rudy — Citrus Springs
Pendray, Alfred H — Williston
Philippe, D A — The Villages
Piergallini, Daniel E — Plant City
Randall Made Knives, — Orlando
Raymond, Michael — Malabar
Renner, Terry — Palmetto
Robinson, Calvin — Pace
Robinson lii, Rex R — Leesburg
Roddenberry, Charles — Live Oak
Rodkey, Dan — Hudson
Romeis, Gordon — Fort Myers
Russ, Ron — Williston
Schwarzer, Lora Sue — Crescent City
Schwarzer, Stephen — Crescent City
Schuette, Charles — Glen St Mary
Smith, Michael J — Clearwater
Stapleton, William E — Merritt Island
Steck, Van R — Orange City
Stephan, Daniel — Valrico
Stipes, Dwight — Palm City
Straight, Kenneth J — Largo
Tabor, Tim — Lutz
Turnbull, Ralph A — Spring Hill
Vogt, Donald J — Tampa
Watson, Tom — Panama City
Weiland Jr., J Reese — Riverview
Wicker, Donnie R — Panama City
Wilson, Stan — Lithia
Zahm, Kurt — Indialantic
Zinker, Brad — Homestead

GA

Arrowood, Dale — Sharpsburg
Ashworth, Boyd — Powder Springs
Barker, John — Cumming
Barker, Robert G. — Bishop
Beaver, Dirk — Ellijay
Bentley, C L — Albany
Bish, Hal — Jonesboro
Brach, Paul — Cumming
Bradley, Dennis — Blairsville
Busbie, Jeff — Bloomingdale
Cambron, Henry — Dallas
Chamblin, Joel — Concord
Crockford, Jack — Chamblee
Daniel, Travis E — Thomaston
Davidson, Scott — Alto
Davis, Steve — Powder Springs
Fowler, Stephan — Dallas
Frost, Dewayne — Barnesville
Gaines, Buddy — Commerce
Glover, Warren D — Cleveland
Greene, David — Covington
Hammond, Hank — Leesburg
Hammond, Ray — Buford
Hardy, Douglas E — Franklin
Hensley, Wayne — Conyers
Hewitt, Ronald "Cotton" — Adel
Hinson And Son, R — Columbus
Hoffman, Kevin L — Savannah
Hossom, Jerry — Duluth
Kimsey, Kevin — Cartersville
King, Fred — Cartersville
Knott, Steve — Guyton
Landers, John — Newnan
Lockett, Lowell C. — Canton

Lonewolf, J Aguirre	Demorest
Mathews, Charlie And Harry	Statesboro
Mcgill, John	Blairsville
Mitchell, James A	Columbus
Moncus, Michael Steven	Smithville
Parks, John	Jefferson
Poole, Marvin O	Commerce
Powell, Robert Clark	Smarr
Prater, Mike	Flintstone
Price, Timmy	Blairsville
Ragsdale, James D	Ellijay
Roghmans, Mark	LaGrange
Sangster, Joe	Vienna
Sculley, Peter E	Rising Fawn
Sharp, Chris	Oxford
Snow, Bill	Columbus
Sowell, Bill	Macon
Stafford, Richard	Warner Robins
Surls, W. Allen	Buford
Thompson, Kenneth	Duluth
Tomey, Kathleen	Macon
White, Lou	Ranger
Whittaker, Wayne	Clarksville
Wright, Robert A	Savannah

HI

Evans, Vincent K And Grace	Keaau
Gibo, George	Hilo
Lui, Ronald M	Honolulu
Mann, Tim	Honokaa
Matsuoka, Scot	Mililani
Mayo Jr., Tom	Waialua
Mitsuyuki, Ross	Honolulu
Onion, Kenneth J	Kaneohe
Ouye, Keith	Honolulu
Salter, Gregg	Waikoloa
Watanabe, Melvin	Kailua
Zakabi, Carl S	Mililani Town

IA

Adkins, Wes	Council Bluffs
Brooker, Dennis	Chariton
Brower, Max	Boone
Clark, Howard F	Runnells
Cockerham, Lloyd	Denham Springs
Helscher, John W	Washington
Lainson, Tony	Council Bluffs
Lewis, Bill	Riverside
Mckiernan, Stan	Lamoni
Miller, James P	Fairbank
Thie, Brian	Burlington
Trindle, Barry	Earlham
Westberg, Larry	Algona
Zscherny, Michael	Ely

ID

Alderman, Robert	Sagle
Bair, Mark	Firth
Bloodworth Custom Knives,	Meridian
Burke, Bill	Boise
Durbin, Jerry	Middleton
Eddy, Hugh E	Caldwell
Farr, Dan	Post Falls
Hackney, Dana A.	Naples
Hawk, Grant And Gavin	Idaho City
Hogan, Thomas R	Boise
Horton, Scot	Buhl
Howe, Tori	Athol
Mann, Michael L	Spirit Lake
Metz, Greg T	Cascade
Patton, Dick And Rob	Nampa
Quarton, Barr	McCall
Rohn, Fred	Coeur d'Alene
Sawby, Scott	Sandpoint
Souther, Michael	Coeur D' Alene
Sparks, Bernard	Dingle
Steiger, Monte L	Genesee
Tippetts, Colten	Hidden Springs
Towell, Dwight L	Midvale
Trace Rinaldi Custom Blades,	Plummer

IL

Armour, Dave	Auburn
Bloomer, Alan T	Maquon
Camerer, Craig	Chesterfield
Cook, Louise	Ozark
Cook, Mike	Ozark
Detmer, Phillip	Breese
Dicristofano, Anthony P	Melrose Park
Eaker, Allen L	Paris
Hall, Scott M.	Geneseo
Hawes, Chuck	Weldon
Heath, William	Bondville
Hill, Rick	Maryville
Kovar, Eugene	Evergreen Park
Kulis, David S.	Chicago
Leone, Nick	Pontoon Beach
Markley, Ken	Sparta
Meers, Andrew	Carbondale
Meier, Daryl	Carbondale
Myers, Paul	Wood River
Myers, Steve	Carlinville
Nowland, Rick	Waltonville
Pellegrin, Mike	Troy
Pritchard, Ron	Dixon
Roosevelt, Russell	Albion
Rosenbaugh, Ron	Crystal Lake
Rossdeutscher, Robert N	Arlington Heights
Rzewnicki, Gerald	Elizabeth
Schneider, Craig M	Claremont
Smale, Charles J	Waukegan
Smith, John M	Centralia
Todd, Richard C	Chambersburg
Veit, Michael	LaSalle
Voss, Ben	Victoria
Werth, George W	Poplar Grove
West, Charles A	Centralia
Wheeler, Robert	Bradley

IN

Ball, Ken	Mooresville
Barkes, Terry	Edinburgh
Barrett, Rick L. (Toshi Hisa)	Goshen
Bose, Reese	Shelburn
Bose, Tony	Shelburn
Chaffee, Jeff L	Morris
Claiborne, Jeff	Franklin
Cramer, Brent	Wheatland
Crowl, Peter	Waterloo
Curtiss, David	Granger
Damlovac, Sava	Indianapolis
Darby, Jed	Greensburg
Davis, John H	Freetown
Fitzgerald, Dennis M	Fort Wayne
Fraps, John R	Indianapolis
Good, D.R.	Tipton
Harding, Chad	Solsberry
Imel, Billy Mace	New Castle
Johnson, C E Gene	Chesterton
Kain, Charles	Indianapolis
Keeslar, Steven C	Hamilton
Keeton, William L	Laconia
Kinker, Mike	Greensburg
Largin, Ken	Connersville
Mayville, Oscar L	Marengo
Miller, Levi	Howe
Minnick, Jim & Joyce	Middletown
Patton, Phillip	Yoder
Quakenbush, Thomas C	Ft Wayne
Robertson, Leo D	Indianapolis
Seib, Steve	Evansville
Shull, James	Rensselaer
Smock, Timothy E	Marion
Thayer, Danny O	Romney
Young, George	Kokomo

KS

Bradburn, Gary	Wichita
Burrows, Stephen R	Humboldt
Chard, Gordon R	Iola
Craig, Roger L	Topeka
Culver, Steve	Meriden
Darpinian, Dave	Olathe
Dawkins, Dudley L	Topeka
Dick, Dan	Hutchinson
Evans, Phil	Columbus
Finley, Jon M.	Leawood
Hegwald, J L	Humboldt
Herman, Tim	Olathe
Keranen, Paul	Tacumseh
King Jr., Harvey G	Alta Vista
Kraft, Steve	Abilene
Lamb, Curtis J	Ottawa
Magee, Jim	Salina
Petersen, Dan L	Auburn
Stice, Douglas W	Wichita

KY

Addison, Kyle A	Hazel
Baskett, Barbara	Eastview
Baskett, Lee Gene	Eastview
Bybee, Barry J	Cadiz
Carter, Mike	Louisville
Downing, Larry	Bremen
Dunn, Steve	Smiths Grove
Edwards, Mitch	Glasgow
Finch, Ricky D	West Liberty
Fister, Jim	Simpsonville
France, Dan	Cawood
Franklin, Mike	Maysville
Frederick, Aaron	West Liberty
Greco, John	Greensburg
Hibben, Daryl	LaGrange
Hibben, Gil	LaGrange
Hoke, Thomas M	LaGrange
Holbrook, H L	Sandy Hook
Jeffries, Mike	Louisville
Keeslar, Joseph F	Almo
Pease, W D	Ewing
Pierce, Harold L	Louisville
Rados, Jerry F	Columbia
Richerson, Ron	Greenburg
Rigney Jr., Willie	Bronston
Smith, Chris	Burgin
Smith, John W	West Liberty
Soaper, Max H.	Henderson
Steier, David	Louisville
Vance, David	West Liberty
Wallingford Jr., Charles W	Union

LA

Blaum, Roy	Covington
Caldwell, Bill	West Monroe
Calvert Jr., Robert W (Bob)	Rayville
Capdepon, Randy	Carencro
Capdepon, Robert	Carencro
Chauvin, John	Scott
Dake, C M	New Orleans
Dake, Mary H	New Orleans
Durio, Fred	Opelousas
Faucheaux, Howard J	Loreauville
Fontenot, Gerald J	Mamou
Gorenflo, James T (Jt)	Baton Rouge
Graves, Dan	Shreveport
Johnson, Gordon A.	Choudrant
Ki, Shiva	Baton Rouge
Laurent, Kermit	LaPlace
Lemaire, Ryan M.	Abbeville
Leonard, Randy Joe	Sarepta
Lee, Ethan	Gonzales
Mitchell, Max Dean And Ben	Leesville
Phillips, Dennis	Independence
Potier, Timothy F	Oberlin
Primos, Terry	Shreveport
Provenzano, Joseph D	Ponchatoula
Randall Jr., James W	Keithville
Reggio Jr., Sidney J	Sun
Tilton, John	Iowa
Trisler, Kenneth W	Rayville
Wilson, P.R. "Regan"	Scott
Winn, Marvin	Sunset

MA

Banaitis, Romas	Medway
Cooper, Paul	Woburn
Dailey, G E	Seekonk
Dugdale, Daniel J.	Walpole
Gedraitis, Charles J	Holden
Grossman, Stewart	Clinton

Hinman, Theodore	Greenfield
Jarvis, Paul M	Cambridge
Johnson, Timothy A.	Worcester
Khalsa, Jot Singh	Millis
Klein, Kevin	Boston
Kubasek, John A	Easthampton
Lapen, Charles	W. Brookfield
Little, Larry	Spencer
Martin, Randall J	Bridgewater
Mcluin, Tom	Dracut
Moore, Michael Robert	Lowell
Rebello, Indian George	New Bedford
Rizzi, Russell J	Ashfield
Rua, Gary	Fall River
Saviano, James	Douglas
Siska, Jim	Westfield
Smith, J D	Melrose
Stuart, Mason	Mansfield
Vining, Bill	Gardner

MD

Aylor, Erin Lutzer	Myersville
Bagley, R. Keith	White Plains
Barnes, Aubrey G.	Hagerstown
Clarke, Ed	Hampstead
Cohen, N J (Norm)	Baltimore
Dement, Larry	Prince Fredrick
Fuller, Jack A	New Market
Gossman, Scott	Whiteford
Hart, Bill	Pasadena
Heard, Tom	Waldorf
Hendrickson, Shawn	Knoxville
Kreh, Lefty	"Cockeysville"
Mccarley, John	Taneytown
Mcgowan, Frank E	Sykesville
Merchant, Ted	White Hall
Nicholson, R. Kent	Monkton
Nuckels, Stephen J	Hagerstown
Presti, Matt	Union Bridge
Smit, Glenn	Aberdeen
Sontheimer, G Douglas	Gaithersburg
Spickler, Gregory Noble	Sharpsburg
St. Clair, Thomas K	Monrovia
Walker, Bill	Stevensville

ME

Bohrmann, Bruce	Yarmouth
Breda, Ben	Hope
Ceprano, Peter J.	Auburn
Coombs Jr., Lamont	Bucksport
Gray, Daniel	Brownville
Hillman, Charles	Friendship
Leavitt Jr., Earl F	E. Boothbay
Oyster, Lowell R	Corinth
Sharrigan, Mudd	Wiscasset
Steingass, T.K.	Bucksport

MI

Ackerson, Robin E	Buchanan
Alcorn, Douglas A.	Chesaning
Andrews, Eric	Grand Ledge
Arms, Eric	Tustin
Behnke, William	Kingsley
Booth, Philip W	Ithaca
Carr, Tim	Muskegon
Carroll, Chad	Grant
Cashen, Kevin R	Hubbardston
Cook, Mike A	Portland
Cousino, George	Onsted
Cowles, Don	Royal Oak
Doyle, John	Gladwin
Ealy, Delbert	Indian River
Erickson, Walter E.	Atlanta
Gordon, Larry B	Farmington Hills
Gottage, Dante	Clinton Twp.
Gottage, Judy	Clinton Twp.
Haas, Randy	Marlette
Harm, Paul W	Attica
Harrison, Brian	Cedarville
Hartman, Arlan (Lanny)	Baldwin
Hoffman, Jay	Munising
Hughes, Daryle	Nunica
Lankton, Scott	Ann Arbor
Lark, David	Kingsley
Logan, Iron John	Leslie
Marsh, Jeremy	Ada
McConnell, David	Kaklkaska
Mills, Louis G	Ann Arbor
Morris, Michael S.	Yale
Nevling, Mark	Owosso
Noren, Douglas E	Springlake
Parker, Robert Nelson	Royal Oak
Repke, Mike	Bay City
Rose Ii, Doun T.	Fife Lake
Sakmar, Mike	Howell
Sandberg, Ronald B	Brownstown
Tally, Grant	Flat Rock
Van Eizenga, Jerry W	Nunica
Vasquez, Johnny David	Wyandotte
Viste, James	Hamtramck
Webster, Bill	Three Rivers
Welling, Ronald L	Grand Haven
White, Richard T	Grosse Pointe Farms
Wood, Webster	Atlanta
Zowada, Tim	Boyne Falls

MN

Andersen, Karl B.	Warba
Burns, Robert	Carver
Davis, Joel	Albert Lea
Fredeen, Graham	Petersburg
Hagen, Doc	Pelican Rapids
Hansen, Robert W	Cambridge
Hebeisen, Jeff	Hopkins
Johnson, Jerry L	Worthington
Johnson, Keith R.	Bemidji
Johnson, R B	Clearwater
Knipschield, Terry	Rochester
Leblanc, Gary E	Little Falls
Maines, Jay	Wyoming
Mesenbourg, Nick	Inver Grove Heights
Metsala, Anthony	Princeton
Mickley, Tracy	North Mankato
Poling, Jim	Alvarado
Ritchie, Adam	Bloomington
Rohde, Daniel S.	Winona
Rydbom, Jeff	Annandale
Shadley, Eugene W	Grand Rapids
Taber, David E.	Winona
Voorhies, Les	Faribault

MO

Abernathy, Lance	North Kansas City
Allred, Elvan	St. Charles
Andrews, Russ	Sugar Creek
Braschler, Craig W.	Zalma
Buxton, Bill	Kaiser
Chinnock, Daniel T.	Union
Cover, Jeff	Potosi
Cover, Raymond A	Mineral Point
Dippold, Al	Perryville
Duncan, Ron	Cairo
Eaton, Frank L Jr	Farmington
Ehrenberger, Daniel Robert	Mexico
Engle, William	Boonville
George, Les	Blue Springs
Hanson, Kyle S.	Success
Hanson Iii, Don L.	Success
Harrison, Jim (Seamus)	St. Louis
Kinnikin, Todd	Pacific
Knickmeyer, Hank	Cedar Hill
Knickmeyer, Kurt	Cedar Hill
Krause, Jim	Farmington
Knox, Jeff	Baldwin
Martin, Tony	Arcadia
Mccrackin, Kevin	House Spings
Mccrackin And Son, V J	House Spings
Miller, William (Bill)	Warsaw
Mosier, David	Independence
Mulkey, Gary	Branson
Muller, Jody	Goodson
Newcomb, Corbin	Moberly
Ramsey, Richard A	Neosho
Rardon, A D	Polo
Rardon, Archie F	Polo
Riepe, Richard A	Harrisonville
Robbins, Howard P	Flemington
Robbins, Landon	Crane
Royer, Kyle	Clever
Schow, Lyle	Harrisonville
Scroggs, James A	Warrensburg
Seaton, David D	Rolla
Smith, Debbie & Jerry	Willow Springs
Sonntag, Douglas W	Nixa
Sonntag, Jacob D	St. Robert
Sonntag, Kristopher D	Nixa
Steketee, Craig A	Billings
Stormer, Bob	Dixon
Waide, Rusty	Buffalo
Warden, Roy A	Union
Whitesell, J. Dale	Stover
Willis, Bill	Ava

MS

Black, Scott	Picayune
Boleware, David	Carson
Cohea, John M	Nettleton
Davis, Jesse W	Coldwater
Davison, Todd A.	Kosciusko
Evans, Bruce A	Booneville
Flynt, Robert G	Gulfport
Jones, Jack P.	Ripley
Lamey, Robert M	Biloxi
Lebatard, Paul M	Vancleave
May, Charles	Aberdeen
Mayo Jr., Homer	Biloxi
Nichols, Chad	Blue Springs
Phillips, Donavon	Morton
Pickett, Terrell	Lumberton
Provost, J.C.	Laurel
Robinson, Chuck	Picayune
Shiffer, Steve	Leakesville
Smith, J.B.	Perkinston
Taylor, Billy	Petal
Tribble, Skylar	Leakesville
Vandeventer, Terry L	Byram
Vardaman, Robert	Hattiesburg
Wehner, Rudy	Collins
White, Russell D.	Rienzi
Wilson, Vic	Olive Branch
Wingo, Perry	Gulfport
Winston, David	Starkville

MT

Barnes, Jack	Whitefish
Barnes, Wendell	Clinton
Barth, J.D.	Alberton
Beam, John R.	Kalispell
Beaty, Robert B.	Missoula
Behring, James	Missoula
Bell, Don	Lincoln
Bizzell, Robert	Butte
Brooks, Steve R	Walkerville
Caffrey, Edward J	Great Falls
Campbell, Doug	McLeod
Carlisle, Jeff	Simms
Christensen, Jon P	Stevensville
Colter, Wade	Colstrip
Conklin, George L	Ft. Benton
Conti, Jeffrey D	Judith Gap
Crowder, Robert	Thompson Falls
Curtiss, Steve L	Eureka
Dunkerley, Rick	Lincoln
Eaton, Rick	Broadview
Ellefson, Joel	Manhattan
Fassio, Melvin G	Lolo
Forthofer, Pete	Whitefish
Fritz, Erik L	Forsyth
Gallagher, Barry	Lincoln
Harkins, J A	Conner
Hintz, Gerald M	Helena
Hulett, Steve	West Yellowstone
Kauffman, Dave	Clancy
Kelly, Steven	Bigfork
Mcguane Iv, Thomas F	Bozeman
Mckee, Neil	Stevensville
Moyer, Russ	Havre
Nedved, Dan	Kalispell
Olson, Joe	Great Falls

Parsons, Pete	Helena
Patrick, Willard C	Helena
Peele, Bryan	Thompson Falls
Pursley, Aaron	Big Sandy
Rodewald, Gary	Hamilton
Ruana Knife Works	Bonner
Smith, Josh	Frenchtown
Stahl, Kim	St. Louis
Taylor, Shane	Miles City
Thill, Jim	Missoula
Weinand, Gerome M	Missoula
Yashinski, John L	Red Lodge

NC

Baker, Herb	Eden
Barefoot, Joe W.	Wilmington
Best, Ron	Stokes
Bisher, William (Bill)	Denton
Brackett, Jamin	Fallston
Britton, Tim	Winston-Salem
Busfield, John	Roanoke Rapids
Craddock, Mike	Thomasville
Crist, Zoe	Flat Rock
Drew, Gerald	Mill Spring
Gaddy, Gary Lee	Washington
Gahagan, Kyle	Moravian Falls
Gingrich, Justin	Wade
Goode, Brian	Shelby
Greene, Chris	Shelby
Gross, W W	Archdale
Hall, Ken	Waynesville
Hege, John B.	Danbury
Hoffman, Liam	Newland
Johnson, Tommy	Troy
Livingston, Robert C	Murphy
Maynard, William N.	Fayetteville
Mcghee, E. Scott	Clarkton
Mclurkin, Andrew	Raleigh
Mcrae, J Michael	Mint Hill
Neely, Jonathan	Greensboro
Nichols, Calvin	Raleigh
Novinc, Kevin	Gastonia
Parrish, Robert	Weaverville
Patrick, Chuck	Brasstown
Patrick, Peggy	Brasstown
Pica, Daniel	Pittsboro
Randall, Steve	Lincolnton
Rapp, Steven J	Marshall
Salyers, Billy	Rutherfordton
Santini, Tom	Pikeville
Scholl, Tim	Angier
Simmons, H R	Aurora
Sirois, Darrin	Fayetteville
Sterling, Murray	Mount Airy
Summers, Arthur L	Concord
Sutton, S Russell	New Bern
Vail, Dave	Hampstead
Wacholz, Doc	Marble
Wagaman, John K	Selma
Walker, Don	Burnsville
Warren, Daniel	Canton
Whitley, L Wayne	Chocowinity
Wiggins, Bill	Canton
Williamson, Tony	Siler City
Wilson, Mike	Hayesville
Winkler, Daniel	Blowing Rock

ND

Kommer, Russ	Fargo
Pitman, David	Williston

NE

Archer, Ray And Terri	Omaha
Hielscher, Guy	Alliance
Jokerst, Charles	Omaha
Lyons, William R. (Bill)	Palisade
Marlowe, Charles	Omaha
Moore, Jon P	Aurora
Sloan, David	Diller
Suedmeier, Harlan	Nebraska City
Syslo, Chuck	Omaha
Tiensvold, Alan L	Rushville
Tiensvold, Jason	Rushville

Till, Calvin E And Ruth	Chadron

NH

Hudson, C Robbin	Rochester
Jonas, Zachary	Wilmot
Saindon, R Bill	Goshen
Ward, Tom	Wilmot
White, Caleb A.	Hooksett

NJ

Ascolese, Sal	New Brunswick
Fisher, Lance	Pompton Lakes
Grussenmeyer, Paul G	Cherry Hill
Knowles, Shawn	Great Meadows
Lesswing, Kevin	Bayonne
Licata, Steven	Boonton
Mccallen Jr., Howard H	So Seaside Park
Nadeau, Brian	Stanhope
Pressburger, Ramon	Howell
Riggi, Nick	Bayville
Sheets, Steven William	Mendham
Slee, Fred	Morganville
Yeskoo, Richard C	Summit

NM

Aldridge, Donald	Albuquerque
Black, Tom	Albuquerque
Burnley, Lucas	Albuquerque
Chavez, Ramon	Belen
Cherry, Frank J	Albuquerque
Cordova, Joey	Bernalillo
Cordova, Joseph G	Bosque Farms
Cumming, Bob	Cedar Crest
Digangi, Joseph M	Los Ojos
Duran, Jerry T	Albuquerque
Dyess, Eddie	Roswell
Fisher, Jay	Clovis
Garner, George	Albuquerque
Goode, Bear	Navajo Dam
Gunter, Brad	Tijeras
Hartman, Tim	Albuquerque
Hethcoat, Don	Clovis
Kimberley, Richard L.	Santa Fe
Leu, Pohan	Rio Rancho
Lewis, Tom R	Carlsbad
Lynn, Arthur	Galisteo
Macdonald, David	Los Lunas
Meshejian, Mardi	Santa Fe
Reid, Jim	Albuquerque
Rogers, Richard	Magdalena
Schaller, Anthony Brett	Albuquerque
Stalcup, Eddie	Gallup
Swearingen, Kurt	Cedar Crest
Terzuola, Robert	Albuquerque
Trujillo, Albert M B	Bosque Farms
Walker, Michael L	Pueblo Sur Taos
Wescott, Cody	Las Cruces

NV

Barnett, Van	Reno
Cameron, Ron G	Logandale
Dellana,	Reno
George, Tom	Henderson
Hrisoulas, Jim	Henderson
Kreibich, Donald L.	Reno
Nishiuchi, Melvin S	Las Vegas
Rougeau, Derick	Sparks
Thomas, Devin	Panaca
Washburn, Arthur D	Pioche

NY

Baker, Wild Bill	Boiceville
Castellucio, Rich	Amsterdam
Cimms, Greg	Pleasant Valley
Daly, Michael	Brooklyn
Davis, Barry L	Castleton
Gregory, Matthew M.	Glenwood
Hobart, Gene	Windsor
Johnson, Mike	Orient
Johnston, Dr. Robt	Rochester
Lamothe, Jordan	Granville
Lamothe, Jordan	Granville
Levin, Jack	Brooklyn

Loos, Henry C	New Hyde Park
Ludwig, Richard O	Maspeth
Lupole, Jamie G	Kirkwood
Manaro, Sal	Holbrook
Maragni, Dan	Georgetown
Mccornock, Craig	Willow
Meerdink, Kurt	Barryville
Merola, Jim	Brooklyn
Miller, Chelsea Grace	Brooklyn
Nazz, Theo "Rock"	New York
Page, Reginald	Groveland
Rachlin, Leslie S	Elmira
Rappazzo, Richard	Cohoes
Rotella, Richard A	Niagara Falls
Scheid, Maggie	Rochester
Schippnick, Jim	Sanborn
Serafen, Steven E	New Berlin
Skiff, Steven	Broadalbin
Smith, Lenard C	Valley Cottage
Smith, Raymond L	Erin
Summers, Dan	Whitney Pt.
Szilaski, Joseph	Pine Plains
Turner, Kevin	Montrose
Welling, William	West Valley
Zieba, Michael	Brooklyn

OH

Batdorf, Jason	Wauseon
Busse, Jerry	Wauseon
Coffee, Jim	Norton
Collins, Lynn M	Elyria
Coppins, Daniel	Cambridge
Cottrill, James I	Columbus
Crews, Randy	Patriot
Downing, Tom	Cuyahoga Falls
Downs, James F	Powell
Etzler, John	Grafton
Francis, John D	Ft. Loramie
Gittinger, Raymond	Tiffin
Glover, Ron	Cincinnati
Greiner, Richard	Green Springs
Hinderer, Rick	Shreve
Humphrey, Lon	Newark
Imboden Ii, Howard L.	Dayton
Johnson, Wm. C. "Bill"	Enon
Jones, Roger Mudbone	Waverly
Kiefer, Tony	Pataskala
Landis, David E. Sr.	Galion
Longworth, Dave	Felicity
Maienknecht, Stanley	Sardis
Marshall, Rex	Wilmington
Mcdonald, Rich	Hillboro
Mcgroder, Patrick J	Madison
Mercer, Mike	Lebanon
Morgan, Tom	Beloit
Munjas, Bob	Waterford
O'Machearley, Michael	Wilmington
Panak, Paul S	Andover
Potter, Billy	Dublin
Roddy, Roy "Tim"	Hubbard
Rose, Derek W	Gallipolis
Rowe, Fred	Amesville
Salley, John D	Tipp City
Schuchmann, Rick	New Richmond
Sheely, "Butch" Forest	Grand Rapids
Shinosky, Andy	Canfield
Shoemaker, Carroll	Northup
Shoemaker, Scott	Miamisburg
Spinale, Richard	Lorain
Strong, Scott	Beavercreek
Summers, Dennis K	Springfield
Thomas, Kim	Seville
Thourot, Michael W	Napoleon
Tindera, George	Brunswick
Trout, George H.	Wilmington
Votaw, David P	Pioneer
Williams, Robert	East Liverpool
Worley, Joel A., J.S.	Maplewood
Wright, L.T.	Wintersville
Yurco, Mickey	Canfield
Stidham, Daniel	Gallipolis

OK

Baker, Ray	Sapulpa
Cleveland, Mike	Mustang
Coye, Bill	Tulsa
Crenshaw, Al	Eufaula
Crowder, Gary L	Sallisaw
Damasteel Stainless damascus,	Norman
Darby, David T	Cookson
Dill, Dave	Bethany
Duff, Bill	Poteau
Dunlap, Jim	Sallisaw
Gepner, Don	Norman
Haze, Jeff	Skiatook
Heimdale, J E	Tulsa
Kennedy Jr., Bill	Yukon
Kirk, Ray	Tahlequah
Lairson Sr., Jerry	Ringold
Martin, John Alexander	Okmulgee
Mcclure, Jerry	Norman
Menefee, Ricky Bob	Blanchard
Midgley, Ben	Wister
Miller, Michael E	Chandler
Parsons, Larry	Mustang
Pridgen Jr., Larry	Davis
Schreiner, Terry	Duncan
Shropshire, Shawn	Piedmont
Spivey, Jefferson	Yukon
Stanford, Perry	Broken Arrow
Tomberlin, Brion R	Norman
Williams, Michael	Broken Bow
Wingo, Gary	Ramona

OR

Allen, Jim	Bend
Bell, Gabriel	Coquille
Bell, Michael	Coquille
Berg, Lee	Roseburg
Bochman, Bruce	Grants Pass
Brandt, Martin W	Springfield
Buchanan, Thad	Powell Butte
Buchanan, Zac	Eugene
Buchner, Bill	Idleyld Park
Busch, Steve	Oakland
Carter, Murray M	Hillsboro
Cook, Chuck	Dundee
Coon, Raymond C	Damascus
Dixon Jr., Ira E	Cave Junction
Emmerling, John	Gearheart
Frank, Heinrich H	Newport
Goddard, Steve	Eugene
Goddard, Wayne	Eugene
Harsey, William H	Creswell
House, Cameron	Salem
Kelley, Gary	Aloha
Lake, Ron	Eugene
Lewis, Mike	Coquille
Little, Gary M	Broadbent
Magruder, Jason	Medford
Martin, Gene	Williams
Ochs, Eric	Sherwood
Olson, Darrold E	McMinnville
Pruyn, Peter	Grants Pass
Richard, Raymond	Gresham
Richards, Chuck	Salem
Rider, David M	Eugene
Sarganis, Paul	Jacksonville
Scarrow, Wil	Gold Hill
Schoeningh, Mike	North Powder
Schrader, Robert	Bend
Sevey Custom Knife,	Gold Beach
Sheehy, Thomas J	Portland
Sibert, Shane	Gladstone
Smith, Rick	Rogue River
Spake, Jeremy	Portland
Squire, Jack	McMinnville
Stucky, Daniel	Springfield
Tendick, Ben	Eugene
Thompson, Leon	Forest Grove
Thompson, Tommy	Portland
Tuch, William	Portland
Turner, Mike	Williams
Vallotton, Rainy D	Umpqua

Vallotton, Thomas	Oakland
Ward, Ken	Grants Pass
Warren, Alan And Carroll	Portland
Kurt, David	Molalla

PA

Anderson, Gary D	Spring Grove
Anderson, Tom	Manchester
Appleby, Robert	Shickshinny
Bennett, Brett C	Reinholds
Besedick, Frank E	Monongahela
Blystone, Ronald L.	Creekside
Candrella, Joe	Warminster
Clark, D E (Lucky)	Johnstown
Corkum, Steve	Littlestown
Darby, Rick	Levittown
Evans, Ronald B	Middleton
Frey Jr., W Frederick	Milton
Fry, Dean	Wellsboro
Godlesky, Bruce F.	Apollo
Goldberg, David	Ft Washington
Gottschalk, Gregory J	Carnegie
Harner Iii, "Butch" Lloyd R.	Littlestown
Heinz, John	Upper Black Eddy
Hendrickson, E Jay	East Berlin
Johnson, John R	New Buffalo
Kolenko, Vladimir	Huntingdon Valley
Krammes, Jeremy	Schuylkill Haven
Malloy, Joe	Freeland
Marlowe, Donald	Dover
Mensch, Larry C	Milton
Miller, Rick	Rockwood
Moore, Ted	Elizabethtown Morett, Donald Lancaster
Nealy, Bud	Stroudsburg
Neilson, J	Towanda
Nguyen, Mike	Pittsburgh
Ogden, Bill	Avis
Parker, J E	Clarion
Root, Gary	Erie
Rose, Bob	Wagontown
Rupert, Bob	Clinton
Sass, Gary N	Sharpsville
Scimio, Bill	Spruce Creek
Sinclair, J E	Pittsburgh
Steigerwalt, Ken	Orangeville
Stroyan, Eric	Dalton
Takach, Andrew	Elizabeth
Wetten, Bobby	Hershey
Whittaker, Robert E	Mill Creek
Zima, Douglas	Lancaster

RI

Dickison, Scott S	Portsmouth
Jacques, Alex	Providence
Olszewski, Stephen	Coventry
Williams, Jason L	Wyoming
Wright, Richard S	Carolina

SC

Beatty, Gordon H.	Seneca
Branton, Robert	Awendaw
Cox, Sam	Gaffney
Denning, Geno	Gaston
Estabrook, Robbie	Conway
Frazier, Jim	Wagener
Gainey, Hal	Greenwood
George, Harry	Aiken
Gregory, Michael	Belton
Hendrix, Jerry	Clinton
Hendrix, Wayne	Allendale
Hucks, Jerry	Moncks Corner
Kay, J Wallace	Liberty
Knight, Jason	Harleyville
Kreger, Thomas	Lugoff
Langley, Gene H	Florence
Lutz, Greg	Greenwood
Manley, David W	Central
Miles Jr., C R "Iron Doctor"	Lugoff
Odom Jr., Victor L.	North
O'Quinn, W. Lee	Elgin
Page, Larry	Aiken
Parler, Thomas O	Charleston

Peagler, Russ	Moncks Corner
Perry, Johnny	Inman
Smith, Ralph L	Taylors
Thomas, Rocky	Moncks Corner
Tyser, Ross	Spartanburg

SD

Boley, Jamie	Parker
Boysen, Raymond A	Rapid Ciy
Ferrier, Gregory K	Rapid City
Thomsen, Loyd W	Custer
Watts, Rodney	Hot Springs

TN

Accawi, Fuad	Oak Ridge
Adams, Jim	Cordova
Bailey, Joseph D.	Nashville
Bartlett, Mark	Lawrenceburg
Breed, Kim	Clarksville
Brend, Walter	Etowah
Burris, Patrick R	Athens
Byrd, Wesley L	Evensville
Canter, Ronald E	Jackson
Casteel, Dianna	Monteagle
Claiborne, Ron	Knox
Conley, Bob	Jonesboro
Coogan, Robert	Smithville
Corby, Harold	Johnson City
Ewing, John H	Clinton
Fitz, Andrew A. Sr. And Jr.	Milan
Hale, Lloyd	Pulaski
Hughes, Dan	Spencer
Hurst, Jeff	Rutledge
Hutcheson, John	Chattanooga
Johnson, David A	Pleasant Shade
Johnson, Ryan M	Signal Mountain
Kemp, Lawrence	Ooltewah
Kilroy, Kyle	Knoxville
Kistner, Dee	Crossville
Levine, Bob	Tullahoma
Mccarty, Harry	Blaine
Mcdonald, W.J. "Jerry"	Germantown
Moulton, Dusty	Loudon
Oates, Lee	Bethpage
Peters, Daniel	Woodlawn
Raley, R. Wayne	Collierville
Ridge, Tim	Crossville
Sampson, Lynn	Jonesborough
Smith, Newman L.	Gatlinburg
Soileau, Damon	Kingsport
Taylor, C. Gray	Fall Branch
Vanderford, Carl G	Columbia
Wall, Greg	Michie
Ward, W C	Clinton
Wheeler, Gary	Clarksville
Williams Jr., Richard	Morristown

TX

Alexander, Eugene	Ganado
Aplin, Spencer	Brazoria
Appleton, Ron	Bluff Dale
Ashby, Douglas	Dallas
Baker, Tony	Allen
Barnes, Marlen R.	Atlanta
Barr, Judson C.	Irving
Batts, Keith	Hooks
Blackwell, Zane	Eden
Blum, Kenneth	Brenham
Bradley, Gayle	Weatherford
Bratcher, Brett	Plantersville
Brewer, Craig	Killeen
Broadwell, David	Wichita Falls
Brooks, Michael	Lubbock
Brown, Douglas	Fort Worth
Bryson, David	Jarrell
Budell, Michael	Brenham
Bullard, Randall	Canyon
Burden, James	Burkburnett
Buzek, Stanley	Caldwell
Callahan, F Terry	Boerne
Carey, Peter	Lago Vista
Carpenter, Ronald W	Jasper
Carter, Fred	Wichita Falls

Champion, Robert	Amarillo
Chase, John E	Aledo
Chelette, Gary	Spring
Chew, Larry	Weatherford
Childers, David	Lampasas
Churchman, T W (Tim)	Bandera
Cole, James M	Bartonville
Connor, John W	Odessa
Connor, Michael	Winters
Cooke, Mark	Spring
Cornett, Brian	McKinney
Costa, Scott	Spicewood
Crouch, Bubba	Pleasanton
Crowner, Jeff	Plano
Darcey, Chester L	College Station
De Mesa, John	Lewisville
Dean, Harvey J	Rockdale
Debaud, Jake	Plano
DeDominicis, Ronnie	Huntsville
Delong, Dick	Centerville
Dietz, Howard	New Braunfels
Dobson, Richard	Gainesville
Dominy, Chuck	Colleyville
Dyer, David	Granbury
Eldridge, Allan	Ft. Worth
Elishewitz, Allen	New Braunfels
Epting, Richard	College Station
Erdlac, Jr. Richard	Midland
Eriksen, James Thorlief	Garland
Evans, Carlton	Fort Davis
Fant Jr., George	Atlanta
Ferguson, Jim	San Angelo
Fisher, Josh	Murchison
Fivecoat, Rocky	Seagoville
Flanagan, Burt	Tom Bean
Foster, Al	Magnolia
Foster, Jared	Colorado City
Foster, Norvell C	Marion
Fritz, Jesse	Slaton
Fry, Jason	Wolfforthy
Fuller, Bruce A	Blanco
Gabriel, Bastian	Houston
Gann, Tommy	Canton
Gatlin, Steve	Schertz
Graham, Gordon	New Boston
Green, Bill	Sachse
Griffin, John	Hockley
Grimes, Mark	Bedford
Guinn, Terry	Eastland
Halfrich, Jerry	San Marcos
Hamlet Jr., Johnny	Clute
Hand, Bill	Spearman
Hawkins, Buddy	Texarkana
Hawkins Jr., Charles R.	San Angelo
Hawley, Troy G.	Ivanhoe
Haynes, Jerry	Gunter
Hays, Mark	Austin
Hemperley, Glen	Willis
Hicks, Gary	Tuscola
Hill, Steve E	Spring Branch
Horrigan, John	Burnet
Howell, Jason G	Lake Jackson
Hudson, Robert	Humble
Hughes, Lawrence	Plainview
Hunt, Raymon E.	Irving
Huse, James D. Ii	Buda
Jackson, Charlton R	San Antonio
Jaksik Jr., Michael	Fredericksburg
Jangtanong, Suchat	Dripping Springs
Keller, Bill	San Antonio
Lance, Dan	Weatherford
Laplante, Brett	McKinney
Lay, L J	Burkburnett
Lemcke, Jim L	Houston
Lennon, Dale	Alba
Lister Jr., Weldon E	Boerne
Love, Ed	San Antonio
Lovett, Michael	Mound
Luchak, Bob	Channelview
Luckett, Bill	Weatherford
Majors, Charlie	Montgomery
Martin, Michael W	Beckville
Mcconnell Jr., Loyd A	Marble Falls
Merz Iii, Robert L	Katy
Minchew, Ryan	Midland
Mitchell, Wm Dean	Warren
Moen, Jerry	Dallas
Moore, James B	Ft. Stockton
Morman, Kelly	Lubbock
Neely, Greg	Bellaire
Noake, Brett	Spring
O'Brien, Mike J.	San Antonio
Ogletree Jr., Ben R	Livingston
Ott, Ted	Elgin
Overeynder, T R	Arlington
Ownby, John C	Murphy
Packard, Ronnie	Bonham
Pardue, Joe	Hillister
Patterson, Pat	Barksdale
Payne, Travis	Telephone
Pierce, Randall	Arlington
Pollock, Wallace J	Cedar Park
Polzien, Don	Lubbock
Powers, Walter R.	Lolita
Ralph, Darrel	Forney
Ray, Alan W	Lovelady
Richardson, Percy	Lufkin
Richardson Iii, Percy (Rich)	Lufkin
Richardson Jr., Percy	Lufkin
Roberts, Jack	Houston
Rucker, Thomas	Spring
Ruple, William H	Pleasanton
Ruth, Michael G	Texarkana
Ruth, Jr., Michael	Texarkana
Schorsch, Kendall	Jourdanton
Self, Ernie	Dripping Springs
Shewmaker, Bob	Farmersville
Shipley, Steven A	Richardson
Sloan, Shane	Newcastle
Smart, Steve	McKinney
Stokes, Ed	Hockley
Stone, Jerry	Lytle
Stout, Johnny	New Braunfels
Swenson, Luke	Lakehills
Thuesen, Ed	Damon
Truncali, Pete	Nevada
Van Reenen, Ian	Amarillo
Vickers, David	Montgomery
Ware, Tommy	Onalaska
Watson, Daniel	Driftwood
Watts, Johnathan	Gatesville
Weever, John	Glen Rose
White, Dale	Sweetwater
Whitley, Weldon G	Odessa
Wilkins, Mitchell	Montgomery
Williams, Robert	New Braunfels
Wilson, Curtis M	Burleson
Wolf Jr., William Lynn	Lagrange
Zboril, Terry	Caldwell
Zermeno, William D.	Houston

UT

Allred, Bruce F	Layton
Black, Earl	Salt Lake City
Carter, Shayne	Payson
Ence, Jim	Richfield
Ennis, Ray	Ogden
Erickson, L.M.	Ogden
Hunter, Hyrum	Aurora
Johnson, Steven R	Manti
Jorgensen, Carson	Mt Pleasant
Lang, David	Kearns
Nell, Chad	St. George
Nielson, Jeff V	Monroe
Nunn, Gregory	Castle Valley
Palmer, Taylor	Blanding
Peterson, Chris	Salina
Ramos, Steven	West Jordan
Ricks, Kurt J.	Trenton
Strickland, Dale	Monroe
Szczerbiak, Maciej	St. George
Velarde, Ricardo	Park City
Weeks, Ryan	Bountiful
Winn, Travis A.	Salt Lake City
Young, John	Ephraim
Jenkins, Mitch	Manti
Johnson, Jerry	Spring City

VA

Apelt, Stacy E	Norfolk
Arbuckle, James M	Yorktown
Ball, Butch	Floyd
Ballew, Dale	Bowling Green
Barnhill, Wess	Spotsylvania
Batson, Richard G.	Rixeyville
Beverly Ii, Larry H	Spotsylvania
Catoe, David R	Norfolk
Davidson, Edmund	Goshen
Foster, Burt	Bristol
Goodpasture, Tom	Ashland
Harley, Richard	Bristol
Harris, Cass	Bluemont
Hedrick, Don	Newport News
Hendricks, Samuel J	Maurertown
Holloway, Paul	Norfolk
Jones, Barry M And Phillip G	Danville
Jones, Enoch	Warrenton
Kearney, Jarod	Swoope
Klein, Kieran	Check
Martin, Herb	Richmond
McCoun, Dylan	DeWitt
Mccoun, Mark	DeWitt
Metheny, H A "Whitey"	Spotsylvania
Mills, Michael	Colonial Beach
Murski, Ray	Reston
Norfleet, Ross W	Providence Forge
Parks, Blane C	Woodbridge
Pawlowski, John R	Barhamsville
Schlueter, David	Madison Heights
Schwartz, Aaron	Woodbridge
Vanhoy, Ed And Tanya	Abingdon
Vestal, Charles	Abingdon
Ward, Ron	Rose Hill

VT

Bensinger, J. W.	Marshfield
Haggerty, George S	Jacksonville
Kelso, Jim	Worcester

WA

Amoureux, A W	Northport
Ber, Dave	San Juan Island
Berglin, Bruce	Mount Vernon
Bromley, Peter	Spokane
Brothers, Robert L	Colville
Brunckhorst, Lyle	Bothell
Buckner, Tom	Olympia
Bump, Bruce D.	Walla Walla
Butler, John R	Shoreline
Campbell, Dick	Colville
Chamberlain, Jon A	E. Wenatchee
Conway, John	Kirkland
Crowthers, Mark F	Rolling Bay
D'Angelo, Laurence	Vancouver
Davis, John	Selah
De Wet, Kobus	Yakima
Diaz, Jose	Ellensburg
Diskin, Matt	Freeland
Erickson, Daniel	Snohomish
Ferry, Tom	Auburn
Gray, Bob	Spokane
Gray, Robb	Seattle
Greenfield, G O	Everett
Hansen, Lonnie	Spanaway
House, Gary	Ephrata
Keyes, Geoff P.	Duvall
Leeper, Dan	Olympia
Lisch, David K	Yelm
Norton, Don	Port Townsend
O'Malley, Daniel	Seattle
Padilla, Gary	Bellingham
Pedersen, Ole	Monroe
Podmajersky, Dietrich	Seatlle
Rader, Michael	Bothell
Roeder, David	Kennewick
Rogers, Ray	Wauconda
Sanford, Dick	Chehalis
Schempp, Ed	Ephrata
Schempp, Martin	Ephrata

Shoger, Mark O — Kalama
Stegner, Wilbur G — Rochester
Sterling, Thomas J — Coupeville
Straub, Salem F. — Tonasket
Swyhart, Art — Klickitat
Thomas, Bob — Ferndale
Wheeler, Nick — Castle Rock
Wright, Kevin — Quilcene

WI

Boyes, Tom — West Bend
Brandsey, Edward P — Janesville
Bruner, Fred Jr. — Fall Creek
Carr, Joseph E. — Menomonee Falls
Coats, Ken — Stevens Point
Delarosa, Jim — Waterford
Deyong, Clarence — Sturtevant
Franklin, Larry — Stoughton
Haines, Jeff — Mayville
Hoffman, Jess — Shawano
Johnson, Richard — Germantown
Kanter, Michael — New Berlin
Kohls, Jerry — Princeton
Kolitz, Robert — Beaver Dam
Lary, Ed — Mosinee
Lerch, Matthew — Sussex
Maestri, Peter A — Spring Green
Martin, Cory — Racine
Martin, Peter — Waterford
Mikolajczyk, Glen — Caledonia
Millard, Fred G — Richland Center
Montgomery, Stephen R. — Madison
Nelson, Ken — Racine
Niemuth, Troy — Sheboygan
Ponzio, Doug — Beloit
Rabuck, Jason — Springbrook
Revishvili, Zaza — Madison
Ricke, Dave — West Bend
Rochford, Michael R — Dresser
Roush, Scott — Washburn
Schrap, Robert G — Wauwatosa
Steinbrecher, Mark W — Pleasant Prairie
Wattelet, Michael A — Minocqua
Zimmerman, Nathan — Waukesha

WV

Derr, Herbert — St. Albans
Drost, Jason D — French Creek
Drost, Michael B — French Creek
Elliott, Jerry — Charleston
Groves, Gary — Canvas
Jeffries, Robert W — Red House
Liegey, Kenneth R — Millwood
Maynard, Larry Joe — Crab Orchard
Morris, Eric — Beckley
Pickens, Selbert — Dunbar
Reynolds, Dave — Harrisville
Small, Ed — Keyser
Tokar, Daniel — Shepherdstown
Wilson, Rw — Weirton
Wyatt, William R — Rainelle

WY

Amos, Chris — Riverton
Ankrom, W.E. — Cody
Banks, David L. — Riverton
Barry, Scott — Laramie
Casey, Kevin — Lander
Deveraux, Butch — Riverton
Draper, Audra — Riverton
Draper, Mike — Riverton
Fowler, Ed A. — Riverton
Friedly, Dennis E — Cody
Kilby, Keith — Cody
Oliver, Todd D — Cheyenne
Rexroat, Kirk — Banner
Reynolds, John C — Gillette
Rodebaugh, James L — Carpenter
Ross, Stephen — Evanston
Spragg, Wayne E — Lovell
Whipple, Wesley A — Thermopolis

ARGENTINA

Ayarragaray, Cristian L. — Parana, Entre Rios
Bertolami, Juan Carlos — Neuquen
Gibert, Pedro — San Martin de los Andes, Neuquen
Kehiayan, Alfredo — Maschwitz, Buenos Aires
Montenegro, Facundo — Merlo (5881) San Luis
Rho, Nestor Lorenzo — Junin, Buenos Aires
Santiago, Abud — Buenos Aires

AUSTRALIA

Barnett, Bruce — Mundaring, WA
Bennett, Peter — Engadine, NSW
Brodziak, David — Albany, WA
Crawley, Bruce R — Croydon, VIC
Cross, Robert — Tamworth, NSW
Del Raso, Peter — Mt. Waverly, VIC
Fludder, Keith — Tahmoor, New South Wales
Gerner, Thomas — Walpole, WA
Giljevic, Branko — New South Wales
Green, William (Bill) — View Bank, VIC
Harvey, Max — Western Australia 6149
Hedges, Dee — Bedfordale, WA
Husiak, Myron — Altona, VIC
K B S, Knives — North Castlemaine, VIC
Maisey, Alan — Vincentia, NSW
Mcintyre, Shawn — Hawthornm, E VIC
Phillips, Alistair — Amaroo, ACT
Tasman, Kerley — Pt Kennedy, WA
Zemitis, Joe — Cardiff Heights, NSW

BELGIUM

Dox, Jan — Schoten
Laurent, Veronique — Brussels
Lurquin, Samuel — Binches
Monteiro, Victor — Maleves Ste Marie
Veronique, Laurent — Bruxelles

BRAZIL

Bodolay, Antal — Belo Horizonte, MG
Boeck, Sandro Eduardo — Cachoeira do Sul - RS
Bossaerts, Carl — Ribeirao Preto, SP
Campos, Ivan — Tatui, SP
Cecchini, Gustavo T. — Sao Jose Rio Preto SP
Dionatam, Franco — Ibitinga-SP
Dionatam, Franco — Jardim Filadelfia, Ibitinga-SP
Dorneles, Luciano Oliverira — Nova Petropolis, RS
Gaeta, Angelo — Centro Jau, SP-CEP: 14.201310
Garcia, Mario Eiras — Caxingui, SP
Glasser, Roger Cesar — 679 - Sao Paulo - SP
Goncalves, Luiz Gustavo — 124A -Sao Paulo - SP
Ikoma, Flavio — Presidente Prudente, SP
Lala, Paulo Ricardo P
 And Lala, Roberto P. — Presidente Prudente, SP
Neto Jr., Nelson And
 De Carvalho, Henrique M. — Braganca Paulista, SP
Paulo, Fernandes R — Lencois Paulista, SP
Petean, Francisco And Mauricio — Birigui, SP
Ricardo Romano, Bernardes — Itajuba MG
Sfreddo, Rodrigo Menezes — Nova Petropolis, RS
Vilar, Ricardo — Mairipora, SP
Vilar, Ricardo Augusto Ferreira — Mairipora, SP
Villa, Luiz — Itaim Bibi, SP
Zakharov, Gladiston — Jacaret-SP

CANADA

Arnold, Joe — London, ON
Beauchamp, Gaetan — Stoneham, QC
Beets, Marty — Williams Lake, BC
Bell, Donald — Bedford, NS
Berg, Lothar — Kitchener ON
Beshara, Brent (Besh) — NL
Boos, Ralph — Edmonton, AB
Bourbeau, Jean Yves — Ile Perrot, QC
Bradford, Garrick — Kitchener, ON
Bucharsky, Emil — Spruce Grove, Alberta
Chambers, Grant — Ottawa, Ontario
Daley, Mark — Waubaushene, Ontario
Dallyn, Kelly — Calgary, AB
De Braga, Jose C. — Trois Rivieres, QC
Debraga, Jovan — Quebec
Deringer, Christoph — Cookshire, QC
Desaulniers, Alain — Cookshire, QC

Diotte, Jeff — LaSalle, ON
Doiron, Donald — Messines, QC
Doucette, R — Brantford, ON
Doussot, Laurent — St. Bruno, QC
Downie, James T — Ontario
Friesen, Dave J — British Columbia
Frigault, Rick — Golden Lake, ON
Ganshorn, Cal — Regina, SK
Garvock, Mark W — Balderson, ON
Gilbert, Chantal — Quebec City, QC
Haslinger, Thomas — British Columbia V1B 3G7
Hayes, Wally — Essex, ON
Henshaw, Craig — Huntsville, ON
Hindmarch, Garth — Carlyle, SK
Hofer, Louis — Rose Prairie, BC
Jobin, Jacques — Levis, QC
Kaczor, Tom — Upper London, ON
Keith, Greg — Montague Gold Mines, NS
Lambert, Kirby — Regina, SK
Langley, Mick — Qualicum Beach, BC
Lay, R J (Bob) — Clearwater, BC
Leber, Heinz — Hudson's Hope, BC
Lemelin, Stephanie — Brossard
Lightfoot, Greg — Kitscoty, AB
Linklater, Steve — Aurora, ON
Loerchner, Wolfgang — Bayfield, ON
Maneker, Kenneth — Galiano Island, BC
Marchand, Rick — Lunenburg, Nova Scotia
Marzitelli, Peter — Langley, BC
Massey, Al — Mount Uniacke, NS
Mckenzie, David Brian — Campbell River, BC
Miville-Deschenes, Alain — Quebec
Moeller, Harald — Parksville, BC
Moizis, Stan — Delta, British Columbia (BC)
Nease, William — LaSalle, ON
Niro, Frank — Kamloops, B.C.
O'Hare, Sean — Grand Manan, NB
Olson, Rod — Nanton, AB
Painter, Tony — Whitehorse, YT
Patrick, Bob — S. Surrey, BC
Pepiot, Stephan — Winnipeg, MB
Piesner, Dean — Conestogo, ON
Poirier, Rick — New Brunswick E4V 2W7
Rassenti, Peter — Quebec J7P 4C2
Ridley, Rob — Sundre, AB
Robert, Ulysse — Frelighsburg, QC
Ross, Tim — Thunder Bay, ON
Schoenfeld, Matthew A — Galiano Island, BC
St. Amour, Murray — Beachburg, Ontario
Stancer, Chuck — Calgary, AB
Storch, Ed — Mannville, AB
Stuart, Steve — Gores Landing, ON
Sylvester, David — Compton, QC
Tedford, Steven J. — Colborne, ON
Tighe, Brian — St. Catharines, ON
Toner, Roger — Pickering, ON
Van de Bruinhorst, Jacco — Tavistock, ON
Vanderkolff, Stephen — Mildmay, ON
Whitenect, Jody — Elderbank, NS
Yelle, Jeremy — Sherbrooke, QC
Young, Bud — Port Hardy, BC

CZECH REPUBLIC

Kislinger, Milos — Dobronin 314 58812
Rusnak, Josef — 323 00 Plzen
Sevecek, Pavel — Brodek U Konice
Tesarik, Richard — 614 00 Brno

DENMARK

Andersen, Henrik Lefolii — Fredensborg
Anso, Jens — Sporup
Rafn, Dan C. — 7400 Herning
Strande, Poul — Dastrup
Vensild, Henrik — Auning
West, Michael — Hobro
Willumsen, Mikkel — S Copenhagen

ENGLAND

Bailey, I.R. — Colkirk
Barker, Stuart — Wigston, Leicester
Boden, Harry — Derbyshire
Ducker, Brian — Colkirk
Farid, Mehr R — Kent

directory

Harrington, Roger	East Sussex
Nowacki, Stephen R.	Southampton, Hampshire
Orford, Ben	Worcestershire
Price, Darrell Morris	Devon
Stainthorp, Guy	Stroke-on-Trent
Wardell, Mick	N Devon
Wise, Donald	East Sussex
Wood, Alan	Brampton
Wylie, Tom	Sutton-In-Ashfield, Notts

FINLAND

Hankala, Jukka	39580 Riitiala
Nylund, Erik	65320 Vaasa
Palikko, J-T	00190 Helsinki
Ruusuvuori, Anssi	Piikkio
Tuominen, Pekka	Tossavanlahti
Vilppola, Markku	Turku

FRANCE

Bennica, Charles	Moules et Baucels
Chomilier, Alain And Joris	Clermont-Ferrand
Doursin, Gerard	Pernes les Fontaines
Grangette, Alain	23210 Azat-Chatenet
Graveline, Pascal And Isabelle	Moelan-sur-Mer
Headrick, Gary	Juan Les Pins
Laroche, Jean-Marc	78160 Marly le Roi
Madrulli, Mme Joelle	Salon De Provence
Regel, Jean-Louis	Saint Leger de Fougeret
Reverdy, Nicole And Pierre	Romans
Thevenot, Jean-Paul	Dijon
Viallon, Henri	Thiers

GERMANY

Boehlke, Guenter	56412 Grobholbach
Borger, Wolf	Graben-Neudorf
Dell, Wolfgang	Owen-Teck
Drumm, Armin	Dornstadt
Faust, Joachim	Goldkronach
Fruhmann, Ludwig	Burghausen
Greiss, Jockl	Schenkenzell
Hehn, Richard Karl	Dorrebach
Herbst, Peter	Lauf a.d. Pegn.
Joehnk, Bernd	Kiel
Kressler, D F	D-28832 Achim
Rankl, Christian	Munchen
Rinkes, Siegfried	Markterlbach
Selzam, Frank	Bad Koenigshofen
Steinau, Jurgen	Berlin
Tritz, Jean-Jose	Hamburg
Wirtz, Achim	Wuerselen
Wulf, Derrick	Wilhelm-von-Miller Weg
Zirbes, Richard	Niederkail

GREECE

Ioannis-Minas, Filippou	Athens
Zafeiriadis, Konstantinos	Marathon Attiki

IRELAND

Brennan, Patrick	Thomastown, Kilkenny
Moore, Davy	Quin, Co Clare

ISRAEL

Shadmot, Boaz	Arava

ITALY

Ameri, Mauro	Genova
Ballestra, Santino	Ventimiglia
Bertuzzi, Ettore	Bergamo
Bonassi, Franco	Pordenone
Esposito, Emmanuel	Buttigliera Alta TO
Fogarizzu, Boiteddu	Pattada
Frizzi, Leonardo	Firenze
Garau, Marcello	Oristano
Giagu, Salvatore And Deroma Maria Rosaria	Pattada (SS)
Mainolfi, Dr. Riccardo	Positano (SA)
Moro, Corrado	Torino
Mura, Denis	Cascina (Pi)
Puddu, Salvatore	(Cagliari) Sardinia
Ramondetti, Sergio	CHIUSA DI PESIO (CN)
Riboni, Claudio	Truccazzano (MI)
Rovatti, Andrea	Verona

Scordia, Paolo	Roma
Simonella, Gianluigi	Maniago
Toich, Nevio	Vincenza
Tschager, Reinhard	Bolzano

JAPAN

Aida, Yoshihito	Tokyo
Ebisu, Hidesaku	Hiroshima
Fujikawa, Shun	Osaka
Fukuta, Tak	Gifu
Hara, Koji	Gifu
Hirayama, Harumi	Saitama
Hiroto, Fujihara	Hiroshima
Isao, Ohbuchi	Fukuoka
Ishihara, Hank	Chiba
Kagawa, Koichi	Kanagawa
Kanki, Iwao	Hyogo
Kansei, Matsuno	Gifu
Kato, Shinichi	Aichi
Katsumaro, Shishido	Hiroshima
Keisuke, Gotoh	Oita
Koyama, Captain Bunshichi	Aichi
Makoto, Kunitomo	Hiroshima
Matsuno, Kansei	Gifu-City
Matsusaki, Takeshi	Nagasaki
Michinaka, Toshiaki	Tottori
Narasada, Mamoru	NAGANO
Ryuichi, Kuki	Saitama
Shigeno, Mamoru	Saitama, 350-1320
Shinozaki, Akio	Fukuoka-ken
Sugihara, Keidoh	Osaka
Sugiyama, Eddy K	Oita
Tamatsu, Kunihiko	Kochi-ken
Toshifumi, Kuramoto	Fukuoka
Uchida, Chimata	Kumamoto
Wada, Yasutaka	Nara
Waters, Glenn	Hirosaki City
Yoneyama, Chicchi K.	Tokyo
Yoshihara, Yoshindo	Tokyo
Yoshikazu, Kamada	Tokushima
Yoshio, Maeda	Okayama

MEXICO

Scheurer, Alfredo E Faes	Distrito Federal
Sunderland, Richard	Puerto Escondido, OA
Ware, J.D.	Merida, Yucatan
Young, Cliff	San Miguel De Allende, GJ

NAMIBIA

Naude, Louis	Okahandja

NETHERLANDS

Brouwer, Jerry	Alkmaar
Noot, Alexander	Oss
Sprokholt, Rob	Gatherwood
Van De Manakker, Thijs	Holland
Van Den Elsen, Gert	Tilburg
Van Eldik, Frans	Loenen
Van Ryswyk, Aad	Vlaardingen

NEW ZEALAND

Bassett, David J.	Auckland
Gunther, Eddie	Auckland
Jansen Van Vuuren, Ludwig	Dunedin
Knapton, Chris C.	Henderson, Aukland
Pennington, C A	Kainga Christchurch
Reddiex, Bill	Palmerston North
Sandow, Brent Edward	Auckland
Sands, Scott	Christchurch 9
Van Dijk, Richard	Harwood Dunedin

NICARAGUA

Morales, Ramon	Managua

NORWAY

Bache-Wiig, Tom	Eivindvik
Sellevold, Harald	Bergen
Vistnes, Tor	Svelgen

RUSSIA

Kharlamov, Yuri	Tula

SLOVAKIA

Albert, Stefan	Filakovo 98604

Bojtos, Arpad	98403 Lucenec
Kovacik, Robert	Tomasovce 98401
Mojzis, Julius	98511 Halic
Pulis, Vladimir	96701 Kremnica
Santa, Ladislav "Lasky"	97637 Hrochot

SOUTH AFRICA

Arm-Ko Knives,	Marble Ray , KZN
Baartman, George	Bela-Bela, LP
Bauchop, Robert	Munster, KN
Beukes, Tinus	Vereeniging, GT
Bezuidenhout, Buzz	Malvern, KZN
Boardman, Guy	New Germany, KZN
Brown, Rob E	Port Elizabeth, EC
Burger, Fred	Munster, KZN
Burger, Tiaan	Pretoria, GT
Culhane, Sean K.	Horizon, Roodepoort, 1740
Dickerson, Gavin	Petit, GT
Fellows, Mike	Riversdale 6670
Grey, Piet	Naboomspruit, LP
Harvey, Kevin	Belfast, MP
Herbst, Gawie	Akasia, GT
Herbst, Thinus	Akasia, GT
Horn, Des	Onrusrivier, WC
Klaasee, Tinus	George, WC
Kojetin, W	Germiston, GT
Lancaster, C G	Free State
Liebenberg, Andre	Randburg, GT
Mackrill, Stephen	Johannesburg, GT
Mahomedy, A R	Marble Ray, KZN
Mahomedy, Humayd A.R.	Marble Ray, KZN
Mitchell, Alan	Randburg, Gauteng
Oelofse, Tinus	Glenstantia, Pretoria
Owen, David J.A.	Johannesburg
Pienaar, Conrad	Free State
Prinsloo, Theuns	Free State
Rietveld, Bertie	Magaliesburg, GT
Russell, Mick	Port Elizabeth, EC
Schoeman, Corrie	Free State
Schutte, Neill	Bloemfontein
Smith, Stuart	Gauteng
Steyn, Peter	Freestate
Thorburn, Andre E.	Warmbaths, LP
Van Den Berg, Neels	Pretoria, Gauteng
Van Der Westhuizen, Peter	Mossel Bay, SC
Van Heerden, Andre	Pretoria, GT
Watson, Peter	La Hoff, NW

SOUTH AUSTRALIA

Edmonds, Warrick	Adelaide Hills

SPAIN

Goshovskyy, Vasyl	Castellon de la Plana

SWEDEN

Bergh, Roger	Bygdea
Eklund, Maihkel	Farila
Embretsen, Kaj	Edsbyn
Hedlund, Anders	Brastad
Henningsson, Michael	430 83 Vrango (Gothenburg)
Hogstrom, Anders T	37011 Backaryd
Johansson, Anders	Grangesberg
Lundstrom, Jan-Ake	Dals-Langed
Lundstrom, Torbjorn (Tobbe)	Are
Nilsson, Jonny Walker	93391 Arvidsjaur
Nordell, Ingemar	FSrila
Persson, Conny	Loos
Styrefors, Mattias	Boden
Vogt, Patrik	Halmstad

SWITZERLAND

Roulin, Charles	Geneva

UNITED KINGDOM

Hague, Geoff	Quarley, Hampshire
Horne, Grace	Sheffield
Maxen, Mick	Hatfield, Herts

URUGUAY

Gonzalez, Leonardo Williams	Maldonado
Symonds, Alberto E	Montevideo

ZIMBABWE

Burger, Pon	Bulawayo

The firms listed here are special in the sense that they make or market special kinds of knives made in facilities they own or control either in the U.S. or overseas. Or they are special because they make knives of unique design or function. The second phone number listed is the fax number.

sporting cutlers

A.G. RUSSELL KNIVES INC
2900 S. 26th St
Rogers, AR 72758-8571
800-255-9034
fax 479-631-8493
ag@agrussell.com; www.agrussell.com
The oldest knife mail-order company, highest quality. Free catalog available. In these catalogs you will find the newest and the best. If you like knives, this catalog is a must

AL MAR KNIVES
PO Box 2295
Tualatin, OR 97062-2295
503-670-9080; fax 503-639-4789
info@almarknives.com;
www.almarknives.com
Featuring our Ultralight™ series of knives. Sere 2000™ Shrike, Sere™, Operator™, Nomad™ and Ultralight series™

ATLANTA CUTLERY CORP.
2147 Gees Mill Rd., Box 839
Conyers, GA 30013
770-922-7500; fax 770-918-2026
custserv@atlantacutlery.com;
www.atlantacutlery.com
Outdoor sporting and hunting knives, mail order

BARK RIVER KNIVES
6911 County Road 426 M.5 Road
Escanaba, MI 49829
906-789-1801
jacquie@barkriverknives.com
www.barkriverknifetool.com
Family-owned business producing bushcraft, hunting, Canadian, deluxe game, professional guide, search & rescue and EDC knives

BEAR & SON CUTLERY, INC.
111 Bear Blvd. SW
Jacksonville, AL 36265
256-435-2227; fax 256-435-9348
www.bearandsoncutlery.com
Bear Jaws®, three sizes of multi-tools, cutlery, hunting and pocketknives in traditional and innovative patterns and designs

BECK'S CUTLERY & SPECIALTIES
51 Highland Trace Ln.
Benson, NC 27504
919-902-9416
beckscutlery@embarqmail.com;
www.beckscutlery.com

BENCHMADE KNIFE CO. INC.
300 Beavercreek Rd
Oregon City, OR 97045
800-800-7427
info@benchmade.com;
www.benchmade.com
Sports, utility, law enforcement, military, gift and semi custom

BERETTA U.S.A. CORP.
17601 Beretta Dr.
Accokeek, MD 20607
301-283-2191
www.berettausa.com
Full range of hunting & specialty knives

BLACKHAWK PRODUCTS GROUP
6160 Commander Pkwy.
Norfolk, VA 23502
757-436-3101; fax 757-436-3088
cs@blackhawk.com
www.blackhawk.com
Leading manufacturer of tactical sheaths and knives

BLADE-TECH INDUSTRIES
5530 184th St. E, Ste. A
Puyallup, WA 98375
253-655-8059; fax 253-655-8066
tim@blade-tech.com
www.blade-tech.com

BLUE GRASS CUTLERY, INC.
20 E Seventh St, PO Box 156
Manchester, OH 45144
937-549-2602; 937-549-2709 or 2603
sales@bluegrasscutlery.com;
www.bluegrasscutlery.com
Manufacturer of Winchester Knives, John Primble Knives and many contract lines

BOKER USA INC
1550 Balsam St.
Lakewood, CO 80214-5917
800-992-6537; 303-462-0668
sales@bokerusa.com; www.bokerusa.com
Wide range of fixed-blade and folding knives for hunting, military, tactical and general use

BROUS BLADES
POB 550
Buellton, CA 93427
805-717-7192
contact@brousblades.com
www.brousblades.com
Custom and semi-custom knives

BROWNING
One Browning Place
Morgan, UT 84050
800-333-3504; Customer Service:
801-876-2711 or 800-333-3288
www.browning.com
Outdoor hunting & shooting products

BUCK KNIVES INC.
660 S Lochsa St
Post Falls, ID 83854-5200
800-326-2825; Fax: 800-733-2825
www.buckknives.com
Sports cutlery

BULLDOG BRAND KNIVES
P.O. Box 23852
Chattanooga, TN 37422
423-894-5102; fax 423-892-9165
Fixed blade and folding knives for hunting and general use

BUSSE COMBAT KNIFE CO.
11651 Co Rd 12
Wauseon, OH 43567
419-923-6471; 419-923-2337
www.bussecombat.com
Simple & very strong straight knife designs for tactical & expedition use

CAMILLUS C/O ACME UNITED CORP.
60 Round Hill Rd.
Fairfield, CT 06824
800-835-2263
orders@shopatron.com
www.camillusknives.com

CANAL STREET CUTLERY
30 Canal St.
Ellenville, NY 12428
845-647-5900
info@canalstreetcutlery.com
www.canalstreetcutlery.com
Manufacturers of pocket and hunting knives finished to heirloom quality

CAS IBERIA
650 Industrial Blvd
Sale Creek, TN 37373
800-635-9366
www.casiberia.com
Extensive variety of fixed-blade and folding knives for hunting, diving, camping, military and general use. Japanese swords and European knives

CASE, W.R. & SONS CUTLERY CO.
50 Owens Way
Bradford, PA 16701
800-523-6350; Fax: 814-368-1736
consumer-relations@wrcase.com
www.wrcase.com
Folding pocket knives

CHRIS REEVE KNIVES
2949 S. Victory View Way
Boise, ID 83709-2946
208-375-0367; Fax: 208-375-0368
crkinfo@chrisreeve.com;
www.chrisreeve.com
Makers of the Sebenza, Umnumzaan and Mnandi folding knives, the legendary Green Beret knife and other military knives

directory

COAST CUTLERY CO
8033 N.E. Holman
Portland, OR 97218
800-426-5858; Fax: 503-234-4422
www.coastportland.com
Variety of fixed-blade and folding knives and multi-tools for hunting, camping and general use

COLD STEEL INC
6060 Nicolle St.
Ventura, CA 93003
800-255-4716 or 805-642-9727
sales@coldsteel.com
www.coldsteel.com
Wide variety of folding lockbacks and fixed-blade hunting, fishing and neck knives, as well as bowies, kukris, tantos, throwing knives, kitchen knives and swords

COLONIAL KNIFE, A DIVISION OF COLONIAL CUTLERY INT.
61 Dewey Ave.
Warwick, RI 02886
401-421-6500; Fax: 401-737-0054
stevep@colonialknifecorp.com
www.colonialknifecorp.com
Collectors edition specialty knives. Special promotions. Old cutler, barion, trappers, military knives. Industrial knives-electrician.

CONDOR™ TOOL & KNIFE
7557 W. Sand Lake Rd., #106
Orlando, FL 32819
407-458-9396; Fax: 407-458-9397
rtj2@att.net; www.condortk.com

COLTELLERIE MASERIN SNC
Via Dei Fabbri n.19
33085 MANIAGO (PN)– ITALY
tel. +39 0427 71335
fax +39 0427 700 690
info@maserin.com
www.maserin.com
Gentlemen's knives, and high-tech, hunting, classic, outdoor, military, rescue, kitchen and sommelier models

CRAWFORD KNIVES, LLC
205 N Center
West Memphis, AR 72301
870-732-2452
www.crawfordknives.com
Folding knives for tactical and general use

CRKT
18348 SW 126th Place
Tualatin, OR 97062
800-891-3100; fax 503-682-9680
info@crkt.com; www.crkt.com
Complete line of sport, work and tactical knives

CUTCO CORPORATION
1116 E. State St.
Olean, NY 14760
716-372-3111
www.cutco.com
Household cutlery / sport knives

DPX GEAR INC.
2321 Kettner Blvd.
San Diego, CA 92101
619-780-2600; fax: 619-780-2605
www.dpxgear.com
Hostile environment survival knives and tools

EMERSON KNIVES, INC.
1234 254th St.
Harbor City, CA 90710
310-539-5633; fax: 310-539-5609
www.emersonknives.com
Hard use tactical knives; folding & fixed blades

ESEE KNIVES
POB 99
Gallant, AL 35972
256-613-0372
www.eseeknives.com
Survival and tactical knives

EXTREMA RATIO
Mauro Chiostri/Maurizio Castrati
Via Tourcoing 40/p
Prato (PO) 59100
ITALY
0039 0576 584639; fax: 0039 0576 584312
info@extremaratio.com
Tactical/military knives and sheaths, blades and sheaths to customers specs

FALLKNIVEN
Granatvägen 8
S-961 43 Boden
SWEDEN
46-(0)-921 544 22; Fax: 46-(0)-921 544 33
info@fallkniven.se; www.fallkniven.com
High quality stainless knives

FAMARS USA
2091 Nooseneck Hill Rd., Ste. 200
Coventry, RI 02816
855-FAMARS1 (326-2771)
www.famarsusa.com
FAMARS has been building guns for over 50 years. Known for innovative design, quality and craftsmanship. New lines of gentleman's knives, tactical fixed blades and folders, hunters and utility pieces.

FOX KNIVES USA
9918 162nd St. Ct. E, Ste. 14
Puyallup, WA 98375
303-263-2468
www.foxknivesusa.com
Designer, manufacturer and distributor of high-quality cutlery

FROST CUTLERY CO
PO Box 22636
Chattanooga, TN 37422
800-251-7768
www.frostcutlery.com
Wide range of fixed-blade and folding knives with a multitude of handle materials

GATCO SHARPENERS/TIMBERLINE
PO Box 600
Getzville, NY 14068
716-646-5700; fax: 716-646-5775
gatco@gatcosharpeners.com;
www.gatcosharpeners.com
Manufacturer of the GATCO brand of knife sharpeners and Timberline brand of knives

GERBER LEGENDARY BLADES
14200 SW 72nd Ave
Portland, OR 97223
503-403-1143; fax: 307-857-4702
www.gerbergear.com
Knives, multi-tools, axes, saws, outdoor products

GINSU/DOUGLAS QUIKUT
118 E. Douglas Rd.
Walnut Ridge, AR 72476
800-982-5233; fax: 870-886-9162
www.douglasquikut.com
Household cutlery

GROHMANN KNIVES
PO Box 40
116 Water St
Pictou, Nova Scotia B0K 1H0
CANADA
888-7KNIVES; Fax: 902-485-5872
www.grohmannknives.com
Fixed-blade belt knives for hunting and fishing, folding pocketknives for hunting and general use. Household cutlery.

H&B FORGE CO.
235 Geisinger Rd
Shiloh, OH 44878
419-895-1856
www.hbforge.com
Special order throwing knives and tomahawks, camp stoves, muzzleloading accroutements

HALLMARK CUTLERY
POB 220
Kodak, TN 37764
866-583-3912; fax: 901-405-0948
www.hallmarkcutlery.com
Traditional folders, tactical folders and fixed blades, multi-tools, shotgun shell knives, Bad Blood, Robert Klaas and Chief brand knives, and Super Premium care products

HISTORIC EDGED WEAPONRY
1021 Saddlebrook Dr
Hendersonville, NC 28739
828-692-0323; fax: 828-692-0600
histwpn@bellsouth.net
Antique knives from around the world; importer of puukko and other knives from Norway, Sweden, Finland and Lapland; also edged weaponry book "Travels for Daggers" by Eiler R. Cook

JOY ENTERPRISES-FURY CUTLERY
Port Commerce Center III
1862 M.L. King Jr. Blvd
Riviera Beach, FL 33404
800-500-3879; fax: 561-863-3277
mail@joyenterprises.com;
www.joyenterprises.com;
www.furycutlery.com
Fury™ Mustang™ extensive variety of fixed-blade and folding knives for hunting, fishing, diving, camping, military and general use; novelty key-ring knives. Muela Sporting Knives. Fury Tactical, Muela of Spain, Mustang Outdoor Adventure

KA-BAR KNIVES INC
200 Homer St
Olean, NY 14760
800-282-0130; fax: 716-790-7188
info@ka-bar.com; www.ka-bar.com
Manufacturer of law enforcement, military, hunting and outdoor knives

KAI USA LTD.
18600 S.W. Teton Ave.
Tualatin, OR 97062
800-325-2891; fax 503-682-7168
info@kai-usa.com
www.kershawknives.com
Manufacturer of high-quality, lifetime-guaranteed knives. Kai USA brands include Kershaw Knives for everyday carrying, hunting, fishing and other outdoor use; Zero Tolerance Knives for professional use; and Shun Cutlery, providing premium-quality kitchen knives

KATZ KNIVES, INC.
10924 Mukilteo Speedway #287
Mukilteo, WA 98275
480-786-9334; fax 460-786-9338
katzkn@aol.com; www.katzknives.com

KELLAM KNIVES WORLDWIDE
7789 S Suncoast Blvd
Suite 142
Homosassa, FL 34446
800-390-6918
info@kellamknives.com;
www.kellamknives.com
Largest selection of Finnish knives, handmade and production

KLOTZLI (MESSER KLOTZLI)
Hohengasse 3 CH 3400
Burgdorf
SWITZERLAND
41-(34)-422-23 78
info@klotzli.com; www.klotzli.com
High-tech folding knives for tactical and general use

KNIGHTS EDGE LTD.
5696 N. Northwest Highway
Chicago, IL 60646-6136
773-775-3888; fax 773-775-3339
sales@knightsedge.com;
www.knightsedge.com
Medieval weaponry, swords, suits of armor, katanas, daggers

KNIVES OF ALASKA, INC.
Charles or Jody Allen
3100 Airport Dr
Denison, TX 75020
903-786-7366; fax 903-786-7371
info@knivesofalaska.com;
www.knivesofalaska.com
High quality hunting & outdoorsmen's knives

KNIVES PLUS
2467 Interstate 40 West
Amarillo, TX 79109
800-359-6202
www.knivesplus.com
Retail cutlery and cutlery accessories since 1987; free catalog available

LANSKY KNIFE, TOOL & SHARPENERS
POB 800
Buffalo, NY 14231
716-877-7511; fax 716-877-6955
cfire@lansky.com
www.lansky.com
Knives, multi-tools, survival axes, sharpeners

LEATHERMAN TOOL GROUP, INC.
12106 N.E. Ainsworth Cir.
Portland, OR 97220-0595
800-847-8665; fax 503-253-7830
info@leatherman.com;
www.leatherman.com
Multi-tools

LONE STAR WHOLESALE
3220 Church ST
Amarillo, TX 79109
806-356-9540
sales@lswtexas.com
www.lswtexas.com
Great prices, dealers only, most major brands

MANTIS KNIVES
16530 E Laser Dr
Suite 6
Fountain Hills, AZ 85268
480-809-4537
480-809-4536 (fax)
gwest@mantis.bz
www.mantisknives.com
Manufacturer of utility, karambit, fixed and folding blades, and Neccessikeys

MARBLE ARMS C/O BLUE RIDGE KNIVES
166 Adwolfe Rd.
Marion, VA 24354-6664
276-783-6143
onestop@blueridgeknives.com
www.blueridgeknives.com

MASTER CUTLERY INC
700 Penhorn Ave
Secaucus, NJ 07094
888-227-7229; fax 888-271-7228
www.mastercutlery.com
Largest variety in the knife industry

MEYERCO USA
4481 Exchange Service Dr.
Dallas, TX 75236
214-467-8949; fax 214-467-9241
www.meyercousa.com
Folding tactical,rescue and speed-assisted pocketknives; fixed-blade hunting and fishing designs; multi-function camping tools and machetes

MICROTECH KNIVES
300 Chestnut Street Ext.
Bradford, PA 16701
814-363-9260; Fax: 814-363-9030
info@microtechknives.com
www.microtechknives.com
Manufacturers of the highest quality production knives

MISSION KNIVES
13771 Newhope St.
Garden Grove, CA 92843
714-638-4692; fax 714-638-4621
info@missionknives.com
www.missionknives.com
Manufacturer of titanium and steel knives and tools with over 20 years in business. Tactical, combat, military, law enforcement, EOD units, survivalist, diving, recreational straight blades, folding blades and mine probes, and more.

MOKI KNIFE COMPANY LTD.
15 Higashisenbo
Seki City GIFU
Pref JAPAN
575-22-4185; fax 575-24-5306
information@moki.co.jp
www.moki.co.jp
Pocketknives, folders, fixed-blade knives and gent's knives

MUSEUM REPLICAS LTD.
P.O. Box 840, 2147 Gees Mill Rd
Conyers, GA 30012
800-883-8838; fax: 770-388-0246
www.museumreplicas.com
Historically accurate and battle-ready swords and daggers

NEMESIS KNIVES, LLC
2753 E. Broadway Rd.
Suite 101-300
Mesa, AZ 85204
562-594-4740
info@nemesis-knives.com
www.nemesis-knives.com
Semi-custom and production kinves

ONTARIO KNIFE CO.
26 Empire St.
Franklinville, NY 14737
800-222-5233; fax 716-676-5535
knifesales@ontarioknife.com
www.ontarioknife.com
Fixed blades, tactical folders, military and hunting knives, machetes

OUTDOOR EDGE CUTLERY CORP.
9500 W. 49th Ave., #A-100
Wheat Ridge, CO 80033
800-447-3343; 303-530-7667
moreinfo@outdooredge.com;
www.outdooredge.com

PACIFIC SOLUTION MARKETING, INC.
1220 E. Belmont St.
Ontario, CA 91761
Tel: 877-810-4643
Fax: 909-930-5843
sales@pacificsolution.com
www.pacificsolution.com
Wide range of folding pocket knives, hunting knives, tactical knives, novelty knives, medieval armor and weapons as well as hand forged samurai swords and tantos.

PARAGON SPORTS
867 Broadway at 18th St.
New York, NY 10003
800-961-3030 or 212-255-8889
customerservice@paragonsports.com
www.paragonsports.com
Folders, fixed blades, hunters, multi-tools, tool knives, handmade fixed blades and folders from top makers

PRO-TECH KNIVES LLC
17115 Alburtis Ave.
Artesia, CA 90701-2616
562-860-0678
service@protechknives.com
www.protechknives.com
Manufacturer specializing in automatic knives for police, military and discriminating collectors

QUEEN CUTLERY COMPANY
507 Chestnut St.
Titusville, PA 16354
814-827-3673; fax: 814-827-9693
jmoore@queencutlery.com
www.queencutlery.com
Pocketknives, collectibles, Schatt & Morgan, Robeson, club knives

RANDALL MADE KNIVES
4857 South Orange Blossom Trail
Orlando, FL 32839
407-855-8075; fax 407-855-9054
grandall@randallknives.com;
www.randallknives.com
Handmade fixed-blade knives for hunting, fishing, diving, military and general use

REMINGTON ARMS CO., INC.
870 Remington Drive
Madison, NC 27025-0700
800-243-9700
www.remington.com

RUKO LLC.
PO Box 38
Buffalo, NY 14207-0038
800-611-4433; fax 905-826-1353
info@rukoproducts.com
www.rukoproducts.com

SANTA FE STONEWORKS
3790 Cerrillos Rd.
Santa Fe, NM 87507
800-257-7625
knives@rt66.com
www.santafestoneworks.com
Gemstone handles

SARCO KNIVES LLC
449 Lane Dr
Florence AL 35630
256-766-8099; fax 256-766-7246
www.TriEdgeKnife.com
Etching and engraving services, club knives, etc. New knives, antique-collectible knives

SARGE KNIVES
2720 E. Phillips Rd.
Greer, SC 29650
800-454-7448; fax 864-331-0752
sales@sargeknives.com
www.sargeknives.com
High-quality, affordable pocketknives, hunting, fishing, camping and tactical. Custom engraving for promotional knives or personalized gifts

SOG SPECIALTY KNIVES & TOOLS, INC.
6521 212th St SW
Lynnwood, WA 98036
425-771-6230; fax 425-771-7689
sogsales@sogknives.com
www.sogknives.com
SOG assisted technology, Arc-Lock, folding knives, specialized fixed blades, multi-tools

SPARTAN BLADES, LLC
625 S.E. Service Rd.
Southern Pines, NC 28387
910-757-0035
contact@spartanbladesusa.com
www.spartanbladesusa.com
Tactical, combat, fighter, survival and field knives

SPYDERCO, INC.
820 Spyderco Way
Golden, CO 80403
800-525-7770; fax 303-278-2229
sales@spyderco.com
www.spyderco.com
Knives, sharpeners and accessories

STONE RIVER GEAR
75 Manor Rd.
Red Hook, NY 12571
203-470-2526; fax 866-258-7202
info@stonerivergear.com
www.stonerivergear.com
Fighters, tactical, survival and military knives, household cutlery, hunting knives, pocketknives, folders and utility tools

SWISS ARMY BRANDS INC.
15 Corporate Dr.
Orangeburg, NY 10962
800-431-2994
customer.service@swissarmy.com
www.swissarmy.com
Folding multi-blade designs and multi-tools for hunting, fishing, camping, hiking, golfing and general use. One of the original brands (Victorinox) of Swiss Army Knives

TAYLOR BRANDS LLC
1043 Fordtown Road
Kingsport, TN 37663
800-251-0254; fax 423-247-5371
info@taylorbrandsllc.com
www.taylorbrandsllc.com
Smith & Wesson Knives, Old Timer, Uncle Henry and Schrade.

TIMBERLINE KNIVES
7223 Boston State Rd.

Boston, NY 14075
800-liv-sharp; fax 716-646-5775
www.timberlineknives.com
High technology production knives for professionals, sporting, tradesmen and kitchen use

TRU-BALANCE KNIFE CO. EAST
PO Box 807
Awendaw, SC 29429
843-928-3624
Manufacturing and sale of throwing knives

UNITED CUTLERY
475 U.S. Hwy. 319 S
Moultrie, GA 31768
800-548-0835; fax 229-551-0182
customerservice@unitedcutlery.com
www.unitedcutlery.com
Wholesale only; pocket, sportsman knives, licensed movie knives, swords, exclusive brands

WILLIAM HENRY STUDIO
3200 NE Rivergate St
McMinnville, OR 97128
503-434-9700; Fax: 503-434-9704
www.williamhenry.com
Semi-production, handmade knives

WUU JAU CO. INC
2600 S Kelly Ave
Edmond, OK 73013
405-359-5031; fax 405-340-5965
mail@wuujau.com; www.wuujau.com
Wide variety of imported fixed-blade and folding knives for hunting, fishing, camping and general use. Wholesale to knife dealers only

XIKAR INC
3305 Terrace, PO Box 025757
Kansas City MO 64111-3637
888-266-1193; fax 917-464-6398
info@xikar.com; www.xikar.com
Gentlemen's cutlery and accessories

importers

A.G. RUSSELL KNIVES INC
2900 S. 26th St.
Rogers, AR 72758-8571
800-255-9034
fax 479-631-8493
ag@agrussell.com; www.agrussell.com
The oldest knife mail-order company, highest quality. Free catalog available. In these catalogs you will find the newest and the best. If you like knives, this catalog is a must. Celebrating over 40 years in the industry

ADAMS INTERNATIONAL KNIFEWORKS
8710 Rosewood Hills
Edwardsville, IL 62025
Importers & foreign cutlers

ATLANTA CUTLERY CORP.
P.O.Box 839
Conyers, Ga 30012
770-922-7500; Fax: 770-918-2026
custserve@atlantacutlery.com;
www.atlantacutlery.com
Exotic knives from around the world

BAILEY'S
PO Box 550
Laytonville, CA 95454
800-322-4539; 707-984-8115
baileys@baileys-online.com;
www.baileys-online.com

BELTRAME, FRANCESCO
Fratelli Beltrame F&C snc Via dei Fabbri
15/B-33085 MANIAGO (PN)
ITALY
39 0427 701859
www.italianstiletto.com

BOKER USA, INC.
1550 Balsam St
Lakewood, CO 80214-5917
800-992-6537; 303-462-0668
sales@bokerusa.com; www.bokerusa.com
Ceramic blades

CAMPOS, IVAN DE ALMEIDA
R. Stelio M. Loureiro, 205
Centro, Tatui
BRAZIL
00-55-15-33056867
www.ivancampos.net

C.A.S. IBERIA
650 Industrial Blvd
Sale Creek, TN 37373
800-635-9366; fax 423-332-7248
mhillian@casiberia.com; www.casiberia.com

CATOCTIN CUTLERY
PO Box 188
Smithsburg, MD 21783

CLASSIC INDUSTRIES
1325 Howard Ave, Suite 408
Burlingame, CA 94010

COAST CUTLERY CO.
8033 N.E. Holman
Portland, OR 97218
800-426-5858
staff@coastcutlery.com;
www.coastcutlery.com

COLUMBIA PRODUCTS CO.
PO Box 1333
Sialkot 51310
PAKISTAN

COLUMBIA PRODUCTS INT'L
24 Beverly Lane
Lincoln Park, NJ 07035
201-310-6181, 201-528-3350, 973-832-7999
nycolumbia@aol.com; http://www.
columbiaproducts.homestead.com/cat.html
Pocket, hunting knives and swords of all kinds

COMPASS INDUSTRIES, INC.
104 E. 25th St
New York, NY 10010
800-221-9904; Fax: 212-353-0826
jeff@compassindustries.com;
www.compassindustries.com
Imported pocket knives

CONAZ COLTELLERIE
American Office
4179 Cristal Lake Dr.
Deerfield Beach, FL 33064
561-809-9701 or 754-423-3356
Fax: 954-781-3693
susanna@consigliscarperia.com;
www.consigliscarperia.it
Handicraft workmanship of knives of the ancient Italian tradition. Historical and collection knives

CONSOLIDATED CUTLERY CO., INC.
696 NW Sharpe St
Port St. Lucie, FL 34983
772-878-6139

CRAZY CROW TRADING POST
PO Box 847
Pottsboro, TX 75076
800-786-6210; Fax: 903-786-9059
info@crazycrow.com; www.crazycrow.com
Solingen blades, knife making parts & supplies

DER FLEISSIGEN BEAVER
(The Busy Beaver)
Harvey Silk
PO Box 1166
64343 Griesheim
GERMANY
49 61552231; 49 6155 2433
Der.Biber@t-online.de
Retail custom knives. Knife shows in Germany & UK

EXTREMA RATIO
Mauro Chiostri; Mavrizio Castrati
Via Tourcoing 40/p
59100 Prato (PO)
ITALY
0039 0576 58 4639; fax 0039 0576 584312
info@extremaratio.com;
www.extremaratio.com
Tactical & military knives manufacturing

FALLKNIVEN
Granatvagen 8
S-961 43 Boden
SWEDEN
+46 (0) 921 544 22; fax +46 (0) 921 544 33
info@fallkniven.se
www.fallkniven.com
High quality knives

FANEEMA CUTLERY
444 E Roosevelt Rd #284
Lombard, IL 60181
469 388 7343
janice@faneema.com
www.faneemacutlery.com

FREDIANI COLTELLI FINLANDESI
Via Lago Maggiore 41
I-21038 Leggiuno
ITALY

GIESSER MESSERFABRIK GMBH, JOHANNES
Raiffeisenstr 15
D-71349 Winnenden
GERMANY
49-7195-1808-29
info@giesser.de; www.giesser.de
Professional butchers and chef's knives

HIMALAYAN IMPORTS
3495 Lakeside Dr
Reno, NV 89509
775-825-2279
unclebill@himalayan-imports.com; www.
himilayan-imports.com
Kukris and swords

IVAN DE ALMEIDA CAMPOS-KNIFE DEALER
R. Xi De Agosto
107, Centro, Tatui, Sp 18270
BRAZIL
55-15-251-8092; 55-15-251-4896
campos@bitweb.com.br
Custom knives from all Brazilian knifemakers

JOY ENTERPRISES
1862 Martin Luther King Jr. Blvd.
Riviera Beach, FL 33404
561-863-3205; fax 561-863-3277
mail@joyenterprises.com;
www.joyenterprises.com
Fury™, Mustang™, Hawg Knives, Muela

directory

KELLAM KNIVES WORLDWIDE
7789 S Suncoast Blvd.
Ste. 142
Homosassa, FL 34446
561-588-3185 or 800-390-6918
info@kellamknives.com;
www.kellamknives.com
Knives from Finland; own line of knives

KNIFE IMPORTERS, INC.
11307 Conroy Ln
Manchaca, TX 78652
512-282-6860, Fax: 512-282-7504
Wholesale only

KNIGHTS EDGE LTD.
5696 N Northwest Hwy
Chicago, IL 60646
773-775-3888; fax 773-775-3339
www.knightsedge.com
Exclusive designers of our Rittersteel, Stagesteel and Valiant Arms and knightedge lines of weapon

LEISURE PRODUCTS CORP.
PO Box 1171
Sialkot-51310
PAKISTAN
L. C. Ristinen
Suomi Shop
17533 Co Hwy 38
Frazee MN 56544
218-538-6633; 218-538-6633
icrist@wcta.net
Scandinavian cutlery custom antique, books and reindeer antler

LINDER, CARL NACHF.
Erholungstr. 10
D-42699 Solingen
GERMANY
212 33 0 856; Fax: 212 33 71 04
info@linder.de; www.linder.de

MARTTIINI KNIVES
PO Box 44 (Marttiinintie 3)
96101 Rovaniemi
FINLAND

MATTHEWS CUTLERY
POB 2768
Moultrie, GA 31776
800-251-0123; fax 877-428-3599
www.matthewscutlery.com
Wholesale of major brands

MESSER KLÖTZLI
PO Box 104
Hohengasse 3, 3400 Burgdorf
SWITZERLAND
0041 (0)34 422 23 78; fax 0041 (0)34 422 76 93; info@klotzli.com; www.klotzli.com

MUSEUM REPLICAS LIMITED
2147 Gees Mill Rd
Conyers, GA 30012
800-883-8838; fax 770-388-0246
mrw@museumreplicas.com
www.museumreplicas.com
Subsidiary of Atlanta Cutlery. Battle-ready swords and other historic edged weapons, as well as clothing, jewelry and accessories.

NICHOLS CO.
Pomfret Rd
South Pomfret, VT 05067
Import & distribute knives from EKA (Sweden), Helle (Norway), Brusletto (Norway), Roselli (Finland). Also market Zippo products, Snow, Nealley axes and hatchets and snow & Neally axes

NORMARK CORP.
Craig Weber
10395 Yellow Circle Dr
Minnetonka, MN 55343

PIELCU
Parque Empresarial Campollano
Avenida 2a Numero 25 (esquina con C/E)
02007 Albacete
SPAIN
+34 967 523 568; fax +34 967 523 569
pielcu@pielcu.com; www.grupopielcu.com
Tactical, outdoor, fantasy and sporting knives

PRODUCTORS AITOR, S.A.
Izelaieta 17
48260 Ermua
SPAIN
943-170850; 943-170001
info@aitor.com
Sporting knives

PROFESSIONAL CUTLERY SERVICES
9712 Washburn Rd
Downey, CA 90241
562-803-8778; 562-803-4261
Wholesale only. Full service distributor of domestic & imported brand name cutlery. Exclusive U.S. importer for both Marto Swords and Battle Ready Valiant Armory edged weapons

SMOKY MOUNTAIN KNIFE WORKS, INC.
2320 Winfield Dunn Pkwy
PO Box 4430
Sevierville, TN 37864
800-564-8374; 865-453-5871
info@smkw.com; www.smkw.com
The world's largest knife showplace, catalog and website

SVORD KNIVES
Smith Rd., RD 2
Waiuku, South Auckland
NEW ZEALAND
64 9 2358846; fax 64 9 2356483
www.svord.com

SWISS ARMY BRANDS INC.
15 Corporate Dr.
Orangeburg, NY 10962
800-431-2994 or 914-425-4700
customer.service@swissarmy.com
www.swissarmy.com
Importer and distributor of Victorinox's Swiss Army brand

TAYLOR BRANDS, LLC
1043 Fordtown Road
Kingsport, TN 37663
800-251-0254; fax 423-247-5371
info@taylorbrandsllc.com;
www.taylorbrandsllc.com
Fixed-blade and folding knives for tactical, rescue, hunting and general use. Also provides etching, engraving, scrimshaw services.

UNITED CUTLERY
475 U.S. Hwy. 319 S
Moultrie, GA 31768
800-548-0835 or 229-890-6669; fax 229-551-0182
customerservice@unitedcutlery.com www.unitedcutlery.com
Harley-Davidson ® Colt ® , Stanley ®, U21 ®, Rigid Knives ®, Outdoor Life ®, Ford ®, hunting, camping, fishing, collectible & fantasy knives

U.S. GLADIUS
www.usgladius.com
Knives based on the design of the Roman gladius, the standard arm of the Roman Legions.

VICTORINOX SWISS ARMY, INC.
7 Victoria Dr.
Monroe, CT 06468
203-929-6391
renee.hourigan@swissarmy.com
www.swissarmy.com
Genuine Swiss Army Knives and Swiss Watches

WORLD CLASS EXHIBITION KNIVES
Cary Desmon
941-504-2279
www.withoutequal.com
Carries an extensive line of Pius Lang knives

ZWILLING J.A. HENCKELS LLC
171 Saw Mill River Rd
Hawthorne, NY 10532
914-747-0300; fax 914-747-1850
info@jahenckels.com;
www.jahenckels.com
Zwilling, Henckels International, Miyabi, Staub, Demeyere kitchen cutlery, scissors, shears, gadgets, cookware, flatware

knifemaking supplies

AFRICAN IMPORT CO.
Alan Zanotti
22 Goodwin Rd
Plymouth, MA 02360
508-746-8552; 508-746-0404
africanimport@aol.com
Ivory

ALABAMA DAMASCUS STEEL
PO Box 54
WELLINGTON, AL 36279
256-310-4619 or 256-282-7988
sales@alabamadamascussteel.com
www.alabamadamascussteel.com
We are a manufacturer of damascus steel billets & blades. We also offer knife supplies. We can custom make any blade design that the customer wants. We can also make custom damascus billets per customer specs.

ALASKAN FOSSIL IVORY
Jerry & Diana Kochheiser
1109 W. Hanley Rd.
Mansfield, Ohio 44904
419-564-8781
jkochheiser@neo.rr.com
Selling fossil walrus ivory, mammoth ivory, stag tapers, stag scales and oosik.

ALPHA KNIFE SUPPLY
425-868-5880; Fax: 425-898-7715
chuck@alphaknifesupply.com;
www.alphaknifesupply.com
Inventory of knife supplies

AMERICAN SIEPMANN CORP.
65 Pixley Industrial Parkway
Rochester, NY 14624
585-247-1640; Fax: 585-247-1883
www.siepmann.com
CNC blade grinding equipment, grinding wheels, production blade grinding services. Sharpening stones and sharpening equipment

ANKROM EXOTICS
Pat Ankrom
613 W. Maple Street
Centerville, IA 52544
641-436-0235
ankromexotics@hotmail.com
www.ankromexotics.com
Stabilized and resin cast handle material. Exotic burls and hardwoods from around the world. Stabilizing services also available.

ATLANTA CUTLERY CORP.
P.O.Box 839
Conyers, Ga 30012
770-922-7500; Fax: 770-918-2026
custserve@atlantacutlery.com;
www.atlantacutlery.com

BLADEMAKER, THE
Gary Kelley
17485 SW Phesant Ln
Beaverton, OR 97006
503-649-7867
garykelley@theblademaker.com;
www.theblademaker.com
Period knife and hawk blades for hobbyists & re-enactors and in dendritic D2 steel. "Ferroulithic" steel-stone spear point, blades and arrowheads

BOONE TRADING CO., INC.
PO Box 669
562 Coyote Rd
Brinnon, WA 98320
800-423-1945; Fax: 360-796-4511
bella@boonetrading.com
www.boonetrading.com
Ivory of all types, bone, horns

BORGER, WOLF
Benzstrasse 8
76676 Graben-Neudorf
GERMANY
wolf@messerschmied.de;
www.messerschmied.de

BOYE KNIVES
PO Box 1238
Dolan Springs, AZ 86441-1238
800-853-1617 or 928-272-0903
boye@citlink.net
www.boyeknives.com
Dendritic steel and Dendritic cobalt

BRONK'S KNIFEWORKS
Lyle Brunckhorst
2020 Maltby Road
Suite 7, Box180
Bothell, WA 98021
425 478-6809
bronks@bronksknifeworks.com;
www.bronksknifeworks.com
Damascus steel. Home of the Xross Bar Lock folder line.

CRAZY CROW TRADING POST
PO Box 847
Pottsboro, TX 75076
800-786-6210; Fax: 903-786-9059
info@crazycrow.com; www.crazycrow.com
Solingen blades, knife making parts & supplies

CULPEPPER & CO.
Joe Culpepper
P.O. Box 690
8285 Georgia Rd.
Otto, NC 28763
828-524-6842; Fax: 828-369-7809
info@culpepperco.com
www.knifehandles.com
www.stingrayproducts.com
www.oldschoolknifeworks.com
Mother of pearl, bone, abalone, stingray, dyed stag, blacklip, ram's horn, mammoth ivory, coral, scrimshaw

CUTLERY SPECIALTIES
6819 S.E. Sleepy Hollow Lane
Stuart, FL 34997-4757
772-219-0436 or 800-229-5530
Dennis13@aol.com
www.restorationproduct.com
Exclusive distributor for Renaissance Wax/Polish and other restoration products. Also a dealer and purveyor.

DAMASCUS USA
149 Deans Farm Rd
Tyner, NC 27980-9718
252-333-0349
rob@damascususa.com;
www.damascususa.com
Sporting cutlery. All types of damascus cutlery steel, including 100 percent finished damascus blade blanks.

DAN'S WHETSTONE CO., INC.
418 Hilltop Rd
Pearcy, AR 71964
501-767-1616; fax 501-767-9598
questions@danswhetstone.com;
www.danswhetstone.com
Natural abrasive Arkansas stone products

DIAMOND MACHINING TECHNOLOGY, INC. (DMT)
85 Hayes Memorial Dr
Marlborough, MA 01752
800-666-4DMT
dmtcustomercare@dmtsharp.com;
www.dmtsharp.com
Knife and tool sharpener—diamond, ceramic and easy edge guided sharpening kits

DIGEM DIAMOND SUPPLIERS
7303 East Earll Drive
Scottsdale, Arizona 85251
602-620-3999
eglasser@cox.net
#1 international diamond tool provider. Every diamond tool you will ever need 1/16th of an inch to 11'x9'. BURRS, CORE DRILLS, SAW BLADES, MILLING SHAPES, AND WHEELS

DIXIE GUN WORKS, INC.
1412 West Reelfoot Ave.
Union City, TN 38281
731-885-0700; Fax: 731-885-0440
www.dixiegunworks.com
Knife and knifemaking supplies

EZE-LAP DIAMOND PRODUCTS
3572 Arrowhead Dr
Carson City, NV 89706
775-888-9500; Fax: 775-888-9555
sales@eze-lap.com; www.eze-lap.com
Diamond coated sharpening tools

FINE TURNAGE PRODUCTIONS
Charles Turnage
1210 Midnight Drive
San Antonio, TX 78260
210-352-5660
info@fineturnage.com
www.fineturnage.com
Specializing in stabilized mammoth tooth and bone, mammoth ivory, fossil brain coral, meteorite, etc.

FLITZ INTERNATIONAL, LTD.
821 Mohr Ave
Waterford, WI 53185
800-558-8611; Fax: 262-534-2991
info@flitz.com; www.flitz.com
Metal polish, buffing pads, wax

FORTUNE PRODUCTS, INC.
2010A Windy Terrace
Cedar Park, TX 78613
800-742-7797; Fax: 800-600-5373
www.accusharp.com
AccuSharp knife sharpeners

GALLERY HARDWOODS
Larry Davis, Eugene, OR
www.galleryhardwoods.com
Stabilized exotic burls and woods

GILMER WOOD CO.
2211 NW St Helens Rd
Portland, OR 97210
503-274-1271; Fax: 503-274-9839
www.gilmerwood.com

GIRAFFEBONE KNIFE SUPPLY
3052 Isim Rd.
Norman, OK 73026
888-804-0683
sandy@giraffebone.com;
www.giraffebone.com
Exotic handle materials

GLENDO CORPORATION/GRS TOOLS
D.J. Glaser
900 Overlander Rd.
Emporia, KS 66801
620-343-1084; Fax: 620-343-9640
glendo@glendo.com; www.grstools.com
Engraving, equipment, tool sharpener, books/videos

GRINDING STEEL, LLC
Antonio Valcarcel
210-544-2563
www.GrindingSteel.com
sales@grindingsteel.com
Abrasive belts

HALPERN TITANIUM INC.
Les and Marianne Halpern
PO Box 214
4 Springfield St
Three Rivers, MA 01080
888-283-8627; Fax: 413-289-2372
info@halperntitanium.com;
www.halperntitanium.com
Titanium, carbon fiber, G-10, fasteners; CNC milling

HAWKINS KNIFE MAKING SUPPLIES
110 Buckeye Rd
Fayetteville, GA 30214
770-964-1023
Sales@hawkinsknifemakingsupplies.com
www.HawkinsKnifeMakingSupplies.com
All styles

HILTARY INDUSTRIES
6060 East Thomas Road
Scottsdale, AZ 85251
Office: 480-945-0700
Fax: 480-945-3333
usgrc@usgrc.biz, eglasser@cox.net
OEM manufacturer, knife and sword importer, appraiser, metal supplier, diamond products, stag, meteorite, reconstituted gems, exotic wood, leather and bone

HOUSE OF TOOLS LTD.
#54-5329 72 Ave. S.E.
Calgary, Alberta
CANADA T2C 4X
403-640-4594; Fax: 403-451-7006
www.houseoftools.net

INDIAN JEWELERS SUPPLY CO.
Mail Order: 601 E Coal Ave
Gallup, NM 87301-6005
2105 San Mateo Blvd NE
Albuquerque, NM 87110-5148
800-545-6540; fax: 888-722-4172
orders@ijsinc.com; www.ijsinc.com
Handle materials, tools, metals

INTERAMCO INC.
5210 Exchange Dr
Flint, MI 48507
810-732-8181; 810-732-6116
solutions@interamco.com
Knife grinding and polishing

JANTZ SUPPLY / KOVAL KNIVES
PO Box 584
309 West Main
Davis, OK 73030
800-351-8900; 580-369-3082
jantz@jantzusa.com
www.knifemaking.com
Pre shaped blades, kit knives, complete knifemaking supply line

JMD INTERNATIONAL
2985 Gordy Pkwy., Unit 405
Marietta, GA 30066
678-969-9147; Fax: 770-640-9852
knifesupplies@gmail.com;
www.knifesupplies.com;
Serving the cutlery industry with the finest selection of India stag, buffalo horn, mother-of-pearl and smooth white bone

JOHNSON, R.B.
I.B.S. Int'l. Folder Supplies, Box 11
Clearwater, MN 55320
320-558-6128; 320-558-6128
www.foldingknifesupplies.com
Threaded pivot pins, screws, taps, etc.

JOHNSON WOOD PRODUCTS
34897 Crystal Rd
Strawberry Point, IA 52076
563-933-6504

K&G FINISHING SUPPLIES
1972 Forest Ave
Lakeside, AZ 85929
928-537-8877; fax: 928-537-8066
csinfo@knifeandgun.com;
www.knifeandgun.com
Full service supplies

KOWAK IVORY
Roland and Kathy Quimby
(May-Sept): PO Box 350
Ester, AK 99725
907-479-9335
(Oct-April)
Green Valley, AZ 85662
520-207-6620
sales@kowakivory.com;
www.kowakivory.com
Fossil ivories

LITTLE GIANT POWER HAMMER
Roger Rice
6414 King Rd.
Nebraska City, NE 68410
402-873-6603
www.littlegianthammer.com
Rebuilds hammers and supplies parts

LIVESAY, NEWT
3306 S Dogwood St
Siloam Springs, AR 72761
479-549-3356; 479-549-3357
Combat utility knives, titanium knives, sportsmen knives, custom made orders taken on knives and after market Kydex© sheaths for commercial or custom cutlery

M MILLER ORIGINALS
Michael Miller
3030 E. Calle Cedral
Kingman AZ 86401
928-757-1359
mike@mmilleroriginals.com;
www.mmilleroriginals.com
Supplies stabilized juniper burl blocks and scales, mosaic damascus, damascus

MARKING METHODS, INC.
Sales
301 S. Raymond Ave
Alhambra, CA 91803-1531
626-282-8823; Fax: 626-576-7564
sales@markingmethods.com;
www.markingmethods.com
Knife etching equipment & service

MASECRAFT SUPPLY CO.
254 Amity St
Meriden, CT 06450
800-682-5489; Fax: 203-238-2373
info@masecraftsupply.com;
www.masecraftsupply.com
Natural & specialty synthetic handle materials & more

MEIER STEEL
Daryl Meier
75 Forge Rd
Carbondale, IL 62903
618-549-3234; Fax: 618-549-6239
www.meiersteel.com

NICO, BERNARD
PO Box 5151
Nelspruit 1200
SOUTH AFRICA
011-2713-7440099; 011-2713-7440099
bernardn@iafrica.com

NORRIS, MIKE
Rt 2 Box 242A
Tollesboro, KY 41189
606-798-1217
Damascus steel

NORTHCOAST KNIVES
17407 Puritas Ave
Cleveland, Ohio 44135
www.NorthCoastKnives.com
Tutorials and step-by-step projects. Entry level knifemaking supplies.

OSO FAMOSO
PO Box 654
Ben Lomond, CA 95005
831-336-2343
oso@osofamoso.com;
www.osofamoso.com
Mammoth ivory bark

OZARK CUTLERY SUPPLY
5230 S. MAIN ST.
Joplin, MO 64804
417-782-4998
ozarkcutlery@gmail.com
28 years in the cutlery business, Missouri's oldest cutlery firm

PARAGON INDUSTRIES, L.P.
2011 South Town East Blvd
Mesquite, TX 75149-1122
800-876-4328 or 972-288-7557
info@paragonweb.com;
www.paragonweb.com
Heat treating furnaces for knifemakers

POPLIN, JAMES / POP'S KNIVES & SUPPLIES
1654 S. Smyrna Church Rd.
Washington, GA 30673
706-678-5408
www.popsknifesupplies.com

POUL STRANDE
Søster Svenstrup Byvej 16
4130 Viby Sjælland
Denmark
45 46 19 43 05; Fax: 45 46 19 53 19
www.poulstrande.com

PUGH, JIM
PO Box 711
917 Carpenter
Azle, TX 76020
817-444-2679; Fax: 817-444-5455
Rosewood and ebony Micarta blocks, rivets for Kydex sheaths, 0-80 screws for folders

RADOS, JERRY
134 Willie Nell Rd.
Columbia, KY 42728
606-303-3334
jerryr@ttlv.net
www.radosknives.com
Damascus steel

REACTIVE METALS STUDIO, INC.
PO Box 890
Clarksdale, AZ 86324
800-876-3434; 928-634-3434; Fax: 928-634-6734
info@reactivemetals.com; www.reactivemetals.com

R. FIELDS ANCIENT IVORY
Donald Fields
790 Tamerlane St
Deltona, FL 32725
386-532-9070
donaldbfields@earthlink.net
Selling ancient ivories; Mammoth, fossil & walrus

RICK FRIGAULT CUSTOM KNIVES
1189 Royal Pines Rd.
Golden Lake, Ontario
CANADA K0J 1X0
613-401-2869
jill@mouseworks.net
www.rfrigaultknives.ca
Selling padded zippered knife pouches with an option to personalize the outside with the marker, purveyor, stores-address, phone number, email web-site or any other information needed. Available in black cordura, mossy oak camo in sizes 4"x2" to 20"x4.5"

RIVERSIDE MACHINE
201 W Stillwell Ave.
DeQueen, AR 71832
870-642-7643; Fax: 870-642-4023
uncleal@riversidemachine.net
www.riversidemachine.net

ROCKY MOUNTAIN KNIVES
George L. Conklin
PO Box 902, 615 Franklin
Ft. Benton, MT 59442
406-622-3268; Fax: 406-622-3410
bbgrus@ttc-cmc.net
Working knives

SAKMAR, MIKE
903 S. Latson Rd. #257
Howell, MI 48843
517-546-6388; Fax: 517-546-6399
sakmarent@yahoo.com
www.sakmarenterprises.com
Mokume bar stock. Retail & wholesale

SANDPAPER, INC. OF ILLINOIS
P.O. Box 2579
Glen Ellyn, IL 60138
630-629-3320; Fax: 630-629-3324
sandinc@aol.com; www.sandpaperinc.com
Abrasive belts, rolls, sheets & discs

SCHMIEDEWERKSTATTE
Markus Balbach e.K.
Heinrich-Worner-Str. 1-3
35789 Weilmunster-Laubuseschbach,
Germany
06475-8911 Fax: 912986
Damascus steel

SCHNEIDER, CRAIG M.
5380 N. Amity Rd.
Claremont, IL 62421
217-377-5715
rafetownslame@gmail.com
www.grindhaus.org
Offering dyed giraffe, camel and cattle bone, various horn, antler and teeth

SENTRY SOLUTIONS LTD.
PO Box 214
Wilton, NH 03086
800-546-8049; Fax: 603-654-3003
info@sentrysolutions.com;
www.sentrysolutions.com
Knife care products

SHEFFIELD KNIFEMAKERS SUPPLY, INC.
PO Box 741107
Orange City, FL 32774
386-775-6453; fax: 386-774-5754
email@sheffieldsupply.com;
www.sheffieldsupply.com

SHINING WAVE METALS
PO Box 563
Snohomish, WA 98291
425-334-5569
info@shiningwave.com;
www.shiningwave.com
A full line of mokume-gane in precious and non-precious metals for knifemakers, jewelers and other artists

SMITH'S
747 Mid-America Blvd.
Hot Springs, AR 71913-8414
501-321-2244; Fax: 501-321-9232
sales@smithsproducts.com
www.smithsproducts.com

SMOKY MOUNTAIN KNIFE WORKS, INC.
2320 Winfield Dunn Pkwy
PO Box 4430
Sevierville, TN 37864
800-564-8374; 865-453-5871
info@smkw.com; www.smkw.com
The world's largest knife showplace, catalog and website

STAMASCUS KNIFEWORKS INC.
Ed VanHoy
24255 N Fork River Rd
Abingdon, VA 24210
276-944-4885; Fax: 276-944-3187
stamascus@centurylink.net
www.stamascusknifeworks.com
Blade steels

STOVER, JEFF
PO Box 43
Torrance, CA 90507
310-486-0976
edgedealer@aol.com;
www.edgedealer.com
Fine custom knives, top makers

TEXAS KNIFEMAKERS SUPPLY
10649 Haddington Suite 180
Houston TX 77043
713-461-8632; Fax: 713-461-8221
sales@texasknife.com;
www.texasknife.com
Complete line of knifemaking supplies, equipment, and custom heat treating

TRU-GRIT, INC.
760 E Francis St., Unit N
Ontario, CA 91761
909-923-4116; Fax: 909-923-9932
www.trugrit.com
The latest in Norton and 3/M ceramic grinding belts. Also Super Flex, Trizact, Norax and Micron belts to 3000 grit. All of the popular belt grinders. Buffers and variable speed motors. ATS-34, 440C, BG-42, CPM S-30V, 416 and Damascus steel

TWO FINGER KNIFE, LLC
4574 N. Haroldsen Dr.
Idaho Falls, ID 83401
208-523-7436; Fax: 208-523-7436
twofingerknife@gmail.com www.
twofingerknife.com
USA-forged and hand-ground finished damascus blades, and blades in 5160, 1095, 52100, D2, 440C, ATS 34, ELMAX and other steels. Finishes sword blades, sword-cane blades, damascus bar stock and tomahawk heads. Offers folder kits, custom sheaths, in-house heat treating.

WASHITA MOUNTAIN WHETSTONE CO.
PO Box 20378
Hot Springs, AR 71903-0378
501-525-3914; Fax: 501-525-0816
wmw@hsnp

WEILAND, J. REESE
PO Box 2337
Riverview, FL 33568
813-671-0661
rwphil413@verizon.net
www.reeseweilandknives.com
   Folders, straight knives, etc.

WILSON, R.W.
PO Box 2012
113 Kent Way
Weirton, WV 26062
304-723-2771
rwknives@hotmail.com

WOOD CARVERS SUPPLY, INC.
PO Box 7500
Englewood, FL 34295
800-284-6229
teamwcs@yahoo.com
www.woodcarverssupply.com
   Over 2,000 unique wood carving tools

WOOD LAB
Michael Balaskovitz
2471 6th St.
Muskegon Hts., MI 49444
616-322-5846
woodlabgroup@gmail.com
www.woodlab.biz
   Acrylic stabilizing services and materials

WOOD STABILIZING SPECIALISTS INT'L, LLC
2940 Fayette Ave
Ionia, IA 50645
800-301-9774; 641-435-4746
mike@stabilizedwood.com;
www.stabilizedwood.com
   Processor of acrylic impregnated materials

ZOWADA CUSTOM KNIVES
Tim Zowada
4509 E. Bear River Rd
Boyne Falls, MI 49713
231-881-5056
tim@tzknives.com; www.tzknives.com
   Damascus, pocket knives, swords, Lower case gothic tz logo

mail order, sales, dealers and purveyors

A.G. RUSSELL KNIVES INC
2900 S. 26th St
Rogers, AR 72758-8571
800-255-9034 or 479-631-0130
fax 479-631-8493
ag@agrussell.com; www.agrussell.com
   The oldest knife mail-order company, highest quality. Free catalog available. In these catalogs you will find the newest and the best. If you like knives, this catalog is a must

ARIZONA CUSTOM KNIVES
Julie Maguire
3670 U.S. 1 S, Suite 260-F
St. Augustine, FL 32086
904-826-4178
sharptalk@arizonacustomknives.com; www.arizonacustomknives.com
   Color catalog $5 U.S. / $7 Foreign

ARTKNIVES.COM
Fred Eisen Leather & Art Knives
129 S. Main St.
New Hope, PA 18938
215-862-5988
fredeisen@verizon.net
www.artknives.com
   Handmade knives from over 75 makers/high-quality manufacturers, leather sheath maker

AUSTRALASIAN KNIFE COLLECTORS
PO BOX 149 CHIDLOW 6556 WESTERN AUSTRALIA TEL: (08) 9572 7255; FAX: (08) 9572 7266. International Inquiries: TEL: + 61 8 9572 7255; FAX: + 61 8 9572 7266; akc@knivesaustralia.com.au, www.knivesaustralia.com.au

ATLANTA CUTLERY CORP.
P.O.Box 839
Conyers, Ga 30012
770-922-7500; Fax: 770-918-2026
custserv@atlantacutlery.com;
www.atlantacutlery.com

BECK'S CUTLERY SPECIALTIES
51 Highland Trace Ln.
Benson, NC 27504
919-902-9416
beckscutlery@embarqmail.com;
www.beckscutlery.com
   Knives

BLADE HQ
400 S. 1000 E, Ste. E
Lehi, UT 84043
888-252-3347 or 801-768-0232
questions@bladehq.com
www.bladehq.com
   Online destination for knives and gear, specializing in law enforcement and military, including folders, fixed blades, custom knives, asisted-opening folders, automatics, butterfly knives, hunters, machetes, multi-tools, axes, knife cases, paracord, sharpeners, sheaths, lubricants and supplies

BLADEART.COM
14216 S.W. 136 St.
Miami, FL 33186
305-255-9176
sales@bladeart.com
www.bladeart.com
Custom knives, swords and gear

BLADEGALLERY.COM
107 Central Way
Kirkland, WA 98033
425-889-5980 or 877-56BLADE
info@bladegallery.com;
www.bladegallery.com
Bladegallery.com specializes in handmade, one-of-a-kind knives from around the world. We have an emphasis on forged knives and high-end gentlemen's folders

BLADEOPS
1352 W. 7800 S
West Jordan, UT 84088
888-EZ BLAD (392-5233)
sales@bladeops.com
www.bladeops.com
Online dealer of all major brands of automatic knives, butterfly knives, spring-assisted folders, throwing knives, manual folders, survival and self-defense knives, sharpeners and paracord

BLUE RIDGE KNIVES
166 Adwolfe Rd
Marion, VA 24354
276-783-6143; fax 276-783-9298
onestop@blueridgeknives.com;
www.blueridgeknives.com
Wholesale distributor of knives

BOB'S TRADING POST
308 N Main St
Hutchinson, KS 67501
620-669-9441
bobstradingpost@cox.net;
www.bobstradingpostinc.com
Tad custom knives with Reichert custom sheaths one at a time, one of a kind

BOONE TRADING CO., INC.
PO Box 669
562 Coyote Rd
Brinnon, WA 98320
800-423-1945; Fax: 360-796-4511
bella@boonetrading.com
www.boonetrading.com
Ivory of all types, bone, horns

CARMEL CUTLERY
Dolores & 6th
PO Box 1346
Carmel, CA 93921
831-624-6699; 831-624-6780
sanford@carmelcutlery.com;
www.carmelcutlery.com
Quality custom and a variety of production pocket knives, swords; kitchen cutlery; personal grooming items

CLASSIC CUTLERY
66 N. Adams St., Ste. 1
Manchester, NH 03104
classiccutlery@earthlink.net
www.classiccutleryusa.com
Private-label zip-up knife cases and all brands of production cutlery and outdoor gear

CUTLERY SHOPPE
3956 E Vantage Pointe Ln
Meridian, ID 83642-7268
800-231-1272; Fax: 208-884-4433
orders@cutleryshoppe.com;
www.cutleryshoppe.com
Discount pricing on top quality brands

CUTTING EDGE, THE
2900 South 26th St
Rogers, AR 72758-8571
800-255-9034; Fax: 479-631-8493
ce_info@cuttingedge.com;
www.cuttingedge.com
After-market knives since 1968. They offer about 1,000 individual knives for sale each month. Subscription by first class mail, in U.S. $20 per year, Canada or Mexico by air mail, $25 per year. All overseas by air mail, $40 per year. The oldest and the most experienced in the business of buying and selling knives. They buy collections of any size, take knives on consignment. Every month there are 4-8 pages in color featuring the work of top makers

DENTON, JOHN W.
703 Hiawassee Estates Dr.
Hiawassee, GA 30546
706-781-8479
jwdenton@windstream.net
www.boblovelessknives.com
Loveless knives

EDGEDEALER.COM
PO BOX 43
TORRANCE, CA 90507
310-532-2166
edgedealer1@yahoo.com
www.edgedealer.com
Antiques

EPICUREAN EDGE
107 Central Way
Kirkland, WA 98033
425-889-5980
info@epicedge.com
www.epicedge.com
Specializing in handmade and one-of-a-kind kitchen knives from around the world

EXQUISITEKNIVES.COM
770 Sycamore Ave., Ste. 122, Box 451
Vista, CA 92083
760-945-7177
mastersmith@cox.net
www.exquisiteknives.com and
www.robertloveless.com
Purveyor of high-end custom knives

FAZALARE INTERNATIONAL ENTERPRISES
PO Box 7062
Thousand Oaks, CA 91359
805-496-2002
ourfaz@aol.com
Handmade multiblades; older Case; Fight'n Rooster; Bulldog brand & Cripple Creek

FROST CUTLERY CO.
PO Box 22636
Chattanooga, TN 37422
800-251-7768
www.frostcutlery.com

GODWIN, INC. G. GEDNEY
PO Box 100
Valley Forge, PA 19481
610-783-0670; Fax: 610-783-6083
sales@gggodwin.com;
www.gggodwin.com
18th century reproductions

GPKNIVES, LLC
2230 Liebler Rd.
Troy, IL 62294
866-667-5965
info@gpknives.com
www.gpknives.com
Serving law enforcement, hunters, sportsmen and collectors

GRAZYNA SHAW/QUINTESSENTIAL CUTLERY
POB 11
Clearwater, MN 55320
320-217-9002
gshaw@quintcut.com
www.quintcut.com
Specializing in investment-grade custom knives and early makers

GUILD KNIVES
Donald Guild
320 Paani Place 1A
Paia, HI 96779
808-877-3109
don@guildknives.com;
www.guildknives.com
Purveyor of custom art knives

HOUSE OF BLADES
6451 N.W. Loop 820
Ft. Worth, TX 76135
817-237-7721
sales@houseofblades.com
www.houseofbladestexas.com
Handmades, pocketknives, hunting knives, antique and collector knives, swords, household cutlery and knife-related items.

JENCO SALES, INC.
PO Box 1000
11307 Conroy Ln
Manchaca, TX 78652
800-531-5301; fax 800-266-2373
jencosales@sbcglobal.net
Wholesale distributor of domestic and imported cutlery and sharpeners

KELLAM KNIVES WORLDWIDE
POB 3438
Lantana, FL 33465
800-390-6918; 561-588-3185
info@kellamknives.com;
www.kellamknives.com
Largest selection of Finnish knives; own line of folders and fixed blades

KNIFEART.COM
13301 Pompano Dr
Little Rock AR 72211
501-221-1010
connelley@knifeart.com
www.knifeart.com
Large internet seller of custom knives & upscale production knives

KNIFECENTER
5201 Lad Land Dr.
Fredericksburg, VA 22407
800-338-6799 or 301-486-0901
info@knifecenter.com
www.knifecenter.com

KNIFEPURVEYOR.COM INC
919-295-1283
mdonato@knifepurveyor.com
www.knifepurveyor.com
Owned and operated by Michael A. Donato (full-time knife purveyor since 2002). We buy, sell, trade, and consign fine custom knives. We also specialize in buying and selling valuable collections of fine custom knives. Our goal is to make every transaction a memorable one.

KNIVES PLUS
2467 I 40 West
Amarillo, TX 79109
806-359-6202
salessupport@knivesplus.com
www.knivesplus.com
Retail cutlery and cutlery accessories since 1987

KRIS CUTLERY
2314 Monte Verde Dr
Pinole, CA 94564
510-758-9912 Fax: 510-758-9912
kriscutlery@aol.com; www.kriscutlery.com
Japanese, medieval, Chinese & Philippine

LONE STAR WHOLESALE
2401 Interstate 40 W
Amarillo, TX 79109
806-836-9540; fax 806-359-1603
sales@lswtexas.com
www.lswtexas.com
Nationwide distributor of knives, knife accessories and knife-related tools

MATTHEWS CUTLERY
PO Box 2768
Moultrie, GA 31776
800-251-0123; fax 877-428-3599
www.matthewscutlery.com

MOORE CUTLERY
PO Box 633
Lockport, IL 60441
708-301-4201
www.moorecutlery.com
Owned & operated by Gary Moore since 1991 (a full-time dealer). Purveyor of high quality custom & production knives

MUSEUM REPLICAS LIMITED
2147 Gees Mill Rd
Conyers, GA 30012
800-883-8838
www.museumreplicas.com
Historically accurate and battle ready swords & daggers

NEW GRAHAM KNIVES
560 Virginia Ave.
Bluefield, VA 24605
276-326-1384
mdye@newgraham.com
www.newgraham.com
Wide selection of knives from over 75 manufacturers, knife sharpening and maintenance accessories

NORDIC KNIVES
404 South 8th Street
St L115
Boise, ID 83704
208-202-2913; fax 805-688-1635
info@nordicknives.com
www.nordicknives.com
Custom and Randall knives

PARKERS' KNIFE COLLECTOR SERVICE
6715 Heritage Business Court
Chattanooga, TN 37421
423-892-0448; fax 423-892-9165
www.bulldogknives.org
Online and mail order dealer specializing in collectible knives, including Bulldog Knives, Weidmannsheil and Parker Eagle Brand. Parkers' Greatest Knife Show On Earth

PLAZA CUTLERY, INC.
3333 S. Bristol St., Suite 2060
South Coast Plaza
Costa Mesa, CA 92626
866-827-5292; 714-549-3932
dan@plazacutlery.com;
www.plazacutlery.com
Now only online! Selling Randall, Medford, Chris Reeve as well as many fine hand made knives. Exclusive projects with Chris Reeve and Medford such as the "Dog Paw" and "Halloween" series of knives. Selling fine knives since 1948.

ROBERTSON'S CUSTOM CUTLERY
4960 Sussex Dr
Evans, GA 30809
706-650-0252
customknives@comcast.net
www.robertsonscustomcultery.com
World class custom knives, custom knife entrepreneur

RUMMELL, HANK
10 Paradise Lane
Warwick, NY 10990
845-769-7273
hank@newyorkcustomknives.com;
www.newyorkcustomknives.com

SCHENK KNIVES
4574 N. Haroldsen Dr.
Idaho Falls, ID 83401
208-523-2026
zane@schenkknives.com
www.schenkknives.com
High-performance factory custom knives. All models offered in the USA forged from damascus steel, forged 52100 bearting steel and ELMAX stainless steel.

SMOKY MOUNTAIN KNIFE WORKS, INC.
2320 Winfield Dunn Pkwy
PO Box 4430
Sevierville, TN 37864
800-564-8374; 865-453-5871
info@smkw.com; www.smkw.com
The world's largest knife showplace, catalog and website

TRUE NORTH KNIVES
2455 Hollywood Blvd
Suite 201
Hollywood, FL 33020
1-866-748-9985
info@truenorthknives.com
www.TrueNorthKnives.com
Custom and production knife purveyor

VOYLES, BRUCE
PO Box 22007
Chattanooga, TN 37422
423-238-6753
bruce@jbrucevoyles.com;
www.jbrucevoyles.com
Knives, knife auctions

knife services

appraisers

Levine, Bernard, P.O. Box 2404, Eugene, OR, 97402, 541-484-0294, brlevine@ix.netcom.com

Russell, A.G., Knives Inc, 2900 S. 26th St., Rogers, AR 72758-8571, phone 800-255-9034 or 479-631-0130, fax 479-631-8493, ag@agrussell.com, www.agrussell.com

Voyles, J. Bruce, PO Box 22007, Chattanooga, TN 37422, 423-238-6753, bruce@jbrucevoyles.com, www.jbrucevoyles.com

custom grinders

McGowan Manufacturing Company, 4720 N. La Cholla Blvd., #190, Tucson, AZ, 85705, 800-342-4810, 520-219-0884, info@mcgowanmfg.com, www.mcgowanmfg.com, Knife sharpeners, hunting axes

Peele, Bryan, The Elk Rack, 215 Ferry St. P.O. Box 1363, Thompson Falls, MT, 59873

Schlott, Harald, Zingster Str. 26, 13051 Berlin, GERMANY, 049 030 9293346, harald.schlott@T-online.de, Custom grinder, custom handle artisan, display case/box maker, etcher, scrimshander

Wilson, R.W., P.O. Box 2012, Weirton, WV, 26062, 304-723-2771 rwknives@comcast.net, www.rwwilsonknives.com

custom handles

Alaskan Fossil Ivory, Jerry and Diana Kochheiser, 1109 Hanley Rd. W., Mansfield, OH 44904, 419-564-8781, jkochheiser@neo.rr.com, selling high color fossil walrus ivory, mammoth ivory, stag tapers, stag scales and oosik.

Cooper, Jim, 1221 Cook St, Ramona, CA, 92065-3214, 760-789-1097, (760) 788-7992, jamcooper@aol.com

Boone Trading Co. Inc., P.O. Box 669, Brinnon, WA, 98320, pre-1972 white and fossil walrus ivory and oosik, hippo tusks. 800-423-1945 www.boonetrading.com

Burrows, Chuck, dba Wild Rose Trading Co, 102 Timber Ln., Durango, CO, 81303, 970-317-5592, chuck@wrtcleather.com, www.wrtcleather.com

Culpepper & Company, 8285 Georgia Rd., Otto, NC, 28763 828-524-6842, info@culpepperco.com, www.knifehandles.com

Fields, Donald, 790 Tamerlane St, Deltona, FL, 32725, 386-532-9070, donaldfields@earthlink.net, Selling ancient ivories; mammoth & fossil walrus

Grussenmeyer, Paul G., 310 Kresson Rd, Cherry Hill, NJ, 08034, 856-428-1088, 856-428-8997, pgrussentne@comcast.net, www.pgcarvings.com

Holland, Dennis K., 4908-17th Pl., Lubbock, TX, 79416

Imboden II, Howard L., Hi II Originals, 620 Deauville Dr., Dayton, OH, 45429, 513-439-1536

Kelso, Jim, 577 Collar Hill Rd, Worcester, VT, 05682, 802-229-4254, (802) 229-0595

Marlatt, David, 67622 Oldham Rd., Cambridge, OH, 43725, 740-432-7549

Mead, Dennis, 2250 E. Mercury St., Inverness, FL, 34453-0514

Myers, Ron, 6202 Marglenn Ave., Baltimore, MD, 21206, 410-866-6914

Schlott, Harald, Zingster Str. 26, 13051 Berlin, GERMANY, 049 030 9293346, harald.schlott@T-online.de, Custom grinder, custom handle artisan, display case/box maker, etcher, scrimshander

Snell, Barry A., 4801 96th St. N., St. Petersburg, FL, 33708-3740

Vallotton, A., 621 Fawn Ridge Dr., Oakland, OR, 97462, 541-459-2216

Watson, Silvia, 350 Jennifer Lane, Driftwood, TX, 78619

Wilderness Forge, 315 North 100 East, Kanab, UT, 84741, 435-644-3674, bhatting@xpressweb.com

Williams, Gary, (GARBO), PO Box 210, Glendale, KY, 42740-2010 270-369-6752, scrimbygarbo@gmail.com, www.scrimbygarbo.com

display cases and boxes

Bill's Custom Cases, P O Box 603, Montague, CA, 96064, 541-727-7223, billscustomcases@earthlink.net, www.billscustomcases.com

McLean, Lawrence, 12344 Meritage Ct, Rancho Cucamonga, CA, 91739, 714-848-5779, lmclean@charter.net

Miller, Michael K., M&M Kustom Krafts, 28510 Santiam Highway, Sweet Home, OR, 97386

Miller, Robert, P.O. Box 2722, Ormond Beach, FL, 32176

Retichek, Joseph L., W9377 Co. TK. D, Beaver Dam, WI, 53916

Robbins, Wayne, 11520 Inverway, Belvidere, IL, 61008

S&D Enterprises, 20 East Seventh St, Manchester, OH, 45144, 855-876-9693, 937-549-2602, sales@s-denterprises.com, www.s-denterprises.com, Display case/ box maker. Manufacturer of aluminum display, chipboard type displays, wood displays. Silk screening or acid etching for logos on product

Schlott, Harald, Zingster Str. 26, 13051 Berlin, GERMANY, 049 030 9293346, harald.schlott@T-online.de, Custom grinder, custom handle artisan, display case/box maker, etcher, scrimshander

engravers

Adlam, Tim, 1705 Witzel Ave., Oshkosh, WI, 54902, 920-235-4589, www.adlamengraving.com

Alcorn, Gordon, 10573 Kelly Canyon Rd., Bozeman, MT 59715, 406-586-1350, alcorncustom@yahoo.com, www.alcornengraving.com

Alfano, Sam, 45 Catalpa Trace, Covington, LA, 70433, alfano@gmail.com, www.masterengraver.com

Baron, David, Baron Engraving, 62 Spring Hill Rd., Trumbull, CT, 06611, 203-452-0515, sales@baronengraving.com, www.baronengraving.com, Polishing, plating, inlays, artwork

Bates, Billy, 2302 Winthrop Dr. SW, Decatur, AL, 35603, bbrn@aol.com, www.angelfire.com/al/billybates

Blair, Jim, PO Box 64, 59 Mesa Verde, Glenrock, WY, 82637, 307-436-8115, jblairengrav@msn.com, www.jimblairengraving.com

Booysen, Chris, South Africa, +27-73-284-1493, chris@cbknives.com, www.cbknives.com

Christensen, Bruce, 3072 W. Millerama Ave., West Valley City, UT 84119, 801-966-0805, cengraver@gmail.com

Churchill, Winston G., RFD Box 29B, Proctorsville, VT 05153, www.wchurchill.com

Collins, Michael, 405-392-2273, info@michaelcollinsart.com, www.michaelcollinsart.com

Cover, Raymond A., 1206 N. Third St., Festus, MO 63010 314-808-2508 cover@sbcglobal.net, http://learningtoengrave.com

DeLorge, Ed, 6734 W Main St, Houma, LA, 70360, 985-223-0206, delorge@triparish.net, http://www.eddelorge.com/

Dickson, John W., PO Box 49914, Sarasota, FL, 34230, 941-952-1907

Dolbare, Elizabeth, PO Box 502, Dubois, WY, 82513-0502 edolbare@hotmail.com, http://www.scrimshaw-engraving.com/

Downing, Jim, PO Box 4224, Springfield, MO, 65803, 417-865-5953, handlebar@thegunengraver.com, www.thegunengraver.com, engraver and scrimshaw artist

Duarte, Carlos, 108 Church St., Rossville, CA, 95678, 916-782-2617 carlossilver@surewest.net, www.carlossilver.com

Dubber, Michael W., 11 S. Green River Rd., Evansville, IN, 47715, 812-454-0271, m.dubber@firearmsengraving.com, www.firearmsengraving.com

Eaton, Rick, 313 Dailey Rd., Broadview, MT 59015, 406-667-2405, rick@eatonknives.com, www.eatonknives.com

Eklund, Maihkel, Föne Stam V9, S-820 41 Färila, SWEDEN, info@art-knives.com, www.art-knives.com

Eldridge, Allan, 7731 Four Winds Dr., Ft. Worth, TX 76133, 817-370-7778

Ellis, Willy B, Willy B's Customs, 1025 Hamilton Ave., Tarpon Springs, FL, 34689, 727-942-6420, wbflashs@verizon.net, www.willyb.com

Flannery Gun Engraving, Jeff, 11034 Riddles Run Rd., Union, KY, 41091,

859-384-3127, engraving@fuse.net, www.flannerygunengraving.com

Gournet, Geoffroy, 820 Paxinosa Ave., Easton, PA, 18042, 610-559-0710, ggournet@yahoo.com, www.gournetusa.com

Halloran, Tim, 316 Fenceline Dr., Blue Grass, IA 52726 563-260-8464, vivtim@msn.com, www.halloranengraving.com

Hands, Barry Lee, 30608 Fernview Ln., Bigfork, MT 59911, 406-249-4334, barry_hands@yahoo.com, www.barryleehands.com

Holder, Pat, 18910 McNeil Ranch Rd., Wickenburg, AZ 85390, 928-684-2025 dholderknives@commspeed.net, www.dholder.com

Ingle, Ralph W., 151 Callan Dr., Rossville, GA, 30741, 706-858-0641, riengraver@aol.com

Johns, Bill, 1716 8th St, Cody, WY, 82414, 307-587-5090, http://billjohnsengraver.com

Kelso, Jim, 577 Collar Hill Rd, Worcester, VT, 05682, 802-229-4254, jimkelsojournal@gmail.com, www.jimkelso.com

Koevenig, Eugene and Eve, Koevenig's Engraving Service, Rabbit Gulch, Box 55, Hill City, SD, 57745-0055

Kostelnik, Joe and Patty, RD #4, Box 323, Greensburg, PA, 15601

Kudlas, John M., 55280 Silverwolf Dr, Barnes, WI, 54873, 715-795-2031, jkudlas@cheqnet.net, Engraver, scrimshander

Lark, David, 6641 Schneider Rd., Kingsley, MI 49649, Phone: 231-342-1076 dblark58@yahoo.com

Larson, Doug, Dragon's Fire Studio, Percival, IA, Phone: 402-202-3703 (cell) dragonsfirestudio@hotmail.com

Limings Jr., Harry, 5793 Nichels Ln., Johnstown, OH, 43031-9576

Lindsay, Steve, 3714 West Cedar Hill, Kearney, NE, 68845, Phone: 308-236-7885 steve@lindsayengraving.com, www.lindsayengraving.com

Lurth, Mitchell, 1317 7th Ave., Marion, IA 52302, Phone: 319-377-1899 www.lurthengraving.com

Lyttle, Brian, Box 5697, High River AB CANADA, T1V 1M7, Phone: 403-558-3638, brian@lyttleknives.com, www.lyttleknives.com

Lytton, Simon M., 19 Pinewood Gardens, Hemel Hempstead, Hertfordshire HP1 1TN, ENGLAND, 01-442-255542, simonlyttonengraver@virginmedia.com

Markow, Paul, 130 Spinnaker Ridge Dr. SW, B206, Huntsville, AL 35824, 256-513-9790, paul.markow@gmail.com, sites.google.com/site/artistictouch2010/engraving

Mason, Joe, 146 Value Rd, Brandon, MS, 39042, 601-519-8850, masonjoe@bellsouth.net, www.joemasonengraving.com

McCombs, Leo, 1862 White Cemetery Rd., Patriot, OH, 45658

McDonald, Dennis, 8359 Brady St., Peosta, IA, 52068

McLean, Lawrence, 12344 Meritage Ct, Rancho Cucamonga, CA, 91739, 714-848-5779, lmclean@charter.net

Meyer, Chris, 39 Bergen Ave., Wantage, NJ, 07461, 973-875-6299

Minnick, Joyce, 144 N. 7th St., Middletown, IN, 47356, 765-354-4108

Morgan, Tandie, P.O. Box 693, 30700 Hwy. 97, Nucla, CO, 81424

Morton, David A., 1110 W. 21st St., Lorain, OH, 44052

Moulton, Dusty, 135 Hillview Ln, Loudon, TN, 37774, 865-408-9779, dusty@moultonknives.com, www.moultonknives.com

Muller, Jody & Pat, 3359 S. 225th Rd., Goodson, MO, 65663, 417-852-4306/417-752-3260, mullerforge2@hotmail.com, www.mullerforge.com

Nelida, Toniutti, via G. Pasconi 29/c, Maniago 33085 (PN), ITALY

Nilsson, Jonny Walker, Akkavare 16, 93391 Arvidsjaur, SWEDEN, +(46) 702-144207, 0960.13048@telia.com, www.jwnknives.com

Parke, Jeff, 1365 Fort Pierce Dr. #3, St. George, UT 84790, Phone: 435-421-1692 jeffrey_parke@hotmail.com, https://www.facebook.com/jeff.parke1

Patterson, W.H., P.O. Drawer DK, College Station, TX, 77841

Peri, Valerio, Via Meucci 12, Gardone V.T. 25063, ITALY

Pilkington Jr., Scott, P.O. Box 97, Monteagle, TN, 37356, 931-924-3400, scott@pilkguns.com, www.pilkguns.com

Pulisova, Andrea, CSA 230-95, 96701 Kremnica, Slovakia, Phone: 00421 903-340076 vpulis@gmail.com

Rabeno, Martin, Spook Hollow Trading Co, 530 Eagle Pass, Durango, CO, 81301

Raftis, Andrew, 2743 N. Sheffield, Chicago, IL, 60614

Riccardo, David, Riccardo Fine Hand Engraving, Buckley, MI, Phone: 231-269-3028, riccardoengraving@acegroup.cc, www.riccardoengraving.com, Instagram @riccardoengraving, Facebook: Riccardo Fine Hand Engraving

Roberts, J.J., 7808 Lake Dr., Manassas, VA, 20111, 703-330-0448, jjrengraver@aol.com

Robidoux, Roland J., DMR Fine Engraving, 25 N. Federal Hwy. Studio 5, Dania, FL, 33004

Rosser, Bob, Bob Rosser Hand Engraver, Inc. 2809 Crescent Ave Ste 20, Birmingham, AL, 35209, 205-870-4422, brengraver1@gmail.com, www.hand-engravers.com

Rudolph, Gil, 20922 Oak Pass Ave, Tehachapi, CA, 93561, 661-822-4949

Rundell, Joe, 6198 W. Frances Rd., Clio, MI, 48420

Schönert, Elke, 18 Lansdowne Pl., Central, Port Elizabeth, SOUTH AFRICA

Shaw, Bruce, P.O. Box 545, Pacific Grove, CA, 93950, 831-646-1937, shawdogs@aol.com

Simmons, Rick W., 3323 Creek Manor Dr., Kingwood, TX, 77339, 504-261-8450, exhibitiongrade@gmail.com www.bespokeengraving.com

Slobodian, Barbara, 4101 River Ridge Dr., PO Box 1498, San Andreas, CA 95249, 209-286-1980, fax 209-286-1982, barbara@dancethetide.com. Specializes in Japanese-style engraving.

Small, Jim, 2860 Athens Hwy., Madison, GA 30650, 706-818-1245, smallengrave@aol.com

Smith, Ron, 5869 Straley, Ft. Worth, TX, 76114

Smitty's Engraving, 21320 Pioneer Circle, Harrah, OK, 73045, 405-454-6968, mail@smittys-engraving.us, www.smittys-engraving.us

Soileau, Damon, P.O. Box 7292, Kingsport, TN 37664 423-297-4665, oiseaumetalarts@gmail.com, www.oiseaumetalarts.etsy.com

Spode, Peter, Tresaith Newland, Malvern, Worcestershire WR13 5AY, ENGLAND

Swartley, Robert D., 2800 Pine St., Napa, CA, 94558

Takeuchi, Shigetoshi, 21-14-1-Chome kamimuneoka Shiki shi, 353 Saitama, JAPAN

Theis, Terry, 21452 FM 2093, Harper, TX, 78631, 830-864-4438

Valade, Robert B., 931 3rd Ave., Seaside, OR, 97138, 503-738-7672, (503) 738-7672

Waldrop, Mark, 14562 SE 1st Ave. Rd., Summerfield, FL, 34491

Warenski-Erickson, Julie, 590 East 500 N., Richfield, UT, 84701, 435-627-2504, julie@warenskiknives.com, www.warenskiknives.com

Warren, Kenneth W., P.O. Box 2842, Wenatchee, WA, 98807-2842, 509-663-6123, (509) 663-6123

Whitmore, Jerry, 1740 Churchill Dr., Oakland, OR, 97462

Winn, Travis A., 558 E. 3065 S., Salt Lake City, UT, 84106, 801-467-5957

Zima, Russ, 7291 Ruth Way, Denver, CO, 80221, 303-657-9378, rzima@rzengraving.com, www.rzengraving.com

etchers

Baron Engraving, David Baron, 62 Spring Hill Rd., Trumbull, CT, 06611, 203-452-0515 sales@baronengraving.com, www.baronengraving.com

Fountain Products, 492 Prospect Ave., West Springfield, MA, 01089, 413-781-4651

Hayes, Dolores, P.O. Box 41405, Los Angeles, CA, 90041

Holland, Dennis, 4908 17th Pl., Lubbock, TX, 79416

Kelso, Jim, 179 Worcester Village Road Worcester, VT 05682, 802-229-4254, jimkelsojournal@gmail.com, www.jimkelso.com

Larstein, Francine, Francine Etched Knives, 368 White Rd, Watsonville, CA, 95076, 800-557-1525/831-426-6046, francine@francineetchedknives.com, www.francineetchedknives.com

Lefaucheux, Jean-Victor, Saint-Denis-Le-Ferment, 27140 Gisors, FRANCE

Myers, Ron, 6202 Marglenn Ave., Baltimore, MD, 21206, (acid) etcher

Nilsson, Jonny Walker, Akkavare 16, 93391 Arvidsjaur, SWEDEN, +(46) 702-144207, 0960.13048@telia.com, www.jwnknives.com

Schlott, Harald, Zingster Str. 26, 13051 Berlin, GERMANY, 049 030 9293346, harald.schlott@T-online.de, Custom grinder, custom handle artisan, display case/box maker, etcher, scrimshander

Vallotton, A., Northwest Knife Supply, 621 Fawn Ridge Dr., Oakland, OR, 97462

Watson, Silvia, 350 Jennifer Lane, Driftwood, TX, 78619

heat treaters

Bodycote Inc., 443 E. High St., London, OH 43140 740-852-5000, chris.gattie@bodycote.com, www.bodycote.com

Kazou, Okaysu, 12-2 1 Chome Higashi, Ueno, Taito-Ku, Tokyo, JAPAN, 81-33834-2323, 81-33831-3012

O&W Heat Treat Inc., One Bidwell Rd., South Windsor, CT, 06074, 860-528-9239, (860) 291-9939, owht1@aol.com

Pacific Heat Treating, attn: B.R. Holt, 1238 Birchwood Drive, Sunnyvale, CA, 94089, 408-736-8500, www.pacificheatreating.com

Paul Bos Heat Treating c/o Paul Farner, Buck Knives: 660 S. Lochsa St., Post Falls, ID 83854, 208-262-0500, Ext. 211 / fax 800-733-2825, pfarner@buckknives.com, or contact Paul Bos direct: 928-232-1656, paulbos@buckknives.com

Progressive Heat Treating Co., 2802 Charles City Rd, Richmond, VA, 23231, 804-717-5353, 800-868-5457, sales@pecgears.com

Texas Heat Treating Inc., 155 Texas Ave., Round Rock, TX, 78680, 512-255-5884, buster@texasheatreating.com, www.texasheatreating.com

Texas Knifemakers Supply, 10649 Haddington, Suite 180, Houston, TX, 77043, 713-461-8632, sales@texasknife.com, www.texasknife.com

Tinker Shop, The, 1120 Helen, Deer Park, TX, 77536, 713-479-7286

Valley Metal Treating Inc., 355 S. East End Ave., Pomona, CA, 91766, 909-623-6316, ray@valleymt.net

Wilson, R.W., P.O. Box 2012, Weirton, WV, 26062, 304-723-2771 rwknives@comcast.net, rwwilsonknives.com

leather workers

Abramson, David, 116 Baker Ave, Wharton, NJ, 07885, 973-713-9776, lifter4him1@aol.com, www.liftersleather.com

Burrows, Chuck, dba Wild Rose Trading Co, 102 Timber Ln., Durango, CO 81303, 970-317-5592, wrtc@wrtcleather.com, www.wrtcleather.com

Clements' Custom Leathercraft, Chas, 1741 Dallas St., Aurora, CO 80010, Phone: 303-364-0403, chasclements@comcast.net

Cole, Dave, 620 Poinsetta Dr., Satellite Beach, FL 32937, 321-773-1687, www.dcknivesandleather.blademakers.com. Custom sheath services.

CowCatcher Leatherworks, 2045 Progress Ct., Raleigh, NC 27608, Phone: 919-833-8262 cowcatcher1@ymail.com, www.cowcatcher.us

Cubic, George, GC Custom Leather Co., 10561 E. Deerfield Pl., Tucson, AZ, 85749, 520-760-0695, gcubic@aol.com

Dawkins, Dudley, 221 N. Broadmoor Ave, Topeka, KS, 66606-1254, 785-817-9343, dawkind@reagan.com, ABS member/knifemaker forges straight knives

Evans, Scott V, Edge Works Mfg, 1171 Halltown Rd, Jacksonville, NC, 28546, 910-455-9834, fax 910-346-5660, support@tacticalholsters.com, www.tacticalholsters.com

Genske, Jay, Genske Knives 283 Doty St., Fond du lac, WI 54935-2246 920-238-5353, jaygenske@yahoo.comGreen River Leather, 1098 Legion Park Road, PO BOX 190, Greensburg, KY, 42743, Phone: 270-932-2212 fax: 270-299-2471 email: info@greenriverleather.com

John's Custom Leather, John R. Stumpf, 523 S. Liberty St, Blairsville, PA, 15717, 724-459-6802, 724-459-5996, www.jclleather.com

Kravitt, Chris, Treestump Leather, 443 Cave Hill Rd., Waltham, ME, 04605-8706, 207-584-3000, sheathmkr@aol.com, www.treestumpleather.com, Reference: Tree Stump Leather

Layton, Jim, 2710 Gilbert Avenue, Portsmouth, OH, 45662, 740-353-6179

Lee, Sonja and Randy, P.O. Box 1873, 270 N 9th West, St. Johns, AZ, 85936, 928-337-2594, 928-337-5002, randylee.knives@yahoo.com, info@randyleeknives.com, Custom knifemaker; www.randyleeknives.com

Long, Paul, Paul Long Custom Leather, 108 Briarwood Ln. W, Kerrville, TX, 78028, 830-367-5536, PFL@cebridge.net

Lott, Sherry, 1098 Legion Park Road, PO BOX 190, Greensburg, KY, 42743, Phone: 270-932-2212 fax: 270-299-2471 email: info@greenriverleather.com, sherrylott@alltel.net

Mason, Arne, 258 Wimer St., Ashland, OR, 97520, 541-482-2260, (541) 482-7785, am@arnemason.com, www.arnemason.com

Metheny, H.A. "Whitey", 7750 Waterford Dr., Spotsylvania, VA 22551, 540-582-3228 Cell 540-842-1440, fax 540-582-3095, hametheny@aol.com, http://whitey.methenyknives.com

Morrissey, Martin, 4578 Stephens Rd., Blairsville, GA, 30512

Niedenthal, John Andre, Beadwork & Buckskin, Studio 3955 NW 103 Dr., Coral Springs, FL, 33065-1551, 954-345-0447, a_niedenthal@hotmail.com

Neilson, Tess, 187 Cistern Ln., Towanda, PA 18848, 570-721-0470, mountainhollow@epix.net, www.mountainhollow.net, Doing business as Neilson's Mountain Hollow

Parsons, Larry, 539 S. Pleasant View Dr., Mustang, OK 73064 405-376-9408 l.j.parsons@sbcglobal.net, www.parsonssaddleshop.com

Red's Custom Leather, Ed Todd, 9 Woodlawn Rd., Putnam Valley, NY 10579, 845-528-3783, redscustomleather@redscustomleather.com, www.redscustomleather.com

Rowe, Kenny, Kenny Rowe's Leather, 3219 Hwy 29 South, Hope, AR, 71801, 870-826-2873, rowesleather@yahoo.com, www.rowesleather.com

Schrap, Robert G., Custom Leather Knife Sheaths, 7024 W. Wells St., Wauwatosa, WI, 53213, 414-771-6472, fax 414-479-9765, rschrap@aol.com, www.customsheaths.com

Strahin, Robert, 401 Center St., Elkins, WV, 26241, 304-636-0128, rstrahin@copper.net, *Custom Knife Sheaths

Walker, John, 17 Laber Circle, Little Rock, AR, 72210, 501-455-0239, john.walker@afbic.com

miscellaneous

Robertson, Kathy, Impress by Design, Evans, GA, 30809-1367, 706-650-0982, (706) 860-1623, impressbydesign@comcast.net, graphic design/marketing/advertising

Strahin, Robert, 401 Center St., Elkins, WV, 26241, 304-636-0128, rstrahin@copper.net, *Custom Knife Sheaths

photographers

Alfano, Sam, 36180 Henery Gaines Rd., Pearl River, LA, 70452

Allen, John, Studio One, 3823 Pleasant Valley Blvd., Rockford, IL, 61114

Bilal, Mustafa, Turk's Head Productions, 908 NW 50th St., Seattle, WA, 98107-3634, 206-782-4164, (206) 783-5677, info@turkshead.com, www.turkshead.com, Graphic design, marketing & advertising

Bogaerts, Jan, Regenweg 14, 5757 Pl., Liessel, HOLLAND

Box Photography, Doug, 1804 W Main St, Brenham, TX, 77833-3420

Brown, Tom, 6048 Grants Ferry Rd., Brandon, MS, 39042-8136

Butman, Steve, P.O. Box 5106, Abilene, TX, 79608

Calidonna, Greg, 205 Helmwood Dr., Elizabethtown, KY, 42701

Campbell, Jim, 7935 Ranch Rd., Port Richey, FL, 34668

Cooper, Jim, Sharpbycoop.com Photography, 9 Mathew Court, Norwalk, CT 06851, jcooper@sharpbycoop.com, www.sharpbycoop.com

Courtice, Bill, P.O. Box 1776, Duarte, CA, 91010-4776

Crosby, Doug, RFD 1, Box 1111, Stockton Springs, ME, 04981

Danko, Michael, 3030 Jane Street, Pittsburgh, PA, 15203

Davis, Marshall B., P.O. Box 3048, Austin, TX, 78764

Earley, Don, 1241 Ft. Bragg Rd., Fayetteville, NC, 28305

Ehrlich, Linn M., 1850 N Clark St #1008, Chicago, IL, 60614, 312-209-2107

Etzler, John, 11200 N. Island Rd., Grafton, OH, 44044

Fahrner, Dave, 1623 Arnold St., Pittsburgh, PA, 15205

Faul, Jan W., 903 Girard St. NE, Rr. Washington, DC, 20017

Fedorak, Allan, 28 W. Nicola St., Amloops BC CANADA, V2C 1J6

Fox, Daniel, Lumina Studios, 6773 Industrial Parkway, Cleveland, OH, 44070, 440-734-2118, (440) 734-3542, lumina@en.com, lumina-studios.com

Francesco Pachi, Loc. Pometta 1, 17046 Sassello (SV) ITALY Tel-fax: 0039 019 724581, info@pachi-photo.com, www.pachi-photo.com

Freiberg, Charley, PO Box 42, Elkins, NH, 03233, 603-526-2767, charleyfreiberg@tds.net

Gardner, Chuck, 116 Quincy Ave., Oak Ridge, TN, 37830

Gawryla, Don, 1105 Greenlawn Dr., Pittsburgh, PA, 15220

Goffe Photographic Associates, 3108 Monte Vista Blvd., NE, Albuquerque, NM, 87106

Hanusin, John, Reames-Hanusin Studio, PO Box 931, Northbrook, IL, 60065 0931, 847-564-2706

Hodge, Tom, 7175 S US Hwy 1 Lot 36, Titusville, FL, 32780-8172, 321-267-7989, egdoht@hotmail.com

Holter, Wayne V., 125 Lakin Ave., Boonsboro, MD, 21713, 301-416-2855, mackwayne@hotmail.com

Hopkins, David W, Hopkins Photography inc, 201 S Jefferson, Iola, KS, 66749, 620-365-7443, nhoppy@netks.net

LaFleur, Gordon, 111 Hirst, Box 1209, Parksville BC CANADA, V0R 270

Lear, Dale, 6544 Cora Mill Rd, Gallipolis, OH, 45631, 740-245-5482, dalelear@yahoo.com, Ebay Sales

LeBlanc, Paul, No. 3 Meadowbrook Cir., Melissa, TX, 75454

Lester, Dean, 2801 Junipero Ave Suite 212, Long Beach, CA, 90806-2140

Leviton, David A., A Studio on the Move, P.O. Box 2871, Silverdale, WA, 98383, 360-697-3452

Long, Gary W., 3556 Miller's Crossroad Rd., Hillsboro, TN, 37342, 931-596-2275

Martin, Cory, 4249 Taylor Harbor #7, Racine, WI 53403, 262-352-5392, info@corymartinimaging.com, www.corymartinimaging.com

McCollum, Tom, P.O. Box 933, Lilburn, GA, 30226

Mitch Lum Website and Photography, 22115 NW Imbrie Dr. #298, Hillsboro, OR 97124, mitch@mitchlum.com, www.mitchlum.com, 206-356-6813

Moake, Jim, 18 Council Ave., Aurora, IL, 60504

Moya Inc., 4212 S. Dixie Hwy., West Palm Beach, FL, 33405

Norman's Studio, 322 S. 2nd St., Vivian, LA, 71082

Owens, William T., Box 99, Williamsburg, WV, 24991

Pachi, Francesco, Loc. Pometta 1, 17046 Sassello (SV) ITALY Tel-fax: 0039 019 724581, info@pachi-photo.com, www.pachi-photo.com

Palmer Studio, 2008 Airport Blvd., Mobile, AL, 36606

Payne, Robert G., P.O. Box 141471, Austin, TX, 78714

Pigott, John, 9095 Woodprint LN, Mason, OH, 45040

Professional Medica Concepts, Patricia Mitchell, P.O. Box 0002, Warren, TX, 77664, 409-547-2213, pm0909@wt.net

Rasmussen, Eric L., 1121 Eliason, Brigham City, UT, 84302

Rhoades, Cynthia J., Box 195, Clearmont, WY, 82835

Rice, Tim, PO Box 663, Whitefish, MT, 59937

Richardson, Kerry, 2520 Mimosa St., Santa Rosa, CA, 95405, 707-575-1875, kerry@sonic.net, www.sonic.net/~kerry

Rob Andrew Photography, Rob Szajkowski, 7960 Silverton Ave., Ste. 125, San Diego, CA 92126, 760-920-6380, robandrewphoto@gmail.com, www.robandrewphoto.com

Ross, Bill, 28364 S. Western Ave. Suite 464, Rancho Palos Verdes, CA, 90275

Rubicam, Stephen, 14 Atlantic Ave., Boothbay Harbor, ME, 04538-1202

Rush, John D., 2313 Maysel, Bloomington, IL, 61701

Schreiber, Roger, 429 Boren Ave. N., Seattle, WA, 98109

Semmer, Charles, 7885 Cyd Dr., Denver, CO, 80221

Silver Images Photography, 2412 N Keystone, Flagstaff, AZ, 86004

Slobodian, Scott, 4101 River Ridge Dr., P.O. Box 1498, San Andreas, CA,

95249, 209-286-1980, (209) 286-1982, www.slobodianswords.com

Smith, Earl W., 5121 Southminster Rd., Columbus, OH, 43221

Smith, Randall, 1720 Oneco Ave., Winter Park, FL, 32789

Storm Photo, 334 Wall St., Kingston, NY, 12401

Surles, Mark, P.O. Box 147, Falcon, NC, 28342

Third Eye Photos, 140 E. Sixth Ave., Helena, MT, 59601

Thurber, David, P.O. Box 1006, Visalia, CA, 93279

Tighe, Brian, 12-111 Fourth Ave., Ste. 376 Ridley Square, St. Catharines ON CANADA, L2S 3P5, 905-892-2734, www.tigheknives.com

Towell, Steven L., 3720 N.W. 32nd Ave., Camas, WA, 98607, 360-834-9049, sltowell@netscape.net

Verno Studio, Jay, 3030 Jane Street, Pittsburgh, PA, 15203

Ward, Chuck, 1010 E North St, PO Box 2272, Benton, AR, 72018, 501-778-4329, chuckbop@aol.com

Wise, Harriet, 242 Dill Ave., Frederick, MD, 21701

Worley, Holly, Worley Photography, 6360 W David Dr, Littleton, CO, 80128-5708, 303-257-8091, 720-981-2800, hsworley@aol.com, Products, Digital & Film

scrimshanders

Adlam, Tim, 1705 Witzel Ave., Oshkosh, WI, 54902, 920-235-4589, ctimadlam@new.rr.com, www.adlamengraving.com

Alpen, Ralph, 7 Bentley Rd., West Grove, PA, 19390, 610-869-7141

Anderson, Terry Jack, 10076 Birnamwoods Way, Riverton, UT, 84065-9073

Ashworth, Boyd, 1510 Bullard Pl., Powder Springs, GA 30127, 404-583-5652, boydashworthknives@comcast.net, www.boydashworthknives.com

Bailey, Mary W., 3213 Jonesboro Dr., Nashville, TN, 37214, Phone: 615-889-3172 mbscrim@aol.com

Baker, Duane, 2145 Alum Creek Dr., Cambridge Park Apt. #10, Columbus, OH, 43207

Barrows, Miles, 524 Parsons Ave., Chillicothe, OH, 45601

Brady, Sandra, Scrimshaw by Sandra Brady, PO Box 104, Monclova Ohio 43542, 419-261-1582 sandy@sandrabradyart.com, www.sandrabradyart.com

Beauchamp, Gaetan, 125 de la Riviere, Stoneham, QC, G3C 0P6, CANADA, 418-848-1914, fax 418-848-6859, knives@gbeauchamp.ca, www.gbeauchamp.ca

Bellet, Connie, PO Box 151, Palermo, ME, 04354 0151, 207-993-2327, phwhitehawk@gwl.net

Benade, Lynn, 2610 Buckhurst Dr, Beachwood, OH, 44122, 216-464-0777, llbnc17@aol.com

Bonshire, Benita, 1121 Burlington Dr., Muncie, IN, 47302

Bryan, Bob, 1120 Oak Hill Rd., Carthage, MO, 64836

Burger, Sharon, Glenwood, Durban KZN, South Africa, cell: +27 83 7891675, scribble@iafrica.com, www.sharonburger-scrimshaw.co.za/

Byrne, Mary Gregg, 1018 15th St., Bellingham, WA, 98225-6604

Cable, Jerry, 332 Main St., Mt. Pleasant, PA, 15666

Caudill, Lyle, 7626 Lyons Rd., Georgetown, OH, 45121

Cole, Gary, PO Box 668, Naalehu, HI, 96772, 808-929-9775, 808-929-7371

Collins, Michael, Rt. 3075, Batesville Rd., Woodstock, GA, 30188

Conover, Juanita Rae, P.O. Box 70442, Eugene, OR, 97401, 541-747-1726 or 543-4851, juanitaraeconover@yahoo.com

Courtnage, Elaine, Box 473, Big Sandy, MT, 59520

Cover Jr., Raymond A., 1206 N. 3rd St., Festus, MO, 63010, Phone: 314-808-2508 cover@sbcglobal.net, learningtoengravecom

Cox, J. Andy, 116 Robin Hood Lane, Gaffney, SC, 29340

Dietrich, Roni, Wild Horse Studio, 1257 Cottage Dr, Harrisburg, PA, 17112, 717-469-0587, ronimd@aol

Dolbare, Elizabeth, PO Box 502, Dubois, WY, 82513-0502

Eklund, Maihkel, Föne Stam V9, S-82041 Färila, SWEDEN, +46 6512 4192, info@art-knives.com, www.art-knives.com

Eldridge, Allan, 1424 Kansas Lane, Gallatin, TN, 37066

Ellis, Willy B., Willy B's Customs by William B Ellis, Tarpon Springs, FL, 34689, 727-942-6420, wbflashs@verizon.net, www.willyb.com

Fisk, Dale, 2202 Ridge Rd, Council, ID, 83612, dafisk@ctcweb.net

Foster Enterprises, Norvell Foster, P.O. Box 200343, San Antonio, TX, 78220

Fountain Products, 492 Prospect Ave., West Springfield, MA, 01089

Gill, Scott, 925 N. Armstrong St., Kokomo, IN, 46901

Hands, Barry Lee, Barry Lee Hands Engraving 1836 Falchion Drive, Borrego Springs, CA 92004, 406-249-4334, barry_hands@yahoo.com, www.barryleehands.com

Hargraves Sr., Charles, RR 3 Bancroft, Ontario CANADA, K0L 1C0

Harless, Star, c/o Arrow Forge, P.O. Box 845, Stoneville, NC, 27048-0845

Harrington, Fred A., Summer: 2107 W Frances Rd, Mt Morris MI 48458 8215, Winter: 3725 Citrus, St. James City, FL, 33956, Winter 239-283-0721, Summer 810-686-3008

Hergert, Bob, 12 Geer Circle, Port Orford, OR, 97465, 541-332-3010, hergert@harborside.com, www.scrimshander.com

Hielscher, Vickie, 6550 Otoe Rd, P.O. Box 992, Alliance, NE, 69301, 308-762-4318, g-hielsc@bbcwb.net

High, Tom, 5474 S. 112.8 Rd., Alamosa, CO, 81101, 719-589-2108, rmscrimshaw@gmail.com, www.rockymountainscrimshaw.com, Wildlife Artist

Himmelheber, David R., 11289 40th St. N., Royal Palm Beach, FL, 33411

Holland, Dennis K., 4908-17th Place, Lubbock, TX, 79416

Hutchings, Rick "Hutch", 3007 Coffe Tree Ct, Crestwood, KY, 40014, 502-241-2871, baron1@bellsouth.net

Imboden II, Howard L., 620 Deauville Dr., Dayton, OH, 45429, 937-439-1536, Guards by the "Last Wax Technic"

Johnson, Corinne, W3565 Lockington, Mindora, WI, 54644

Johnston, Kathy, W. 1134 Providence, Spokane, WA, 99205

Karst Stone, Linda, Kerrville, TX, 78028-2945, 830-377-9916, linda@karstone.com, www.karstone.com

Kelso, Jim, 577 Collar Hill Rd, Worcester, VT 05682, 802-229-4254 kelsomaker@gmail.com, www.jimkelso.com

Koevenig, Eugene and Eve, Koevenig's Engraving Service, Rabbit Gulch, Box 55, Hill City, SD, 57745-0055

Kostelnik, Joe and Patty, RD #4, Box 323, Greensburg, PA 15601

Lemen, Pam, 3434 N. Iroquois Ave., Tucson, AZ, 85705

Martin, Diane, 28220 N. Lake Dr., Waterford, WI, 53185

McDonald, René Cosimini-, 14730 61 Court N., Loxahatchee, FL, 33470

McFadden, Berni, 2547 E Dalton Ave, Dalton Gardens, ID, 83815-9631

McGowan, Frank, 12629 Howard Lodge Dr., Winter Add-2023 Robin Ct Sebring FL 33870, Sykesville, MD, 21784, 863-385-1296

McGrath, Gayle, PMB 232 15201 N Cleveland Ave, N Ft Myers, FL, 33903

McLaran, Lou, 603 Powers St., Waco, TX, 76705

McWilliams, Carole, P.O. Box 693, Bayfield, CO, 81122

Mitchell, James, 1026 7th Ave., Columbus, GA, 31901

Moore, James B., 1707 N. Gillis, Stockton, TX, 79735

Ochonicky, Michelle "Mike", Stone Hollow Studio, 31 High Trail, Eureka, MO, 63025, 636-938-9570, www.stonehollowstudio.com

Ochs, Belle, 124 Emerald Lane, Largo, FL, 33771, 727-536-3827, contact@oxforge.com, www.oxforge.com

Pachi, Mirella, Localita Pometta 1, 17046 Sassello (SV), ITALY, +39 019 72 00 86, www.pachi-photo.com

Parish, Vaughn, 103 Cross St., Monaca, PA, 15061

Peterson, Lou, 514 S. Jackson St., Gardner, IL, 60424

Pienaar, Conrad, 19A Milner Rd., Bloemfontein 9300, SOUTH AFRICA, Phone: 027 514364180 fax: 027 514364180

Poag, James H., RR #1 Box 212A, Grayville, IL, 62844

Polk, Trena, 4625 Webber Creek Rd., Van Buren, AR, 72956

Pulisova, Andrea, CSA 230-95, 96701 Kremnica, Slovakia, Phone: 00421 903-340076 vpulis@gmail.com, www.vpulis.host.sk

Purvis, Hilton, P.O. Box 371, Noordhoek, 7979, SOUTH AFRICA, 27 21 789 1114, hiltonp@telkomsa.net, http://capeknifemakersguild.com/?page_id=416

Ramsey, Richard, 8525 Trout Farm Rd, Neosho, MO, 64850

Ristinen, Lori, 14256 County Hwy 45, Menahga, MN, 56464, 218-538-6608, scrim@loriristinen.com, www.loriristinen.com

Roberts, J.J., 7808 Lake Dr., Manassas, VA, 22111, 703-330-0448, jjrengraver@aol.com, www.angelfire.com/va2/engraver

Rudolph, Gil, 20922 Oak Pass Ave, Tehachapi, CA, 93561, 661-822-4949

Rundell, Joe, 6198 W. Frances Rd., Clio, MI, 48420

Satre, Robert, 518 3rd Ave. NW, Weyburn SK CANADA, S4H 1R1

Schlott, Harald, Zingster Str. 26, 13051 Berlin, +49 030 929 33 46, GERMANY, harald.schlott@web.de, www.gravur-kunst-atelier.de

Schulenburg, E.W., 25 North Hill St., Carrollton, GA, 30117

Schwallie, Patricia, 4614 Old Spartanburg Rd. Apt. 47, Taylors, SC, 29687

Selent, Chuck, P.O. Box 1207, Bonners Ferry, ID, 83805

Semich, Alice, 10037 Roanoke Dr., Murfreesboro, TN, 37129

Shostle, Ben, 1121 Burlington, Muncie, IN, 47302

Smith, Peggy, 676 Glades Rd., #3, Gatlinburg, TN, 37738

Smith, Ron, 5869 Straley, Ft. Worth, TX, 76114

Steigerwalt, Jim, RD#3, Sunbury, PA, 17801

Stuart, Stephen, 15815 Acorn Circle, Tavares, FL, 32778, 352-343-8423, (352) 343-8916, inkscratch@aol.com

Talley, Mary Austin, 2499 Countrywood Parkway, Memphis, TN, 38016, matalley@midsouth.rr.com

Thompson, Larry D., 23040 Ave. 197, Strathmore, CA, 93267

Toniutti, Nelida, Via G. Pascoli, 33085 Maniago-PN, ITALY

Trout, Lauria Lovestrand, 1136 19th St. SW, Vero Beach, FL 32962, 772-778-0282, lovestranded@aol.com

Tucker, Steve, 3518 W. Linwood, Turlock, CA, 95380

Tyser, Ross, 1015 Hardee Court, Spartanburg, SC, 29303

Velasquez, Gil, Art of Scrimshaw, 7120 Madera Dr., Goleta, CA, 93117

Williams, Gary, PO Box 210, Glendale, KY, 42740, 270-268-7888, scrimbygarbo@gmail.com, scrimbygarbo.com

Winn, Travis A., 558 E. 3065 S., Salt Lake City, UT 84106, 801-467-5957

Young, Mary, 4826 Storeyland Dr., Alton, IL, 62002

organizations

AMERICAN BLADESMITH SOCIETY
c/o Office Manager, Cindy Sheely; P. O. Box 160, Grand Rapids, Ohio 43522; cindy@americanbladesmith.com; (419) 832-0400; Web: www.americanbladesmith.com

AMERICAN KNIFE & TOOL INSTITUTE
Jan Billeb, Executive Director, AKTI, 22 Vista View Ln., Cody, WY 82414; 307-587-8296, akti@akti.org; www.akti.org
Advocacy organization

AMERICAN KNIFE THROWERS ALLIANCE
c/o Bobby Branton; POB 807; Awendaw, SC 29429; akta@akta-usa.com, www.AKTA-USA.com

ART KNIFE COLLECTOR'S ASSOCIATION
c/o Mitch Weiss, Pres.; 2211 Lee Road, Suite 104; Winter Park, FL 32789

CALIFORNIA KNIFEMAKERS ASSOCIATION
c/o Clint Breshears, Membership Chairman; 1261 Keats St; Manhattan Beach CA 90266; 310-372-0739; breshears1@verizon.net
Dedicated to teaching and improving knifemaking

CUSTOM KNIFE COLLECTORS ASSOCIATION
c/o Kevin Jones, PO Box 5893, Glen Allen, VA 23058-5893; E-mail: ckca.blade@gmail.com; Web: www.ckca.com
The purpose of the CKCA is to recognize and promote the artistic significance of handmade knives, to advnace their collection and conservation, and to support the creative expression of those who make them. Open to collectors, makers purveyors, and other collectors. Has members from eight countries. Produced a caledndar which features custom knives either owned or made by CKCA members.

CUTTING EDGE, THE
2900 S. 26th St., Rogers, AR 72758; 479-631-0130; 800-255-9034; ce_info@cuttingedge.com, www.cuttingedge.com
After-market knives since 1968. We offer about 1,000 individual knives each month. The oldest and the most experienced in the business of buying and selling knives. We buy collections of any size, take knives on consignment or we will trade. Web: www.cuttingedge.com

JAPANESE SWORD SOCIETY OF THE U.S.
PO Box 712; Breckenridge, TX 76424, barry@hennick.ca, www.jssus.org

KNIFE COLLECTORS CLUB INC, THE
2900 S. 26th St, Rogers, AR 72758; 479-631-0130; 800-255-9034; ag@agrussell.com; Web: www.k-c-c.com/

The oldest and largest association of knife collectors. Issues limited edition knives, both handmade and highest quality production, in very limited numbers. The very earliest was the CM-1, Kentucky Rifle

KNIFE RIGHTS
Doug Ritter, Chairman and Executive Director, P.O. Box 657 Gilbert, AZ 85299-0657; 866-889-6268, 602-476-2702, www.kniferights.org
Advocacy organization

KNIFEMAKERS' GUILD, THE
c/o Gene Baskett, Knifemakers Guild, 427 Sutzer Creek Rd., La Grange, KY 42732; 270-862-5019; Web: www.knifemakersguild.com

KNIFEMAKERS GUILD OF SOUTHERN AFRICA, THE
c/o Andre Thorburn; PO Box 1748; Bela Bela, Warmbaths, LP, SOUTH AFRICA 0480; +27 82 650 1441 andrethorburn@gmail.com; Web: www.kgsa.co.za

MONTANA KNIFEMAKERS' ASSOCIATION, THE
1439 S. 5th W, Missoula, MT 59801; 406-728-2861; macnancymclaughlin@yahoo.com, Web: www.montanaknifemakers.com
Annual book of custom knife makers' works and directory of knife making supplies; $19.99

NEW ENGLAND CUSTOM KNIFE ASSOCIATION
Vickie Gray, Treasurer, 686 Main Rd, Brownville, ME 04414; Phone: 207-965-2191, Web: www.necka.net

NORTH CAROLINA CUSTOM KNIFEMAKERS GUILD
c/o Tim Scholl, President, 1389 Langdon Rd., Angier, NC 27501; 910-897-2051, tschollknives@live.com, Web: www.ncknifeguild.com

NORTHEAST CUTLERY COLLECTORS ASSOCIATION
Web: www.ncca.info

OREGON KNIFE COLLECTORS ASSOCIATION
Web: www.oregonknifeclub.org

TEXAS KNIFEMAKERS' GUILD
www.texasknifemakersguild.com

THE WILLIAM F. MORAN JR. MUSEUM & FOUNDATION
4204 Ballenger Creek Pike, Frederick, MD 21703, info@billmoranmuseum.com, www.williammoranmuseum.com

publications & editorial websites

AUTOMATIC KNIFE RESOURCE
c/o Lantama Cutlery, POB 721, Montauk, NY 11954; 631-668-5995; info@latama.net, Web: www.thenewsletter.com,
Unique compilation and archive for the switchblade/automatic knife fan.

BLADE MAGAZINE
5600 West Grande Market Drive, Suite 100, Appleton, WI 54913; 920-471-4522; www.blademag.com, www.bladeshow.com, www.shopblade.com
The world's No. 1 knife magazine. The most in-depth knife magazine on the market, covering all aspects of the industry, from knifemaking to production knives and handmade pieces.

KNIFENEWS.COM
www.knifenews.com
Covers new releases, industry news, current events.

KNIFE MAGAZINE
PO Box 3395, Knoxville, TN 37927; Phone: 865-397-1955, knifepub@knifeworld.com, www.knifeworld.com
Since 1977, a monthly knife publication covering all types of knives

KNIVES ILLUSTRATED
22840 Savi Ranch Pkwy. #200, Yorba Linda, CA 92887; Phone: (800) 764-6278; customerservice@engagedmediainc.com; www.knivesillustrated.com
All encompassing publication focusing on factory knives, new handmades, shows and industry news

THE CUTTING EDGE
http://blog.knife-depot.com
Editorial presence of Knife Depot, an online retailer, that covers industry news, history, technical info and more.

THE LEATHER CRAFTERS & SADDLERS JOURNAL
222 Blackburn St., Rhinelander, WI 54501; Phone: 715-362-5393; info@leathercraftersjournal.com, www.leathercraftersjournal.com
Bi-monthly how-to leathercraft magazine